**Everyone
Who Is Gone
Is Here**

Everyone Who Is Gone Is Here

The United States, Central America, and the Making of a Crisis

Jonathan Blitzer

PICADOR

First published 2024 by Penguin Press
An imprint of Penguin Random House LLC

First published in the UK 2024 by Picador
an imprint of Pan Macmillan
The Smithson, 6 Briset Street, London EC1M 5NR
EU representative: Macmillan Publishers Ireland Ltd, 1st Floor,
The Liffey Trust Centre, 117–126 Sheriff Street Upper,
Dublin 1, D01 YC43
Associated companies throughout the world
www.panmacmillan.com

ISBN 978-1-5290-3931-3 HB
ISBN 978-1-5290-3932-0 TPB

Copyright © Jonathan Blitzer 2024

The right of Jonathan Blitzer to be identified as the
author of this work has been asserted by him in accordance
with the Copyright, Designs and Patents Act 1988.

Brief portions of this work originally appeared, in different form,
in articles published in *The New Yorker* from 2017 to 2022.

Humberto Ak'abal, "I Walk Backwards," trans. Deborah T. Levenson,
in *The Guatemala Reader*, eds. Greg Grandin, Deborah T. Levenson and Elizabeth Oglesby, pp. 499.
Copyright © 2011 by Duke University Press. All rights reserved.
Republished by permission of the copyright holder, and the Publisher. www.dukeupress.edu.

Grateful acknowledgment is made to the Roque Dalton Fundación for permission to translate into
English the first stanza from "El Gran Despecho" by Roque Dalton, originally published in Spanish
in *Taberna y Otros Lugares* by Roque Dalton (Havana, Cuba: Casa de las Américas, 1969).
Translated and reprinted by permission of the Roque Dalton Fundación.

Image credits appear on page 507.

All rights reserved. No part of this publication may be reproduced,
stored in a retrieval system, or transmitted, in any form, or by any means
(electronic, mechanical, photocopying, recording or otherwise)
without the prior written permission of the publisher.

Pan Macmillan does not have any control over, or any responsibility for,
any author or third-party websites referred to in or on this book.

1 3 5 7 9 8 6 4 2

A CIP catalogue record for this book is available from the British Library.

Printed and bound by CPI Group (UK) Ltd, Croydon, CR0 4YY

This book is sold subject to the condition that it shall not, by way of
trade or otherwise, be lent, hired out, or otherwise circulated without
the publisher's prior consent in any form of binding or cover other than
that in which it is published and without a similar condition including
this condition being imposed on the subsequent purchaser.

Visit **www.picador.com** to read more about all our books
and to buy them. You will also find features, author interviews and
news of any author events, and you can sign up for e-newsletters
so that you're always first to hear about our new releases.

To Alex and Ben, and to my parents

Country of mine you don't exist
you're just my bad silhouette
a word that I got the enemy to believe.

—Roque Dalton,
"El Gran Despecho"

Now and then
I walk backwards.
It is my way of remembering.
If I only walked forward,
I could tell you
about forgetting.

—Humberto Ak'abal,
"I Walk Backwards"

Contents

Introduction   *1*

PART 1

1. The Heart Doctor	9
2. The True Identity of the People of God	13
3. The General and His Boots	25
4. Spanish for Vietnam	37
5. Something Immigrant and Hungry	47
6. Pro Bono Coyotes	53
7. We Can't Stop, but Do We Have Any Other Choice?	61
8. They Don't Even Let You Fuck in Peace	72
9. The Guatemalan Solution	77
10. The Red Bishop	84
11. Living as Long as the Republic Does	94
12. Smugglers with a Conscience	99
13. Stepsister of the Government	107
14. The Heart Doctor Speaks	115
15. A Park Called Pain	124
16. Sanctuary Goes to Trial	134

CONTENTS

17. Nothing More Permanent Than a Temporary Immigrant — *143*
18. The Doctor and the General — *147*

PART 2

19. Half Anthropologist, Half Wannabe Hood — *155*
20. Gang Wars — *159*
21. La Clínica del Pueblo — *171*
22. Hispanics versus Blacks versus Whites — *180*
23. War Zones — *188*
24. Operation Blockade — *198*
25. Above the Rest — *206*
26. The Third Rail of American Politics — *213*
27. Fast Eddie — *222*
28. The Sisters — *235*
29. The Trial — *250*
30. Homieland — *259*
31. The Reformers — *270*

PART 3

32. The Voice of God — *281*
33. Deporter in Chief — *290*
34. Border Emergency — *300*
35. Memory Card — *307*
36. Trump — *318*
37. Killing Fields — *330*
38. Los Nerds — *343*
39. La Pastora — *352*
40. Stay at Your Own Risk — *362*
41. Do I Have to Come Here Injured or Dead? — *370*
42. The Highlands at the Border — *375*
43. We Need Concrete Information — *383*

44. The Caravan	389
45. Solidarity 2000	396
46. Remain in Mexico	403
47. Rewriting Asylum	415

PART 4

48. The Heart Doctor	425
49. The Wuhan of the Americas	430
50. Eddie and Juan	436
51. Keldy	441
52. Lucrecia	448
53. Simply Not Who We Are	456
54. Home	460
Acknowledgments	465
Note on Sources	471
Notes	473
Bibliography	503
Image Credits	507
Index	509

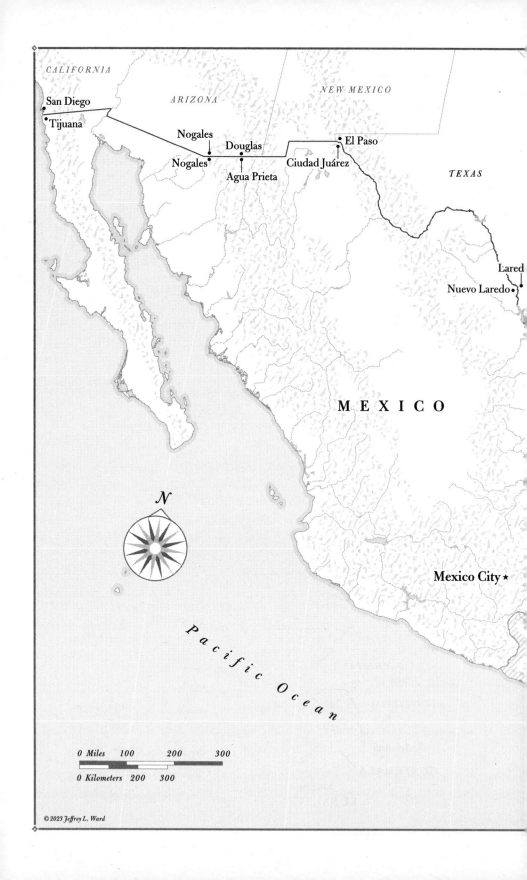

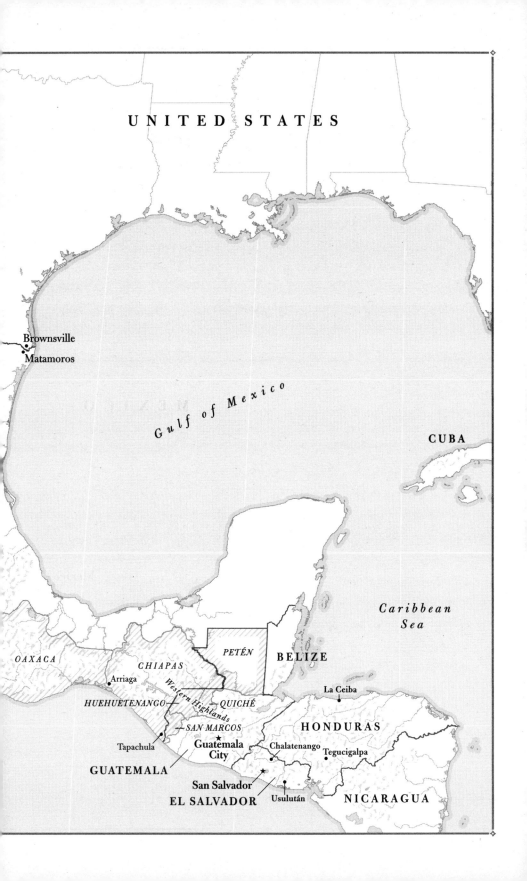

Everyone Who Is Gone Is Here

Introduction

On a bright, humid evening in early August 2019, ten Honduran migrants met to pray in the basement of a Mexican housing complex called Solidarity 2000. They were far from home and farther from their destination. Most had previously been deported from the United States, but none of them could stay in Honduras, so they were making the journey again. Their reasons varied. One was being hunted by criminals. Another had been going hungry. When I met them, they were biding their time in Tapachula, a city along the Guatemalan border, squatting in a semi-abandoned building.

Many members of the prayer group had been to Tapachula before. They knew people in the city—friends they had made in American immigration jails, or in the country they had left behind. Honduras was no longer home. Home had become the route they had to tread, and retread, through Guatemala, Mexico, and the US detention system. The migrants in Tapachula may have been Honduran, but more important, they were deportees and asylum seekers with very low odds of being admitted to the United States. Their immigration status had become a defining, immutable fact of who they now were. In news stories about "surges" or "floods" of migrants massing toward the US, these were the people whose faces were blurred and anonymous. Eventually, they would become numbers on government spreadsheets and talking points at election time. They were "removables," in the cold bureaucratic language of homeland security. Those who managed to traverse Mexico and cross the US border would earn yet another new status for their trouble. By law, they would be repeat offenders, and thus felons.

The room in Solidarity 2000 was small and dimly lit, with pocked floors and bare walls. A pink fan wheezed in a corner. I had come at the invitation of the pastor leading the prayer session, a woman I'd met in a Texas detention center a year earlier. The group went around in a circle to introduce themselves. Where they came from, no one was untouched by immigration, even those who stayed behind. Some could afford to remain at home only because family members had already emigrated, sending money back to pay for necessities. But these were the lucky ones. The families I sat with in Mexico saw a single, stark possibility. The people they knew who were still in Honduras were either infirm, trapped, or resigned; anyone with any sense was leaving. "Even Juan Orlando is going to leave when his term is up," one young man said, referring to the Honduran president. "Just watch. He'll ask for asylum in the US, too."

Everyone that evening had an American story—a trauma, a memory, or, in some cases, a memento. One man, a burly extrovert in a red T-shirt and a flat-brimmed hat tilted to the side, took out a photograph from Eloy, the detention center in Arizona where he had been held the year before. For a few dollars at the commissary, you could get a photo of yourself and your friends posing in the *yarda*. Seeing it, the pastor's nephew pulled out his own version of the same photo from his wallet. They compared poses and swapped stories about the jail.

For more than a century, the US has devised one policy after another to keep people out of the country. For more than a century, it has failed. The past decade has proven the futility of this ambition and laid bare its incalculable human cost. More people are on the move than ever before, uprooted by war, famine, persecution, natural disasters, pandemic, climate change, corrupt regimes, and economic collapse. A new era of mass migration is well underway. Politicians have won elections by stoking fears of open borders and irreversible demographic change. Immigration, a White House official recently told me, has become a "democracy issue": if liberal-democratic governments across the world fail to address the situation, it will continue to fuel the rise of populist authoritarianism.

From the 1980s to the early 2000s, the story of the southern border was about the United States and Mexico. At the time, migrants entering the US tended to be single Mexican men looking for work. But around 2014, a different population started to arrive on a scale Americans had never before seen. These were children and families from El Salvador, Guatemala, and Honduras—the so-called Northern Triangle of Central America—traveling north to seek asylum. In just about every respect, the US was unprepared for this shift. Two inescapable realities collided. First, living conditions in Central America had gotten so bad that many people couldn't remain even if they wanted to; the region was in the free fall of an exodus. Second, the US immigration system was capable only of flailing triage.

On July 31, 2019, a few days before the Hondurans gathered to pray, another group assembled, this one at the US embassy in Guatemala City, where the acting secretary of the US Department of Homeland Security was hosting a select group of Guatemalan politicians, business leaders, and journalists. He was pitching the American government's latest gambit: a deal that would force any migrant traveling to the US through Guatemala to apply for asylum there instead. Top officials at DHS would soon be having the same conversations with the leaders of El Salvador, Honduras, and Panama. The goal, in effect, was to shift the US border farther south—some called it the "invisible wall."

The Americans felt they were running out of options. More immigrants than ever before were trying to enter the US and had fewer legal means to do so. By the end of 2019, one million migrants—most of them from Central America—would be arrested at the southern border, a 90 percent increase from the year before and the highest total in twelve years. "These are numbers no immigration system in the world is designed to handle," said the head of Customs and Border Protection. American officials believed the system was being abused. Only a fraction of those who applied for asylum would receive it, the acting secretary pointed out at the embassy in Guatemala City. The legal standards were exacting and esoteric. Fleeing a gang, for example, was legally distinct from fleeing a repressive government, even if the gang controlled a country like a shadow state. Leaving a country that had become too dangerous wasn't the basis for asylum; leaving it under specific threats of imminent death or torture was.

Fending off starvation didn't count as a form of persecution. Immigration law didn't align with the muddled exigencies of the region, and most applicants, however sympathetic, would find their entry barred.

The last time Congress had reformed the immigration system was 1990, and that effort had been piecemeal. The asylum system became one of the final open doors for legal immigration—and it was open only a crack. But the federal bureaucracy was incapable of handling so many people, and the mechanisms of government were buckling. In 2009, when Barack Obama took office, there was a backlog of half a million asylum cases. By the end of the Trump administration, the queue had reached 1.3 million. On average, it took about twenty-four months to resolve an asylum claim. In the meantime, more asylum seekers arrived. Some were allowed to enter the country on the grounds that they would eventually appear before a judge; others were jailed, summarily deported, or expelled straight into Mexico. The randomness of the system was a cruelty all its own.

Immigration policy is governed by a politics of permanent crisis, with the border as its staging ground. One of the core premises of US immigration policy—true under Democrats as well as Republicans—is deterrence: turn away enough people, and others will stop trying to come. The practice is called the Consequence Delivery System, a term with an Orwellian charge. In 2018, the Trump administration decided to separate parents and children who arrived together seeking asylum. The idea originated from a furious government brainstorming session during a border emergency in 2014, but top officials had dismissed it as inhumane. Under Trump, the government delivered the most brutal consequence imaginable, but migrants were undeterred. Staying home was worse than leaving and facing the punishment.

I happened to be en route to Tapachula when I learned of the meeting in Guatemala City and rerouted in the Mexico City airport. As a result, I spent one day with DHS personnel in Guatemala, and the next in Mexico with the very people DHS was trying to discourage. These two worlds were deeply intertwined, and yet they seemed barely to touch. It is the mission of this book to be a kind of go-between: to tell each side's story to the other; to find a way to bring the Homeland Security officials into the housing-complex basement;

and to allow the migrants in the basement to participate, for once, in the privileged backroom conversations that decide their fate.

◇—◇

Each of the last three American presidents dealt with a major humanitarian emergency at the border, and each time the American public experienced it as a separate incident. One came in 2014, the next in 2019, the third in 2021. The latest crisis was always the worst, until the next one. But these were all different chapters of the same story, which went back to 1980.

That was the year the US first codified refugee and asylum law, while also deepening its involvement in two major civil wars in Central America. The first asylum seekers were escaping regimes the US was arming and supporting in the name of fighting communism. American immigration policy still largely focused on legalizing the undocumented and dealing with the arrival of Mexicans at the border. But US foreign policy was changing that. The government was creating new categories of immigrants and, in turn, reshaping American life from Los Angeles to Washington, DC. Immigrants have a way of transforming two places at once: their new homes and their old ones. Rather than cleaving apart the worlds of the US, El Salvador, Guatemala, and Honduras, the Americans were irrevocably binding them together.

In the 1980s, administrations in Washington saw Central America through the totalizing prism of the Cold War. Over the next few decades, the fear of the spread of leftism morphed into a fear of the spread of people. A straight line extends between the two, pulled taut during the intervening years of forced emigration, mass deportation, and political expediency. Immigration laws draw sharp boundaries around citizenship and identity, casting this history aside. Politics is a form of selective amnesia. The people who survive it are our only insurance against forgetting.

Part 1

1.
The Heart Doctor

As a boy in Usulután, in eastern El Salvador, Juan Romagoza grew up knowing that one day he would become either a doctor or a priest. The church called first, with the casual force of inevitability. The signs of a future life in the Catholic ministry were everywhere, starting on the street where he lived, in a Spanish colonial house with his parents, eight siblings, grandparents, an aunt, and an uncle. It was just around the corner from the city's main church, a simple but imposing building with two towers and a broad front staircase. Early each morning, the family attended mass. On Sundays, at the house of Juan's great-grandparents, the bishop would often visit for lunch. He was a stiff, corpulent man, who dressed in a flowing white robe. Jewelry covered his hands and neck. The adults used to summon Juan and the other children to kneel before him and kiss one of his rings. The whole family was *muy beata*, neighbors used to say; they were church folks, pious in the extreme. In 1964, when Juan was thirteen, he announced to the family that he wanted to leave home to attend the seminary, in the nearby mountain town of Santiago de María. "One less mouth to feed and one more saint in the family," his mother said.

It didn't take him long to realize his mistake. Juan loved Usulután's pulsating sense of community; neighbors were linked together in an atmosphere of friendly complicity. The seminary felt closed off and drained of communal life.

It was also treacherous in ways he hadn't foreseen. At night, he learned to wrap himself tightly in his bedsheets and blankets to avoid the attentions of one priest who was notorious among the young seminarians for making rounds after dark. When Juan came home, six months later, he not only refused to return to the seminary; he thought he might be an atheist.

Medicine became Juan's enduring religion. As with the church, his attraction to it ran deep, dating from the day he watched his fifty-two-year-old grandfather die of a heart attack. Juan was eight at the time, and he clung to his grandfather's side while the family waited three hours for a doctor to arrive. Untreated ailments addled other family members. They developed chronic debilitations—blindness in an eye, a bad limp, a lifetime of stomach trouble. "A doctor is really a kind of high priest," he told his family as he grew older. The profession answered to a higher calling.

Juan was short and scrawny, with wispy dark hair, olive skin, and alert eyes. Quiet charisma hung off him like a loose shirt. At school, and on the streets, he always found his way to the center of group activity. There were soccer matches and neighborhood pranks in his boyhood, and, as he got older, demonstrations organized against local authorities. The prevailing attitude in town was a ready sympathy for the *obreros* and *campesinos* in their midst—the workers and the peasants—and a corresponding coolness toward men of overweening authority. Church figures were a sometimes polarizing exception.

Juan's mother was a seamstress, his father a gym teacher. They could only afford to send one child at a time to college, but Juan, who was his school's valedictorian, earned a scholarship from the Casa Presidencial, in San Salvador. In 1970, he arrived at the University of El Salvador to study medicine, a seven-year degree that wound up lasting ten.

El Salvador's politics were dominated by an alliance between the business elite and the armed forces, which grew increasingly turbulent during the 1970s as the broader public rebelled. Protests and protracted worker strikes led to government crackdowns. The university kept closing for months on end. During these stoppages, Juan would volunteer in different hospitals across the country—in places like Usulután and Sonsonate, where he knew people—and this way got some training in before school reopened. He had already chosen his subspecialty. He wanted to be a heart surgeon.

The surgery residency came near the end of his education, one of the last rotations before completing the degree. This was why, on a hot, humid evening in February 1980, Juan found himself at the San Rafael National Hospital, in Santa Tecla, twenty miles west of San Salvador. It was his fourth week at the facility, and he was beginning to feel comfortable there. The building was old but charming; a single story, it was organized around an interior courtyard, with a facade made of stone painted white and blue, the national colors, and lined with deep-set windows and decorative columns. Like any medical resident, Juan spent more time at the hospital than he did at the garret-size room he rented in San Salvador. He worked long hours and took naps where and when he could, in between assignments assisting with surgeries and running down doctors' requests.

At around five p.m. a gurney came crashing through the doors of the emergency room. On it was the bloodied, unmoving body of a student protester. Juan later learned the identity of the patient. He was the leader of an association of high school students called the Movimiento Estudiantil Revolucionario Salvadoreño (MERS), a junior offshoot of the teachers union. It frequently mobilized in anti-government demonstrations around the capital.

The student had been strafed in the neck and stomach by police gunfire and rushed by his friends away from the scene of the shooting to his parents. But they had all been reluctant to bring him to a hospital. The state security forces had a reputation for searching hospitals after violent incidents and dragging out injured protesters. Often, these protesters would never be heard from again, or else their mutilated bodies would be deposited a day or two later on a street corner as a warning to their confederates. The family had decided to take him to San Rafael because the hospital was just outside the city and therefore, they hoped, beyond the immediate watch of the police.

For four hours, Juan assisted with the surgery, and eventually the student was stabilized and transferred from the operating room. At San Rafael, the intensive care ward was a single rectangular-shaped hall, with beds arranged in rows and cordoned off from one another with curtains. Juan pulled a chair up to the patient's bed. He checked his blood pressure, adjusted his catheter, and recorded his vital signs. It was after ten p.m. by the time Juan was done with the first round of tasks, and the hospital had grown quiet. Only Juan and a nurse remained in the ward. Sitting upright alongside the bed, he drifted off, lulled to sleep by the sound of the nurse padding along the tile floor.

A thumping sound jolted him awake a few minutes later. The intensive care ward was in the eastern wing of the hospital, and the emergency room and parking lot were on the western side. It took Juan a few seconds to realize that he was hearing the rhythm of soldiers' boots marching the length of the hospital, down the colonnaded archway, toward where he sat with his patient.

"They're coming for you," he found himself saying aloud to the boy sleeping beside him. He rose and spotted the nurse, who was standing up, ramrod straight. Before either of them could do anything, there was a loud, guttural shout. Juan wheeled around to see a group of a half dozen men masked in balaclavas and armed with rifles and pistols coming through the door. Some wore the green uniforms associated with the national security forces; others were dressed like civilians.

"Get on the ground. We'll shoot you if you try to get up," one of them yelled. Juan dropped to the floor. He kept his eyes on their boots as the men walked toward his patient, stopping right in front of the bed. They knew their target. A member of the hospital staff had likely tipped them off.

Without saying a word, the men opened fire. Spent cartridges rained down around him, pinging off the floor. The bed rocked and rattled from the force of the bullets. Then, just as swiftly as they had entered, the gunmen left, marching off the way they had come.

"Did they leave?" Juan called out to the nurse. She was in her fifties, calm and experienced, but she was crying. "I think so," she replied. He jumped to his feet and gratuitously grabbed the wrist of his patient to feel for a pulse that wasn't there. Juan's eyes were on the window, and he moved toward it cautiously before looking out. In the parking lot, he could see a fleet of green trucks before their taillights flickered on—a flash of red in the dark—and they peeled out into the night. Juan began picking up the cartridges, which were still hot to the touch.

"Why are you taking those?" the nurse asked.

"To remember this," he replied.

2.

The True Identity of the People of God

A single event, known as La Matanza, or the Massacre, defined modern Salvadoran history. On January 22, 1932, agricultural laborers in the western part of the country, armed with machetes and hoes, staged an insurrection against the nation's coffee-growing elite, which had been subjugating the rural poor for decades. In the late 1870s, much of the arable land in El Salvador had been in public hands. It belonged to individual communities whose population depended on it for their survival. The rise in global coffee prices, together with the need for an exploitable labor force, prompted the government to seize and privatize these holdings. There was too much money to be made, so it began auctioning off the plots to the wealthy owners of large plantation-style estates known as *fincas*. Hundreds of thousands of peasants were dispossessed, then forced to work for nothing on land that used to belong to them.

In 1932, one American diplomat in El Salvador, writing to his superiors at the State Department, saw a backlash as inevitable, if also futile. "A farm animal is of more general value than the worker, for there is generally a plentiful supply of the latter," he wrote. A cobbler and labor organizer named Miguel Mármol founded the Salvadoran Communist Party in 1930, a year after the global financial crash. He traveled the countryside to survey the damage, finding that peasants were "being treated like slaves, by slaveholders on plantations and estates," and were forced to endure "starvation wages, arbitrary and inconsistent wage reductions, massive unjustified firings, evictions . . . and direct and fierce repression by the national guard in the form of imprisonment, expulsions from homes, burning of houses."

The revolt in 1932 sputtered in a matter of days, but the repression it provoked went on for weeks. The military intervened on the side of the landowners. They were joined by members of the National Guard, who had been suppressing labor disputes for years. Together the soldiers slaughtered some thirty thousand people—roughly 2 percent of the Salvadoran population. Anyone who looked vaguely Indigenous or dressed like a peasant was branded a rebel and executed. Corpses were dumped in public or left hanging to instill terror. In one town, troops rounded up prisoners in groups of fifty and brought them before firing squads.

La Matanza froze the country in time for the next four and a half decades. The government replaced the real story of what had happened with lavish propaganda about how the military had fended off bloodthirsty communist hordes. The National Library removed references to the events from its records. Newspaper accounts were destroyed. Government files from the time were hidden or burned. What remained, the American historian Thomas Anderson wrote in 1971, was a "paranoiac fear of communism that has gripped the nation ever since. This fear is expressed in the continual labeling of even the most modest reform movements as communist or communist inspired." Roque Dalton, the Salvadoran poet and activist, put it more succinctly: "We were all born half dead in 1932."

By the time Juan Romagoza went to the seminary, in the early 1960s, it was estimated that seventy-five people from twenty-five families controlled 90 percent of El Salvador's wealth. The elite had expanded its reach from coffee to other cash crops, including cotton and sugarcane, and it had also moved into banking. As a teenager, Juan traveled back and forth between Usulután and the university in San Salvador. He'd spend much of the week in the capital, then return home by bus on weekends.

When *campesinos* from the countryside visited Juan's home city, he noticed that their fingers and hands were almost always purpled, gnarled, and bruised. Their battered limbs and missing digits were a sign of torture. They had demanded higher wages, tried to organize a union, or simply struck the authorities as suspicious. The state security forces had identified broad categories of people whom they considered to be a threat to the social order, including rural schoolteachers, Catholic catechists, and residents of a zone of the country populated by known political activists.

There was a taxonomy of uniforms that Juan learned to spot and avoid. The National Guard, which patrolled the countryside, wore green fatigues, helmets, leather leg guards, and large brass belt buckles. The National Police, in charge of the cities, had short-sleeve shirts and olive pants. The Treasury Police, tasked with combating illegal smuggling, used khaki jackets and hats bearing the insignia PH, for Policía de Hacienda. All of them received training and weapons from the United States. Throughout the late 1950s and 1960s, American military advisers helped restructure the Salvadoran police academy. They also wrote a manual for the Treasury Police, and trained members of the National Guard and National Police in riot control.

The US government had never taken a serious interest in El Salvador, but after the Cuban Revolution, in 1959, concern over the spread of communism led to a new posture in the region. The Kennedy administration created a military command center, called SOUTHCOM, to coordinate so-called counterinsurgency operations carried out by special forces throughout Latin America. Modeled on American maneuvers in Vietnam, these activities were conceived as "guerrilla" actions "in support of the state." The American paradigm posed an immediate dilemma for ordinary Salvadorans. The state itself was wildly repressive, but the US advisers who were training and arming it considered any public opposition to be grounds for a militarized response. "Insurgency," the US Joint Chiefs of Staff wrote in 1962, was defined as any "illegal opposition to an existing government." In El Salvador, that included worker strikes, unionization efforts, and public demonstrations.

One of Juan's first encounters with the state security forces began with an innocent celebration in the main square in Usulután, on a warm evening in 1968. The city had just held its mayoral elections, and Juan was at home waiting for the results when he heard shouts and cheers on the streets. Putting on a pair of sandals, he ran outside, where he found crowds of his neighbors assembling in celebration. People were dancing and playing music, throwing homemade firecrackers that popped in short, staccato bursts. Their candidate had defeated his opponent from the Partido de Conciliación Nacional (PCN), the party backed by the military government. Juan had just joined the festivities when truckloads of troops from the National Guard pulled up.

The soldiers assembled on the outskirts of the plaza and set up a barricade to intimidate the revelers. Then, a few of them started shoving a group of elderly women who were placidly taking in the evening's euphoric air from a ring of park benches. The *señoras* were practically sacred in Usulután; revered and looked after, they were like grandmothers to everyone. When Juan and some of his friends saw what was happening, they rushed over to intercede. The soldiers responded by firing their weapons in the air, causing the crowds to scatter. Because Juan's house was nearby, he led people inside to wait out the disturbances.

A few days later, the winning mayoral candidate was replaced by a member of the PCN. In 1972, a coalition called the Unión Nacional Opositora, which represented a broad array of leftists, was leading in the polls when the government abruptly stopped the vote count. After a mysterious delay, an announcement was made that the military's preferred candidate, from the PCN, had won. A group of disgruntled officers mounted a coup in vain. National protests followed in which the military shot and killed two hundred demonstrators, while the opposition candidate was taken into custody and beaten. By the time he went into exile, a few days later, his nose and cheekbone had been shattered.

One of the ironies of the government repression was that it galvanized, rather than cowed, the opposition. Before the 1972 elections, the public still had some measure of faith in the electoral process. As a result, armed elements of the far left drew few adherents. There was just one guerrilla organization, and it was too small and disorganized to carry out kidnappings or direct attacks on government officials. But as the government interfered with elections and committed further abuses against the public, the ranks of guerrilla groups and grassroots organizations grew, pulling in university students, labor leaders, peasants, and members of the Catholic Church. "The guerrilla groups, the revolutionary groups, almost without exception began as associations of teachers, associations of labor unions, *campesino* unions or parish organizations which were organized for the definite purpose of getting a schoolhouse up on the market road," an American diplomat observed. "When they tried to use their power of association to gain their ends, first they were warned and then they were persecuted and tortured and shot."

◇—◇

Juan carried the bullet casings in his pocket for the rest of the week. He knew the risks. If a police officer stopped and searched him on the street, under even the flimsiest pretext, he was doomed. Either he would be identified as the witness to a military murder or would stand accused of being a subversive himself. In San Salvador, in 1980, people were killed for much less. On Sunday morning, he set out to deliver the bullets to the one person he thought could help: Óscar Romero, the archbishop of San Salvador.

It would be decades before Romero achieved sainthood, but his stature, even then, was unmatched. He was known in El Salvador as the "voice of the voiceless," for his unyielding defense of the poor. He opened churches to thousands who'd been displaced, and exposed acts of aggression by the government and its right-wing allies. In a country darkened into total indecipherability by oppression and misinformation, his clarion statements became a national and international reference point. They showed the reality of a country descending into civil war.

The Metropolitan Cathedral was a majestic cement and brick structure painted white in the heart of downtown, which Juan always regarded with awe. This time, rather than pause at the front entrance to take it in, he entered through a side door. It was early, an hour before the morning mass. Juan was alone, pacing anxiously outside the door of the sacristy in anticipation of Romero's arrival. A few minutes later, Romero strode down the hallway, a thin, diminutive man who wore his gray hair combed back, with a pair of thick-framed glasses. When Romero saw him, he said, "Something bad has happened, hasn't it?"

HE AND JUAN HAD a history together—two histories, really. The first began in 1974, when Romero was the bishop of Santiago de María, a municipality in Usulután. Home from university for the weekend, Juan met the new bishop at his great-grandparents' house on a Sunday. When he arrived, Romero was sitting in a hammock surrounded by people, with a plate of food on his lap. Following the custom, Juan knelt to kiss his ring and noticed that it was the only article of jewelry Romero wore; otherwise, the bishop's hands were bare. Juan watched him seek out a family friend from the countryside, a *campesino* in late middle age, who kept to the periphery of the gathering. The man was disheveled, and his hands were grimy and callused from his work, which consisted of carving small sculptures of the saints from wood. Romero looked the man in the eye while they spoke.

But something else had still unsettled Juan about the bishop. Romero championed the poor in his sermons and in his writings, yet he was more conciliatory when it came to matters of governance. He was reluctant to openly confront the country's president or to call for land reforms.

Juan spent the 1970s moving in the opposite direction, toward outright political engagement. Right next to the university in San Salvador was a series of slums that had filled with *campesinos* who'd fled their homes in the countryside because of the worsening repression. Many of them wandered the streets of the city barefoot and disoriented. They staggered into traffic at major intersections around the university, causing accidents. Juan joined a group of medical students who opened a clinic to give them free health care. The patients had been tortured and maimed by state security forces and by the death squads of the far right. They'd lost family members to disappearances and assassinations.

The more abiding relationship between Juan and Romero started later, in the nation's capital, as fellow activists responding to the new state of emergency. In 1977, when Romero became the archbishop, state violence was spinning out of control. Hundreds of priests and Catholic workers across the country had been murdered, injured, or threatened, including one especially prominent victim: a forty-nine-year-old Jesuit priest and celebrated advocate for the poor, named Rutilio Grande. A close personal friend of Romero's, he was gunned down by right-wing assassins a month before Romero moved to San Salvador.

Grande's assassination disabused Romero of the promise of gentler diplomacy with the government. Romero never sounded the same afterward. His speeches were forthright and bold, delivered in a voice that rumbled with an otherworldly drum of urgency. He decried the violence and called for a national land reform to give the rural poor a fighting chance at survival. When Romero learned of the work that Juan and the other medical students were doing, he requested a meeting. "I want you to help me tend to this population," he told a group of them. "And I want you to help bring me information about what's been happening to them. You are my eyes and ears." The medical students started to drop by the church every few weeks, bringing pages of handwritten notes replete with the names of people who'd been tortured or killed. Working at the clinic gave them direct access to the victims, and the archbishop frequently cited the information they brought him in his sermons.

Juan came to Romero before the morning mass because there was nowhere else to report a crime. The government denied to the press that its soldiers had killed anyone earlier that week. No stories of the incident ran in local newspapers. It was as though the murder had never happened.

"I was a witness, Father. I was there," Juan said. He recounted the sound of the boots marching down the hallway, the shouts, the gunfire. "These are the bullets they used," he added, digging them out of his pocket. Juan noticed tears on Romero's face. "Children, they're just children," the archbishop said, more to himself than to Juan. He was preparing for the mass now, but promised to register the incident with Socorro Jurídico, a human rights monitor associated with the church. Juan left the bullets with Romero in the sacristy and went to find a place in the chapel.

Whenever Romero led mass, the church would be full. There were everyday worshippers, dressed in neat but modest clothes, as well as *campesinos* in dustier, tattered attire, having traveled in from the countryside to hear him. In the back of the chapel, identifiable by their starched shirts and small personal entourages, were diplomats, opposition politicians, and, invariably, news reporters.

Each Romero sermon was a virtuoso literary feat in three sections. The first was the most directly theological, a ranging biblical exegesis interspersed with contemporary commentary. Next came a section that he called "The Life of the Church," with announcements about church initiatives and activities, many of which were coming under direct threat from the death squads. But it was the final part, which Romero titled "The Events of the Week," that drew the most attention. Part forensic analysis of state terror and part legal indictment, it was, above all, an impassioned personal plea to the government for mercy. Here the

Archbishop Romero leaving the Metropolitan Cathedral after Sunday mass in San Salvador, El Salvador, 1979.

sermon grew dense with information about the violence and mayhem overtaking the country. For half an hour, sometimes longer, he would methodically list the names of people who'd been killed or disappeared, the dates of murders and mass arrests, and the locations of recent crackdowns.

These reports were widely seen as the most definitive accounts of the ongoing repression, and they drew notice around the world. For those who couldn't attend in person, the sermons were broadcast by radio. They reached three quarters of the population in the countryside and nearly half of all city residents. During his Sunday sermons, which could run up to two hours, a person could hear every word while strolling down the street. Each home would have it playing loudly on a transistor radio.

Juan was seated near the middle of the pews when Romero walked out wearing a white robe. In a steady, booming voice, he congratulated everyone in attendance. By being there in the chapel, he said, they were "impressing on this moment the true identity of the people of God." Conservative critics often accused Romero of turning his masses into political meetings. "I am in no way attempting to practice politics," he said, by way of introduction. The church was silent, the attendees rapt. He started to speak louder; his cadence quickened. "If

I shed some light on the politics of my country because the moment calls for it, I do so as a pastor, using the light of the Gospel."

Beyond Romero's public prominence, Juan credited him with a more personal achievement: the miracle of restoring Juan's belief in God. Romero's own conversion to activism had been the impetus for it. With his own risk-taking mirrored and amplified in the actions of the archbishop, Juan began to see himself and his activism differently. He was no longer an isolated humanitarian trying to find his way through the chaos on instinct. What gave him the greatest faith was that Romero had allowed himself to change. He'd gone from being an uncommonly thoughtful, but canny, country bishop to being a national leader who put everything on the line.

"How much worse can a civil war be than what we're already experiencing, with people being killed everywhere you look?" Romero continued. He paused to cough, but before he could resume everyone in the church erupted into applause. The previous several months had been the most violent in decades. State security forces had killed hundreds of civilians—159 in October 1979, 281 in December, and 320 in January 1980.

What made the bloodletting even more tragic was that there'd been an unprecedented, but doomed, effort to reform the military from the inside that very fall. On October 15, 1979, dozens of junior officers staged a coup to force some of the most extreme hardliners out of the military and to establish civilian rule for the first time since before La Matanza. A ruling council, known as the junta, would then replace the government and restaff the upper ranks of the cabinet. In theory, their demands were straightforward. They called for the abolition of ORDEN, the country's most notorious death squad, which had ties to senior officials in the military; the recognition of the rights of *campesinos* to organize; and the passage of an agrarian reform law that could facilitate, in their words, an "equitable distribution of national wealth."

Within hours of the coup, however, a cadre of conservative senior officers wrested control of the new junta. At least one of them was on the payroll of the CIA. When it became clear to the far right that the top military brass was reconsolidating its power, there was a rash of further killings and reprisals. A power struggle ensued inside the junta. Romero had been advising the members of the new government, but the chasm between the military and civilian factions was becoming unbridgeable. Senior military officers refused to take orders from anyone but the minister of defense. By early January, after a wave of resignations by civilian leaders who lacked any real power, the government collapsed.

The one that replaced it was arguably worse. Brokered by the US State Department, the new junta was a union between the military and a center-left party known as the Christian Democrats, whom the Americans liked because of their outspoken anti-communism. The Christian Democrats were divided over whether to enter a government that was effectively run by the military. Half the party distrusted the arrangement, while the other half, hungry for power that had eluded them for years, wanted to forge ahead. The skeptics were proved right: with the patina of legitimacy conferred by the Christian Democrats, the military soon redoubled its repression.

"Political power is in the hands of unscrupulous military officers," Romero said in the sermon, to more applause. Most of those in attendance would have known who he was talking about. Officers on the far right were working directly with death squads to plot clandestine hits on opposition politicians and organizers. But Romero was also referring to the military's top officials who pleaded ignorance of the worst atrocities. There was Carlos Eugenio Vides Casanova, the clever, wealthy head of the National Guard, and José Guillermo García, the brasher minister of defense and de facto president. Both knew that members of the military were participating in extrajudicial killings. And each, in his way, condoned them by stonewalling investigations and refusing to punish the officers involved. Such violence was too useful for them to try to stop. The far right was doing their dirty work by exterminating their political rivals. At the same time, the rising death toll served as the military's pretext for preserving power. Without the military hierarchy intact, they claimed, the country would succumb to chaos.

"The present government has no popular support and depends only on the armed forces and certain foreign powers," Romero told the churchgoers. "This concern has moved me to be bold enough to write a letter to President Carter himself, and I'm going to send it to him after you tell me your opinion of it." He began to read it aloud. "Señor Presidente," he said. "Because you are a Christian and because you have shown that you want to defend human rights, I venture to set forth for you my pastoral point of view."

Without consulting the civilian members of the junta, the US had been giving direct aid to the military. The latest waves of killings hadn't dissuaded Washington. American money went toward gas masks, bulletproof vests, and other supplies, which the US president rationalized as forms of "nonlethal aid." Romero wanted to correct Carter's misapprehension. Now the security forces were simply better equipped and "even more violent in repressing the people," he said, quoting his letter in progress. If Carter truly cared about human rights, Romero went on, he could do two things. The first was "to forbid that military aid be given to the Salvadoran government." The second was to guarantee that the US would not interfere in the "destiny of the Salvadoran people."

On the campaign trail, in 1976, Jimmy Carter built his foreign policy platform on the idea that his administration would respect international human rights. As a Christian, running in the aftermath of Watergate and Vietnam, Carter liked to quote the theologian Reinhold Niebuhr: "The sad duty of politics is to establish justice in a sinful world." There was support for this vision both among the electorate and in Congress. Earlier that year, legislators required the State Department to issue annual reports on human rights in each of the countries receiving American military aid. If any of them displayed a "pattern of gross violations," Congress would freeze the money.

When Carter assumed office, he vowed that "our commitment to human rights must be absolute." Yet his administration struggled to define human rights violations and to prescribe appropriate sanctions. Because of the earlier congressional mandate, a few countries—such as Uruguay and Ethiopia—lost American aid at the start of Carter's presidency. Several other countries, including El Salvador, chose to reject American aid altogether rather than submit to congressional scrutiny. At first, this gave Carter some breathing room in Central America. His commitment made more tangible and immediate sense in the context of the Soviet Union. The White House defended dissidents and welcomed Jewish refugees. But the agenda grew considerably more complicated elsewhere in the world. Billions of dollars of US aid were at stake, and regardless of Carter's avowals, entrenched geopolitics prevailed. Cold War orthodoxies were sacrosanct. In July 1979, left-wing Sandinistas in Nicaragua overthrew the dictator Anastasio Somoza, a US ally. Officials in the upper echelons of the State Department, the CIA, and the Defense Department wondered whether El Salvador might fall next. The view in Washington was that the military needed American support for the center to hold in El Salvador.

Salvadoran soldiers, meanwhile, came up with a new name for an old torture technique. A victim was tied up by his hands and feet, while his interrogators applied intense pressure to the man's testicles with a wire. They called it "the Carter."

3.

The General and His Boots

On the evening of March 24, 1980, Juan was working at the student clinic when he heard someone screaming. The shouts came from another room, and all he could make out at first were the words "What has happened? What has happened?" There was a commotion and, a few seconds later, an answer delivered in a tremulous voice wracked by sobs: "They've killed Romero."

He didn't have time to process the news beyond its immediate imperative. If Romero had just been shot, the military and the death squads were probably in the midst of a broader, citywide assault. In moments like these, soldiers sometimes went directly to the university to round up students. Juan and the others in the clinic rushed to finish what they were doing and close the office.

The streets were empty as Juan hurried home, and car traffic was thinning. The cab drivers had seemed to cut short their evening shifts. It was like the city was under an unofficial curfew, Juan thought. When he arrived at the small rooming house where he lived, he went directly to the apartment of a neighbor, an elderly woman who had a television. The news was on by the time he entered, and her face was ashen. The assassination had occurred in the chapel of a hospital called Divine Providence, where Romero had been presiding over a small, serene gathering that began around six p.m., with the door left open for the breeze. A red car pulled up, and a gunman stepped out with a rifle. No one noticed him until he took aim at Romero and shot him in the chest.

"If they can get to Romero, no one can be saved," Juan's neighbor said, her voice flat. She was too stunned to cry. Juan didn't know it at the time, but American officials shared her assessment. Cables sent from the US embassy in San Salvador had described the prospect of Romero's killing as the likely end of a "moderate solution" to the country's political crisis; all that remained was a "military solution," the prospect of untrammeled terror.

The assassination marked the beginning of a crisis that was profound even by the country's macabre standards. More patients showed up at the clinic in critical condition with torture wounds. A female professor had been left for dead in a dumpster, having been covered in hot tar, with burn marks all over her body and bleeding from her nipples, vagina, and rectum. A high school student turned up with scarring over his genitals from an electric prod. He was too traumatized to speak.

Juan attended protests with a small medical bag. Being a doctor was the profession that brought you closest to God, he'd always thought. But often he would find people injured beyond his ability to help them. There was a young woman he tried to lift from her slump only to realize that the back of her head had been blown away. Activists gulped down their final breaths before expiring in his arms.

At a certain point, he and his colleagues got word that their names were on a hit list assembled by the death squads and distributed among officers in the military. As one American official put it at the time, "If your name happens to be on the list and you are taken prisoner, your future life expectancy is about one hour." At the hospital, Juan began coming and going at odd hours, frequently in disguise. He wore an orderly's uniform, a large sombrero, or the outfit of an electrician. When he could, he hitched a ride in the back of an ambulance to sneak into the emergency room through the hospital garage. Colleagues stood watch on street corners, warding him off with hand signals if they noticed security personnel milling around the hospital entrance.

For Juan it was all tactics and survivalist calculations, but nothing like an actual reckoning with the real danger he was in. If you moved fast enough, and worked constantly, as he did, it was possible to risk your life without feeling much of an accompanying fear. The barrage of daily threats came to seem like quotidian encumbrances, routine problems to skirt and solve. He had a partner in these moments. For the past year, he'd been in a relationship with another medical student and activist, named Laura, an outspoken woman from a conservative family in Santa Ana, who had the uncompromising intensity of a convert with something to prove. She was shorter than Juan, and plump, with dark hair and clear skin. Where Juan was soft-spoken and reserved, Laura was direct and exacting; they were like a revolutionary odd couple.

In the spring of 1980, they were marching on the street one morning with a bunch of *universitarios* when Laura leaned in to share some news. She was pregnant. Juan was so elated that he began to shout right there in the middle of the crowd. Immediately grasping his excitement, the other activists joined in. For a minute or two, it was like the group had forgotten its somber reason for assembling, and the demonstrators hugged and celebrated. Later that night, and in the following months, Juan and Laura were left to face a discomfiting reality: What did it mean to bring a new life into their current world? There was no ready answer, but they came to regard Laura's due date as a deadline of sorts by which to make every possible social improvement to the world awaiting their baby.

BETWEEN JANUARY AND MARCH, government forces had killed at least nine hundred civilians, more than in all of 1979. Late in February, the country's attorney general, a Christian Democrat named Mario Zamora, was murdered at home, in the middle of a dinner party. Several days afterward, civilian members of the government resigned in protest. The far right had hatched an especially sinister strategy: because the military brass needed the top leaders of the Christian Democrats to remain in government for political cover, the death squads selectively assassinated members of the party's rank and file. It was a plan to "domesticate" the party, according to a former officer; Zamora was one of sixty-four Christian Democrats killed that year. The new American ambassador, an unusually clear-eyed diplomat named Robert White, who started the job in

Mourners in the plaza outside the Metropolitan Cathedral during Romero's funeral. San Salvador, El Salvador, March 30, 1980.

The plaza after state security forces opened fire on crowds of mourners during Romero's funeral. San Salvador, El Salvador, March 30, 1980.

mid-March, sent a cable to the State Department: "The major immediate threat to the existence of this government is the right wing violence."

Six days after Romero's assassination, on Palm Sunday, a funeral was held at the Metropolitan Cathedral. The day was stiflingly hot—bright and breezeless. Some two hundred priests and clergy from more than a dozen other countries assembled inside the front doors of the church, while a group of bishops stood outside, next to the casket, which rested on an altar ringed in flowers facing the square. Tens of thousands of Salvadorans gathered in the heat to pay their respects, with thousands more spilling onto the streets nearby.

Juan and the other medical students expected violence, but they didn't know how, or when, it would strike. They arranged with a group of taxi drivers for a rapid-response unit to treat casualties and bring them to safety. Carrying bottles of water and bicarbonate, in case there was tear gas, each of them wore a black T-shirt, under which was a second shirt of a different color. If they were being followed, they'd shed the top shirt to make it harder for their pursuers to identify them in the crowd. The group stationed itself on the north side of the cathedral, by a taxi stand on a small street that snaked out onto a main thoroughfare.

Twenty minutes before noon, a Mexican cardinal was eulogizing Romero when a sudden explosion rocked the far edge of the plaza. Gunfire followed, then another series of explosions. The panicked crowds stampeded for safety. Hundreds rushed the front steps of the cathedral, while the priest and bishops pushed the altar away from the door and dragged Romero's casket inside. Juan darted among the bodies outside in the square. He reached an elderly woman who'd been trampled and led her to a taxi, which sped off toward the university clinic. The sidewalks were littered with shoes, articles of clothing, and large palm fronds that mourners had brought with them for the occasion and then discarded in their shock. He came upon others who were wounded, with blood spattered on their clothes and around the pavement while they sat, doubled over, in a daze. When there were no more taxis left to carry away the casualties, the students brought them into the cathedral through a side door.

There were now so many people inside that Juan couldn't fit through the main entrance. Someone had to pull, then lift him across the threshold to get him inside. For two hours, dead bodies were carried in and out. When the terror subsided, by the middle of the afternoon, the death toll was at least forty, with hundreds more injured.

◇—◇

On the night of the US election, November 4, the American embassy hosted a watch party at the Hotel El Presidente, in San Salvador. The American diplomats were dejected as the returns came in, but their Salvadoran guests celebrated. In attendance were members of the business community and military officers, who took turns firing their guns into the air outside in jubilation. When a group of American envoys left to go home, the wife of one businessman in attendance accosted them. "Get out of here, Communists," she shouted. Others chimed in, "Death to White. Viva Reagan!"

Attitudes on the Salvadoran right were already hardening when a group from Ronald Reagan's transition team made its first official visit to El Salvador and Guatemala to announce the end of Carter's human-rights policy. The military would no longer need to keep up appearances about exercising restraint. In mid-November, General García, the minister of defense, summoned the civilian members of the junta to the Casa Presidencial, where he delivered a long presentation detailing the results of what he claimed was a military investigation. All the nuns and priests in Chalatenango, a volatile region north of the capital, he said, were in league with the guerrillas and needed to be dealt with accordingly. A few weeks later, a man arrived at a Chalatenango parish late one night with a message: everyone there, including four American missionaries doing relief work, was on government death lists. "This very night, we will begin," he said.

In El Salvador, the political left extended well beyond the Christian Democrats, and included a spectrum of smaller parties ranging from armed guerrilla groups to nonviolent Marxists, socialists, and unionists whose views fell to the left of the governing junta. On November 27, six leaders of the non-guerrilla left—formally called the Frente Democrático Revolucionario (FDR)—were preparing to deliver a statement at a Jesuit high school in San Salvador. They had decided to negotiate with the junta, which was significant, because the Christian Democrats in the government had been struggling for support from the country's leftists. Before the leaders could speak, however, two hundred officers from the state's combined security forces surrounded the school, while two dozen men stormed the building and kidnapped them. Soon afterward, their bodies were found near Lake Ilopango, just east of the capital, showing signs of torture. CIA cables at the time cited intelligence that García and other high-ranking military officials had backed the operation. Ambassador White sent a message to Washington: "The military have explicitly rejected dialogue and heralded a policy of extermination."

On the evening of December 2, Dorothy Kazel, an Ursuline nun, and Jean

Donovan, a lay missionary, arrived at the San Salvador airport. They were picking up two Maryknoll Sisters in their forties named Maura Clarke and Ita Ford, who were returning from a conference in Nicaragua. The funeral of the murdered FDR leaders was being held the next day. The four women had just merged onto the highway outside the airport when a truck full of National Guardsmen pulled them over and placed them under arrest. They were raped and murdered later that night, their bodies thrown in a ditch by the side of the road.

The head of the National Guard, General Vides Casanova, denied any knowledge of the murders. But it was inconceivable that lower-ranking soldiers would commit such a crime without an order from superiors. Vides Casanova's own cousin was the colonel in charge of the territory near the airport where the women were abducted.

Eventually, Stanley Pimentel, the FBI's top legal attaché in Central America, partnered with an American embassy official to narrow down a list of five suspects. Pimentel visited Vides Casanova at the headquarters of the National Guard to ask him to hand over the weapons used in the killings. He would then send the rifles to an FBI laboratory, where forensic analysts could dust them for fingerprints and examine the bullets collected from the crime scene. Vides Casanova was tight-lipped but obliging. Several days later, though, Pimentel learned that Vides Casanova had ordered subordinates to hide the weapons, planning to replace them with different rifles to share with the Americans.

Years later, a CIA cable, citing a source whose name was redacted, would confirm that Vides Casanova's cousin had given the order for the churchwomen's murders. But in December 1980, with violence mounting in El Salvador and the US government lurching through a presidential transition, a renewed pall of impunity descended. In El Salvador, investigations were promised, then slow-walked. After a brief interruption, American aid money to the military continued. The sums grew larger as the outgoing Carter team sought to preempt criticism that it had been soft on the guerrilla left.

Jeane Kirkpatrick, a political science professor at Georgetown, already notorious for her unapologetic neoconservatism, was one of President Ronald Reagan's top foreign policy advisers. After the assassination of the FDR leaders, she quipped to journalists that their slaying was a "reminder that people who choose to live by the sword die by the sword." When asked the views of the incoming administration on the brutal murder of the American churchwomen, she replied, "The nuns were clearly not just nuns. The nuns were also political activists."

◇——◇

Several days after the churchwomen were killed, Juan set out for a small hamlet in Chalatenango with a group of six other doctors and nurses. It was early on a Saturday morning, and the trip consisted of a bus ride followed by a two-and-a-half-hour hike along craggy, rock-strewn paths. Every few days, they visited a different town in the countryside to perform medical exams for villagers who were trapped because of skirmishes between government forces and leftist guerrillas. For each outing, Juan and the others learned where to go, and how to arrive there, from church activists.

This time, Juan had received special instructions about an injured resident who needed abdominal surgery. He knew only that the man had been shot twice in the stomach. The less Juan knew, the better, for his own safety. Yet it meant filling his medical bag with extra instruments and medications to cover different surgical contingencies. Juan and the others were supposed to arrive in town right after morning mass, and to treat patients from a makeshift clinic that operated out of someone's home, just off the main square. When the time was right, someone would lead Juan on another hike, two hours farther west, to a tiny home in an even smaller village along the Honduran border. After performing the operation, he would spend the night there, and return to the capital the next morning.

Mass had just ended when they arrived. The streets were overrun with children and families celebrating an annual festival in honor of the Virgin of Guadalupe. Piñatas hung from the branches of trees lining a small square by the church, and tables were covered with platters of tamales and pupusas. A small procession was underway, in which residents paused by the church. Many of them drifted away from the larger groups and filed into the house for their medical consults.

As he began conducting the medical exams, Juan spotted two olive-green trucks that looked like military vehicles. A ripple of nervous chatter moved through the crowd. Just as the doctors stepped outside to urge the patients to stay, the truck doors opened and a unit of soldiers emerged with their weapons drawn. They began spraying the crowd with gunfire. A bullet fragment grazed Juan's forehead, opening a superficial but bloody wound. Another bullet struck him squarely in the right ankle. The force of the impact blew off his boot. He fell to the ground.

A soldier approached Juan to finish the job, pressing the barrel of his pistol against Juan's temple. Juan's chest tightened, his vision blurring with panic. There was a quick click as the soldier pulled the trigger. The safety was on.

Grunting, the soldier flipped the switch off. He was cocking the gun a second time when he noticed Juan's shoes. One was still on his foot; the other lay beside him on the ground. They were a pair of sturdy hiking boots, a gift from a cousin in the Boy Scouts. Their high quality gave the soldier pause. Then he caught sight of Juan's medical bag; some of its contents had spilled out. "Medical equipment," Juan tried to explain, but the soldier didn't believe him. He'd never seen pincers or forceps before. The instruments looked like pieces of a weapon that had been disassembled.

"You're a guerrilla commander, aren't you?" he asked Juan. Juan frantically denied the accusation, insisting he was a doctor and fumbling for his medical credentials. But the soldier had already called over a few others. Together they hoisted Juan to his feet and carried him to the truck.

He was tossed onto the floor in the back and covered with a canvas tarp. Five minutes passed before the vehicle came to a halt. The soldiers transferred him to a helicopter. While they were in the air, the soldiers opened the door of the cabin, threatening to throw Juan out.

When they landed, he learned he was at a military garrison in Chalatenango called El Paraíso. There he was stripped down to his underwear, blindfolded, and placed on a cement slab. The interrogations would last twenty-four days. Nothing he said or did seemed to matter; the punishment was preordained. They would ask him a question about his secret involvement with the guerrillas, he would deny it, and they would beat him and shock him with electrodes. His bullet wounds festered, and the pain numbed him into a disembodied state. He saw himself the way a doctor might a patient, offering a dispassionate prognosis. He observed that he would likely lose his right leg.

A day after arriving in El Paraíso, he was flown to the capital, and brought to the National Guard headquarters, which he glimpsed through a gap in the fabric of his blindfold. "We're taking you to the best hotel in El Salvador," one of the soldiers told him.

The torture methods grew more elaborate and baroque in San Salvador. Juan was tied to iron rungs on the floor, in a position designed to further inflame his wounds. Soldiers sodomized him with a metal rod; shocked him; put out cigarettes all over his body; hung him by his fingers, wrists, and legs until the wires they'd used to string him up severed his skin and pierced the bones and muscles in his fingers and toes.

The sounds of screams and howls from other interrogation rooms blared in and out as he lost and regained consciousness. Each morning, around dawn, he could hear a military band in the distance practicing its daily rendition of the national anthem. One day, his torturers took a pistol and shot him through his left forearm, shattering it. "This is the mark you'll have for helping those people," a soldier told him. "You'll always be marked as a leftist. This is so that you will never practice medicine again."

Shortly after Christmas, the soldiers told Juan he would be receiving a very important visitor, whom they referred to as "the boss." He was led from his cell while it was cleaned in anticipation of the man's arrival, and for the first time a medic took a perfunctory look at the bullet wounds in his leg and arm. Juan, chained to the floor by both arms and his left leg, was splayed awkwardly on his side when the guest arrived.

The first thing he glimpsed through the small gap in his blindfold was the man's newly shined boots, and the clean, crisp cuffs of his pants. The fabric, freshly pressed, was richer and denser than the flimsy khaki uniforms worn by Juan's other interrogators. This was clearly a man of high rank. The other voices in the room grew quiet and deferential.

"You stink of death," the man said, to obsequious laughs. Juan recognized the voice from the TV news. It belonged to Carlos Eugenio Vides Casanova, the head of the National Guard.

THE GENERAL AND HIS BOOTS

Caspar Weinberger (right), former US secretary of defense, walks with El Salvador's then minister of defense, Carlos Eugenio Vides Casanova (left), in front of Salvadoran troops. San Juan Opico, El Salvador, September 7, 1983.

Tall, with a head of dark hair and green eyes, Vides Casanova had a stately, aristocratic manner. He exuded a sense of restrained power that the Americans took as proof of his moderation. Within the security forces, though, he was known as an obsessive who kept close tabs on his colleagues and pored over minute details concerning personnel and operations. His credentials were impeccable: second in his class at the military academy, the top performer on the officers' examinations, followed by a prestigious assignment as commanding instructor at the academy. But he was extremely conservative, and the professional polish and poise couldn't always disguise his true feelings. A year before, at a meeting at the Casa Presidencial where civilian and military leaders had gathered to discuss the future of the country after the October coup, he'd said, "We've been running this country for fifty years, and we are quite prepared to keep on running it." The killings of La Matanza, he'd added, had been a necessary measure that could, and should, be repeated "to keep the country from going communist."

Unlike Juan's other interrogators, who repeated the same slate of generic questions and insinuations, Vides Casanova wanted to know about his family. Juan's two uncles on his mother's side were colonels in the military. In a country as small as El Salvador, this wasn't uncommon, and family relations had sometimes been strained but always civil as Juan's activism increased during the 1970s. Vides Casanova knew, and trusted, one of Juan's uncles, but he harbored suspicions about the other.

The uncle Vides Casanova liked was an odontologist and the deputy director of the country's main military hospital. He had once studied in London with one of Vides Casanova's brothers. The other uncle, with whom Juan was closer, was a trained economist named Manuel Rafael Arce. Six years earlier, his oldest son had snuck off from the family's home one night and joined the ranks of the guerrillas in the countryside. He never spoke to his parents again. This complete severance of contact probably saved his father's life—proof that he'd had nothing to do with his son's decision to fight against the government. But from then on Arce was ostracized and alone. His colleagues never trusted him again. A few years later, they watched him carefully to see how he reacted when the military captured and killed his son. The test was whether Arce would stay silent, which he did.

Vides Casanova wasn't the trusting type. He grilled Juan about Arce, searching for any hint that the two of them were in league. He wanted to know whether they were siphoning off weapons from the military and giving them to the guerrillas. Juan denied this so forcefully that his own voice began to sound alien to him. When Vides Casanova paused, the other soldiers kicked Juan in the ribs and chest. Someone had taken out a stiff-bristle brush and ran it over the rotting bullet wound in Juan's right ankle. Worms emerged from the wound, and the soldiers, laughing, flicked them onto his chest while Vides Casanova watched.

The torture worsened in the days after Vides Casanova's visit. One morning, when the soldiers informed him he would be moved one last time, Juan was convinced that he'd finally be killed. He thought of his family in Usulután, as well as Laura and their child, who'd been moving between the university clinic in San Salvador and medical outposts in Chalatenango. All of them must have assumed he was already dead.

The soldiers led him down a hallway and into a larger room, where they removed his blindfold. The space was wide and cavernous, bare except for a few coffins in the middle of the floor. They opened the lid of one of them and pushed him in.

4.

Spanish for Vietnam

The letter arrived on a Thursday in April 1976. Margo Cowan, the twenty-six-year-old head of a social services organization in Tucson called the Manzo Area Council, was being fired. It was addressed to her personally, from the government-run agency that controlled Manzo's budget. She had discredited the agency, the letter said. Her behavior was "disloyal" and "incompatible" with its mission. They would give her thirty days to clear out her belongings from an office she'd been running for three years.

The next afternoon, she was at the home of a friend across town, trying to make sense of her firing, when the phone rang. It was one of Cowan's staffers, in a state of panic. A dozen federal officers from the Immigration and Naturalization Service, the Border Patrol, and the US Attorney's office had just arrived at the Manzo Area Council's office, a single-floor stucco building that used to be a grocery store on Tucson's west side. "Some of the guys here are wearing suits," she said. They were carting off ten boxes of documents. Inside were nearly eight hundred client files, including five hundred immigration applications. The assistant US attorney was accusing the council of harboring undocumented immigrants and helping them sign up for welfare. A few of the agents had taken brooms and were sweeping stray papers off the floor, to be sure that nothing had escaped their attention.

The Manzo Area Council was a small, scrappy outfit with a permanent staff of four, a group of about a dozen loyal volunteers, and a budget that barely reached twenty-seven thousand dollars a year. It had been founded in the 1960s, with funding from Lyndon Johnson's War on Poverty, and by the time Cowan took over, in 1973, its staff half expected that the Nixon administration would end the operation at any moment. To their relief, and perpetual surprise, he never did. On it went, modestly but implacably, through the presidency of Gerald Ford. Daily tasks included brokering meetings between the community and local police, preparing welfare and other social-service applications, and helping senior citizens. The group's activism tended to be higher profile. Members of the council staged protests at a private golf course to have the mayor turn it into a public park. When a group of high school students held a walkout to improve bilingual education in neighborhood schools, members of Manzo were on hand to assist.

For the first few years of Cowan's tenure, Manzo hadn't done immigration work. There was never much of a need. The community Manzo served was primarily Mexican American, and it didn't matter that many residents on the west side, who had lived there for decades, had at some point either let their legal status lapse or never bothered to apply in the first place. What good were documents if no one was asking for them? In a city like Tucson, just sixty miles north of Mexico, most families had deep binational ties. They switched easily between English and Spanish, speaking both with a lilting border accent. The two countries weren't separated by an enforceable dividing line so much as linked by a revolving door, crossed unthinkingly and often, in both directions, for work, school, shopping, and family visits. Physically there was little separating the two countries or marking the border itself, beyond some bands of concertina wire that local authorities had fastened to wooden posts next to the port of entry between Douglas and Agua Prieta.

In 1974, this all changed: Border Patrol agents began showing up. In their green uniforms, with holstered revolvers, the patrolmen were an unfamiliar presence in Tucson. In the past, they'd kept to their scattered checkpoints along the interstate, or roved around the austere border towns of Ajo and Douglas. But now they were sitting outside in parked cars, waiting for mass to let out at St. Margaret's church, in a neighborhood called Barrio Hollywood. When the parishioners filed out, the agents were ready with handcuffs. They broke up neighborhood soccer games, leading the players into the backs of green trucks. One morning, an immigration raid took place at El Rio Bakery, a neighborhood mainstay just down the block from Manzo's headquarters on Grande Avenue.

In Tucson, the spate of arrests seemed to come out of nowhere, but two thousand miles away, in Washington, policymakers were reaching a new consensus that the border was becoming overrun. The number of people crossing illegally into the US was increasing in the 1970s, from 420,000 every year to roughly a million, while the personnel at the Immigration and Naturalization Service (INS), the federal agency in charge of enforcing immigration laws, hovered around ten thousand agents nationwide, plainly inadequate to deal with the situation. "The INS simply does not know the number of illegal aliens, or who or where they are," the General Accounting Office wrote.

INS did know one thing: most of the people crossing the southern border were Mexicans coming north for predictable reasons. Mexico's population was surging past seventy million people, well beyond what the country's anemic economy could sustain. In Mexico City, the minimum wage amounted to roughly four dollars a day, half of what a factory worker in an American city could make in a single hour; subsistence farmers in rural Mexico could fetch forty dollars a month for their crops, the same amount of money as one day's earnings on an American farm. At one point, in 1975, the Supreme Court ruled that Border Patrol was justified to use a person's appearance as legitimate grounds to make an arrest for illegal entry, since "the likelihood that any given person of Mexican ancestry is an alien is high."

Law enforcement had all sorts of leeway to police the border. The US had been "outmanned, under-budgeted, and confronted by a growing, silent invasion of illegal aliens," Nixon's outgoing INS head, a former marine commander named Leonard Chapman, wrote in a portentous essay in *Reader's Digest*, in 1976. Immigration officials were not alone in hyping the perils of a porous border. William Colby, the head of the CIA, called the transit of undocumented Mexicans into the country "a greater threat to the future of the United States than the Soviet Union."

Residents started coming to Manzo for legal help, and Cowan and the others began a crash course in the immigration system. Mainly, they filed paperwork—hundreds of pages of documents at a time, in dizzying and expensive configurations—meant to formalize the status of children, parents, and spouses who had family ties to the US. The cost of filing an individual immigration application was typically a thousand dollars, but the staff at Manzo processed them for free. It was arduous, plodding work. By the spring of 1976, only twenty-five applications, of the five hundred that they filed, had been successfully submitted.

A few days after the raid, Border Patrol started going door-to-door across the neighborhood, arresting and harassing people who had submitted paperwork to Manzo. A Mexican mother of four, who had a green card, was told she had a week to send two of her children back to Mexico because they didn't have residency permits. A man in his fifties, who'd lived in Tucson for many years and was married to a US citizen, was given a month to leave the country. A sixteen-year-old who had an American fiancé and had just given birth to a son learned that she had a single week to finalize her marriage papers, even though it took several weeks for the government to process them. These visits and ultimatums seemed like a monstrous breach to the residents who had trusted Manzo, but the head of the Border Patrol's anti-smuggling unit made no secret of what his agents were doing. "With that information, we are bound under the law to find out what their status is," he said. "Depending on the case, we apprehend them, process them, and send them to Mexico." By the summer, Border Patrol had deported fifty people, all of them Mexican.

The situation made Cowan angry but methodical. A Tucson native, she had a practiced, disciplined appetite for social combat. She had spent the early part of the decade in California, making twenty-five dollars a week working under Cesar Chavez and Dolores Huerta at the union of the United Farm Workers. She had been beaten on a picket line and charged with inciting a riot; Teamsters had taunted and threatened her. "I learned about nonviolence from Cesar," Cowan once told a local reporter. "And also not to be defensive." Residents of west Tucson rallied to her cause, staging a handful of protests to get Cowan reinstated. The community board that oversaw Manzo relented and held a vote; within days, she was back in her old post.

There was still the more intractable problem of how to recover the confiscated files. This was a slower fight, waged in the courts over the spring and summer, with mixed results. Lupe Castillo was a graduate student at the University of Arizona, and a member of a campus activist group called the Mexican-American Liberation Committee. A few years later, she and Cowan would become a couple as well as collaborators, a recognizable duo who traveled together through Mexico and the borderlands to represent immigrants. But in 1976, Castillo, like many other activists in Tucson, saw the raid on Manzo as an attack on the Mexican community, and the next day she decided to get involved with the council.

To Castillo and Cowan, the responses of Border Patrol and the assistant US attorney were proof that their work had been making an impact. But no one had expected the deportations that followed. They continued daily as Manzo tried to convince a judge to force the government to return the files.

Relief came when Jimmy Carter won the presidency, and the leadership of the Immigration and Naturalization Service turned over. By then, Cowan and four others at Manzo had been indicted by a grand jury for aiding undocumented immigrants in evading capture. They were awaiting trial. In late 1977, however, the charges were dropped, and William Vogel, the assistant US attorney who had led the prosecution, was fired. The front page of the *Tucson Citizen* summarized the outcome in soaring, loaded terms. "It was inevitable that the lines would be sharply drawn between those who 'want the wetbacks stopped or shipped out' and those who believe that 'undocumented workers are entitled to every right under our law and to a helpful welcome as well,'" the paper's editors wrote. Vogel, "the hardliner," had "lost" to Cowan, the humanitarian. Leonel Castillo, the new head of the INS under Carter, took the additional step of providing Manzo with a formal certification so that they could represent undocumented immigrants in their legal proceedings. The whole protracted, ugly incident, in the end, had ironically liberated Manzo, allowing it to become a licensed outfit for immigrant defense.

⋄—⋄

On July 4, 1980, temperatures in the Organ Pipe Cactus National Monument, a five-hundred-square-mile expanse of desert between Yuma and Tucson, reached upward of 120 degrees. Crossing it, from Mexico, were twenty-seven Salvadoran refugees trying to reach the US. These weren't typical borderland travelers. The women wore skirts and heels, and the men carried suitcases. They were middle-class professionals, university students, housewives, a cobbler, some factory workers. Most of them had had direct confrontations with Salvadoran security forces or the death squads, and the others had watched as their livelihoods crumbled in the blur of strikes, shutdowns, and violent chaos that roiled the country. Smuggling operations had cropped up in El Salvador during the months before the official outbreak of civil war. Each member of the group had seen an advertisement in a small newspaper placed by a twenty-six-year-old coyote who ran his business out of a television repair shop in the capital. The deal was twelve hundred dollars a head for a bus trip through Guatemala that was supposed to be followed by a flight from Mexico to Los Angeles.

The travelers were disabused of the idea that this was a reliable operation when the bus continued straight through Mexico. It stopped, four days later, at Sonoyta, a dingy border town in Sonora, where a local smuggling outfit called Los Muñecos (The Dolls) was waiting to lead them on the final and most difficult leg of the journey. A day later, having already been paid, their Mexican guides abandoned them. There wasn't enough food or water for the group to advance any farther. The Salvadorans had reached the US, but they were lost. In every direction, for miles, were scrub brush, clusters of cactuses, wispy paloverde trees that afforded no shade.

By the second day, a few members of the group had begun to die of thirst. The rest stripped off their clothes, drank their own urine, and filled their mouths with pebbles to keep the saliva flowing. Their skin was scorched by the sun, their hands and arms covered in welts and cuts from the spines of the cactuses they reached for while trying to keep themselves upright. The group scattered in search of help. On the third day, Border Patrol agents encountered two of the stragglers, and eventually closed in on the broader group. Only half the travelers were still alive. The survivors were rushed to a hospital emergency room in Tucson.

Margo Cowan and Lupe Castillo were among the first to hear the news. They had never helped anyone like the Salvadorans before. It was one thing for someone to walk into the Manzo office and tell them about an injustice in Barrio Hollywood. But it was quite another for a Salvadoran, in a hospital bed, to describe the predations of the death squads and the intricacies of a foreign government's security apparatus.

Having been exposed to the broader context of US involvement in Central America as part of her graduate studies, Castillo could prime Cowan and the others. The US was propping up a war machine in El Salvador, she told them; it had long treated the region as a geopolitical laboratory. The CIA had overthrown the Guatemalan government in 1954 at the behest of an American corporation that, among other things, wanted bigger tax breaks abroad. Honduras had come to be known in the region as the USS Honduras, a de facto American military installation. For years, the US's man in Nicaragua was a dictator. In Castillo's circles, as the saying went, El Salvador is Spanish for Vietnam.

As the survivors slowly recovered in the hospital, the Salvadoran consul, a man named Hugo Orantes, flew in from Los Angeles. He showed up at the office of the Pima County Sheriff, where he immediately struck the sheriff and his deputies as suspiciously solicitous. Orantes kept asking for photographs of the people who had died. When the sheriff asked him why the photos mattered so much, the consul said something about needing to publish them in Salvadoran newspapers so that the victims' families could come forward. Yet at the same time, a message had also arrived at the sheriff's office from El Salvador, sent by five relatives of those who'd died asking for the bodies to be cremated rather than sent back to the country for identification. Something was clearly amiss. After the sheriff politely put the consul off, Orantes stormed out of the office, saying that "something bad" was going to happen and that "the State Department was going to do it." When the sheriff gave a statement to local reporters, he said nothing about Orantes, but made his own position plain. "The tragedy unfolding here in the desert is due in part to social and political problems in El Salvador," he said. "This is not an ordinary illegal entry situation. I don't think the legalistic approach would be the appropriate response from our government."

The arrival of the Salvadorans wasn't a complete surprise to Cowan and

Castillo. They'd begun hearing stories about Salvadorans who were approaching the US border, causing a bottleneck in Northern Mexico. But their main source of information was a friend named Ramón Dagoberto Quiñones, a bespectacled Mexican priest in his forties who ran a church called the Sanctuary of Our Lady of Guadalupe. It occupied a white stucco chapel perched on a small hill in Nogales, within view of the Arizona border.

For months, Salvadorans had been showing up in Nogales, and Quiñones offered them food and shelter as they planned their crossing into the US. Each day, the church's maid would climb up a pair of rickety stairs to the second floor of the church, beside a modest bell tower, and keep watch for the moment when the US Border Patrol agents took their lunch break. "OK, they're gone," she'd shout down, and dozens of Salvadorans, with their possessions packed, would emerge from the church's dormitories and living quarters to cross the border. Quiñones worked with Cowan and Castillo on Manzo's immigration cases, often helping locate Mexican documents, like birth certificates and custody papers, that were necessary for legal residency applications. He had a heart condition, and his doctor was based in Tucson, so every few months he'd visit Cowan and Castillo while he was in town.

That summer, the two activists received a phone call from someone in Ajo with a tip. A pair of Salvadoran teenagers were stranded in the desert on their way to Phoenix. Through a contact at Manzo, Cowan had heard that their mother, who was still in El Salvador, had sent her children north for their safety. Cowan and Castillo picked them up one afternoon at an A&W Root Beer stand in the desert. A few days later, another woman from El Salvador came directly to Manzo's office, on Grande Avenue, with a bullet lodged in her hip. She was covered in blood, having made the trip through Mexico by bus without stopping. Salvadoran cases were picking up in Tucson; in a span of months, the volume of asylum seekers had grown by the hundreds. Castillo decided to drop out of graduate school to devote herself full time to immigration work.

The Border Patrol separated migrants apprehended along the border into two categories: Mexicans, who made up 80 percent of all the people they caught crossing the border, and everyone else. Mexico loomed so large for border enforcement that it was built into the agency shorthand for the rest of the world:

migrants from anywhere else—India, Brazil, or El Salvador; it didn't matter—were all known as OTMs, "other than Mexican." There was a practical reason for making such a broad distinction. The protocol for dealing with Mexicans caught crossing into the US wasn't to formally deport them, which would involve first detaining them, then marking down the infraction on their record. Instead, in a process that took about five minutes from start to finish, agents simply dropped them back off across the border. There was virtually no paperwork at the office, just a few cursory notes written by hand in the field.

OTMs were much more difficult for Border Patrol. The agents couldn't merely shunt them across the border. They needed to detain them while they took down their information and readied their deportations. The paperwork alone took the agents hours to complete. At the Border Patrol station in Douglas, there were generally four agents on duty policing sixty miles of the border. When one or two of the agents arrested a group of Salvadorans, everyone on the next shift would stay in the office, on the first floor of the three-story government building at the port of entry, and take positions on an improvised assembly line. The fastest typist manned the office's only typewriter, another handled the fingerprints, while a third took Polaroid photographs for each file. A supervisor in Tucson had to be called for authorization to set bond. The Salvadorans sat on the floor for hours on end. Sometimes one of the agents would call a local burger joint to feed everyone in custody, placing an order for a "green meal," which got charged to the INS tab.

Castillo spent her days driving among Border Patrol stations, county jails, and other facilities where the authorities were holding Salvadorans. Everywhere she went she carried a stack of forms called G-28s, which a migrant had to sign to be represented by legal counsel. It wasn't enough for Castillo or Cowan to demand to see all the Salvadorans in custody; agents would turn them away unless they had a person's full name and official detainee number. Only then could they get people to sign the G-28s and begin the process of posting the money to bond them out.

Manzo had a reputation for taking swift and decisive action in the Arizona desert, so phone calls would come from family members in the US or El Salvador, or from Quiñones, in Nogales. Each call brought a lead—a name, detainee number, and a location. Castillo and Cowan scrambled to arrange the money for the bonds, then drove out to the detention facilities. But in the final months of 1980, as INS reported an increase in new arrivals from El Salvador, the women from Manzo encountered a problem. Often when they made it to a government holding station along the border, the migrants they had come to bond out were already gone.

5.

Something Immigrant and Hungry

Throughout the twentieth century, American leaders touted the US as a nation of immigrants, but for most of that time the country never had a formal refugee or asylum policy written in law. It wasn't until 1965, with the passage of the Immigration and Nationality Act (INA), that Congress officially contemplated the idea. But the measures were paltry: each year, 17,400 people were given "conditional entry," as long as they were either fleeing communism or trying to escape a country in the Middle East. The Cold War, rather than any principle of law or humanitarianism, accounted for the narrowness of these terms. Hundreds of thousands of refugees from the rest of the world were left out; another provision of the INA granted the attorney general the power to "parole" foreigners into the US on an ad hoc basis. By the late 1970s, a million refugees had entered the US this way. The rationale for which people the attorney general could admit, and when, was an uncodified matter of geopolitics. The US preferred to accept people leaving countries that were leftist or socialist, and to ignore dissidents from strategic allies. There were 38,000 Hungarians, displaced by Soviet invasion, in 1956; 240,000 Cubans between 1959 and 1962; 1,500 Ugandans in the early 1970s; nearly 80,000 Soviet Jews in the 1970s; and, in 1975, 130,000 Vietnamese and Cambodian refugees.

Paroling immigrants into the US didn't automatically put them on a path to legal status. For that, Congress needed to pass an "adjustment act" anytime the attorney general admitted a new population into the country, so that they could apply to stay. Several such acts followed: a Hungarian adjustment act, the Cuban Adjustment Act, a series of Indo-Chinese adjustment acts.

In March 1980, Congress and the Carter administration put an end to the policy chaos and passed the Refugee Act. By then, the US was admitting, on average, roughly ninety thousand refugees each year. Now the government would have an actual blueprint, bringing US law into step with long-standing international compacts. It began with some definitions. According to the act, a refugee was someone outside his homeland, unable or unwilling to return because of either outright persecution or a "well-founded fear of persecution." Such persecution was defined as being based on "race, religion, nationality, or membership in a particular social group or political opinion." Immigration lawyers, judges, lawmakers, and government officials would spend decades fighting over the underlying ambiguities. But for the time being, the act represented an unqualified advance in American legal practice. As one congressman pointed out, on the House floor, these definitions identified refugees by "a more universal standard based on uprootedness rather than ideology."

Since refugee law was new in Washington, the principal officials in the federal bureaucracy who first began to shape it became accidental protagonists in a drama of which they were only dimly aware. Immigration mattered as a political issue, but it wasn't yet top drawer; in the 1970s, those who worked on such policy came to it through a combination of happenstance, intuition, and luck.

Doris Meissner, who was twenty-nine when she arrived in Washington, wasn't sure at first whether her luck was good or bad. In 1973, she began as a White House fellow assigned to the attorney general's office, a prestigious job that lasted a year. The year of her fellowship happened to coincide with Watergate. A month into her term was Nixon's Saturday Night Massacre—the rapid resignation of the attorney general and deputy attorney general, the firing of a special prosecutor—and then the president's own resignation the following August.

Meissner was a calm presence in an office shaken by upheaval. Fiercely competent, with a plainspoken and forthright manner, she could be firm in her convictions but also diplomatic with the male powerbrokers who dominated the halls of government. After her fellowship was up, the new attorney general asked her to stay on. She served for the next thirteen years, through the Ford and Carter administrations and into Reagan's second term.

When the Carter White House began its talks with Senate Democrats on the Refugee Act, Meissner was working at the Justice Department, as the deputy associate attorney general. INS fell under her office's purview, and the refugee policy was assigned to her. She was hardly a newcomer to the topic of immigration, or to politics. Meissner grew up in Milwaukee, the daughter of German immigrants, and attended the University of Wisconsin, where she met her husband, an economist who would later work at the World Bank. When he left for a tour in Vietnam, she stayed in Madison, earning a master's degree in political science and managing a political campaign. Her candidate, for the State Assembly, was a progressive woman running on an anti-war platform who went on to defeat a twenty-year incumbent. In Washington, DC, where Meissner moved once her husband returned, she helped found and head the National Women's Political Caucus; its mission was to support female congressional candidates whom both the Democratic and Republican establishments turned down as unlikely to succeed.

Meissner had served in the Justice Department in the spring of 1975, when Saigon fell, ending the Vietnam War and creating hundreds of thousands of refugees who had been loyal to the US-backed government of South Vietnam. The humanitarian crisis, which lasted for years, was a further blight on American involvement in the region. The State Department desperately tried to convince other governments to accept displaced people. But to do so the US had to prove its own commitment to resettle the refugees. The details fell to the attorney general's office and, before long, to Meissner herself.

To prepare for the Refugee Act, there were marathon meetings with officials from the State Department, Health and Human Services, and the INS, followed by tactical discussions with staffers on the Hill, with an eye to congressional vote tallies. While they were finalizing the terms of the bill, one issue struck everyone as tangential. When the US resettled refugees, the government vetted them and brought them into the country. The people who arrived on US soil seeking asylum were another story. The US couldn't control the size or composition of this population.

Members of the administration decided to enshrine the principle of asylum in the statute, making it the first congressional act to mention the concept. The question was, how many people who'd been granted asylum could adjust their legal status each year to become permanent residents? Over the previous decade, roughly two thousand asylum seekers showed up on American soil each year; managing their numbers seemed doable. "Let's be really expansive," Meissner told her counterparts at the State Department. "We'll double it, and then some." The number they arrived at was five thousand. In March 1980, it seemed inconceivable that all those slots could be filled in a single year.

FOUR WEEKS AFTER THE PRESIDENT signed the Refugee Act, Dick Gullage, the deputy chief of the INS's Miami office, began to hear rumors that a few American boats docked in Florida were setting sail for Cuba. Earlier that month, in Havana, ten thousand Cubans had stormed the gates of the Peruvian embassy and refused to leave without a guarantee of safe passage out of the country. The boats leaving Florida were piloted by Cuban Americans who wanted to help. By the time they set off, the State Department had learned that Fidel Castro was planning to allow some of the dissidents to leave from Mariel, a coastal city twenty-five miles west of Havana. "If he does that, we're going to have every boat in South Florida on the way to Cuba, if they can get their relatives out that way," Gullage said.

On April 21, two boats, the *Dos Hermanos* and *Blanche III*, returned to Key West with forty-eight Cubans. A day later, a sixty-foot shrimper called the *Big Baby* returned with two hundred more. Soon, the causeway from Miami to the Florida Keys was jammed with cars hauling boats of every size and shape, from small dinghies to cabin cruisers.

Meissner arrived in Key West in late April, on the orders of the attorney general. By then, several thousand Cubans had arrived. It was becoming clear that Castro was deliberately flooding the Florida ports. The storming of the Peruvian embassy had initially been an embarrassment to the Castro regime, an unsightly display of dissent. But in the middle of an election year, it was Carter who was most vulnerable. The US couldn't deport Cubans because Castro refused to accept them, and the Marielitos, as they were soon called, were coming without identification documents, records, or even verifiable names.

Dozens of INS agents from Chicago, Detroit, El Paso, and San Diego converged on Key West, along with officials from the Federal Emergency Management Agency (FEMA). Together they erected and staffed makeshift holding centers in Key West and at an air force complex in the northern part of the state. When those facilities were filled a few weeks later, agents used the Orange Bowl stadium in Miami and a blimp hangar in Opa-locka.

In a government sedan, Meissner and her colleagues drove right up to the harbor and watched in astonishment as more Cubans than they could count emerged from rafts, fishing vessels, and powerboats. Witnessing the swell of new arrivals, Meissner stared straight at a policy paradox. How did you deal with this, she wondered, without immediately undercutting the principle that migrants had the right to seek protection, a right she had just fought to enshrine in law?

By early May, there were more than fifteen thousand Marielitos, and American authorities were realizing something even more alarming: Castro hadn't simply allowed the ten thousand dissidents who'd amassed at the Peruvian embassy to leave. He was emptying prisons and psychiatric institutions, mixing criminals and mental health patients in with the groups headed for the US. One hundred and twenty-five thousand Cubans arrived in the ensuing six months, and according to the State Department, some forty thousand of them had criminal records. Fewer than half of all the Cubans who arrived had families to receive them; the rest were on their own, meaning US authorities had to figure out where to send them as the crisis continued. The Department of Defense had space for twenty thousand Marielitos at army bases in Wisconsin, Pennsylvania, and Arkansas.

Politically, this was immediately and lastingly toxic. Nineteen thousand Marielitos were being held at a base called Fort Chaffee, in Arkansas. One weekend in May, hundreds of Cubans protesting the prisonlike conditions set fire to the barracks and managed to overtake the gates, escaping down the road. "A lot of those refugees are just thugs," the sheriff of Sebastian County, which included Fort Chaffee, told the public.

Guard posts and additional fencing were installed on the orders of the governor, a thirty-one-year-old, first-term Democrat named Bill Clinton. His Republican opponent for the governor's race that fall, Frank White, had already accused him of failing to "stand up" to the federal authorities. Politicians everywhere were warning their constituents about "undesirable immigrants," and police departments from Los Angeles to New York blamed Marielitos for rising crime rates. For the first time, city and state law enforcement agencies requested partnerships with the INS, sending along the names of prison inmates who were immigrants and thus might be deportable when their criminal sentences expired.

The imagery of rageful, dangerous killers was more than just a political specter used to scare up votes; it swiftly crossed over into the iconography of popular culture. Soon the young movie star Al Pacino—already known for such seminal roles as an idealistic cop, a brooding mob boss, and a rookie bank robber—added a new character to his résumé: Tony Montana, in *Scarface*, a snarling Cuban delinquent with a cocaine addiction and a murderous temper, who comes to Florida during the Mariel boatlift. The movie had been made in the 1930s, by Howard Hawks, with Al Capone as its inspiration; the plotline was updated to track with the times. "When I watched him in rehearsals," Oliver Stone, who wrote the script, later said, "I saw how he turned Tony Montana into something very feral, something immigrant and hungry and decadent."

In the fall of 1980, Clinton lost his bid for reelection—the first, and last, electoral defeat of his career. His vulnerability on immigration wasn't a political experience he'd soon forget. Fourteen years later, when he was president, there'd be another spike in Cuban arrivals as the island's economy cratered. "No new Mariel," White House officials said to each other at the time. "Remember Fort Chaffee."

6.

Pro Bono Coyotes

There was a simple reason Margo Cowan and Lupe Castillo couldn't find the recently arrested Salvadorans in the county jails and Border Patrol outposts in the summer and fall of 1980. The INS was transferring them five hours west to a detention center in a remote patch of Southern California called El Centro, where 85 percent of the detainees were from El Salvador.

The facility was a sparse complex of low-slung buildings. Inside were barracks with two hundred bunk beds, a television, and a single watercooler. But this shaded space was closed during the day, forcing everyone into what passed for a recreation yard: a small square of dirt, with a partial aluminum awning that left most of the six hundred detainees exposed to the elements. The bathrooms and living quarters were not cleaned. Abusive guards were unsupervised, and basic medical services barely existed. Some of the detainees had been stuck there for close to two years, but the fate of most of those who passed through El Centro was swift and unceremonious deportation. Two San Diego–based immigration judges heard seven hundred cases a week, issuing rulings in batches of twenty at a time. In the fall of 1981, when a congressional investigator finally made it to the facility, he reported deportations at a rate of fifty per hour.

The first few times Cowan and Castillo entered the facility, they returned to the parking lot to find the tires of their van slashed. The culprits were INS agents who resented the intrusion of outsiders. These same men observed what the young activists were there to do and belligerently thwarted their work. When the women sat down with clients in a small side office, the guards paraded the center's unruliest detainees outside, making it impossible to talk over the din. Then they crammed so many immigrants inside the room, which was only about a hundred square feet in size, that there wasn't space for the volunteers and translators. Some days, meeting hours were abruptly and inexplicably suspended; without warning, the guards would take two full hours for roll call.

El Centro wasn't a place that typically attracted visitors. A thuggish order prevailed. Many of the judges who came to El Centro to hear cases wore sidearms in a show of bravado.

"Being an American citizen protects you," Cowan said. "When the US picks a fight with you, and you're on the TV saying, 'We're not afraid of you,' then people who are the victims of terrible abuse come to you." This boldness helped them overcome the overwhelming newness of the task at hand, a job for which there was no model or clear legal precedent. Their aim was to stop deportations to El Salvador at all costs. The only way to achieve that was to bond out of detention as many people as they possibly could. "What's the equivalent of throwing a glass on the floor, to stop everything?" Cowan said. "People are telling us terrible things that happen to them and their family members. The first question is how do I protect you?" That required money, between five hundred and a thousand dollars per detainee, and Manzo fundraised with local churches and aid groups in Tucson. To cover shortfalls, the activists took out liens on their homes, trailers, cars, and property.

Every Sunday, a dozen volunteers, led by Cowan or Castillo, would assemble in Tucson and board the Manzo van, a giant Dodge emblazoned with the words *Basta con la migra* (No More Immigration Police). They'd drive all night to a dilapidated roadside motel in the town of El Centro called the Golden West—a ring of rooms around a grimy pool—where they'd set up workstations. The rooms and narrow balconies became makeshift offices, with legal papers piled in mounds on beds and typewriters passed around impatiently so the activists could fill out forms. Some sixty volunteers rotated in and out of the motel in shifts lasting up to two weeks at a time.

None of this was possible, however, without coordination from inside El Centro. Because the representatives from Manzo could only meet with detainees whose full names and alien numbers they had, the Salvadorans in detention needed to smuggle their information beyond the facility's walls to get help. A former student who had first arrived in Tucson in the early months of 1980 contacted Manzo before traveling to Los Angeles to reunite with members of his family. Border Patrol apprehended him on the way and sent him to El Centro. From there he called Cowan and Castillo, who traveled to California to file his asylum application and post his bond. By then he had told the other Salvadorans inside about the two women and had drawn up lists of names and numbers. "This guy who had been an organizer in El Salvador began to organize in El Centro," Castillo said. The earliest waves of asylum seekers tended to be social and political activists in El Salvador. The skills that had led to their persecution helped stave off deportation.

When Cowan and Castillo arrived at El Centro, they requested meetings with the others on the list. Those people, in turn, signed the G-28 forms to make Cowan and Castillo their legal representatives. From then on, a trade took place whenever a volunteer from Manzo entered El Centro to have a client sign a G-28: the detainee would get legal representation, and Manzo would receive more names of future clients, often written on torn-out Bible pages and cigarette wrappers, whatever the detainees had on hand.

Deportation wasn't the only danger Salvadorans faced inside El Centro. There were forms that, if signed, waived the legal right to apply for asylum. Unless they'd been forewarned, the Salvadorans who turned up in El Centro didn't know to insist on applying for asylum, often in the face of intimidating resistance. INS officers rarely asked the new arrivals if they feared deportation and wanted to apply for relief in the US. Much more frequently, they told asylum seekers explicitly that no such right existed, threatening those who objected with indefinite detention or solitary confinement.

The Salvadorans were handed a form in English with a dense block of small English text and a line at the bottom for a signature. The paper was not an asylum application or some sign of impending relief, but an administrative sleight of hand called a "voluntary departure," which immediately fast-tracked their expulsion to El Salvador without an immigration hearing. Not realizing they were waiving their rights, many signed the forms. Hours later, they were on a plane back to San Salvador.

Between 1980 and 1981, this had happened to more than ten thousand of the thirteen thousand Salvadorans apprehended at the border. In October, a woman named Doria Elia Estrada, who'd been arrested near Calexico, California, demanded time to read the full form before signing it. When she was done, she refused to pick up the pen shoved in front of her by the INS agent. In response, he told her that she would be stuck in jail for "a long period of time" and left to fend for herself in a cell filled exclusively with men. It didn't matter what rights she thought she had, he said. Her application for asylum would eventually be rejected anyway, and the US government would share her information with "the authorities in El Salvador."

Inside the detention center, the organizers' most urgent task was to keep people from signing the voluntary-departure documents and to protect those who refused. Cowan and Castillo were developing a broader strategy based on an appropriately jaded appraisal of the INS. They were filing hundreds of asylum applications at a time, even though, as Castillo said, "the government couldn't be trusted in immigration matters." Their own experience at Manzo— the office raid, Cowan's indictment on trumped-up charges, the Border Patrol's use of confidential attorney-client communications—had convinced them to adopt a more oppositional stance to the legal system. It should be subverted rather than abandoned. "We need to push the law to the limits," Castillo said. Cesar Chavez had once told Cowan, "Don't do the same thing twice. They'll know you're coming." Asylum law was still relatively undeveloped. Even with the creation of the Refugee Act, the terms of who should apply for asylum— and how—hadn't yet been defined in practice. "We were not pushing asylum to win," Castillo said. "We were doing it to prevent deportations, to prevent people from being killed."

On an early visit to El Centro, she once asked an official at the facility about a sheet that had appeared in a client's asylum file. It was on State Department letterhead, from an office called the Bureau of Human Rights. The document offered a dry, one-sided synopsis of the situation in El Salvador, with extended references to leftist guerrillas and a besieged government. The information appeared to be based on the American embassy's sources on the ground, but it was at conspicuous odds with the stories the activists had been hearing from newly arrived Salvadorans.

Although the INS officially granted asylum, the State Department controlled the process. These write-ups were the State Department's conclusions about "country conditions" in El Salvador. Couched as recommendations, the reports were supposed to inform the INS officers who made the individual decisions about asylum. In fact, they provided a rationale for the INS to deny asylum and claim the agency's hands were tied. The language was always the same: "Upon careful review of the information submitted, it is our view that the subject has failed to establish a well-founded fear of being persecuted upon return to El Salvador within the meaning of the United Nations Protocol Relating to the Status of Refugees." The Refugee Act was supposed to standardize the terms by which the INS administered asylum law. But, paradoxically, it also supplied the government with a legal pretext for issuing denials. According to the INS, asylum was available only to individuals facing persecution. A crippled economy and an atmosphere of generalized violence were not enough. As the agency's commissioner went on to say, "Basically everyone in the world would be better off in the US."

What struck Castillo wasn't the document itself, or even the central role of the State Department in immigration decisions. It was that the El Centro official had blithely told her about a mimeograph they kept in one of the back offices. "We run these forms off," the official had said. INS was issuing boilerplate responses to reject Salvadorans' asylum applications en masse.

This gave Cowan an idea. If the INS was overloaded with applications, the agency couldn't immediately rule on each case; she could buy her clients time and avert deportations by filing as many as possible, and appealing them to a body called the Board of Immigration Appeals. "The government won't decide if we win or lose" in individual cases, she said. "We'll define success for ourselves. We'll get our clients out of custody" and into the orbit of friends and family members. She called it "moving people off the border."

By the summer of 1981, the activists had secured the release of 150 asylum seekers after paying more than $16,000 in bond and raising an additional $175,000 in collateral. Some of the Salvadorans joined Cowan, Castillo, and the others on buses to Los Angeles and San Francisco, where they reunited with their families. The rest returned with the volunteers to Arizona.

In Tucson, a network of supporters was creating a movement—it lacked a name but already had a cast. One of the main characters was John Fife, a forty-year-old pastor with a salt-and-pepper beard and a penchant for cowboy boots and turquoise belt buckles. At six feet, four inches tall, he was a towering, charismatic presence who resembled, in the words of the journalist Ann Crittenden, "a cowboy dressed in clerical drag." Originally from Western Pennsylvania, Fife had a long history of civil rights and Vietnam War activism. He had first arrived in Tucson a decade earlier to lead Southside Presbyterian, a hardscrabble church on a desolate lot, and had become committed to a host of local causes.

Central America was new to Fife. But in the summer of 1980, he received a call about the disaster at the Organ Pipe Cactus National Monument. The survivors at the hospital in Tucson wanted to speak to a pastor, so he went, expecting to say a few prayers and offer generic words of condolence in broken Spanish. Instead, the survivors shared the stories of why they'd fled El Salvador. It was the first time he'd heard about the death squads and the state security forces. Appalled, he returned to Southside determined to learn more. Through a contact at the Presbyterian church, he located a Salvadoran minister based in San Francisco, who gave Fife a tutorial by phone every few weeks. The conversations revolved around the heroism of Óscar Romero and the tenets of liberation theology, a religious movement within the Catholic Church that took root in Latin America in the late 1960s; at its center was a fierce defense of the poor and an embrace of grassroots activism.

One afternoon in 1981, Fife visited the headquarters of INS in Tucson to ask for advice. He had no reason at first to distrust the immigration authorities, and even less cause for concern after his encounter there. The district director of the office was Bill Johnston, an affable man in his forties with an unlikely profile for the job. A former New York City cabbie, he held a degree in Latin American studies from the University of Texas. His daughter went to high school with Fife's son. "What do we need to do to help people?" Fife asked him. "Well, we have political asylum here," Johnston replied. "You need to form some sort of legal aid organization and help them apply for asylum. Go through the judicial process. That's the best way." The two men struck an agreement. If Fife could file asylum applications on behalf of apprehended Salvadorans, Johnston would release them from custody and allow them to stay in Fife's church while they waited for a hearing.

For months, the arrangement worked as planned, and Southside began to fill up with Salvadoran asylum seekers. It started slowly, with Fife opening a small apartment situated in the back of the church building; as the numbers grew, many slept on the floor of the chapel. While Cowan and Castillo were working to spring Salvadorans from detention, Fife became their conduit to the religious community in Tucson and to a coalition of clergy called the Tucson Ecumenical Council. With their help, he raised thousands of dollars for bond, and found churches and religious centers that could house the Salvadorans who'd been released from custody.

Another spirited participant in these early maneuvers was James Corbett, a diminutive, middle-aged Quaker and rancher with a Harvard divinity degree, who wanted to help Salvadorans stuck in Nogales cross into the US. At Manzo, Castillo showed him how to fill out the G-28 forms and took him across the border to meet Quiñones at Our Lady of Guadalupe church. His Spanish was a bit ragged, spoken with an ungainly American accent, but he made himself understood. After shadowing Quiñones on a visit to the local prison, he began making the trip himself, dressed in black so the prison guards would assume he was a minister. He introduced himself as Padre Jaime.

Corbett found hundreds of Central Americans who'd been caught in Northern Mexico. Mexican authorities would automatically send them to the Guatemala border, even though some had valid travel visas. In a few instances, Corbett met Salvadorans whom Border Patrol agents had apprehended within a few miles of Mexico and simply handed off to the Mexicans for swifter deportation. Corbett came away from his trips to Nogales convinced that Border Patrol was illegally preventing Salvadorans from asking for asylum at the ports of entry. In the borderlands, far from any form of oversight or public scrutiny, the disconnect between the law and its practice was stark, so Corbett decided to game the broken system. He prepared asylum applications for the Salvadorans he met in Mexico, then shuttled the migrants across the border himself—straight to the Tucson INS office, where Johnston had his ongoing agreement with Fife.

In the summer of 1981, two things upended Fife's and Corbett's plans. The first involved the asylum applications filed with the INS: all of them were being rejected. Learning this was a particular blow to Fife and Corbett, who were newcomers to legal advocacy and hadn't expected such a total failure through official channels. (More experienced, Cowan and Castillo were disappointed but hardly surprised.) The second development was even more dramatic. On June 27, Corbett took three Central Americans to INS headquarters to lodge their asylum claims. Rather than release the men as he had before, Johnston took them into custody, setting bond at three thousand dollars per person and sending them to El Centro. According to Johnston, the State Department had given the order.

Corbett became convinced that he, Fife, and the others had to go underground to protect the asylum seekers who arrived in the American borderlands. This would be a pro bono coyote operation, Corbett said. The activists would help Salvadorans cross into the US, then hide them in people's homes and in churches until there was a safe way to transport them into the interior of the country, where immigration enforcement was scant. Fife was skeptical at first, but he came around to the idea that October.

One evening, the two men were standing on Corbett's ranch, a dusty expanse with trailers and adobe *casitas*. Twenty-one Salvadorans were staying on the property, crammed into one of the houses and sharing a single bathroom. "I don't think we have any choice," Corbett told Fife. The two agreed that the other strategies—the bond push, flooding the immigration system with asylum claims—bought them time, but not enough; the deportations would inevitably ramp up within months.

"So, how the hell do you figure, Jim?" Fife asked. He understood what Corbett wanted to do and couldn't think of a better alternative himself. The two men were close, and each knew how to draw the other out. Corbett shifted the conversation away from logistics and toward history. He mentioned the abolitionist movement and the creation of the underground railroad. "As I read history, those folks were faithful. They were the ones who got it. They got the faith right," Corbett said. He mentioned the Holocaust and how the church had failed to protect the Jews in the 1930s and '40s; it was an indelible case of the church "getting it wrong."

"That's how I read history, too, Jim," Fife replied.

Corbett looked him in the eye. "I don't think we can allow that to happen on our border in our time, can we?"

7.

We Can't Stop, but Do We Have Any Other Choice?

The Carter administration had been full of reluctant Cold Warriors—officials who envisioned a human rights–driven foreign policy but still had conventional fears about the rise of socialism. Reagan had no such ambivalence. He entered office spoiling for a fight in Central America and wasted no time filling his administration with hardliners and ideologues who would declare total war against communism in the president's name.

His choice for secretary of state, the brash, barrel-chested general Alexander Haig, had been a commander in Vietnam and an instigator of Nixon's Saturday Night Massacre. He saw Soviet diplomacy as a "test of wills" that the US had been failing since the fall of Saigon. "The fires of insurrection fed by the Soviets and fanned by their surrogates, the Cubans, spread unchecked in Central America," he said. The region was a "strategic choke point" in the wider war with the Soviet Union, a "hinge area for vital American interests." The two countries of greatest concern to Haig were Nicaragua and El Salvador. In Managua, it had been more than a year since the leftist Sandinistas had overthrown the dictator. The White House wanted to dislodge them from power. Three hundred miles west, in San Salvador, American allies were in charge, but at war.

In January 1981, Salvadoran guerrillas from the Farabundo Martí National Liberation Front (FMLN) launched a major offensive to make gains on the battlefield before Reagan—"that fanatic," they called him—took office later in the month. The effect of their incursion, however, was to make Carter skittish in his final days. Top officials in his administration had grown alarmed that the Salvadoran government might collapse and that the outgoing White House would be blamed for it. After years of withholding lethal military assistance over human rights concerns, the State Department reversed itself, freeing up the Pentagon to ready $6 million. Carter invoked emergency provisions in the Foreign Assistance Act to deliver the money without congressional authorization.

The guerrillas had hoped to spark popular insurrections in urban areas throughout the country, just as the Sandinistas had in Nicaragua a year and a half earlier. But the ranks of the military didn't split apart; while some progressive officers defected the majority stood firm. The FMLN changed tack, aiming to cause chaos and bleed the military of money and resources. They cut power lines, burned crops, and attacked isolated garrisons of soldiers. The Salvadoran army had seventeen thousand troops nationwide, a substantial edge in manpower and in resources. Yet these men were poorly trained and often unmotivated; the military brass was easily flummoxed. The generals defended major cities and towns while ceding large parts of the countryside to the guerrillas, whose power grew by the day.

In February, when American military advisers analyzed the situation, the Defense Department concluded that the Salvadoran regime was simply "not organized to fight an insurgency." It had "no hope" of outlasting the guerrillas unless military leadership was completely overhauled. The US had been propping up a corrupt and openly repressive officer corps out of fear that reforming the military would risk destabilizing it. The result, one US official wrote at the start of Reagan's term, was an army "sitting in garrisons abusing civilians" rather than combating the guerrillas.

The Reagan administration did not care about human rights, but it was preoccupied by the operational shortcomings of its Salvadoran partners; the issues were related. Whole divisions of the army were little more than fronts for the death squads, and military conscripts, many of whom were poor teenage peasants who'd been threatened and tortured into joining, were undisciplined soldiers.

Haig was so frustrated that he entertained the possibility of invading Cuba to disrupt its support for the FMLN. "You just give me the word," he told the president. "I'll turn that fucking island into a parking lot." It took the secretary of defense and the joint chiefs of staff—unlikely voices of restraint—to override him. By the fall of 1981, the National Security Council had come up with a temporary solution: the US would give up to $300 million in economic aid to governments in Central America and the Caribbean, as well as a large share of emergency military funds to El Salvador and Honduras, which was becoming the staging ground for military operations in El Salvador and Nicaragua. The US would increase its military training program in El Salvador and bring Salvadoran troops and officers to the US for further instruction.

One recipient of this infusion of money and advisers was an elite unit inside the Salvadoran military called the Atlacatl Battalion. US personnel trained the outfit in counterinsurgency operations, making it the first of its kind in El Salvador. The Atlacatl's stated mission was to serve as a "rapid deployment infantry" brigade that crisscrossed the country in response to guerrilla incursions. But Salvadoran military officials saw the matter in grander terms. "The subversives like to say they are the fish and the people are the ocean," one group of officers told a US delegation in February 1981. "What we have done in the north is dry up the ocean so we can catch the fish easily." Commanding troops in the Cabañas Department, near the Honduras border, was an officer named Sigifredo Ochoa Pérez. The Americans loved him for his fierce reliability. "He has the best organized patrols in the country, loyal to a man and tougher than lizard lips," a US Army senior adviser to the Salvadorans said at the time. On November 11, Ochoa led twelve hundred troops into the hamlet of Santa Cruz on the pretense of rooting out guerrillas. Over the next two weeks, they annihilated multiple villages in the area. Women and children fled en masse, hiding in the surrounding hillsides from helicopter and airplane fire. Scores of innocent villagers were killed, and dozens more crossed into Honduras.

The American military knew about operations like these—it had assigned at least ten military advisers to monitor the actions of the Atlacatl Battalion—but looked the other away. On the morning of December 8, three thousand Salvadoran troops led by the Atlacatl Battalion entered a string of remote mountain hamlets in the Morazán Department, in the eastern reaches of the country. It was part of a counterinsurgency campaign called Operation Rescue, aimed at reclaiming parts of the countryside from the guerrillas. Peasants in rural areas regularly ran the risk of being targeted by the military as guerrilla sympathizers, but in several of the towns, including one called El Mozote, residents felt they were protected. They'd always distanced themselves from the guerrillas, not wanting to provoke the government. When they learned that soldiers were closing in, they decided to stay put rather than abandon their homes.

The Salvadoran colonel in charge of the operation was a slight, wispy officer with a dark complexion and big ears who hardly looked the part. His name was Domingo Monterrosa. He was something of a cultish figure inside the Salvadoran military. On tactical matters, he cultivated a philosophical air, which he matched with a high-wire sense of bravado in the field. He invited reporters with him onto his helicopter, posed for photographs, and dilated colorfully at impromptu press conferences. In the words of one fawning US military attaché, he was "a hotshot strategist . . . whom I'd put up against any American hotshot."

It was around five in the morning, on December 11, when the soldiers began rounding up the villagers of El Mozote and separating the men from the women and children. The men were marched to the village's lone church and eventually lined up and executed; the women were taken to the hills, where they were raped and burned alive. On Monterrosa's orders, the soldiers advanced to the other villages over the next two days, killing everyone they encountered and setting fire to the homes. Monterrosa had a word for such an operation—it was, he told his subordinates, a *limpieza*, or cleansing. By the end of the campaign, at least 978 people were dead, including 477 children under the age of twelve.

A thirty-eight-year-old mother of two named Rufina Amaya, whose children and husband were killed in front of her, was the lone survivor of the massacre at El Mozote. A month later, she met two war reporters—Raymond Bonner, an American working for *The New York Times*, and Mexican journalist Alma Guillermoprieto, a freelancer for *The Washington Post*. Each had traveled independently to El Mozote, where they found scenes of devastation: homes razed, the church destroyed, scattered corpses rotting in the sun. At the center of El Mozote, beside a demolished sacristy, bones, severed limbs, and pieces of flesh jutted from the rubble; the corpses of children were still clothed. The soldiers hadn't bothered to bury any of their victims, or to hide the evidence of their atrocities.

Both newspapers ran the story on their front pages on January 27, 1982, the day before Ronald Reagan was planning to send a formal notice to Congress announcing that El Salvador was "making a concerted and significant effort to comply with internationally recognized human rights." Every six months, the president needed to provide an official reassurance, known as "certification," to lawmakers; in exchange, they sent millions of dollars of aid money to the Salvadoran government. The back-and-forth was pure theater. There was a slate of conditions with which the Salvadorans had to comply, including a vow to exercise "substantial control" over the military. But it was the White House's responsibility to confirm that these terms were being met, and Congress had to take the president's word for it. The Democrats had been too timid to challenge the White House on foreign policy, so they had never pushed for a legislative veto of the president's determination. Now, in the middle of this biannual, face-saving charade, the American press was reporting about a massacre perpetrated by soldiers who'd been specially trained and overseen by the US military.

Human remains from the El Mozote massacre.
Morazán Department, El Salvador, 1982.

The pushback from the administration was swift and ruthlessly effective. It denied everything, pointing to an obscure cable written by two American embassy officials who, "as the eyes and ears" of the US government, traveled with Salvadoran military personnel to evaluate the reports. The Americans were skittish about visiting areas controlled by the guerrillas, so they didn't get close to any of the killing sites. Afterward, they wrote that "it is not possible to prove or disprove excesses of violence." The ambiguous language of the cable served as the justification the administration officials needed. In their telling, reports about the massacre were little more than guerrilla propaganda disseminated on the eve of the certification process to embarrass the president. There had likely been a "firefight" between the army and guerrillas, but "no evidence" of a massacre, according to Elliott Abrams, the assistant secretary of state for Human Rights and Humanitarian Affairs. He attacked the veracity of the *Times* and *Post* stories and questioned the credibility of the reporters who wrote them. The certification went forward. Within a few months, the executive editor of the *Times* had ordered Bonner back to New York.

The title of Abrams's post at the State Department was something of a misnomer by the time Reagan took office. His predecessor in the job, under Carter, was Patricia Derian, a southerner who had spent her pre-government years working as a civil rights activist in Mississippi. With her at the helm, the office grew and gained stature during the four years of Carter's presidency. But when Abrams assumed control, the human rights bureau adopted an overtly political mission. A Harvard-educated lawyer from New York, Abrams was Reagan's chief combatant. He was a disaffected Democrat, alienated by Carter's foreign policy, who saw Central America as his proving ground. In the early 1980s, much of Abrams's work consisted of rebutting, before Congress and in the press, evidence of atrocities committed by the Salvadoran government.

He was also denying another growing body of evidence that began to dog the US government: an ever-larger number of Salvadorans being deported from the US were being killed upon their return. By the end of 1981, stories were beginning to appear in newspapers and human rights digests that government soldiers were murdering deportees. Soldiers lay in wait for planes to touch down. The bodies were discarded along the highway near the airport. Abrams rejected the claims as supposition. But, unlike the evidence of faraway massacres, which was easier for Washington to obfuscate, the proof of the deportee murders came directly from the mouths of Salvadoran soldiers themselves.

One of them was José Rosales, a twenty-seven-year-old sergeant from a poor corner of Santa Ana. The son of peasants, he joined the army in 1970, at the age of sixteen, and stayed on mostly because he had never met or heard of anyone who'd left the military alive. As he moved up the ranks, his responsibilities grew, and with them came opportunities to befriend other members of the officer corps. The death squads, he learned, were referred to simply as military missions; they were routine. When he volunteered for one detail, in March 1980, a National Guardsman gave him his orders and an army colonel conducted the mission. The man they apprehended was thirty-seven, under suspicion of something, but Rosales was never told what. He watched as the others drove a nail through the man's nostril, broke all his fingers, and stabbed him with a hypodermic needle. The torture lasted for two hours before they shot him and stole his watch.

Afterward, Rosales realized that one reason so many soldiers volunteered for the death squad missions was for the chance to rob their victims. Over time, he came to feel that all young men in El Salvador, from teenagers to thirty-year-olds, ran the risk of persecution at the hands of the military. Having volunteered for the army, Rosales was an exception. It was much more common for the military to kidnap teenagers right off the streets, often outside movie theaters or eateries, and then to torture them on army bases until they agreed to serve. Anyone who didn't was killed on the spot.

The dangers were magnified for deportees. At the end of 1979, one of Rosales's superiors explained the logic to him while they were stationed at the San Salvador airport. Together with a group of soldiers, he was supposed to wait for a plane to land with nine deportees who were being returned from Mexico. If someone was deported it confirmed that he'd first tried to escape El Salvador, which meant he was presumed to be a leftist, an immediate death sentence. The protocol was to take deportees into custody for an "investigation." A seasoned soldier like Rosales would have understood the translation: forced disappearances, which began with torture and ended in death. A few days later, the body would appear by the roadside and local newspapers would publish photographs that family members used to identify the remains.

The new US Refugee Act—designed to help immigrants persecuted for their membership in a "particular social group"—was marking the Salvadorans who sought protection under it. To have set foot in the US, then been cast back out into the war zone, led straight to government-sanctioned murder. Whatever Elliott Abrams told Congress or the press, the Reagan administration knew the reality. INS heard it firsthand from Rosales in the fall of 1981 when the young soldier gave a signed and sworn affidavit to officials in San Mateo, California. Unable to stomach the daily operations of the Salvadoran military, he had decided to flee, and was now seeking asylum himself.

◇—◇

The toughest hurdle for Fife to clear in his early days as a "pro bono coyote" was the inevitability that he'd be caught. He didn't know how or when it would happen, but to do the work, he could not have illusions about getting away with it. For every "alien" he helped cross, the punishment consisted of a two-thousand-dollar fine and up to five years in prison. Yet he was smuggling Central Americans across the border because their lives depended on it. The urgency of the mission was liberating. When he thought about it as an imperative, not a gamble, his nervousness solidified into resolve.

The group's main activity took place in Nogales, where members of Father Quiñones's church knew the border better than anyone. They could show the Salvadorans the best spots to cross at breaks in the fencing or along patches that the Border Patrol tended to neglect. (Agents "were easy to fool," Cowan said. "They were like Texas Rangers who got lost. They acted with a lot of bravado and machismo, but it was very easy to move people.") The destination for the immigrants was the tallest landmark on the Arizona side: the bell tower of the Sacred Heart church, where they were instructed to wait under the care of the local pastor while Fife and the others drove in from Tucson to pick them up. If they were caught, the migrants had received a simple directive: claim to be Mexican, so that the agents would drop them off across the border rather than deport them.

The activists usually worked in pairs. Manning what they called the "scout car," one driver would serve as a lookout for Border Patrol checkpoints along the highway to Tucson. That person would call the church from a pay phone along the route to confirm that it was safe to proceed. Twice a week, Fife took his white Chevy LUV pickup truck.

In mid-December 1981, an attorney for the INS approached Margo Cowan at a hearing at the federal courthouse in Tucson. "We know what you're doing," he had told her. Agents had been arresting migrants who were carrying Corbett's phone number in their pockets. A few days later, Cowan, Castillo, Corbett, and a few other members of the Tucson Ecumenical Council held an emergency meeting in Fife's living room.

"We can't stop, but do we have any other choice?" Fife asked the group. Everyone agreed that they needed to go public. But how could they generate attention without immediately getting blocked by the INS? The idea came to Fife as a recollection rather than as a revelation. A few months earlier, he had received a letter from a Lutheran pastor in Los Angeles who described an incident in East LA. INS agents had chased a Salvadoran teenager into his church, eventually dragging him out in handcuffs. Members of the church were outraged that the agents had violated a sacred space, and when the pastor wrote the local INS office to complain, the district director apologized and promised to forbid his agents from making arrests in churches, schools, or hospitals. "This order, in essence, is saying the church is a sanctuary, but it is not established as law," the pastor wrote. Fife had initially thrown out the letter on account of its final few paragraphs: the pastor had traced the history of church sanctuary all the way back to the Middle Ages, which struck Fife as academic and naive. But now the concept made more sense. They could continue to help Central Americans cross the border, then give them sanctuary. Using the church as a public platform would be a form of protection and a statement of principle.

In January, at the annual meeting of his congregation, Fife brought the proposal up for a vote, but not before his parishioners asked a string of unanswerable questions. Was it possible the whole church might be prosecuted for breaking the law? He had to admit he wasn't sure. Could other churches join Southside, so that it didn't have to act alone? "I hadn't even thought of

Reverend John Fife speaks outside the Southside United Presbyterian Church in Tucson, Arizona, announcing the start of the Sanctuary Movement, on March 24, 1982. He is joined by "Alfredo" (left), a Salvadoran refugee using a pseudonym for his own protection.

that," Fife replied. "But that's a great idea." After four hours of discussion, followed by a secret ballot, the proposition passed—with fifty-nine people in favor, two against, and four abstentions. Members of the Tucson Ecumenical Council contacted several other churches across the country that had also been unofficially housing Central American refugees. The institutions were in liberal enclaves far from Tucson—San Francisco, Boston, Washington, DC, and Berkeley, California. All the churches agreed to hold a public ceremony announcing their intention to provide sanctuary. The date they selected was March 24, 1982, the second anniversary of the assassination of Óscar Romero.

When the day finally came, Fife and the others had already contacted reporters and sent out letters announcing their plans to the attorney general, the US attorney in Arizona, the state's congressmen, and the heads of the INS and Border Patrol. "We take this action because we believe the current policy and practice of the United States Government with regard to Central American refugees is illegal and immoral," the letters said. "We believe our government is in violation of the 1980 Refugee Act and international law by continuing to arrest, detain, and forcibly return refugees to terror, persecution, and murder in El Salvador and Guatemala." The activists also proposed a moratorium on deportations for the duration of the war, known as "extended voluntary departure," which Fife and Corbett had first heard about from Bill Johnston, the INS official in Tucson. Until their terms were met, the letters stated, "we will not cease to extend the sanctuary of the church to undocumented people from Central America," adding, "Obedience to God requires this of us all."

That morning, at a table set up in front of Southside's chapel, Fife, Cowan, and Corbett were joined by a thirty-year-old Salvadoran man dressed in a cowboy hat with a bandanna covering his face. He went by the pseudonym Alfredo—a necessary precaution, Fife told the assembled press, because the Salvadoran military might attack his family at home. Alfredo would be staying in Southside as its first official beneficiary of sanctuary. In El Salvador, he had worked for the government agency in charge of agrarian reform, making him the target of death threats from members of the military and the far right. (A year before, the Salvadoran head of the land reform program was murdered by military gunmen while having dinner at the Sheraton Hotel in San Salvador with two Americans affiliated with the AFL-CIO who were also killed.) The *Tucson Citizen* wrote afterward that Alfredo was "one of the most publicized undocumented aliens here ever."

8.

They Don't Even Let You Fuck in Peace

Juan Romagoza spent forty-eight hours in the coffin, cocooned in total darkness. His right leg and left arm throbbed with sharp, stabbing pains. The cuts on his forehead burned. It had been nearly three weeks since his arrest. He weighed seventy-five pounds. He started to go limp; his mind unstuck itself from his body. It felt like he was levitating, his limbs and torso floating and bobbing through space. He knew he was still alive because he kept asking himself the same question: *Am I still alive?* As long as it was still a question, he had his answer.

Suddenly there was a rustling sound followed by a flood of blinding light. A door had opened. Juan couldn't see what was happening, but he felt a pair of hands grab him from under his arms and lift him up. Squinting through the glare, he made out the face of one of his uncles—Manuel Rafael Arce, the economist and lieutenant colonel.

His uncle didn't say a word as he held Juan to his chest. They moved from the coffin room into a long hallway and then a parking lot, where a car was waiting. Juan struggled to focus over Arce's shoulder, but managed to spot his other uncle, the medical doctor, standing alongside Vides Casanova, who stared back impassively.

When the government had contacted Juan's parents, an official from the National Guard had told them he was dead but didn't elaborate. The night before coming to San Salvador they had asked for a ride from a friend with a spacious car, to make room for a casket. Juan's mother brought a sheaf of identification documents to claim the body. She and her husband were waiting across the street, beyond the view of the military barracks. Only when Juan emerged in his uncle's arms did they discover he was alive.

Being freed from the military's custody did not mean Juan was out of danger. Usually, a prisoner's official release was merely a prelude: within days, if not hours, soldiers in the death squads would finish the job. Juan's uncles could not protect him from what was coming.

Arce took him to the house of Juan's oldest brother, Enrique, near the university in San Salvador. Enrique lived with his wife, her mother, and the family's three children. It was risky for anyone to be caught helping Juan after his release, so Enrique decided to keep him in the house for a single night before driving him to Usulután, where a wider network of friends could provide clandestine shelter. When Juan's parents arrived, they were beaming with relief. They hugged him, said a litany of prayers, then left. They needed to get back to Usulután to plan for hiding Juan the next day.

Juan and Enrique traveled by ambulance to the hospital where their aunt worked as a lab supervisor. She was waiting in a white coat with a colleague from Usulután when they arrived. There wasn't time for a full examination, and Juan couldn't risk being seen. In between a series of blood tests, his aunt wheeled him around on a gurney under a pile of blankets, while he pretended to be unconscious. The wound on his foot was infected and festering, but he'd have to seek treatment later. When he and Enrique set out the following morning in his brother's old car, he sat slumped in the back seat, with a full cast on his left arm, a splint and IV bag with antibiotics attached to his ankle, and bandages wrapped around his head.

Juan arrived in Usulután on January 6, 1981, just four days before the FMLN guerrillas launched their counteroffensive against the government forces. Once the fighting began, a curfew went into effect: no one was allowed out after six in the evening. The army had a large barracks in the city from which soldiers increased their street patrols.

Juan's family planned to move him every few days to a different house, avoiding the obvious places, such as his parents' home, where the death squads would come to look for him. He started with his twin sister, Morena Guadalupe, an executive secretary with a family of her own, who agreed to protect him for a few days in her house in a commercial district in the center of town. Juan taught her a technique to dress his wounds that stabilized his ankle with a splint while keeping it exposed to the air. There were no orthopedic specialists in Usulután, and it was worryingly obvious that some drastic surgical intervention was necessary to save his foot from amputation.

Two doctors he knew visited every few days, dressed as domestic workers with white smocks over their clothes. They couldn't do much beyond removing some of the dead and rotting tissue where the bullet had first entered his foot. When it was time for Juan to move to the next safe house, someone would carry him to a waiting car. They'd set out just after dawn, when the streets were still empty.

Over the next two months, Juan's life followed an excruciating rhythm. Long bouts of interminable boredom, days on end bedridden and befogged by pain, followed by a morning adrenaline rush as he moved to a new location, where the waiting would begin again. Each place he went had its advantages and disadvantages. A family friend, who owned a pharmacy, was on good terms with local members of the National Guard. Her residence was comparatively safe, but unusually cramped. Another neighbor lived in a more spacious home right next to the army barracks, where the obvious risks of proximity were balanced by an element of surprise: the security forces would never expect Juan to stay so close.

It was here, at the house of an old friend called Marta Molina, where his cover was almost blown. One day, several guerrilla fighters, who made periodic stun raids on government posts throughout the department, crept into the city and launched a fusillade of bazooka blasts at the army barracks. Troops went door-to-door in the neighborhood to see who was harboring the shooters.

When Molina heard them coming, she instructed Juan to strip down to his underwear and cover himself with a blanket. She unlocked the front door, took off her shirt, and climbed into bed with him. The soldiers stormed in without knocking, entering to find Molina and Juan together under the covers. "Damn it," she shouted. "Here they don't even let you fuck in peace!" The soldiers left, stammering apologies.

The wounds worsened. Juan's only option was to go to Mexico for emergency medical treatment. But how to get there? A lifeline materialized in the form of a close family friend named Margarita Ortíz, a savvy forty-year-old merchant with a discreet reputation for smuggling activists, unionists, and catechists out of the country for their safety. She transported people while delivering goods in her truck to markets in Guatemala and Mexico, and she was, Juan knew, an expert in the *mordida*, or bribe.

Customs officials at the border as well as soldiers at each country's internal checkpoints tended to be corrupt and exacting. The only way past them was to pay up. The slightest pause communicated doubt or intransigence, reminding the soldiers of the unadulterated power they wielded over civilian travelers. Ortíz lulled the agents by talking in relaxed circles and exuding confidence. She could be firm, coquettish, and vulgar in equal measure. As she darted around in conversation, she would nonchalantly hand over her passport with cash folded neatly inside.

Ortíz presented the plan for Juan's escape. It would take place during Holy Week, in April, when the streets of the city were filled with people. Juan would hide in the back of her pickup truck, under dozens of bags of onions, which she would bring to a market in the middle of Guatemala City. Two other men would join him: a tailor in his sixties who had once belonged to the Communist Party and was now on a government hit list, and a high school activist. They would stop in Guatemala so Ortíz could unload the onions and buy wares to take to Mexico City to sell; she'd leave the three men in the care of her nephew, who'd been living there for months after he himself had fled, also with Ortíz's help.

The evening before Juan left, he relocated to his parents' house to spend one final night with them. He hadn't seen them since January 5, when they briefly reunited in Enrique's apartment in San Salvador. In the three months since then, Juan's mother had prepared food for him every day, and had different people deliver it to him in hiding.

When Juan arrived at his childhood home it was just before the evening curfew, and the sun was sinking. His mother fussed over Juan's favorite dinner—corn tamales with frijoles and queso fresco—and the gentle thrum of activity helped calm everyone down.

This was both a homecoming and a departure, a reunion and a rupture. They tried to talk about the affairs of the town and the latest news involving their friends and neighbors—anything to keep the conversation from the topic of when they might see each other again. Their gestures underlined everything that was amiss. Chiefly, there was Juan's own family, his girlfriend and their five-month-old daughter, who were unreachable in Chalatenango, a combat zone. There was no way to send them word that he was alive, or to confirm that they were. All Juan could hope for was to recuperate in Mexico and for the war to die down so he could seek them out.

That night, Juan slept outside under the mango tree where he used to hide out as a boy when his grandmother got angry with him. Its branches had grown since then and extended into the neighbors' yard. This was one last precaution in case soldiers turned up at the house. If they did, he'd climb the tree just as he used to do as a child, and sneak over the back wall of the property.

9.

The Guatemalan Solution

There were two powers running Guatemala after the Second World War, and only one of them was the government. The other was an American corporation called the United Fruit Company, known inside the country as the Octopus because it had tentacles everywhere. It was Guatemala's largest employer and landowner, controlling the country's only Atlantic port, almost every mile of the railroads, and the nation's sole telephone and telegraph facilities. US State Department officials had siblings in the upper ranks of the company. Senators held stock. Running United Fruit's publicity department in New York was a legendary adman who claimed to have a list of twenty-five thousand journalists, editors, and public figures at his beck and call. They formed, in his words, "an invisible government" with "true ruling power" over the US, to say nothing of the countries under American sway.

By 1952, the president of Guatemala, Jacobo Árbenz, only the second democratically elected president in the country's history, was trying to get United Fruit to pay taxes on its vast holdings. Not only had the company been exempt for decades; it had also secured a guarantee to pay its employees no more than fifty cents a day. In response, United Fruit unleashed a relentless lobbying campaign to persuade journalists, lawmakers, and the US government that Árbenz was a Communist sympathizer who needed to be overthrown. It didn't matter that in a country of some three million people, the Communist Party had only about four thousand members. The start of the Cold War made American officials into easy marks. "We should regard Guatemala as a prototype area for testing means and methods of combating Communism," a member of Dwight Eisenhower's National Security Council said, in 1953.

Over the following year, the CIA and the United Fruit Company auditioned figures to lead a "Liberation" force against the government. They eventually landed on Carlos Castillo Armas, a rogue Guatemalan military officer with dark, diminutive features and a toothbrush mustache, who came across as flighty and dim. "He looked like he had been packaged by Bloomingdale's," one commentator said at the time. His chief qualification was his willingness to do whatever the Americans told him. In June 1954, after an invasion staged with American bombers and choreographed by the US ambassador, he was rewarded with the presidency. Árbenz was flown into Mexican exile, but not before Castillo Armas forced him to strip to his underwear for the cameras as he boarded the plane. The State Department helped select the members of Castillo Armas's cabinet.

Castillo Armas availed himself of American help for the short time he clung to power. In August 1954, with the CIA providing technical support, his government passed a "Law against Communism" that created a blacklist of some seventy thousand suspected leftists. The legal charge was a "grave presumption of dangerousness," which the government invoked to ban them from employment and detain them indefinitely. Naturally, this was a pretext for rounding up enemies, critics, and anyone else who might arouse the suspicions of the exceedingly paranoid men in the National Palace. The database used for the blacklist remained intact through the 1980s, and was eventually known as the Diario Militar, although Castillo Armas didn't live to use it. He was assassinated in 1957—replaced by another right-winger handpicked by the Americans.

The prevailing ideology was less a belief structure than a blueprint for a police state. In 1963, the CIA intervened again, this time to prevent Juan José Arévalo, Árbenz's predecessor and political mentor, from returning to the country to run for reelection. Three years later, on the eve of another election, in which the front-runner was a civilian reformer, the agency sent one of its "fixers" to work alongside the Guatemalan military on a campaign known as *La Limpieza*, a social cleansing that consisted of arrests, tortures, and executions. "The counterinsurgency campaign is out of control," a US intelligence report acknowledged in 1967. At the same time, a State Department official praised the Guatemalan military for its "successful use of terror" in disappearing "real and alleged communists."

Armed resistance to the military was perhaps inevitable; the irony was in who led it. The first revolutionaries to emerge in the 1960s weren't leftist ideologues but military officers who felt that the regime had sacrificed the country's sovereignty to the US. At first the fighting was confined almost entirely to a few towns in the east. The overall threat to the military was minimal, but the government's disproportionate response ignited a broader uprising in the capital among students, professors, and union leaders. The effect was a feedback loop in which the military, seeing threats everywhere, redoubled its crackdown.

From the Americans, the Guatemalan army received extensive training, napalm, radar technology, and planes—a good deal of them transferred to the country directly from US installations in Vietnam. Local bombing operations in Guatemala were frequently run out of US bases in Panama. The guerrillas fought back with targeted kidnappings, assassinations, and bank robberies, but were quickly overwhelmed. By the end of the decade, the revolutionary movement was in shambles, with whole segments of the urban opposition decimated. The military and its death squads had murdered almost the entire leadership of the labor movement as well as the upper ranks of the moderate political parties.

IN 1976, Juan traveled to Guatemala for the first time and barely made it out alive. Determined to finish his medical degree, he had decided to leave San Salvador, where federal troops had once again occupied the university, and to travel to Mexico City to enroll at the National Autonomous University of Mexico. On his way, he stopped in Guatemala City to visit a friend, another medical student driven to leave El Salvador a few years before. One night walking to dinner in the center of the city's downtown, Juan was stopped by a group of police officers, who asked him for his identity papers. He was carrying an ID card from medical school. "So you're a student," one of them said. "A communist."

He was eventually taken to a new facility on the outskirts of the capital. It was called Pavón, which the Guatemalan government was touting as one of the biggest prisons in the region, capable of holding a thousand prisoners at a time. After the prison guards learned he was a medical student, Juan was made to conduct medical exams on the other inmates. This was a privilege and a form of protection. He was granted, for example, a spot on the floor where he could lie down each night, unlike the others, who were packed together so tightly in their cells that they had to sleep sitting up. But the guards found other ways of tormenting him. Most of the time, he was ordered to perform gratuitous rectal exams. The full-time doctors showed up every few weeks. In a metal bowl in the infirmary, syringes were collected to be reused. Many of the people who entered the facility never left. Juan was saved by some well-placed calls made by his uncles in El Salvador, but he was there for three months.

The ride to Guatemala in the spring of 1981 was long, bumpy, and uncomfortable, and the three men in the back of Margarita Ortíz's truck spent the journey in silence. Nothing could distract them from the thought of where they were. To be on the lam in Guatemala was only a modest improvement on hiding out in El Salvador. Guatemala's security forces weren't just allies of the Salvadoran military; they were the envy of the Salvadoran officer corps, many of whom dreamed of a form of governance modeled on what they called the "Guatemalan solution," a state of total, unchecked military control.

ORTÍZ DROVE TO A run-down commercial district of Guatemala City made up of gas stations, strip clubs, and decrepit old buildings. She left Juan and the others to go sell her onions at a nearby market and returned a few hours later with the first of several batches of artisanal crafts and trinkets. In 1976, an earthquake measuring 7.5 on the Richter scale devastated the country, killing more than twenty thousand people and wounding some seventy thousand. The epicenter was about a hundred miles from Guatemala City, but the wreckage was still visible on the streets half a decade later. Buildings were in disrepair. Residents who had been displaced from the shanties ringing the city were seeking out new places to sleep. The electrical grid, water supply, and telephone system worked intermittently. Juan split a room with the other men at a fleabag motel near a loud, crowded bus station and commercial hub called La

Terminal. They would spend a few weeks there while Ortíz plotted the next leg of their trip.

Three years before, Fernando Romeo Lucas García, an army general and former defense minister, won a sham election and initiated one of the most violent periods of repression in decades. His civilian vice president, a liberal-minded international law expert, joined the ticket thinking he could dilute the influence of the military, but within two years he'd fled both the administration and the country, saying that in Guatemala "there are no political prisoners, only political corpses." Between March and September 1980, more than a hundred lawyers, teachers, and university students had been killed; by the start of the following year, thirty-six opposition politicians had been assassinated. But the crackdowns were more discreet than in El Salvador, where dead bodies lay on street corners and military trucks circled the roadways. In Guatemala, the judicial police might pick someone off in broad daylight, and it would happen so fast, with so little fanfare, that passersby might not even notice. A witness would observe the seamless way quotidian life sealed back up around the disturbance, leaving a trace so slight it felt like a taunt.

The guerrillas, for their part, would respond in kind, often choosing to strike in swankier neighborhoods. But Juan and the others never had any occasion to visit these sorts of places. In an upscale suburb of the city, shortly before Juan arrived, a group of wealthy onlookers were watching a softball game one afternoon when three guerrillas walked onto the field, shot the second baseman, and kidnapped the shortstop, who was the son of one of the country's richest families.

One reason a full-fledged war wasn't immediately obvious was because the main theater had shifted from the capital to the countryside. The military had feared that the guerrillas would mobilize the Indigenous Maya against the government. They made up more than 60 percent of the national population, and in a country with a poverty rate of nearly 90 percent, they were the poorest and worst-off by far. After the revolutionary skirmishes of the 1960s, the guerrillas and the military came to the realization more or less simultaneously: it was only a matter of time before the Indigenous population took up arms. The guerrillas—who were primarily westernized, Spanish-speaking, and members of the country's dominant social caste—eventually overcame their own racism to make their movement more representative and inclusive.

Circumstances conspired to help them force the issue. The military repression had ebbed in the first half of the 1970s, but the Indigenous population was a permanent underclass on the Pacific coast at a time when agribusiness and large landowners were squeezing them from both sides. In the country's interior, corrupt members of the military were also stealing communal land set aside for growing subsistence crops. On May 29, 1978, in a remote area of the northern state of Alta Verapaz called Panzós, fifty Maya Q'eqchi' land activists staged a demonstration with the help of the Guatemalan Labor Party to protest the government's theft of their land. The military sent troops who machine-gunned the crowds, killing several dozen people on the spot. "Those seeking real change will have no alternative but the violent left," the US ambassador observed afterward.

Instead of relying on targeted assassinations, as it had before, the army was increasingly engaging in mass murder. In 1980, members of a major Indigenous organization called the Peasant Unity Committee (CUC, by its Spanish acronym), which had formed two years earlier, took over the Spanish embassy in Guatemala City to call attention to government abuses. Activists from the department of El Quiché were joined by students from the University of San Carlos, the country's flagship public university; together they had alerted members of the Spanish embassy ahead of time. It was supposed to be a nonviolent event, but when Lucas García learned of it he called for the immediate extermination of the participants. ("Take them out as you can," he told his interior minister.) The police locked the building's doors from the outside and attacked the structure with grenades and firebombs. Nearly everyone inside was killed: thirty-nine activists, embassy staff, Spanish diplomats, even the Guatemalan foreign minister who'd been sent inside as a negotiator.

Guatemala City was divided into different zones with numbers that sometimes belied their proximity to one another. The Spanish embassy fell in Zone 9, a tony area of Spanish-colonial-style buildings and broad, tidy streets populated by diplomats and international businessmen. Just a few blocks north were La Terminal and a motley assortment of dives and budget motels, in Zone 4, where Juan and the others rarely ventured out. When they did, it was to grab food or run quick errands. By the evening, the restaurants closed and the streets became deserted. Cherokee Chief station wagons, the preferred car of the death squads, were usually a sign of some impending horror.

One morning, Juan limped out of his hotel on a single crutch for a meal down the block. He had just returned, relieved to have made it back, when a loud noise startled him. A group of police officers were trudging down the hotel stairs with someone in handcuffs. Juan shuddered as they spun around to look at him. With his crutch, he must have seemed too abject for the trouble. They marched past him to their cars.

Ten days later, the time came for the twelve-hour ride to Mexico. Ortíz drove up the Pan-American Highway, wending her way west toward the Pacific coast while skirting the dreaded highlands, with their whispers of catastrophe. The truck kicked and rattled along the pocked roadways. Each hour was an eternity as Juan lay contorted among the bags of handcrafts, his legs cramping. After a while, the growl of the motor subsided and the vehicle came to a halt. Juan could hear the crescendo of Ortíz's voice as she talked to the agents at a checkpoint. He imagined the *mordida*—the cash gently handed off, her look of steely nonchalance. When the engine came rumbling back a few minutes later, he knew they were making progress.

10.

The Red Bishop

In the spring of 1981, when Juan arrived in Mexico City, he started using the pseudonym Blanco—literally blanking out his last name. The region was lousy with Salvadoran intelligence agents. If Mexican immigration authorities ever caught and deported him, this was his only shot at escaping immediate execution back in El Salvador. In Usulután, all his friends were accustomed to using nicknames, slang, and code words to communicate in case a phone was tapped or an informer, or *oreja*, was listening.

The first order of business was getting him to a hospital, where he underwent a rapid succession of operations to save his foot and repair the damage to his arm. The doctors reconstructed his foot by grafting tissue, muscle, and skin around the infected wound; they replaced the rotted bone in his ankle with a copper prosthesis. His forearm and hand were easier to treat, but the nerve damage was permanent. His torturers had made good on their vow that he would never perform surgery again. For the rest of his life, beginning the day he left the hospital in Mexico City, four months after entering it, his fingers would tremble, ache, and then fizzle into numbness when he tied his shoes or buttoned his shirt.

Home for the three newly arrived Salvadorans was a white two-story house in a quiet residential neighborhood on the northern fringes of the city, called San Juan de Aragón. The property was at the end of a broad street, tucked away behind a low perimeter wall; it had a garden, a front and back patio, and a large basin outside for washing clothes. The owner of the residence was a Mexican woman who worked at a relief agency for refugees and rented the property at a steep discount to ten Salvadorans, including Ortíz's nephew.

Nearly everyone who lived there was from Usulután, so they nicknamed the residence the Usulután embassy, or the embassy for short. It functioned as a collective, with each of the residents in charge of a rotating set of domestic chores. Together they grew vegetables in the garden and kept a pen of rabbits, which they slaughtered, skinned, and sold for extra money.

Juan worked for three months as a land surveyor in the desert of Hidalgo. The grueling work began early each morning before the midafternoon heat made it too strenuous, and Juan had little choice but to work through his injuries. "Physical therapy," he called it. He lugged a theodolite under one arm, using the other to manage his single crutch; if he balanced himself just right, he could jot down the measurements on a clipboard, while gazing through a viewfinder set up on a tripod.

He was the only man on the crew who could barely walk, but in the end they suffered equally. The day the men were supposed to be paid, their contractor disappeared. They returned to Mexico City with nothing. It was Juan's initiation into the cruel rites of immigrant disposability. Without papers, there was no recourse. What choice did he have but to take such jobs? Another opportunity arose through a friend at the embassy. A café on the opposite side of Mexico City, near the university where Juan once dreamed of studying, needed a bookkeeper. By then, he knew enough to tell the owner that he had vast experience in accounting.

Mexico was full of generosity and solidarity, but also contradictions. A few months after Juan arrived, Mexico and France became the first two countries to recognize the FMLN guerrillas in El Salvador as a legitimate "representative political force." This was a castigation of the Salvadoran military. Still, Mexico's political leadership had little influence over the country's immigration authorities or police force. Officers routinely preyed on migrants—robbing, extorting, and deporting them any chance they got, often in exactly that order.

Juan was an optimist by nature and by necessity. He considered himself lucky to have been assaulted only twice, because both times he was able to avoid arrest. Once, on the Metro, a policeman stole his boots because Juan didn't have enough money to pay a bribe. He limped home on his crutches, relieved to be merely shoeless. Another time, he was stopped as he got off a *pesero*, one of the city's cheap buses; when the officers learned that he was on his way to work they accompanied him, demanding his paycheck from the office.

At the embassy, the Salvadorans had contingency plans if the police ever arrived. The most sacrosanct house rule was never to give up the address in San Juan de Aragón. If you got arrested, you owed it to everyone else to stay silent.

Juan learned that speaking aloud in public could attract unwanted attention. If he did speak—on a bus, to ask for change at a kiosk—he had to do it in a voice that wasn't his own. The Salvadorans studied Mexican Spanish to sound like natives. Maybe it was obvious they weren't from the capital, but Mexico was a giant country, full of small towns and idiosyncratic backwaters, a whole geography of potential covers and pretexts.

At the embassy, they prepared as though for a university exam. It wasn't just linguistics, but a kind of theater. An authentic Mexican, for instance, would be scandalized if an arresting officer questioned whether he was from abroad, so Juan developed a routine. *"Chinga tu madre. Yo soy mexicano, de Chiapas,"* he used to say, careful not just to get the curses right ("go fuck your mother"), but also to shorten his syllables, pinching the words so they fell out of the sides of his mouth in that trademark macho staccato. A common exercise for all of them was to memorize the lyrics of the Mexican national anthem, and to learn all the local landmarks in whatever town they claimed to be from. The Salvadorans who'd been there the longest had picked up these details from others, and the names of schools, unmarked roads, and churches in Chiapas, Guerrero, and Oaxaca were passed down among them like old crib sheets. Policemen were known to quiz the people they arrested on anything.

The struggle to get news from El Salvador was another reminder of the group's precarious position. Calling home was an arduous, hours-long proposition that required the use of a phone at a neighbor's house in San Juan de Aragón. Juan spoke to his parents once a week, but they didn't have their own phone. He had to call the town's lone telecommunications office, run by a government agency called ANTEL, and a messenger would hop on a bicycle to retrieve his parents, who lived a block away. The conversations themselves were clipped and self-conscious because no one could be sure how closely ANTEL was monitoring the lines. "How was the piñata yesterday?" Juan would ask his mother, using one of their makeshift codes for the war. She'd reply, "It was fine, there were only small sweets." *Dulces* meant pistols, no heavy artillery.

In Mexico, the Salvadorans could follow the war at home from news broadcasts and underground radio. They were amateur sleuths, cobbling together clues about the fighting in Usulután by reading between the lines of Salvadoran outlets that parroted government talking points. When the battles picked up in the town of Berlin, in 1983, the Salvadorans at the embassy read about the death toll among the guerrillas in the country's mainstream papers. If there was no mention of military casualties, they knew the damage to the government was steep.

While Juan and the others made these basic inferences, the US government could never seem to learn how to penetrate the doublespeak of the Salvadoran military. The US government had direct and regular contact with the upper echelons of the Salvadoran armed forces, but access wasn't the problem; these military men simply fed them lies, spin, and insinuations that they could only half believe most of the time. The Usulután embassy also had a more reliable— if humbler—source of human intelligence: the continual stream of Salvadorans fleeing to Mexico. Every weekend, they would gather in a corner of the Chapultepec Park, in Mexico City, a sprawling lush forest with walking paths, lakes, pavilions, and a zoo. The city's buildings peeked through the canopy in the distance. At a long line of wooden stalls, the Salvadorans sold homemade food and handcrafts; there were musical performances and dancing. Refugees pumped one another for information and argued about politics.

One morning, several months after Juan arrived in Mexico, he was working at one of the stalls in the park, selling goods made at the embassy, when he spotted a short young man with dark features and hooded eyes. The man was squinting back at Juan, his face suddenly bright with a look of astonishment. "Chicho?" he shouted. This was the nickname both Juan and his father had in Usulután—he hadn't been called that in nearly a year. The man was stammering. "But you're dead. You're not dead?" Juan recognized him instantly as an old friend and fellow medical student named Giovanni. Because Juan had disappeared into military custody, then went into hiding once he was released, most of his old university colleagues had assumed he was dead. Giovanni had attended a wake in San Salvador for the person he was now hugging in Chapultepec Park.

⋄—⋄

The bishop of Cuernavaca was tall and thickset, with a broad bald head that he kept shaved. His stature made him into an icon and a target. One day, in the early 1970s, he had just returned from Chile, where he'd attended a summit called Christians for Socialism, when a group of teenagers accosted him in the Mexico City airport, dousing him with a large can of red paint. His name was Sergio Méndez Arceo, but after the incident he became better known as the "red bishop," a conservative insult that he took as a compliment.

When Juan Romagoza met him, on a Sunday afternoon in the fall of 1982, Méndez Arceo was in his midseventies and in the final year of his episcopacy. He had been an influential participant in the Second Vatican Council, a staunch defender of the Mexican student protesters of the 1960s, an unrepentant socialist, a champion of the Sandinistas, and an outspoken exponent of liberation theology. Juan knew about these distinctions, but to his mind they paled beside another: in March 1980, Méndez Arceo had attended Óscar Romero's funeral.

Juan wandered into the cathedral for mass partly by accident. Cuernavaca was only an hour outside Mexico City, and he had decided to take a day trip with three friends. The cathedral had been built in the sixteenth century, in the baroque style, with a plain stone facade and an elegantly domed bell tower. A single nave inside was lined with stained glass windows, but there were no images of the saints anywhere among the side altars. In the 1950s, Méndez Arceo had removed them because he felt they were a distraction. All that was left inside the church was a rendering of Christ on the cross. Several years before the Second Vatican Council modernized church practice, Méndez Arceo had already been at the liturgical vanguard. He held mass in Spanish (rather than in Latin) and replaced the traditional German organ music with mariachis who played songs from Latin America.

From the pulpit, Méndez Arceo sounded a lot like Romero. He spoke passionately about biblical imperatives to help the poor, assailing the traditionalism that walled the church off from the wider world. "In our brothers and sisters we encounter God," he once said. "It is toward them that our true pilgrimage should move." The day Juan first heard Méndez Arceo preach in Cuernavaca, the bishop was calling for solidarity with refugees from El Salvador and Guatemala. "We have to introduce ourselves to him," Juan told his friends.

Méndez Arceo invited them to lunch. After learning that Juan had trained as a doctor, he asked for his help with a church initiative. The bishop had created a medical clinic for a group of Indigenous refugees from Guatemala. These were families who'd been displaced twice: first from their homelands in the western highlands and then again from southern Mexico, where they came to seek protection. Tens of thousands were living in refugee camps along Mexico's border with Guatemala, in the rugged, mountainous state of Chiapas. The Mexican government often looked the other way while Guatemalan soldiers crossed the border to conduct raids, air strikes, and executions. Maps used by the Guatemalan army labeled the refugee camps in southern Mexico as part of the "guerrilla infrastructure." Meanwhile, the US, Mexico, and Guatemala were having clandestine talks to create "repatriation zones" in Guatemala, where the Mexican government could return the refugees once and for all.

Of tens of thousands of refugees, a few hundred stragglers reached Cuernavaca. A network of Mexican clergy and lay activists were responsible for helping the most vulnerable get to safety. The work of transporting them north, away from the Guatemalan border, prefigured the American sanctuary movement, and operated in tandem with it. Méndez Arceo was connected to the Mexican borderlands by Samuel Ruiz, a bishop in Chiapas who also practiced liberation theology. Both men used their seminaries to train priests as community organizers and to support parishioners who set up "base communities" that paired Bible study with local activism to serve the poor.

The Guatemalans in Cuernavaca typically had personal ties that pulled them north. Left to their own devices, few of them would have considered the United States a desirable destination at all. The peasants in the highlands were often reluctant to relocate even to cities within Guatemala because of the racism they faced outside their own close-knit communities. They were strangers everywhere they went.

In an isolated mountain hamlet, however, it only took a single neighbor or family member who had wound up in the US and could report back that it was strange but survivable, with steady work and solid wages. That was enticement enough. Staying put while the war raged in Guatemala wasn't an option. Small clusters of Guatemalans were slowly forming in Central Florida, where they found seasonal work that roughly resembled their agricultural livelihoods back home. Others settled together in housing complexes in urban centers like Houston or Los Angeles, creating islands of community where they kept to themselves.

Méndez Arceo wanted Juan to treat the families who arrived at the clinic each weekend and to travel with them to the US border. Juan agreed straightaway. During the week, in Mexico City, he was working extra hours at a restaurant to raise money to help his siblings escape El Salvador. The owners of the establishment, a Jewish family with leftist political ties, were generous with overtime pay, and he took on additional shifts as often as he could. In Cuernavaca, the work was unpaid. Every Friday night, Juan would leave by bus, returning to Mexico City by Sunday or early Monday. He'd be gone for only a few days, but each of these spells outside the capital had an outsize effect on his spirit. Sometimes, he'd come back from a weekend spent traveling to the US border from Cuernavaca and go straight to the restaurant to work. To get home, he took the subway, followed by a *pesero* bus. He felt too restored to his old sense of purpose for the lack of sleep to slow him down.

In Cuernavaca, he stayed in a small dormitory on the church grounds, where he slept and dined with the Guatemalans and their families. In El Salvador, the Indigenous population had virtually disappeared with La Matanza in the 1930s. Those who weren't murdered had assimilated. In Guatemala, the Indigenous Maya didn't hide, and couldn't even if they wanted to. There were more than twenty different ethnic groups spread across the western highlands and into the north, and most of them spoke their own languages, which had nothing in common with Spanish. At the clinic, some of the church workers could translate for Juan, but he enjoyed trying to make himself understood using gestures and props, exchanging vocabulary over dinner.

His patients were grateful to him, and in their remote, laconic way protective, too. After a group of them learned that Juan had been separated from his young daughter they started to send their own children to welcome him each weekend. When they made the long trips to the US border, sitting together in the back of the church van, the Guatemalans would sing Juan songs from their hometowns, while he responded with folk songs he used to listen to in El Salvador. His favorite, which he sang in a diffident voice that cracked and caught, was called "Milonga del fusilado," about a fallen revolutionary. His listeners couldn't understand the lyrics, but they sensed that he needed to sing it for himself.

Juan identified himself as a doctor, yet in Cuernavaca he began to understand himself as a patient, a survivor, and a torture victim. Physically, this was obvious in his ragged limp and his gnarled, tingly left hand. He referred to his *dedos fregados*, or bum fingers—five digits that negated a decade of study and training.

But the damage ran deeper than that, and it announced itself to Juan in nightmares that began in Guatemala. One night, in their motel in Zone 4, Ortíz heard him screaming from down the hall and had to wake him up before he caused a disturbance. At the Usulután embassy, it was a common occurrence for the residents to jolt each other awake from sleep with their moans and howls. No one liked to talk about it. Weakness among the men was derided as a *mariconada*—"gay shit"—so the pain would get buried under the surface of manful denials and jokes. "Keep it up and you'll have to sleep in the bathroom tonight," they told Juan. The memories and flashbacks, however, continued to flicker, like there was some mysterious trick of subterranean wiring that he couldn't unplug.

At first, he tried to banish all thoughts that caused him the worst grief—the torture sessions he endured in San Salvador, or the blurry face of his month-old daughter. But with every attempt, his body, rather than his conscious mind, came roaring back in refutation. There were cramps, migraines, night sweats, body aches. Juan lived in a haze of constant ailments. They flared up the farther away he got from El Salvador, just as he let his guard down, a tether he couldn't break.

The Guatemalan refugees he was treating also showed physiological signs of deep underlying trauma. Their symptoms were varied but unmissable:

muscle spasms, joint pain, insomnia, depression, and high blood pressure. Through gritted teeth, the older men confessed to feeling an overwhelming urge to cry. Their children would act out, or struggle to focus on simple tasks. The worst part, in Juan's view, was that emotions were taboo among these patients. None of them would talk about what they'd seen and suffered. If Juan asked, the response would be silence, and he'd watch his patient recede into a kind of catatonia. This had nothing to do with the macho stoicism displayed by the men in the Usulután embassy. Keeping quiet—suffering inwardly—was more ingrained among members of the highland communities, a habit as much as an ethos. They had also just lived through something unspeakable. In Guatemala, the early 1980s came to be known as La Violencia, a deliberately suggestive understatement; to Juan's patients, it was simply *la situación*.

They were fleeing a genocide. The worst of the massacres occurred between 1981 and 1983, in parts of the countryside with the highest concentrations of Indigenous residents. In the northwest, in the lush, mountainous highland departments of El Quiché and Huehuetenango, were the Maya Q'anjob'al, the Chuj, the Ixil, and the K'iche'; and in the Verapaces, farther east, were the Achi. The Lucas García government adopted a policy that one general called "blindness and madness," in which the military killed, tortured, and raped as many Maya as it could to instill terror and diminish support for the guerrillas. "The

Suspected of being "subversives," a mother and her child are interrogated by soldiers in Chajul, Quiché, Guatemala, 1983.

great Indian masses," as the army called them, were the "social base" of opposition to the military. The premise followed from American counterinsurgency doctrine, but the execution exceeded even the US government's capacity for geopolitical rationalizations. The Carter administration had cut off aid to the Guatemalan military in 1977; Reagan was trying to restart it. At the same time, hundreds of villages were destroyed, and two hundred thousand people were killed and disappeared. More than a million Indigenous residents were displaced, with tens of thousands fleeing to Mexico. At one point, after the military burned down entire forests to make whole swaths of the highlands uninhabitable, villagers reported changes in rainfall patterns and climate.

In March 1982, an evangelical Christian general named Efraín Ríos Montt staged a coup and took over the Guatemalan government. He systematized the attacks begun by his predecessor, whose biggest failure, in the eyes of Ríos Montt, had been his disorganization. The massacres continued under the auspices of a new campaign to "pacify" the rural Maya. He dubbed it Victoria 82. Lucas García had prosecuted the counterinsurgency by charging the military with "one hundred percent random slaughter," according to the historian Virginia Garrard-Burnett. An adviser to Ríos Montt, carrying out the new initiative, "called for a thirty percent 'total kill' in the zones of conflict." The remaining 70 percent of his operations involved efforts to relocate displaced peasants to specific zones where they were wholly dependent on the army for food and basic medical care. (Fusiles y Frijoles, or Bullets and Beans, was the name of one program.) As a US cable put it, "the rural populace is ordered to move to villages where the army has outposts. A scorched earth policy is then applied to the surrounding area." The military also created a "civil patrol system," in which villagers were forced to conduct sweeps of their own neighbors, responding to tips and insinuations about who might harbor antipathy toward the government. Years later, a truth commission run by the Catholic Church would attempt to quantify and catalog the full scale of the devastation. But there was no taxonomy for everything they found. "In what category does being forced to kill one's own brother fall?" the researchers wrote. "What concept should be applied to public ceremonies where everyone is obligated to beat the victim over the head with a stick until he dies?"

11.

Living as Long as the Republic Does

J uan never crossed the US border with the Guatemalans, and he was never tempted to try. The Americans seemed to find their way to him. In Cuernavaca, he met a young nun from Sacramento named Sister Bernadette, who first told him about the sanctuary movement in Tucson, Berkeley, and San Francisco. On his trips north he had realized that American activists were waiting on the other side of the border to receive the Guatemalans. But that was all he knew. Sister Bernadette often mentioned the name of John Fife, in Tucson. It was an easy one to remember—two crisp syllables of encouragement that Juan could file away as a hint of American solidarity with the cause.

At the Usulután embassy, a Salvadoran woman moved into a bedroom on a corner of the second floor. Her boyfriend was an American musician she'd met at Chapultepec Park. He and his friends, who were amiable and chatty, would sometimes be at the embassy when Juan returned from his weekends in Cuernavaca. When the topic of the war in El Salvador inevitably came up, they asked questions that led Juan to two conclusions. First, there was a difference between Americans and their government. Second, very few people in the US seemed to know what was really happening in El Salvador and Guatemala. Juan showed them his own scars, and thought, "If the tools of war are flowing from the US, maybe these are the people we should be setting straight."

While the Guatemalans were moving north, Juan's own family was coming to Mexico City. After a year at the restaurant, he had raised enough money for his siblings to escape El Salvador with their families. One brother came by bus, another by plane. His sister, Morena Guadalupe, arrived with her husband and their two children. Everyone stayed in the Usulután embassy in Mexico, and eventually Juan's parents visited for the holidays. Then, one by one, they started to scatter. Juan's parents returned home. They were old enough not to arouse the suspicions of the military, and Juan's mother used her brothers to secure travel visas. A brother left for Australia to seek asylum, and another departed for Nicaragua. Later, Morena Guadalupe took her family to San Francisco, where an aunt had been living since the 1950s, working as a nurse.

Juan continued making trips to the border, learning more about the routes through Northern Mexico. Most of the Guatemalans went to Tijuana because the trip allowed them to avoid hundreds of miles of scorching desert. California, the state with the most Spanish speakers, had the reputation of being the most welcoming of the American border states. The Guatemalans who chose to cross in El Paso or in Tucson tended to have a family member on the East Coast.

When Juan dropped off another group at the border, someone in the party would always turn to him and ask, "Why not just cross now yourself? You're right here." Each time, he replied, "Not right now. In Mexico, I can be closer to El Salvador."

It had now been two years since Juan had had contact with Laura and their daughter. His life in Mexico had the unexpected virtue of impermanence: he didn't have to foreclose the possibility of returning home. For as long as Juan's family was in El Salvador and he wasn't, it didn't matter where he was. They were either alive or not; finding them depended entirely on the situation in Chalatenango. But to leave Mexico for the United States implied a lapse of faith.

Around noon on a Sunday, in November 1982, he received the dreaded news, in the form of a short notice from one of the bulletins that were mimeographed and distributed in Chapultepec Park. There had been a military strike in Chalatenango and among the list of the presumed dead was "Carolina," a "student in her last year of medical school." This had been Laura's pseudonym from her days as an activist. Juan had never met the rest of her family because they had disapproved of the political life he shared with their daughter. Laura's sister and mother had left the country sometime in 1980 and moved to Puebla, Mexico. But Juan didn't have an address or a phone number. According to the bulletin, the body hadn't been found. There was no mention of Juan's daughter.

Later that month, a Salvadoran bishop announced that the pope would be visiting El Salvador in February or March of the following year. Catholic missions from across Latin America arranged trips to the country for the pope's visit. Seeing an opportunity, Juan devised a plan. It was possible that the news about Laura had been wrong. Through his contacts in the Church, he would pose as a Mexican seminarian, traveling with a religious delegation to San Salvador for a tour of the city on the eve of the pope's arrival. Once he got there, he would split from the group and try to sneak into Chalatenango. If he could smuggle himself into the department—past the government checkpoints and military patrols—he might find out for sure.

He arrived by bus with a delegation of Mexican priests one afternoon in March. Wearing the brown robe and white cincture of a Franciscan friar, he carried a fake foreign visa and spoke in an affected Mexican accent. It was as though he had and hadn't returned home.

A few days later, when the others began a tour of the city's churches, Juan went to a market to buy a loaf of bread and a small basket of fruit. He had worked out a script ahead of time, committing the story to memory. The idea was to board a bus to Chalatenango on the pretext that he was a Mexican priest with a Salvadoran congregant in Mexico City who couldn't travel because of the war; he was visiting her family on her behalf, bringing the food as a gift.

Ordinarily the drive from the capital would take about two hours, but the roads were interrupted by checkpoints. Soldiers waited in guard stations on the outskirts of the capital, in Apopa, Aguilares, and finally at the entrance to Chalatenango, in the zone called El Paraíso, where Juan had first been detained at the barracks. The soldiers were instructed to turn away anyone who didn't have papers proving that he lived in the area. Getting past them would be difficult but not impossible.

Juan took a seat by the window in the back right corner of the bus. The countryside rose and fell in waves of thick vegetation that occasionally gave way to cleared fields scorched by the sun. Gazing out at the landscape, Juan thought about all the troops he couldn't see but who he knew were there, hidden in the surrounding ravines and forests. This was rebel territory, and it was swarming with spies and lookouts from both sides of the conflict.

Informers were most likely on the bus with him, so he had to stay in character, projecting a demeanor of calm, priestly reserve. The younger passengers were most likely aligned with the guerrillas. Those who were older and dressed slightly better, in leather boots or unripped jackets, might be working with the military. Juan scouted certain tells. In his experience, *campesinos* tended to forgo wearing their traditional broad-brimmed hats when they traveled. Anyone who fit the general description of a government informer, and who also wore a hat on the bus, registered with Juan as suspicious. He took note of those with slight discordances in their posture. A person's eyes might dart around while his body remained still. That could be a sign of someone who didn't want to be noticed. But it was just as likely that the other passengers were sizing up Juan with the same misgivings. He exercised every muscle in his face to appear relaxed. To pass the time, he recited prayers in his head until he ran out and began making up his own.

The first few checkpoints came and went, but at the last one, before Chalatenango, the bus slowed to a crawl. On the right side of the road, grassy areas had been converted into firing ranges for the troops. On the opposite side, a green wall topped with razor wire marked the beginning of the military installation. A slogan had been painted on it: "The Army will live for as long as the Republic does." Juan could make out the parapet of El Paraíso. A soldier got on the bus and said something to the driver, who nodded. He pulled at the gearshift and began to turn the vehicle around.

Juan tried again the next morning and once more on the afternoon of the following day. Each time, he made it past the first checkpoints, but soldiers stopped them at El Paraíso.

On one of the desolate afternoons he spent back in San Salvador, trying to rethink his plans, he visited a friend of his and Laura's who had studied medicine with them at the university. Her name was Mercedes Grijalva, and she lived in a small neighborhood in an adjacent, working-class town called Mejicanos. Juan went to her house dressed in his brown robe, waiting a few hours for her to return from work.

"You're not a priest," she said when she arrived. The house, which she shared with her family, was too small for the two of them to talk privately. They went to a nearby park bench, where she told him that Laura's body had been found. Soldiers had stormed the hamlet in Chalatenango where Laura had been tending to patients. Everyone had fled, but she ran back to fetch her medical bag. She got caught in the crossfire and was taken into custody. Her corpse had shown signs of torture. Their daughter, Maria, was now with Laura's family in Puebla.

A few days later, when the church delegation returned to Mexico City, Juan joined them. He returned to the Usulután embassy feeling morose and drained, but, in an unexpectedly liberating twist, he found that he was no longer in purgatory. There were choices he had to make. If he traveled north, maybe there was some chance of doing something, however slight, that could pressure Washington to help wind down the conflict. Of the two lives he began to imagine for himself—as an undocumented immigrant in the US or in Mexico—the American one seemed to involve a fight. He came to think of it as the only true path back home.

12.

Smugglers with a Conscience

Peggy Hutchison was tugging at a pair of rusted cables on the barbed wire fence between the US and Mexico when the group arrived, on a fall morning in 1982. They were coming from Agua Prieta—two mothers, their four young daughters, and a baby. Everyone was breathing heavily, in gasps that were short and shallow. With Hutchison holding open the wires, they pushed through a small gap in the fence. A minute later, they were all in Douglas, Arizona, trudging toward Hutchison's car, a beat-up yellow Toyota Corona with bucket seats and peeling upholstery. She'd left it running by the side of the road.

Behind the wheel, she leaned forward and pulled the gearshift into drive, squinting through oversize plastic eyeglasses to check for oncoming traffic. The green jeeps from Border Patrol were easy to spot, perched high on their tires like sentries. But the morning was dark and rainy, and a mist rose off the road. She pulled onto the highway and toward the safehouse in town, where a pastor and several activists were waiting.

Hutchison was twenty-seven years old, tall and slender, with an air of coiled intensity. Originally from the Bay Area, in California, she had come to Tucson a few years earlier, to work in the border ministry for the desert southwest conference of the United Methodist Church. It wasn't long before she visited the ratty prison in Nogales, Mexico, where she met Father Quiñones and James

Corbett. By the end of 1982, she'd become a reliable member of the sanctuary movement. Margo Cowan and Lupe Castillo specialized in legal services. John Fife secured church space for the migrants. Corbett traveled to southern Mexico to recruit a network of activists. Hutchison devoted herself to the crossings themselves.

She used different cars for the trips, most of them borrowed from the other volunteers. The first time, she got nervous and, with a car full of Salvadorans, made a wrong turn onto Fort Huachuca, a military base. Every crossing presented new challenges. Once, a refugee was sitting next to her in the front seat when they were forced to slow down at a checkpoint on the passenger's side. She coaxed the woman to slump out of sight, while waving vigorously to the Border Patrol agent. He motioned the car through; they never even came to a stop. Another time, she circled the back alleys of Douglas as two migrants she'd come to pick up were being chased by a team of Border Patrol agents. The two men ran out from a side street, spotted Hutchison, and piled into her back seat before the agents turned the corner. Usually, people coming through Agua Prieta made the first leg of the trip on their own. They'd hike through the mountains, snaking along a patch of New Mexico before emerging in Arizona, on the fringes of a bird sanctuary. Hutchison and the others would be waiting, posing as birders. For women with children, though, that trip was too risky.

They had barely driven a mile down the highway when the Border Patrol trucks appeared. Two of them emerged from the fog, their lights barreling toward the car. They dwarfed Hutchison's Corona, then whipped past it in a blur. One of the children in the car started hyperventilating, and the others began to cry. To the mothers and children, who were from El Salvador, the Border Patrol trucks resembled the ones driven by the Salvadoran military. Everyone in the car was panicking, and all the sobbing and heavy breathing were fogging up the windows.

Through the early 1980s, Border Patrol had been setting up motion sensors along the fence, and Hutchison guessed that one of them had gone off when she helped the women through. If they were arrested, the Salvadorans were supposed to admit who they were and what they were doing. Hutchison would explain that she was helping them seek asylum. She was unsettled by the unequal consequences they faced. "What's going to happen to you if you're caught is nothing like what's going to happen to them," she used to tell herself.

Hutchison kept checking the rearview mirror as she neared Douglas, expecting to see the Border Patrol vehicles speeding after her, but they never appeared. There were other agents on the road. She smiled at them as they drove past. One lesson she'd learned making these runs was to appear confident and untroubled at the sight of law enforcement. Officers saw a young, bespectacled white woman, not a human smuggler.

A few blocks away, the other activists were conferring nervously with the pastor. They were sitting in his living room at the parsonage—the safe house for the day's operation—debating what to do. They'd seen a caravan of Border Patrol trucks speed off to the outskirts of town where they knew Hutchison had made the crossing.

Hutchison circled the block once, as planned. On her second pass, she slowed down and gazed at the parsonage. Peering out from behind a corner of the curtains was the face of one of the other activists. A few seconds later the garage door opened. Hutchison pulled into the driveway, easing the car into the garage. She and her passengers got out only when the door closed behind them.

By the mid-1980s, there were close to seventy thousand members of the sanctuary movement in the United States. One of its strengths was that membership could take a range of forms. Some participants, like Hutchison, were full-fledged activists, crossing and sheltering refugees at substantial personal risk. But most of the others volunteered in more modest ways. They voted to make their churches "sanctuary" spaces, which could mean anything from being actual places of shelter to being symbols of solidarity. Certain Catholic archdioceses across the country distributed literature for prospective congregations, listing steps in a "discernment process" for congregants to decide how they wanted to participate. Some people welcomed refugees in their homes and churches; others sponsored events about Central America, or donated clothes, food, and money to churches more directly involved in providing relief to the migrants. To call the entire network an underground railroad, as many observers did, was scarcely an exaggeration. But the whole undertaking operated in plain sight, which is how it continued to draw supporters. More than 150 congregations joined the movement, spanning both coasts, the borderlands, and the Midwest.

From the day Southside Presbyterian declared sanctuary, in 1982, John Fife and James Corbett had become the face of the movement at the border. Both were comfortable and charismatic before the cameras, and they saw the press as a tool. Spreads appeared in local, national, and international papers, from *The Arizona Daily Star* to *Newsweek*, *The Washington Post*, and the London *Times*. Reporters occasionally turned up when Hutchison and the others crossed Central Americans at the border; cameramen sometimes milled around the participating churches.

Their presence bothered Hutchison. From the beginning, she had wrestled with what it meant for her—a white woman and US citizen—to intervene on behalf of a group of Central Americans. "I could learn to live with atrocity, or I could stand with the oppressed and the persecuted and respond to these sojourners in my midst," she wrote in the *United Methodist Reporter*, in the spring of 1983. But to be an American was to reckon with a guilty conscience. Indirectly but unequivocally, Hutchison's government was responsible for driving hundreds of thousands of people from their homes. What she couldn't figure out personally was how to manage the practical realities of the work (logistics, operations, strategy) without muzzling the people she was supposed to be helping. "They need to be able to make decisions for themselves," she said. But those decisions depended on factors—such as where and when to travel; if and how to address the press—that the Americans were often in a better position to understand.

Hutchison and another activist once arrived at the border to bring a group of Salvadorans across, only to find two reporters from *The Sacramento Bee* who were already there waiting for them. "Did anyone ask these Salvadorans if they were OK with this?" Hutchison asked. There was no time to rehash the verbal agreements that had been brokered back in Tucson. The priority was getting the families into the US. The reporters were sympathetic, even valuable to the general cause, but now Hutchison had to make an extra set of arrangements for them. Did they need another car for the crossing? Who would travel with whom? How should they explain to the asylum seekers who these strange men with notebooks and cameras were?

In the winter of 1982, *60 Minutes*, one of the most prominent primetime news shows in the country, devoted a segment to asylum. To represent the position of the Reagan administration, CBS showed an old interview with Elliott Abrams from the State Department. "They come here for better jobs, but that doesn't entitle them to asylum," he said. "Asylum is a very special thing which we give to people who can prove that they have a well-founded fear of persecution." The broadcast intercut his inert, legalistic assertions with the moving testimony of a Salvadoran woman living in LA without papers. "I never wanted to come to the United States," she said. "But this looked like the only choice." If she were ever deported, she continued, "I am more than sure I'll be killed."

The coverage was damning for the government, and staffers in the Western Regional Office of the INS, in California, started trading cables with their counterparts in Arizona. For the first time, one of the men broached the possibility of arresting Corbett, who had appeared in the segment. "Phoenix anti-smuggling unit is designated as control office in this matter and Tucson anti-smuggling unit will provide available data, intelligence, and support to the control office as requested," another official responded.

Fife and Corbett commanded a large share of the public attention, but they needed help beyond Tucson. "The phone was going off the wall day and night with refugees getting in touch with us," Fife told one reporter at the time. "We discovered refugees we didn't even know existed in Tucson, let alone all along the border." Corbett approached a group called the Chicago Religious Task Force on Central America, an association of lay activists that formed in January 1981, after members of the Salvadoran National Guard had raped and killed the four American churchwomen. The task force represented two dozen humanitarian and religious groups in the Chicago area. It was a powerful engine for signing up participating churches and enlisting activists across the Midwest. Within two years, owing to appeals made by the task force, another two hundred churches, synagogues, and Quaker meeting houses opened sanctuary spaces. The activists in Chicago also published and distributed some thirty thousand copies of booklets and instruction manuals on sanctuary.

From the start, the sanctuary workers in Chicago had misgivings about what was happening in Tucson, and it wasn't hard to see why. The activists in Tucson were on the front lines of a low-grade humanitarian crisis. Each day was an exercise in triage. Fife and Corbett, who were hardly defenders of American foreign policy, thought that politicizing the work undercut its moral appeal. To the activists in Chicago, that thinking was precisely backward. They put out a Statement of Faith, in which they wrote, "The sanctuary movement seeks to uncover and name the connections between the US government and the Salvadoran death squads. . . . To stop short of this is to betray the Central American people and the refugees we now harbor." The activists in Chicago wanted to screen at least some of the refugees they helped based on their political beliefs. If the refugees were going to testify while in sanctuary, the activists wanted their narratives to be aligned with the movement.

One afternoon in the late fall of 1982, Fife received a phone call from a friend north of Tucson who was concerned about a young Indigenous couple from Guatemala. They were teenagers who'd fled a small village in the western highlands and found jobs picking cotton in Arizona, where they stood out among the field hands. They were shorter than the Mexicans toiling alongside them, and darker skinned. "They're going to get picked off by the INS," Fife's friend said. "Can you come and get them?" When Fife picked them up, they spoke about their village, which had been bombed and burned to the ground. The couple blamed the guerrillas. "They dropped leaflets that said so," the young man told Fife. Eventually he found someone to take them to Chicago, while he left on a trip to Central America. On his return, a few weeks later, a letter was waiting for him from some of the activists in the Chicago Religious Task Force explaining that the two Guatemalans had been returned to Arizona. They hadn't demonstrated a "proper analysis of the conflict in Central America."

When Reagan became president, his administration effectively ignored the 1980 Refugee Act. The result wasn't just a legal and political jumble but also a kind of operational vacuum that the sanctuary workers tried to fill. Both admirers and detractors of the movement often portrayed it as an exercise in mass civil disobedience. Yet the activists were trying to act on the law and make practical sense of its untested principles. The ambiguity between "economic migrants" and legitimate asylum seekers was the most obvious area of confusion. It was made more complicated by the fact that Central Americans were often fleeing persecution while simultaneously seeking work to survive on the run. International human rights law, which the 1980 act was meant to follow, made further distinctions between a situation of general violence and one of specific persecution. Only the latter was supposed to trigger asylum protections.

On one occasion, Hutchison was traveling in Nogales, about an hour from Tucson, when she came across a group of Nicaraguan men. She stopped and discussed their situation with them. They'd left the country because the Sandinista government had conscripted them to fight against the Contras. They generally supported the government but were unwilling to fight in a war. She gave them some money as well as a few tips on how to evade Border Patrol, but helping them cross, she said, was out of the question. It was one thing to escape a country wracked by general violence, and another to flee persecution. She later told the other activists about them, and Corbett, a Quaker, disagreed with her decision. He felt they should be helping everyone. Hutchison countered that the movement was focused on El Salvador and Guatemala. "It puts the movement at risk if we start transporting people who aren't asylum seekers," she said.

Other times, Hutchison conducted short interviews with Central Americans in Mexico to decide who to bring across the border. She and the other activists tried to gauge the "level of danger" someone faced if he were to be returned to his home country; they relied on screening procedures modeled on guidance from the UN High Commissioner for Refugees. There were three categories a refugee could fall into. The first was "high-risk": these migrants had to either have documents from an established human rights organization, have a letter of recognition from the UNHCR, or be able to show torture marks on their bodies. "Medium-risk" refugees belonged to groups that typically faced persecution, such as catechists, former political prisoners, unionists, and army deserters. "Low-risk" migrants were simply fleeing violence.

Hutchison entered Mexican jails with a pad and pen. The state authorities would wait until the cells filled up with enough people to bus them back to Guatemala, to justify the expenditure of gas. The Salvadorans and Guatemalans

Hutchison met inside often wanted to share their full stories, but there was never time. She felt they needed an explanation of what would happen next: since it was likely they'd be deported, she tried to help them make contingency plans. The pages of her notebooks filled up with the phone numbers of their relatives, which Hutchison took down in a special code in case she got stopped. Next to each digit, she wrote the name of a different food so that her notes would resemble grocery lists.

13.

Stepsister of the Government

In the spring of 1981, Reagan's advisers were so divided on immigration policy that they could agree only that the president should avoid the subject altogether. It was a "no win issue," one of his counselors wrote in a memo. "Given the difficulties that can be expected," another noted, White House action "may be more detrimental to domestic standing than living with the current situation."

The current situation was this: There were somewhere between three million and six million people living without legal documentation in the US, and another four hundred thousand to a million migrants crossing the border that year. The budget of the INS was less than half that of the Philadelphia police department. "Nothing short of a Berlin Wall could keep illegals out," one of Reagan's advisers confessed. The country was in a recession, which further inflamed the public against immigrants who were seen as competitors for their jobs. The president also had to think about his core political supporters. Growers, industrial farming operations, hotels, restaurants, and manufacturers along the border and in the Sunbelt depended on cheap labor, and already there was a shortage of unskilled workers in the Southwest. In May, a well-connected California farmer sent an angry letter to William French Smith, Reagan's attorney general, complaining about INS activity in Fresno. Arrests by Border

Patrol, he claimed, were costing him an average of seventeen hundred workers each month. He was losing crops.

Reagan himself maintained a permissive, laissez-faire view of immigration that put him closer to the US Chamber of Commerce than to the populist wing of his party. His cabinet was divided along the same lines as the GOP itself. On one side was Smith, the attorney general, who worried that the US had "lost control of its borders." Increased enforcement, employer sanctions, and more stringent ID requirements for job seekers were the only way, he argued, to resurrect the public's "faith in our laws." On the other side of the divide were White House officials opposed to any form of government "interference" in the labor market. Regulating immigration with a heavy hand, as one of them told the president, "would disrupt an established pattern of employment." At meetings in the White House, Reagan was withdrawn, sitting silently and looking bored while his advisers carped among themselves. "Good Lord," Reagan interjected after the discussion turned, once more, to the subject. "We're back to immigration already!"

The issue was particularly difficult for Reagan to downplay because a panel of lawmakers and public officials had just produced a detailed report offering concrete solutions. Formed by an act of Congress in 1978, the group was called the Select Commission on Immigration and Refugee Policy. In the 1970s alone, two immigration bills had passed the House but died in the Senate. A third, which had an amnesty provision to legalize the undocumented, failed to make it to the House floor. The commission consisted of sixteen members picked by the president, the Speaker of the House, and the president pro tempore of the Senate. Its director was Theodore Hesburgh, a Roman Catholic priest and the head of the University of Notre Dame, who'd been an adviser and bipartisan confidant to American presidents for more than two decades.

The Washington establishment was usually indifferent to the labors of obscure commissions, but this one set new standards of seriousness and relevance. In addition to its sixteen members, the commission relied on a team of some fifty staff members and consultants, who compiled briefing papers and held hearings. They consulted academics, public-policy experts, and officials across multiple cabinet agencies. When the commission's findings were released, only a month and a half after Reagan took office, they took up thirteen volumes, some of which were hundreds of pages long. *The New York Times* called them "a permanent contribution to the debate" and the "most authoritative Government study of the issue."

The recommendations were built around a premise that neither political party could easily dismiss—as Hesburgh put it, "closing the back door to undocumented-illegal immigration" and "opening the front door a little more to accommodate legal migration in the interests of the country." The government needed to enhance border enforcement by increasing its annual funding. But it also had to reduce the size of the undocumented population in the US by legalizing millions of immigrants living in the country. The third and most politically complicated recommendation was to penalize employers who knowingly hired workers without legal papers.

The clarity of the proposals compounded the political dilemma for the White House. The president bought himself a few extra months by appointing his own task force, which gave his advisers until August to extricate him from the conundrum of employer sanctions. But with the terms of the policy debate already set, Congress was getting involved.

Leading the effort in the Senate was Alan Simpson, a Republican from Wyoming who was six feet, seven inches tall and had a reputation for wrestling lofty, intractable policies to the ground. His partner in the House was an Italian American Democrat from Kentucky named Romano Mazzoli, whose father, a bricklayer, had come to the US through Ellis Island. Reagan's task force eventually produced its own wish list—a watered-down version of the commission report. But the president quietly ceded ground to Simpson and Mazzoli. They introduced a bill in 1982 that passed the Senate but languished in the House, then reintroduced a version of it three more times in the next four years.

A viable immigration bill was a kind of legislative Rubik's Cube. Organized labor approved of employer sanctions but bristled at expanded legal immigration. Mexican American advocacy groups, which supported legalization of the undocumented, opposed employer sanctions for fear of discrimination against Hispanic workers. For every law-and-order type championing increased enforcement, there was another congressman whose most powerful constituents depended on cheap, undocumented labor.

After four years serving in the Carter administration, Doris Meissner put her professional life expectancy under Reagan at about two weeks. Yet by the winter of 1981, it was dawning on her that the new team at the Justice Department wasn't ready to let her go. Since Meissner had already been working on the Hesburgh commission from inside the Justice Department, the attorney general wanted her to be around to brief people in February, when the findings were finally released.

Meanwhile, in another accident of timing, Meissner received an unexpected promotion. Leonel Castillo, the head of the INS during the Carter years, had stepped down in the fall of 1979. His replacement as acting commissioner was the agency's general counsel, an attorney whom the incoming administration saw as a Carter loyalist. Meissner was well respected and one of the most experienced hands on immigration inside the Justice Department. Serving under Republicans and Democrats put her beyond the partisan suspicions of her boss, a crucial qualification. Rather than getting sacked at the start of the Reagan era, Meissner became the acting commissioner of the INS.

The position was more of a burden than a reward. The agency was understaffed and short on resources—"the stepsister of the government," Meissner called it. But the INS was still the biggest organization she had ever run. Her greatest challenge was interpreting the mixed signals sent from the White House.

The fallout from Mariel, for instance, was ongoing. There were thousands of Cubans stuck in jails and military bases because they had criminal records, but there was no place for the Reagan administration to move them without causing further outcry. In Arkansas, where gubernatorial elections were held every two years, the Republican incumbent Frank White, who had won election in 1980 by lambasting Clinton over the refugees at Fort Chaffee, was now on the receiving end of the same attacks. It was Clinton's turn, this time as White's challenger, to blame the governor for doing nothing about immigrant criminals in the state. "I don't need to tell you how important it is to the Republican Party and to my own political future that these people be moved," White told one of Reagan's advisers in the summer of 1981.

The cataclysm of Mariel had also eclipsed a growing exodus from Haiti.

Some eight thousand Haitians fled the country for the US throughout the 1970s, arriving in small boats and flotillas. But in 1980 alone close to twenty-five thousand more landed at American ports. The Carter administration detained a large share of them, and Reagan spent months transferring them from one facility to another across the country to free up more space. After the Department of Justice moved one population of Haitian detainees to a holding center in Big Spring, Texas, the state's senior Republican senator, John Tower, called the White House in a rage. "You have tripled the black population of Big Springs [sic], Texas," he said, "and not even advised me in advance."

Faced with overlapping policy dilemmas, Reagan's advisers opted to make an example of asylum seekers. In July, the president's immigration task force announced a tough new enforcement regime. There had been, the president said, "sudden influxes of foreigners," and the government had to "establish control." From that moment forward, the US would jail any migrant who showed up seeking asylum. The US would dispatch the Coast Guard to intercept anyone fleeing Haiti; those who made it through the abbreviated hearings on government boats would be placed in detention. "For any exclusion program to have significant deterrent effect," the assistant attorney general wrote his boss, "the illegal aliens must be held in custody."

Meissner had to explain the new policy to Congress. Reagan's initial statement didn't mention detention, and officials at the Justice Department acted as though detaining asylum seekers was merely a continuation of past practice. It was "really quite the opposite of that," she explained in one hearing. The government had ended the policy of mass detention of immigrants in 1954. Meissner saw no reason to pretend the policy options were appealing. "In the future, undocumented aliens arriving in the United States who do not choose to depart voluntarily will be placed in administrative detention pending the determination of their admissibility," she said. "We are just pulling this all together now to be certain that it is uniform because some of these things, as you know, have developed along different streams."

At the end of September, the president finally nominated an INS commissioner—a forty-eight-year-old Cadillac salesman and campaign contributor from Miami named Norman Braman. He freely admitted to knowing nothing about the issue, but called himself, as the son of Romanian and Polish parents, "the product of a good, sane immigration policy." Then, in November, Braman suddenly withdrew. Senate staffers were still reviewing Braman's business records in anticipation of his confirmation hearing. The only explanation Braman gave was that he wanted to return to Florida.

In his place, Reagan settled for an old crony from California, Alan Nelson, whom Meissner then helped prepare for confirmation. When the Senate confirmed him, in February 1982, Nelson asked Meissner to stay on to deal with asylum issues that had arisen in the year since Reagan took office. He created a special position for her, the "executive associate commissioner," and made her the agency's third most powerful person.

The higher Meissner rose in the halls of government, the more acute the contradictions of US asylum policy appeared. The Refugee Act didn't protect people equally, and the Justice Department, which oversaw the INS, barely pretended that it did. The government's treatment of Haitians was a case in point. Through the 1960s and early seventies, before Meissner was in government, large numbers of Haitians started coming to the US in flight from the repressive regime of François "Papa Doc" Duvalier. Their numbers increased when he died and his son, Jean-Claude, took power, just two years before Meissner started her White House fellowship. The Duvaliers were no friends of the US government, but by the blunt logic of the Cold War they weren't enemies, either. This geopolitical ambiguity raised legal questions in immigration court. When, in December 1972, a boat with sixty-five Haitian men, women, and children arrived in Pompano Beach, Florida, *The Miami Times* ran an editorial that framed the matter clearly:

> A moment of truth has arrived for our local immigration officials who so casually go about their almost daily task of processing Cuban citizens landing in South Florida after having escaped the Castro regime. Should the procedure be any different for the dark-skinned Haitians?

While Cubans were immediately admitted and set on a path to permanent residency within a year, the Haitians were thrown into detention centers. The INS set bond between five hundred and a thousand dollars, and the detainees were relegated to a separate legal track known as an "exclusion hearing," an expedited form of deportation predicated on the legal fiction that they'd never, technically, entered the US. Their initial asylum interviews were often held late at night, in an immigration jail near Miami called Krome. Each one lasted twenty minutes, without lawyers or interpreters present. If Haitians cleared this first hurdle, the government erected others. On an August morning in 1981, Steve Forester, an immigration attorney representing Haitian asylum seekers, had twenty-nine hearings scheduled in three separate courts. "I had four people deported because I couldn't get there," he said afterward.

Eventually, in response to a class-action lawsuit filed on behalf of four thousand Haitians, a federal judge intervened, finding that the conditions in Haiti were "stark, brutal, and bloody," and that deportees from the US were in "substantial danger" of being tortured or killed. The INS, he ruled, had violated the Constitution in denying the Haitians the semblance of a fair hearing. "Those Haitians who came to the United States seeking freedom and justice did not find it," he wrote. "Instead, they were confronted with an Immigration and Naturalization Service determined to deport them. The decision was made among high INS officials to expel Haitians, despite whatever claims to asylum individual Haitians might have."

By then, Meissner was herself one of the agency's top officials, and had come to understand how the system worked. The INS was organized into thirty-three different districts, each with its own director. Meissner outranked them all, but did not have direct authority over them in the institutional chain of command. She was also a woman and a career official; the field belonged to tough-talking lawmen who were contemptuous of legal niceties. The district directors were potentates controlling every aspect of their offices' operations. Because INS was the lone immigration body inside the Justice Department, the district offices were responsible for everything from making arrests to processing applications for legal status. Each office handled asylum requests in its own way, with local officials conducting a preliminary interview and then sending the applications along to the State Department for an expert opinion. The ultimate decision would be delivered on INS letterhead, signed by the district director, but the decision was essentially made in Washington.

Among immigration lawyers it was obvious that Salvadorans and Guatemalans were being rejected at suspiciously high rates. The sanctuary movement, which was growing in stature, helped force the conversation in newspapers and on television. Meissner was deputized to respond. She'd crisscross the country dressed in the crisp suits that were her uniform in Washington and debate people like John Fife, who strode in with turquoise belt buckles and cowboy boots.

Unlike Elliott Abrams, whose press junkets were tightly controlled, his condescension palpable, Meissner treated each of these encounters with the studied seriousness of a congressional visit. Squaring off on television programs, in town halls, and at local libraries, she was peppered with questions by members of church groups and reporters.

Fife found that he was developing a grudging respect for Meissner. Before their face-offs, they began to greet each other like old friends forced into opposite corners of a familiar argument. Meissner never would have admitted it to him in public or private, but she was becoming increasingly convinced that there was truth to what Fife was saying. Central Americans were not receiving adequate protection in the US, yet many of their cases, she'd tell colleagues, were "textbook" examples of political persecution.

Meissner was watching government attorneys and State Department officials strain to create legal openings to resettle Southeast Asians at the same time that they were deliberately ignoring straightforward asylum cases from Latin America. The State Department's Bureau of Human Rights endorsed political asylum much more often to Nicaraguans fleeing the Sandinistas than to Salvadorans or Guatemalans hounded by American allies.

Back in Washington, behind closed doors, she began to raise objections. The agency's own statistics left nothing to the imagination. By 1984, at a time when 25 percent of asylum seekers were obtaining a positive result, Salvadorans and Guatemalans were being rejected at a rate of 98 and 99 percent. When she broached the discrepancy with agency lawyers, they grew defensive. A probing report she put together was aggressively dismissed as the "Big Red Book," and the INS general counsel—a former real estate lawyer and ardent Reaganite named Maurice Inman—told her to "deep six it." In 1986, she resigned.

14.

The Heart Doctor Speaks

The six men were locked in a makeshift cell in the basement of a house in Los Angeles. It was May 5, 1983. The smugglers had shut them in and left four big dogs to roam around on the other side of the metal bars, just in case any of the captives tried to squeeze out through the lone, window-size opening at the edge of the cage. Among the men inside, eyeing the dogs, was Juan Romagoza. Thirty years old now, he was still trim and youthful-looking, but his face was weathered in subtle ways that showed around his eyes. They seemed deeper, receding ever so slightly into a new sort of watchfulness.

Reaching the US had been the easy part. The church activists from Cuernavaca had offered to help Juan cross with sanctuary workers, but he declined. "I've been living in Mexico now for two years," he told them. "I'm pretty much Mexican at this point. I talk like a Mexican. I have Mexican papers. There are other people who don't. You should help them." Early one morning in April, Juan joined a group of migrants who had lined up along the Tijuana–San Diego border and waited for the moment when the Border Patrol agents sitting in their pickup trucks started to nod off.

Around four o'clock, while the sky was still dark, he and a bunch of others bolted across. By the time the floodlights came on, he was clear of the border, hiding in a ditch near the interstate. He didn't know where he was, however, and didn't have money for bus fare. Later that morning, he came upon a caravan of migrants loading into a truck driven by a pair of smugglers and joined them. He knew they would probably hold him until he came up with the money for their payment, which he couldn't afford. A cousin and her husband lived in Los Angeles, but he had no idea where. Once they arrived in LA, the smugglers wanted to see his cousin's phone number, so Juan took the number of the restaurant where he used to work in Mexico City and added an LA area code. Each time he called, with the smugglers standing nearby to supervise, he shrugged after a few rings and hung up. "They must be out working," he said.

Two weeks passed, and gradually the other immigrants paid their money and were released. The group of twenty men crammed into the basement dwindled to Juan and a few Guatemalans. On that May night, sometime after they ate dinner, the Mexicans keeping watch had decided to leave for a party. They gave Juan and the others a bottle of tequila and a paper bag full of churros.

Juan and the other men huddled together as soon as their captors were gone. One person suggested tossing the churros to the dogs and then rushing out through the opening in the cell. Another said the dogs would eat the food too fast for the men to get away. A third man suggested something else: What if they soaked the churros in the tequila, then tossed them to the dogs? No one objected; they were too all desperate. Pouring the tequila over the churros, they dangled them through the bars.

Half an hour later the dogs curled up and went to sleep. Juan and the others made a break for it. They burst out of the basement, running up the stairs of the house and out the front door. Once they were far away from the house, they asked someone on the street in Spanish how to reach the one landmark in LA that they knew—MacArthur Park.

◇—◇

One morning near the end of June, officials at the Phoenix INS office received a memo with a curious title: "El Salvadorian Underground Railroad." Its author was an anti-smuggling agent in his early forties named James Rayburn, a Texan from the borderlands and a Vietnam veteran known at the agency for his diligence as an investigator. The document, like the man who wrote it, was dry and to the point. "I strongly recommend that for the present, the 'El Salvadorian Underground Railroad' be assigned to a centralized intelligence office," he wrote. In his view, the sanctuary activists weren't religious figures engaged in a crisis of conscience but rather political combatants who were becoming dangerously untouchable. If the INS arrested the activists, there could be a backlash against the agency. The claims of the sanctuary workers "are well orchestrated to the news media." His suggestion was to increase the agency's surveillance.

Rayburn's dogged approach to the job didn't always accord with the political realities of immigration enforcement. In the mid-1970s, he led an investigation into a smuggling network at the center of the Florida citrus industry that resulted in two high-profile convictions and dozens of arrests. But a group of politically connected Florida growers complained to the Justice Department, and state congressmen halted the prosecutions. A few years later, he was helping to prepare the case against the Manzo Area Council—Margo Cowan's outfit in Tucson—when the Carter administration took office and decided to drop the charges.

In the spring of 1982, he started a file of press clippings on the sanctuary movement. In it was a *People* magazine article about Corbett, the transcript of the *60 Minutes* episode, articles in the local and national newspapers, and the publications of the Chicago Religious Task Force on Central America. He analyzed and annotated each of these documents. The article in *People*, for instance, "created an aura of martyrdom" around Corbett by "drawing the reader's attention to Subject Corbett's poor health and ever-present pain." (Corbett suffered from lupus.) In the spring of 1983, Rayburn watched one of the public debates between John Fife and Doris Meissner with alarm. The activists were now trying "to force US immigration to take them to court on either harboring charges or transportation charges," Rayburn wrote, adding that the "movement will then use the trial as their stage to challenge both U.S. policy on Central American and [INS] policy."

In January 1984, Rayburn's new boss in Phoenix brought orders from the powerful director of the INS's western district, Harold Ezell, a Reagan donor who had previously been the vice president of a California hot-dog chain called Wienerschnitzel International. On the Hill, testifying before Congress, Ezell described his enforcement agenda as "catch 'em . . . clean 'em, and fry 'em." "If the sanctuary movement continues to spread," he told one reporter, it "is going to damage the future of this nation." He told Rayburn to open an investigation, called Operation Sojourner, the following spring.

Rayburn enlisted two undercover operatives to infiltrate the sanctuary movement. His first hire was Salomon Graham, an undocumented Mexican with a criminal record. He'd been arrested twice for illegal entry in the early 1970s, twice more a few years later for alien smuggling, and another time for illegal entry. After he was deported in 1978, he returned under a pseudonym. He and Rayburn had worked together before. In exchange for information about smuggling operations, the government overlooked Graham's felony offenses. Rayburn paid him two hundred dollars in cash to attend events sponsored by advocacy groups opposed to the US involvement in Central America.

While Graham was in his forties and raffish, with dark hair and a thin mustache, Rayburn's other agent, Jesus Cruz, had a more disarming profile. He was in his midfifties, portly, and avuncular. His priors were similar to Graham's, though their legal status was different. A naturalized citizen who was born in Mexico, he began smuggling migrants across the border in the late 1970s. He was caught moving Mexican farmworkers into Iowa in the summer of 1978. They were deported, and he became a government informant. Over the next several years he participated in eight other INS operations. His modus operandi was to insinuate himself into a group of smugglers, then tape them using a bug he wore under his shirt.

When Cruz first showed up at Southside Presbyterian church on a spring day in 1984, the activists were immediately put off. Something seemed odd about the man. Even among a group of passionate altruists he came across as being unusually generous with his time. He seemed young to be a retiree, which he claimed he was, and he was constantly offering to give people rides in his pickup truck. His schedule was always wide open; not once did it seem to interfere, as it did for everyone else. He "just didn't fit," Corbett told the others. There wasn't a clear consensus on this, however. When the activists held a meeting to discuss Cruz, no one could justify casting out a volunteer because of an unconfirmed suspicion.

So Cruz lingered, and the other activists came to rely on him. It helped that the group was constantly short on cars and people. He showed up to meetings and planning sessions, he traveled to Mexico to deliver food to Father Quiñones's church, and before long, he brought reinforcements, in the form of Graham and two other agents, whom he introduced as friends and fellow volunteers. By the summer of 1984, Cruz and the other INS operatives were crossing migrants and traveling as far as California to reunite children with their parents. Their recorders were running the whole time, and they sent the tapes to Rayburn at headquarters—an old post office building in Phoenix, where neither the directory nor the office's outer doors gave any indication that INS was inside.

In the late winter of 1984, agents made two high-profile arrests of sanctuary activists in South Texas. The first led to the conviction of a twenty-nine-year-old sanctuary activist named Stacey Merkt; she received two years' probation after a jury found her guilty of "transporting illegal aliens." The other involved the dramatic apprehension of a peace activist named Jack Elder, who ran a migrant shelter for Central Americans in Brownsville called Casa Óscar Romero.

The materials Cruz, Graham, and the other agents amassed while undercover advanced the agency's investigation into the nucleus of the sanctuary movement in Tucson. But the main breakthrough happened by accident that spring. Two young activists were making a run just before midnight, setting out from the Sacred Heart church, in Nogales, with four Salvadorans on their way to Tucson. A scout car rode ahead of them to check the road for Border Patrol, and the driver called the church to confirm that the coast was clear. Driving late at night posed more risks because that was when professional smugglers tended to work. The activists were also using the only vehicle available that day, a low-riding 1976 Ford station wagon with tinted windows. It was a smuggler's car.

Behind the wheel was Phil Conger, a twenty-seven-year-old Methodist activist from San Diego who'd worked with Peggy Hutchison at the Tucson Metropolitan Ministry. He was chatting with the three Salvadorans in the back seat when he spotted a Border Patrol cruiser lurking by the side of the interstate, about ten miles outside Nogales. When Conger gently pumped the brakes, the siren came on.

Afterward, a judge would rule that the patrolmen had stopped and searched Conger's car unlawfully. But by then the Salvadorans had been placed in deportation proceedings, and government agents had already rifled through Conger's backpack, where they found a thick and detailed document written by Corbett. It was called "Some Proposals for Integrating Smuggling, Refuge, Relay, Sanctuary, and Bailbond Networks." The pages contained details about safe houses, phone numbers, and addresses.

MacArthur Park sat like a shimmering green island in the middle of Central Los Angeles, sliced into two crescents by Wilshire Boulevard. In the northern part of the park were sports fields and a band shell. The lower portion consisted of an oblong lake surrounded by clusters of palm trees and crisscrossing footpaths. Juan knew the general geography from the stories swapped back at the Usulután embassy. "Go to MacArthur," he was told. "You'll find Salvadorans there who can help you."

Over the course of the civil war, the number of Salvadorans living in Los Angeles grew tenfold, to three hundred thousand people, by the end of the decade. In March 1983, Reagan was issuing public warnings that El Salvador was "on the front line of the battle that is really aimed at the very heart of the Western Hemisphere, and eventually at us." He was right that the fates of the US and Central America were entwined, but wrong about why. The Americans were helping to unleash a regional exodus. More than a million Salvadorans were displaced by 1984. Almost a quarter of the country's population would eventually be living in the US. Tens of thousands of them lacked legal status because the American government refused to recognize their legitimate claims to asylum. When Juan arrived, relatively early in this process, the Pico Union and Westlake neighborhoods, which were near MacArthur Park, were already growing dense with Central American transplants.

Juan walked into the southern corner of the park, where streetlamps cast a dim glow. Following the instructions he'd received in Mexico, he picked out an unimposing man standing near a group chattering in Spanish and asked where he could find the Salvadorans from Usulután.

This nook of the park observed an unofficial but distinct order. The area was divided into unmarked zones that corresponded to the different regions of El Salvador. Beside one tree were Salvadorans from Chalatenango. In a small clearing, only a few yards away, were refugees from Santa Ana and the capital. An uninitiated passerby might see cliques of foreign men. But to Juan it was as though the map of his country had been compressed, spliced, and superimposed onto a few hundred square feet of Los Angeles park space. The man waved him over to a copse within view of the lake, where twenty men from Usulután were lounging around—some asleep on the grass, others talking quietly, and still more drinking tequila from paper bags.

It didn't take long for Juan to find someone in the group who knew his cousin and could give him directions to her house. The next day he found her and her husband. Shocked to see him, they immediately drove him back to MacArthur Park, this time to take care of some paperwork. In a different section of the park, hawkers sold fake social security cards, work authorization forms, and identity documents for five dollars apiece. Juan would need these to find a job, but his cousin insisted that he start by taking English classes at a small language school. Juan disagreed, wanting to waste no time making money he could send home to the rest of his family. Because he planned on returning to El Salvador soon, he didn't see the point in learning a new language. His cousin, who'd been in Los Angeles for several years and claimed to know better, did not relent. He was staying in her house and spending her family's money to get on his feet; eventually, he capitulated. For the next three weeks, he started his days in a small, overheated ESL classroom crammed behind a desk alongside dozens of other recent arrivals. Around two thirty, class let out, and he'd walk over to MacArthur Park to spend the rest of his afternoon getting to know his new surroundings.

The Salvadorans in the park—all men—had each narrowly escaped murder, unlike so many of their friends, relatives, and spouses. Other family members had stayed behind because traveling north was too dangerous, expensive, and uncertain. A large contingent of the men drank and raged and lurched around in a fog. Others drifted into a quieter, nightly oblivion, having spent the day working menial jobs to the point of exhaustion.

Juan was magnetic and approachable, with his wide, dark eyes radiating candor, and his limp suggesting both vulnerability and endurance. One day, a ragged man with a pallid, haggard face confessed to Juan that the sound of his own screaming was waking him up every night. He and his brother-in-law had worked together on a construction crew in San Salvador, and both belonged to a union. They were kidnapped one day after work, detained together while National Guardsmen tortured the brother-in-law. The man told Juan that the soldiers had made him watch when they finally shot his brother-in-law in the head. The survivor's guilt was almost worse than the memory itself. "Something similar happened to me, too," Juan said, without elaborating.

Each day, he returned to the park and carried on the conversation with the man and a few others. Juan's cousin disapproved of his trips. She called the men there *chusma*—riffraff—which Juan interpreted less as judgment than as an expression of fear. To her, the whole point of coming to the US was to escape political dangers, not to relive them.

A turning point came one afternoon when Juan arrived at the park earlier than usual, determined to get in a few hours of uninterrupted conversation before the drinking began that evening. He and a few others were sitting under a tree and reminiscing about Usulután. Exile made these reminiscences painful. The participants would go around the circle naming mutual friends and trying to ascertain if they were alive or dead. Most of the time the names were met with one-or-two-word responses: *lo mataron* (they killed him), *desaparecido* (disappeared), or *nadie sabe* (no one knows). This time someone began to cry, and the conversation came back to Juan. "You were also a prisoner at one point, weren't you?" someone asked him. "What happened?"

Juan sat back and narrated the story of his final months in El Salvador. With a steady, unwavering voice, he lifted his eyes every few sentences to meet those of his listeners. Usually, when conversations turned to dark subjects, the men leapt to their feet as though scalded, and the spell would be broken. A soccer ball would roll into view, or someone would pluck a guitar string. This time no one moved. Instead of receding into their customary silence, the men began to ask questions. It was as though his listeners couldn't stand for him to pause between the answers. What was the worst torture he experienced? What sorts of questions did his torturers ask him? Who did they ask him about?

Who was doing the asking? At a certain point, Juan had to tell them to raise their hands. "I promise I'll answer each of your questions," he said.

He noticed that they began referring to him reverently as "doctor." Eventually, Juan ended the session, announcing it was time for soccer. "The doctor is our goalie," one of them said, protectively. It was the only position Juan could play with his injured leg.

15.

A Park Called Pain

Juan knew soon after arriving in Los Angeles that eventually he'd travel north to San Francisco. After three months, it was time. An aunt had been living there since the end of the Second World War, and through her as well as some old friends from Usulután Juan saw it as the main hub for Central Americans on the West Coast. Los Angeles had several Latino barrios, where, as the city's most recent arrivals, Salvadorans occupied the lower rungs of an unforgiving urban hierarchy. In San Francisco, which had drawn Salvadorans for decades, one main neighborhood, the Mission District, was dominated by Spanish speakers. At its western edge was Dolores Park, where Juan spent his first two weeks, sleeping outside in the crisp, foreign air of the Bay Area. He followed the lead of the other Salvadorans camped out in the park, picking up bedding and blankets from a nearby church.

If Tucson was ground zero of the sanctuary movement, San Francisco had been its vanguard in the early 1970s when conscientious objectors partnered with the city's more activist congregations to oppose the Vietnam War. Local clergy also got involved in housing Chilean refugees fleeing the newly installed regime of Augusto Pinochet, who had overthrown the previous government in the fall of 1973, with the help of the US State Department and the CIA.

What distinguished the activists in San Francisco, beyond their unusual organizational sophistication, was their proximity to power. The Catholic Church wasn't merely sympathetic to the causes of social justice in Latin America; its archbishop, John Quinn, an eloquent, silver-haired Californian in his midfifties, was at the forefront of the opposition to the American war effort. He also happened to be the president of the National Conference of Catholic Bishops in the late 1970s. In March 1980, he attended Óscar Romero's funeral in San Salvador, where he was caught in the stampede of mourners after gunmen had opened fire on the crowds. When the Salvadoran government blamed the left for the incident, Quinn used his prominence in the US to rebut the charges. "There is a tendency to blame the leftists for all things," he told a reporter that April. "The leftist elements, which we all saw clearly from the altar where I was standing, were peaceful. . . . The first bomb was thrown at them." He went on to urge Jimmy Carter to end military aid to the Salvadoran government, and in the years after turned his attention to the failures of American immigration policy. At the California Governor's Prayer Breakfast in January 1982—ordinarily a somnolent, apolitical affair—he rattled attendees with a forceful speech about deportations. "Large numbers of Salvadoran men, women, and children are regularly being shipped back to El Salvador and an almost certain death," he said.

In Dolores Park, Juan continued the work he'd begun in MacArthur, organizing homeless Salvadorans into therapy groups. They sat in circles—jittery and skittish about talking, but desperate and therefore patient—as Juan gently coaxed them into opening up. The setting was appropriate for their mission, he liked to say: *dolores*, in Spanish, meant pain. "I'm going to have the faith to share my *dolores* with you," he said. "You should, too." Afterward, he'd walk around the neighborhood, down Eighteenth Street heading west toward the Castro. On the streets, vendors ducked into laundromats and dollar stores selling pupusas from small carts, while women stationed themselves on the corners with baskets of tamales and fresh cheese. Used clothing folded neatly for sale sat in piles on blankets unfurled on the sidewalk.

One afternoon, a woman came up to Juan in Dolores Park with a mysterious request. Someone at Casa El Salvador wanted to talk with him. Casa El Salvador was one of a handful of Central American organizations across the country opposing US involvement in the region. It also worked closely with church groups and relief agencies to provide services for newly arrived refugees. Juan's reputation in the park had reached the organizers, and they wanted to vet him to lead an independent group, separate from Casa El Salvador's political operation, to aid Salvadorans and Guatemalans who needed medical attention, food, and shelter in San Francisco.

The emissary in the park was a sign of caution. For the past several years, the FBI had been surveilling any group with ties to the Central American left. The Committee in Solidarity with the People of El Salvador (CISPES), one of the bigger advocacy groups, had at least 180 chapters across the US; some twenty-three hundred Americans associated with these offices were the subjects of sustained surveillance. Agents infiltrated their meetings just as the INS had done with the sanctuary movement, though the FBI took its investigations further. They broke into rectories, NGO offices, and private residences. The burglaries started to fit a recognizable fact pattern: agents would filch pamphlets, address books, contact lists, and photographs, while leaving behind the sorts of valuables that would typically attract the attention of petty criminals. One *Boston Globe* reporter, working the crime beat in Cambridge in late 1984, was initially dispatched to cover a string of church break-ins; by the time he grasped the full range of the incidents, he'd chronicled nearly two hundred reported cases from Phoenix, Berkeley, and Dallas to Louisville and Detroit.

The INS investigators had received strict instructions to stick to domestic targets, but the FBI was coordinating directly with the Salvadoran National Guard. Around the time that Juan arrived in Mexico, a series of meetings was taking place in El Salvador. An FBI recruit named Frank Varelli, a naturalized Salvadoran living in Dallas, traveled to San Salvador to meet with General Vides Casanova. Their relationship was personal. Varelli's father, a former colonel in the Salvadoran army, was a close friend and admirer of Vides Casanova; now, with the White House's blessing, Vides Casanova was on the verge of becoming the country's next defense minister. Six years later, a Senate investigation uncovered the nature of Varelli and Vides Casanova's partnership: together they generated a large body of information, almost all of it fabricated, in which Salvadoran intelligence sources identified members of CISPES as part of international "terrorist support" groups working in the US as agents of a foreign power. These leads became the FBI's basis for launching deeper investigations.

"Politics can be a barrier to people here," Juan told the organizer at Casa El Salvador, an engineer in his early twenties named José Artiga. They met at the corner of Twentieth Street and Mission. "There are Salvadorans on the streets who aren't all sympathetic to the FMLN. It's best for me to stay neutral, and to help them as refugees." It was exactly what Artiga had wanted to hear. He'd spent the past three years in the US watching the Reagan administration brand asylum-seeking Salvadorans as communists and agitators. "We'll want you to keep your distance," he told Juan. "You can't be seen with an FMLN flag, or wearing red clothes. We need a strict split."

Juan started to lead a small group of a dozen immigrants that he called the *comité de refugiados*—or CRECE, the Central American Refugee Committee. There wasn't an office in its early days, so each weekend Juan set up a table in the hallway of the Most Holy Redeemer church, on Diamond Street near the Castro. He was already a familiar presence there, having recently moved into one of the small apartments at the back of the building that the church used to provide sanctuary.

The work itself was constant and intense, an endless improvisation. Salvadoran immigrants would turn up at all hours of the day. Some of them hadn't eaten; others lacked clothes or housing. Everyone was looking for work and legal advice. There was hot food on a rotating daily basis at St. Teresa of Avila church, St. Anthony's, and the Buen Pastor; weekly clothing drives at St. Mary's; and legal consultations at St. John's, a Lutheran church on Twenty-second Street. Juan led group therapy sessions, and the committee referred Central Americans to health clinics in the Mission and to hospitals that offered free services.

For the first time, Juan was beginning to think of himself as a health administrator. Working in the undocumented immigrant community required dealing with a whole universe of complicated logistics. If someone walked into the church with a condition like diabetes, it wasn't enough to schedule a full exam. Juan himself couldn't conduct it because he lacked an American medical license. But if further testing was needed, or if additional symptoms arose, he'd have to make separate arrangements with another provider, cobbling together pro bono offerings from different doctors and clinics across the city. None of his patients had insurance, and few had social security cards. Their precariousness reminded him of the *campesinos* he had treated in Chalatenango and on the fringes of San Salvador. There was no official system they could access, no legal tools for them to use; they depended, in essence, on ad hoc acts of generosity.

Life in the US was a daily collision of all the accumulated injuries that had brought them there. Medical appointments were pointless if the patients never showed, and it took concerted effort to convince Salvadorans who were frantic to find work that their debilitating migraines or insomnia were physical manifestations of deeper emotional pain. In El Salvador, they might have been hunted by death squads and federal troops, but in San Francisco they lived under the threat of arrest and deportation.

Juan recruited a team of Spanish-speaking psychology students from the University of California, Berkeley, to help with counseling a few days a week. It was from them that he learned about an emerging strain of medical literature on a condition called post-traumatic stress disorder. It had first appeared in the third edition of the American Psychiatric Association's *Diagnostic and Statistical Manual of Mental Disorders*, in 1980. Through the latter part of the 1970s, PTSD was known as "Post-Vietnam syndrome" because its most conspicuous victims were American veterans.

SINCE ARRIVING IN THE US, Juan had been using the generic last name Pérez, but on the streets of the Mission he was known simply as "Doctor." He'd quickly earned the kind of status of a town elder. People stopped him to ask for advice or to thank him for his work; sometimes they pressed small gifts into his hands— a piece of pastry, a loaf of bread. He moved around the neighborhood with a cane and a pronounced limp, and the teeming streets parted in his path.

Juan was also becoming more active in San Francisco's sanctuary movement, speaking out at church gatherings and to the press. He led caravans of immigrants to cities in the area (San Jose, Sacramento), where other churches put them up for a few days and publicized their stories. Articles about his work were published in the *San Francisco Chronicle*, the *Lodi News-Sentinel*, *The Daily Californian*, *The Mercury News*. His name would be written as Juan Pérez, or just Juan. The photos showed a short, athletic-looking man in his thirties wearing a white cowboy hat, sneakers, and a T-shirt with the face of Óscar Romero emblazoned across the chest; his mouth was almost always open—mid-shout—a fist in the air. When people asked him if he was scared doing all this as an undocumented immigrant, he replied, "Part of the therapy is shedding our fear."

Juan Romagoza leads a group marching from San Jose to San Francisco to protest US support for the Salvadoran military, March 1984.

Juan resting with a group of Salvadoran refugees during an annual caravan to celebrate the life of Óscar Romero and to protest American involvement in the Salvadoran civil war. San Francisco, March 1985.

Each week at the church, he gathered with other members of the *comité de refugiados* in a room with a television. In 1983 and 1984, the American president was often on the screen speaking in bold, unapologetic terms about Central America. You wouldn't know it from his sparkling delivery, but his cabinet remained divided between hardliners at the Defense Department, the National Security Council, and the Department of Justice and moderates at the State Department. At one point, that August, the US military conducted a series of air and naval exercises near Nicaragua in a clear attempt to intimidate the Sandinistas. William Clark and Caspar Weinberger, at the National Security

Council and the Pentagon, orchestrated the operation without consulting George Shultz, the secretary of state. They were suspicious because Shultz and his subordinates, with the backing of a few sympathizers at the White House, were developing a "two-track" approach in El Salvador that combined more military aid with efforts to start talks between the government and the FMLN rebels. The ideologues dismissed these plans as a sign of weakness; the moderates considered the ideologues ignorant and impractical. One White House aide complained to *The Washington Post* that the administration's internecine struggles were leading to a "guerrilla war" of constant leaks, sabotage, and recriminations.

The situation on the ground in El Salvador was growing more muddled for the Americans. Acting on a US plan originally drawn up for South Vietnam, the Salvadoran military initiated a new campaign to drive the guerrillas from a few key departments. The FMLN lay low for several months, then struck back. They overran the government's forces in December at the El Paraíso military base in Chalatenango, which the Americans had long considered impenetrable. A hundred government troops were killed, and another 160 were captured. The Salvadoran government buried its casualties with bulldozers to hide their losses. In private, officers acknowledged what the Americans did not: all the weapons, money, and military advisers from the US were prolonging the fighting without changing the outcome. In 1980, the Salvadoran military had twelve thousand troops; four years later, boosted by American largesse of $1 million in aid a day, it had forty-two thousand. But on the battlefield, they were still fighting to preserve a stalemate. "The only way to salvage the situation is to give the troops something to fight for," one of the Salvadoran officers admitted to a reporter from *The Christian Science Monitor*. "Until that time, we cannot be saved, no matter how much military equipment arrives from the United States."

Juan followed the news from friends and family in El Salvador, and every few days Casa El Salvador released bulletins with updates on the fighting. All through the summer and fall, the Salvadoran death squads rampaged against Christian Democrats and trade unionists. The Salvadoran Assembly was prepared to pass a law that the US had come to see as essential to justify its investment in the Salvadoran political system. It was a measure known as land reform, to redistribute more than three hundred agricultural estates to peasant cooperatives and to grant 125,000 tenant farmers and sharecroppers smaller plots. The aim was to level the gross social inequalities that had given rise to the civil war. But now far-right members of the armed forces were openly murdering and threatening American partners in the effort. Officials at the State Department frantically met with the Salvadoran president, whom they had virtually handpicked for the job two years before. But when he tried to talk to the military brass, they rebuffed him. "I have no power, no authority," he subsequently told the Americans. Reagan, meanwhile, was undercutting his own diplomats. First, he vetoed a bill that would have kept in place the minimal human rights certification requirements in El Salvador. Then, a month later, he publicly defended the death squads. "I'm going to voice a suspicion I've never said aloud before," he said. "I wonder if all this is rightwing, or if those guerrilla forces have not realized that . . . they can get away with these violent acts, helping to try to bring down the government, and the rightwing will be blamed for it."

When Juan heard Reagan adopt the line of the Salvadoran far right, he redoubled his sanctuary work. The caravans he helped organize in California were growing, and he traveled with larger groups to farther-flung cities, such as Seattle, Chicago, and Washington, DC. The advocates were now trying to get municipal governments to declare themselves sanctuary jurisdictions in solidarity with the Central Americans living there. The premise was to have local police departments limit their dealings with the INS, so that arrests for petty crimes wouldn't automatically end in a person's deportation. Church activists courted the support of union heads, school-board directors, and other power players in local politics. Juan would be called in to add a face to the proposition, steeling himself in front of unfamiliar audiences to recount his story of fleeing El Salvador, in a mix of Spanish and broken English.

A second strategy was tied to legislation recently introduced in the US Congress to suspend deportations during the Salvadoran civil war. Its chief authors were an Arizona senator named Dennis DeConcini and the Boston-based congressman Joe Moakley. Each had entered the fray because of sanctuary activists.

DeConcini was a former prosecutor who'd previously been wary of causes involving undocumented immigrants. But he'd also worked as a county attorney in Tucson, and he knew John Fife. He visited Southside Presbyterian church and spoke to some of the Salvadorans seeking sanctuary there. After listening to their stories, he decided to travel to El Salvador to meet with members of the leftist opposition, and dispatched staffers to the immigration jail at El Centro, in California, to document allegations of mistreatment.

The first Moakley heard about the plight of the Salvadorans was when a bunch of constituents showed up to tell him about it. It was a Friday, in 1983, and he was holding a regular constituent meeting at a post office in the Boston neighborhood of Jamaica Plain. "Congressman, you really need to listen to these folks," one of the attendees he knew told him. A small group came forward and introduced themselves as members of the Ecumenical Social Action Committee. For the rest of the decade, Moakley became Congress's most implacable fighter for the rights of Salvadorans. But the bills he and DeConcini introduced languished in the usual fashion. Most Republicans opposed them, and a large share of Democrats were scared to take on Reagan.

Every March 24, Juan led a caravan of activists to commemorate the day of Óscar Romero's assassination, but in 1984 the atmosphere was unusually charged. The next day, El Salvador was holding elections. If the Christian Democrats backed by the Americans won, the Reagan administration would be validated; if they lost, the White House strategy would be up for grabs. Juan and the other activists were ambivalent. While the Christian Democrats were politically moderate—a far cry from the violent supremacy of the extreme right—their role in the government gave cover to the military. The generals were still the ones in charge. A victory for the Christian Democrats was a victory for Reagan—and thus the status quo. "One thing Congress can't resist is an election," a senior administration official said at the time. "Assuming we have a fair and open one that elects Duarte"—the leader of the Christian Democrats—"we should be able to prevail in getting more aid for El Salvador."

This was exactly what happened. José Duarte eventually won, and in the spring, he came to Washington to lobby for more aid. His visit overshadowed another, simultaneous event: the US government had to evacuate the American ambassador in San Salvador after uncovering a death-squad plot to assassinate him. On May 9, Reagan delivered a prime-time address on Central America, urging Congress to act. "This Communist subversion poses the threat that 100 million people, from Panama to the open border on our south, could come under the control of pro-Soviet regimes," he said. He also warned that the consequences could involve "hundreds of thousands of refugees fleeing Communist oppression." The Democrats caved, and Congress gave the president what he wanted—$200 million in military aid, nearly two and a half times the previous year's appropriation.

On the night of November 6, 1984, Juan turned off the TV early as the election returns came in. Reagan won in a landslide.

16.

Sanctuary Goes to Trial

On January 14, 1985, the government indicted sixteen people involved in the Arizona sanctuary movement. A few of them had limited connections to the cause, and they pleaded out. The wider group—eleven others who were directly involved in the border operations—planned to go to trial. None of these holdouts surprised the government. They included John Fife; James Corbett; Peggy Hutchison; Phil Conger; a Catholic priest from Nogales, Arizona, named Anthony Clark; and Darlene Nicgorski, a nun who'd previously worked in Guatemala and Nicaragua. Ramón Quiñones and a congregant at his church named María del Socorro Pardo de Aguilar were Mexican, and thus could ignore the charges. But they decided to face them in the US with their peers.

There were seventy-one counts in the indictment, which alleged a criminal conspiracy to smuggle and harbor illegal aliens. The charges carried real consequences for the activists, including potential prison time, but as always, the migrants faced the greatest risks. Fifty-five Salvadorans and Guatemalans who'd passed through Tucson between March and November 1984 and were now living in the US were named as "illegal alien unindicted co-conspirators." The government offered to drop the criminal charges against them if they testified at the trial, but it was putting them into deportation proceedings regardless. INS agents began the roundups immediately.

Before the indictment had been announced, a conference to discuss the state of the movement had been scheduled for January 24 at a synagogue in Tucson. Some of the organizers had billed the event as a "shoot-out" between the Tucson and Chicago chapters, which were increasingly at odds. At the start of the month, three hundred people were registered to attend; after the indictment, the guest list swelled to fifteen hundred. The movement had quickly raised more than $1 million for the National Sanctuary Defense Fund. Topflight trial attorneys offered their services, as well as seasoned lawyers from prominent civil rights groups and firms in New York and San Francisco. At the conference, a Salvadoran minister and a Maya K'iche' activist from Guatemala spoke about the political situation in the region. William Sloane Coffin of the Riverside Church, in New York City, gave a rousing speech about the necessity of activism, and Elie Wiesel, the Holocaust survivor and Nobel laureate, delivered the keynote. "Woe to our society if to be human becomes a heroic act," he said.

Among the attendees was Juan Romagoza, an admirer of Fife and the Tucson activists since his days in Mexico, when their names were bywords for the American resistance. He traveled to Tucson with a small contingent from San Francisco and stayed in a convent near the St. Augustine Cathedral for the duration of the conference. It was the first time he'd been to Tucson; to him the city was an almost mythic place.

The grave national implications of the trial, scheduled for the following fall, obscured the deepening fissures at the heart of the movement. These tensions threatened the activists nearly as much as the US attorneys. The Chicago activists criticized the Tucson chapter for referring only 5 percent of the migrants they crossed for what was called "public sanctuary." This was the network of which Juan was a part: the Central Americans who told their stories to the press and at public events. For their part, Fife and Corbett never forgave the Chicago activists for their absolutism. After the indictment, members of the Tucson chapter had further cause for complaint. The INS investigators had used publications released by the Chicago Religious Task Force to make the case that the sanctuary movement was built around politics and not morals. Members of the Tucson chapter had tried to keep their messaging clear: they were defending laws like the 1980 Refugee Act, which the government itself was flouting. The government investigators, however, amassed contradictory documents and statements published in Chicago. Citing the explicit doctrines of the Chicago Religious Task Force, the prosecutors portrayed the movement as being primarily anti-Reagan.

Juan and Eileen Purcell, a close friend and fellow activist who had been central to the earliest stages of the sanctuary push in the Bay Area, attended one of the breakout sessions at the conference. They sat together in a half circle of folding plastic chairs in a Sunday-school classroom. The American activists tended to speak first, making their cases; then the confrontational spirit would ebb, and someone would remember to say, "What do the refugees here think?"

Juan spoke in one of these lulls. "During the day, we do our jobs and support sanctuary, but at night we all dream that we're home, in our own country," he said. His remarks didn't slot neatly into the zero-sum terms of the Chicago-Tucson standoff. He resided in San Francisco, but never stopped living in El Salvador. "The dream is to reunite with our families. But to be able to go back, to be able to have contact, we need there to be peace," he continued. One of Juan's strengths as a speaker was to be disarmingly plainspoken—argument without artifice—like he was talking to himself and allowing others to listen in. The movement *had* to take on Reagan, he said. "If we don't ask about all that, then what is it that we want? How can we protect the people who are still there?"

Oral arguments began on November 15, 1985, but in a key sense the trial was over before it began because of the judge, a curmudgeonly Arizonan nominated to the federal bench by Jimmy Carter who had a reputation for unpredictability. His name was Earl Carroll, and neither the defense nor the prosecution was happy about drawing him. But it didn't take long for both parties to recognize that the defendants had the bigger problem.

When the government issued its indictment, it also submitted a long and detailed request on everything it wanted the judge to exclude from the case—namely, all the context that explained the motivations of the sanctuary activists. They requested that he impose tight restrictions on testimony about the conditions in El Salvador and Guatemala; the likelihood of deportations leading to death; the suspiciously high rejection rates for asylum claims coming from these countries; the US role in the region's wars; the INS's glaring record of mistreating asylum seekers; the tenets of international law; and the terms of the 1980 Refugee Act. All the government was bringing before the court was the narrow question of whether the sanctuary workers had helped cross and harbor undocumented immigrants.

By the start of November, as the two sides were finalizing jury selection, Judge Carroll announced his decision to exclude any testimony or material that went beyond the most immediate question at hand. As he put it, only the attorney general of the United States had the power to admit immigrants as asylees. All the witnesses the defense lawyers had planned to call—human rights experts, legal scholars, church figures—could no longer testify. There'd be no point in putting any of the defendants on the stand either, because the judge wouldn't allow them to explain their thinking. As Miriam Davidson, who covered the trial for *The Christian Science Monitor*, wrote in her book *Convictions of the Heart*:

> The only real defense he left open was if the sanctuary workers could say they didn't know that a person hadn't been presented to the INS. If that were the case, they did not "knowingly and willfully" break the law. But the point was they *did* know—they knew they couldn't present a person to the INS because to do so would only speed up his or her deportation. And that point they were not allowed to explain.

In the eight-month trial, the defendants called no witnesses and barely mounted their own case. Given the restrictions imposed by Judge Carroll, there was little they could say. Donald Reno Jr., the US attorney trying the case for the government, knew that his main vulnerabilities were the people employed by the INS to conduct the investigation. Salomon Graham, for instance, had once faced allegations of pimping women out to undocumented field hands in Florida. He had ignored the INS's instructions and secretly recorded the sanctuary activists while they were in church and in Mexico. The leader of the operation, James Rayburn, had an obvious personal animus. These men were kept off the stand during the trial. Of the seventeen witnesses called by the government, only one, an INS agent named John Nixon, was an American citizen. The rest were the Salvadorans and Guatemalans who'd been named as "illegal alien unindicted co-conspirators" and Jesus Cruz, a Mexican.

In mid-January 1986, a forty-four-year-old Salvadoran labor leader who went by the name Alejandro Rodríguez took the stand. He was a husband and father of four, who had worked as an industrial electrician in El Salvador and had been the secretary of a large construction union. State security forces had jailed and tortured him for his work, and he fled with his family to Mexico. ("We're not going to get into ears and eyes and individual tortures," Judge Carroll warned from the bench.)

The US government had put Rodríguez in a bind, and he was testifying grudgingly. He and his family were living in Rochester, New York, when the INS found them. Reno wanted Rodríguez to name the sanctuary worker who'd helped him and his family get across the border. She "was the only person who offered me a roof over my head when I was most in need," Rodríguez said. Each time he strayed from Reno's script, according to reporting by Davidson, the attorney interrupted his own witness to ask Judge Carroll to strike the answer.

These exchanges grew more awkward when the defense began its questioning. Rodríguez was the exemplar of the kind of asylees the US government was supposed to be helping. In El Salvador, his wife worked as the comptroller of a Salvadoran subsidiary of an American corporation, and the couple owned a farm, two homes, and a bus, which generated more earnings; they made roughly forty thousand dollars a year in El Salvador, a respectable, middle-class income. When they fled, it wasn't in search of money but of protection. They had had to abandon everything they owned. In Mexico City, Rodríguez had gone directly to the UN High Commissioner for Refugees and submitted to a three-hour interview. UNHCR gave him a document confirming his status as a political refugee. The plan was to wait for the US, the Netherlands, Belgium, Canada, or Switzerland to admit the family. But after four months without word, Rodríguez began to worry that their papers would expire and that they could get arrested and deported. That was when he decided to enter the US.

Frequently, after Reno rose to object during Rodríguez's testimony, Judge Carroll would instruct the jury to forget what it had just heard. This was a metaphor not just for the whole trial, but for the blinkered approach the US took on asylum: the government suppressed any facts that chafed with its agenda.

Why, Reno wanted to know, hadn't Rodríguez applied for asylum as soon as he set foot in the US?

Rodríguez replied that he'd needed time to gather documentation. He started to explain what his lawyer had told him: the government was rejecting Salvadoran asylum applications at an exceptionally high rate. But before he could finish his sentence, Reno objected. Carroll stopped the testimony.

In early 1985, around the time of the indictments, a group of lawyers in San Francisco and New York were discussing how to defend the sanctuary workers in court. Many of them were immigration lawyers who had already been working together to find ways to protect asylum seekers from mistreatment by the INS in the 1970s and early '80s. Representing hundreds of clients from dozens of different countries, they had come to know the agency well and could identify trends in the government's treatment of Central Americans compared with other nationalities.

In San Francisco, two young attorneys were at the forefront of these efforts— Marc Van Der Hout, who practiced immigration law full time from an office in Redwood City, and Carolyn Patty Blum, who worked at an immigrants' rights group before starting an asylum clinic at the University of California, Berkeley. Both had been involved in the sanctuary movement themselves and had close relationships with religious leaders, faith workers, and other progressive legal organizations. This network brought them into contact with Ellen Yaroshefsky, a staff lawyer at the Center for Constitutional Rights, and Lucas Guttentag, the director of the Immigrants' Rights Project at the ACLU in New York. It was a heady time to work on immigration. The situation in Central America was front-page news, and the Refugee Act had introduced a wide new field of legal possibilities.

For the past few years, the lawyers had been trying to use individual cases to fashion collective protections for Central American asylum seekers. The work was mostly trial and error. It began with a project that Van Der Hout and Blum called "the young male case" in the early 1980s. Young men from their late teens to their midthirties were routinely coerced into fighting for the Salvadoran government and killed as guerrilla sympathizers if they resisted or deserted. Just being young and male in El Salvador made someone a target for persecution, so the two American lawyers zeroed in on the language of the 1980 Refugee Act to craft an argument. According to the law, a migrant eligible for protection was someone persecuted for his "race, religion, nationality, or membership in a particular social group or political opinion." The category of "particular social group" was usefully open-ended. Van Der Hout and Blum applied the phrase to young, working-class Salvadoran men of military age who would refuse to enlist in the armed forces. Their general political views were irrelevant; the young men's identity alone led the government to make a specific—and often fatal—assumption that they opposed the regime. A judge rejected the argument, but momentum for similar challenges was building.

In another case filed at the same time, *Orantes-Hernandez v. Smith*, a different group of lawyers urged a federal court to stop the INS from forcing immigrants to sign voluntary departure forms. The practice amounted to clear coercion of asylum seekers to abandon their legal claims. This time, a judge sided with the plaintiffs, but the INS, which was unaccustomed to judicial checks, dragged its feet. The legal wrangling continued for years. Later, in Los Angeles, a separate case, *Mendez v. Reno*, challenged the INS officials tasked with holding asylum interviews. They "were not trained and were ignorant of applicable asylum law"; "interpreters were not provided"; and "sessions were rushed with little privacy." An ancillary aim of the case was to compel government officials to sit down for depositions. Under oath, asylum officials whose job was to execute the terms of the Refugee Act were forced to admit that they couldn't name any of the legal grounds for asylum.

In May 1985, a group of eighty religious, refugee, and legal assistance organizations responded to the sanctuary indictments by filing a lawsuit—*American Baptist Churches in the USA v. Meese*—in a federal court in Northern California. Representing them were Van Der Hout, Blum, Guttentag, and Yaroshefsky, who together identified Reagan's attorney general, the commissioner of the INS, and the secretary of state as defendants. The religious organizations made two arguments. They claimed that the First Amendment protected their right to give sanctuary to refugees. And, on behalf of individual refugees, they accused the government of discriminating against asylum requests made by Salvadorans and Guatemalans. The lawyers cited the INS's own data showing that Salvadorans and Guatemalans were rejected at a much higher rate than asylum seekers from other countries.

For half a decade now, the position of the Reagan administration had been categorical: "It's not enough to be fleeing a civil war," Elliott Abrams said just weeks before the lawyers filed the American Baptist Churches (ABC) lawsuit. "You have to show that you, personally, are a target." But the INS numbers exposed a bias. If the government was preemptively ruling out claims brought by Salvadorans and Guatemalans, then applying for asylum was a foregone conclusion. On average, the US granted asylum to 23 percent of everyone who applied. But the grant rate for Nicaraguans was 14 percent, 34 percent for Poles, and 60 percent for Iranians. For Salvadorans it was less than 3 percent; for Guatemalans, less than 1 percent.

The ABC lawsuit and the sanctuary case overlapped in substance, but they proceeded along vastly different timelines. The Tucson trial dominated the headlines, as the ABC lawsuit plodded through procedural motions. On May 1, 1986, the Tucson jury found eight of the eleven defendants guilty on smuggling and conspiracy charges. Judge Carroll said, "The [immigration] system works. It works slowly, but that's not the fault of the system. It's the fault of the people who use it." Nevertheless, in July, he sentenced the sanctuary workers to probation—a notably lenient outcome.

Over the next four years, the government tried three separate times to convince a judge to throw out the American Baptist Churches lawsuit. The First Amendment component was eventually dismissed, but the discrimination claims withstood each of the challenges. In September 1989, a federal judge ruled that that case could proceed, and he certified as a nationwide class the Salvadorans and Guatemalans who'd been denied asylum.

By then, after a decade of delays, the government was on the verge of approving a series of regulations for implementing the Refugee Act. Advocates had long been pushing for these changes, which created a corps of government officials trained to handle asylum claims and established clearer standards to ensure that applicants were treated equally regardless of their home countries. "Too often in recent years we have tolerated a double standard, under which asylum has been unfairly denied to legitimate refugees for fear of embarrassing friendly but repressive governments," said Ted Kennedy, the chairman of the Senate Judiciary's subcommittee on immigration. Faced with having to share documents and to sit for depositions in the ABC lawsuit, government lawyers opted to settle. The case was now called *ABC v. Thornburgh*, renamed for George H. W. Bush's attorney general. In 1991, a settlement was reached, allowing some three hundred thousand Salvadorans and Guatemalans to remain in the US and reapply for asylum.

17.

Nothing More Permanent Than a Temporary Immigrant

Juan Romagoza had never met a Salvadoran or Guatemalan who received asylum in the US, and by the time he was running CRECE very few immigrants bothered to ask about it. The prospect of winning a case was too remote. The close ties between the US and Salvadoran governments scared away anyone who hadn't already been put off by the odds. Juan heard constantly that Salvadorans in San Francisco might be risking the safety of their families back home anytime they attended a rally or church event. Most of the time he could reassure them, but applying for asylum involved handing over personal information to a government they didn't trust.

In 1985, as the Arizona activists were preparing for trial, cities across the country were declaring themselves sanctuary jurisdictions. Chicago, Berkeley, and Saint Paul did so in March; followed by Cambridge in April; Madison, Wisconsin, in May; and New York, Los Angeles, and Olympia, Washington, in the fall. In December, after months of intense lobbying, the San Francisco board of supervisors held a vote on its own measure.

On the morning of December 18, wearing a pair of khakis and a button-down shirt, Juan stood before the eleven members of the city board of supervisors. There were more than a dozen people testifying in support of the sanctuary resolution, but he was the only refugee. The day's program listed him, simply, as "Juan (pseudonym), Central American Refugee Community." It had been two years since he had first told his story in MacArthur Park, and now his audience consisted of the top American officials in his adopted city, including the mayor herself, Dianne Feinstein, a rising Democrat. He calmed his nerves with a mantra he'd honed after leaving El Salvador: "I am here to do this."

On Christmas Eve, the board of supervisors voted eight to three to adopt the sanctuary resolution, making it the thirteenth city nationwide to do so. There was also bigger news in Washington. After four years of touch-and-go negotiations and multiple failures, an immigration reform bill was lumbering toward a vote in Congress. Talks centered on three sweeping areas of legislation: tougher border enforcement, penalties for employers who knowingly hired undocumented workers, and a plan to legalize three million immigrants living in the US.

In January 1986, one group of House Democrats was meeting privately to revive talks on temporary agricultural workers, a subject that had split apart the caucus, while other members were trying to broaden the scope of the legalization policy. A comprehensive bill provided a cutoff date—January 1, 1982—for when someone must have arrived in the US to qualify for citizenship. Because tens of thousands of Central Americans had arrived before then, the measure would have a huge impact on the Salvadoran and Guatemalan communities in the US. But Juan hadn't arrived until 1983, too late to be eligible.

The Moakley-DeConcini proposal on extended voluntary departure was introduced as an amendment to the larger bill, but it had powerful foes from the start. The Reagan administration lobbied hard against it, with Alan Nelson, the INS commissioner, warning that there'd be "an invasion of feet people" if it were ever adopted. "There are forty wars raging in the world," he said. The "bill will open the door to all of them." Alan Simpson, who was now the sponsor of the comprehensive bill, said, "There's nothing more permanent than a temporary immigrant. . . . They come here, they have a child and that child is an American citizen, and then when you do try and deport them . . . it's impossible."

On September 24, 1986, after months of renewed optimism about the passage of the immigration bill, followed by sputtering talks, Republicans in the House dealt it another blow. This time, a small group of Democrats joined them in their opposition to an important rule proposal. The bipartisan block formed in partial response to two new provisions—one to legalize undocumented farmworkers and the other to include extended voluntary departure.

Several days later, however, the bill reemerged after influential House Democrats made a series of concessions to Republicans on the legalization of farmworkers. When the House negotiators shared their revised terms, just two weeks after many of them had written off the legislation as unsalvageable, they reached a tentative deal. The bill, one Democratic representative said, was "like Rasputin—it refuses to die." Keeping the Moakley-DeConcini amendment alive, however, was proving untenable. In early October, a vote to kill it failed by only two votes. Then, while the bill was being finalized in a conference committee, Reagan's attorney general, Edwin Meese, called a top Democrat in the House with a threat: "If Moakley's amendment goes through, the whole bill is dead." At that point, Moakley relented and pulled the measure.

THE ROOSEVELT ROOM AT the White House was already full of senators and representatives standing stiffly along a wall covered in presidential portraits when Ronald Reagan entered. On a wood table, next to a podium, sat a thick sheaf of paper and four pens, neatly laid out in a column. It was November 6, 1986, and the atmosphere was collegial and congratulatory. The president was there to sign the Immigration Reform and Control Act (IRCA) into law—"the most comprehensive reform of our immigration laws since 1952," he said, reading from a prewritten speech in which he praised Congress for its "truly successful bipartisan effort." Some three million undocumented immigrants would be legalized. The legislation had been years in coming, he added, joking that the final stretch was up to him. "Hope nothing happens to me between here and the table," he said.

There was hearty applause as he signed the bill, but something happened in between the podium and the door. A reporter shouted, "Mr. President?" Reagan turned to the press gallery. "Do we have a deal going with Iran of some sort?" It was a reference to a story that had surfaced earlier that week and would soon gain traction as the so-called Iran-Contra Affair, a window into the

White House's continued obsession with Central America. In contravention of Congress and an explicit arms embargo, the administration was covertly selling weapons to Iran in order to send the proceeds to the Contra forces fighting to overthrow the Sandinista government in Nicaragua.

The room grew instantly quiet, as the president paused. "No comment," he said.

18.

The Doctor and the General

Juan never applied for asylum because he had no intention of staying in the US, so he was caught off guard when a lawyer friend told him, one afternoon in the winter of 1987, that he should try. Mark Silverman was a Californian in his early thirties and a staff attorney at the Immigrant Legal Resource Center, in San Francisco. He'd first met Juan in the close-knit community of Bay Area sanctuary activists. Pro bono lawyers such as Silverman frequently visited churches for legal consults. In a few short months, Juan had become a fixture not just at the Most Holy Redeemer, but in the whole of the Mission. Before long, the two of them were together speaking on panels, appearing on local news shows, and arranging meetings for Central American immigrants who'd just arrived. Silverman had grown close enough to Juan to have an idea about how to persuade him to file for asylum. As the head of CRECE, Silverman told him, Juan could motivate others to apply for asylum by example. They worked into the night preparing the application. Silverman filed it the next day at a local INS office, and Juan, expecting nothing, promptly forgot about it.

That March, he traveled east by car with a group of other activists to Washington, DC. The city's mayor had already issued a decree limiting the authority of local police officers to stop people and ask for their legal papers. Now the city council was considering a bill to declare itself a sanctuary jurisdiction. The symbolism of the declaration being made in the nation's capital drew Bay Area activists to lend their support.

The night he arrived was cold and windy. A small delegation of Washington activists bundled in heavy coats and scarves waited for Juan and the others near the church where they were staying. "Where are the people who've just arrived?" Juan asked one of them. He set out for a homeless shelter in a rough neighborhood of low-slung buildings and boarded-up storefronts called Mount Pleasant. Everything about the area—the distrustful glances traded on the street between Blacks and Latinos, the biting chill, the dark alleys—was a rebuke to the comforts of San Francisco. But inside the shelter he walked into a homecoming. When the Salvadorans there introduced themselves, he could tell from their accents and softer, indrawn cadences that they were from his part of the country. These weren't the city dwellers from San Salvador and its environs who tended to congregate on the West Coast of the US; they were *campesinos* from the departments around where he grew up: Usulután, San Miguel, La Union.

At around nine o'clock, a group of them left the shelter for a place they called La Clínica. It was a medical clinic on Irving Street, near Fifteenth Street Northwest, that offered free services to the undocumented. Staffed by a single doctor and only a few nurses, it was mostly run by volunteers—members of the community, medical residents from George Washington University, and social workers. Joining the Salvadorans from the shelter, Juan arrived at a three-story row house, where he climbed the stairs to the top floor.

The place was packed with people spilling into the stairwells and hallways. Everyone was speaking in Spanish, and a few were cheerily selling pupusas and frijoles from small baskets slung over their arms. There were only three private examining rooms, and volunteers were doing intake with clipboards out in the open, in makeshift stalls that someone had hastily built with cheap wood and curtains.

After a week in Washington, Juan returned to San Francisco, as planned, but he could not stop thinking about La Clínica. The more he learned about the place the stronger its hold on him became. The full name of the operation was La Clínica del Pueblo, and it had been founded in 1983 by an East Coast chapter of the Central American Refugee Center (CARECEN), a group Juan worked with in San Francisco. It was the sort of bootstrap operation he'd dreamed about in El Salvador and had tried to create ever since, in Mexico and on the West Coast.

Later that spring, two developments wrested him from his Washington reverie. The first was a phone call from Mark Silverman. "You've been granted asylum," Silverman told him. Juan was stunned. His first thought was that it would now be easier for him to return to his family in El Salvador because he'd have a passport and a place where he could legally retreat should he need it.

The second development came a few weeks later. La Clínica del Pueblo was on the verge of closing because there was simply too much work for its army of volunteers to perform on their own. Unless they could find someone to run the clinic's daily operations and coordinate the welter of logistics, staffing, and budgeting, there wasn't a way for the place to continue to function. A Salvadoran friend of Juan's at CARECEN in San Francisco told him the news, then confessed to an ulterior motive. She had a proposal: Would he want to run La Clínica? On July 4, 1987, Juan Romagoza boarded a flight for Washington.

In early 1988, roughly five years after becoming the Salvadoran minister of defense and a year before retiring from the military, Carlos Eugenio Vides Casanova applied for an American green card. He had a strong case based on family ties. His wife of nine years was the daughter of an American citizen who lived in Baltimore. She had studied in Houston in the mid-1970s; visited the US throughout the 1980s; and became a permanent resident that March. When Vides Casanova began planning to leave El Salvador, there was a family address he could list on his application: 44 Colonial Court, a ranch house on a quiet cul-de-sac in Palm Coast, Florida.

"What is Vides?" a former member of the Salvadoran government asked around that time. "A reactionary, a progressive? He is a soldier who has to preserve his institution. He'll do what he has to. So you can't classify him politically very well." During the 1980s, the Americans tried and failed to classify him. Vides Casanova had spent the start of the decade leading the National

Guard when the government was killing more civilians than at any other point in the war. Yet by the spring of 1983, when the Americans tired of the country's then defense minister, José Guillermo García, they accepted Vides Casanova, who was forty-four, as the next in line. He was a "gentleman," one FBI informant had put it. "His eyes do not have the ferocious kind of look that many commanders have."

While García had openly ignored the human rights concerns of the Americans, Vides Casanova was careful to plot a stealthier course. He cared just as little as his predecessor had about the military's abuses, but he knew he had to navigate between the US and the warring factions inside the Salvadoran officer corps. This was something the Americans understood only dimly. The Salvadoran military had its own equivalent of political parties constantly forming alliances and jockeying for primacy. What defined them was the system put in place at the country's military academy, where each graduating class was known as a *tanda*. The officers felt intense loyalty to their own *tandas*, and they often moved through the ranks of the military hierarchy together. Vides Casanova had been in the *tanda* of 1957, García in that of 1956.

By the time the two men were in the top military positions, another class had already risen to prominence and wielded unusual power because of its unprecedented size. For this reason, it was called the *tandona*, and it included some of the most violent right-wing personalities of the 1980s. One of them was Roberto D'Aubuisson, who was responsible for the assassination of Óscar Romero and, in 1982, managed to win election as speaker of the Constituent Assembly. (He was too extreme even for some of the Americans at the State Department, and the Reagan administration intervened to prevent him from taking the presidency.) The others would become known to the public years later, after committing some of the most brazen acts of the war.

All through the eighties, Vides Casanova quietly formed alliances with members of the *tandona*, covering for the abuses of individual cadets and allowing officers to assume an expanding number of command posts. It was a matter of survival. He made the arrangements with the same alacrity with which he reassured Vice President George H. W. Bush, in December 1983, that he'd bring the death squads to heel once and for all. (Convinced of his loyalty, Reagan later thanked him by awarding him a Legion of Merit.) But it had become clear to Vides Casanova, by 1988, that this new crop of officers didn't care about appearances and couldn't be corralled.

On August 21, 1989, his plane arrived in the Miami Airport. At customs, he presented his passport and a crisp, new American visa. He was a resident of the US now—in his early fifties, with a monthly pension from the Salvadoran government, and his wife and four children waiting for him. In the next several months, the only outward signs of his time at the helm of the Salvadoran military would be the photos of him smiling proudly alongside three American presidents hanging on the wall of his home.

Nearly two months later, on an early afternoon in October, General José Guillermo García stepped off a TACA Airlines flight arriving in Miami with roughly two hundred other passengers. The planes didn't have a first-class cabin in those years, so the VIP passengers tended to sit up front, allowing them to be the first among the travelers to set foot on US soil.

García was not as well connected as Vides Casanova, whose wife's family had been among the wealthiest in El Salvador, so his arrival had required different preparations. He had an entry visa and a plan that was already arranged with lawyers and approved by the US government. He was applying for political asylum.

Part 2

19.

Half Anthropologist, Half Wannabe Hood

Eddie Anzora liked to say that he "made sense with everybody." There were the Black guys from the Rollin 20s Bloods and the Brims. They dressed in baggy shades of red, with cocked hats and oversize T-shirts. In South Los Angeles, during the late 1980s, every big gang had a bunch of local outfits, defined by the street corners where they dealt drugs, drank forties, and roughed people up. The city grid dictated do-or-die enmities and alliances. Eddie lived on the Bloods' turf, at the intersection of Thirtieth and Kenwood. But his school was on a stretch of Vermont Avenue that fell under the sway of the Harpys, a Chicano gang whose local clique was called the Dead End. The older brothers of a bunch of his friends ran with them, teenagers who ironed their corduroys and wore button-down shirts and Vans. "Footies" were in style: colored socks with little pom-poms that dangled around the ankle. Everyone's footsies were red where Eddie lived, which showed who was in charge. Style accented muscle. The wardrobes concealed knives and pistols.

Eddie was a survivor before he knew what he was surviving. He used to bike around a four-story brick building on a corner near the King's Swap Meet, an indoor flea market on a large lot next to a high school. This was close to the Pico Union section of the city, a Central American enclave. A giant 18 had been sprayed in thick black paint on one of the walls and was visible for blocks. The 18th Street gang was already well established and growing fast. They swore fealty to a more powerful organization called the Mexican Mafia. At the restaurant where his mother worked as a cook, a hole-in-the-wall called La Chapalita, Eddie sometimes shot pool with a guy who had a tattoo of the number eighteen spidering up his arm.

Closer to home, Eddie did laundry amid plumes of weed smoke, the aroma of his early childhood. The Harpys had a banner emblazoned with their name in block letters outside the laundromat. The place's owner, known to all the gangsters as Popeye, had a Jheri curl and kept a bandanna tied around his forehead. While Eddie folded his clothes, the older kids passed around joints and bottles, and the ground rumbled from a stereo almost half as tall as Eddie was. It was 1988, the year of N.W.A and Ice-T, of "Dope Man" and "I'm Your Pusher," which blared out of boomboxes and blasted from the open windows of Chevy Monte Carlos that bounced and swooned on hydraulics.

Eddie was ten years old. He thought he was Mexican, because that's what you were if you weren't Black in his corner of the city. But he had been born in El Salvador. Seven years earlier, when he was three and his brother Carlos was two, their mother, Victoria, brought them with her to San Francisco. They stayed for a year, in a small apartment on the Mission, where Eddie's father lived. He drank and cheated and disappeared for days on end. Victoria eventually relocated them to South Central Los Angeles to live with her siblings. The place on Thirtieth and Kenwood was so beat-up, almost cartoonishly derelict, that Eddie thought it looked like a haunted house.

Nothing really scared him, though. He, Carlos, their baby brother Michael, and Victoria rented the top floor, along with two aunts, their three children, and an older uncle. Another family occupied the unit downstairs. The whole situation could be chaotic—that many people under a single roof, in a house without a yard, on a rough corner in one of the most dangerous cities in America. Yet Eddie knew no different; because he was young, and crafty, he roamed freely around the neighborhood. Victoria worked around the clock. Carlos, meanwhile, was the wilder of the two older boys, and filched money from the family's rent stash to buy a BB gun at an army surplus store and Garbage Pail Kids from a stall at the swap meet. School bored Eddie, but he was a ravenous student of American slang, music, and gangland fashions. He was half anthropologist, half wannabe hood. If someone shoved him, he swung back. But he was more of a talker than a brawler, and he paid close attention to everything. Copying the older brother of a friend, he started using bobby pins to affix the cuffs of his pants to his shoes so that they never dragged on the ground.

One morning, he was playing football on the street with his friends, which was a regular ritual. In addition to Eddie were Quincy, Tutu, and Gerardo—the mainstays from Vermont Avenue Elementary. A few others ducked in to shout taunts and wing a pass before moving along. A crowd of older guys, most of them Black, were chatting in front of someone's house. The block was filled with its usual sounds and rhythms. The music never seemed to stop—Big Daddy Kane, Salt-N-Pepa, and LL Cool J on a loop—but every few minutes the lyrics would get drowned out by the growl of a truck revving its engine nearby.

The ball was floating in the air when a piercing noise spun everyone around. An old Pinto burst into view, screeching, and wobbled around the corner of Kenwood before straightening out and peeling down the block. Smoke poured from its wheels, and the sour odor of burning rubber filled the air.

One of the older guys shouted, "They're gonna shoot." Eddie and his friends dove to the ground and took cover under parked cars. Several teenagers were visible in the Pinto. Long-haired, wearing dark T-shirts, they looked like goth rockers. Eddie thought he could see the muzzle of a gun poking out of a rear window, but just as he was straining to make it out a second car sped around the corner. It was a Monte Carlo that belonged to a neighborhood teenager named Whino, from the Harpys. The car careered down the block with its windows open. A few shots sprayed out toward the Pinto. No one was hit, but there were shouts and the sound of shattering glass. Eddie lowered his head when he heard the pop of the guns. When he looked up, Whino's Monte Carlo was speeding out of view. The goth rockers, in their battered Pinto, were long gone.

The boys with the long hair were newer to the neighborhood. They went by a name that Eddie had heard for the first time only recently: Mara Salvatrucha, or MS. This was Salvadoran slang—a portmanteau meant to convey scrappiness and savagery. *Mara* referred to a gang or group of close-knit guys; the word first became popular in El Salvador in the 1950s, as part of a loose translation of a widely seen Charlton Heston movie called *The Naked Jungle*. *Salva* was a nod to the country, but it also suggested something savage (like the Spanish word *salvaje*), and *trucha* meant street-smart. Eddie spoke some Spanish with his mother at home, and he understood a lot of what he overheard on the streets, where some of the Mexican American gangsters would pepper their speech with stray phrases. But these two words were beyond Eddie's streetwise vocabulary. Then he started noticing the letters scrawled in permanent marker on the clothes of one of his neighbors, Christian, an eight- or nine-year-old who lived in the downstairs unit of his house. The MS appeared on Christian's jeans and on his shoes. Christian's older brother—a slender teenager with hooded eyes and a faint accent who went around wearing Iron Maiden T-shirts—was in the gang. When Eddie mentioned the letters on Christian's clothes to his friend Gerardo, whose brother was a Dead End Harpy, Gerardo said, "Fuck MS."

The gang wars were often refracted through sibling relationships, with the younger kids imitating the mannerisms and the snarls of their elders. The boys would all be hanging out, when suddenly one of them would throw a gang sign. It was pure show, but everyone got inculcated early. It was never too early to declare allegiances. Eddie took note when Christian and his brother eventually had to move away because they were getting into too many fights.

After the shoot-out, Eddie and the others emerged from their hiding places, chatting excitedly about what they'd just witnessed. If they'd been scared by the gunfire, no one would admit it. These were quotidian skirmishes. The warring gangsters were neighbors or the brothers of schoolmates—respected, familiar faces. Whino and the Harpys drove back around a few minutes later and parked the car on the side of the street. They greeted everyone and joined the football game.

20.

Gang Wars

In Eddie's neighborhood, anyone worth emulating was Black or Chicano; there were no white people where he lived, and the Central Americans, who were now arriving by the thousands every month, were unassimilated newcomers at the bottom of an already vicious racial hierarchy. Black and Mexican street gangs brutalized many of them. It would be a few more years before Eddie fully understood what it meant to be Salvadoran himself. No one had bothered to explain his origin story to him. Whether his family meant to keep it from him or simply forgot to spell it out, the elision helped shield him from the tribalism on the streets. By the early 1990s, gang-related killings accounted for more than a third of all homicides in Los Angeles County, and at least 55 percent of the victims were Latino. Salvadoran teenagers were trapped: to be unaffiliated was to be the enemy of everybody, but "jumping in," as an outsider, was an extreme act that incurred other dangers.

Some of the refugees tried banding together in self-defense. There were two options, and 18th Street was the more established one. The gang got its name from a span of three blocks between Arapahoe and South Bonnie Brae streets, in Pico Union. It had started small, in the late 1950s and 1960s, as a mostly Chicano outfit with a retro flair for suits and fedoras—a callback to the zoot suits of the early 1940s. But over the years what distinguished 18th Street was its inclusiveness. Other Chicano gangs active in Southern California tended to reject anyone who wasn't Mexican American, including would-be members born in Mexico. The gangsters from 18th Street welcomed immigrants and cultivated a more ecumenical Latino identity. This wasn't exactly a matter of altruism: 18th Street grew faster, and more fearsome, than most of its rivals; its members went on to call it La Grandota—the big one.

The same could not be said of the Mara Salvatrucha. In the early to mid-1980s, MS was a band of outcasts and misfits populated with new arrivals from Central America. Members called themselves the MS Stoners and stood out for their style in a city dominated by gangster rap and baggy cholo fashions. They wore tight-fitting jeans torn at the knees and black T-shirts; their hair was long, like the heavy-metal rockers of Black Sabbath, AC/DC, and Megadeth. The trademark MS gang sign was the index and pinkie finger extended out like devil's horns. Sometimes they added the number thirteen to their tag because of its evil associations. Every gang fronted a bit, performing an identity, but MS's emphasis on dark, Satanic symbols was unique. Many of its members spoke, looked, and acted like foreigners and would not have been able to blend in if they tried; even their Spanish was different, full of clunky profanities (like *cerote*, "piece of shit") or earnest-sounding pronouns (*vos* instead of *tú*). "The Salvatruchas didn't force themselves to talk like Chicanos or to renounce their origin," journalists Carlos Martínez and José Luis Sanz wrote. "They carried it on in the name of their gang." Outnumbered and outgunned everywhere they went, MS started using machetes. Macabre stories of decapitations started to spread.

Small cliques cropped up across the city, each one tied to a different set of street corners. The bigger gangs were selling drugs and extorting local businesses and dealers; MS was still too slight to realize these sorts of ambitions. Their MO was mostly to protect their own, pick fights, and thus make a name for themselves as the purveyors of staggering acts of violence. On the west side were the Normandie Locos, the Coronado Locos, the Hollywood Locos, and the Leeward Locos, all of them named after streets or intersections.

In the summer of 1984, the Los Angeles Police Department did these cliques a favor. Four years before, the US had boycotted the 1980 Olympics because they were held in Moscow; now, in July, Los Angeles was hosting the summer games. To clean up the streets in anticipation, the police made high-profile arrests, nabbing some of the bigger players from the more established street gangs. The vacuum that resulted inflamed the violence in and around Pico Union. MS had a fighting chance to gain some ground.

In these gangs' early, inchoate years it wasn't always possible to tell who was or was not a member of MS. A careful observer of appearances, Eddie started to realize there were things he couldn't see. His aunt Gladys, whose son was five years older than Eddie and a member of 18th Street, was dating a Guatemalan man named Oscar. Oscar was a former soldier in his thirties, muscular and stern, who liked to wear a lot of gold jewelry. He had fled Guatemala several years before and now lived in the neighborhood, working at a liquor store. To Eddie, the most interesting thing about Oscar was his red mini-truck, which had a black retractable hardtop roof that he left open when he drove the boys around the city.

One evening, with the boys in the back of the car, a driver cut Oscar off, forcing him to drive up on the curb to avoid a collision. Both vehicles stopped. Oscar kicked open the door and strode around to the trunk. The two men in the other vehicle were getting out, in the loping, deliberate manner of fighters preparing to attack. One had a machete, the other a crowbar. Eddie's eyes were fixed on them, so he was startled to see Oscar hurtling into his field of vision wielding a baseball bat. Oscar swatted away the machete from one man and struck him in the knee before advancing on the other guy, who backed away. Oscar turned his attention to their car. He circled it, smashing it up, swing by swing, in a methodical rhythm. He then returned to his truck, readjusted the rearview mirror, and drove everyone to dinner. Oscar, Eddie soon learned, was a member of MS.

IN 1989, when Eddie was eleven, his mother had decided that the family needed to move. The crack epidemic, which had been worsening for years, was reaching an almost warlike level of intensity. Each night, police helicopters circled loudly overhead, and people were routinely breaking into the house on Kenwood to steal things to sell for drug money. A few times, Eddie's uncle Jaime had to chase out intruders with a knife. But the family noticed that small trinkets and jewelry were going missing anyway. Jaime himself had started to use.

Outside it was as if the neighborhood were possessed. Familiar faces grew hollow and vacant; neighbors seemed to age overnight, emerging in the morning looking mangy and haggard. There were more fights, and they were bloodier; the rough but once intelligible logic of street grudges became unpredictable—drive-by shootings, muggings in broad daylight, altercations right in the middle of street traffic.

One afternoon later that year, Victoria took time off work one afternoon to go apartment hunting with her sons in the San Fernando Valley. Spanning some 250 square miles, from upper Los Angeles to the Santa Susana Mountains in the north, and the Simi Hills in the west, the valley was home to more than a million people. Its more iconic associations (movie studios, palatial malls, gated communities) didn't apply where the Anzoras were looking. When they got off the bus, after a half-hour drive from South Central, they emerged into the neighborhoods of Van Nuys, Arleta, Reseda—hardscrabble pockets with valley trappings like swimming pools attached to dingy apartment complexes. Another family passed the three of them on the street and offered to give them a ride. They were house hunting, too, they said. In the car, Victoria gave them the address of some apartments where friends had suggested she look. "I'll take you there, but it's not a good neighborhood," the driver warned. Victoria replied, "Oh, we're going to check it out. We've been living in South Central."

They moved into an apartment on Langdon Avenue, right off Sepulveda Boulevard. "Gangville," one of Eddie's friends called it. The rest of the family—the aunts, uncles, and cousins—settled down nearby. At Langdon Avenue Elementary School, Eddie set out to learn a new social code, something he had come to expect and that he treated with a casual confidence. "You gotta be a man quick," he said. The process was universal—first he'd prove his toughness, but the people he fought went by different names than those in South Central. Here some of the stronger kids repped a local gang called Langdon; one guy, Ziggy, approached him in the schoolyard to slug it out. This happened a few more times, with the intensity of combat diminishing from one round to the next. Eddie held his own, and soon he was hanging out with a new group of friends—going to each other's houses for TV, sneaking into neighbors' swimming pools.

Eddie studied the tics and styles of the gangs, but their ferocity put him off.

The violence and air of malcontent seemed pointless. If you were in a gang, you felt proud and protected, but in the eyes of a rival population you barely knew, you were always in the wrong. He fell in with a lower-key crowd of Mexican, Salvadoran, and Asian hustlers, who were known as taggers. Graffiti appealed to Eddie's sense of street etiquette: he would rove around the city and hone his signature on public property. He liked to sign his name as some variation of Take or Taker; the combination of letters looked sharp, and the moniker described someone claiming his due. His crew went by the name of MCP, which, depending on who was asking, stood for Mexicans Causing Panic, Marking City Property, or Making Crime Prime.

San Fernando was a dream canvas for a tagger. Eddie used to take the bus with friends to swanky places or the vast neglected stretches of public walls under traffic-clogged freeways and get to work. When he was twelve years old, in 1990, he and a fellow MCP tagger went up and down Melrose Avenue, covering everything they could with their initials like they were marketing a new brand. The cops showed up and his friend darted away. But Eddie panicked and froze. He spent a night at Central Juvenile Hall.

The crack epidemic was turning into a national political campaign, with Los Angeles as its epicenter. In 1986, *Time* magazine called it "the issue of the year," while *Newsweek* described the drug problem as the biggest story since Vietnam and Watergate. In the summer of 1986, Len Bias, a twenty-two-year-old basketball star from the University of Maryland, who was drafted second by the Boston Celtics and had been compared to Michael Jordan, died of a cocaine overdose. The tragedy fed a growing panic ("America discovered crack and overdosed on oratory," according to a *New York Times* editorial), and the Democratic Speaker of the House, Tip O'Neill, called for legislation that eventually became the Anti–Drug Abuse Act. Passed less than a month before IRCA, Reagan's immigration law, it created stiff, mandatory prison terms for anyone convicted of drug possession, establishing a notorious disparity for sentencing in which crack triggered substantially harsher punishments than powder cocaine. This was a ploy to target Black suspects, which law enforcement officers never bothered to conceal. The casual drug user "ought to be taken out and shot," the head of the Los Angeles Police Department said a few years later, in testimony before the Senate Judiciary Committee.

Eddie Anzora (left), joined by a friend, tagging a wall with graffiti in Santa Fe Yards. Los Angeles, California, 1992.

Eddie Anzora tagging in Venice. Los Angeles, California, 1996.

On Langdon Avenue, drugs were turning the block into a cauldron of dealers and thugs who hawked and stole rock cocaine. As Eddie got older, he was starting to grasp the ubiquity of addicts in his orbit. "Everyone's looking skinny, dirty, cracked out," he'd observe to his friends, who knew the reality better than he did; several of them were losing their parents to drugs. Eddie sometimes saw them when he visited their houses, adults splayed on couches or in bed, in a state of catatonia.

Victoria worked constantly, piling up shifts in a small restaurant and taking on stray catering jobs. Her sister tipped her off to some extra work operating a food truck. She'd get up each morning at three forty-five to serve burritos and breakfast sandwiches outside some of the *fábricas* and garages in the area. Her strategy was to spend no more than ten minutes in one spot. She built her schedule around the workers' shifts and break times. She was the sole provider for the family, bringing home about $175 every week, and was hardly ever home. Unsupervised, Eddie and his brother often cut school and got into trouble.

Neither participated in the hard-core gangs, but crossing paths with them was unavoidable. On Langdon Avenue, mortal enemies posted up within feet of each other, on opposite sides of the street or in adjacent housing units. "You'd be so close you could flip them off," as one resident put it. On the corner of Roscoe and Sepulveda, in an apartment complex behind a McDonald's, a group of MS members, thirty or forty guys strong, would throw bottles or fire warning shots with low-caliber pistols at anyone who wandered too close. On Langdon and Nordhoff, just up the block, the Langdon Gang was in regular combat with the Columbus Boys and, occasionally, a smaller group called the TJ Locos. Eddie and his friends would sometimes hang out at a neutral spot, the Donut Shop on Roscoe Boulevard, where the owner had set up arcade games. Drug dealers milled around while the boys played *Street Fighter*. The sound of gunshots would scatter everybody, like a dinner bell at the end of the day. When they reconvened, hours or days later, someone would be there to offer an account of the latest skirmish. On one occasion, a small-time dealer made the rounds to show off his newest battle scars. Another guy had shot him through the cheek, blowing off the lower part of his jaw. He popped out a pair of dentures to prove his stoicism.

MS was evolving. It was beginning to look like the other Chicano street outfits. Shorter, close-cropped hair replaced the rocker look; clothes got baggier; and tattoos flowered on members' arms, necks, and chests. More of its ranks were winding up in prison. The state penitentiaries set the standards for street life, dictating everything from the shifting alliances and feuds to the fashions and moneymaking ventures of everyone on the outside. There was a reason for this, and members of MS, like the gangsters in the decades before them, were learning it the hard way. Serving time was an inevitability, something everyone had to expect and plan for. The MS gangsters had worked hard to scare people in Pico Union and Westlake, but when they reached prison there weren't enough of them to fend off beatings and rapes. They needed protection, which required affiliating themselves with one of the big prison gangs.

Inmate factions were decided by race—the Aryan Brotherhood, the Black Guerrilla Family—but for Latinos there were two options, depending on where someone came from. An imaginary border ran through a midsize city called Bakersfield, a historic oil and agriculture hub about one hundred miles from LA: to the north were members of a gang called Nuestra Familia and to the south was the Mexican Mafia, better known as La Eme. In the late 1960s, the two gangs started a riot at San Quentin that was later called the Shoe War, begun when a *soldado*, or foot soldier, from La Eme stole the shoes of a Nuestra Familia member. By the time authorities quelled the fighting, nineteen inmates had been stabbed, and one had been killed; from then on, the groups were sworn enemies. The 18th Street gang aligned itself with the Mexican Mafia. In exchange for protection inside the state's prisons, members of 18th Street paid a portion of the money from their drug deals and extortions of neighborhood businesses to La Eme. The partnership existed on a knife's edge—any slipup from 18th Street, whether an unpaid tax or a perceived slight, and the Mafia would punish them for it.

By the end of the decade, MS had also fallen into line. Upstart MS members had often gravitated toward the number 13, because it seemed sinister and diabolical. Some of them started calling the gang MS-13. Now, the 13 was being repurposed: it was an homage to La Eme, the thirteenth letter of the alphabet.

◇—◇

On the night of August 1, 1988, a twenty-one-year-old named Raymond Carter was nearing home with a pizza when a police officer pulled him over. The officer walked up to the driver's-side window and asked, "Where do you live?" Carter gave the address where he lived with his mother, an apartment in a building at the corner of Thirty-ninth Street and Dalton Avenue in South Central Los Angeles. "You're one of them," the officer replied. "One of what?" Carter asked. "Don't play stupid," the officer said. "You're one of them." Then he placed him under arrest.

A few minutes later, Carter was lying on his stomach in his building's front courtyard, with his hands cuffed behind his back. Sirens were blaring and helicopters swooped low. Dozens of squad cars circled the block, carrying some ninety officers. Carter's neighbors from the building and from three others on the same block were massed together on the street in a state of agitation and alarm. Several, like Carter himself, were handcuffed, others beaten and dazed. In the din, he could make out the voice of his mother pleading with an officer for her blood pressure medication. Their apartment, he said later, looked like it "had been hit by a pack of wild animals." The cops were punching through walls, shattering mirrors, tearing up furniture, and demolishing toilets with hammers. Thirty-three people, all of them Black, were arrested. The property damage, later assessed at roughly $4 million, was so severe that the Red Cross had to provide housing for ten adults and twelve children who were left homeless. Some of the police officers sprayed graffiti on the building where Carter lived: "LAPD Rules. Rollin' 30s Die."

Four months earlier, in April 1988, the Los Angeles Police Department had carried out a new policy called Operation Hammer. It sent more than a thousand officers into neighborhoods with high rates of gang crime to make nearly fifteen hundred arrests in an overwhelming show of force. Already there were special LAPD units outfitted to combat gangs. These operated under a task force called Community Resources against Street Hoodlums, or CRASH. (It was initially called Total Resources against Southeast Hoodlums, or TRASH, but public complaints led to a name change.) Their targets, in theory, were drug dealers and gangbangers, but the police had wide latitude. Soon after the raid at Thirty-ninth and Dalton, the state legislature passed a law called the Street Terrorism Enforcement and Prevention Act, which effectively made it illegal to be "affiliated" with a street gang. Prosecutors could "enhance" a criminal sentence by several years if the defendant was, or had ever been, arrested for gang associations. It was easy to wind up with such an arrest: if an officer frisked someone for drugs or weapons and didn't find anything, he could still write the person up for being a "gang associate." On the streets, there was no such thing as being a gang associate—people were either in a gang or not; partial membership wasn't an option—but that only made it more difficult to disprove.

Los Angeles was at the national vanguard of anti-gang policing, which had more in common with the practices of the US Army than with the protocols of other police forces across the country. This "wasn't policing," according to one historian. It was "anti-insurgency run amok." The idea was to uproot gang members from their strongholds; if that meant decimating whole neighborhoods that gangsters shared with working-class people of color, the collateral damage could be justified in the broader war against crime.

A legal novelty created by the city attorney's office for this purpose was gang injunctions, which introduced a raft of enhanced penalties and, in some cases, allowed the police to arrest people for congregating in public places. It began with the Playboy Gangster Crips, a Black gang that was associated with the intersection of Cadillac Avenue and Corning Street, in West Los Angeles. By multiple police measures, this corner was not the most dangerous in the city, but it happened to fall near the offices of a group of aggressive city prosecutors. Cops kept binders filled with the names, photos, and fingerprints of anyone they suspected to be tied to the gang. One of the prosecutors later explained, "We were not sure if it was ethical or legal. We had a list in our drawer, and if we got this person arrested, fuck 'em as bad as we can no matter what." Other gang injunctions soon followed, including one that identified a clique of the Mara Salvatrucha in Hollywood.

The police raid on Thirty-ninth and Dalton turned up six ounces of weed, less than an ounce of cocaine, and only a single successful prosecution for a minor drug charge. The city would eventually pay damages to Carter, his mother, and others as part of an out-of-court settlement. Compensation like this was rare. Much more often, the police paid, and admitted, nothing.

AT THE START of the 1990s, Eddie could feel the gang culture in San Fernando hardening against the new onslaught from law enforcement. Everyone became more violent and territorial, and even the taggers, who stood outside the usual field of battle, were forced to declare allegiances and fight off attacks. The members of MCP started to argue about what kind of outfit they were. One faction felt it was time to clear the air; they were Mexicans Causing Panic now, not the other names, and that meant that the boys had to be Chicano to stay active. A lot of the local crews were adding the number 13 to their names.

There were some seventy-five active gangs in San Fernando, but only one major MS-13 clique, the Fulton Locos. A wiry twenty-year-old named Ernesto Deras, whose nom de guerre was Satan, was its leader, having arrived in Los Angeles in 1990. Satan was a former Salvadoran soldier with an impressive combat pedigree: his battalion in El Salvador had trained at Fort Bragg, in North Carolina, and thus came to be known in the Salvadoran officer corps as the Gringo Battalion. His first tattoos, on the upper part of his back, weren't the letters of the Mara Salvatrucha but the initials of his rapid-deployment force arrayed around a knife. The weapons he had used to train were all US-made—an M16 assault rifle, an M60 machine gun, an M203 grenade launcher.

In El Salvador, Satan had hunted guerrillas during some of the final offensives of the war, but in Los Angeles he was an insurgent. MS-13 in the San Fernando Valley was every other gang's common enemy. Sometime around 1989, a dispute with the 18th Street gang—once a close, sibling-like ally of MS-13—turned into a full-fledged war. Because the groups had such close ties, with families and friends on both sides, the killings escalated fast. "When an enemy gave the green light to kill somebody, when it basically condemned a rival to death, there was always someone who knew where to find him," Martínez and Sanz wrote. "Each gang knew the other's hiding places and where all the other members lived."

At first the police had focused on Black gangs, but once they turned their attention to the Latino gangs their legal arsenal expanded beyond that of city prosecutors. They could get people deported. Ernesto Deras hadn't legally come to the US, and authorities estimated that at least half a dozen gangs in Los Angeles were made up of mostly undocumented members. By law, the police weren't allowed to arrest immigrants simply for a lack of documents. It was a civil, not criminal, infraction. But in 1986, the INS started to work alongside the officers. "We don't arrest people for being illegal aliens," a spokesperson for the police force told the *Los Angeles Times*. "But it is a pilot program in our campaign to obliterate violence by gangs."

The officers identified gang suspects, and the INS removed them. John Brecthel, the assistant district director for INS investigations in Los Angeles at the time, said, "If a gang member is out on the street and the police can't make a charge, we will go out and deport them for being here illegally if they fit that criteria." Between December 1988 and April 1989, the effort led to 175 deportations for alleged involvement in "gang and narcotics activities," including seventy-seven to Mexico, fifty-six to El Salvador, and fifteen to Honduras. The task force claimed to have "decimated" MS-13 leadership. The initiative also granted the INS access to city and state jails, which its agents helped clean out by deporting anyone with a criminal record. By early 1989, the INS deported roughly nine thousand immigrants with felony convictions from the Western Regional Office alone, including more than two thousand from Los Angeles.

The Anzoras had legal status. Michael, the youngest, was a citizen, having been born in San Francisco. Victoria had applied for citizenship through the 1986 Immigration Reform and Control Act and obtained her green card a few years later. Eddie took this luxury for granted. He was too young—too hard-charging and reckless—to appreciate the advantages it conferred. He and his brother were getting in trouble constantly. In a city where violent crime was spiraling out of control, Eddie kept his distance from the worst of it. But his waywardness was not mellowing. He landed in jail a few more times, for tagging, petty theft, and disorderly conduct. He was cutting school several times a week. The infractions mounted until one day, in 1991, he was forced to appear with his mother before a juvenile judge. All the options were on the table—reform school, a stint in a juvenile facility. But Victoria proposed another idea, which the judge quickly approved. Because Eddie and Carlos couldn't seem to appreciate what it meant to live in the United States, they should experience the life she had spared them in El Salvador. Two of her brothers still lived there, in a town just outside the capital, called Soyapango, and the civil war was starting to wind down. They'd spend a full year there because that was the amount of time the judge would have sentenced them to reform school.

21.

La Clínica del Pueblo

The man was in his midforties, neither tall nor short, with a thick mustache and a slight build—an ordinary-looking person who generally escaped notice. But Juan Romagoza had seen him around during the late winter of 1991, once at a nearby migrant shelter and a few times out on the streets, where he squatted in the abandoned houses that Juan passed on his way to work. He was homeless and an alcoholic, with tattered clothes and sickly, reddened eyes. The Adams Morgan neighborhood around La Clínica del Pueblo was full of people like that, especially Salvadorans and Guatemalans who arrived in the city traumatized, war-haunted, and alone. On Tuesday nights, the only day of the week the clinic was open for general consultations, homeless immigrants entered the open doors of the dilapidated brick building on Irving and Fifteenth Street Northwest and hid out in the basement. They blended in with the crowds of people arriving for appointments. In search of a place to sleep, many of them started on the third floor for medical attention, then slunk off downstairs. At a certain point, usually around one or two in the morning, the clinic's volunteers had to turn everyone out before closing.

Juan's office opened directly onto the waiting room, a big, well-appointed space that had once belonged to a church rector, with old wood wainscoting. It was the only aesthetic flourish at La Clínica. The building's boiler rarely worked, and broken windows were patched with makeshift plastic coverings that hung at angles. The vastness of Juan's office meant that it was constantly packed with supplies and people, rushing in and out for meetings. The chipped tile floor smelled of Pine-Sol.

Beginning his shift one night, Juan glimpsed the man, but didn't have time to introduce himself. Juan never stopped moving. Each night at the clinic was an exercise in chaos control. The appointments started at around six, as soon as the first doctor arrived, and within minutes more than seventy patients showed up. Conversations blared. Juan greeted the patients and introduced them to a team of volunteers with clipboards, who took down their information. Juan made rounds, cleaning, advising, directing. If he saw someone throwing something away, he'd swoop in to inspect it, in case it could be saved or repurposed. Resources were tight. Tables, furniture, and basic medical equipment like blood pressure monitors came through small grants and donations from Catholic and Quaker charities. Diagnostic testing went through the George Washington Medical Center, where some of the volunteer doctors worked by day. The medications came in the pharmaceutical sample sizes that drug reps dropped off in small cartons for doctors. There were no fixed hours at La Clínica, just a continuous run that sometimes didn't end until dawn.

At around ten o'clock, the man with the mustache elbowed his way through the waiting room to reach Juan. "I need to talk to you," he said. He respectfully addressed Juan as *usted*. They moved to a quieter corner of Juan's office. "You were a prisoner. You were beaten and tortured," the man began. "I want to tell you that I was there. I saw what they were doing to you. I was a part of it." He began to cry, explaining that he, too, was from Usulután. The man's name was Pedro. He'd been a member of the National Guard.

EVERYONE WHO FLED THE WAR for the US arrived jilted or debilitated. But of all the refugees Juan observed at La Clínica, the ex-soldiers tended to be in the worst shape. Most of them had become addicts. They lived on the streets and kept to themselves. As a doctor, Juan took an analytic view of their profiles. Many lower-level soldiers had been conscripted and were often tortured if they were caught absconding or disobeying orders. Some of them were *campesinos* themselves, not so much sadists as cowed conformists who'd been indoctrinated during their military service. Juan wasn't naive about the savagery of their past acts. He just felt that the war had victimized everyone in different ways. Pedro, for instance, had become a pariah wherever he went. Among the other immigrants in Washington, he was a villain, but in El Salvador he'd be tortured for desertion.

Sometimes, arguments erupted at La Clínica when a patient revealed he'd served in the military. Many volunteers felt these men didn't deserve treatment, but Juan disagreed. La Clínica had higher responsibilities, he said, in his gentle yet implacable way; its obligations were medical and quasi-religious. His genuineness convinced everyone. Eventually, he organized group therapy sessions exclusively for ex-soldiers, which became the most interesting of his meetings. At the start of his sessions, he introduced himself in a way that made clear he'd never forget the sins of the armed forces. "I was not a part of the army, nor the police. I wasn't even a member of the guerrillas. I was helping *campesinos* who were against the army. I cured them and gave them treatment. But for that this is what happened to me," he said. Then, he held up his deformed hand.

La Clínica was two and a half miles from the White House, and a forty-minute walk straight down Fifteenth Street NW. The halls of American power were practically contiguous with the streets of Adams Morgan and the immigrant neighborhood, called Mount Pleasant, where Juan lived in a small apartment provided by a church. When he wasn't working at the clinic, he was engaging in his usual activities—protests and church events in the name of the sanctuary movement—only now the intended audience felt near at hand.

In 1989, the new occupant of 1600 Pennsylvania Avenue, George H. W. Bush, who had served as Reagan's vice president, did not share his predecessor's ideological zeal. He was a moderate Republican with a cool, patrician reserve and a more pragmatic bent on foreign policy. El Salvador and Guatemala interested him less than Nicaragua, where the US had long been pressuring the Sandinistas to relinquish power. He also inherited a situation clouded by scandal. In response to Reagan's arms sales to Iran, congressional Democrats cut off direct American aid to the Contras. By the spring, Bush had signed a bipartisan agreement. After eight years sparring over aid to the Contras, Democrats in Congress and the Republican White House were "like two punched-out prizefighters staggering in a clinch," the historian William LeoGrande later wrote. "As much out of exhaustion as conviction," they "decided to call it a draw." The US would give the Contras $4.5 million in nonmilitary aid each month until February 1990, at which point Daniel Ortega, the Sandinista president of Nicaragua, had agreed to hold national elections. A senior White House official told a reporter, in March, that diplomacy under Reagan had been "a cover story for what we were really trying to do," but "the cover story has become real."

Juan hadn't changed his message since arriving in DC. He was still publicizing human rights abuses in Central America and campaigning to end both US military aid to El Salvador and the deportation of immigrants back to a war zone. He visited Capitol Hill to corner congressmen who didn't support a deportation moratorium. After government bombing raids in El Salvador, he led prayer vigils outside the Salvadoran embassy and at the Pentagon. At one point, he and a handful of other activists staged a weeklong hunger strike at St. John's Episcopal Church, across the street from the White House. Juan was undeterred by the grueling monotony of these efforts. His tactics hadn't changed but the setting had. "The capital of the world" is what Juan called Washington; or, more emphatically, "the capital of the empire that drove me from my home."

A series of regional peace talks, led by the president of Costa Rica, Óscar Arias, had been underway since early 1987. But they were delayed by bursts of renewed fighting. At this point, the civil war in Guatemala was nearing the end of its third decade, while the one in El Salvador was coming to the end of its first.

The new American administration refused to change course, partly out of stubbornness and partly because of the vast sum of money already sunk into the cause. Bush was convinced that US military aid—roughly $90 million a year; $1 billion total since the start of the conflict—was edging the Salvadoran military toward victory. In fact, the Americans were financing the final and arguably bloodiest phase of a stalemate. Almost every setback was rationalized. That included the ouster of the Christian Democrats, two months after Bush himself took office. The longtime American hope, José Napoleón Duarte, who'd once enjoyed bipartisan support on the Hill, was suffering from terminal cancer. His party, unpopular after so many years of fealty to the US, was falling apart.

A new party representing the far right emerged in its place, favored by 54 percent of Salvadoran voters. Founded by a member of a death squad who was involved in the murder of Óscar Romero, it was called the Alianza Republicana Nacionalista, or ARENA. Its leader was a polished businessman named Alfredo Cristiani. He had been educated at Georgetown and was the brother-in-law, by marriage, of General Vides Casanova, the former head of the National Guard and minister of defense, who had interrogated Juan Romagoza in a San Salvador cell in 1980. Cristiani wore tailored suits and smoked thick cigars; when he spoke, his voice had the understated but firm quality of a discreet dealmaker. Members of ARENA had direct ties not only to the death squads but also to the most recalcitrant hardliners in the armed forces. By comparison, Cristiani was a moderate, and he convinced the Americans that he would negotiate for peace.

On November 11, 1989, two days after the fall of the Berlin Wall, the FMLN launched a surprise offensive in six neighborhoods in the northern part of San Salvador. The goal was to bruise the army one final time and bring it to the negotiating table. Cristiani claimed to want peace, but politically he lacked the strength to overcome resistance from the military brass. The army responded by indiscriminately bombing the neighborhoods, leading to more than a thousand civilian casualties. Of the seventy-five thousand people killed over the entire course of the war in El Salvador, some thirteen thousand died during the FMLN offensive in November.

Eventually, the guerrillas pulled back to the countryside, and a cabal of army officers exacted their revenge. Inside the armed forces there was a newfound sense of alarm that the guerrillas were unbeatable. Feeling they might not be able to get away with it for much longer, members of the death squads launched attacks against journalists, students, and activists. But the most decisive action came from the military's high command. Early in the morning, on November 16, a few dozen soldiers from the Atlacatl Battalion, armed with AK-47s, stormed the campus of the José Simeón Cañas Central American University (La UCA), one of the country's most prominent institutions. It was run by a group of Jesuit priests who the extreme right believed were too close to the

FMLN. Before dawn, the soldiers forced their way into the rector's residence, where they found five Spanish priests, their Salvadoran housekeeper, and her fifteen-year-old daughter. The soldiers ordered them to lie facedown on the ground outside and executed them. When they came across a sixth priest, from El Salvador, they killed him, too. Before leaving, they scrawled graffiti on a sign, just as the LAPD officers had done on Dalton Avenue, in Los Angeles, in 1988. The aim was to doctor the crime scene to implicate the guerrillas: "FMLN executed those who informed on it. Victory or death."

For weeks after the killings, there was intense international outrage, but also confusion. At first, the American embassy bought the army's line and suggested the FMLN was responsible. Eventually the evidence grew murky, then damning. By January 1990, the US military learned that the Atlacatl Battalion was behind the murders. Cristiani admitted as much and ordered the arrest of five soldiers and four officers. There was little question these men carried out the attacks, but who had given the order? The Speaker of the US House appointed a task force to investigate. Unlike Reagan, Bush wasn't keen on making public excuses for a murderous Cold War ally. But he wasn't clamoring for answers, either. To be the task force's chair, the Speaker chose the congressman from South Boston, Joe Moakley, one of the most fervent Beltway champions of human rights in El Salvador.

MOAKLEY WAS A CASE STUDY in calibrated political theatricality. A talker, fighter, schemer, and strategic self-mythologizer, he downplayed his considerable legislative talents to his perpetual advantage. He liked to say, for instance, that his "idea of foreign affairs" was going to East Boston for an Italian sub. In truth, he'd been all over the world and, together with his young aide Jim McGovern, had studied the situation in El Salvador. Depending on his audience, Moakley even liked to vary the story of how he first became aware of the humanitarian crisis there. A group of peace activists had approached him at a constituent meeting in Jamaica Plain one morning in January 1983. But he was always careful to broadcast his association with a wider array of sympathetic allies. In his telling, it began as an encounter with a group of nuns at a post office. He was savvy and adaptable. When the State Department refused to share documents, Moakley told fibs to trick Salvadoran officials into sharing material directly. Once, to obtain a classified letter from the US Defense Department, he barged into the office of a Salvadoran military officer and asked him to make a copy because he'd left his own at the hotel. In public he was a "regular Joe," a college dropout and navy veteran who grew up aspiring to a union job as a sheet-metal operator. But in his homely, unostentatious way he had also risen to become the chair of the House Rules Committee, an immensely powerful position that made his opponents reluctant to cross him.

On February 11, 1990, Moakley and the task force took a trip to El Salvador on a fact-finding mission that put them in direct conflict with the Salvadoran high command. The officer served up as the ringleader of the plot was a colonel who wasn't known to freelance or act alone; there were several reasons to doubt that the killings were solely his idea. Cristiani was right to arrest the killers in El Salvador, Moakley said in a speech, but "this is not the final curtain—it's only the first act. . . . Those who ordered or otherwise consented to the crime must also be brought to justice."

Two weeks after Moakley left on his trip, another development in the region supplanted El Salvador in the headlines of American news. On February 25, an opposition coalition led by a journalist and prominent political widow named Violeta Chamorro soundly defeated the Sandinistas in the Nicaraguan elections. The result was a major victory for the Bush administration, which could lift a long-standing embargo against the country and restart aid. This was the president's second triumph in as many months. In January, American troops who had invaded Panama removed the country's president, Manuel Noriega, a former US ally who'd been on the payroll of the CIA before clashing with Bush. After his surrender, the Americans flew him to a Miami courthouse. The White House called the military campaign Operation Just Cause.

In the winter and spring of 1990, Moakley's staff traveled back and forth between the US and El Salvador, chasing down leads. In the end, there was too much working against them for a clear breakthrough. But Moakley did succeed in demonstrating that neither the Salvadoran government nor the White House sought the full truth. The investigation the Salvadorans had promised was "at a standstill," the task force wrote in a report that April, and the State Department and CIA were giving it cover. It would take decades to bring the full cast of killers to justice. By then declassified US cables—from the embassy, Department of Defense, and CIA—revealed that the Salvadoran military had orchestrated the killings, while US officials had "foreknowledge" of the plot.

The search for answers in the Jesuit case was only part of Moakley's agenda for El Salvador. Since 1983, he'd been pushing his bill to create a temporary status for Salvadorans living in the US that would protect them against deportation during the war. "It's our bombs, our guns, and our mines that made these people refugees," he said. Yet each time he and his Senate colleague Dennis DeConcini introduced the measure, it died in committee.

There was a fresh opportunity in the form of an immigration bill moving through the Senate, shaped by immigrants' rights advocates and sponsored by Ted Kennedy. It was seen, to quote one observer, as "the obvious vehicle for fixing IRCA's loose ends." In 1986, IRCA had been intended as a comprehensive bill to deal with legal *and* illegal immigration to the US. In effect, it dealt only with the latter, legalizing 2.8 million undocumented immigrants in exchange for tougher enforcement measures. Now members of Congress were looking to expand legal avenues for entering the US—creating several new visa categories, changing the availability of green cards, and raising caps on overall immigration.

The Immigration Act of 1990, as the bill was called, was also a chance to resurrect the plan to protect Salvadorans from deportation. Moakley called it temporary protected status (TPS), and while, in theory, it could apply to immigrants from anywhere who were stranded in the US during periods of upheaval in their home countries, Moakley singled out Salvadorans. In the spring of 1980, 92,000 Salvadorans were living in the US, according to the Pew Research Center; by 1990, there were 459,000. Moakley's measure was immediately opposed not just by conservatives but also by Democrats like Kennedy, who worried that it would doom his broader bill. This time Moakley had leverage, as chair of the Rules Committee and as head of a prominent task force investigating human rights abuses in El Salvador. If the Salvadoran issue "goes," Moakley told Senate leadership, "then there'll be no fucking bill."

In late October 1990, a bipartisan group of House members and senators brought the measure up for final debate in a conference meeting. Moakley addressed Alan Simpson directly. "What do you need, Senator Simpson? Just tell me." Before the senator could answer, according to an account by author Charles Kamasaki, the chair of the House Judiciary Committee, Jack Brooks, a grizzled Texan with a thick drawl, interjected. A cigar protruded from the corner of his mouth. He addressed Simpson with an air of exaggerated courtesy. "I would like to remind you, sir, over here in the House, Mr. Moakley is chairman of the Rules Committee. And that makes Mr. Moakley a very important person when we want to pass bills." There was a long silence after Brooks finished.

Inside the chamber, in addition to the representatives themselves, were staffers and immigrants' rights advocates, sitting along the periphery. Everyone stared expectantly at Simpson, whose reply was slow and deliberate. "Are you really serious about putting teeth into this thing?" he asked. "Because if you are, we can have our staffs work out the language." The eventual compromise spared close to half a million Salvadorans currently living in the US. The trade-off—the "teeth" Simpson wanted—was that TPS holders did not have a path to permanent residency. Their protection against deportation allowed them to live and work in the US, but it had to be renewed every eighteen months.

The 1990 act was the last major immigration reform package the US Congress would pass. In the following two decades, the only other significant measures to become law involved enforcement: tools to increase deportations, funding bills to expand border security, and an act to overhaul the Immigration and Naturalization Service. TPS holders would become permanently stuck with a status that was meant to be provisional. Republican and Democratic administrations found it easier to renew their TPS status every two years than to create an actual route to citizenship for those who had built lives in the US over decades. Ironically, the Salvadorans who ultimately benefited from TPS received the protection as a result not of the civil war itself but of a series of earthquakes that struck the country in 2001. Many whose asylum petitions had been denied or delayed were pursuing legal relief through the *American Baptist Churches* litigation; others went underground or eventually availed themselves of TPS when it became available. A quarter of the Salvadorans living in the US ultimately obtained TPS.

22.

Hispanics versus Blacks versus Whites

The first medical director of La Clínica was Peter Shields, a bright and blunt-mannered doctor in his twenties with a day job. He was a resident at the George Washington University Hospital. When he wasn't on a rotation, and sometimes even when he was, he crammed in whatever he could do for the clinic; it was a passion project that had morphed into an obsession. He did diabetes screenings, administered vaccines, and conducted pap smears. When a cancer patient showed up having been kicked out of a nearby hospital because he couldn't pay, Shields took charge of his care. He procured dialysis machines for patients with kidney disease, arranged visits with specialists, recruited volunteer doctors, sent out lab work, and rounded up medical supplies. He also managed La Clínica's books, with Quicken.

When Shields first heard the news of Juan's arrival he was relieved to have help. But it confused him that this other man who was supposedly so vital to La Clínica's future couldn't draw blood, administer tests, or conduct full exams, and that he didn't have an American medical license and barely spoke English. Shields didn't speak Spanish.

Shields used to joke graciously that he had a "North American filter" in those years—a doctor's bias against unconventional practices, many of which migrated to La Clínica with Juan. One of them was a model Juan had learned in El Salvador during the early years of the war, in which some of the patients themselves would provide medical care. They were known as *promotores de salud*, or health promoters, and after taking a weeks-long training course they did everything from nursing tasks to office administration and community outreach. Those who spoke English formed a corps of translators to accompany patients on their appointments with outside specialists.

Washington's foreign-born Latino population was expanding rapidly through the 1980s and early '90s, from 60,000 people in 1980 to more than 160,000 in 1990. The overwhelming majority of them were from El Salvador; the DC area's Salvadoran community was the second largest nationwide after that of Los Angeles. But the city was still overwhelmingly monolingual and largely inaccessible to the war refugees. Social and political life in Washington, which had been notoriously segregated for decades, revolved around a rigid racial dichotomy of Black and white; local officeholders and members of the police force were usually one or the other. Latinos didn't yet factor into the equation. The Salvadoran immigrants were in a similar situation to that of the *campesinos* Juan used to treat in the countryside. They were so far removed from health services that they didn't seek out treatment of any kind. "Official" institutions scared them.

The medical records at La Clínica were kept in locked file cabinets in case of INS raids, and each chart, with its list of symptoms tied to stress and fear, told a story of the failed promise of the 1986 immigration reform. At that time, when IRCA passed, somewhere between five hundred thousand and a million Salvadorans were estimated to be living in the US. About half of them had arrived before 1981, which was the cutoff for legalization under IRCA. In Washington, DC, however, 90 percent of Salvadorans had arrived after that date. The legislation thus triggered a panic. Ten percent of Salvadoran students enrolled in DC public schools withdrew after the bill was passed; there was a 20 to 30 percent drop in ESL courses, and local charities reported a spike in hunger that coincided with mass firings of immigrant workers. Sylvia Rosales-Fike, who'd hired Juan at La Clínica, told *The Washington Post*, "Everybody is selling cars. They are ready to leave, but they don't know where to go." For the first time ever, American employers who knowingly hired undocumented staff faced financial penalties. They had until June 1988—eighteen months—before the government began enforcing the new rules.

Shields's skepticism of Juan dissipated within a few months, once he saw how Juan anchored La Clínica to the immigrant community in Washington. The *promotores* joined Juan in setting up tables at church events, cookouts, and street fairs, where they encouraged people to get medical tests and register for appointments. The numbers of patients at La Clínica grew as more people recognized Juan and the other volunteers from their own neighborhoods. There was also a sizable contingent of people who'd been medical professionals in El Salvador but had to look for new lines of work in kitchens and at construction sites with payment under the table, because of either the language barrier or professional licensing regulations. At La Clínica, Juan enlisted their help, with Shields's supervision. One of them had been an emergency nurse in Guazapa, another a doctor who had also been tortured by the Salvadoran military. They came on Tuesdays, Saturdays, and Sundays, and formed a group to which Juan assigned a dignified and galvanizing name: the National Association of Latin American Health Professionals.

La Clínica was staying open a few days every week, and its resources were growing. It had been receiving special funds from the city because the doctors were doing HIV testing and providing care for patients with AIDS. Another grant came when La Clínica agreed to provide physical exams to a large group of newly resettled Vietnamese refugees. The money went toward additional staff hires, including a part-time nurse who helped tend to the Central American patients. All the medical services at La Clínica remained free, regardless of the patients' needs or legal status.

The sprawling community operation was what Juan had dreamed of bringing to Usulután before the war. But his position was unpaid, so he had to take a separate job to earn a living. There was a Salvadoran man in town who ran a cleaning

Juan with a group of volunteers at a health fair held by La Clínica to administer blood tests and treat common medical conditions affecting the Latino community in Washington and Maryland.

company that was known around Mount Pleasant for hiring immigrants. Through him, Juan took a shift as a janitor at an office building on K Street. He had to clean all the bathrooms, but because of his experience in El Salvador he'd developed a phobia of small, enclosed spaces. The elevators were therefore out of the question. Each night, Juan lugged his cart brimming with mops, brooms, cleaning products, toilet paper, and trash bags up and down the building's stairwells. The shift started at seven p.m. and ended at five a.m. There were benefits to working fast. If he finished around two a.m., he could spend the final three hours of his shift sleeping on a couch in one of the offices he'd cleaned.

In 1991, Cinco de Mayo fell on a Sunday, and the Central Americans of Mount Pleasant treated the day, which was technically a Mexican holiday, as a grander-than-usual occasion to unwind. People milled around outside, and families strolled with their children. A large contingent of young men, ranging in age from their late teens to early forties, congregated on street corners to drink. Sundays were typically their only day off, and they picked up one-dollar bottles of beer from the bars and mini-marts on Mount Pleasant Street, the main artery running diagonally through the heart of the neighborhood. Drinking outside was common among some of the immigrants living in Mount Pleasant, but it was also contentious. There were complaints, lodged mostly by white residents, that the drinkers were rowdy and belligerent. The police increased foot patrols in the area, but the drinking would eventually pick back up. Store owners themselves were divided. Sometimes they wouldn't sell to people who were already drunk, but much more often they simply gave their customers a paper go-cup with every bottle.

Most of the drinkers were Salvadoran, but there were also Mexicans, Nicaraguans, and Guatemalans. They had certain things in common: each had come to the US alone, ahead of his family, to make enough money to send back home or to bring a spouse, children, and parents north. Together these men were part of the tense and changing demographics of the area. Mount Pleasant had a population of roughly fourteen thousand people—35 percent were white, 30 percent Black, and almost 25 percent Latino. Adams Morgan and Columbia Heights, the neighborhoods to the south and east, were predominantly Black. There were dividing lines that everyone knew not to cross, invisible tripwires that could detonate hostilities. One of them ran down Fourteenth Street and Columbia Road; another was a matter of timing. On Friday evenings, when undocumented immigrants would get paid in cash, the streets would become treacherous. With nowhere to stash their money but in their socks—*el banco del calcetín*, or the sock bank, it was called—they would get mugged by assailants with baseball bats. When they fought back, usually with knives, other residents started to worry about their own safety. "It's Hispanics versus Blacks versus whites," one resident said at the time.

At around seven thirty in the evening on May 5, at the corner of Seventeenth and Lamont streets, two beat cops arrested four Salvadorans who were drunk and staggering near a restaurant called Don Juan. (The establishment's owner, who was a Cuban immigrant, had recently stopped selling liquor to go, telling people, "I want to attract more Americans.") There was a small tract of park space, which came to a sharp point at the corner of the block, where the men were loitering in a group. The two officers included a Black rookie on the force named Angela Jewell. Neither she nor her partner, who was white, spoke Spanish, and the men they were arresting didn't speak English. Jewell and her partner had three of them in handcuffs, when a fourth pulled away and started cursing. A small crowd gathered as the police officers tried to wrangle him. He lunged at them, and Jewell saw the glimmer of a knife. She pulled out her pistol and shot him in the chest.

An ambulance came, and the man—a thirty-year-old Salvadoran—was taken away. He would survive, but several days passed before the news spread. For more than an hour, the police didn't call to the scene Spanish-speaking officers to calm the increasingly angry crowd. There weren't many of them *to* call—on a force of four thousand about a hundred spoke Spanish. The rumors were that the police had shot and killed a drunk man in handcuffs. Later that night versions of the account circulated in distant corners of Mount Pleasant, and rioting began. Looting started at a 7-Eleven on Mount Pleasant Street and at a clothing store farther away, on Columbia Road. The police set up a loose cordon at the top of a hill, half a mile from the initial shooting. They were clearly reluctant to enter the fray.

The next day the situation got worse—more looting, vandalism, and clashes with police officers, who'd finally been sent in to control the crowds. Two stores were burned down, along with nineteen police cars and a city bus. People from all over the city started coming to Mount Pleasant to riot. "Everybody who doesn't like the police participated," one Black resident said. "There's no color on that." Washington's mayor, Sharon Pratt Dixon, was the first Black female mayor of a major city. She imposed a curfew, and arrests multiplied, mostly of Black agitators from nearby neighborhoods.

Juan Romagoza first heard about the disturbances late Sunday night, and on Monday morning he attended a meeting of local Latino leaders in the basement of the Sacred Heart church, down the street from Don Juan restaurant. Their priority was to stop the destruction of local businesses. A group of community mainstays, including Juan and a priest from the church, went out into the streets to march. They walked arm in arm through the crowds, imploring the rioters to redirect their rage. "Where are we going to go after this?" Juan shouted. "This is our home." A fog of tear gas shot by policemen blanketed the streets. At one point, Juan pulled slightly ahead of the priest, and when he turned around a canister of gas rolled onto the sidewalk where they were standing. The priest began coughing heavily and collapsed. Juan and the others took him to an apartment complex. Outside, they soaked the priest with a hose. Someone else left and came back with a change of clothes, and they led him upstairs, while Juan returned to the streets.

The curfew kept La Clínica from opening the next day, and most of the people who were injured on the streets were too scared to go to a hospital. On Tuesday and the first part of Wednesday, Juan and La Clínica's volunteers made house calls, and did quick consultations on the streets. Juan carried his small medical bag, just as he had in his days tending to protesters in El Salvador.

WITHIN THREE DAYS, the riots had largely died down, and a fragile period of collective introspection followed. More than two hundred people had been arrested, most of them for violating the curfew; some of the rioters faced stiffer sentences for destroying property and assaulting officers. But the city could no longer pretend that Latinos were marginal to Washington's identity. A

The second night of riots in the Mount Pleasant neighborhood of Washington, DC, 1991.

moribund Latino Civil Rights Task Force restarted its work in earnest, and the city opened up an office for police-Latino community relations on Columbia Road and Fourteenth Street Northwest, a street many of the Latino residents of Mount Pleasant had previously been reluctant to cross.

Later that spring, Juan was invited to a police precinct to explain what had happened. He was a recognizable figure, in good standing with residents and local authorities alike, but he still spoke little English, because to him learning the language had always implied accepting the US as his permanent home. A young volunteer from La Clínica named Catalina Sol, a college student whose sister had also worked with Juan, came with him to translate. Until that moment, Catalina knew very little about Juan, despite the time she spent at La Clínica. To her, he seemed reserved and a bit mysterious, an old-timer with a remote past who kept his personal life separate from his work.

They entered a conference room filled with officers in uniform—some sitting, others standing in the back. Catalina stood by his side as he spoke. The purpose of his address, he began, was to enumerate some of the reasons so many Central American residents feared men in uniform. Take him, he said. "When I see a police officer, my body starts to tremble."

Juan was used to sharing aspects of his own story, but he could never be sure whether he'd lose his composure once he started getting into the details.

He spoke slowly, careful not to raise his voice beyond a controlled pitch, as though gently testing his limits of self-exposure. The cops were drawn in. A stillness filled the room. Juan liked to think he could read situations with a clinician's eye for certain physical cues. He noticed a few audible exhales among the officers as he spoke; some of them were beginning to make eye contact with him. When Juan referred to the Salvadorans as *campesinos* from the countryside, one of the officers interjected. "*Campesinos* from Mexico, you mean?" Juan corrected him. "I thought all the people we were seeing were Mexican," another one said.

23.

War Zones

The list of things that Eddie Anzora considered "ghetto" was long and varied: Kenwood Avenue in South Los Angeles; the swap meet; the haunted house where Eddie and everyone lived; the apartment on Langdon Avenue where they had moved. He assigned this label to most of the objects and places in his world. And yet it couldn't be applied to what he was seeing now. That "wasn't even ghetto." There wasn't a word or a readily available idea to capture the force of his observations when he, Carlos, and their mother arrived in Central America, in December 1991. The scale of everything was off. The natural surroundings were all bigger: the flora, the verdant hills, the humidity. The human aspect was smaller: the cars, the clothes, the streets, even the people. He felt towering and dizzy at once, superior for a second, then brought low by the general strangeness.

Victoria had wanted to prepare her boys for this leap into a new reality, so they stopped in Guatemala City on the way to El Salvador. They would take a bus for the final leg of the trip. At the station, she took out a large plastic grocery bag she'd stowed away in her luggage and began unloading packets of grapes and articles of clothing. Groups of children crowded around her as she distributed the items. Money was always tight in California, but she'd saved enough for some modest donations. Years later Eddie would finally understand that she was proud, as an immigrant who'd made it north and now had a green card, to help in such an immediate, assertive way. At the time, he and his brother were annoyed, even slightly embarrassed. At one point, when Carlos spotted a kid sneaking his hand into his mother's purse, he shouted at her, rather than at the would-be thief. "What are you doing, Mom? They're stealing from you!"

Once they reached El Salvador, the three of them spent a month together in the house of Victoria's brother Lito, in Soyapango, just east of San Salvador. The fighting had mostly abated, and the guerrillas and the government were on the verge of signing peace accords. Eddie spotted bullet holes in the facades of crumbling buildings, and heaps of rubble where grenades and other explosives had gone off. On the corner of certain streets were sandbags piled to create bunkers. He rarely walked far without seeing a man in uniform, which lent his surroundings a haunting, unfinished air, like they were part of a half-built museum to something not yet in the past.

Two weeks later, after Victoria left, the reality of the situation set in. Eddie and Carlos would be going to school in San Salvador, at a private academy called Liceo Canadiense. They had to wear uniforms (khakis and white polo shirts), which was a sartorial equalizer. When they weren't in school, which was often, they stood out in outrageous ways. Their style was a cultural non sequitur in wartime El Salvador, all LA cholo flash and bravado. Eddie wore pants with thirty-eight- and forty-two-inch waists, sagging and cinched with a belt; running sneakers; and oversize shirts. He was listening to Kris Kross and Cypress Hill in those days. At first, he was a joke to the other kids, who wore tighter-fitting and more conservative clothes (shirts with collars, dressier shoes, or work boots). They'd see him and shout, "Ding-dong, ding-dong," mocking the bagginess of his clothes and his pendulous tough-guy gait. But they were also intrigued, the girls especially. Being from the US brought him instant cachet. His every move was a novelty, down to his gawky Spanish.

At school, the dominant group of boys always found some excuse to start a shoving match. One day, shortly after they began, Eddie and Carlos were jawing and swinging and stepping out into the schoolyard for a fight. A circle formed around them, and then, just as quickly, evaporated. Eddie heard the voice telling everyone to get lost before he saw the speaker. It was deep and booming, but relaxed, amplified by the power of someone who didn't have to speak loudly to be understood. The schoolboys scattered to reveal a handsome teenager with short, dark hair and a gap-toothed smile. He wasn't a student at the *liceo* but everyone seemed to know, or at least to fear, him. He was dressed more like Eddie than the others. In smooth, unaccented English, he introduced himself as Psycho, but Eddie would later learn that he preferred to be called Duke. "Let's go to my hood," he told them.

His hood was a *colonia* on the eastern edge of the city called Amatepec. It would become a regular haunt for Eddie and his brother. Duke was living out of the apartment of a distant family member, in a dilapidated complex with an asphalt sports field covered in dust and sand. Hip-hop played from a boombox. People came and went in a rhythm that reminded Eddie of LA—always moving but never in a rush. It turned out Duke was an Angelino himself. Recently deported as a member of 18th Street, he was starting up his own clique. In El Salvador, there were all sorts of small gangs, a lot of them connected to the local schools, but they were insular and informal. Locals used the word *mara* to describe them, in the literal sense of the word meaning a band of friends, not the newly hyped American usage associated with savagery.

For a few weeks after meeting Duke, Eddie smoked weed from joints wrapped in toilet paper while Duke "jumped in" a new crop of recruits in the afternoons. "I just got two people I gotta do," he said. "Give me a second." Duke beat up each one while someone counted to ten. At the end, the victim was winded and heaving, but Duke helped him to his feet and clapped him on the back. He kept a small tattoo gun in his apartment. Each initiate followed him inside to get inked up.

For whatever reason, Duke never pressured Eddie or his brother to join the gang. He regarded them with the bemused, protective spirit of an older sibling. After three months, Carlos got tired of the cramped conditions at Lito's house and moved in with another relative, in Usulután. Eddie went to spend some time with his grandmother, in a rural area not far from Lito's called Alta Vista. He milked cows and helped with farming. But everywhere he went he saw glimmers of his old LA life. There'd be a kid dressed in baggy clothes, jumpy and ill at ease. He and Eddie would exchange knowing glances, the commiseration of American transplants. Sometimes, the faces he saw were familiar and specific. He was downtown in San Salvador when a teenager in oversize jeans and Nike Cortez sneakers called out to him by name. "What's up, Holmes?" He was from Eddie's old block in South LA, an MS guy. "They deported my ass," he told Eddie. Another day he ran into two others—twins named William and Edwin—who used to sell drugs for MS on Langdon Avenue.

Eddie's social circle expanded with the unexpected cast of old acquaintances from Los Angeles. Some of them were hardened criminals when Eddie had first met them, the kind of people he'd be amiable with on the streets of San Fernando but whom he'd otherwise try to avoid. In El Salvador, they hung out because they all spoke English.

Ideally, the FMLN would have participated in El Salvador's legislative elections in March 1991, but the peace talks had stalled. The main problem, for the government and the guerrillas, was what to do with the military. The FMLN wanted to reduce its size and the government to establish a new civilian police force to replace the repressive state security apparatus. The military wouldn't countenance it, and Alfredo Cristiani was trapped between the two sides. The elections went ahead as scheduled, without the FMLN, but the results changed the picture entirely. A leftist coalition, known as the Democratic Convergence, tripled its vote share from the 1989 presidential race. This galvanized members of the FMLN by showing there was a constituency waiting for them to give up their weapons and enter politics. To Cristiani and members of the political right, the public tide appeared to be shifting, which put a premium on swifter negotiations. As did the American position: a year earlier, a cadre of Democratic congressmen—including Joe Moakley in the House—slashed aid to the Salvadoran military by 50 percent.

At the end of the year, the negotiators reached a breakthrough. There would be a truth commission to investigate abuses perpetrated by the armed forces. Cristiani agreed to cut the size of the military by half, and the government would also create a police force staffed mainly by civilians.

Juan was following the developments from Washington, optimistic but incredulous. After twelve years of fighting, some seventy-five thousand civilians were dead, and more than 20 percent of the surviving population was now living in the US. At La Clínica, Juan treated patients whose medical cases seemed like a microcosm of the country's prospects. Shell-shocked and battered, they were trapped between war and recovery. Was it possible, Juan sometimes wondered, to predict political outcomes from the symptoms of individual citizens? What was the prognosis for a whole country that had been traumatized? The first words of his patients were always some version of *Está bien, no pasa nada*. They minimized or rejected the very idea of a problem. For a country, that sort of denial could be fatal.

On December 31, 1991, the outlook brightened. Cristiani and the FMLN came to a near-final agreement in a meeting at the United Nations, in New York. When they did, Juan, who now had a green card but hadn't yet received his US citizenship, began preparing a trip home. His mother and father happened to be visiting Juan's sister in California at the time, which was how he wanted it. He felt better knowing that his parents were far away and safe. At La Clínica and in Mount Pleasant, there was no shortage of skeptics who pleaded with Juan not to go, but he couldn't be dissuaded. He took ten days off work and, with a small entourage of Americans and Salvadorans from La Clínica, returned to El Salvador for the first time since 1982.

When they touched down in the San Salvador airport, Juan's body registered the homecoming before his mind could. His breath steadied in the humid, tropical air. He said later that his life in El Salvador had been like a cassette tape, paused but never ejected from the player. Now that it was unspooling again, the familiar smells and sounds settled him: the smoky scent of tortillas cooked on iron skillets, the gently sour aroma of sliced-open coconuts, the rhythmic shouts of vendors hawking wares.

Still, there were absences everywhere: close friends who hadn't survived, gaps and silences left by death and emigration. Every fresh glimpse of the country doubled as a record of loss. "I knew we'd be finding *vacíos*," or holes, he told the nurses and doctors who joined him.

Laura had been dead for a decade, and after years of trying to locate his daughter, Maria, they had finally made contact in 1990. Juan's in-laws still blamed him for their daughter's death. The thought of showing up in Puebla unannounced and being turned away in Maria's presence was unbearable, so he had deputized a friend who traveled through Mexico for work, to help him find an address and phone number. It took Juan dozens of phone calls to persuade Maria's grandmother and aunt that he had no intention of taking his daughter from them. They worried he was coming to reclaim her. She was a teenager at the time, smart but introverted. His long absence made her suspicious of him. Their relationship over the next two years consisted of halting phone conversations; he asked her questions about herself that she answered in guarded monosyllables. These single words, exchanged weekly, were Juan's only defense against feeling forgotten. The fact that so many of his and Laura's mutual friends in El Salvador were gone contributed to the impression that a large part of his life was in the process of being erased.

One of his companions had rented a car so they could drive around to attend events and parties. The streets were full of jubilant people shedding years of fear and paranoia. Juan was staying at the home of one of his brothers, in San Salvador, while the others took rooms in a nearby hostel. They set out early each morning with ambitious itineraries, traveling around the country like tourists making impossible plans. They attended mass at the chapel where Romero was murdered, and visited the campus of La UCA, where the soldiers of the Atlacatl Battalion had executed the Jesuits. There wasn't enough time to visit people in Usulután, so Juan settled for a rushed walk through the town square before jumping into the car and racing back to the capital for another event. One afternoon, the group was in a mountain town called La Palma, near the Honduran border, when a man recognized a member of La Clínica. The man had gone there once as a patient, he said. Someone else fetched a thin mattress from a nearby house and set it down on two rocks to serve as an examination table. Juan, two nurses, and an American chiropractor spent the next few hours giving medical advice and massages to townspeople.

At other towns in Chalatenango, the guerrillas were beginning to descend from the mountains to hand over their weapons. They were dressed in their combat fatigues, lugging large packs. Crowds of aid workers mixed in with the locals to cheer them on. Juan and the others heard about one of these ceremonies, at a municipal park in the town of San José Las Flores. By the time they arrived, the formal *entrega*, or handoff, had given way to a party. A musical group assembled with guitars, violins, and an accordion, and the guerrillas danced to *la chanchona*, festive country music with a sharp, two-step rhythm from the rural east. Someone pressed an horchata into Juan's hands as he watched, stupefied by the sight of men in uniforms who were unarmed.

The war officially ended on January 16, 1992, in a ceremony in Mexico City. Besuited and beaming, Cristiani stepped down from a dais at a nineteenth-century neoclassical castle in the middle of Chapultepec Park, and shook hands with the leaders of the FMLN. "The conflict is behind us," he said. A massive rally followed in San Salvador, where a sea of people wearing red kerchiefs around their necks screamed with elation. The cathedral and government buildings were festooned in the red-and-yellow flags of the FMLN.

Juan spun through the crowds in tears. He paused near a tree, breathing heavily and trying to calm his emotions, when an older woman approached him. He recognized her from Usulután. She was the mother of a close friend of his from medical school, a student by the name of Mauricio Pérez Saravia, who'd joined the guerrillas shortly after Juan left the country. He was killed in a firefight while Juan was in Mexico. His mother had thought Juan was dead, too. All she wanted now, she said as she embraced him, was to know where they'd buried her boy. Could he help her?

When Eddie wasn't doing chores for his grandmother, or hanging out with Duke and the other deportees, he went tagging. His favorite spots were the abandoned trenches made by the guerrillas. He felt like he was adding his name to a smoldering relic of history: Taker from LA meets the old country. The signing of the peace accords was news everywhere, and Eddie grasped the enormity of the moment. But he was distracted by what was happening in his actual hometown. Just as the war was ending in El Salvador, another one was starting in Los Angeles.

On March 3, shortly after the Anzoras left for El Salvador, a Black man named Rodney King was hurtling down Interstate 210, drunk and speeding. When the police caught up with him near an apartment complex in the San Fernando Valley, there were more than two dozen officers on hand. King emerged from the car, laid down on the ground, then stood back up. He wobbled a bit, and staggered toward one of them before the beating began. The officers formed a circle, while three of them took turns kicking him and hitting him with batons. They landed fifty-six blows in all—shattering one of King's eye sockets, fracturing his cheekbone, breaking his leg, and knocking multiple fillings from his teeth. From across the street, a resident with a camcorder captured everything, including the scream of an onlooker: "Oh, my god, they're beating him to death."

In the weeks and months after the incident, snippets of the video footage were shown on a loop on local news, and city officials announced charges against the officers. The King beating was the latest in a series of city tragedies. A handful of police brutality cases had left several Black Angelinos injured, dead, or dispossessed. A predictable set of acquittals had followed. One of them was of three officers who faced misdemeanor charges for destroying the apartments of Black and Latino residents at Thirty-ninth Street and Dalton Avenue, during the raids a few years before. They were acquitted in June 1991, three months after the King footage surfaced. The following month, a commission appointed by the mayor, a Black political veteran and former cop named Tom Bradley, released the findings of an extensive investigation into police misconduct. "There is a significant number of officers in the LAPD who repetitively use excessive force against the public," its authors wrote. By then, Bradley was openly feuding with the white police chief, Daryl Gates, whom he was trying to oust. There were calls for Gates to resign, but there was resistance inside the department. In August, three Korean markets in South Central were firebombed, including one where a Korean grocer had shot and killed a Black teenager she'd accused of shoplifting. In November, a judge granted the grocer probation rather than jail time, which unleashed a wave of street protests.

Bradley and Gates hadn't spoken for a full year when, on April 29, 1992, a jury reached a verdict on whether the three officers shown on the video beating Rodney King, along with their supervisor, were guilty of violating his civil rights. The acquittal was announced that afternoon, from a courtroom in Simi Valley. It struck like an earthquake. Within hours, rioting had broken out across the city. At six forty-five p.m., a group of Black men pulled a white truck driver out of his vehicle on the corner of Florence and Normandie avenues and beat him, bashing his head with a brick. An hour later, a liquor store nearby went up in flames. The city had become a hotbed of tribalism and racial tension: Blacks against Koreans, Latinos against Blacks, the police against everybody. The King verdict lit the fuse of an all-out war. Store owners armed themselves with pistols. People were attacked at random. Shoplifters ran through streets, clouded with plumes of smoke, carrying whatever they could take. Others drove in to haul their loot in the trunks of their cars or strapped to the roofs.

For the first twenty-four hours, pandemonium descended on all corners of the city; news choppers shot live video of what looked like a war zone. The one group conspicuously absent from the melee in its earliest and ugliest hours was the LAPD itself. Officers were outnumbered and unprepared; ranking members of the force ordered whole units to pull back. South LA was destroying itself. By the second day of rioting, there were more than five hundred reported injuries, hundreds of fires, and close to $250 million in estimated damage. The conflagration, which began to lap at other parts of the city, soon persuaded state and federal authorities to send in troops—six thousand National Guardsmen and a thousand federal agents. Two hundred of those agents belonged to a special operations force of the US Marshals that President Bush had recently dispatched to Panama to arrest Manuel Noriega.

In Alta Vista, two thousand miles from LA, no one had their own landline, but there were two public telephones. They hung from weathered metal booths just outside a general store, with a daily queue of expectant callers waiting out front. Each day, Eddie got in line to call his mother and cousins. Only a few of his neighbors in El Salvador had televisions, but the images of American mayhem still reached him. The cousin he had always looked up to was seven years older, and a member of the 18th Street gang. He was in San Fernando, clear of the riot's epicenter. But, like Eddie, he was well connected among the residents of their old neighborhood on Kenwood Avenue. He reeled off the intersections

Los Angeles riots in 1992.

to Eddie on the phone: Seventy-first and Normandie, Thirty-sixth and Vermont Avenue, Florence and Normandie. It was a running inventory of the destruction, a roll call of old landmarks, such as the swap meet, that had been wiped out overnight.

The LA gangs had wildly divergent reactions to the riots. The Bloods and the Crips were enemies but agreed to a temporary truce in the name of racial solidarity. Members of the Mexican Mafia and other Chicano street gangs in East LA were alarmed by the destruction, and for the most part urged those among their ranks not to participate. The attitude was different among many of the Central Americans who belonged to MS-13. Those in South LA joined the mobs, destroying property, stealing weapons, and raiding stores. In San Fernando, Ernesto Deras, of the Fulton Locos, saw an opportunity. "While the police is tied up over there, in the city, let's get started over here," he told the reporter Carlos García. "Who wants Nike sneakers? I do, I do. Let's go strong."

When Eddie got off the phone, his friends wanted to know the latest news about the riots. For the deportees and their growing retinue of Salvadoran acolytes, LA was the main reference point, eclipsing the heady new moment in El Salvador. One of the boys, looking at Eddie with unusually wide-eyed candor, said, "Hey, man, you sure you want to go back there to all that? It sounds dangerous."

24.

Operation Blockade

In the summer of 1992, executives at the Salvadoran airline TACA had a mysterious problem. Every time a plane would arrive in the Los Angeles airport, its toilets would be clogged. At first, they assumed it was a matter of plumbing. They cleaned out the pipes and considered replacing the toilets. Eventually, the flight attendants figured out what was happening. A few hours into the flight, passengers would start lining up to use the bathrooms. Inside, one after another, the passengers were tearing up their passports and flushing the pages down the toilet. The airline began to station a flight attendant outside each of the plane's lavatories to make passengers hand over their passports before using the facilities.

TACA Airlines wasn't alone in finding passports flushed down toilets. It was happening at major American airports as well, from LAX to JFK. Immigration officials across the country started calling those who arrived without passports "flushers." Travelers who couldn't sneak away to the bathroom before reaching customs found other ways to destroy or conceal their identity documents. They hid them in their carry-on luggage or, in cases of desperation, tried eating through the pages. Whatever their means of disposal, everyone had wised up to the same strategy: without a passport to confirm a country of origin, there was no way for INS officials to initiate the deportation process. These travelers requested asylum, and because there was limited space for detention, the INS often released them with a work-authorization form and a future court date.

By the early 1990s, the asylum system was in a state of disarray. After passing the Refugee Act, in 1980, legislators mostly lost interest in the issue; the chaos of Mariel was followed by a period of steady asylum applications (between sixteen and twenty-six thousand each year) but no accompanying sense of political urgency. For most of the decade, the Reagan administration was denying asylum applications with such regularity it saw no need to bolster the government's resources. Under George H. W. Bush, however, there were new geopolitical considerations, which US asylum policy started to reflect. With growing concern about government repression in Beijing, the US expanded protections for Chinese émigrés fleeing the country's one-child policy. The resulting wave of applications, coupled with old inefficiencies, meant unresolved asylum claims mounted. Soon there was a backlog of more than a hundred thousand cases.

ONE OF THE ENTRIES in the backlog dated to 1988, and it belonged to Carmelina Cadena and her mother. In the early 1990s, they were living together in Arcadia, Florida. The orange groves had drawn them to the state, which was a good place to work, considering the alternatives. When they had first arrived in the US from Guatemala, in 1983, Carmelina's mother found a sewing job in Los Angeles, but lost it when her employers demanded papers. She didn't know how to get them. Her Spanish was bad, but her English was worse. In San Miguel Acatán, their hometown in the mountains of Huehuetenango, Guatemala, everyone spoke a language called Akateko. From Los Angeles, they relocated to Colorado—odd jobs in Denver, cleaning mushrooms in Alamosa. They spent the nights sleeping in the trunk of a car to avoid the workers' cabins, which were filled entirely with men, about thirty of them in all. In Oregon they picked onions; in Idaho, potatoes. In New York, during the fall, they picked apples, though this task was especially strenuous for the mother and daughter, who were four feet nine and four feet six, respectively. By the time they reached Florida, there were about twenty thousand Indigenous Maya living in the state, most of them clustered about a hundred miles farther east in a sparsely populated agrarian community with citrus groves and vegetable farms called Indiantown. It was "a good omen we happened to find a place with this name," one Indigenous leader said. Most Floridians assumed the newcomers were Mexican, so they were baffled to encounter a language that didn't sound anything like Spanish. Nurses at one hospital tried to treat a Maya woman who, they later reported, appeared to be "speaking in tongues."

Almost all the Indigenous Guatemalans in Florida at the time had come from somewhere in the Cuchamatán mountains, in small groups beginning in the early 1980s, as the repression in the western highlands of the country grew more intense. More than a million Maya fled to Mexico and the United States during those years. But their legal standing was difficult to discern. Carmelina lost an aunt, an uncle, and nineteen cousins to military murders; her father was so traumatized by the killings that he began to drink after the family reached Mexico, and he eventually landed in jail. Yet Carmelina and her mother, like most of the others who reached the US, were reluctant to speak about what they'd suffered. They figured their best move was to prove their willingness to work; the first words in English that many of them learned was the phrase "I need a good work." This made it even easier for the government to write them off as "economic migrants." Those who applied for asylum were almost all rejected. Between 1983 and 1986, close to a hundred thousand Guatemalans reached the US, but only fourteen asylum petitions were granted. The denials didn't stop the flow of people heading north. They simply clouded any understanding of who was coming and why.

An irony of the dysfunctional asylum system was that it led to more applications. You didn't apply for asylum expecting to get it. The odds were too long. But because the government was running so far behind, it was granting asylum seekers work authorization while their applications were pending. In 1991, there were 56,000 recently filed asylum applications; understaffed INS offices completed 16,000 of them. In 1992, there were 103,000 additional applications, only 21,000 of which were completed. "By the 1990s," one historian later wrote of the Guatemalans, "the earlier stream of 'war refugees' gave way to a chain of migration of 'economic refugees' drawing on family and village ties." Advertisements placed by *notarios* and small law firms started cropping up in local newspapers. One of them, in a Spanish daily in Central Florida, read:

"Work Authorization (Political Asylum)." Another advertised "Work Permits," and added, in smaller font, "through political asylum."

Carmelina's mother had a work permit that she had to renew each year. She had applied for asylum but never heard back. It had been fourteen years. She and her daughter would take the bus to an INS office in Miami to update her documents. One afternoon, strolling down Calle Ocho, near the corner of Twenty-seventh Avenue, Carmelina, who was now fourteen, saw a flyer describing a court settlement. It was called *American Baptist Churches v. Thornburgh*. It seemed that she and her mother could call an 800 number associated with the government and get their name on a list. Lawyers had brought the class action because the government had unfairly dismissed the asylum petitions of Salvadoran and Guatemalan applicants. The Justice Department was acknowledging that it had done wrong. According to the terms of the agreement, any Guatemalan who'd arrived in the US before October 1, 1990, could reapply. Carmelina called the number to share her family's information. She had no idea if she and her mother would be eligible.

Several years passed before an immigration lawyer whom the family could finally afford found their names in the settlement agreement. The *ABC v. Thornburgh* case may have represented a belated victory for the principle of asylum, but it added hundreds of thousands more applications for the INS to review. By the end of 1994, the backlog had grown to more than four hundred thousand cases.

Doris Meissner was working at the Carnegie Endowment for International Peace when Bill Clinton offered her the job to head the INS. She accepted knowing the downsides. The agency had a modest budget and a sprawling mission. Its responsibilities put it squarely in the political fray. What the agency needed was ambition and leadership. What it had was the indifference of presidents who saw immigration policy as a political liability.

Clinton was wary of the issue, and even so, his learning curve was steep. On the campaign trail, he attacked George Bush over a policy his administration had adopted in May 1991, in which the US turned away tens of thousands of

Haitian asylum seekers who were trying to reach the US by boat. After a coup the following September, the human rights group Amnesty International estimated that the new government had killed at least fifteen hundred people whom it considered loyal to the old regime. The number of Haitians fleeing to the US increased. As it did, the American policy intensified, with the Coast Guard intercepting US-bound vessels at sea. Clinton called it "appalling" and vowed to give each Haitian an asylum hearing once he was president. But as the president-elect he now faced the reality of an impending humanitarian crisis. In late December, a seventy-foot wooden freighter that was crammed with 392 Haitians en route to South Florida sank; eight survived. "What if in the first few days of the Clinton administration, thousands more refugees cast off and died during their perilous voyage?" one reporter wrote in the *Chicago Tribune*. By the time of Clinton's inauguration, some twelve hundred new boats were reportedly under construction, with tens of thousands of Haitians preparing to set out. Fearing a repeat of Mariel, Clinton reversed himself, telling Haitians that they should stay at home "for the time being."

Clinton officially entered the White House on Wednesday, January 20, 1993. On Friday, his nominee for attorney general, a corporate lawyer named Zoë Baird, withdrew from consideration. A *New York Times* report had recently revealed that she'd employed an undocumented Peruvian couple to work as a nanny and chauffeur. Three days later, around eight in the morning, a Pakistani national named Mir Aimal Kansi pulled up to a traffic light on Route 123, across the street from the entrance to CIA headquarters, in Virginia. He opened the door of a brown Datsun station wagon and fired an AK-47 into oncoming traffic, killing two CIA employees and injuring several others. When authorities investigated, they learned that he'd applied for asylum; because of the backlog, he had obtained a work permit while his application was pending. On February 6, Clinton's new pick for attorney general, Kimba Wood, a federal judge, bowed out after admitting that she, too, had employed an undocumented nanny. The Washington press corps called this side plot Nannygate.

On February 26, just a month into Clinton's first term, two terrorists bombed the World Trade Center, one of whom had gained entry after applying for asylum. The urgency grew on June 6 when a ship called the *Golden Venture* crashed ashore along the Rockaway peninsula in New York, between Brooklyn and Queens. Two hundred eighty-six Chinese immigrants were on board, each having paid roughly thirty thousand dollars to reach the US from the province of Fujian. The *Golden Venture* was the twenty-fourth ship to reach the US from China in the previous twenty-two months, according to William Slattery, the New York district director of the INS. "The Third World has packed its bag, and it's moving," he said. "The aliens have taken control."

BY THE TIME CLINTON announced his nomination of Doris Meissner to lead the INS on June 18, 1993, she'd already assembled a working group to make plans for reforming the asylum system. The problems were obvious (endemic delays, staff shortages, tangled bureaucracy), and the recent incidents at the CIA headquarters and the World Trade Center raised national security concerns. There was talk in conservative circles on the Hill that new legislation should pare back the Refugee Act.

The reform agenda had three major components. The first step was to disincentivize frivolous applications by refusing to grant immediate work permits to asylum applicants. The government would commit to resolving each case within six months; if it couldn't, only then would the applicant be eligible for temporary work authorization. To stick to this timeline, the INS would decide the most recently filed applications first; this was the next prong of Meissner's plan. The older cases in the queue tended to be harder to close because of stale evidence, address changes, and other glitches. The idea was to send a new message to *prospective* asylum applicants: the government was speeding up the process, which would make the system much more difficult to game. The last part of the reform was territorial. The INS would finally wrest control of the asylum process from the State Department, and a dedicated corps of asylum officers, working exclusively on the issue, would eventually take over from the INS district directors. Backed up by their own research staff, these officers would spend four days a week hearing asylum cases and the fifth day reviewing human rights reports and government documents detailing the conditions in different countries.

A few weeks after being confirmed, Meissner presented the asylum plan to the president's top advisers, who authorized its funding through the 1994 crime bill. Under Clinton, Meissner quickly learned, the emphasis would always be on demonstrating toughness. The president and his political advisers were obsessed with charting a centrist course. The White House wanted to preempt criticism from the right. Leading and policing the strategy was Rahm Emanuel, a short, pugnacious young adviser in his early thirties. Some of his colleagues called him "Rahmbo." He once mailed a pollster a dead fish in a box, because the man had been slow to send Emanuel the latest returns. Another time, while campaign hands gathered to celebrate Clinton's victory in the 1992 election, Emanuel grabbed a knife and started reeling off the names of politicians who had "fucked us." After saying each name, he'd growl, "Dead man," and slam down the knife.

The new asylum policy started showing results soon after the government implemented it. The pace of applications slowed, and approval rates increased; far fewer applicants submitted dubious claims. When Meissner shared the good news at a White House meeting, Emanuel seemed distracted. They'd all been sitting around a table; as the group broke up, he took her aside. "That's fine," he said of the asylum policy. "When are you going to come to me with something about the border?"

◇—◇

On September 19, 1993, while Doris Meissner was preparing for her confirmation hearings in the Senate, a Border Patrol chief in West Texas named Silvestre Reyes lined up four hundred agents roughly fifty yards apart. They assembled along the most heavily trafficked parts of the border, in downtown El Paso and Ciudad Juárez. Reyes wanted to discourage people from attempting to enter the US by diverting them to more remote stretches of the desert, where it was physically harder to cross the border. Those who did anyway received an additional punishment. They were not deported straight across the border to Juárez, as in the past. Instead, the Border Patrol drove them sixty miles west of El Paso, into New Mexico, and dumped them in Palomas, Chihuahua. From there, the deportees had to find their way back to Juárez—hitching rides, sleeping on the streets as they scrounged for money, or trekking east on foot.

El Paso was the second-largest city on the US-Mexico border, smaller only than San Diego. But that designation overstated the size and remoteness of the place. Fewer than seven hundred thousand residents lived there, and the nearest American cities were hundreds of miles away. The Border Patrol sector was much vaster than the city itself. It covered 268 miles of the border, including the two westernmost counties in Texas as well as the entirety of New Mexico.

In the late 1980s and early '90s, when the US government was trying to contain Mexican border crossers, agents in El Paso responded by racially profiling residents. Because they couldn't catch everyone who entered the US, the patrolmen stopped anyone they could within the city limits, from grandmothers to high schoolers, demanding to see their papers. This posed a special problem in a county that was 75 percent Hispanic. There was a lawsuit; the controversial local head of the Border Patrol retired; and his replacement, Silvestre Reyes, brought an idea that would revolutionize border policy for the next three presidential administrations. He called it Operation Blockade.

Reyes's superiors in Washington were skeptical until they saw the results. Over the following year, there was a 72 percent drop in apprehensions in the sector. These figures would later prove to be deceiving. Migrants were continuing to cross—they were just doing it farther from the major ports of entry. An increasing number of them were dying in the desert. But fewer arrests counted as a clear success by the low standards of immigration enforcement. The INS scaled up the operation in other locations along the border. In San Diego, there was Operation Gatekeeper; in Arizona, Operation Safeguard; and in South Texas, Operation Rio Grande. The government began speaking about a concept it was calling "prevention through deterrence."

25.

Above the Rest

One morning at the end of the winter, in 1993, Eddie Anzora rounded the corner of Roscoe Boulevard, in Los Angeles, careful to avoid the McDonald's, an old MS-13 haunt. Turning onto Sepulveda, he loped toward a bus stop. Back from El Salvador only a few months, he was on his way to James Monroe High School, where he was starting the ninth grade. As Eddie walked down the sidewalk, a city bus on a different route came into view. Hanging out of open windows toward the back were a dozen of his friends shouting and waving to get his attention.

Before Eddie had left the year before, they had all joined a new outfit, called ATR. The acronym stood for Above the Rest, but its members considered themselves part of an underground. This was less a gang than a confederacy of gang skeptics. Everyone in it had drifted away from the other street crews. The gangsters were the city's main power brokers—they were to be studied and respected, but the boys in ATR didn't see a reason to emulate them. The lives of these kingpins seemed defined by arbitrary grudges begun over clothing colors, attacks against strangers, endless posturing. Eddie and his friends preferred to take their cues from hip-hop. The lyrics of songs like "I'm Your Pusher" and "Children's Story," by Slick Rick, which they all knew by heart, sent a message of resistance. To survive was to move against the grain, to keep a lower profile.

To ward off the gangs, however, the ATR guys had to form their own. MS-13, 18th Street, and the Langdon Gang were voracious recruiters who did not view membership as a choice. "We were just going to get eaten up," said Joel Orozco, one of Eddie's oldest friends. "All they wanted to do was take people as members. We didn't allow it, because we had our own thing." They thought of themselves as looking like "non-gangster gangsters," Eddie said later. Rather than Nike Cortez sneakers, an identifiable gang shoe, they wore shell-toe Adidas or cross-trainers; their pants, already several sizes too big, were creased at the top to look even broader. Members of ATR thought of their "beefs" as being in the service of their own survival, fighting that was necessary and not gratuitous. But that distinction didn't always apply. When Eddie left for El Salvador, ATR was still mostly about graffiti—"getting your name up everywhere," he said. When he returned, his friends gave him a long list of other street gangs. "These are the crews we don't get along with anymore," they told him.

Eddie ran over to the bus and jumped on. The seats and windows were caked in graffiti. The other passengers were nervously pressed together toward the front. Eddie didn't have to ask the others where they were going. One of them shouted out the details as Eddie made his way to the back. They were headed in the direction of Birmingham High School, to hunt down a bunch of "enemies" who were supposed to be standing around outside a doughnut shop.

The bus stopped, and someone spotted the targets across the street. The crew tore off in pursuit. The crowd outside the doughnut shop fanned out, leaving behind a few stragglers to fight. It was hard to run in such baggy pants. Eddie was halfway across the street, still far from the action, when the police arrived. By then, two of the rival boys were hurt—one of them bloodied by a punch, the other writhing on the ground with a screwdriver sticking out of his leg.

Instead of arriving at Monroe High School that morning, Eddie landed in Central Juvenile Hall. The first thing the other boys would ask a newcomer when he arrived was: Which crew do you represent? Depending on the answer, opposing factions might sneak into his room afterward to attack him while the guards were on break or distracted. When the question was put to Eddie, he told them he was with ATR. His interrogators replied, "What the fuck is that?"

THE RIOTS IN APRIL 1992 changed everything in and around Los Angeles. By the time Eddie returned from El Salvador, there was a new mayor and a new police chief. The anti-gang units of the LAPD were in ascendance, and racial recriminations were all-consuming. Sixty-one percent of the "arrested looters" were Latino, according to the police. The areas hit hardest by the rioting in South Central Los Angeles were Black neighborhoods filled with Latinos. But the destruction also spread to other parts of the city with large populations of newly arrived immigrants from Central America and Mexico: Pico Union, Koreatown, East Hollywood. The more established Latino communities—in East Los Angeles, for instance—had tried to keep their distance from the mayhem, giving rise to other anxieties and resentments. In the *Los Angeles Times*, a Chicano journalist wrote, "Yes, Central American immigrants and Chicanos might both be termed 'Latino.' But the ethnic link between the two groups is thin." The article ran with the headline, "Should Latinos Support Curbs on Immigrants? A Question Left by the Riots Is Whether New Arrivals Threaten Second- and Third-Generation Mexican-Americans." Elana Zilberg, a professor at the University of California, San Diego, later wrote, "Whites pointed at Blacks, who pointed at Latinos, who in turn pointed at Central American immigrants."

Back in California, after his stint in El Salvador, Eddie caught glimpses of the shifting social order. The ATR guys spent their teenage years in and out of juvenile lockups. When they were home, in San Fernando, they cut school and traveled around the city stealing things to resell. They called it racking. A typical day would involve striking a deal with mom-and-pop shop owners, mostly Chinese or Indian guys with heavy accents, who would place orders for pilfered goods such as twenty sticks of deodorant. The boys would go to Ross, a department store, and stuff their pockets full of merchandise. Their pants and shirts were so baggy that the security guards didn't notice the bulging items when they left. Another trick was to wear sweatshirts with tapered cuffs, so they could stash the goods in their sleeves and not have to worry about them tumbling out. Later they would return to the original shop, to trade in their spoils for cash.

Eddie was charismatic and smooth-talking, a natural leader at ease around people; his sharp intelligence was wily and entertaining. ATR was growing, with members across the valley. Joining had initially felt like a narrow and personal decision to Eddie, a quiet pact made among friends on Langdon Avenue. But later, in a correctional facility, there were reminders of how their ranks had changed. Once, leaving the shower, he noticed a stranger with an ATR tattoo. "I'm from ATR, too," he said. "They call me Take, or Eddie." The boy replied, "Oh, *you're* Eddie! They told me I was going to run into you."

By the mid-1990s, ATR had close to two hundred members. When they would meet up, every couple of months, the crew's de facto headquarters tended to be wherever Eddie lived. At the time, he was dating a girl from a neighboring housing complex whose mother was connected to the Mexican Mafia. (Her brother, who was in prison, was a high-ranking member.) Listening to her, Eddie was in his element—hungry for fresh information, relaxed in his questions, irresistibly interested in the world. At her apartment one night, Eddie learned that La Eme planned to reduce drive-by shootings, effectively cleaning up the neighborhoods under its sway. The riots and their aftermath were bad for business. "In a couple of months," she told him, "this whole place is going to be controlled. No one's going to be able to fuck around anymore."

ATR would have to be much more careful about tagging. The Mexican Mafia was putting out a "green light" on taggers—the criminal equivalent of an all-points bulletin, enforceable by beatings or even killings—because residents were complaining. It bothered the mob's top people that the taggers didn't represent a single neighborhood at which they could strike back to punish them. Eddie and the others began to cover up their tattoos, mostly by inking new designs (spiders, clowns) over the letters *ATR*. They also participated in a series of gatherings overseen by the Mexican Mafia that were held at parks around the city. Different street crews had fistfights to thrash out their disagreements. These were like controlled detonations, to satisfy the pride and territoriality of the city's Latino gangs without additional casualties. ATR wasn't big enough to draw an invitation to the most consequential of these meetings, which was held on the afternoon of September 18, 1993, at Elysian Park, near Dodger Stadium, in Los Angeles. With a thousand gangsters in attendance, Mafia members handed down an inviolable edict: crews could still fight, but if they did, it had to be face-to-face. Police officers formed a broad cordon around the park but kept their distance; some metro reporters showed up with their notebooks. "This is for *la raza*, the Mexican people," a gang member told one of them. "If you have to take care of business," the gangster went on, "at least do it with respect, do it with honor and dignity."

At seven on the morning of April 13, 1994, Eddie was at home in bed when the police arrived with a warrant. Officers from the Community Tagger Task Force—a group drawn from divisions of the Los Angeles and San Fernando police departments—were arresting him on felony vandalism charges. He was one of five members of ATR accused of causing thirty-eight thousand dollars in damages with their graffiti, including eleven thousand dollars' worth of damage to an off-ramp of a Simi Valley freeway. While the officers searched the house, they found a video that Eddie had made documenting one of his tagging escapades. It was entered into evidence.

He spent a month at Sylmar Juvenile Hall, an austere redbrick facility twenty-five miles north of the city, before being sentenced. An eighteen-year-old ATR member faced a year of jail time and a thousand-dollar fine. Eddie was sent to the Juvenile Camp Louis Routh, where teenagers were offered an alternative to time behind bars. Earning a dollar a day, they fought forest fires and slept in cabins in the hills around Big Tujunga canyon, twenty miles north of the city. The training consisted of timed runs up a steep trail that was called Kill 'Em Quick, because it climbed a thousand feet in less than a mile. Two dozen switchbacks twisted among desert brush and loose rocks up to a picturesque ridgeline, and the boys often wore their firefighting gear for practice: hard hats, white-and-blue uniforms, canvas packs, and occasionally chain saws. Eddie found the atmosphere intensely motivating. The probation officers were stern but encouraging, and admonished the boys to think about their future in a way that Eddie took seriously. On Langdon Avenue, he and his friend Joel had often talked about starting a career in music, brainstorming ways to convert the street hustle into more durable prospects. Their conversations had always been interrupted by an arrest or a skirmish. Now Eddie decided to train for the LA Marathon, on March 5, 1995. While at Routh, he also received his GED, which he called his "good enough diploma."

He was released near the end of 1995, a few months shy of his eighteenth birthday, with enough money to put a down payment on a used lowrider

Chevy Caprice. In the years after his release, he still socialized with friends from ATR, but he took a job at an animal hospital in Sherman Oaks. "All these people you meet," he said later, *"vienen del otro camino de la vida.* Their stress is different from your stress." Some of the veterinarians, for instance, had their own cars and homes; they didn't want for material possessions, yet they were crippled by social anxiety. They'd often ask Eddie to take them out to bars and clubs so he could help them talk to women. He was drawn by the way they spoke: sentences were free of cursing and spoken entirely in English, unspun from the bravura cadences of the street. As he once did with the fashions and mannerisms of the South Los Angeles gangsters, Eddie began to study these newer figures in his life—the veterinarians, the well-heeled pet owners, the polished receptionists.

In 1997, Eddie was twenty years old and living with his brother and Joel in an apartment on Langdon Avenue. It faced the street and was on a low floor, and they worried about stray bullets flying inside. They bought a sheet of scrap metal from a workshop by the railroad tracks and propped it up against the windows when they were home.

One night after dinner, Joel objected when Eddie announced that he was going to step outside. It was dark, and they generally tried to stay off Langdon Avenue at night. Crime was one risk, but it paled beside the threat of the anti-gang police squads that patrolled the streets in full force. Residents had come to believe that the officers arrested whomever they could, often nabbing innocent people because they lived alongside gang members in the same housing units. A few years later, in 1999, one of the worst scandals in the history of the LAPD roiled the department and the city. The Rampart Division of the LAPD's anti-gang unit was exposed by an officer within its ranks as a criminal enterprise. Some of the agents had been involved in gang-related moneymaking schemes of their own; to keep up appearances, and to curb potential rivals, many of them had been fabricating and planting evidence for years. At one point, when the department reopened cases to investigate, detectives were forced to fly to Central America to look for people who'd been wrongfully deported. Langdon Avenue fell in a different jurisdiction, outside the LA city limits, but the practice still applied. The Rampart scandal confirmed for Eddie and his friends that they were right to distrust the authorities.

But every so often Eddie's intelligence betrayed him with a false sense of invincibility. This time, he decided to leave the apartment. He was walking toward his car with a friend when he spotted a group of officers making an arrest down the block. If he hurried back into his building, it would arouse more suspicion. Steadying himself, he advanced calmly toward his car and got in. He was beginning to drive away when the officers ordered him to stop and get out. While he and his friend stood next to the car with their hands pressed against the hood, the officers conducted a search. In the glove compartment, they found an ounce of weed, which belonged to Eddie; his friend was carrying a packet of meth, which he dropped on the floor of the car. The officers booked them both for drug possession.

26.

The Third Rail
of American Politics

I n 1994, when Janet Murguía started her job in the Clinton White House, it was impossible to attend a meeting without polling data spread across a desk or waved around by a gesticulating hand. Fresh printouts would circulate every few hours. The president's advisers weren't just content to know where the American public stood on a particular issue; they needed to know where the public stood on that issue at every hour of the day.

Murguía was thirty-two years old, a Mexican American from Kansas. She'd spent the previous seven years as a legislative aide to Jim Slattery, a moderate Democrat from her home state, and in that time amassed experience on a range of topics, from health care policy to foreign affairs. (At one point, as part of a congressional delegation, she met the head of the Contras in a Honduran military camp.) She considered the agenda of the Clinton White House to be "ultra centrist." The practical possibilities of a Southerner who knew how to make a play for moderates and conservatives appealed to Murguía. The issue for her, and for the president she now served, was timing.

Shortly after Murguía joined the administration, a cantankerous congressman from Georgia named Newt Gingrich became the Speaker of the House. He had just been elected with a wave of other Republicans on a platform they called the Contract with America. It was the first time the Republicans had held a House majority in forty years, and they controlled both chambers of Congress as Clinton's reelection campaign approached.

The field generals inside the White House were in overdrive—poll-obsessed and reeling. In addition to Emanuel there was another adviser, roughly the same age, named Bruce Reed. An impeccably educated, lifelong political junkie, Reed was cerebral and high-minded. In person, he came across as genial and mild-mannered, but behind his unimposing facade was the author of the president's most forceful campaign slogans. Emanuel was loud and profane, Reed more subdued. But together they were convinced that the president needed to "cut to the right." The only way he could win reelection was if he got something done, and the only way he could do that was by working with Republicans, signing *their* bills into law. The key was to temper their legislation without seeming to obstruct it.

In the summer of 1996, Murguía found herself squarely in the middle of the president's dilemma. She was the chief House liaison, which made her Clinton's main go-between among Democrats and Republicans on the Hill. Dealing with the GOP was unpleasant but predictably so; the real problem was having to break so much bad news to members of her own party, then plead for their votes. She was working long hours in the East Wing of the White House and paying regular visits to congressional offices, where she wheedled, cajoled, and updated staffers on two major bills that were under negotiation at the same time. The first involved welfare reform, the second immigration.

Welfare reform was the more complicated bill for the president. Clinton had campaigned on "ending welfare as we know it"—a line written by Bruce Reed—before getting blindsided by the Republican Congress. The first two welfare-reform bills that reached his desk were harsh even by his own malleable standards. He vetoed both. (As soon as he did, Bob Dole, the Senate majority leader and Clinton's opponent in November, was ready with a punch line: The president stood for the "end of welfare reform as we know it.") Another bill passed Congress in August 1996 and went to the president for his signature. This one, he complained to his advisers, was "a decent welfare bill wrapped in a sack of shit." The law slashed the welfare rolls and unraveled the social safety net, but perhaps the most controversial aspect of it was how the bill funded job training programs to wean people from government support. Almost half of the total funding—some $23 billion—came from cutting aid to legal immigrants. For years, permanent residents and green-card holders had received federal relief. The bill would end that, making them ineligible for welfare, aid to families with dependent children, supplementary security income, food stamps, and Medicaid. Up until this moment, there was a clear fault line for immigrants in the realm of public policy: legal immigrants were considered upstanding and thus largely protected, while "illegal" immigrants were treated as reprehensible. The welfare reform bill drew a distinction between legal immigrants and citizens.

Cecilia Muñoz, an immigrants' rights advocate with an organization called the National Council of La Raza, was roughly the same age as Murguía. She was a young mother pregnant with her second child as early drafts of the welfare bill circulated in the summer of 1995. The daughter of Bolivian parents who'd immigrated to the Detroit suburbs, she'd spent much of her childhood discussing Latin American politics at the dinner table. One evening, her high school boyfriend was over when he heard her father complaining about US policy in El Salvador and Nicaragua. It was the late 1970s. "If we do end up in a war," the boyfriend told her, "your parents should be interned. I couldn't know where their loyalties lay." The moment was an epiphany for Muñoz: in the eyes of some Americans, her parents would never be full citizens. Years later, she would cite her ex-boyfriend's remark as motivation, in part, for the accelerated course of her career. After getting a master's degree in Latin American studies, she moved to Chicago to work as an organizer and soon landed a top job with the city's Catholic charities. IRCA had just passed, and the archdiocese was running a program to help immigrants apply for legal status. Millions of undocumented immigrants were eligible under the new law, but many of their children, siblings, and parents didn't qualify for amnesty. Because they'd entered the US after the law's eligibility deadline, some were getting deported. Muñoz had lobbied the Bush administration to create a "family unity" policy, before getting involved in shaping the 1990 Immigration Act.

Six years later, the welfare reform bill reminded Muñoz of what had first pushed her into organizing. Millions of legal immigrants spent years of their lives paying taxes and starting families, only to see the political debate suddenly shift. To Muñoz's mind, it was as though Congress were telling them,

"You're not us yet." Muñoz's parents were already citizens, but when she heard Republicans talk about how noncitizens didn't "deserve" these protections, she nevertheless thought of her own family. She was reminded of a story her parents had told her about having once been threatened with eviction from an apartment for being overheard "speaking Mexican."

Murguía was Muñoz's conduit into the administration. She was sympathetic to Muñoz but outgunned inside the White House by Emanuel and Reed. In the first half of 1996, she would return from the Hill with messages from left-leaning Democrats alarmed by the president's plans. Their votes mattered less to the White House than those of conservative Democrats, however. Muñoz and her peers in the advocacy community tried to document, in painstaking detail, the suffering the president's policy would cause. Murguía shared as much of this information as she could with administration insiders, but she was so deep in the haggling, vote counting, and technical aspects of the negotiations that she could not fully survey the potential damage. There were allies in the administration, but no one powerful enough to override the president's survival instincts. At one point, an official at the Office of Management and Budget named Ken Apfel gave a presentation to Clinton, laying out the bill's monumental impact on legal immigrants. It didn't dissuade Clinton from endorsing the bill, but it made a mark that would prove consequential. On August 22, 1996, Clinton signed the bill into law, but at a press conference several days earlier he had promised to find some way to eventually undo the damage. "I am deeply disappointed that the congressional leadership insisted on attaching to this extraordinarily important bill a provision that will hurt legal immigrants in America," he had said from a dais at the White House. "This provision has nothing to do with welfare reform; it is simply a budget-saving measure, and it is not right."

Muñoz was cutting out articles from local, state, and national newspapers and keeping them in a file that was growing thicker as the welfare policy was finalized. The government was beginning to send out notices informing legal immigrants that their relief checks would stop coming. One clip in Muñoz's folder included an account of a seventy-five-year-old Mexican-born farmworker named Ignacio Muñoz. He'd lived in the US for forty years and had been receiving four hundred dollars in supplemental security income each month.

When a government letter reached him at his home in Stockton, California, he bought a gun and shot himself in a canal bed under a local bridge. Around this time, one of Cecilia Muñoz's colleagues at La Raza gave her a glass jar that she called "Cecilia's Moments of Joy." She instructed Muñoz to write, on small strips of paper, short descriptions of moments that made her happy, because the outlook was getting worse by the fall of 1996.

Rahm Emanuel and Bruce Reed didn't have an ideological aversion to immigration—they just thought that anything short of toughness on the issue was a political loser in an election year. Emanuel would later call immigration "the third rail of American politics." You could fault him for being too calculating but not for misreading the political forecast. In 1994, Californians voted overwhelmingly to approve a ballot measure, called Proposition 187, that barred undocumented immigrants from using public health care or education services. A federal court eventually struck down the measure as unconstitutional, but Washington took note. For much of the 1994 campaign, the state's incumbent governor, a Republican named Pete Wilson, was trailing his Democratic opponent by a wide margin. Seeing the passion generated by Proposition 187, he claimed the cause as his own. He aired a video of men darting past cars while sneaking across the border onto Interstate 5 in San Diego; as they scurried under a highway overpass, music played in a minor key and a somber voice intoned, "They keep coming." He won reelection by fifteen points.

Clinton won California's fifty-four electoral votes in 1992, but the state was hardly a Democratic lock. In 1988, George H. W. Bush had won it convincingly, and four years later Clinton beat him with less than 50 percent of the vote. Thousands of people, most of them Mexican, were crossing the border between San Diego and Tijuana on foot. At dusk each day, hundreds would line up together and run across; onlookers on the Mexican side cheered them on and shouted "goal" each time someone eluded a Border Patrol agent and made it through. Two months before the election, the INS announced a $4 million plan to "get results within sixty days."

In Washington, Gingrich hadn't made immigration a central plank of his Contract with America, but Pete Wilson's victory persuaded him that the hardliners in his caucus should run with the issue. The result was the second piece of legislation that Murguía and Muñoz spent the summer trying to fight off. It was an overweening measure crafted by Alan Simpson, in the Senate, and Lamar Smith, the new chair of the immigration subcommittee in the House. Simpson was still smarting from his lost fight over the 1990 Immigration Act, which expanded legal immigration over his objections. With the Republicans in the majority, he wanted to reinstitute restrictions. One part of the 1990 act supplied him with a pretext: it had created another commission on immigration reform, headed by a Black former congresswoman named Barbara Jordan, who was known as a leading civil rights figure as well as an opponent of immigration. Her recommendations included everything from the creation of a national ID card to curb worker fraud to cutbacks on asylum protections and the reduction of legal immigration by a third. Simpson, who championed all these policies, had the imprimatur of the commission.

Smith shared Simpson's passion on immigration but lacked his policy experience. When Smith took over the immigration subcommittee, he hired an attorney named Cordia Strom, who had served as the legal director of a far-right anti-immigration organization called the Federation for American Immigration Reform (FAIR). The brainchild of a white supremacist ophthalmologist from Michigan named John Tanton, FAIR had been operating at the fringes of US politics since its founding in the late 1970s. Tanton's goal was to "infiltrate the judiciary committees," he wrote in 1986. "Think how much different our prospects would be if someone espousing our ideas had the chairmanship!" Smith turned the bill writing over to Strom, who authored it in isolation and then made revisions during conference committee meetings, while the House and Senate versions of the bill were being reconciled. Democrats didn't see the changes Strom made until four days before the final vote. One immigrants' rights advocate told *The Texas Observer*, "We would start to lobby on it, and when we went to offices, some of them would say, 'we didn't even know this provision was in there.'"

Cecilia Muñoz was spending almost all her time dealing with welfare reform, but a legion of other advocates—from the ACLU to La Raza and the National Immigration Forum—focused on the immigration bill. Their main strategy reflected collective pessimism: between the White House and an emboldened Republican Congress, tougher penalties and enforcement protocols directed at undocumented immigrants seemed inevitable. They fought against the measures limiting legal immigration—"Split the bill," they called it. There was a reason why Simpson had failed to achieve his goal in 1990, and it was still true. Middle-of-the-road figures in both parties were reluctant to block legal immigrants from coming into the country. Some had principled reasons for this, others had economic ones; the labor market needed more workers across a range of different sectors, from growers in the Sunbelt and the West to the rapidly expanding service sector everywhere else. Inside the White House, the president's chief of staff, Leon Panetta, had previously served as a congressman from the San Joaquin Valley, in Central California. There were some lines he wasn't comfortable crossing. "We all understand the problem of illegal immigrants," he said at the time. "We're all trying to ensure that we have additional enforcement to protect against illegal immigrants. But I, for the life of me, do not understand why we need to penalize legal immigrants in that process."

The advocates succeeded in sinking the provisions of the bill that would have restricted legal immigration and undermined asylum law. But the rest of the bill remained intact. Without the politically unpopular elements threatening legal immigration, it was essentially unstoppable. The measures that went to the president for his signature in September were almost too harsh and far-reaching to survey. The journalist Dara Lind, writing two decades later, said, "it was a bundle of provisions with a single goal: to increase penalties on immigrants who had violated US law in some way (whether they were unauthorized immigrants who'd violated immigration law or legal immigrants who'd committed other crimes)." The law, called the Illegal Immigration Reform and Immigrant Responsibility Act of 1996 (IIRIRA), established mass deportation as the new centerpiece of American immigration policy.

At INS, where she and her colleagues were tasked with implementing it, Doris Meissner found the new law extremely disconcerting. Most of them had opposed many of the provisions but hadn't been consulted. In meetings throughout the fall of 1996, she learned that IIRIRA would mean deporting tens of thousands of people who otherwise would be allowed to stay in the country because they'd either lived here for a long time, had families who depended on them, or faced "undue hardship" in their native countries. The discretion once exercised by INS agents and immigration judges no longer applied. According to the law, the government had to detain everyone it could possibly deport; once a person was in deportation proceedings no one could intervene to stop them in the event of extenuating circumstances. At the same time, the law expanded the list of crimes that could lead immigrants, including those with green cards and permanent residency, to be deported, even if they'd already served jail time. These crimes were called "aggravated felonies," and they ranged from drug offenses to acts of so-called moral turpitude. Writing a fake check, evading taxes, and stealing a purse out of a parked car could trigger deportation.

The worst part was that the government could punish offenders retroactively, so if someone had committed an aggravated felony five or ten years before the law was passed he would still be deported. In a memo, from November 1996, Rahm Emanuel recommended that the president make use of the new law to burnish his image as being tough on crime. If Clinton took advantage of the opportunities afforded by IIRIRA, Emanuel wrote, he could "claim and achieve record deportations of criminal aliens."

◇—◇

When Eddie Anzora turned eighteen, his juvenile record was expunged, giving him a clean slate. The drug arrest on Langdon Avenue now counted as his first criminal offense, and while he faced two charges—for drug possession and "intent to sell"—neither he nor the public defender representing him was concerned, especially since he'd never been caught with drugs before. The advice he received was to plead guilty and accept probation; he'd be back home to resume his regular life in a matter of months.

In the weeks after his arrest, he waited in a county jail, where inmates, as a matter of course, traded speculation about the legal system. Someone mentioned the new law that Clinton had signed, but no one could say for sure what it meant. "You've been here," another detainee reassured Eddie. "I'm sure you're a citizen." Eddie replied, "It's true. I got my documents."

A few days after Eddie had entered the jail, a guard took him to meet some visitors from the immigration service. Having never heard of the INS before, Eddie had to ask what the acronym stood for. They sat in a dimly lit, sparsely furnished room at the facility, where the agents asked him a list of pro forma questions: his full name, date of birth, home address. His mind was starting to drift when one of them capped his pen and closed the file. "You're going to get deported," he said.

EDDIE'S MOTHER brought a bundle of his school diplomas to the first hearing in his deportation proceedings. Her eyes were bloodshot and twitching. His own shock, together with his mother's anguish, seemed to weigh on the judge, who granted him bail. Eddie resumed his day job at the animal hospital and spent his evenings with his brother and Joel in their apartment on Langdon Avenue. His mother helped him find an immigration lawyer. They paid the attorney five hundred dollars every two months; in exchange Eddie was free to think about his legal situation less. Every six months, he was required to check in with INS agents at an immigration court in downtown Los Angeles. This went on for four years.

One morning, in 2001, he arrived outside the courtroom a few minutes before his meeting. This time, his lawyer stopped him before he could reach for the door. "If you walk in there right now, they'll cuff you and put you on a plane," the lawyer said. He told Eddie to tear up his Social Security card, and not to mention their conversation to anyone. Eddie was now on the run.

27.

Fast Eddie

In 1996, when Scott Mechkowski joined the INS, everything about the job put him off, starting with the training. At the instructional academy in Georgia, he had the distinct impression that working for the government meant getting lectured by bureaucrats and lawyers who spent more time telling you what you couldn't do than what you could. The scene at the Newark, New Jersey, office, where he reported for his first day, was cramped and claustrophobic; his new colleagues, all of them wearing suits, struck him as rather too pleased to be sitting behind their desks pushing paper. Everyone punched out at five.

An army reservist who'd been detailed to the Drug Enforcement Administration, Mechkowski was in his midtwenties, a hulking presence at nearly six and a half feet tall and 240 pounds, with a buzz cut and arms like pylons. His background in law enforcement made him a seemingly typical recruit—a tough guy, ready to get to work—but there was more to his upbringing than met the eye. His mother, who was Puerto Rican, adopted him when he was a toddler. She was a dark-skinned woman who raised him to speak English and Spanish but struggled to pronounce her own son's name. Cotty, rather than Scotty, is what she called him. Other people were always baffled when she addressed him. Throughout childhood, his school friends would meet him—this towering, athletic white boy—then visit his house to find a short woman with a thick accent who introduced herself as his mom.

The family grew up poor, in a New Jersey township called Colonia, where Mechkowski (whose father, a truck driver, was Polish) heard his mother called everything from the N-word to a "spic." She didn't have a profession, exactly: she worked at a hair salon, sold jewelry, opened a shop with knickknacks. She was always hustling, her finances forever on the brink. As a teenager, he enlisted in the army for the money. It was that or pushing shopping carts at the A&P; his enlistment came with an eight-thousand-dollar signing bonus.

INS had been hiring new field agents with funding from the 1994 crime bill. Mechkowski assumed he would be doing police work for the agency. In one of his first days on the job, walled in at his desk by stacks of files, he made a loud show of standing up and heading out. He'd been reading through the rap sheet of a Jamaican drug dealer and decided to try to find him. His boss intercepted him at the door. "OK, tough guy," he said. "Don't you do anything." From that moment forward, in the sleepy Newark office, he was known as a cowboy.

He couldn't believe his restlessness caused such a stir. The government was paying him forty-five thousand dollars a year, with benefits, and all he was doing was typing on a computer. He'd get home each night, after marking seventy files with humdrum updates, and ask himself what he had been doing all day. There were case folders to check for the relevant documents: the notice to appear in court (NTA), the judge's sign-off on a person's voluntary departure, the arrest report, known as an I-213. Once he confirmed its contents, he filed the folder away. He didn't know where these people were—if they'd left the country or were still here. It embarrassed him.

In 1997, when the immigration law IIRIRA went into effect, Mechkowski felt liberated. He was freer to go out onto the streets, and there were new tasks to perform. Anyone who fit the description of an aggravated felon would go straight into detention. INS lawyers told the rank and file to "NTA" everyone: once they were in court, immigration attorneys could no longer prevent the inevitable. At office-wide trainings, he learned about a tool called expedited removal, which allowed the government to deport someone apprehended near the border without bringing him before a judge, if the person had been in the US for less than two years. In Mechkowski's eyes, the government was finally letting INS take control.

But at the same time, the law's conservative authors were starting to have second thoughts, which they brought to the INS. In 1999, twenty-eight House members—including Lamar Smith—wrote a letter to Doris Meissner and the attorney general, requesting that the administration interpret the law's language more forgivingly. "Cases of apparent extreme hardship have caused concern," the representatives wrote. "Some cases may involve removal proceedings against legal permanent residents who came to the United States when they were very young, and many years ago committed a single crime . . . but have been law-abiding ever since, obtained and held jobs and remained self-sufficient, and started families in the United States." A year before, in Smith's home state of Texas, the INS had launched a raid around Labor Day called Operation Last Call, which targeted immigrants with past felony convictions for driving while intoxicated. They arrested five hundred people. When the Mexican consulate in El Paso managed to interview ninety-one of them, who were in local detention, officials found that the average time they'd lived in the US was more than twenty-one years. Ninety-one percent of them held jobs, and 81 percent had children who were US citizens. These outcomes had been entirely predictable, and constituents were complaining. In 2000, Meissner issued enforcement guidelines to allow agents to exercise some limited discretion in deciding whom they went after.

In Newark, the supervisors were agency veterans, relics of an older, more passive order; the young guys, like Mechkowski, wanted to make arrests. The supervisors could no longer hold them back. Mechkowski's reputation as a hard charger was beginning to earn him some respect, though he continued to nurse a sense of aggrievement. The INS still seemed like the knockoff of a federal law enforcement agency. It irritated his sense of pride, but he wasn't the type to retreat. He worked harder, kept longer hours, arrested more people. He'd never met Meissner, but he considered her a bleeding heart. She didn't even want immigration officers to carry a gun.

Eddie Anzora's life changed the day he realized he was on borrowed time. His legal situation wouldn't stop him from moving ahead, he decided; to the contrary, he was now determined to move faster than ever, to achieve more. He wanted to get serious, so much so that his friends gave him the nickname

"Fast Eddie," after Paul Newman in *The Hustler*. It was like some surging ambition and hunger had been unleashed in him. He rushed to transform all his vague plans into something real enough to call his own. Years later, he'd put it this way: "Before, I was just a ghetto kid from around the way—just another kid from the hood, hanging out. But after that it was 'Do as much as you can, before you find yourself in El Salvador.' I lived that life. I lived the real fast life."

Paradoxically, the fast life meant starting slowly. At the animal hospital, he'd begun on the lowest rung, as a cleaner who did the work no one else wanted—spraying down the cages, mopping up the shit and the vomit, scrubbing out the stenches. He made his mark with quiet dependability and was promoted to veterinary technician. At night, to formalize his new position, he took classes at Pierce College, where he was studying for a veterinary degree. Friends drove him wherever he had to go. He entered the buildings at school and at the animal hospital through the back and side doors, keeping watch over his shoulder just in case the INS was on his tail.

It was impossible to talk to Eddie without getting magnetized by his charm. He had a bright, untroubled affect that made him seem wise to the world, but also inured against darker moods. Job offers sometimes materialized unsolicited. A manager at the animal hospital told him about a gig at the Playboy Mansion, where Hugh Hefner needed someone to tend to his dogs. For ten dollars an hour, he rode over to the plush, gated grounds, feeding and walking the menagerie each morning.

He also plotted grander plans, which revolved around music, a dream he shared with his childhood friend, Joel Orozco. They met a woman at a dance club whose two Rottweilers had a stomach virus called parvo and needed medication from the animal hospital. When he brought it to her house in Beverly Hills the next day, she told him about her husband, a music executive who offered to give Eddie studio time as payment for the veterinary help. Standing over the microphone a few days later, in a small square room in Hollywood, he froze when it was his turn to sing. From then on, he left the rapping to Orozco, who had a clear talent, while he pursued his true calling as a producer and impresario, a man who made things happen.

One morning, in September 2001, he was working in one of the back rooms of the animal hospital when a voice came over the loudspeaker. "Eddie, we need you to fix something in cage seven." He bolted upright and made his way for the exit. This was a code he had devised with the help of one of the receptionists at the front desk, in case immigration authorities ever came to arrest him.

He tried to run for it, to the hospital's back lot. As he swung open the door, an officer waiting on the other side lunged at him. He wriggled away, doubling back into one of the hallways. The INS agents had the front and back doors under surveillance, but they hadn't realized there were other ways out. In a dead sprint, Eddie wended through a series of passageways to an animal shelter next door. Bursting through an unguarded door, he barreled into the sunlight, tearing down Ventura Boulevard. Cars whizzed by him. Eventually, he reached a residential building and ducked inside, galloping up a flight of stairs to reach the roof. Once he made it through the door leading outside, at the very top of the building, he fell to his knees and gasped for breath. A few seconds later, the door creaked open behind him. A woman's voice broke the silence. "What are you doing on the top of our roof?" she asked.

Realizing that he was still wearing his scrubs from the animal hospital, he replied that he was looking for an escaped cat. The woman sighed and offered to get him a glass of water. When she disappeared, he called his brother to come pick him up.

Later that night, he crashed with a coworker—it wasn't safe to return home. Her name was Vanessa, and she had an extra room in her apartment. Early the next morning, he woke to the sound of her banging on his door. His first thought was that the immigration agents had found him again. But through the closed door, Vanessa shouted, "You won't believe this. You gotta come here." The television in the living room was on when he entered. The screen showed an image of the Twin Towers aflame.

⋄—⋄

In his early days at the agency, when Mechkowski struggled to convince local cops to share information and leads with the INS, some of them hadn't realized that his agency worked anywhere other than the southern border. Mechkowski's job description bemused them. But in the fall of 2001, when he passed through their precincts in New Jersey, many of these same officers treated Mechkowski with disdain. "You guys don't do shit," they told him. "*Now* you're working. So it took an act of terrorism!"

All nineteen of the hijackers had been living in the US on temporary visas. Four of them had violated the terms of those visas by the time of the attack. In March 2002, an INS service contractor mistakenly sent out by US mail visa extensions for two of the dead hijackers. It was a bureaucratic snafu of little material consequence, but it further concentrated public and political ire against the agency. Mechkowski found it rich that the INS had become the subject of routine, bipartisan excoriation. But that didn't mean he disagreed with the criticisms.

By the spring of 2002, members of both parties were proposing to overhaul the agency. Their calls followed a spate of legislation in the wake of the terrorist attacks. The previous October, the US Congress passed the Patriot Act, which vastly expanded the government's ability to surveil anyone on US soil without probable cause. Immigrants were the main source of the government's concern. In September 2002, the Justice Department launched a program called the National Security Entry-Exit Registration System, or NSEERS, which required immigrants from twenty-five countries—selected, with the exception of North Korea, based on the size of their Muslim populations—to submit their names to a government database that vetted them for involvement with terrorism. By the following May, with 138,000 immigrants registered, the program hadn't led to a single successful terrorism prosecution, but twelve thousand people had been placed in deportation proceedings. On April 17, 2003, attorney general John Ashcroft ruled that undocumented immigrants could be held indefinitely without bond in the interest of national security. This was in response to a case involving David Joseph, a Haitian asylum seeker who had arrived in Miami on a boat, along with 215 others, on October 29, 2002. Joseph was eighteen and had no ties to terrorism, but his release on bond, Ashcroft wrote, "would create a perception in Haiti of an easing in U.S. policy" that would lead to "future surges in illegal migration . . . diverting valuable Coast Guard and DOD resources from counterterrorism and homeland security responsibilities."

In April 2002, two bills to restructure INS were moving through the House and Senate. When one of them passed the House, by a vote of 405 to 9, Ashcroft said, "It is time to separate fully our services to legal immigrants, who helped build America, from our enforcement against illegal aliens, who violate the law." The main point of consensus, shared by Republicans and Democrats, was that the government needed to treat immigration enforcement as a matter of national security, and to accord it the resources and institutional heft typically reserved for military defense.

Within months, the White House provided a more detailed plan that earned swift congressional support. On November 25, 2002, George W. Bush signed the Homeland Security Act, creating a new federal department to house more than twenty different subagencies and, eventually, more than 250,000 employees. Each agency dealt with national security in some form, whether it was the Secret Service, the Coast Guard, or the Federal Emergency Management Agency. But immigration policy was the department's raison d'être. Border Patrol merged with Customs in a new hybrid agency called Customs and Border Protection. Administering the legal immigration system went from the INS to Citizenship and Immigration Services. Enforcement fell to a new body called Immigration and Customs Enforcement, or ICE, which had a section dedicated to arresting and deporting immigrants in the country unlawfully. This last group, called Detention and Removal Operations, was where Mechkowski was assigned, in early 2003.

He was having mixed feelings about the atmosphere at work, not because he had any reservations about the new vigilance, but because it looked to him like politics was making yet another incursion into the field. One day he was sent to arrest an Egyptian immigrant, because the agency was prioritizing people from the Middle East. But when Mechkowski looked at the case file, he saw that the man was a Coptic Christian who'd overstayed an H-1B visa for skilled foreign workers. It didn't take any great power of deduction to see that his target was not a national security threat. During the hours he spent canvassing the man's neighborhood in Jersey City, Mechkowski bumped into a Mexican guy he'd been after once before. The man recognized Mechkowski and surrendered his wrists. "You caught me," he conceded, in Spanish. Mechkowski waved him off, pulling out a photo of the Egyptian. Had he seen this man?

Mechkowski's work at DHS was called fugitive operations. Anyone who could be deported was considered a fugitive. Mechkowski was asked to teach training courses for recent recruits, then was promoted in New York in 2004. One of his colleagues called him the Great White Hunter. He led a fugitive operations team, one of two in the state.

Despite the air of sobriety and reevaluation in Washington, there was something about "the fugitives" that most policymakers took for granted. The population of undocumented immigrants in the US was growing in large part because of the 1996 immigration law, which trapped them in the country. According to its strictures, an undocumented person couldn't get on a path to legal status through marriage or sponsorship by a family member. If she had been in the US without documentation for six months, she'd have to leave the country for three full years before reapplying for entry; if she had lived in the US without papers for a year, she'd be required to leave for another ten before returning. (These came to be known as the three- and ten-year "bars.") A large share of immigrants used to travel back and forth across the border, to be with family or to work seasonal jobs, but now they were stuck. The sociologist Douglas Massey estimated that because of the bars the undocumented population more than doubled, from five million before the law went into effect to about twelve million.

There were six people on Mechkowski's team: four deportation officers to hit the streets, a detention officer in charge of arrestees, and an office clerk. Mechkowski's boss at ICE, John Torres, was visiting the Hill and fielding questions from congressional appropriators. The representatives couldn't give the agency money fast enough, but ICE needed to quantify its progress so that members of Congress could feel confident that their massive new appropriations were going to good use. As usual, Mechkowski thought, none of the parties involved knew the realities of fugitive operations. Congress was just "polishing a turd," he said. "It was obsessed with labels. DUIs and shoplifting meant someone was a 'criminal.' The deportation machine *had* to start working." Torres made grand promises to rustle up money for his agents, but he was dealing with people who seemed to think that racking up arrests was straightforward. They wanted each fugitive operations team to arrest one thousand immigrants per year. It was an impossible number, and every agent on every fugitive operations team knew it. Each unit had five agents in the field who would take sick days and breaks for vacation. There were federal holidays.

Given all the hours that went into tracking down people on the run, the annual quota looked a lot like they were being set up to fail.

In 2003, the first year of the new fugitive operations model, Mechkowski and the others were told to go after "dangerous" criminals. By the start of the following year, 30 percent of arrests involved immigrants with criminal records. The rest were guilty of administrative violations such as entering the country unlawfully or overstaying a visa.

That would be the high-water mark for fugitive operations. In 2006, under pressure from Congress, ICE instituted the annual arrest quotas, and, unsurprisingly, agents started arresting far fewer people with criminal records and far more of what they called "ordinary status violators." Previously, if Mechkowski had been pursuing one person and encountered other undocumented immigrants along the way, he would ignore them, sticking to his original target. But because the arrest numbers were the key to unlocking more money for the agency, he and the other agents began making "collateral arrests." They rounded up anyone they could. By the end of 2006, only 17 percent of all arrests made by fugitive operations involved immigrants with criminal records. The percentage was roughly half that the following year.

Friends used to ask Mechkowski if he ever felt bad. He would answer with a rhetorical question: "You don't think I ever feel like shit if I had to arrest some guy and I knew he had kids?" Mechkowski was a father himself. The work grated on him, but he took an apolitical stance. The laws might change, or a judge might issue a new precedent from the bench; department superiors could unveil a different policy or agency priorities could shift. His sole source of reassurance was that the people he was arresting had final orders of removal, so he could tell himself that they'd "had their day in court." Otherwise, he kept moving, trying not to overthink his work, because one question usually led to a cascade of others. Was a couple he was investigating engaged in a real marriage, or a contrived one for the purposes of skirting immigration laws? Was the man he was cuffing in front of his son a good father or a bad one? The job was draining enough without disentangling these ludicrously subjective questions. Before long, he was using an expression common among agency veterans: "Sure, the work pulled on the heartstrings."

Living in San Fernando, Eddie's best friend Joel Orozco tended to think that his bad luck came in reliable doses—neither too much nor too little at any moment. He could not say the same for Eddie, who managed to have the *worst* bad luck and the *best* good luck, often at the same time. Take his life on the lam. On the one hand, it was unthinkable that after spending his whole life in California Eddie could suddenly be deported. On the other, Eddie had been on the run since 2001, about six years, and except for the close call at the animal hospital had avoided any run-ins with the law. Orozco got pulled over every week—a broken taillight, speeding, refusing to yield at a sign, any pretext would do. Meanwhile, Eddie had managed to buy a Chevy Tahoe with the dealership tags still on it, which other people drove him around in. Somehow it never piqued the interest of the traffic patrol.

Fast Eddie had also bought a house, making the down payment with a credit card. An old friend of his named James showed him how to build his credit score. ("After school, he took the real estate route," Eddie said. "I took the everything-else route.") When Eddie sold it, he used the profits to open a small recording studio in his old neighborhood, on the corner of Sepulveda and Magnolia. Under someone else's name, he built a music-promotion business called Above Ground Entertainment. He opened another studio on Ventura Boulevard; put out singles; organized concerts; and spun off a fashion line. Eddie was even publishing a culture magazine, called *The Stash*. There were photos of the legendary LA actor Danny Trejo posing with a copy of it. ("He knows me; he knows what I'm about," Eddie said.) In a city notorious for its rigid racial caste, Eddie had become a Latino heavyweight in hip-hop circles. At one point, the rapper the Game used his studio to record some early songs, and 50 Cent dropped by but stayed in the parking lot. "*Cabron* didn't come inside," Eddie said.

He was making enough money to help his mother, too, and he had several deals in the works that were each potentially worth thousands of dollars. But this was where Orozco had a point. The greater Eddie's success, the more he had to lose. The thought of being deported haunted him constantly. He had a longtime girlfriend, and they wanted kids, but he was scared of being separated from them.

Eddie Anzora with his recording equipment, 2009.

The day finally came, in January 2007, when Eddie decided to drive himself to a local barber for a haircut. He settled into the front seat of his Tahoe, adjusted the rearview mirror, and there it was: a dark sedan hovering at the corner of the parking lot. He stepped on the gas pedal, reversing at a sharp angle to speed out past the waiting car. But the Tahoe banged into it, which boxed him in. The agents got out and approached. One of them pulled open the driver's side door. Eddie slammed it shut, trying to escape out the passenger's side, but he was surrounded. The whole situation was both an agony and a strange relief. He knew his luck had its limits. Unbeknownst to him, the brother of a business partner was involved with a Mexican gang that had killed a police officer. Eddie was caught in a dragnet that ICE had set up for someone else.

TRYING TO GET AWAY, he had committed another crime. When he had collided with the agents' vehicle, then shut the door on one of the officers in pursuit, he had engaged in assault with a deadly weapon (his own car). Before being deported, he spent nine months in an LA County jail. His mother visited, along with his aunts, cousins, friends, and girlfriend. Not one to waste an opportunity, he used the time to prepare himself for El Salvador.

His experience in the juvenile system had taught him how to move around the facility. None of the menacing rituals intimidated him or diminished his sense of purpose. He had three options: declare himself either a *paisa* (a Spanish speaker with no gang ties), a resident (a Southern Californian without an affiliation), or a member of a particular gang, which he would then have to name.

Eddie said only that he was from Southern California, at which point the real vetting began. Different inmates would stop by his bed asking questions: What was his full name, where was his old neighborhood, who were his acquaintances? The process culminated on a Friday night, when Eddie had to write down for everyone his prisoner ID number and gang affiliation (complicated in his case, as an ex-member of ATR, which was never really a gang). The other inmates would run their own background checks on him, making calls to contacts on the outside before sharing information among themselves on balled-up pieces of paper passed around the cells. If Eddie had ever ratted someone out or committed an especially grisly crime (rape or an act of pedophilia, for example), he would pay. But the quasi-systematic checks gave him confidence that there'd be some measure of due process.

He took advantage of all the human intel surrounding him for information about El Salvador. Mixed among the Hispanic population in the facility were Central Americans. The ones who spoke bad English were of the greatest interest to Eddie, because they seemed better connected to where he was headed. He wanted to know everything about El Salvador: the neighborhoods to avoid, any scraps of detail about criminal elements. A rail-thin, dark-skinned Honduran covered in tattoos told Eddie he was surprised by the number of American inmates who were ostentatiously inked up. He couldn't have been older than eighteen or nineteen, and he looked even younger. "Most of the time people get tats to look cool," Eddie said. "That's different from Honduras," the young man replied. "You gotta earn your tattoos." He started pointing out some of his own. "In the United States, you act tough for a little bit, and then you figure out your life. You become a construction worker or a plumber," Eddie thought. "It's different there. You live with that thing that one of those days I'm going to get killed."

The hardest part of being locked up before his deportation was learning that his life was being disassembled. Once people found out that Eddie was going to be deported, old acquaintances, rivals, and even former friends started pilfering equipment and other valuables from his studios. Each one of them had some rationalization (an unpaid debt, an owed favor), which Eddie heard through his brother, who was trying and failing to keep everyone at bay. "Lot of people started doing me wrong once they saw I was in jail coming over to El Salvador," Eddie said. "You do a lot for people, and when you hit bottom nobody's there for you."

There were people he could count on in El Salvador, starting with his extended family. But some of them were running from their own risks. He'd been corresponding with an old friend, Cesar, who had been deported many years before. Cesar's girlfriend still lived in Los Angeles, and she'd told him about Eddie's situation. It was Cesar who got in touch first, writing him an email. "I hear you might end up here," it began. "My lady told me you were running from INS." (It would take several years before everyone corrected themselves and called the agency by its new name. Eddie joked with them that he was one of the first targets ICE ever had.) Cesar told him he had a car and a place where Eddie could crash, and Eddie wrote back to thank him and ask a few follow-up questions.

Five days passed, then seven, then nine—no response. Eddie wrote Cesar's girlfriend, who broke the news. Some gangsters had accosted him at church one Sunday and tried to steal his truck. When he fought back, they killed him.

28.

The Sisters

Myrna Mack Chang and her younger sister, Helen, had a tacit agreement never to discuss politics. Two years apart in age, they were extremely close, and wanted to keep it that way. But their lives had led them down different ideological paths—Myrna's to the left, Helen's to the right. In Guatemala, in the late 1980s, everyone had grown accustomed to living with certain lacunae. Some subjects you simply didn't mention, because you never knew who might be listening. "To get into politics was to be stigmatized," Helen once said. "As long as the violence did not touch you, why get involved?"

By the end of the decade, the Macks were living together with their parents in a simple but spacious house near Morazán Park, in Zone 2 of Guatemala City, a leafy, tranquil middle-class enclave. In her late thirties and separated from her partner, Myrna had a teenage daughter named Lucrecia. The family patriarch, Yam Jo Mack, had immigrated to Guatemala in the 1930s, from China. He had planned to return home eventually, but when his family lost their land during the Maoist revolution, he decided to stay, buying up a few hundred acres near the Pacific coast to raise cattle and cultivate sugarcane. Then the Árbenz government began its agricultural reform campaign, and a wave of land confiscations followed. Yam Jo Mack landed in jail, with a death sentence. A few days before he was supposed to face a firing squad, in the summer of 1954, the CIA toppled the government. He had been a staunch anti-communist ever since. But when it came time to educate his daughters, he sent them to a boarding school run by Maryknoll nuns, a liberal order; the Mack sisters would make their own way.

Helen began a career in business administration, taking a job at a construction company, while Myrna trained as an anthropologist in England. Myrna became a student of leftist causes, starting with Nicaragua, the subject of her doctoral dissertation. Her partner—Lucrecia's father—was a surgeon and activist. In 1984, he moved to Mexico, where he performed medical operations for Indigenous Guatemalans who had fled the war and relocated to Chiapas. When Lucrecia asked him why the family wasn't all together, in Guatemala City, he replied, "*Mija*, we have to be where we're most needed." Like many other Guatemalans in Mexico, he was living without papers, so when Lucrecia went to visit him there were strict rules for preserving their identity: no talking in crowded public places, avoiding Guatemalan slang, and memorizing the Mexican national anthem.

Back in Guatemala, where Myrna was most needed, another set of strictures applied. Lucrecia was to avoid talking about her mother's research in Nicaragua, or the fact that her father was living in Mexico. They had friends who appeared in the Diario Militar, the government registry of suspected subversives. At home, the result was an atmosphere at once tight-knit and riddled with silences. As a teenager, Lucrecia associated the dry air of repressed confidences with her mother, who could be withholding by nature and was passionately obsessed with her work.

Myrna wrote and edited political pieces for a Central American news service called Inforpress Centroamericana, which covered the ongoing government repression. Years later, when Lucrecia thought of her mother, she would always hear the typewriter clacking into the night. Myrna's mothering was caring but reserved, and she inculcated her daughter with a spirit of flinty independence. Once, before Lucrecia turned fifteen, she asked Myrna if they might throw her a party. "Ah, *mija*," her mother replied. "Do you really want to have a party that will take three months to prepare and that will be over in five hours? Think about it. What would be better would be a trip, or an encyclopedia."

In 1985, after decades of military rule, a civilian president won the national elections—Vinicio Cerezo, an avowed liberal, who was the leader of a party known as the Christian Democrats. Behind the scenes, little changed. He was a front to legitimize the military's operations. A few years before, the military had acknowledged that there were limits to its power of repression. "With only military and police operations, it is not possible to definitively annihilate subversive activity," one planning document stated. Guatemala had grown isolated—starved of defenders and, more important, financial backers— and the economy was failing. With a civilian at the helm and a new constitution, the Americans could champion Guatemala's "democratization," just as they had when the Christian Democrats took office in El Salvador. Money from foreign governments and the private sector could flow back into the country.

Myrna, Lucrecia, and Helen Mack, in Trafalgar Square, London, 1975.

No one at the Mack residence had any illusions about this ambiguous new period, but a sense of opportunity prevailed. In 1986, together with some colleagues from Inforpress, Myrna formed an organization called AVANCSO, or the Association for the Advancement of Social Sciences in Guatemala. It generated the sort of research, writing, and analysis that had once come out of the universities before most of the intellectuals had been killed or forced into exile. Lucrecia was entering high school now, and she was beginning to perceive a slight opening around her. The silences at home seemed less enveloping than before.

Around this time, Myrna was moving away from journalism and back toward anthropology, traveling to the highlands departments of Huehuetenango, El Quiché, and Alta Verapaz for fieldwork. She was often gone for weeks on end, and in her absence Helen cared for Lucrecia. Neither one of them fully grasped what Myrna was doing—the pathbreaking nature of her research, or the danger it was putting her in.

A million Indigenous Guatemalans had been displaced in the early part of the decade, and most remained uprooted by the late 1980s. More than a hundred thousand were still in Mexico, either because they no longer had homes or because they feared being attacked by the military upon their return. In the northern reaches of El Quiché, another fifteen thousand war refugees were hiding out in the mountains, while the military launched bombing raids to smoke them out.

Myrna's work focused on the enormous population of the "internally displaced," a phrase she helped popularize. Where the repression had been the worst, with entire communities destroyed, the army rebuilt villages to maximize its control. As one historian later put it, there was the "war of extermination" during the early 1980s, and the "war of reconstruction" that followed. The military assigned Orwellian names to these locales: they were "model villages," "development poles," or "strategic hamlets." Two dozen of them were installed across the countryside. Daily life in these villages resembled that of a reeducation camp or low-security prison. In one hillside hamlet in Alta Verapaz, which had a population of 570, a sign overlooking the town welcomed people to "An Ideologically New, Anti-Subversive Community." The residents of another village said they lived "all piled up on top of each other . . . like chickens in a coop." Everyone had to register with the army, and all movements were closely monitored. To travel anywhere required a special pass stating a destination and itinerary. In so-called security zones, where the military demanded hypervigilance, residents were forced to interrupt their work for an entire week to serve on civilian defense patrols, policing themselves for signs of subversion.

Myrna would pack a bag full of notebooks wrapped in plastic, a small lantern, a sleeping bag, a voice recorder, cigarettes, and a bottle of whiskey—then travel by bus to some of the most remote corners of the country. These included the model villages of Barillas, San Matteo Ixtatán, and an especially perilous place, swarming with military personnel, known as the Ixil Triangle. Soldiers waited along the bus routes to interrogate travelers, inspecting papers and searching belongings. A group of American anthropologists associated with AVANCSO joined Myrna on the trips. Foreigners were granted slightly more leeway, especially Americans; harming them could lead to questions, so the soldiers had to muster a modicum of restraint. One American member of the team likened these trips to "waving a red flag in front of the army," and considered herself a kind of "shield" to help protect Myrna while she worked. The military was still conducting operations in rural areas, and anytime Myrna and the other researchers arrived in a new place, they had to present themselves to the local authorities.

In their extreme geographic and cultural isolation, these swaths of the countryside were a world apart, unseen and unheard. "The development poles in the Ixil Triangle and Alta Verapaz began as reception camps for the displaced who returned in 1982 and 1983," Myrna wrote in a report called "Assistance and Control." "One army official estimates that the military regime attended 42,000 people in the Ixil Triangle alone. This figure represents the entirety of the population in the affected area; in other words, virtually 100 percent of the population there was relocated into the reconstructed villages." Invoking the military jargon, she described El Quiché as the "red zone" of the country, where, according to one resident she interviewed, "you simply don't see, feel, or notice that there exists in Guatemala a civilian government."

The villagers themselves used to change out of their traditional garb—colorful handwoven wraps and dresses—when they traveled between hamlets or to larger towns, because wearing it put them at immediate risk of being attacked by soldiers. Myrna, who needed a translator to conduct interviews in the Indigenous dialects, was one of the first people to expose the true situation. The work found an immediate and eager international audience. Georgetown University funded much of it, and the United Nations International Conference on Central American Refugees distributed her drafts and used them as the basis for new policies. The bishop of El Quiché sought her out for advice on how the church could help the population.

Sometimes, while Myrna worked, word got back to her that it was time to leave. The threats were oblique but clear—a hovering presence trailing her at a distance, or the lingering gaze of a villager. These whispers betrayed screamingly imminent dangers. In the Ixil Triangle, someone from the military base was going around asking people about a certain "Chinese woman." On two occasions—in August and early September 1990—she met with the bishop to tell him that she was being followed. Eventually, she returned to the offices of

AVANCSO, on 12 Calle in Zone 1 of Guatemala City, where her colleagues suspected that they also were being surveilled.

One night in the late summer of 1990, Helen and Lucrecia were at home, when the maid stepped out to buy a newspaper. She returned looking pale. The vendor at the kiosk was a genial man named Virgilio, who had been selling newspapers to the Mack family for fifteen years. He had just told her that three men had been staking out the house. One of them was following Helen on a motorcycle each time she left. Lucrecia was sixteen now, and her high school graduation was a few weeks away. She was beginning to understand the gravity of what was happening around her. In the past few years since Cerezo took office, political assassinations had increased, following a pattern: each killing was a targeted message to a sector of the opposition such as journalists or labor leaders. But in a country nearing its fourth decade of civil war, acts of intimidation were routine. Lucrecia was less scared than baffled. Later that night, Myrna told her, "Look, the following that they were doing to your aunt is really about me."

On the evening of September 11, around six o'clock, Myrna called Lucrecia at home to say she was about to leave the office. Forty-five minutes later, she stepped out onto a street lined with low-slung buildings that had facades of yellow, turquoise, and white. Some street vendors were congregated at the end of the block, near its intersection with 12 Avenida. Myrna had just emerged when a small group of undercover agents swarmed around her. There was no time to run. Witnesses could not confirm how many men attacked her. She was stabbed twenty-seven times and died, alone, on the street.

Immediately after Myrna was murdered, the police called Helen to say there'd been a traffic accident. The official explanation was a robbery. Helen had generally trusted the government, but she found the explanations absurd—not just because of the pattern of surveillance that had preceded the murder but also because of Myrna's body, which the family retrieved later that night. Helen, her parents, and Lucrecia were washing and preparing it for the funeral.

The white dress the family had initially selected wouldn't work because of all the visible slashes and half-sutured wounds left by the coroner.

The police investigation moved slowly and erratically, despite the immediate international outcry. On September 29, a well-regarded homicide investigator named José Mérida Escobar submitted his first report on the murder to the director of the police. The findings were unambiguous: Myrna Mack had been murdered for her work on the internally displaced population in the countryside; at least three perpetrators had attacked her outside the AVANCSO offices earlier that month. The lead suspect was Noel de Jesús Beteta Álvarez, an agent working for a highly placed military unit called the Archivo. He was in his midtwenties and slender, with an angular face, dark mustache, and arching eyebrows. One of Mérida Escobar's government sources warned him not to proceed with the investigation because it would implicate the military high command. Sharing this view, the director of the police shelved the report. On November 4, 1990, a different version was entered into the court file, identifying the crime as a robbery with no known suspects.

About a month after the murder, as the official investigation was stalling, Helen made a life-altering decision. She started interviewing witnesses herself. She traveled to the scene of the crime. She visited the newspaper kiosk near her house to gather details about the men who'd been surveilling them. With the exception of a brief period during Myrna's marriage, Helen had lived with her sister her entire life. Without her, she sought answers with a relentlessness that went beyond politics and defied the social pressures that kept most well-heeled Guatemalans silent.

"I had the *desconfianza*"—distrust—"of both sides," Helen said. Myrna had introduced her to some of her leftist friends over the years, but she was an outsider in those circles. Her more conservative acquaintances wanted nothing to do with her crusade. She was undergoing a political conversion in plain sight. "I recognized the terror that existed in Guatemala," she said. "I learned the people of Guatemala were being subjected to repression and intimidation that made you a victim all over again."

In August 1991, Mérida Escobar, the police investigator, was gunned down on the street outside a police station, shot four times in the face. His partner and their immediate boss fled to Canada. All the witnesses to Myrna Mack's murder had also left the country. The suspect, Beteta Álvarez, had already snuck into the US, where he was living in Long Beach, California, working for a rental-boat company. One day, apparently by mistake, he appeared in a Telemundo newscast, and a Guatemalan viewer who recognized him placed a call to an FBI tip line. He was arrested for an immigration infraction, in December 1991, deported to Guatemala, and taken into custody. He eventually confessed to the crime and named a cadre of officers who'd ordered him to commit the murder. After first slow-walking the case, the government prosecuted Beteta Álvarez, seeming to assume that the investigation would end with him.

No political murder had ever been adjudicated in the Guatemalan justice system, and no precedent existed for prosecuting such a high-profile case in the country's labyrinthine and sclerotic courts. Helen Mack—a political neophyte, with no legal training—was mostly doing it on her own. In the middle of a war, she was bringing a case against the country's military. It was, she'd later say, "amid the contradictions" of her life "where your faith becomes clear." The threats came by phone, mail, and word of mouth; agents followed her around; and a military smear campaign alleged that Myrna had engaged in black-market misdeeds.

Helen's strategy turned on a novel legal tool: she would serve as the *querellante adhesiva*, or a private accuser, who had standing on her sister's behalf. Helen was interested in the "intellectual authors" of the crime. Beteta Álvarez was a foot soldier and a thug. The men she was accusing were among the most powerful in Guatemala: Edgar Augusto Godoy Gaitán, the head of the Presidential General Staff, which oversaw the Archivo; Juan Valencia Osorio, director of the Presidential Security Department; and Juan Guillermo Oliva Carrera, the deputy head of the Presidential Security Department. All of them had been mentioned in the initial, suppressed police report.

It took about two years to secure Beteta Álvarez's conviction, but at first the courts dismissed the case against his superiors. Helen appealed multiple times before getting another shot. By February 1994, when the case against the military officers finally started, the government was stonewalling the prosecution. Helen needed information about the organization of the high command, which the military refused to turn over in any form. Her recourse came from an unexpected place: the archives of the US State Department, the CIA, and the

Pentagon. The US government had stopped giving direct aid to Guatemala in 1977, but remained in regular contact with the military. Hundreds of cables from the war years, written by US officials, offered detailed descriptions of government strategy. Kate Doyle, an American researcher at the National Security Archive, in Washington, DC, filed public records requests on Helen's behalf, and dislodged a cable written by Thomas Stroock, the US ambassador to Guatemala at the time of Myrna's murder. "The sort of hit discussed here," he wrote, "is carried out or directed by individuals who are members of the security forces, often military intelligence." The attacks were ordered at a "senior level," he continued, but "'death squad' personnel might often not appear on the official rosters of the security services and do not report for duty to official installations; they wait at home for orders, usually via the phone, or at times are picked up without prior notice to perform a job. They operate in cells so it is difficult to trace the orders up the hierarchy."

THE SILENCES OF LUCRECIA'S childhood grew more pronounced after her mother's murder. She was in shock, which muted her immediate grief. In the general chaos that befell the Mack family, Lucrecia's aunt and grandparents decided she should stick to the plans made before the tragedy. In October 1990, Lucrecia graduated from high school, and was due to start a medical degree at the public university in Guatemala City, in January. Myrna had arranged a trip for her to live with a host family in Canada during the intervening months. "The assassination didn't generate any change in the plans, or any questioning about whether they made sense," Lucrecia said. In retrospect, it was clear that the Macks were all overwhelmed, but at the time carrying on seemed like an homage to Myrna.

The first disruption came just before she was supposed to start school. Lucrecia had dreamed of studying at the University of San Carlos, the country's flagship public institution, known for its student activism. Both her parents had spent time there. Growing up, Lucrecia particularly admired the work of her father. She saw medicine as the most direct form of social action, and San Carlos as the logical place to start that career. Many of its students and professors were military targets during the 1980s. Lucrecia's grandmother told her,

"I'll pay for you to go to a private university. But you're not to go to San Carlos. They'll kill you just like they did your mother." Under the circumstances, Lucrecia could hardly accuse her of paranoia, and she was crestfallen when she arrived that January at Francisco Marroquín University, a notoriously conservative place.

She lasted one year and considered her time an exercise in earning the right to rebel. At the start of 1992, when Lucrecia enrolled at the University of San Carlos, her mother's case was starting to move through the justice system. It would be a few more years before the full weight of her loss registered with Lucrecia. But a necessary precondition was reckoning with the magnitude of her mother's work. In 1992, Rigoberta Menchú, a Maya activist whose father had died in the Spanish embassy fire twelve years earlier, won the Nobel Peace Prize, and Helen was given the Right Livelihood Award, another prestigious international citation for human rights advocacy. Lucrecia started to scour the books in Myrna's library. One was called *Guatemala: Eternal Spring, Eternal Tyranny*, by the American photojournalist Jean-Marie Simon, an exposé of government repression in the countryside during the 1980s. It put Myrna's fieldwork in context and helped Lucrecia fill in the gaps left by her mother's silences.

Lucrecia's relationship with her aunt, meanwhile, grew more complicated. Helen had always been a second mother to her, and they became even closer after the murder. But as Lucrecia was learning more about Myrna's life, Helen was trying to shield her from the facts surrounding her death. "My logic was protection," Helen said. "Her logic was different. It was to know everything she could about her mother." Helen and Lucrecia were both undergoing radical personal transformations, and theirs was a relationship of *silencios* and *reclamos*—silences and complaints—Helen said. Still, she saw no other way to shield Lucrecia from the danger that was lurking everywhere. Beteta Álvarez, for instance, had once acted as an *oreja*, or spy, at the university.

In 1993, with funding from her recent award, Helen established the Myrna Mack Foundation. Its headquarters was on the floor of an apartment building in Zone 10. The ongoing legal case was the organization's defining project, but the foundation was also becoming a national reference point during the heady and unstable period approaching the end of the war. In the spring of 1993, Cerezo's successor as president, another civilian, named Jorge Serrano, dissolved

Congress and the Supreme Court, and suspended the constitution in a power grab known as the Serranazo. ("It was the first time I smoked a cigarette," Lucrecia, who joined a group of San Carlos students in taking to the streets, said later.) For a week, the country was in upheaval, but the military complied when a judge on the country's Constitutional Court issued an order invalidating the president's move. The judge, Epaminondas González Dubón, who was also involved in the Myrna Mack case, was killed a year later in a drive-by shooting, after he approved the extradition of a military officer to the US. Around that time, an assassination plot against Helen was exposed, and she briefly had to leave the country.

And yet Guatemala was as close as it had ever been to peace. Government representatives were meeting with members of the Unidad Revolucionaria Nacional Guatemalteca (URNG) to negotiate the terms, first of a cease-fire and then of an end to the armed conflict. At San Carlos, Lucrecia was a member of a student group at the medical school, and she was dating a charismatic sociologist who belonged to a university chapter of a guerrilla group called the Fuerzas Armadas Rebeldes (FAR); she was suspicious of the dogmatism and general high-mindedness of the outfit, but eventually joined in the final year before the accords were signed, once the group renounced violence. One of the terms of the peace accords—which had the lofty name of "Firm and Lasting Peace"—was that the former guerrilla forces could become a legitimate political party.

Lucrecia eventually grew tired of the rigid, hierarchical caste of the organization's rank and file. Just after the accords were signed, in December 1996, the URNG held rallies to celebrate the start of a new era. As her party members crowded into a plaza to cheer, they called to the group's leader, who'd just signed the accords on behalf of the URNG, and shouted, "Comandancia general, give us orders!" These last words put her off. If they were entering a democratic era, why was *order* still the operative word? A phrase that bothered her more was a euphemism people used to rationalize the top-down approach: *verticalismo democrático*. After about a year, she drifted away from both the URNG and partisan politics, considering herself "a political orphan."

The shifting political climate wasn't enough for the government to change its approach to the Myrna Mack case. Helen's only tool for applying pressure, beyond filing endless motions in the Guatemalan courts, was to advance a parallel legal effort in a regional body known as the Inter-American Court of Human Rights. Based in Costa Rica, it consisted of seven judges elected to six-year terms by the general assembly of the Organization of American States. Its judgments were not binding, but they carried weight in the countries that had signed a compact known as the American Convention on Human Rights. This applied to almost all of Latin America, including Guatemala. In March 2000, at a public hearing of the court, in San José, lawyers for the Guatemalan government recognized the country's "institutional responsibility" for Myrna Mack's murder. The problem was getting the state to allow the criminal case against the officers to proceed. When a judge on the Guatemalan high court ruled that it could, in 1999, he was forced into exile.

The peace accords may have brought relief after decades of bloodshed, but they also exposed what the country's politicians already knew: the military had lost none of its influence. In principle, the government had agreed to address the systemic problems that led Guatemala into civil war in the first place: gross inequality, overt racism, and the overwhelming need for land reform. But in practice these were open-ended promises that depended on flagging political will. Crossing the military, or threatening its bottom line, was suicide. A large contingent of the senior officer corps turned to organized crime—smuggling, graft, and especially drug trafficking. The top generals in the intelligence services during the war were known as the *cofradía*, or the brotherhood; as their reach grew, corruption extended into the private sector as well as certain quarters of the civilian government.

The US was aware of the problem because it kept close tabs on the military, but the fallout was also reaching the US-Mexico border. By the late 1990s, the Drug Enforcement Administration determined that 75 percent of all the cocaine that reached the US passed through Guatemala. According to the State Department, Guatemala was the "preferred transit point in Central America for onward shipments of cocaine." In *The Texas Observer*, investigative journalist Frank Smyth wrote, "What distinguishes Guatemala from most other nations is that some of its military suspects are accused not only of protecting large criminal syndicates but of being the ringleaders behind them." Across the border from McAllen,

Texas, ex-members of the Guatemalan special forces—the Kaibiles—were training hitmen from the Zetas cartel in paramilitary operations.

Seeking accountability for crimes of the past was its own high-wire act. The terms of the peace accords did not explicitly address the question of justice or recompense, but two major research projects had begun as part of the broader, postwar reconciliation. One was an international body created by the United Nations called the Commission for Historical Clarification. A staff of three hundred people spent two years conducting thousands of closed-door interviews, reviewing government documents, and reconstructing information on the atrocities of the war years. The commission would go on to publish a twelve-volume account that supplied some of the most definitive facts of the conflict: 200,000 civilians had been killed; there were 669 massacres; 83 percent of the victims were Maya; 93 percent of the crimes committed during the war years involved members of the military.

For Helen Mack and others, however, the effort was tarnished by one principal shortcoming. The UN commission could not name individual people or military units or assign blame for any of the documented murders. None of the testimony could be used for future prosecutions in court. A second commission emerged as a complement to the international investigation, but it wound up finishing first. It was run by the Guatemalan archdiocese's office of human rights, and overseen by the outgoing bishop, a strikingly tall seventy-five-year-old named Juan Gerardi. Gerardi had a long and tormented history with the military. After confronting soldiers when he was bishop of El Quiché, in 1980, he faced several assassination attempts. One led him to close the diocese altogether, and another landed him in exile in Costa Rica for several years. Gerardi was close with the Mack family, and each September on the anniversary of Myrna's death, he led prayer vigils. Sometimes they were held on 12 Calle at the scene of the crime, but often everyone convened at the church of San Sebastian, where he was the parish priest. Painted a pale yellow, with white Corinthian columns and a set of heavy wooden doors, the church was within walking distance of the Macks' home.

The report published by the archdiocese's office—called *Guatemala: Never Again!*—combined historical analysis, a vast inventory of data points, and extended testimony of victims, who were quoted at length. It was released in April 1998. The report was explosive because it included specific details about the structure and personnel of the military intelligence services. In certain instances, the authors named military units and individual officers responsible for specific crimes. Four days after the report's release, Gerardi was murdered in the garage of the church.

Among those who gathered at San Sebastian the night of his slaying was Helen Mack. She brought a forensics specialist with her, then spent the rest of the night smoking cigarettes in angry silence. "Those military pieces of shit," she was overheard saying. "Those assholes did it."

THE MYRNA MACK MURDER trial began on September 3, 2002, at nine in the morning, in a special auditorium of the country's Supreme Court. Because of the crowds, the judges needed the largest space available—in this case, three hundred seats arranged in two sections, separated by a long aisle running down the middle of the hall. Three magistrates sat on the bench. On the right side of the room, facing the judges, were Helen Mack and the lawyers for the prosecution; on the left were the three defendants. Behind them were the two camps squaring off in the case. Civil-society organizations, diplomats, and international observers filled the rows behind the prosecution. Military officers, veterans, and their families occupied those behind the defendants.

The hearings lasted a month, against a backdrop of regular intimidation. After leaving the country for her own protection, Helen returned in time to find her lead lawyer sending away his own family. A gunman had shot up their house, and the lawyer's son was receiving text messages that said, "You'd better be frightened because you're really going to die." Staff from the foundation were being followed. In the country's major newspapers, an organization of prominent military veterans—called the Military Veterans Association of Guatemala—was taking out full-page ads warning soldiers and officers that it was "open season" on them. The message was recycled on TV spots and radio broadcasts, and the country's main roadways were decorated with yellow ribbons meant to symbolize solidarity with the armed forces.

The trial itself proceeded with minimal intrusions, although the judges were under armed guard and police had been stationed around the courtroom.

The verdict came a month later, on the evening of October 3. It was around six thirty when the judges took their seats. The auditorium was crammed with people. That morning, the chief judge had tried to clear the court, but the defendants' supporters refused to move. Pro-military students from the polytechnic school piled in, two to a seat, behind the prosecution's table, crowding out the Mack supporters who returned to the court later that afternoon. Guards were checking ID at the door, but soon the hall was overrun. Taunts sailed like darts between the two camps, but no one dared get physical. Two court clerks started reading the verdicts aloud. The recitation took nearly two hours, and the second clerk, taking over from the first, read so fast that everyone in the hall strained to comprehend the words.

Two of the three officers were acquitted for lack of evidence. The third—Juan Valencia Osorio, director of the Presidential Security Department—had given Beteta Álvarez the assassination order. He was found guilty and received a maximum sentence of thirty years in prison. His wife let out a sob when the clerk read this part of the decision, and she swooned, nearly falling to the floor. The judges were split two to one. After the verdict was read, the lone dissenter took the microphone to explain that all three of the officers should have been acquitted. The room erupted in applause. The military sympathizers gave him a standing ovation, drowning out the chief judge's repeated orders to be quiet.

Helen angled her response midway between victory and defeat. She was "partially satisfied," she told the assembled press. When reporters asked Lucrecia if she believed justice had been served, she replied, "For one of them." It was now around nine thirty p.m. These interviews took place just outside the courtroom, as the attendees filed out, and while Helen was talking, the building's power abruptly went out. A nervous hush descended in the dark. The only source of light emanated from the cameras clustered around Helen, who continued to speak for a few seconds more to finish her thought.

In May 2003, Valencia Osorio was released from custody during an appeal. A court ordered him back to prison in late January 2004, to commence his sentence. But by then he had fled the country and was never seen again.

29.

The Trial

On the morning of June 24, 2002, Juan Romagoza was in the witness chair at a federal courthouse in West Palm Beach, Florida. He raised his right hand and swore an oath into a microphone before a jury. Across from him, at the table for the defense, were the two men he blamed for the worst suffering of his life: José Guillermo García, El Salvador's minister of defense from 1979 to 1983, and Carlos Eugenio Vides Casanova, García's successor, the former head of the National Guard, and one of Juan's interrogators from December 1980. Now in their midsixties, they wore suits and sat rigidly upright, blank expressions on their faces.

Juan focused on his lawyer, who asked him a series of biographical questions. Where did he live? ("In Washington, DC.") What did he do for a living? ("I am working as director of the Clínica del Pueblo.") Where was he born? ("Usulután, El Salvador.") For months they had prepared for this. The rhythm of simple responses created a gentle momentum. His testimony would last two days. He had described the torture before—often to complete strangers—in California parks, at sanctuary events, and in the offices of La Clínica. On each of those occasions, he had excluded certain details for the sake of concision and the sensitivities of his audience. This time, he planned to spare nothing. He wore a dress shirt and a tie. That morning, at dawn, he attended mass at a church near his hotel.

Juan had always suspected that the generals had emigrated to the US. "Where else are they supposed to live?" he told a reporter for *The Washington Post*. "They had an open door to come here." One day in 1999, he found out where they'd been living. An old friend and attorney named Shawn Roberts, who worked at the Center for Justice and Accountability, a human rights organization in San Francisco, shared the news. She had called Juan to ask if he would participate in a landmark case to seek redress. The center was building a litigation strategy around a law that allowed US courts to hear cases involving international incidents of torture, killings, and crimes against humanity. At issue was civil, not criminal, liability. Perpetrators would have to pay damages to their victims. The center's lawyers went after top-ranking government officials by demonstrating that they had exercised "command responsibility" for atrocities committed by their subordinates.

Having heard Juan tell his story in public, Roberts knew he would make an ideal plaintiff, but she felt ambivalent as his friend. "Litigation can be horrible," she said. It could dredge up old traumas, provoke threats, and invite unflattering press. There were two cases in development. Vides Casanova and García were the defendants in both. Juan would serve as a plaintiff in the second. The first was being filed on behalf of the four American churchwomen raped and murdered on December 2, 1980. The brother of one of the victims, Bill Ford, was adamant that his sister would have wanted her case to include Salvadoran victims. In 1998, Ford had convinced attorneys at the Lawyers' Committee for Human Rights to travel to El Salvador to interview four National Guardsmen who'd been arrested and imprisoned for the crime. From that trip, the lawyers had learned the whereabouts of Vides Casanova and García. At least a thousand war criminals from all over the world were living in the US at the time, including many Salvadoran military officers. One war refugee bumped into his torturer on a public bus in the Bay Area. The man who had killed Óscar Romero sold used cars in Modesto, California. A colonel implicated in the assassination of the Jesuit priests in 1989 had a job at a candy factory outside Boston.

Juan knew immediately that he wanted to testify, but he conferred with his family first. His sister, Morena, who lived in San Francisco, was encouraging. But when he told his mother, she begged him not to get involved. She and her husband were wary of the consequences. They came around only once they realized that Juan was asking for their blessing but not their permission. Some of his siblings in El Salvador, who feared repercussions, were less comprehending.

The most wrenching conversations, though, were with his daughter. After a few years of gingerly phone calls, Juan was making occasional visits to Mexico. At first, they never met in Puebla but in neutral places nearby: Mexico City or towns with pre-Columbian ruins, which they both liked to explore. Maria was studying psychology but had the interests of a budding anthropologist. Their encounters in Mexico were plodding and awkward, though a current of familiarity was building up; their communications had grown regular. But the idea of public exposure unnerved her. She asked Juan why he couldn't leave her dead mother in peace. "I'm doing this for your mother as well," he said. "It's to make her and people like her visible." Maria wasn't convinced by Juan's activist zeal. His strongest argument was ultimately an apolitical one. "This trial is necessary," he said. "Not just for me. It's to share the pain. If I share it, the guilt and the suffering are easier. I can tremble. I can cry. The weight that bears down on me can ease a little." Maria said she understood, but Juan could hear her crying on the phone. She didn't return his calls for several days after that.

The two cases were supposed to be tried together, but the judge split them. The churchwomen's case went to trial first, in October 2000. After a month, the jury returned a verdict in favor of the defense. The lack of living victims who could testify in open court undoubtedly weakened the emotional core of the case. But the generals also succeeded in describing a wartime atmosphere of complete chaos, in which command responsibility hadn't seemed to apply. Death squads colluded with extremists in the army. Cliques of officers showed greater loyalty to their *tandas* at the military academy than to the leadership of the armed forces. In their telling, Vides Casanova and García were moderating influences inside the government. That had been the Reagan administration's argument. The men had commendations from the White House to prove it.

Juan was one of three plaintiffs, along with Neris González and Carlos Mauricio, who had each applied for asylum more than a decade earlier and now lived in Chicago and San Francisco. González was leading a sustainable agriculture program and Mauricio taught high school biology. Both had been brutally tortured: González in December 1979 and Mauricio in June 1983. Like Juan, neither had been charged with a crime, but their associations had made them suspect. González had been active in a base community through her church, while Mauricio had been a trained agronomist with a university professorship. The National Guardsmen who had kidnapped González from a market in San Vicente had taken an especially perverse interest in her. She was then eight months pregnant. The soldiers repeatedly raped her and pushed her down flights of stairs. They withheld food and made her spend the nighttime hours submerged neck-deep in a tub of ice water. They cut her forearm with machetes and put out lit cigarettes on her skin. At one point, they forced her to lie supine under a metal bed frame, which they balanced over her pregnant belly; they took turns standing on opposite ends of it so that the frame rocked back and forth over her abdomen like a seesaw. She gave birth shortly after being left for dead by the side of a road. Her baby had fractures and indentations on his face. He died two months later.

In 2001 and the early months of 2002, the legal team prepared the case and studied the missteps from the previous trial. A key witness, who hadn't testified before, was Terry Karl, a Stanford political scientist widely regarded as one of the world's most knowledgeable experts on the Salvadoran military. She had spent the war years on fact-finding missions to El Salvador, cultivating government sources and interviewing military men. Drawing from US cables and firsthand testimony, she could lay out with encyclopedic clarity how much Vides Casanova and García had really known about the armed forces' rampant abuses given the structure of the high command. The government had been a military dictatorship, she argued: it was impossible to separate the death squads from the small corps of commanders and top brass. They were all in league. "Unified" and "consolidated" were how the former US ambassador, Robert White, described the chain of command. Having warned the State Department about the far right in 1980 and 1981, he was another witness for the plaintiffs. "One word" from the minister of defense, White said, and the worst human rights offenders in the armed forces "would be gone." But that was never the case; Vides Casanova and García had protected the worst abusers.

The legal team included two pro bono litigators from the San Francisco–based law firm of Morrison & Foerster as well as a group of human rights and immigration attorneys. One of them was Carolyn Patty Blum, who'd been involved in the *ABC v. Thornburgh* lawsuit before becoming a professor at Berkeley

Law. She had flown out to meet with Juan in his office at La Clínica in January 1999.

At Juan's desk, undistracted by the buzz of activity outside, they had spoken for hours about what might come up at the trial. In El Salvador an amnesty law passed in 1993 that had granted total immunity to Vides Casanova and García. Yet in the US a federal court was giving Juan an opportunity to confront them directly. He couldn't understand why the case wouldn't focus on the role of the US in the war. It seemed odd for historical and geographic reasons: they were testifying in the US, before an American jury. Why tell only part of the story? Blum had explained that if the generals were the target, the focus had to stay on them. Part of the evidence against them would also come from US government cables, so harping on the Americans could backfire. All of the jurors would be learning this history for the first time at trial.

The most concerted preparations involved the plaintiffs themselves. At the start of 2002, a group of psychologists were on hand as Juan and the others talked through the details of their testimony. They went over it multiple times at meetings with the lawyers. The trauma of recollecting what they had suffered often made them seize up or lose control. A single detail could ignite a bonfire of flashbacks. Roberts worried that Neris González might disassociate and become catatonic. Juan had moments of disorientation himself. It happened when he was recounting how the soldiers had dangled him out the door of the helicopter as they flew him to the National Guard barracks. One night, while an attorney was simulating a harsh cross-examination, his answers grew monosyllabic, his tone flat. Eventually, he stopped responding to the questions. The plan had been for Juan to testify first. But during a break, he confided in Blum that he didn't think he could be the one to open the case. He needed to "warm up" to the situation, he said.

Ever since the start of the churchwomen's case, in the fall of 2000, Juan, González, and Mauricio had been in the public eye. They were reported on by name and associated with both cases because of the original joint filing. By the summer of 2002, when the second trial began, they had been receiving threats. Anonymous notes arrived at La Clínica instructing Juan to remember his family back home. Sometimes people called to say that they knew where he lived and that if he wanted to be tortured again he should go back to El

Salvador. At one point, Juan's mother became too scared to go to church in Usulután. In Mount Pleasant, at his house on Longfellow Street, Juan was sleeping badly and suffering from anxiety attacks. Shortly before the trial began, he thought about pulling out of the case altogether. He wavered for a few days but decided to continue.

Juan's testimony began in the morning and continued into the afternoon. He spoke entirely in Spanish, with a translator sitting next to him. He was narrating his whole life leading up to the day in December 1980 when he had been shot and taken into the custody of the National Guard at El Paraíso. The scenes unspooled like images on a reel. He was both holding the camera and watching as a viewer from the outside. There was his childhood home: "one block away from the central parish church . . . a half block away from the house of my grandparents," he said. He momentarily relived his departure from the seminary as a boy, with his flagging interest in the church. ("I was in disagreement with some of the things at the seminary, and I decided to return to my city.") When his grandfather died, he went on, "there was nothing to help and no doctor." He described his burgeoning passion for medicine, and the lens widened onto his university years and his relationship with Óscar Romero. ("It was a radical change of my beliefs of faith and practice of faith.") He recounted the killing he witnessed as a medical resident at the hospital in Santa Tecla— how he and the nurses "were threatened that we shouldn't turn to look" at the soldiers who had just murdered a patient in the post-op ward.

As he responded to the lawyers' questions, certain patterns of observation emerged. There was, for instance, an uncanny recurrence of footwear: first, the military boots he saw while hiding on the floor of the hospital; second, the interest the National Guardsmen had taken in his own hiking shoes on the day he was shot in the ankle; and finally, General Vides Casanova's freshly polished boots glimpsed through a gap in his blindfold at the headquarters of the National Guard, in San Salvador. "How are you familiar with military boots?" his lawyer asked him. "These were the boots that my uncles would give to my mother so she could shoe all of the boys," he replied.

He kept himself steady while describing the torture, breathing slowly, holding his eyes on his lawyer, summoning courage by thinking about his dead wife and dead friends. The generals were unflinching as they listened. Roberts later described them as "ridiculously poker faced." Their expressions betrayed so little that they became an obsession for the plaintiffs and their attorneys throughout the trial. What were these two men possibly thinking? Was their stoniness a sign of incomprehension or of arrogance? Juan saw them as blurry forms while he testified. The generals were silent and still, but Juan could feel the burning heat of their presence in the courtroom even when he wasn't staring right at them.

Watching Juan as he spoke, Blum realized that he was sharing things that he hadn't yet unlocked from his memory during their pretrial preparations. The courtroom was small, with the two tables for the plaintiffs and defense at the front, situated before the bench. The jury sat parallel to the plaintiffs. A railing separated the legal teams from the gallery, which was partially filled. González's daughter was there, along with Mauricio's wife. Juan had opted to testify without any relatives in attendance. Yet no one could move while listening to him. He spoke in a plangent, unhurried voice.

At one point, near the end of the first day, he described a torture technique the Guardsmen had called "Chinese fingers." They had suspended him from a rafter by his fingers, which were tied by wire. "Hanging there like that, they introduced a stick," he told the court. "A wooden instrument into my rectum. It was an instrument of some sort, it is long, and went as far down to the floor. It would touch on the floor. And they said I have to hold it there. If I dropped it, it would be more electric shocks, it would be more blows."

THE TRIAL LASTED A MONTH. During that time, Juan spent the weekdays in West Palm Beach and the weekends in Washington. On Friday evening, after the hearings concluded, he boarded a plane so that on Saturday he could have more time at La Clínica. He had to catch up on work, but also return to a community. A group of fifteen other Salvadorans—La Clínica regulars—gathered in his office in the evening. They wanted to hear everything about the trial, especially the two generals. How did they respond to each aspect of the testimony? Did they wobble under cross-examination? Did they seem angry or upset? Someone would bring food, and Juan answered their questions and summarized the testimony while they sat around eating homemade pupusas and tamales. Usually, after a few hours, someone took out a guitar, and they tried to relax.

When Juan returned to West Palm Beach, he and the other plaintiffs spent their afternoons and evenings together. They each brought their own psychologist—the Center for Justice and Accountability encouraged it—and Juan practiced yoga and went to church every day before court. At lunch, after exhausting conversation about the trial, the three of them tried to maintain a spirit of levity. Juan made up new lyrics to a popular Dominican merengue about a cuckold, called "El Venao," replacing the chorus with the refrain from the generals' testimony, in which they repeatedly denied knowing anything about the crimes in question. He sang the words with a playful shimmy that made the others laugh: *Yo no sé, yo no sé*, or "I don't know, I don't know."

That summer, Maria had gradually overcome her unease about the trial, and she and Juan were speaking by phone more than ever. She asked him questions about what he'd endured during the war. Until then, family resentments and lingering uncertainties surrounding Juan's long absence from her life had cramped her understanding. Juan basked in this new curiosity. Maria wanted to know why the trial was taking place in Florida, as opposed to El Salvador, and how it was that the generals had come to live in the US. "We were learning together," Juan said.

Juan Romagoza, Neris González, and Carlos Mauricio testified as the plaintiffs in a civil case brought against two Salvadoran generals in West Palm Beach, Florida, 2002.

On the morning of July 17, 2002, General Vides Casanova testified, and when he finished the defense rested. He was just returning to his seat when the judge spoke: "All right. Let me turn back to the plaintiffs." Two days before, a member of the jury had passed a note to the judge, which he had read out loud. "I do not know if this is appropriate," it began, "but may I ask to see the cigarette burns on Ms. González's body, the bullet wound in Dr. Romagoza's arm, and any documentary medical, not psychological evidence, showing the extent and severity of the injury suffered by the plaintiffs?" Photographs of their scars had already been entered into evidence. But the lawyers had conferred with Juan and González, and they agreed to show their wounds to the jury before it deliberated.

"Why don't you have the doctor fold up his sleeve, and when that is done, he can simply walk in front of the jury," the judge said. With González standing beside him, Juan rolled up his shirt. Both were nervous baring themselves before the court. They kept close. From the gallery, it looked as though they were holding each other up. Juan stepped forward to approach the jurors. He didn't feel self-conscious. His surroundings melted away. He had the sensation of leaving his body and floating above himself. He wasn't alone. He was merging with the bodies of the people he knew, those who had died. The mother of his child. Romero. His friends. Family members. Christians. People better than himself. A pressure lifted from his shoulders. A sense of community pervaded his body. The dead were alive and with him. "So many scars in El Salvador, and we have the privilege to show ours," he thought. "Everyone who is gone is here."

SIX DAYS LATER, Juan was in the air, returning to Florida from Washington, when the jury delivered its verdict. By the time his plane touched down, González, Mauricio, Blum, Roberts, and the rest of the legal team were on their way to the airport to share the news. They reached Juan as he was leaving the terminal. The jury had sided with the plaintiffs. The generals were ordered to pay $54 million in damages, including $20 million to Juan. The dollar amounts were abstract; appeals were pending. But none of the plaintiffs cared about the money.

30.

Homieland

On the five-hour flight from Los Angeles to El Salvador, Eddie was handcuffed, with his legs shackled. There were thirty other men on the plane. He was still wearing the same clothes as when he'd been arrested—a tattered T-shirt, cargo shorts, and white Adidas sneakers. An ICE officer had removed the laces. He was too smart not to be scared, but he wasn't about to admit it, least of all to himself. There were angles to play, moves to game out.

It was the evening of September 14, 2007, and the sky was growing dark when the plane touched down in San Salvador. A separate hangar was reserved for deportation flights, which had become a regular occurrence, at least two per week. Eddie was one of nearly twenty-two thousand Salvadorans deported that year, almost double that of the previous year.

The immigration wing of the airport was several hundred yards away from the main terminal and hidden behind a flimsy white fence about seven feet high, which ran the length of an adjacent parking lot. At a small office with crumbling white paint, policemen were waiting to fingerprint the new arrivals and strip off their shirts to inspect them for gang tattoos. Anyone with a pending criminal case in El Salvador was rearrested. But most, including Eddie, were waved into a small room with chairs scattered in untidy rows. At the front of the space was a screen where a short video presentation welcomed everyone to El Salvador. A couple of minutes later, a government agent handed Eddie a packet of condoms and two cold pupusas wrapped in tinfoil. He was free to go. A swarm of vendors, job recruiters, scam artists, friends, and family members waited by a bus stop outside. Eddie skirted the crowd, looking for one of his cousins, who was there to drive him to his apartment in a neighborhood called San Jacinto, on the east side of the city.

Unlike many of the other deportees arriving in El Salvador, some of whom had last been there as small children before the war, Eddie knew something about his surroundings. His time in Soyapango, in 1992, had reacquainted him with the place, though it had changed radically in his absence. Ever since he realized he might get deported, Eddie had kept tabs on the country—asking people about it, scanning news items, touching base with family members. He knew there were neighborhoods to avoid and habits to curb. In the US you fought to prove your strength, and if someone swung at you, or flashed a gang sign, you either came back at him or risked humiliation, which usually led to something worse. "There you get into a little fight and you're cool," he said. "Over here you fight someone and gotta kill the guy." When he spoke, he used a blend of English and Spanish. "I'm American-culturized," he'd say; his Spanish, with its lilting Chicano accent, was "all beat up." Certain words frequently eluded him, and he'd revert to Spanglish to retrieve them. His first words as a toddler had been in Spanish, but it was a second language. LA had made him, and its marks were indelible. "I'm on the native side of English," he said.

The next morning he woke up at his cousin's apartment, his legs dangling over the sides of a small couch. The television was on and the sound of the national anthem, played by a marching band, blared through the speaker. September 15 was Salvadoran Independence Day, and there were parades throughout the city. The peak of a volcano loomed into view through the window. He prepared to step outside and survey the neighborhood when his cousin intercepted him at the door to check his clothes. Anything baggy or sporty would attract attention; the hip-hop fashion that was the lingua franca of California signified that a person had ties to a gang in El Salvador, a potentially fatal association. Eddie was wearing a white T-shirt and a drab, snug-fitting pair of pants. His cousin approved, but as Eddie walked to the door, he caught sight of himself in the mirror. His spare new look was a reminder of the person he no longer was.

Just shy of thirty, the man staring back looked old, like someone who should be settling down rather than starting from scratch. He felt empty-handed, slight. His mind raced through everything that he'd earned for himself in Los Angeles: three cars, a condo, a stable job, his own production company. These were the achievements of the Fast Eddie years. He thought, "This is my life right now? This is what I got to work with?"

There was a reason why Eddie's cousin was so anxious about the clothes. This stretch of San Jacinto belonged to a gang that everyone referred to simply as "the letters," for fear of being overheard. It was a more discreet way of saying MS-13. The same principle applied to "the numbers," a euphemism for 18th Street. Just as the streets of LA and San Fernando had once been carved up and divided among rival crews and cliques, the cities and towns of El Salvador were now defined by patches of gang turf. During the decade and a half Eddie had been building his life in California, the country had become one of the most dangerous places in the world. He'd witnessed the early moments of its transformation firsthand, which only made the situation stranger. In 1992, the LA transplants listening to hip-hop and flaunting cholo fashions enthralled everyone. They were exotic, comparatively rich, worldly. Eddie called them "the New Thing." Basking in his own hard-earned expertise, he'd put it to people this way: "The New Thing had symbolism. It had music. It had money. You throw in a couple of movies"—a gangster flick called *Blood In Blood Out*, for instance—"and it's just brainwashing. Then throw in a couple of songs from Cypress Hill. Cypress Hill fucked everyone up over here." Some of the national newspapers ran multipage articles analyzing the deportees' clothes and English slang. In a daily called *El Diario de Hoy*, a government psychologist wrote at the time, "The style is the gang, and it's an accomplishment, a triumph, to belong to one. For the youth it's a trophy to be marked by a gang, and it signifies power."

Eddie had always grasped the cultural appeal of the gangs, but their utter dominance floored him. American deportation policy had turned local street gangs from LA into an international criminal network. MS-13 and 18th Street fanned across the country and the region; their rivalries spread with them, mutating into something even more violent and ungovernable. The Clinton administration was so eager to demonstrate its toughness on crime that it had deported hardened criminals without warning the Salvadoran authorities. Its disregard was even more egregious because the US embassy, more or less simultaneously, had also been dictating whom the government named to top posts in the national police force. Between 1993 and 1996, four thousand teenagers and young men with thick criminal records were sent to El Salvador. Many of them had been arrested for robberies, kidnappings, and homicides.

After twelve years of civil war, the country was in no state to receive them. Military weaponry was easily accessible. The economy had cratered, and many former soldiers and guerrillas, with experience in kidnapping and extortion, were turning to street crime. One of the terms of the peace accords was that the government would reconstitute the national police. As a theoretical check against its past abuses, patrolling officers were lightly armed with old pistols and nightsticks, while criminals carried M16 rifles. There were budget shortfalls, recruitment problems, and a shortage of jail space.

Members of the new Salvadoran government pleaded with the US ambassador and officials at the State Department to slow the deportations, or at least to help devise a system for screening the most dangerous elements. But the Americans weren't interested. In August 1997, the president of El Salvador told *The New York Times*, "This is a very serious problem. The United States lets these dangerous types out and tells them 'go back to where you came from.' But we have no way to try them or jail them . . . and so we must not only let them in but let them go free."

Cliques from specific corners of Southern California cropped up in El Salvador, with names that corresponded to their original American locales: Hollywood Locos Salvatrucha, Fulton Locos Salvatrucha. "They consumed everything in their path," the anthropologist Juan José Martínez d'Aubuisson observed. "Piecemeal neighborhood gangs saw no choice but to join one of the two for their own survival. The alternative was complete annihilation." Some of the earliest recruits joined on a part-time basis, spending their days at school or working; others spent all day hanging around makeshift gang redoubts called, in English, "destroyers." They made money selling drugs and extorting local businesses, charging taxes (known as *renta*) on stores, food stalls, and public buses. In addition to the transplanted American cliques, new ones emerged, like more virulent strains of a virus. Two of them, MS-13 affiliates called the

Sansivar Locos Salvatrucha and the Harrison Locos Salvatrucha, were thought to be the first spin-offs outside the US. In short order, there were hundreds of others, and while many of them were mortal enemies, certain American rules still applied. Called "southern pacts," in reference to the Mexican Mafia in California, the arrangements allowed for outright war between gangs, but forbade the extortion of businesses that fell in another's neighborhood.

The arcane logic of this new civil war made sense to the participating gangsters, but not to the people caught in the crossfire. Every Salvadoran carried a national identification card necessary for any number of quotidian reasons: to enter work, pick up medicine at the pharmacy, and sign for packages. But because these documents listed home addresses, they also invited scrutiny from upstart gangsters, who could know if an otherwise innocent person happened to live on a rival's turf. To some of the fiercer cliques, which set up checkpoints on the outskirts of their own neighborhoods, someone with a "bad" address was a legitimate target.

In the mid-1990s and early 2000s, deportees associated with MS-13 arrived in San Salvador knowing exactly where to find camaraderie: in the bars across from the Modelo market downtown, where some sixty other "homeboys" would be drinking beers and eating ceviche. Those with ties to 18th Street would go to the middle of Parque Libertad, where they would spot a large group wearing Dickies or Ben Davis overalls and Nike Cortez sneakers. "Where do you come from, *ese?*" someone would say, as if they were all still in California. Others belonged to more obscure offshoots of the two main gangs, such as Shalimar 13 (from Orange County), Pacoimas 13 (from San Fernando), or Mirada Locos 13 (from Hollywood), or they were returning to towns in the countryside where no one knew the meaning of the California cliques. They created their own alliances just as they had in American jails. The 13 next to their names, which once signified their fealty to La Eme in California jails, was the only shred of identity they had left. "A common past of deportation and abandonment unified them," Martínez d'Aubuisson wrote. "They thought El Salvador was a giant, violent California prison."

In September 2007, when Eddie arrived, it had been roughly four years since the right-wing ARENA government of Francisco Flores had unleashed a new anti-gang policy called Mano Dura, or "Strong Hand." It had consisted of massive patrols and gang sweeps launched by combined units of the military and police; with broad new security powers, the government arrested thousands of people, some of whom didn't belong to the gangs but were thought to be associated with them, either because of where they lived, whom they knew, or how they dressed. The measures were timed to precede national elections, to give ARENA an advantage on the main issue preoccupying Salvadoran voters: crime. In 2004, the party's candidate, Antonio Saca, won the presidency handily. After the Supreme Court invalidated key parts of the original anti-gang policy, Saca introduced another version, dubbed Super Mano Dura. The prison population exploded, which further consolidated the power of the gangs. To avoid constant riots, members of MS-13 and 18th Street were kept in separate facilities, but because their leaders were now well protected, they arranged hits and orchestrated extortions with cell phones, commanding an expanding army of foot soldiers who operated outside the prison walls.

Although Eddie considered himself tough and adaptable, his profile put him at substantial risk. The gangs went after Americanized deportees because they were immediately conspicuous. If their clothing didn't expose them, it was their clunky Spanish, the style of their gait, stray expressions, barely perceptible tics and mannerisms—a whole host of tells that they often didn't know they had.

But deportees immediately fell under suspicion from regular Salvadorans who associated all the new arrivals with criminality. Eddie didn't belong to a gang, and he was determined to keep his distance. The same was true of most people deported during the presidency of George W. Bush. The legal tools for sweeping immigration arrests and expulsions had been in place ever since the passage of IIRIRA, in 1996, but it was only in the aftermath of 9/11 that the full bureaucratic machinery got engaged; the deportation numbers had been rising steadily each year since. When Eddie had lived in El Salvador in the early 1990s, fluency in English minted his status and made him endlessly appealing to everyone he met. But now when people heard him speaking English, they lowered their eyes. "Oh, you've been deported," some of them would say gravely before turning away.

Over dinner one night, Eddie and his cousin were talking about money. For his first few weeks in the country, Eddie received a Western Union transfer from his mother, to cover basic living expenses. But he was burning through the cash and needed more. Deportees typically struggled to find work because employers considered them criminals. Eddie's cousin mentioned a company called Sykes, which ran one of the two largest call centers in El Salvador. It was based in Florida, providing customer service and technical support to American businesses, but had call centers in twenty countries, including some three thousand employees in El Salvador.

In 2005, President Saca had finalized the terms of a regional free trade agreement with the US, making El Salvador the first country in Central America to become a party to the deal. Among the myriad foreign companies that began investing in El Salvador were Sykes, AT&T, and Dell, which were outsourcing large shares of their US labor force. Drawn by low operating costs and generous tax incentives, call centers were on the rise, fueled in large part by the influx of English-speaking job seekers.

Deportees were a natural fit for the workforce: they spoke idiomatic American English, were desperate for money, and couldn't find work anywhere else. Deportees were "very loyal," a call-center recruiter once admitted to the news service McClatchy. "They know they won't get another shot." Eddie hadn't known it when he first arrived at the San Salvador airport, but there amid the crowds—in crisp khakis and golf shirts, beaming solicitous smiles—were call center recruiters, rushing to hire deportees almost as soon as they stepped off the planes. In Latin America, the burgeoning industry depended on US immigration policy, which was uprooting tens of thousands of Americanized immigrants each year. The call centers ran the gamut in El Salvador, from large and highly professional ones to midsize firms and smaller, boutique shops. What differentiated them, typically, was the number of accounts each had; at the bigger outfits, there could be as many as three or four American companies spread across multiple floors, farming out different aspects of their operations, from sales to customer support. At many of them, more than half of the employees had been deported. Sykes was known, in English, as "homieland" because of all its deportees.

In October 2007, a few weeks after the conversation with his cousin, Eddie started working for Sykes, in a hulking building in a strip mall. Instructors drilled him on the language of customer service: "sir" instead of "dude," "You're welcome" instead of "It's cool." Eddie had always been a first-rate talker, a natural salesman. He coasted through the lessons and was assigned to take calls for Hotels.com, upselling customers on more expensive rooms. He also performed technical support for Kodak; when callers complained about their printers, he read from a list of basic troubleshooting techniques. Everyone worked out of small cubicles, under harsh fluorescent lights and in front of computer screens and black, shiny phones; cell phones, notebooks, and personal items weren't allowed on the sales floor to ensure that no one could surreptitiously take down a customer's credit card number and smuggle it off the premises.

In the early days Eddie's thoughts about work never strayed from the math: $150 a week—his current earnings—was roughly three times the Salvadoran minimum wage. His mother had wanted to hire a coyote and smuggle him back to the US, but he resisted. He was almost thirty years old now, and if anything went wrong, he could end up in jail—more years of his life burned off in detention. Within two months he could afford his own apartment in San Salvador, a small place that went for $125 a month, on the fourth floor of a raggedy building near Metrocentro, within view of the shopping mall where Sykes was located. Steadily, it began to fill with furniture financed by overtime hours and all-night, graveyard shifts. Sykes wasn't the only place he worked. He added some hours first at a small firm called ExpressTel, which was run by a group of deportees whom Eddie came to feel were "power-tripping"; then at a bigger place called Teleperformance, where, in a fit of pique, he once put an obnoxious four a.m. caller on hold for fifteen minutes while he took a leisurely stroll to the bathroom. There was one extravagance he allowed himself on this lean new salary—a dryer. The Salvadorans he met all had washing machines but hung their clothes to dry in the humid open air; the light smell of mildew, and their perpetually damp touch, became a fixation for Eddie, a line he decided he couldn't cross.

At the Sykes office, he watched the other deportees struggle to adjust. Their stateside experience tended to be in manual labor (construction, landscaping), and the deskbound monotony ate away at their patience. They looked stricken pecking at their keyboards. Tattoos mottled their hands or snaked out from under shirtsleeves. Leaning back in his chair, with his headset on, Eddie stared at his phone and waited for American area codes he could recognize. When a familiar one appeared, the voice of Fast Eddie never failed to materialize in response. He'd start talking in his fluent, beguiling style, cracking jokes and suggesting lines of complicity with the voices on the other end. These calls were his only connection to the country he still considered home. One late-night caller from Hawaii (an 808 number, instantly recognizable) was greeted with an "aloha" and treated to a story of a vacation Eddie had once taken to the islands. The call was for Hotels.com, and the man wanted to book a room in Las Vegas for seven hundred dollars a night.

"What's up, Eddie," the caller said. "Where are you, anyway?" "I'm right here," Eddie replied, tacking on "El Salvador" like it was an afterthought. "What do you do?" he asked Eddie, who answered, without hesitation, "I do publicity." In a series of trips to the airport, Eddie had paid a sympathetic customs agent in cash to let him reclaim five boxes sent by his brother in the US. They contained everything he owned: studio equipment, clothing, video recorders, computers, electronics, and books on Photoshop, US copyright law, and screenwriting. Already Eddie was planning on bringing Above Ground Entertainment, his LA production company, to El Salvador. But there were hitches. One idea, for a spin-off fashion line he was calling ES 503, in recognition of the country's international calling code, got nixed after a gangster who saw him wearing a promotional T-shirt let him off with a warning: "the numbers" were off-limits. Twenty minutes into his phone call with the Hawaiian, they were swapping email addresses. The man told Eddie about a product he was bringing to market, an energy drink called Golden Eagle. "We could work that up over here," Eddie told him. A few weeks later, four boxes of the drink showed up on the sales floor, bearing Eddie's name.

There were times when the call center floor seemed to open directly onto his old life in California. Every few days, a new crop of employees would arrive for a tour of the office, all of them bearing the unmistakable signs of deportees new to Salvadoran soil. They had the stiff, feral, defensive pose of someone who was scared but didn't know from which direction the danger might be coming. They compensated with throwback swagger: puffed-out chests, exaggerated gestures, deliberately languid moves to project an air of calm. Eddie saw right through such theater because it had once been his act, too. When Eddie was in prison, he remembered a similar rhythm. The guards would press a button, and with a loud buzz the cell doors opened; in walked a fresh crop of prisoners, who were immediately aware of being sized up. Sometimes, Eddie would be sitting on his bed when he spotted someone he knew. The worlds of the prison and the neighborhoods where he'd grown up were fluid. More than a decade later, he sat at his desk at the call center, watching as a new group strode out onto the floor.

One day, as he was taking down a hotel reservation, he spotted someone from his past life. The man was tall, with a tattoo of a rose on the back of his neck. His loping stride stood out. Salvadorans didn't walk like that. "Where you from?" Eddie asked, standing up, when the man reached his desk. "Sunland Park," he replied. It was an LA neighborhood. As teenagers, the two of them had gotten into a fistfight there.

Cliques formed at Sykes based on where employees had lived in the United States—the West Coast, Texas, the Tri-State area. They listened to the American accents that others used while answering calls and introduced themselves during breaks. Everybody met at the call centers. In Spanish the word for "deportee" is *deportado*, but the call-center employees preferred to call themselves *deportistas*—"athletes." The *deportistas'* lives revolved around the groups that formed in the office. Later, they gathered at bars near the call center to strategize about life in their new city.

Starting out meant being short on cash, which often forced them to live in run-down and dangerous neighborhoods. One of Eddie's friends moved into an area called Bosques de la Paz, or Forests of Peace. He lasted a week and a half before a few guys approached him with an ultimatum. They were teenagers—scrawny and boyish—but they were covered in tattoos with gothic lettering and carried knives and guns. "We know you're not from the enemy," they said. "But in this place you gotta join us, or you're going to get out of here." A few days later, Eddie and a few others came to help their friend pack up and move out. In the waistbands of their pants, they carried pistols supplied by one of Eddie's relatives, an undercover cop. "I worry more about street guys like the regular gang member than about a narco or a coyote," Eddie said. "Those guys have something to lose. The guys on the street have nothing to lose."

At Sykes, the management posted a memorial photo when an employee was killed. On a bulletin board near the break area were the victim's name and contact information for his family. The other employees milled around glumly, trading speculation about how he "got caught up." Within a few months, the ritual started to repeat with ominous frequency: once a week, three times a week, four times. When the photos started crowding each other off the bulletin board, the memorials ceased. "There were so many employees from Sykes getting killed, they didn't want to talk about it no more," Eddie said. It felt like the world around him was closing in. Of the thirty people on his original deportation flight, fewer than five were still alive. Many of the *deportistas* looked up to Eddie and sought out his advice. "You have guys who got deported who don't change their style," he said. "If you don't change your style, and you go to certain areas, they're going to test you. If you're a tough one, you're going to test them. But you forget. You probably don't have a gun. These guys have guns. And these guys are going to kill you for sure. They're not shooting to scare you. Or they'll cut you up. There's no remorse. Because they get points for all that." The only way to see yourself through to safety, he'd say, was to scan your surroundings with "Salvadoranian eyes." Otherwise, you were as good as blind.

31.

The Reformers

On the morning of June 28, 2007, the US Senate was voting on a comprehensive immigration reform bill that would legalize the status of eleven million people. Cecilia Muñoz had arrived early to stake out a position in the hallway just outside the chamber. But before she had reached the building's front doors, something gave her pause on the manicured front lawn. A group of twenty day laborers were huddled together around a lawyer from an advocacy group called CASA de Maryland. "Repeat after me," the lawyer was saying, in Spanish, before switching into English with the script: "Don't let reform die today." A chorus of accented voices echoed the words.

The atmosphere outside the Senate was charged with expectation, yet Muñoz was trying to fend off a sinking feeling. The day laborers were so close to getting on the "right" side of the law; they were standing outside the country's highest deliberative body, minutes before it was about to hold a crucial vote. The senators began to arrive, entering the building one at a time. It would take sixty of them to wrest these men on the front lawn from their legal limbo. The vote was on something called cloture, and it required more support than the bill would eventually need if it were to become a law: two thirds of the Senate, rather than a simple majority. A yes meant ending debate over dozens of poison-pill amendments and advancing the bill to a final vote; a no allowed opponents to sink the bill by filibuster.

Half a decade of near misses and failed efforts to reform the immigration system had preceded this moment. In the summer of 2001, the Bush administration had been in advanced talks with Mexico to announce a comprehensive plan when 9/11 inverted the agenda. For the next several years Congress funded a harsh enforcement regime in preparation for legalization measures that never materialized. In 2006, a bill sponsored by Ted Kennedy and John McCain passed the Senate but wasn't taken up in the House. The Bush White House supported this latest version, and the Democrats controlled both chambers of Congress. Yet there were other complications. For one, McCain was no longer a sponsor. He was preparing to run in the Republican primary for president and had decided to keep his distance from controversial legislation. The fact that advocates and a bipartisan group of senators were on the verge of giving millions of people a path to citizenship had galvanized the opposition. The congressional phone lines crashed from an onslaught of calls placed by enraged conservative voters, stirred up by representatives on the far right, talk-radio hosts, and Lou Dobbs, a CNN anchor who filled the prime-time slot with nightly rants about "amnesty for illegals."

Muñoz went inside, sensing that some of the senators were avoiding her eyes as they passed her on their way into the chamber. A Democrat from New Mexico, Jeff Bingaman, kept to the far wall of the hallway, with the sunken shoulders and lowered head of someone with a guilty conscience. If his vote were a yes, Muñoz thought, he would look her in the face. At forty-four, she was already something of a veteran organizer, and had recently received a MacArthur "Genius Grant" in recognition of her work. Ten years earlier, with a coalition of advocates and Janet Murguía, in the Clinton White House, she had helped restore 50 percent of the benefits that legal immigrants had lost because of the president's welfare reform. In 1998, thanks to the same contingent of organizers and government allies, 175,000 immigrant children had their food stamps restored.

Muñoz had spent several months working the phones, pressing senators to back the bill. All the while, the Department of Homeland Security had been carrying out immigration raids across the country. ICE officers were barging into people's homes without warrants, arresting parents, leaving behind their children, and rounding up anyone who "looked" undocumented and happened to be within reach. Many undocumented immigrants were used to living paranoid, circumscribed lives, but little could have prepared them for the enhanced tactics adopted under the National Fugitive Operations Program. The agency now had an actual policy sanctioning ruses, whereby officers could effectively trick people into opening the doors of their houses. Claiming to be police was a common ploy. Another was for officers to tell a mother, for example, that her son had been a witness to a crime, and that they needed his help. Other times, officers dispensed with pretext altogether and forced themselves inside, availing themselves of unlocked (or partially cracked) doors.

Workplace raids were also increasing. In December 2006, ICE teams arrested almost thirteen hundred people in a single operation at meat-packing plants in six states. DHS had arrest quotas to fulfill, and the White House wanted to gain credibility with Republicans. To Muñoz and the other advocates pushing for legalization, the country's undocumented population had to be protected even if it meant accepting imperfect legislation. "There's enforcement stuff in here that five years ago we wouldn't have been supporting," Muñoz told a Democratic staffer at one point. "This is all about getting it done."

Some of the day laborers joined Muñoz outside the chamber and recited their scripts to the passing senators. Sam Brownback, a Republican from Kansas, came over to them. He'd long been a supporter of immigrants' rights, until he wasn't. The polling changed. His tortured reversal was the subject of obsessive discussion among reporters and advocates. It was taken as an ominous bellwether of dwindling congressional allies. "Let me tell you what's about to happen," he told the day laborers. From his somber expression, Muñoz had an idea of what he was going to say, but she was surprised by his explicitness. "I'm going to go in there and I'm going to vote yes, and I'm going to watch and see how other people vote. If it looks like this is going to fail, which is what I think is going to happen, I'm going to change my vote so that I can be on the winning side."

Sometimes in the chamber different senators occupied the seat on the raised dais usually reserved for the vice president, and gaveled the session into order. That morning, the job fell to Barack Obama, the junior senator from Illinois who had declared his long-shot candidacy for president four months earlier. The voting began before eleven, and within minutes the final tally was in.

Obama had voted yes to cloture, along with forty-five others, including many Democrats and Republicans. But together they fell well short of the mark. The year before, the Senate had passed a bill that was virtually identical; this one was dead before receiving an up-or-down vote. Obama struck the gavel to conclude the proceedings, while Muñoz turned to the day laborers standing beside her in the hallway. "The hammer of enforcement is going to fall on all these people," she thought.

Nearby, but beyond Muñoz's view, Michael Chertoff, the secretary of Homeland Security, stepped into a circle of reporters to issue a statement. He was thin and bald, with a light gray mustache and a prosecutor's stern intensity. "I have a job to do, which is to enforce the laws," he said. "You will continue to see heart-wrenching examples of families being pulled apart. . . . But in order to regain the credibility with the American people that's been squandered over thirty years, we're gonna have to be tough."

IN RETROSPECT, Muñoz found it striking, if not quite auspicious, that Obama had been the senator wielding the gavel. They had first met in 2006, and he had begun calling her for policy advice during the congressional debates on immigration that winter and spring. There were certain patterns in his thinking—less ideological stances than an overall sensibility—that distinguished him from the usual Democratic crowd. The first was what Muñoz would later call his "civil rights instincts": a group of people was excluded from basic services and subject to racial profiling. At the same time, he pushed Muñoz to bolster his intuitive arguments against predictable counterpoints. "Help me explain how more immigrants coming in doesn't mean fewer jobs for people," he said. Would American workers be displaced? What if the US government couldn't manage its own border? How could he address these questions without fixating on them? He had a few trademark formulations when they sparred during briefings. One was to say: "I get the reflexive progressive position on this but tell me why it's not a problem for this other reason." Another was: "OK, I hear you. Now you tell me how I should explain that to people in Southern Illinois."

Obama's questions to Muñoz grew progressively sharper. Yet, along the way, he still took positions reflecting the mainstream consensus. It was like he was wrestling with himself while Muñoz watched and rooted for the idealist to win out. From the start, though, he'd made his outlook plain: the idealist had to be yoked to the pragmatist if anything were to come of their conversations. Less clear was where the lines of pragmatism blurred into conservatism. In October 2006, just a few months after supporting an immigration-reform bill that passed the Senate, Obama joined an eighty-vote majority to greenlight the construction of seven hundred miles of fencing along the border.

By the end of December 2007, Muñoz had embraced Obama's presidential bid. She didn't formally join the campaign, but she advised him, and her confidence in him grew. In Iowa, there was an annual debate called the Brown and Black Forum, organized by two state legislators, one Latino and the other Black. ("The whole audience was white," Muñoz pointed out.) To prepare, they discussed what Obama should say on the topic of granting undocumented immigrants driver's licenses. As a New York senator, Hillary Clinton, the heavy favorite in the primary, had supported the policy, before reversing herself after a backlash. Obama's advisers were uneasy about staking out a bold position, but he was not. Muñoz said that there was no substantive reason to oppose the licenses, and when Obama agreed, David Axelrod, his chief political adviser, cast a sharp, sidelong glance her way. "David, I know it's not what people want to hear, but that might be exactly why we need to say it," Obama said. The issue never came up at the debate, but Muñoz told herself, "That's why this is my guy."

They needed her less in the general election, which suited her fine. Her mother died in April 2008, and her two daughters were teenagers. Her post at the National Council of La Raza was influential, particularly if a Democrat entered the White House, and she considered herself more effective working a new administration from the outside. John McCain, Obama's Republican opponent, had spent the entirety of the Republican primary running away from his otherwise admirable record of bipartisan advocacy for immigration reform. Obama attacked him for getting cold feet once immigration reform became "politically unpopular." His own rhetoric was that of a reformer with an ear to the grassroots. In one speech, he said, "When communities are terrorized by ICE immigration raids, when nursing mothers are torn from their babies, when children come home from school to find their parents missing, when people are detained without access to legal counsel, when all that is happening, the system just isn't working."

When Obama won, Muñoz started receiving phone calls, beginning with one from John Podesta, who oversaw the presidential transition. He asked her to interview with Rahm Emanuel and Jim Messina, two top advisers, as they began to staff the new administration. "One of my kids was in high school when I was chief of staff," Podesta told her. "It's really hard, but it's possible. You work all the time, and you get one thing besides work; and if that thing is your kids then you've chosen your thing, and you won't do anything else." She was unpersuaded but accepted the interview to collect intel on Emanuel. His aversion to immigration politics was notorious among the advocates. She left that meeting just as uninterested in an administration job. But she was impressed by how specific Emanuel got in counting to 218, the number of votes needed in the House for a reform bill to pass. He already had lists of moderate Republicans the White House could peel off. When Messina called with a job offer, she passed. Then, two days later, on a Friday afternoon, she was in the car with her sister and one of her daughters when a call came in from the 312 area code. It was Emanuel, telling her to hold for the president-elect. "This is Barack Obama," the voice began. "Hillary couldn't say no to me, and neither can you."

In the spring of 2008, Juan Romagoza's body sent him a message. It began with nausea and sharp pains in his stomach, then tightness in his chest, followed by spells of crippling lethargy. An examination led to a diagnosis of colon cancer, and after two surgeries the prognosis remained grim and ambiguous. He was fifty-seven years old. "I have to leave before I die," he told himself. He had spent twenty-five years in a country where he'd never planned to stay more than a few months. Returning to El Salvador had been his dream all along, but life had kept interceding.

La Clínica was no longer the ragtag outfit he'd inherited but was now a fully professional operation with a staff of eighty-five. Juan felt it could use some fresh blood. A fixture in Mount Pleasant and a prominent figure in the

DC Latino community, he had also joined the board of La Raza, the organization where Muñoz worked. The immigration-reform fights in the Capitol made him feel that he was witnessing history at the barricades. The West Palm Beach trial, which ended in 2002, gave way to protests of the Iraq War, rallies in support of mass legalization of undocumented immigrants, and marches against the harsh Republican alternatives. Obama was Juan's immediate favorite in the crowded Democratic primary. But in the heady months of the general election, because of Juan's fragile health, his usual activism was no longer possible. His niece, who was studying at Howard University, moved into his place on Longfellow Street. Juan left to join his mother in Usulután. She was eighty-two years old, a widow, and all alone in the family's large house.

When he returned home in March 2008, his symptoms were worsening, and they combined with a rush of emotions. He couldn't quite shake the old, familiar feeling that he was being followed. When he ran an errand, he would peer outside and survey the street, before darting back inside. Simple tasks like going to the grocery store or the pharmacy would take twice as long because he would stop on the way and cautiously retrace his steps, as he had several decades before. The house itself was roughly how he'd left it, though he now stayed on the second floor rather than on the first, where he had slept as a boy. Each morning at five thirty, he rose with his mother and together they walked a block and a half to church for morning mass. Cousins, uncles, and aunts dropped in throughout the day. They all lived on the outskirts of the departmental capital, and the big empty family house, with its presiding matron, was the hub when they came to town. In the afternoon between two and four, its main parlor would fill with ten octogenarian friends of Juan's mother for a daily meeting of the local church group. They'd call Juan down from his room—where he was now battling fevers, constipation, and body aches—to say a prayer for his health. A month after his arrival, Juan had another surgery, which went better but required a long convalescence.

When Juan regained his strength, five months later, it was the fall of 2008. He occupied himself the only way he knew how—by volunteering at an underfunded medical clinic. The main hospital in the department was in the capital, but the rural poor relied on a patchwork of paltry outposts. To manage costs, the country's Health Ministry contracted out preventive medical services to a group of NGOs. But these outfits didn't have permanent offices, and there was a shortage of doctors and medicine. Juan found a clinic in a place called El Destino. From there he followed up with his patients around the department, roving all the way to the Pacific coast, where he prowled the beaches on the back of a horse, in search of patients.

There were presidential elections the following year, and for the first time, after two decades of unbroken governments run by the right-wing ARENA party, the FMLN fielded a strong candidate. His name was Mauricio Funes, a forty-nine-year-old former television journalist with close-cropped hair and square-framed glasses whose formative experiences came from covering the war. He had lost a brother at the start of the conflict, when the police shot him for being a student activist, but his tone as a campaigner was moderate and ecumenical. He vowed to be the candidate of "safe change." Lula da Silva, in Brazil, would be his governing model, not the Venezuelan populist Hugo Chávez, which put the Americans at ease. The amnesty law, which shielded from prosecution anyone who'd been accused of committing crimes during the war, would remain intact. As one of Funes's advisers told journalists, "We don't want revenge. . . . We want forgiveness and the truth."

Juan was an FMLN man, a leftist of the old school, but what most appealed to him about Funes's candidacy was his stance on public health. Reforming the health-care system was a central plank of the FMLN's agenda, and Funes organized regular forums on the issue during the campaign. A group called the Alianza Ciudadana contra la Privatización—the Citizens' Alliance Against Privatization—helped turn out voters.

In late 2008 and early 2009, Juan volunteered for the Funes campaign, and when Funes won in March, with 51 percent of the vote, a team of public-health experts working for the incoming government published a detailed report titled *Construyendo la esperanza*, or Building Hope. They were trying to create a network of clinics that could provide immediate primary care, free of charge. Two of the leading figures in this effort had served as physicians for the FMLN during the war; in addition to their ambitious plans to increase state funding for universal medical coverage, they also repurposed wartime strategies for community outreach. One of them was a model Juan himself had brought to La Clínica in Washington, *promotores de salud*, or locals trained to work as nurses and health aides in places where residents had come to distrust public institutions. In 2010, with a loan from the Inter-American Development Bank, the Funes administration undertook its new reforms and set out to hire national staff. Overseeing the thirty-four clinics in the twenty-three towns making up the department of Usulután was Juan. Thirty years later, the job he'd dreamed of having since medical school had finally materialized.

Part 3

32.

The Voice of God

It was around dawn in late October 1998 when Keldy Mabel Gonzáles Brebe de Zúniga heard a noise that sounded like an explosion. She was fourteen and lived with her family in a house near the Bonito River, in a port city called La Ceiba, on the northern coast of Honduras. Heavy rains were pelting the roof, and winds lashed at the walls. Everyone at home rushed outside together: Keldy, her mother, a brother, a sister, and a niece. They emerged into the storm in time to see a bridge collapse into the river. Vehicles and their drivers disappeared under the water. One of the trucks had been carrying sacks of oranges, which had spilled out and were bobbing in the current. Scattered bills floated up from the spot where another driver had sunk out of view. "Look at the money," someone shouted, pointing first to the river and then to the sky. "What's happening up there?"

Hurricane Mitch was the deadliest natural disaster to strike Honduras in more than a century. The rains led to floods, the floods to mudslides. Maps became useless overnight because whole networks of roads were wiped out, sealing villages away in sudden isolation. Keldy wasn't especially religious as a child, but the destruction felt otherworldly and ungraspable. Eleven thousand people were confirmed dead and almost as many were missing. Twenty percent of Hondurans lost their homes. Seventy percent of the country's crops were destroyed.

Before the hurricane, La Ceiba's city limits represented the ends of the earth to Keldy; afterward, those boundaries started to crumble. Relatives and neighbors were leaving. The world grew bigger but more desolate. Mitch introduced her to the name of a new city: Denver, Colorado. One of her brothers, Milton, who was twenty years old and had worked at a local airport that was destroyed, decided to go there. All he said to Keldy was *me voy*, like he was leaving for the weekend. She thought Denver must have been another town nearby until his long absence started to make sense.

Keldy was born in the department of Olancho, a vast and rugged ranching state that extended from the Honduran heartland to the Nicaraguan border. She had moved to La Ceiba as a small child after her father died. Her family needed money, so she dropped out of school at thirteen and started to work, spending the week as a personal assistant to a local doctor and the weekends with her mother, Amanda who cooked and sold food at the airport. During the storm, Keldy and Amanda abandoned the house around the time the water started to reach their waists. They relocated to a university nearby that had been converted into a shelter for the displaced. After a month and a half, they returned home to clean up. Her family was among the fortunate ones in the neighborhood of Colonia Primero de Mayo—their house was still there. But to Keldy it seemed to have been "buried standing," packed full of mud and debris.

In the weeks that followed, a pall fell over the *colonia*. Keldy felt it when she walked to the river to fetch drinking water. All the pipes had burst; water no longer came out of the tap, and no one could be sure what was safe to drink.

Honduras had always been the poorest country in the region—"the country of the seventies," a former Honduran president once called it. "Seventy percent illiteracy, seventy percent illegitimacy, seventy percent rural populations, seventy percent avoidable deaths." During the height of the Cold War, the US sent roughly $750,000 a day in aid—some $2 billion over the course of the 1980s—but the money went directly to the military and its business holdings. By the nineties, American largesse was over, and the Honduran government didn't have the means to rebuild itself after the storm. Estimates put Mitch's destruction at close to $6 billion.

Amanda lost her food stall in the storm. Two of Keldy's other brothers eventually followed Milton to Denver. Her eldest brother, Luis Fernando, who was in his midthirties and married with four young children, became the family's lifeline. He supported Amanda and took in Keldy to help care for his children. Luis Fernando could afford to do all this because he was a police officer—one of the only professions that Mitch hadn't decimated.

Cops usually weren't paid well in Honduras, but the country was entering a new political era that brought a high demand for elite law enforcement. In 2002, Ricardo Maduro, an American-educated economist from the conservative National Party, became president. The former head of Honduras's central bank, he entered politics after his twenty-five-year-old son was murdered in a botched kidnapping in San Pedro Sula in 1997. His main campaign slogan was "zero tolerance" for crime. "The mandate of the people has been abundantly clear," he said at his inauguration. "I have been elected to fight first and foremost against insecurity. To fight against murder, against kidnapping, and against robbery." A few days later, his *guerra contra la delincuencia* began, or as it was more widely known, La Mano Dura. The Salvadoran government would eventually adopt Maduro's approach, which relied on the same legal instruments introduced in California more than a decade earlier. Anyone charged with "illicit association" could face up to twenty years in prison. Sixteen-year-olds would be tried as adults. If the police acted "in defense of society," it had carte blanche.

The *maras* who'd been hardened on the streets of American inner cities were beginning to surface in Honduras. There were cliques from California, criminals who drifted over from El Salvador, and those who had already been involved in local petty crime but were graduating to more serious offenses. What unnerved Keldy was that she couldn't identify whom she was supposed to avoid. A friend told her to look out for *pandilleros*, or gangsters. "What's a *pandillero*?" she asked. "They're the people who kill people and who kidnap girls to be their women," the friend replied. At first, none of these predators seemed to dress any differently than regular teenagers. Keldy came to suspect that tattoos were hidden under their clothes, and that they had special powers for concealing their malevolence. She wasn't wrong. But the fact that teenage boys were falling under general suspicion led to police abuses. One ex-policeman who worked in La Ceiba later said that in cases involving kidnappings, "the policy was to exterminate the kidnappers. If a search was legal, the people who were arrested were brought before the Public Ministry, along with the evidence, but there were ten legal searches out of every hundred. Other times, they detained four, eliminated three, and presented one to the Ministry."

Keldy and her friends avoided areas known for being "hot." On the few occasions she visited, before she knew better, she spotted boys with buzz cuts and shaved heads. Other times, Luis Fernando would tell her and the rest of the family when and where the police would be launching raids. There were always big press conferences afterward, with the police officers wearing ski masks to avoid being identified for reprisals. Luis Fernando was rising in the ranks and was invited to participate in bigger operations in San Pedro Sula. "I like doing this cleanup. I like locking up criminals," he once told Keldy. For his family's own protection he was known publicly only as "Brebe." "Never tell anyone you have a family member in the police and definitely not that he works on capturing *pandilleros*," he warned them. "You can't talk about this with anybody. I don't want anything to happen to you." Still, Keldy could recognize him when he appeared on television, masked alongside the other officers. His posture was a dead giveaway, making her wonder if anyone else could spot his tells.

Keldy's future husband, Mino Zúniga, entered her life when she was seventeen. Amanda had started working again, running a mini-mart across from a hotel in the center of town. One afternoon, Mino came sprinting down the block past her store, trying to escape a group of boys with weapons. He was handsome and tall, with dark, bronzed skin and a neat beard. Amanda stepped outside to reprimand the boys in pursuit. This was one of the strange facts of life in La Ceiba: everyone had known even the most dangerous local toughs since they were babies. "Don't touch him, he's my son-in-law," she shouted. Mino and Keldy had never met. When they did, a few weeks later, Keldy had reservations. He was twenty years older, and she already had a son, Alex, a two-year-old whose father had split. Mino's tenderness with Alex, combined with his confident, flirtatious edge with Keldy, eventually won her over.

They had their first son, Patrick, in December 2001; their second, Erick, was born in January 2004. Keldy considered these the luckiest years of her life. Mino was dedicated to Alex and loved him like his own son. The couple had money and a house for their family; their parents and siblings were nearby. At night, wearing spike heels and a glittering silver minidress, Keldy would go out dancing.

Their fortunes changed on December 7, 2006, the day that Keldy turned twenty-three. She was on a bus on her way to visit Luis Fernando in San Pedro Sula, when another passenger, a traveling musician, recognized her, lent her his cell phone, and told her to call her family. "I heard something bad has happened," he said. Because she was too nervous to call Luis Fernando herself, the musician dialed the number and handed her the phone. Luis Fernando was wailing when she pressed it to her ear. Their brother Carlos, a former soldier who drove a bus, had been killed after refusing to pay a tax to a group of thieves on his route. It sounded like standard gang protocol, *pandilleros* demanding their *cuota*. "They killed my Carlos," Luis Fernando kept repeating. He was convinced that Carlos's killers knew who his family was.

A year later, the global recession hit, and the American tourists who came to Mino's company for rafting and hiking trips started to cancel. Those who could still afford to travel were wary for a different reason: the country's violence was increasingly in the news. Keldy was anxious about Carlos's killing, and Mino was growing concerned about their finances. They decided to leave their sons with Amanda and set out for the United States. They would live there for, at most, a few years, enough time to earn money to fund a more stable life in La Ceiba. Keldy's brothers, who were still in Denver, would hire a smuggler to help them cross the border once they made it through Mexico.

Although they never planned to stay in the US for long, they risked everything to make it there. After a grueling bus ride through Guatemala, they boarded a freight train, known as the Beast, in Mexico, near a town in Tabasco called Tenosique. The train, twenty-eight cars long and brimming with threats, was the primary means for migrants to traverse Mexico. Bandits, rapists, and kidnappers lurked on board, scoping out potential victims. Crushed limbs and fatal falls were at least as common as assaults. The cars were packed, forcing many of the travelers to climb up the sides to reach the roof. The wind alone was enough to knock a person to his death. Mino tied Keldy down so she wouldn't fall if she drifted to sleep.

They left the Beast in Tamaulipas and took a bus the rest of the way to the border. In Nuevo Laredo, they were kidnapped by the Zetas, perhaps the most frightening of the Mexican crime syndicates. Known for beheadings and mass killings, these were ex-army commandos and cartel hitmen who had cornered the lucrative market of kidnapping and extorting migrants on their way to the US. Keldy and Mino managed to escape the drop house where they were being held and headed west. But in Sonoyta, across the border from Arizona, Mino's camouflage pants aroused the suspicions of a unit of Mexican soldiers. He was taken into custody, and only released after Keldy persuaded the local commander that he was her husband and not a *sicario*.

After the drama of their journey, their time in Denver was mundane, productive, and brief. Mino painted houses; Keldy prepared and sold food. Some of their earnings went toward renting a small apartment of their own. They sent the rest to Honduras. After a year, they had saved enough to buy some property in La Ceiba. Keldy had her sister Claudia and a brother-in-law visit different lots in town, while Mino shared photos of the type of house they wanted to build.

Around dawn on June 28, 2009, two hundred soldiers entered the Casa Presidencial in Tegucigalpa and pulled Manuel Zelaya, the president, out of bed at gunpoint. Zelaya was a businessman from the Liberal Party, who wore cowboy hats and had a thick mustache. His manner was blustery and self-aggrandizing. When he had entered office, three years before, everyone had expected the conventional politician he'd always been: pro-business and inoffensive to the country's elites. But as president, Zelaya discovered a passion for being a reformer unbothered by legal strictures and bureaucratic politesse. He opposed the privatization of the country's telecommunications industry and raised the minimum wage. To the annoyance of the Americans, he brought Honduras closer to Venezuela and Cuba.

He was a man with enemies. But his costliest move was to insist on holding a national referendum on whether the country should rewrite its constitution. His critics alleged that this was a stealth plot to stay in power. That seemed unlikely. For one thing, the referendum would be nonbinding; for another, two candidates in his own party were already vying to replace him in the next election, in November 2009. Yet when the Supreme Court and Congress blocked the referendum, Zelaya disregarded them and ordered the army to distribute ballots. On the day of the vote, he was put on a plane for Costa Rica. It made one stop—at a US air base—for fuel. The plotters called it a *golpe profiláctico*, a coup to forestall something worse.

Keldy followed the story from Denver, but the political news didn't immediately change her plans. What did, ten months later, was the strength of her desire to return to her children. In April 2010, she and Mino took a bus to Houston and boarded a plane to Honduras. The return trip was much easier than their departure had been. Neither of them expected to visit the US ever again. They hadn't told the rest of their family that they were coming back; it was supposed to be a surprise. "I was the one who got surprised," she later said. In the airport, Keldy received a call that another brother had been killed: Nelsin Obed, an electrician, who was murdered on a road just outside La Ceiba.

His death marked a period of terror in Keldy's life. When she and Mino returned, it was already known around town that they had worked in the US and therefore had money. Their new house was a one-floor, unpainted structure near a paved road and a grocery store, the only one in the area with a perimeter wall fringed in security wire. But the plot was in a *colonia* called Búfalo, in an area that was a short walk from a gang neighborhood. Shootings began shortly after Keldy and Mino had moved their belongings there and settled in. One day, someone came by the house to tell Keldy that he liked their property and wanted it for himself.

The 2009 coup had turned the country into a tinderbox. In the months after Zelaya's ouster, he had twice tried to reenter the country—first by plane, then by foot—but the military blocked him each time. He succeeded on his third attempt, and hid out in the Brazilian embassy, where thousands of supporters flocked in solidarity. Mass arrests and police shootings hardly discouraged them from turning out. The current president was Roberto Micheletti, the leader of the coup. "No matter what the merits of the case against Zelaya, his forced removal was clearly illegal," the US ambassador wrote in a confidential cable to the State Department and White House. "Micheletti's ascendence as 'interim president' was totally illegitimate." Eventually, in late October, the Americans brokered a deal: Zelaya would be restored to power until the country had its scheduled elections at the end of November. When Micheletti reneged, several days later, the US shocked everyone by accepting the outcome of the elections

Soldiers clash with supporters of President Manuel Zelaya after he was ousted in a coup in Tegucigalpa, Honduras, June 29, 2009.

anyway. Massive protests were already raging across the country, but they intensified when the National Party went on to win the election. The new president, Porfirio Lobo, called in troops to police the streets, installing checkpoints and passing a law to create a slush fund for security operations. A new conservative order was installing itself in power. The party deposed four Supreme Court judges and illegally appointed a new attorney general.

In La Ceiba, the coup and its aftermath unleashed another wave of lawlessness. One morning, in November 2011, two men on a white motorcycle parked in front of Keldy and Mino's house and took photographs. They said they would be back later to evict them. Around this time, Keldy received a call from Luis Fernando. "I'm in the middle of something sensitive," he told her. "If you don't hear from me, it's because I can't talk." In January 2012, he and his wife were murdered.

There was no time to mourn. The next month, a series of thefts began, and Keldy frantically filed police reports. Armed men claiming to be in charge of the *colonia* stole cinderblocks and solar panels. Her family members were also being threatened. "I'm asking the authorities to help me," her brother Óscar said, according to a separate report filed in late June. "I don't know what to do and my fear is that they're going to kill me."

On the morning of July 17, 2012, Keldy was walking to Óscar's house when she saw three men running away from the property. Keldy found Óscar on the ground covered in blood, heaving but still conscious. He was able to name his attackers, who had beaten him with stones and a two-by-four. He died at a nearby hospital a few hours later. Keldy filed another set of police reports identifying the men responsible. This led to more direct threats. Other men followed her around town and told her to keep quiet. Keldy's family had a white Toyota Corolla. One day, she and Mino were watching the news and saw that someone with an identical car and a similar license plate had been gunned down while driving.

Keldy and Mino took their boys and fled. They chose to hide out in a small lodge Mino's family owned in the forest of El Naranjo, two hours east of La Ceiba. Keldy's mother and niece joined them but told no one else. It would be two years before they left. The lodge had two floors, made of wood and stone, and was tucked away in a thicket of guava trees. Occasionally, they attended church nearby and ran errands to buy food. But Keldy was starting to feel ill; she had stomach cramps, and her legs went numb. There were days when she couldn't move. Eventually, she consulted a doctor, who suggested she get tested for ovarian cancer.

A few Sundays later, Keldy stayed behind when the rest of the family went to church. Alex kept her company. It was raining outside, the air muggy. Alex was napping on Keldy's legs when she heard a voice, stern and booming. Years later, as she told and retold the story of the religious epiphany that changed her life, the words she heard would always be rendered with perfect, unvarying clarity. God was sending her a message. "I have helped you so much," the voice began. "How many times have I saved you? How many guns have they wanted to fire at you? I've been there to defend you." She roused Alex, and the two hiked through the rain to the church. They arrived soaked and reborn.

Her newfound strength inspired her to take another action from which there'd be no return. She traveled to a court in Tegucigalpa to break the one universal taboo in Honduras. Under oath, she testified against Óscar's killers.

33.

Deporter in Chief

Obama had entered the White House vowing to protect the undocumented and restrain ICE, but deportations increased steadily during his first two years in office. An average of a thousand immigrants were being removed every day, a large share of them the very people the president had promised to spare: parents of American-born sons and daughters; immigrants, known as Dreamers, who had arrived in the country as small children; and those with no criminal records. The president had inherited a deportation system that operated on a scale unknown to his predecessors. The vast legal machinery of the Illegal Immigration Reform and Immigrant Responsibility Act of 1996 had not been fully set in motion until the creation of the Department of Homeland Security, which received gargantuan appropriations from Congress. A few years into Obama's first term, for example, the immigration enforcement budget at DHS was $18 billion—more than the funding for all other federal law enforcement agencies combined. Personnel at Customs and Border Protection had nearly doubled since 2003, as had the number of ICE officers.

The situation put Cecilia Muñoz in a bind. Inside the administration, she considered herself an "outlier with an advantage." The advantage was that she knew the president had picked her for a reason. Her job was the little-known White House director of intergovernmental affairs, in which she served as the main intermediary between the president and state and local governments. When the transition team tapped her for the role, they stipulated that she'd have to recuse herself from immigration issues, because she had previously registered as a lobbyist with the National Council of La Raza. "It doesn't make any sense to do this if I'm recusing myself from the thing that's been my life's work," she countered. At the president's behest, lawyers at the White House eventually filed an ethics waiver, acceding to Muñoz's request. In addition to her portfolio at the Office of Intergovernmental Affairs, she would advise the president on immigration. It would be her responsibility to tell him if the administration was ever "overshooting the runway" on enforcement. She felt he trusted her to be a moral compass.

Still, she was an outlier just the same. The president's inner circle of advisers was not ready to spend political capital on immigration. The country was in the midst of a severe recession, with the economy shedding upward of six hundred thousand jobs a month; the effects of the $780 billion federal stimulus package, which passed in February 2009 despite overwhelming Republican opposition, were materializing gradually. That summer, fissures appeared inside the Democratic Caucus as the president pushed for health-care reform. Seven months after Obama took office, Ted Kennedy died of a brain tumor, leaving the Senate strategy in doubt. The health-care bill that was supposed to pass Congress in August 2009 was delayed until March 2010. As the midterms approached, Democrats in border states faced a Republican onslaught, and, as usual, immigration made them vulnerable. At one point, Gabby Giffords, the Democratic congresswoman from Arizona contacted the White House with a plea. "You have to call up the National Guard on the border," she said. "I'm going to lose my reelection unless I can show that we are serious about border security."

Muñoz's biggest obstacle inside the White House was Rahm Emanuel, Obama's chief of staff. At a staff meeting one morning, in the spring of 2009, he singled her out for telling a *New York Times* reporter that the president wanted to pursue immigration reform in his first term. "I want to know, at a moment when we are only supposed to be talking about the economy, why there is a story about immigration reform on the front page of *The New York Times*," Emanuel said. "And who elected you to decide what our message is going to be today?"

There were other routes to the president—top advisers like Pete Rouse and Valerie Jarrett, Muñoz's most immediate boss, were more open-minded—but she had to use them judiciously. Comprehensive immigration reform was a long game, and she remained convinced that the president shared her convictions. The immediate emergency was the deportations.

The DHS secretary was Janet Napolitano, a poker-faced, canny lawyer who'd spent the previous six years as governor of Arizona. In an electorate dominated by independents, she was known for her obdurate centrism. It won her elections and turned her into an authority on immigration politics. Arizona had become a crucible for the national debate. A succession of its moderate Republicans—John McCain, Jeff Flake, and Jim Kolbe—kept sponsoring reform bills, while the insurgent right, in ascendance in party primaries and the state legislature, pushed countermeasures. The most infamous was a state Senate bill that required law enforcement officers to check someone's immigration status if there was a "reasonable suspicion" that the person might be undocumented. "If you zig, you have to zag," Napolitano told members of the Obama administration. Compassion required some compensatory toughness, and vice versa, as a matter of not just policy but also salesmanship in state capitals.

With a population of eleven million undocumented immigrants living in the US, DHS exercised enormous latitude in whom it went after. One of Napolitano's first moves was to end the workplace raids that had become routine under her predecessor. She also created a task force to study how the department could exercise discretion so that ICE officers would eventually arrest immigrants with serious criminal records and new arrivals who had recently crossed the border. The administration's opening gambit was to accept Congress's lavish appropriations for enforcement, but to use it strategically. ICE had the funds to deport four hundred thousand people a year. In 2009, DHS set a record for annual deportations, at 392,862, with the secretary emphasizing that half of them—195,772; another record—were convicted criminals.

Yet what made someone a "criminal" was much less clear. Under one federal program, the government took significant cues from local police. When officers arrested a person, whether for a serious felony or a traffic infraction, they would check his immigration status and file a "detainer" with DHS for federal agents to take that person into custody if he lacked legal status. There was barely any oversight of the arresting officers, who were often responding to local political pressures. In Las Vegas, for example, 70 percent of these detainers involved people who had committed violent crimes or drug offenses. By contrast, in Cobb County, Georgia, and Frederick County, Maryland, 80 percent of detainers corresponded to arrests for misdemeanors or traffic violations.

The administration also expanded a Bush-era program called Secure Communities, which automatically shared data with ICE anytime someone was booked in jail. If one problem was that law enforcement officers had inconsistent criteria for contacting ICE, Secure Communities swung in the opposite direction: the fingerprints of arrestees went straight to ICE databases, and detainers were immediately issued if there was a match. In principle, this was supposed to make immigration arrests more targeted, by homing in on jails. But in practice large numbers of people were swept up in an expanding dragnet.

Napolitano's closest advisers were from her Arizona years, and they shared her intuition about holding a firm line on enforcement. In their view, there was always a chance that a decision *not* to arrest someone could backfire. At the same time, Napolitano took note when ICE overreached, and she had staff keep files with press reports on troubling arrests that the department should avoid, such as a Dreamer who'd been put in removal proceedings, or a sympathetic parent who had lived in the US for years and had a family.

As Muñoz saw it, Napolitano and her team were being too cautious. At the end of June 2010, the head of ICE formalized the first of a series of "priorities" memos, laying out the different categories of people the agency ought to be pursuing. The groupings were straightforward: national security or public safety threats, followed by those convicted of certain crimes, and then "recent illegal entrants." But the idea behind these categories was to protect the immigrants who fell outside them. Another version of the memo, released the following year, further sharpened the terms. Of the eleven million undocumented immigrants living in the US, three million were prioritized for arrest. Muñoz wanted DHS to move more decisively, to shield more people from deportation. But she couldn't easily intercede; the secretary oversaw these calibrations, and she managed them in close coordination with the head of ICE, who dealt with the rank and file. One top Napolitano staffer later described the process of crafting the enforcement priorities as an exercise in trial and error: when the government saw examples of the "wrong" types of immigrants getting deported, officials went back to the priorities to modify them.

Muñoz, meanwhile, was consumed by thoughts that she wasn't doing enough, yet if she tried to do more she feared she would be sidelined. Already, she was self-conscious about her reputation as a former advocate from La Raza. Some skeptical colleagues in the administration second-guessed her political instincts or insinuated that she was some sort of Latina affirmative-action hire. Her clear conviction about the president could sometimes make things harder. If he was in the room with her, she felt she wouldn't have a problem. But he *wasn't* in the room for many of these discussions—his cabinet secretary was. Obama's intelligence and cool-mindedness could lead him to overestimate his ability to mediate stark disagreements among his staff. At one point, after proposing stronger language in a draft of an enforcement memo, Muñoz got into an argument with Napolitano's chief of staff. Napolitano's deputy defended his principal, telling Muñoz, "It's Janet's name that is going to be on this memo." "But she works for the president," Muñoz said. Through the whole exchange she was thinking, "If they call Rahm, I'm so screwed." To cover herself, she phoned Rouse to ask him to intervene personally if DHS appealed to a higher authority. Often when she approached Rouse for backup, she would tell him, "I need your help on something that I know the president cares about."

On May 10, 2011, the president traveled to El Paso to give a speech on comprehensive immigration reform. It was his first trip to the border since taking office, but his fifth event in a month dedicated to the subject. He spoke from a dais in a park called the Chamizal National Memorial, an expanse of bike paths and grass lawns pressed between a local high school and one of the city's four international bridges leading into Ciudad Juárez. In shirtsleeves and a tie, Obama worked at his usual pitch—charismatic, clear, exuding a sense of passionate reasonableness. "We have gone above and beyond what was requested by the very Republicans who said they supported broader reform as long as we got serious about enforcement," he said. "All the stuff they asked for, we've done. But even though we've answered these concerns, I've got to say I suspect there are still going to be some who are trying to move the goalposts on us one more time."

Outside the administration, Muñoz was becoming a pariah with her former peers, who accused her of being a sellout and an apologist for the president. She served as the face of a White House immigration policy that angered everyone. It fell to her to make statements like this one to *The New York Times*: "The president is concerned about the human cost of separating families. But it's also true that you can't just flip a switch and make it stop."

Janet Murguía, Muñoz's friend and former conduit inside the Clinton White House, had had her own experiences wrestling with the setbacks and disappointments of practical governance. She came to feel that at the end of the day it boiled down to a core question: Do I believe in my president or not? "I didn't see all the elements that were being balanced," Murguía said. "You have to do your own gut check. You have to trust that [the president is] doing the right thing, not just the politically expedient thing." Muñoz believed completely in Obama, but her loyalty isolated her from most people whose politics she shared.

Some of the broadsides were especially unforgiving. One group, called Presente.org, circulated a petition demanding that she "return to her roots." Other, more sympathetic advocates were stung by her evasiveness behind closed doors. In 2010, a group of young immigrants marched from Miami to Washington, DC, calling for a bill to grant them a path to citizenship. They were all outspokenly critical of the president. Muñoz met with them at the White House and cried while trying to defend Obama. One attendee was a twenty-six-year-old Dreamer from Ecuador named Maria Gabriela Pacheco, an early force behind national youth organizing. "She should take a stand against what is happening," Pacheco said afterward. "It really pained me to hear her say that all this is just collateral damage." A member of the congressional Hispanic Caucus groused that Muñoz sounded the same in private as she did in public.

Muñoz had taken the White House job feeling like an impostor, questioning whether she was truly up to the task; the solitude she felt in the role was overwhelming. Her main strategy for coping with the pressure was to organize her critics into two broad categories: those whose opinions mattered to her personally, and everyone else. It made sense that advocates would challenge her, but she had expected people who knew her to give her the benefit of the doubt. The way she saw it, there was a difference between "being righteous" and "being strategic."

Being strategic meant sitting down to an interview with Maria Hinojosa, a well-known Latina journalist anchoring a PBS *Frontline* episode called "Lost in Detention." It was an exposé of ICE detention facilities told through the lives of families that had been separated by deportations carried out by the Obama administration. "You need people who know what I know making policy," Muñoz said later. "And part of the job is defending those choices." Hinojosa began by pointing out that the president was aggressively executing the very laws he had decried as a candidate. "Even broken laws have to be enforced," Muñoz replied. When asked if the administration would continue to deport four hundred thousand people a year, she answered, "As long as Congress gives us the money to deport four hundred thousand people a year, that's what the administration is going to do. That's our obligation under the law."

The show aired in October 2011, at a moment of intensifying speculation about the president's political calculus. Was Obama trying to prove his toughness to earn Republican support for comprehensive reform? "There's no quid pro quo," Muñoz answered, ceding nothing. Hinojosa read a dramatic statement by Obama from the campaign trail, about communities being terrorized by ICE. "I was there when he said that," Muñoz replied. "That's exactly why we need to reform immigration law." But the president, she added, couldn't just ignore the law in the meantime. "That's not how a democracy works." Hinojosa abruptly steered the conversation toward a personal subject. "You received a MacArthur Foundation 'genius' award for your work on immigration," she said. "How do you see your MacArthur genius award given that now you work for an administration that has deported more people than any other president in history?"

UNITED WE DREAM WAS the largest youth-led immigrants' rights group in the country, and for years its members had been setting the Hill on fire. They staged sit-ins at congressional offices, held marches, and hectored the Obama administration, in person and from afar. There had been broad national support for a path to citizenship for Dreamers, ever since a group of Democratic and Republican senators introduced a bill for that purpose in 2001. But eleven years and multiple Congresses later, legislative will had flatlined. More than a million and a half immigrants fit the profile: they had arrived in the US as children and grown up as Americans in every sense but a strict legal one. If the president was going to take executive action to help anyone, this was the most likely population to get relief.

Two teams were working in tandem inside the administration on an idea to formalize protections for Dreamers. One group was led by Napolitano at DHS, who'd become convinced that something dramatic had to be done. The other included Muñoz and a team at the White House. By now Muñoz had ascended to the head of the president's Domestic Policy Council, a first for a Latino. The administration wanted to create a form of prosecutorial discretion by drawing on a clear historical precedent. Every presidential administration since Eisenhower had extended reprieves from deportation, known as deferred action, to certain categories of undocumented immigrants who were considered low priorities for arrest. Beginning in 1981, federal regulations explicitly authorized such immigrants to work. Combining these practices, the government could protect Dreamers from deportation while also making them eligible for work, bank loans, and financial aid to go to college. The proposals came with an additional slate of eligibility requirements. Recipients, for instance, would have to be either students, high school graduates, or members of the armed forces; they couldn't have a criminal record, and there was a strict cutoff date for when they had to have arrived in the country. Roughly eight hundred thousand Dreamers qualified.

The president himself was enthusiastic, but also wary of crossing the legal line of what he could do without Congress. There were long, painstaking discussions with lawyers at the Office of Legal Counsel, and a welter of memos, policy analyses, and internal reviews. On June 15, 2012, after Napolitano signed a memo authorizing it, the president announced Deferred Action for Childhood Arrivals, or DACA, in the Rose Garden. "This is not a path to citizenship," he said. "It's not a permanent fix. This is a temporary stopgap measure that lets us focus our resources wisely while giving a degree of relief and hope to talented, driven, patriotic young people." Inside the White House, Muñoz and her colleagues weren't sure whether the program would get tied up in court, or if centrist Democrats would turn on it going into the 2012 elections. DACA was precisely the calculated risk Muñoz had long been convinced the president would take when the time was right.

ON THE NIGHT OF Obama's second inauguration, in January 2013, Rahm Emanuel told White House officials that now "even a blind person" could steer a comprehensive reform bill through Congress. The highest compliment he could pay the cause was that, for once, it made clear political sense. During the campaign, Obama had criticized his opponent Mitt Romney for swinging too far to the right and alienating Latinos, "the fastest-growing demographic in the country." Romney's refrain on immigration was that the undocumented needed to "self-deport." Democrats and Republicans ultimately agreed that the main reason his candidacy had failed was that, in appealing to hard-right conservatives, he had lost everyone else.

For Muñoz, decades of work finally seemed to be coming to a head. A Democratic president she trusted, in whose administration she served at a high level, had just won reelection and planned to pursue the issue that mattered most to her. Two years earlier, a team had quietly drafted a generous legislative proposal that they could now use. The principal authors were Esther Olavarria, Ted Kennedy's top immigration staffer and now a senior official at DHS; Felicia Escobar, a White House lawyer who'd helped craft DACA; and Tyler Moran, a former senior aide to Senate majority leader Harry Reid.

At the same time, two bipartisan groups were working toward immigration deals in the Senate and House. The Democrats had a majority in the Senate, so the White House decided to start there. But in January 2013, the Democrats involved in the Senate negotiations—members of the so-called Gang of Eight—asked Obama to keep his distance. If the president announced specific measures, the Republicans would oppose them outright. Some officials at the White House had come to a similar conclusion. "If we just rolled out the president's bill it would be target practice," Muñoz said. Obama agreed to coordinate behind the scenes.

In April, the Gang of Eight announced its proposal, which *The New York Times* called "the most ambitious effort in at least 26 years to repair, update, and reshape the American immigration system." The bill would grant legal status and eventually citizenship to millions of undocumented immigrants, while creating two guest-worker programs and a new legal-immigration system for assigning green cards. In exchange, the government would have to spend $6.5 billion in enforcement and border fencing in the following ten years. On June 27, 2013, the bill passed the Senate by a vote of 68 to 32, with the support of fourteen Republicans. The bill's many backers were confident that this emphatic vote would pressure representatives in the House, where the Republicans had a thirty-three-vote majority.

A week before, the Speaker of the House, John Boehner, held a meeting with the GOP conference in the basement of the Capitol. He'd been speaking regularly with Obama about an immigration bill, and officials at the White House believed he was committed to passing legislation. Now, however, he was telling his members that he would bring the bill to a vote on the floor only if a majority of them supported it.

34.

Border Emergency

On Mother's Day weekend 2014, Obama's new secretary of Homeland Security, Jeh Johnson, was returning from California, where he and his wife were visiting their son, when a top official at Customs and Border Protection told him that the situation in South Texas was "out of control." Thousands of unaccompanied children from Central America were showing up at Border Patrol stations, confounding agents and overwhelming the department's resources. There was also a significant spike in the number of parents and children who were arriving together and seeking asylum.

Decades of Central American history were crashing down at the US border. Throughout the 1980s, '90s, and early aughts most immigrants stopped by the Border Patrol were Mexican men, traveling alone and crossing for work. In 2011, signs of an incipient shift began to appear. Agents were encountering more children arriving alone from El Salvador, Guatemala, and Honduras, in search of parents or family members already in the US. The US government developed a $175 million program to house and process them, but few officials in the upper reaches of the administration paid much attention. Everyone was focused on comprehensive immigration reform, which remained stuck in the House.

Johnson and his wife rerouted from Washington, DC, and landed in McAllen, Texas, where the first detention facility they visited was overrun with children. One girl, who couldn't have been older than ten, was sitting at a desk, in tears, waiting for an agent in a green uniform to take down her information. Almost all of the adults around were government personnel. Mylar blankets that looked like oversize sheets of tinfoil were scattered in pens enclosed by metal wiring. Johnson called Muñoz at the White House to deliver the news. "This thing is too big to downplay," he said.

Nearly 69,000 unaccompanied children arrived at the border between October 2013 and September 2014, up from some 39,000 the previous year. Another 68,000 families were seeking asylum, a 200 percent increase. By the summer, in South Texas alone, there were 33,000 children in government custody.

The government rules for how to treat immigrant children at the border were laid out in an obscure court settlement known as the Flores agreement, the result of a lawsuit involving two Salvadoran children who had arrived in California in 1985. According to the agreement, which was later codified into law, immigration authorities could not detain children in borderland facilities for longer than seventy-two hours. Instead, the government was supposed to house them in the "least-restrictive setting" possible. Over the years, a network of shelters was created for this purpose, run out of a branch of the Department of Health and Human Services called the Office of Refugee Resettlement. But the existing system could only accommodate between six thousand and eight thousand children, and the volume of new arrivals was creating a bottleneck at the border. By the end of May, the Obama administration was using emergency shelters to move children out of immigration detention and into the care of HHS. A naval base in Ventura County, California, was used to shelter six hundred children; an air force base in San Antonio provided twelve hundred more beds. Large white buses ferried children from the borderland holding cells to these other facilities.

Inside the White House, Muñoz was caught between overlapping humanitarian and political emergencies. The most immediate pressure was operational: transferring children from Customs and Border Protection to the Office of Refugee Resettlement. Lawyers needed clearance to get the Federal Emergency Management Agency to coordinate the logistics. But the Office of Refugee Resettlement was not a foster-care agency. Although it placed children with family members living in the US, there were no procedures for fully vetting them, such as making home visits, nor did the federal government track the children after their release. It was important that parents and relatives applying to sponsor the children know that the Department of Health and Human Services wasn't sharing their information with ICE, because many of them were undocumented.

If the administration appeared to lose control over the border, its entire immigration agenda would unravel. Republicans were already conflating the reform bill with the influx of new arrivals. The House majority leader, Eric Cantor, was one of the lead negotiators in a backroom effort to revive comprehensive reform in the House. But he was also facing a right-wing challenger in a June primary, so he was sending out campaign mailers accusing Obama and the Democrats of "pushing amnesty to give illegal aliens a free ride." Later that summer, three government buses carrying a group of women and children toward a government facility in Murrieta, California, were blocked by a crowd of angry protesters holding signs that read "Go home!" and chanting "USA! USA!" They'd been tipped off to the route by disgruntled members of the Border Patrol. After a brief standoff, the drivers were forced to turn around and take their passengers elsewhere.

At DHS headquarters, in Washington, there were war-room-style meetings each morning: deputies, career officials, and senior staff crowded around tables to generate ideas for triage. Those who couldn't attend in person were patched in by phone, and the secretary arranged a separate set of briefings with his top staff, frequently peeling off to visit the White House for emergency updates with Muñoz and officials at the National Security Council. The directive at DHS was to "send up" a list of all possible policies, from the harshest to the most humane; having the full range of options was supposed to allow the secretary to find a middle ground.

Thomas Homan, a top official at ICE, first broached the prospect of separating parents and children at the border by charging the adults with a misdemeanor for entering the country illegally. While they were being held on criminal charges, the government would temporarily take custody of their children. It would be painful, he said, but not fatal—a deterrent. This was immediately shot down as inhumane, as was another suggestion that involved ICE arresting parents when they came to claim their children from the Office of Refugee Resettlement. A few advisers, thinking toward longer-term approaches, proposed housing asylum seekers in Mexico with the aid of international relief organizations, rather than trying to detain them in the US. Others suggested mechanisms for handling refugee applications in Central America, to expedite processing and spare vulnerable children from making an overland journey rife with danger.

For all its mammoth budgets devoted to enforcement and detention, the government was not prepared for the kind of demographic shift that was taking place at the border. It wasn't just the mass arrival of unaccompanied children; nationwide, ICE had only ninety-five available beds where it could detain families for an extended period. This meant that DHS had essentially two options, neither of which the administration liked. One was simply to release the families after booking them and assigning them a date in immigration court. The other was to build more detention space. That was what Johnson chose. "We simply cannot have a situation where if you cross the border and are apprehended, you can count on being escorted to the nearest bus station," Jeh Johnson said. He decided to open two new facilities in South Texas while retooling a third, in Pennsylvania.

The spaces would hold some three thousand families: twenty-four hundred at the South Texas Family Residential Center, in Dilley, which would become the largest immigrant detention center in the country; five hundred more at a similar facility nearby, in Karnes City; and another hundred at an ICE complex in Berks County, Pennsylvania. The Texas facilities were to be run by private prison companies—the GEO Group and CoreCivic—which had been involved in immigration detention since the mid-1980s and were profiting from an ever-larger share of DHS contracts.

The view of family detention inside the Obama administration was characterized by an uneasy acceptance of its inevitability. It was impossible to detain all the families arriving at the border, but government officials believed that detaining a small fraction of them would send a message to Central Americans contemplating a similar trip. The facilities themselves would be set up less like prisons than like barracks. The families could move around the premises, and they'd sleep, a dozen to a room, in spaces with bunk beds, refrigerators, televisions, and telephones. There'd be access to regular medical attention, health screenings, and clothing. But confinement could last months: the government would deny them bond until a judge issued a final ruling on their asylum cases.

"I tried to keep it together," Cecilia Muñoz said later. "That summer was the hardest of my life." The humanitarian crisis at the border had blindsided her. When she traveled to South Texas with Jeh Johnson, the first child she met was seven. After being briefed, she learned that the average age of the minors in custody was twelve. There were babies and toddlers traveling with siblings or neighbors, but not their parents. A mother herself, Muñoz was making policy decisions on behalf of mothers who couldn't be with their own children to protect them. The burden of responsibility was overpowering.

The White House, meanwhile, was stuck in a holding pattern caused by Republican gamesmanship. That spring, the president had prepared a new set of executive actions to further regulate ICE activity in the interior of the country. The House Speaker, John Boehner, responded by threatening to kill the reform bill outright. Obama waited for signs of progress, but soon it was clear that there was no point in holding out. On June 10, Eric Cantor lost his primary by eleven points to an economics professor associated with the Tea Party who had assailed him for doing too little to stop illegal immigration. Earlier that day, Mario Díaz-Balart, a Florida Republican involved in House immigration talks, had told Boehner that 140 members—a decisive majority of Republicans—now supported a version of the bill. Díaz-Balart and his staff were celebrating at his apartment when they learned about Cantor. "We lost the whole thing," Díaz-Balart told a Democratic counterpart, according to *The New York Times*. "It's over." Cantor's defeat confirmed the vulnerability of any Republican who refused to toe the populist line. The bill would never come to a final vote.

In the early afternoon of June 30, 2014, Muñoz and Valerie Jarrett sat at a long, rectangular table in the Roosevelt Room of the White House to address a dozen influential immigration advocates from groups such as the Service Employees International Union, America's Voice, and the National Immigration Law Center. The purpose of the meeting was to discuss the White House's immigration agenda, and the crowd was restive. One notable absence summed up the general mood: that of Janet Murguía, who was now the president of the

National Council of La Raza, Muñoz's old organization. A few months before, she coined a phrase that was catching on as a progressive refrain. Obama, she'd said, was the "deporter in chief."

A door opened from the Oval Office, and in walked Obama and his vice president, Joe Biden. Speaking without notes for an hour, the president surprised everyone with his decisiveness. They expected bromides about patience, but instead Obama told them about a conversation he'd had a week before with Boehner, who had finally admitted that he would block a vote on the immigration bill until after the midterms. Boehner had admonished Obama that the votes would be there in the next Congress if the administration refrained from issuing additional executive actions on immigration. "Sorry about that," Obama told him. "I'm going to keep my promise." "He was a different guy," one of the advocates, the veteran organizer Frank Sharry, said later of the president. "He was unplugged." In the coming months, according to Obama, another set of executive actions and enforcement policies would protect some five million more people from immediate deportation.

When the conversation turned to the border, however, the tone grew tense. Gustavo Torres, representing the group CASA de Maryland, was concerned that the administration wanted to expand its powers to deport the newly arrived children from Central America. The president's response—in which he outlined plans for humanitarian assistance and funding requests for Congress to set up temporary housing and provisional immigration courts—led to a blunt intervention from Marielena Hincapié, of the National Immigration Law Center. She told the president he needed to consider the "human tragedy" that was unfolding in Central America.

Muñoz was silent as the conversation reached a familiar impasse. She had once sat on the board of trustees of Torres's organization; Frank Sharry had been at her wedding. For them to ask if the president understood the tragedy of the situation angered her. What were they actually proposing? The advocates around the table—her friends and former allies, all of them like-minded up to a point—surrounded her, but her seat was closest to the president. Despite his muted style, Obama's frustration was palpable. The US *had* to enforce the law, he said; it had to if it wanted people in Central America to think twice before sending their children north on their own.

At this point, Angelica Salas cut in. She was the executive director of the Coalition for Humane Immigrant Rights of Los Angeles, and a close friend of Muñoz. "Mr. President, when my family and I came to the country, I was four years old, and when we were caught crossing the border and were sent back, we didn't give up," she said. Salas, who was born in Mexico, had traveled to the border with her three-year-old sister and an aunt and uncle, who were fourteen and sixteen; Salas's parents were already living in California. "We kept trying until we made it," she said.

What she said next sounded barbed, but she meant it as a concession to the enormity of the president's responsibility, rather than as a reprimand. "I don't know how you can sleep at night," she said. Obama replied, "You know what? I don't really sleep at night, but let me tell you why. It's not just that I worry about these kids from El Salvador. I also worry about kids in Sudan, and in Yemen, and in other parts of the world. And here's my problem: we live in a world with nation states. I have borders. You may believe that it's inherently unfair that a child born in El Salvador has a completely different set of opportunities available and a completely different set of dangers than a child born in the US. And that's because it *is* unfair. I can't fix that for you."

35.

Memory Card

Juliana Ramírez grew up with a single memory of her father. He was sitting in the half-light of evening on the porch of their home, in a small town near San Miguel, El Salvador, while her mother cooked dinner in the kitchen. A man in a black mask emerged from the darkness. Juliana heard three gunshots, and saw her father fall off his chair, vomiting blood. It was 2005, and she was three years old; afterward, she wondered if the killing had really happened. The most tangible detail was the man in the mask, who came to seem more present in her life than her father ever was. Juliana would find her mother by the windows, pulling back a corner of the curtains to be sure that he had not returned. "It was like that man went on living with us," Juliana sometimes thought. One day, when she was older, her mother said that a gang called the Mara Salvatrucha had killed her father for refusing to pay a tax on a deli that he operated out of the house.

For five years after the killing, the family moved every six months, staying with relatives throughout El Salvador, trying to keep ahead of the gang. In 2011, after Juliana's mother, Ramona, testified against the killer, a member of MS-13 tried to stab her at a soccer game, where she was selling refreshments. She escaped and fled the country, leaving Juliana and her two younger sisters at an aunt's house, because she couldn't afford to bring them with her. She went to Brentwood, on Long Island, where she had relatives, and took a job cleaning houses. A few years later, she was returning home from work, when she got a call. "What I need is money," a male voice told her. "I know the people of the neighborhood. I know your family, your kids, your daughter." Several days later, one of Juliana's schoolmates, a sixteen-year-old boy who belonged to MS-13, kidnapped her from her aunt's house; for weeks, she was raped and beaten. She managed to call her mother one afternoon, and together they plotted her escape.

In June 2015, Juliana, who was now thirteen, and her two sisters set off in the back of a truck, covered by a nylon tarp, packed in with other migrants heading north. In a jungle along the border between Guatemala and Mexico, Juliana had an asthma attack and the smugglers almost abandoned her.

In Washington, officials at DHS and the White House were trying to find ways to dissuade migrants like Juliana from making the trip. At one meeting, Jeh Johnson consulted Michael Chertoff, a DHS head under George W. Bush, who reasserted the conventional wisdom. Immigration, he told Johnson, was "a market-sensitive phenomenon." The US government needed to limit the business of smugglers by disrupting the demand of migrants to reach the US. It already had a policy it called the Consequence Delivery System, an elaborate deterrence scheme designed to send strong messages back to the region: expedited removal of migrants at the border, the use of jails to detain recent arrivals, enforcement operations choreographed to generate press attention. Starting in the spring and summer of 2014, it added a regional counterprogramming campaign. If you turned on the radio in the Northern Triangle of Central America, you might hear songs with lyrics like these, from an ad that ran in El Salvador and Honduras: "Hanging on the railcars / Of this iron beast / Migrants go as cattle / To the slaughterhouse." There were TV spots as well, with dramatizations of migrants dying before they could reach the US.

Juliana, who didn't have a television, was focused on more immediate dangers. Six weeks after setting out, when she and her group were arrested in Texas by United States Border Patrol agents, she was relieved. The smugglers had told her what would happen now: it was time to hand herself over and experience the *hieleras*, the cold cells, called "refrigerators" by migrants, in borderland detention centers. It would be unpleasant but temporary. The other children around her had similar plans. They knew the names of towns and local landmarks where family members were waiting for them.

Juliana and her sisters eventually made it to Brentwood and moved in with their mother. The scale of everything was beyond her comprehension. She looked for small, tin-and-mud houses, like those from her hometown, but all she saw were giant suburban ones with geometric lawns. The strip malls, with their big-box stores and air-conditioned restaurants, were inexplicable monstrosities. She followed a simple adolescent maxim: avoid humiliation. She prepared for her first day of seventh grade by memorizing the sentence "I do not speak English." When she arrived at a two-story brick building with dozens of classrooms and long hallways lined with lockers and crammed with students, she had no idea where her classes were, or how to read her schedule. She recited the sentence she'd rehearsed to other kids, but they ignored her or responded unintelligibly. Juliana spotted a teacher who looked Hispanic and asked her for help. *"No hablo español,"* the teacher replied, and then walked away.

After a few months in school, two Salvadoran boys wearing oversize shirts, sagging pants, and light-blue bandannas sat down next to Juliana in her math class. They peppered her with questions in Spanish. Where was she from? Whom did she hang out with back home? Juliana had promised her mother that she wouldn't tell other students her full name so that word of her escape wouldn't reach El Salvador, and as the boys grilled her, she started to panic. When someone talked this way—with heavy slang and a confident tone of casual menace—it often meant that they were in a gang.

Her interrogators belonged to MS-13, the gang that Juliana had fled. She didn't know that MS-13 had started in the US, or that years before she was born, hundreds of West Coast gangsters had moved east to places like Washington, DC, the Maryland suburbs, and Long Island. "They're not supposed to be here," she kept telling herself.

◇—◇

The same year Juliana and her sisters fled El Salvador, some 40,000 unaccompanied children arrived at the border, along with 40,000 families. In 2016, there were 60,000 children and 78,000 families. Deportations generated a separate wave of people, flowing in the opposite direction. In 2015 and 2016, the US deported roughly 42,000 Salvadorans, 42,000 Hondurans, and

67,000 Guatemalans. With this many people in a state of perpetual flux—pushed toward the border, then pushed back again—the dividing line between the US and Central America only grew blurrier.

In San Salvador in 2016, Eddie Anzora had no illusions about living somewhere else. But it could sometimes seem like his universe constituted a third country entirely—not the United States, not El Salvador, but a blend of the two, in which the realities of both places were present in shifting proportions. After several years spent working at call centers, he had saved up enough money to start a family and had already met the woman who would become his wife. Her name was Mayra, a fiery, glamorous single mother from a town called Apopa, on the outskirts of the capital. It was a rough, gang-controlled area that Eddie could visit only with a local chaperone. The two of them had met at the Metrocentro mall, in downtown San Salvador, at a photo shoot he'd arranged for a fashion line he was trying to start. A year after they married, in 2012, they had a son named Christopher.

The long hours Eddie was spending at the call center were wearing on him. He had maxed out on all the raises and promotions that were available to employees. There was no outlet for his ambition. A perk of his current line of work, however, was that he could observe trends. He noticed that the demand for English speakers seemed to be outpacing the supply, so he decided to start his own language school, which he called English Cool. A handful of schools were springing up to meet the needs of call-center work. There was English-4CallCenters, Got English?, Direct English, and English Coach. "English is coming back in style," Anzora told anyone who would listen. "People want to speak it, because it means you can get work." Deportees ran and staffed most of the schools, whose pitch was like that of any other language school: study with a native speaker. "If you want to learn English, a deportee's a really good guy to learn from, because he actually dealt with people from Texas, from California," Eddie said.

English Cool occupied part of a run-down house, flanked by a cell phone repair shop and a garage. Eddie lived above the school with Mayra and their children. On the second floor were two classrooms, each with a whiteboard and a desktop computer linked to a TV. The bookshelves held copies of *The Screenwriter's Bible*, *Photoshop*, and *Run Your Music Business*, vestiges of his LA days.

Another room was filled with all the gear he had accumulated from his side hustles: recording equipment, promotional materials from concerts he'd organized, cameras he used while moonlighting as a wedding photographer, markups of websites he'd sketched as a sporadic graphic designer for hire. There was an unabashed Americanness to the setup. The house was a monument to a man on the make, teeming with plans and backup plans. Some of the other schools were fancier than English Cool and had more polished resources, such as language labs, computers, and break rooms. But none of them could match English Cool's atmosphere of ravenous possibility.

At ten a.m. one Monday in April, eight students arrived at English Cool for the intermediate-level class. Wearing blue jeans and a black English Cool T-shirt, Eddie met them at the door of the classroom. Most of the students were between eighteen and twenty-five, and one man was in his late thirties. Some had low-paying or part-time jobs; others were still in school. The cost of Eddie's course—thirty-six dollars a month—was designed to undercut the competition. (The average for the other schools was sixty dollars.) Still, only about half of the forty students could pay regularly. The rest were on generous installment plans.

"How were your weekends?" Eddie called out. "Pair off and tell your partner what you did." He darted around the classroom, making jokes and spurring on the more tentative students. For a speaking exercise, he posed a question to the group: "When was the last time you were robbed? And what did they take?"

Eddie had learned his teaching methods at English4CallCenters, where he had once worked part time while also taking shifts at a call center. The school, which was founded in 2014 by Rodrigo Galdamez, a twenty-seven-year-old Salvadoran, then had ten locations all over the country, plus two in Guatemala, and a thousand students each term. Galdamez had never been to the United States, so he hired a deportee from Texas, and together they prepared a teaching plan. They realized that the biggest impediment to Salvadorans who wished to work in call centers was attitudinal, not linguistic. The key to preparing them for conversations with demanding American callers was teaching them to be assured and solicitous. Direct English, a high-end competitor to English Cool, had a mock call center, with fifteen computers and headsets, so that students could practice taking phone calls. Its owner, who used to live in Southern

California, set up two big classrooms on the first floor, called the Staples Center and the World Trade Center.

At English Cool, Eddie gave his students a crash course in improvisational swagger. That morning, he led the class in a call-and-response reading of Yelp reviews. Eddie went first. "I tried the Oreo Rice Krispie, toffee cookie, and peanut butter gluten-free cookie," he said. He paused so that his students could repeat after him, as if they were reciting some madcap catechism. "I had my plus-one go back to get more on my behalf," they intoned. A student interrupted with a question: What was a Rice Krispie?

FOR A YEAR and a half, between 2012 and the start of 2014, El Salvador suddenly became safer. Gang killings across the country fell by more than 50 percent, and while the FMLN government of Mauricio Funes was generally credited with this development, the reasons behind it were a secret. In February 2012, a small team inside the country's Ministry of Public Security started clandestine negotiations with representatives of MS-13 and of 18th Street, which had splintered into two rival factions, the Sureños and the Revolucionarios. These talks took place in the bowels of the country's most infamous prison, a six-floor, cement-block building that held some four hundred inmates who weren't allowed to have any sort of physical contact with visitors and could leave their cells for only three hours each week. It was called Zacatecoluca, but better known as Zacatraz. If inmates had to leave the facility for a court hearing or a medical emergency, they were kept in isolation upon their return until they could defecate in front of prison guards to prove that they weren't smuggling anything back in. The most violent gang offenders were held in the lowest and darkest sector of the prison, Sector 6, reserved for "the Heroes," as they were known by the gangsters, where each cell had a single window, roughly ten centimeters wide.

The prime mover of the new strategy was a former general named David Munguía Payés, who fought against the guerrillas during the civil war and had recently been chosen to head the Security Ministry. When Funes named him, members of the FMLN were alarmed that an ex-military man, rather than a civilian, was taking control; choosing him, some of them said, smacked of "a decision that was made somewhere in the US capital." Munguía Payés had vowed to unleash soldiers on gang enclaves across the country. But as a military tactician, he also knew when a battle was unwinnable. Privately, he tapped an ex-guerrilla to start talks: in exchange for perks such as conjugal visits, the transfer of inmates out of Zacatraz, and a pause in military crackdowns in gang neighborhoods, the gangsters would stop killing one another and anyone else who got in their way.

The two political parties had made ad hoc agreements with the gangs before, almost always right before elections—to enforce higher turnout or to periodically blunt the death count—but these talks went further. A Catholic priest was involved, as was an observer from the Organization of American States, a regional oversight body. At the first meeting, nine members of MS-13 and ten from 18th Street gathered around a table for a meal of fried chicken from the fast-food chain Pollo Campero, delivered by the government's main negotiator. One of them was Duke, Eddie's old acquaintance. A gangster broke the silence by asking another to pass the ketchup. The leaders of the rival gangs eventually stood up to shake hands. Both had grown up in Los Angeles, and their first words to each other were in English. "Spanish," the negotiator reminded him. "Not everyone here speaks English."

MS-13 gang members in a prison cell in Chalatenango, El Salvador, September 17, 2018.

History was repeating itself with a different cast. The negotiators of the truce thought of it as a second coming of the Acuerdos de Paz, signed twenty years earlier between the guerrillas and the military. "We're talking about an army of seventy thousand men," one of them said, in reference to the gangs. "There's no army in the region that can combat them." Just like the old guerrillas, many of the gangsters agreed to hand over their weapons in public ceremonies; when they did, authorities found some of the M16s and a Claymore mine that the US government had given the Salvadoran military during the war.

The American embassy, for its part, was displeased by this turn of events. Officials at the State Department, which provided funding for Salvadoran prisons and law enforcement operations, considered the negotiations a capitulation and a security breach. Seven months later, the Treasury Department designated MS-13 a "transnational criminal organization" and began applying sanctions. It was the first time a street gang had received such a label. Anyone caught doing business with MS-13—including, in some cases, those working on community initiatives to coax gangsters away from violence—faced jail time.

The truce was even more controversial in El Salvador. The public was shell-shocked and enraged by the predations of the gangs. Years of Mano Dura–style policies had become the norm. Anything that smacked of vengeance was a reliable vote getter at election time. Funes refused to acknowledge the negotiations in public, leaving his negotiators out on a limb. In 2014, when his successor, Salvador Sánchez Cerén, a fellow FMLN man and the first ex-guerrilla to serve as president, assumed office, he dissolved the agreement and redoubled the old crackdown. "At no time is our government prepared to negotiate with these criminals," he declared. "We are going to hunt them down, capture them and put them on trial." When, as predicted, the homicides spiked, reaching new highs in 2015, the government served up the negotiators as scapegoats. In El Salvador, the attorney general was appointed by Congress rather than by the president; in the spring of 2016, he began arresting government officials who'd been involved in the truce, from the top negotiators down to the undercover policemen tasked with collecting some of the discarded weapons.

During breaks at English Cool, or at night over a pupusa and a Corona, while the rest of his family slept, Eddie watched *Vice* and BBC documentaries on YouTube about the operations of organized crime in Mexico and Colombia. What came to obsess him, because it defied straightforward or even financial logic, was the randomness of the carnage surrounding him in El Salvador. He had a cousin who was a cop, and he messaged him constantly, pumping him for stories and fact patterns. They traded theories about human psychology—How was it possible for a thirteen-year-old to kill a stranger for sport?—and turf-war politics. Between MS-13 and 18th Street, there were some sixty thousand gang-

A fruit vendor murdered on the streets of downtown San Salvador, El Salvador, March 15, 2017.

sters in El Salvador, roughly 1 percent of the overall population. They had a strong presence in 247 of the 262 municipalities and extorted 70 percent of the country's businesses. The Central Reserve Bank of El Salvador estimated that the country lost some $4 billion each year to extortion, yet the gangs themselves were nothing like other organized criminal groups. The US Treasury Department put MS-13 in the company of Mexican drug cartels and the Japanese Yakuza, multibillion-dollar operations. MS-13's annual revenue, by contrast, was $30 million; its members, on average, made about sixty-five dollars a month, which was half the minimum wage of a day laborer in the agricultural sector. The best explanation Eddie could come up with for the ferocity of the violence was that teenage gangsters were so drained of hope and vitality that prison wasn't appreciably worse than ordinary life on the streets.

Early one morning at the start of 2016, Eddie was leaving a graveyard shift at a call center called O'Currance, a compound of white buildings enclosed by a brown metal gate on a quiet street. It was a little after six, the sky still shrouded in predawn gray. He crossed the street at an angle to avoid an alley frequented by gangsters, and came upon a pupusa stand he often visited when working late. The seller, who knew him, immediately started preparing his order, offering him a cup of hot chocolate in a special mug that Eddie liked.

Killings were up across the city. By the end of 2015, there had been at least sixty-six hundred homicides in a population of around six million people, bringing the murder rate higher than it had been during much of the civil war. A few months later, the Supreme Court issued a decision categorizing the gangs as terrorist groups, which gave the police and the military license to be even more aggressive. In Washington, ICE had recently decided to mount a series of so-called Christmas raids to send a message, because the number of asylum seekers at the border was rising once again. The Salvadoran government responded by tweeting out legal advice to Salvadorans living in the US, reminding them of their Fourth Amendment protection against illegal search and seizure. The move was billed as a show of solidarity with the Salvadoran diaspora, but it masked a sense of desperation. Those who were arrested would, in effect, be sent back to a war zone.

Eddie scanned the street in both directions before taking a sip of his hot chocolate. The early morning was usually a safe time. For a moment, he allowed his mind to wander. When he brought the mug down from his mouth, two boys were standing in front of him. They were young and wild looking, with baggy clothes and tattoos on their arms and necks. "You better not run, we got this whole place controlled," one of them said. "You run, we'll kill you right now. But if you walk with us we're just going to check you out."

They moved toward an alleyway shaded by trees. "This is it," Eddie thought. His brain screamed to attention, and as he followed them, he started making contingency plans. Which one would he hit first? The tougher one who threatened him seemed like the leader of the two. But maybe if he dropped the other guy, he'd have more of a fighting chance. Was either one of them carrying a gun? It was hard to make out the bulge of a weapon under their clothes. "Lift up your shirt. Give me your cell phone," the second one said. Eddie knew what was happening now: they were checking him for gang tattoos and scrolling through his photos and contacts to see if they could find anything incriminating. This was an MS-13 neighborhood, so they were looking for evidence of "the numbers." They wanted to see his ID, but Eddie didn't carry it. His old address was still listed, and it corresponded to an 18th Street locale. When he went to work at O'Currance, in MS-13 territory, he made a point of leaving the ID at home.

The interrogation started to assume a good-cop, bad-cop rhythm. The leader cursed at him, calling him *cerote* and muttering threats, while the other stayed quiet. "They're very *professional*," Eddie noted. It was a strange thought to have at a moment like this, but he found himself appreciating their finesse; they'd clearly done this before. *"Bien* military," Eddie observed to himself. *"Estos cabrones* know what's up."

It started to rain, and Eddie reached for a backpack by his feet. He knew to move slowly, to show that he didn't have anything up his sleeve, but they both shouted at him to slow down. Eddie nodded and unzipped the bag. He pulled out a black sweatshirt and offered it to the leader, who was getting wet. "Put this on, it's raining," he said. His tone was sympathetic, but not submissive. The guys smirked, and Eddie felt the danger starting to lift.

"Look, because you did that, you're a cool guy, we're going to let you go this time," the leader said. They started to hand him his stuff back, everything but the cell phone. "But do you really need this?" the other asked, holding it up. Eddie knew he could speak more freely now. Every material possession had a cost. He could afford to replace the phone itself, but not what was on it. There were contacts he'd spent years building up, the names of friends and business associates and people he could call in a pinch. They were the armor around the life he'd rebuilt for himself in El Salvador, his new network of support so that he would no longer have to survive on his own. "Honestly, if you need the phone take it," he said. "But let me grab my memory card."

36.

Trump

On a blustery Thursday morning, in April 2016, Paul Pontieri was hurrying down the main street of Patchogue, New York, on his way to the parking lot behind a performance hall called the Emporium. Patchogue was too small to qualify as a town. It was a seaside village of some thirteen thousand residents on Long Island, about fifty miles east of New York City. Pontieri, a warm man in his sixties, with thinning gray hair and a broad, easy smile, was Patchogue's mayor. Everyone called him by his first name. Being mayor wasn't his only job; he also served as an interim principal at a high school nearby, in Amityville.

A police officer stood watch on the road outside the Emporium. As Pontieri approached, the officer stepped forward. "I'm sorry, where are you going?" he asked. Surprised, Pontieri replied, "I'm Paul," adding, as though reminding himself, "the mayor of Patchogue." The officer hadn't recognized him because he didn't usually work in the village. Patchogue didn't have its own police force, and on this day, county leaders had decided it would be necessary to bring in police from all the neighboring towns. Just seventy-two hours before New York's Republican primary, Donald Trump was delivering a speech at the invitation of the Suffolk County GOP.

In June 2015, Trump had announced his candidacy for president with a calculated broadside against immigrants: "rapists" were entering the country from Mexico. Nine months later, in the spring of 2016, he consolidated his lead in the Republican primary race. Yet his campaign—full of slapdash histrionics and racist taunts—still had the lurid feeling of a sideshow. Long Island Republicans, who idolized him as a native son, were abandoning the party establishment and backing Trump as the new front-runner. "He's being provocative. That's refreshing," said John Jay LaValle, the chair of the local party. All the presidential candidates had been invited to the event at the Emporium, but only Trump had accepted. LaValle saw his candidacy, which Trump had built around a radical opposition to immigration in all forms, as an opportunity for a national catharsis. He said, "We have an immigration problem. Trump's approach is, 'Let's take that to the next level.' They ask me, 'Is he going to build a wall?' And I say, 'Does it matter?'"

It mattered to Pontieri, because many of his constituents and friends were immigrants from Ecuador, El Salvador, and Mexico. The Emporium was a few hundred yards down the block from a memorial to Marcelo Lucero, a thirty-seven-year-old Ecuadorian who had been murdered by a group of teenagers in 2008. The boys had gone out one night looking for immigrants to attack—"beaner hopping," they called it, using a racist slur for Latinos—and came across Lucero returning home from work. Afterward, the federal government intervened to reform the Suffolk County Police Department, which had failed to address pervasive anti-Latino violence. In Patchogue, the local clergy organized prayer vigils, and Pontieri met regularly with Ecuadorians and Salvadorans to communicate his outrage and solidarity. At one point, he traveled to Lucero's hometown in Ecuador to apologize personally for what had happened. While he was there, he bumped into some of the Ecuadorians from Patchogue. They'd learned about his trip and had gone down to welcome him themselves. "You look out for us in Patchogue, we look out for you here," one of them told him.

In the hours before Trump's speech, a circus-like atmosphere engulfed the few blocks that made up downtown Patchogue. Vendors wheeled up carts festooned with souvenirs: foam fingers, bobbleheads, rubber masks with Trump's face. Out-of-towners streamed in, their cars decorated with Trump banners and gaudy paint jobs in red, white, and blue; signs dangled from windows saying

"TRUMP RULES," and T-shirts bore garish slogans such as "This Woman Is Voting for Trump." Tickets for entry started at $150; for a thousand more, attendees could pose for a photo with Trump.

The candidate took the stage around five o'clock, beginning his speech with canned bravado from the stump. A crowd of thirteen hundred people was packed into the Emporium, while a few hundred protesters gathered outside, near Lucero's memorial. Holding signs of their own—"Say No to Trump, Say No to Hate"—like shields, they were neighborhood sentries, defending their community from hostile outsiders. Pontieri paced nervously. Ever since Trump had started gaining in the polls, it seemed to him, personal relationships mattered less than they ever had; long-standing ties were fraying. When he interacted with white, middle-class residents of Patchogue, Pontieri had to make a new distinction, between traditional Republicans and Trump loyalists.

When Trump's script lagged, he brushed the pages off the lectern with an exaggerated thrust of his arm and started a call-and-response. "Who's going to build the wall?" "Mexico," the crowd roared in response. The Emporium shook. He continued, practically screaming, his voice raw but never cracking. A little over an hour later, it was over. The candidate strode off stage into a swarm of bodyguards, who hustled him toward a dark Suburban.

FOR ALL THE PASSION inspired by immigration, it had never before been the defining issue of a winning presidential campaign. In the 1992 Republican primary, the pundit Pat Buchanan challenged George H. W. Bush from the right by using immigration as the central plank of his campaign. He proposed a border wall and a five-year moratorium on legal immigration. Bush "is a globalist, and we are nationalists," he announced on December 10, 1991, in New Hampshire. "When we take America back, we are going to make America great again, because there is nothing wrong with putting America first." Buchanan didn't win a single state primary, but he demonstrated that a nativist platform could appeal to about a third of Republican voters.

Immigration tapped into a rich vein of American outrage, and Trump had an instinct for a galvanizing message. He had found a unified theory that could account for declining factory jobs, the anger and insecurity stoked by far-right media, an opioid epidemic, and the indignity of the country's first Black president. Immigrants could be blamed for everything. By the summer of 2016, a few weeks after he won the New York primary and went on to clinch the nomination, the question was whether Trump's rants on immigration were cynical theater or the inchoate policies of a potential president. To those who were watching the campaign carefully—the people on the outermost fringes of the Republican Party, the ideologues, the establishment castaways—his ideas looked serious, not because of Trump himself but rather because of those who surrounded him.

Most important was Alabama senator Jeff Sessions, the first Republican in the Senate to endorse Trump for president. Of the eleven candidates in the primary field, Sessions had been expected to back Texas senator Ted Cruz, who began the race as the far right's favorite. Sessions, Cruz said, was "the strongest opponent of amnesty in the United States Congress." On February 27, 2016, a week after Trump beat Cruz in the South Carolina primary, Sessions had an hour-long phone conversation with Steve Bannon, the head of Breitbart News. Sessions and Bannon had spent several years on the political margins, scheming to move the party's center of gravity to the far right. In 2013, Bannon had even tried to recruit Sessions to run for president on a nationalist platform built around immigration and trade, but Sessions declined. Two years later, on the morning of June 16, 2015, Bannon was at Breitbart's headquarters, in a Washington town house, watching Trump descend the escalator at Trump Tower to the soundtrack of Neil Young's "Rockin' in the Free World." Soon, he was advising Trump and recruiting other ideologues to the cause. "Trump is a great advocate for our ideas," Sessions admitted to Bannon on the phone in February. His only reservation was whether Trump could break through. "Do you think he can win?" he asked. Bannon replied, "One hundred percent. If he can stick to your message and personify this stuff, there's not a doubt in my mind." The next day, on a stadium stage in Madison, Alabama, Sessions stood next to Trump and said, "This isn't a campaign. This is a movement." With Sessions convinced, others followed. "Sessions was Trump's Good Housekeeping seal of approval," said Mark Krikorian, the head of the influential anti-immigration think tank Center for Immigration Studies.

Sessions was a short, mousy man in his early seventies with an impish smile and a thick Southern drawl. He had spent the entirety of his political career as a lightning rod and a punch line. In 1986, while he was serving as a US attorney in Alabama, Reagan nominated him to be a judge, but allegations of racism blocked his confirmation. At the time, Sessions was the first nominee for a federal district judgeship not to be confirmed in more than thirty years. This was an embarrassing setback, but it also made him an early martyr for white identity politics. He claimed to stand for a "humble and honest populism." Ten years later, he was elected to the US Senate, where his career was defined by his rabid opposition to immigration. In 2007, he attacked George W. Bush for proposing comprehensive immigration reform, and in 2013 he assailed Obama for the same thing. Sessions may have lacked the clout to pass any bills, but he generated enough heat to scuttle them.

In 2015, after the Republicans took control of the Senate, Sessions rebutted the consensus inside the Republican establishment that Mitt Romney had lost the 2012 presidential election because he'd moved too far to the right. In a memo titled "Immigration Handbook for the New Republican Majority," Sessions argued that the GOP had lost the election because it hadn't been aggressive enough. "The last four decades have witnessed the following," he wrote. "A period of record, uncontrolled immigration to the United States; a dramatic rise in the number of persons receiving welfare; and a steep erosion in middle class wages." He went on, "The largest untapped constituency in American politics are the 300 million American citizens who have been completely left out of the immigration debate. Speak to that constituency—with clarity and compassion—and change the issue forever."

Sessions had espoused these views since entering public office, but now someone else was refreshing and bolstering his message. His coauthor was a little-known thirty-year-old speechwriter from Santa Monica, named Stephen Miller. Bald, with a sharp, narrow face, Miller was richer, slicker, and edgier than the senator he served. His parents were Jewish Democrats who had drifted to the right. In the early 1990s, the real estate firm run by Miller's father had faltered, and the family moved from a five-bedroom house to a smaller one near Pico, south of Interstate 10 in California. Miller "was just angry all the time," a high school classmate later told his biographer, Jean Guerrero. "He put on this real victimization attitude." He was a strident conservative by the time he was a teenager, and he defined himself in opposition to the student body at the liberal school he attended. The terrorist attacks of 9/11 took place when he was a junior, further cementing his persona. "Anti-Americanism had spread all over the school like a rash," he wrote in an online essay in 2003. "Osama Bin Laden would feel very welcome at Santa Monica High School." At Duke University, where he studied political science and wrote a column for the student newspaper, he became a fixture on conservative television and radio programs. He opposed left-wing bias in the classroom, invited controversial speakers to campus, and organized "Islamo-Fascism Awareness Week." "America without her culture is like a body without a soul," he wrote in one column. "Yet many of today's youth see America as nothing but a meeting point for the cultures of other nations."

Miller and Sessions may have shared some core convictions, but they approached immigration from different perspectives. During the 1990s and early aughts, immigration had quadrupled in Alabama, and Sessions grew alarmed at the state's increasingly foreign workforce. Miller came to immigration politics through post-9/11 xenophobia. His concerns tended to be more inflammatory, calculated not only to punish immigrants but also to antagonize their liberal defenders. He questioned the ability of Latin Americans to learn English and declared Islam incompatible with American norms. Before he worked for Sessions, Miller had taken a job as press secretary for Michele Bachmann, the Republican representative from Minnesota, who had gained national attention after an undocumented immigrant near her district crashed her car into a school bus, killing four children. Encouraged by Miller, she went on Fox News, describing the tragedy as an example of "anarchy versus the rule of law."

Impressed by Miller's skill at fanning controversy, Sessions hired him in 2009, introducing him to NumbersUSA and the Center for Immigration Studies, think tanks that produced data-laden reports on the societal costs of immigration. Soon, Miller was attending weekly meetings at the Heritage Foundation, the conservative policy institute, with a small group of congressional staff. The attendees came from some of Congress's most conservative offices, but Miller stood out. He was brash, bombastic, and undeniably smart. He spouted extreme views with the practiced fluency of a college debater. Among the other Republican staffers, Miller became known for his mass emails about immigration, full of links to articles from fringe websites such as Breitbart and VDARE, which often published white supremacists. Most of the recipients would delete the emails as soon as they saw Miller's name.

It was a Hill fashion to mock Miller behind his back while avoiding any confrontation with him. Other senators may have had more influence and an air of bipartisan respectability, but Miller and Sessions managed to dominate the immigration debate inside the Republican Party. In 2013 and 2014, they sank the comprehensive reform bill by rendering it too politically toxic for many Republicans to touch. They made a point of attacking the conservative provisions that other members of the caucus were adding to the bill to bolster its support inside the party. It was zero-sum combat for Miller, but also an education. He "got a master's degree in immigration policy during that process," a Republican aide who worked with him at the time later said. "Before that, he didn't have any policy experience at all. It was all communications. In 2013, he learned where all the bodies were buried." Miller studied decades of immigration regulations, rules, and discretionary judgments, which were designed to guide and temper enforcement after the passage of IIRIRA. He fixated on the many loopholes in immigration laws, especially a widespread practice known as "catch and release," which allowed large numbers of migrants to remain in the US while they waited for their cases to be heard by immigration judges. "Miller's response was, 'The laws need to change,'" another aide said. "He was unimpressed by the promises of more Border Patrol agents, or a trillion dollars for a virtual wall. People were taking advantage of laws, not just of a porous border."

In the winter of 2016, a few weeks before Sessions endorsed Trump, Miller switched jobs and joined the campaign. The rallies, with their ecstatic crowds, emboldened him. He often served as a warm-up act for Trump. Pacing the stage with a relaxed smile, he resembled an insult comic, leading chants of "Build the wall." Flashing a peace sign, he'd make way for Trump, who would recite a list of crimes committed by undocumented immigrants. Then, growing somber, Trump would invite the parents of a victim onstage to offer his condolences.

On August 22, 2016, at a rally in Phoenix, Trump delivered a policy speech on immigration, written by Miller. Seventy-seven minutes long, it was raucous and aggressive, full of racist fearmongering, but it also contained a detailed blueprint. "Our immigration system is worse than anyone realizes," Trump began. "Countless Americans who have died in recent years would be alive today if not for the open border policies of this administration." A ten-point list of desired policies followed, including an "end to catch and release," "zero tolerance for criminal aliens," penalties for sanctuary cities, a vow to reverse Obama's executive orders, and a "big-picture" vision for reforming the immigration system "to serve the best interests of America and its workers." Miller told *The Washington Post* that it was "as though everything that I felt at the deepest levels of my heart were now being expressed by a candidate for our nation's highest office."

AFTER TRUMP WON, SESSIONS and Miller got the jobs they wanted: attorney general for Sessions and a role as senior adviser at the White House, with sway over the Domestic Policy Council, for Miller. No one was surprised by Sessions's pick. It had been the fantasy of his long and undistinguished legal career. "I'm just astounded that President Trump made the miraculous intervention, and I'm attorney general of the United States," he said later. Miller had chosen carefully, having spent the entirety of the transition trying to figure out which position in the president's immediate orbit had the most influence over immigration. At the White House, Miller would have close access to Trump, while at the same time enjoying insulation from congressional scrutiny. He wanted to issue orders, not implement them, and his White House credential protected him from having to testify before Congress, a privilege that cabinet secretaries lacked.

Because Cecilia Muñoz had headed the Domestic Policy Council during the Obama years, she was required to brief her successors after the election. Holding out hope that the incoming administration might become more temperate now that the campaign was over, she asked Miller how she could help orient him in the new position. "How do you maneuver so that you're making the decisions and not the NSC?" he replied, adding, "How do you elbow them out of the way so that you are controlling the decision making?"

Immigration restrictionists had had a foothold in Congress for decades, but they hadn't had access to the White House in a century. Miller's approach struck even the ideologues as idiosyncratic—and risky. In his view, the more controversial the administration's immigration policies were, the more easily it could divide and conquer the electorate. He had scared Republican House leaders in 2013 by caricaturing Democrats and moderate Republicans as advocates for "open borders"; now he aimed to send the same message from the White House.

The president's immigration advisory group, which had been formed during the transition, was considering an order to block travelers from several Muslim-majority countries from entering the US. It would also temporarily freeze the processing of all refugees into the country, bar all Syrians, and slash the number of refugees that the government would eventually allow into the US. The group had been preparing for legal challenges when Miller intervened. To him, strategic due diligence was a concession of weakness. "Miller has two impulses that he's warring with," a senior Republican aide said. "One is to be the bomb-thrower he always was. The other is to try to secure victories for the President." In the days leading up to Trump's inauguration, Miller and a close associate named Gene Hamilton, a former Sessions staffer in his midthirties, drafted an executive order called "Protecting the Nation from Foreign Terrorist Entry into the United States"—the travel ban.

When Trump signed the ban soon afterward, none of the top officials at the Department of Homeland Security had been notified in advance, even though they were responsible for enforcing it. Travelers with valid visas were suddenly trapped at American airports, unable to enter the country; refugees who, after years of waiting, had been extensively vetted and approved for entry were turned back. Thousands of protesters and civil rights attorneys began congregating at airports across the country, and Republican senators Lindsey Graham and John McCain, arguably the party's most respected voices on immigration, issued a statement saying, "We should not turn our backs on those refugees who . . . pose no demonstrable threat to our nation, and who have suffered unspeakable horrors."

The next day, the president's senior staff assembled in the Situation Room: John Kelly, the head of DHS; Tom Bossert, the president's Homeland Security adviser; and officials from the State Department. Miller launched into a diatribe. "This is the new world order," he told the attendees. "You need to get on board." The ban was immediately challenged in federal court; it took eighteen months, and three versions of the order, before it passed legal muster, just as the president's advisory group had first warned. But instead of censuring Miller, Trump blamed the courts and lawyers at the Justice Department, including Sessions, for "watering down" the order.

Miller wasn't so much channeling Trump as overtaking him. Inside the White House, he was known as a "walking encyclopedia" on immigration, and the president's political advisers, who acknowledged that campaigning on the issue had been the key to Trump's victory in 2016, deferred to him as an expert. Those with reservations—like Rex Tillerson, the secretary of state, and H. R. McMaster, the national security adviser—had other responsibilities, and were frequently distracted. Miller, whose portfolio was devoted to a single issue, could outmaneuver them if he used the right interagency channels. He sent email sparingly and avoided calling officials directly to issue orders, relaying his messages through intermediaries. Other times, he'd weigh in directly to make a point, then withdraw, relying on surrogates to finish the job.

ON JUNE 5, 2017, officials from several federal departments assembled at the White House to begin the annual process of determining the next year's so-called refugee cap. Since the Refugee Act of 1980, the president was required to have his top policy advisers decide how many refugees the country would accept in the following fiscal year. During the Obama administration, the average was 76,000, and for 2017, Obama increased it to 110,000, for Syrians who were fleeing the ongoing civil war. The cap was not a hard-and-fast requirement but a carefully formulated goal that followed from months of meetings, position papers, and constant recalibrations. Agency experts evaluated the government's capacity for security vetting and analyzed the resources of the country's nine refugee resettlement organizations; they calculated the overall costs to the government and made detailed projections for how, through future taxes and employment, newly arrived refugees would grow the economy. Getting the assessment right was also seen as a foreign policy imperative, because it communicated an American commitment to humanitarianism, which, in turn, influenced how many refugees other international allies would accept. US generals were unfailing supporters of the program, not least because they saw it as a way of building trust among allies in and around international war zones.

In attendance that day were career officials from the State Department, the National Security Council, the Department of Homeland Security, and a White House policy group called the Homeland Security Council. But when the meeting began, Miller stepped forward. "We know how this used to go in the past," he said. "But we also know that the president views this as a homeland security issue."

Records from that meeting were never circulated. Other stakeholder agencies—such as the Joint Chiefs of Staff, the Defense Department, the US Mission to the United Nations, and the Office of Management and Budget—were excluded from subsequent conversations. At another session, in August, someone from the NSC asked why the administration was excluding representatives from the military, the National Counterterrorism Center, and the FBI, all of whom were usually active participants. One of Miller's surrogates replied, "What the hell does DOD have to say about this?"

Meanwhile, the Domestic Policy Council, which had never played a direct role in the policy, was intercepting documents generated by issue experts across the bureaucracy and editing them beyond recognition. Statistics were cherry-picked or replaced outright with figures from reports by the Center for Immigration Studies. One such report maintained that refugees were thirty times more likely than other members of the public to commit acts of terrorism, but this was a pure fabrication. The interagency process had been designed over decades to generate a series of dispassionate analyses outlining the operational costs, needs, and potential outcomes of refugee resettlement. This time, a routine cost-benefit calculation performed by officials at the Department of Health and Human Services was truncated at Miller's behest. All that was stated were the "costs" of resettling refugees, but none of the considerable economic benefits. "The president believes refugees cost more, and the results of this study shouldn't embarrass the president," Miller told them.

By the fall, when the administration presented its final number to Congress, the refugee cap was forty-five thousand, the lowest in the history of the program and below the explicit recommendations made by the State Department, the military, and the vice president's office. Yet the number itself mattered less than the warped new process that had generated it. By the end of Trump's term in office, the cap would drop several more times, to fifteen thousand refugees—so low that refugee resettlement agencies had to lay off much of their staff. Miller was perfecting a strategy that would define his time in government. The key wasn't just to rely on brash edicts and pronouncements from on high; it was to learn how to manipulate the federal bureaucracy, giving policies a veneer of institutional validity and thus foiling subsequent efforts to undo his handiwork.

Because Trump could rarely comprehend the full substance of his own administration's agenda on immigration, Miller could define what victory looked like. One of the president's favorite routines was to play the good cop to Miller's bad cop. He'd smile and say, "Well, that sounds OK to me, but, Stephen, I know you'd never go for it." Meanwhile, Miller invoked the president constantly, especially when he encountered resistance from other officials. "Stephen, what you're trying to do is not possible," he'd be told. "It *is* possible," he replied. "I spoke to the president an hour ago, and he said it had to be done."

For the first seven months of his presidency, Trump vacillated on canceling DACA, the highly popular program that protected from deportation some seven hundred thousand people who had come to the US as undocumented children. Obama had instituted DACA in June 2012, through an executive action, and Trump had campaigned against it, then reversed himself, in a rare acknowledgment of how extreme it would look to target such a sympathetic population. "We are going to deal with DACA with heart," he said, after taking office. "To me, it's one of the most difficult subjects I have, because you have these incredible kids." Later, he added, "We love Dreamers." Miller, however, had always been hostile to the policy. In an email to an editor at Breitbart, he said that expanding the "foreign-born share" of the US workforce was an instance of immigration being used "to replace existing demographics."

In September 2017, under pressure from Miller and other White House advisers, Trump agreed to cancel DACA, setting a six-month deadline for Congress to find a legislative solution. He left the announcement to Sessions, who delivered it on the Tuesday morning after Labor Day. At the press conference, Sessions called Dreamers by a different name. They were, he said, "a group of illegal aliens" who were taking jobs away from citizens, contributing to "lawlessness," and threatening the country's "unsurpassed legal heritage."

37.
Killing Fields

In September 2016, two American teenagers, named Nisa Mickens and Kayla Cuevas, ages fifteen and sixteen, were found dead in the woods of Brentwood, New York, killed with machetes and baseball bats, their bodies mutilated beyond recognition. Thirteen members of MS-13, seven of whom had come to the US as unaccompanied minors, were charged in their murders. Donald Trump learned about the crime as the president-elect. His campaign had turned on the specter of immigrant crime, and now, going into his first term, he had identified public enemy number one.

From 2016 to May 2017, authorities in Suffolk County attributed seventeen killings to MS-13. The county's police department identified at least eighty-nine gang members who were undocumented immigrants; thirty-nine had been placed with family on Long Island by the federal government. These numbers were a minuscule portion of the local immigrant population, which was statistically far more law-abiding than American citizens. There were half a million immigrants on Long Island, and about sixty thousand Salvadorans in Suffolk County. The most expansive estimates made by the Suffolk County Police Department put the gang's membership at around four hundred people. Gruesome gang killings magnified a sense of alarm that did not match the actual threat.

Crime was down overall and ebbing since the 1990s. "This sort of thing is about a feeling," Steve Bellone, the county executive, admitted at the time. "You don't feel that crime is down. Acts like these murders aren't supposed to happen in the suburbs." His predecessor, Steve Levy, a lawyer with a penchant for populist theatrics, had weaponized immigration in the early aughts, as Central Americans became an unmissable presence among the dense suburbs, vegetable farms, vineyards, and valuable beachfront real estate that comprised the county. When Trump visited Patchogue, his audience was primed. Suffolk County was one of the largest suburban areas in the United States to flip from solidly blue, in 2012, to red, four years later. Obama had won it by four percentage points, Trump by seven.

In April 2017, the president was still holding rallies as though the campaign had never ended. At one of them, assembled in support of the National Rifle Association, he asked the crowd, "You know about MS-13? Get them the hell out of here, right? Get them out!" Never had an American president spent so much time talking about an obscure Latino street gang. Trump mentioned it constantly—in State of the Union addresses, on television, during congressional debates. Each time, he recited a litany of the gang's most horrific acts, eclipsing all other policy discussions. Democrats floundered, and moderate Republicans saw a talking point with no political downside. One pollster in New Jersey, who was advising a Republican candidate for governor, took the view that New Jerseyans "don't have a problem with immigration," but they did "have a problem with illegal immigration, and with violent criminals." In Virginia, a party insider named Ed Gillespie—widely regarded as an establishment bulwark against Trumpism—started running attack ads with footage of tattooed gangsters in a Salvadoran prison. MS-13's motto blazed across the screen like opening credits: Kill, Rape, Control.

In July, Trump visited Long Island to deliver a rip-roaring speech in Brentwood. He addressed a sympathetic crowd handpicked for the occasion: local officials, Republican legislators, and a sea of police officers dressed in dark blue uniforms. The venue was a local community college auditorium. The lighting was dim and soft, giving the scene a hazy air. MS-13, Trump said, had "transformed peaceful parks and beautiful, quiet neighborhoods into bloodstained killing fields. They're animals." Waving his arms and shambling around the stage for effect, he suggested that when the police arrested local gangsters, they should rough up "these thugs" as they threw them "into the back of a paddy wagon."

A large contingent of men in blue erupted in laughter, with one conspicuous exception. He was Timothy Sini, a husky, clean-cut lawyer with dark hair, a canny demeanor, and a light Long Island accent. He was the thirty-six-year-old commissioner of the Suffolk County Police Department. A few weeks earlier, Jeff Sessions had come to Central Islip to give a speech about MS-13 and immigration at a federal courthouse. Sini had been there and wasn't pleased. It was his job to keep the peace after the federal officials left town, trailing political talking points in their wake. A former assistant US attorney, Sini had led the department since the fall of 2015, after a prominent sergeant on the force had been arrested for stealing cash from Latino drivers during traffic stops. Sini was a pragmatist. Given the police's wretched reputation in the Latino community, he spoke publicly about the need to rebuild trust, especially if he wanted to root out local gangsters. Most of the victims of MS-13 on Long Island were immigrants themselves, and many had come to the US recently as unaccompanied children. The gangsters and their victims lived together in the same towns, went to the same schools, and vied for the same jobs. Their lives were thoroughly enmeshed. Without cooperation from witnesses (sharing tips, lodging complaints, asking for help), the police were adrift. Trump was complicating Sini's plans to make inroads. "We have to compete now with concerns and anxieties created by other government agencies," Sini thought. "We have to compete with that noise."

THE NOISE WAS ITSELF part of the Trump agenda, and its loudest exponents were members of ICE and Border Patrol. The new head of ICE since January 2017, Thomas Homan, was an agency veteran who'd served under six presidents. Bald and broad-shouldered, with a ruddy face and bulbous nose, he was a lawman's lawman, bullish and gruff. When he was addressing members of the rank and file, he could be gregarious and charming. They respected him for having climbed the hierarchy from its lowest rungs. In the 1980s, Homan began his career as a local cop in upstate New York, policing the US-Canada border; later, he took a job in Border Patrol. After stints in Southern California and Arizona, he moved into the INS, which eventually became ICE. Agency officers had a job to do, he would say, and they would do it without reservation until members of Congress changed the laws.

In 2014, as it was becoming clear that Republicans would oppose comprehensive immigration reform, DHS had overhauled ICE's enforcement priorities, delivering the more rigorous protections that Cecilia Muñoz had wanted. The population of undocumented immigrants prioritized for arrest narrowed further, to some 1.4 million people out of a total of eleven million. (The administration also suspended the Secure Communities program.) There were effectively two Obama presidencies when it came to ICE enforcement: the first from 2009 to 2014, and the second during his final two years in office. Arrests made in the interior of the country dropped substantially, from 300,000 in 2009 to 140,000 in 2016. Homan, who was the head of the agency's Enforcement and Removal Operations division, resented Obama for interfering. By the time Trump took office, Homan was due to retire and had already secured a job in the private sector, at PricewaterhouseCoopers, the international consultancy. One Friday in late January 2017, he was at his going-away party at ICE headquarters when he received a phone call from John Kelly, Trump's first DHS secretary, asking him to stay, with a promotion.

While Homan was unpacking the boxes in his new office at agency headquarters the following Monday, tens of thousands of immigrants across the country were packing their bags, making contingency plans, and even preparing actual escapes. In Queens, a twenty-two-year-old DACA recipient and college senior named Antonio Alarcón returned from school one night to the home he shared with his aunt and uncle to find that they had placed a pile of boxes and suitcases full of their belongings by the door. "We want to be prepared," they told him. Later that winter, reports of an ICE raid in Las Cruces, New Mexico, kept families from going outside. Attendance at the county's public schools dropped by 60 percent. Principals sent social workers to make home visits.

On an afternoon in February, one of them, Julie Kirkes, arrived at a flat-roofed stucco house on the outskirts of town, with a small front window partially visible from the road. As she got closer, she saw that it was covered by a wrinkled white sheet. The address belonged to the family of an elementary school student with a good attendance record who hadn't shown up for more than a week. A middle-aged woman answered the door, and reluctantly led her inside. The house was cavernous and dark. A large blanket was hanging from the ceiling of the hallway, to block the view of a warren of rooms behind it. It took the woman a few minutes to become convinced that Kirkes was there to help. Only then did she call out to the rest of the family. They'd been hiding in the hallway, behind the blanket. "You can come out now," she shouted, and three children, their father, and their grandfather appeared. Other houses Kirkes visited had been abandoned altogether.

"We will now enforce the laws on the books, which we haven't been allowed to do," Homan said in the summer of 2017. Days after becoming president, Trump had rescinded the priorities memos Homan had begrudgingly enforced under the previous administration. In this new era, Homan's primary function was to make combative appearances before Congress and on cable news, under sharp questioning from Democrats and prime-time hosts. The more insistent the opposition, the brasher Homan became. The president bragged that his ICE head looked "very nasty" and "very mean." "No population is off the table," Homan told members of the House in June. "If you're in this country illegally and you committed a crime by being in this country, you should be uncomfortable, you should look over your shoulder. You need to be worried."

Every time federal officials came to Suffolk County to give speeches about MS-13, the undocumented community on Long Island took to their phones. They sent text messages and posted to private Facebook groups, describing the latest sightings of policemen, state cops, and ICE officers, an index of the roads and intersections to avoid. All the law enforcement personnel turned out in full force during the high-profile political visits, and because of all the national attention on MS-13 murders, the state's Democratic governor, Andrew Cuomo, had also sent more patrols to the county. Anyone pulled over for a traffic infraction would have to present a driver's license, which undocumented immigrants weren't allowed to have. Historically, Latinos made up 20 percent of the Long Island population, but almost 50 percent of the cases in traffic court. There was nothing—no law, agency-wide practice, or legal protection of any kind—to stop a driver from being handed over to ICE for deportation.

Juan Gómez had been a policeman in El Salvador, but in 2007, when he had moved to Brentwood as an undocumented immigrant, he took a job in landscaping. He was in his early forties, strapping and chatty, and lived with his wife, Silvia, and their two daughters in a small, wood-framed house on a quiet suburban street. He only spoke in Spanish, with brisk, rapid-fire diction. But when he mentioned MS-13, he did so in English. To his mind, the gang's American incarnation had created a specific dilemma, in which ordinary people were trapped between the gangsters and the authorities who were supposed to be pursuing them.

In March 2016, Gómez's fifteen-year-old daughter disappeared for three days with a teenage boy. When he called the police, they told him that she had probably just run off with a boyfriend. He and Silvia were circling the neighborhood in their car when they spotted her, in tattered clothes, staggering around at a major intersection. Clearly drugged, she had been dumped on the street. The experience made Gómez paranoid and suspicious of his own neighbors. "If you meet someone who just arrived here, especially a kid who came to Long Island alone, avoid him," he told his family. "There's a 50 percent chance he's in the gang."

Gómez and his wife began keeping detailed logs of worrisome encounters or observations, such as an unfamiliar car parked on their block or a hostile run-in with aggressive teenagers at a gas station. They supplemented their records with photographs and videos. These weren't materials they planned on sharing with the police. There was no point; the officers were mostly indifferent to the everyday indicators of mounting danger. The only group Juan and Silvia trusted was called Make the Road New York, an organization based in Manhattan, Queens, Brooklyn, and Long Island that provided support to local immigrants. At least once a week, Juan and Silvia visited the group's offices in Brentwood to share their concerns and to get legal advice. The lead organizer in Suffolk County, Walter Barrientos, a thirty-three-year-old from Guatemala, had grown up in nearby Amityville, in a mixed-status family with some relatives who were documented but others who were not. He was more receptive than any police officer, and infinitely more comprehending. His own view, he told them, was that predictable spikes in gang violence usually followed a pattern—one of them being that girls disappeared. The police often wrote off these disappearances as teenage romance, but in Barrientos's experience the incidents were more often precursors to something worse. He told them, "Not long after someone disappears, even if they eventually return, people turn up dead."

In December 2016, Gómez's daughter disappeared again. Late one morning, a boy led her from school to a waiting cab. A few hours later, when she hadn't returned home, The Gómezes went to the school, where a security guard demanded to see identification. "I have a daughter in this school," Gómez protested. They presented identification cards from Make the Road, but the guard declared them invalid; eventually, Silvia persuaded him to accept a Salvadoran ID card. They met with a school administrator who was reluctant to share any information. When the couple returned home, their daughter was there, unharmed but too scared to say anything about what had happened.

Gómez eventually persuaded her to tell him where the boy had taken her. When he arrived at the small, ramshackle house on the outskirts of town, a woman answered the door and insisted that the boy he was looking for didn't live there. Gómez went home and called the police, who promised to investigate. The family never heard from them again. Several months later, watching the local news, Gómez recognized the house he had visited. Two brothers who belonged to MS-13 lived there; they had just been arrested for the murders of Nisa Mickens and Kayla Cuevas. The police found guns, knives, and drugs on the property. "I thank God that my daughter's OK, but no one else," Gómez said.

After that, Gómez's family traveled around Brentwood in his truck, careful not to stray far from one another. The parents and the children were in a precarious situation, but in different ways—the daughters because of the gang, and Juan and Silvia because they were undocumented. One afternoon, despite his precautions, Gómez was stopped for a traffic infraction and ticketed for driving without a license. In El Salvador, he would have been forfeiting a steady chunk of his paychecks to gangsters demanding *renta*. On Long Island, the money went to the Department of Motor Vehicles, by way of the local police. Over the course of 2017, Gómez spent about a thousand dollars on tickets. He would pay them on days when it was raining, so that he didn't miss landscaping work.

◇—◇

Seven months after arrests were made in the killing of Nisa Mickens and Kayla Cuevas, a sign on a telephone pole outside Brentwood High School still offered a fifteen-thousand-dollar reward for information about their murder. The sign greeted students as they entered the two separate schools that made up Brentwood High. In front was Ross Center, and behind it was Sonderling Center. Students who lived in historically poorer areas of Brentwood, the south and the east, went to Ross; those from the north and the west, which were once slightly better off, attended Sonderling. The entrance hall of Sonderling was gleaming, with a fountain and plants along the walls. At Ross, the linoleum floors were badly scuffed and the hallways dimly lit. The two buildings were linked by a long hallway that students traversed only reluctantly.

Elena Sandoval, a sixteen-year-old who was born on Long Island to Salvadoran parents with temporary protected status, went to Ross. The school hosted Brentwood's main Spanish-language ESL program, and although Sandoval spoke fluent English, she had been in ESL since kindergarten. When students enrolled, the school district would send a form to their families asking them if English or Spanish was the predominant language spoken at home. If it was Spanish, the student was supposed to be interviewed and tested before being placed in an academic program. Sandoval had been overlooked, automatically placed on the Spanish track.

Sandoval was thin and reserved, with a nervous laugh and a faint voice. The name of her ex-boyfriend, Carlos, was tattooed in cursive on her left wrist. He was in prison for the murders of Mickens and Cuevas, but the fact that he was locked away compounded her fears. Ever since the police picked him up, Sandoval had worried that his friends in the gang would come looking for her. MS-13 members were still angry that she'd broken up with him. But she was also scared of his old rivals: to members of the Bloods, who lived on her street, she was guilty of having once associated with MS-13.

A year earlier, they had met at a laundromat—Carlos had come over and started flirting. The intensity of his attention charmed her. Several weeks later, when he revealed that he was in a gang, she thought he was joking. "You're in MS, sure, and I'm president," she had responded. Carlos had arrived from El Salvador in 2015, as an unaccompanied minor. His brother, who lived in Brentwood, belonged to MS-13, and had initiated him into the gang. "I'm a gang member. You can't leave me," he told Sandoval. He often swore at her, and occasionally hit her. When she spoke to other men, even relatives or teachers, he became violently jealous.

Carlos had dropped out of high school and worked as a landscaper, but his friends in MS-13 attended Ross, and they trailed Sandoval around school. The ESL classrooms were on a corridor that everyone called the "Papi and Mami hallway"—the students were mostly from El Salvador and spoke only Spanish. In one corner of the hallway, about twenty boys would gather to "rep" the gang. One of Carlos's friends, who was later suspended for threatening to kill a teacher, took photographs of Sandoval to show Carlos where she went between classes. Carlos had her schedule and called her throughout the day with questions about interactions that his friends had observed.

Sandoval and her parents filed a report with the police, accusing Carlos of harassment. When he found out, he began messaging her several times a day, saying that he was going to kill her parents. He sent her photographs of himself posing with guns, his hand flashing the gang's sign, the shape of an M. One night, he called her with an obscene and inscrutable message. "I'm playing with teeth," he said. Sandoval told herself he was crazy, or high, but she later learned that he had pulled the teeth from the corpse of someone the gang had killed.

One night in the fall of 2016, Carlos called Sandoval to ask if she had heard any rumors about girls who had gone missing. This was the first she'd heard about any disappearances. The next day, the police announced that they had found the bodies of Kayla Cuevas and Nisa Mickens. Sandoval knew Mickens from school, but Carlos forbade her to go to the funeral. A few weeks later, she was walking to the bus stop when a red pickup truck pulled up next to her. Carlos emerged, holding a gun, and told her to get in. With two friends, he drove her to the woods, where MS-13 members had a meeting spot. Carlos kept

Sandoval hostage for three months, moving her among houses in and around Brentwood and Central Islip. At night, they hid in the woods.

She became pregnant and resolved to escape. On a few occasions, she heard the police knocking on the door of Carlos's mother's house, in Central Islip, where she was sometimes stashed during the day. But no one ever came inside. One morning in December, Carlos went to work early, and the friends he had deputized to watch her got into a fight and left the house. Sandoval ran to a friend's place, where she called her mother, who got in touch with the police. They told her to call a taxi to pick Sandoval up.

Sandoval had always distrusted the police, because she felt that they could not protect her from Carlos. After being forced to make her getaway in a taxi, she came to resent them. "Thank God you're alive," one of the officers told her. "Do you have any idea who you were with?"

In January 2017, Sandoval had a miscarriage, and spent a few weeks convalescing at her aunt's house, in Hempstead. When she returned to Brentwood High School, the corner of the Papi and Mami hallway was empty. Most of the MS-13 members who hung out there had been arrested. At school, Sandoval met a sixteen-year-old Salvadoran named Jorge, who had arrived as an unaccompanied minor a year earlier and lived with his sister. He was sensitive and respectful, and even Sandoval's parents, who could be stern and unforgiving, supported their relationship.

In late February, as they left school, they noticed a car idling across the street. Two middle-aged men got out, identifying themselves as detectives. They took photographs of Sandoval and Jorge, asked for their identification, searched their backpacks, and inspected the teenagers for gang tattoos. One detective made a gang sign to see how Jorge would react. But Jorge, who had no connections to MS-13, did nothing, and they were eventually allowed to go. Even so, in July, he was arrested at a body shop where he worked as a mechanic and was sent to a detention center in Texas; he was scheduled to be deported.

During the spring and summer, Sini, the police commissioner, was preparing to run for district attorney. He was a campaigner now, no longer the careful practitioner intent on building an abiding trust with the immigrant community. The gang arrests were a political credential. Sini held a press conference complete with a helicopter and more than a dozen uniformed officers wearing sidearms. In one of his campaign ads, he said, "As Suffolk police commissioner, I declared war on MS-13, and put hundreds of its members behind bars. My message to the rest of them? Get ready, we're coming for you."

While the race was underway, the Suffolk County police were working with federal immigration authorities in the ways that undocumented residents had most feared. "We automatically notify the Department of Homeland Security when we arrest an individual for a misdemeanor or felony who was not born in this country, so that immigration authorities can take appropriate action," Sini told a US Senate subcommittee, in May 2017. In the months that followed, the police and ICE rounded up more than three hundred suspected gang members, touting their own success at press conferences. Specific information about the arrests was rarely made public, and many in the community complained that authorities considered undocumented residents to be gang members without evidence.

Jorge wasn't the only teenager to be arbitrarily accused of belonging to MS-13. At least four other students in Suffolk County were suspended from school because administrators thought that they were involved with the gang. Three of them, students at Bellport High School, twenty miles east of Brentwood, had come to Long Island as unaccompanied minors from Guatemala and El Salvador. One had worn a Chicago Bulls T-shirt to school; MS-13 members used to wear Bulls attire, because the horns of the team's insignia resemble the gang sign. Another had posted a Salvadoran flag, which is mostly blue, on his Facebook page; MS-13's trademark color is light blue. That seemed to be the extent of the evidence in each case, but neither the school nor the police would share any information. In Brentwood, an eighteen-year-old girl from El Salvador, who had come to the US fleeing the gangs, was detained in the immigration wing of a county jail because school officials found marijuana in her locker and had seen her socializing with "confirmed MS-13 members." A judge released her, and she was allowed to return to school. "I'm scared to go back," she told NPR. "Look at everything I went through just for attending that school."

At schools throughout the county, the police posted an employee known as a resource officer, whose job was to provide support to administrators. But they also helped to identify gang members. What constituted membership was nebulous. ICE identified someone as a gang member if he met at least two criteria from a list that included "having gang tattoos," "frequenting an area notorious for gangs," and "wearing gang apparel." Sandoval had observed how Carlos and his friends from MS-13 would change their style of dress in response to the heightened police activity. In the weeks after the murders of Mickens and Cuevas, the gang members at school replaced their Nike Cortez sneakers with Adidas. They mocked the police for being slow to catch on. Immigrant teens without ties to the gang didn't necessarily know which clothes were off-limits because schools never specified. Throughout the summer, a handful of students were expelled on suspicions of gang membership and put into removal proceedings by ICE. According to a federal lawsuit brought by the ACLU, at least thirty-two teens were placed in immigration jails for alleged gang ties. The charges included being "in the presence of MS-13 members" on a town soccer field, being seen at school and in a car with confirmed gangsters, cutting class, and writing the number 503, the international calling code for El Salvador, on a school notebook.

The strategy for combating MS-13 rested on one of the core premises of American immigration enforcement: undocumented immigrants had far fewer rights than citizens did. Dismantling a criminal organization was a complex and painstaking legal task. It was much easier to deport someone than it was to convict him of a crime. In the fall of 2017, ICE launched a new initiative, called Operation Raging Bull, in which the government arrested some three hundred suspected gang members nationwide; in New York, a separate crackdown led to hundreds more arrests. "We're placing people in removal proceedings as a way of disrupting MS-13's efforts," said Angel Melendez, the special agent in charge. In response to a growing number of documented cases in which teenagers faced deportation because of baseless allegations, Melendez simply said, "The removal process continues." Ties to the gang would never have to be proved because the teenagers were guilty of something that was never in dispute: to flee the gang they were now accused of joining, they had entered the country without papers.

In December 2017, Sandoval went to an immigration court in New York City to attend a hearing about Jorge's case. Ever since his arrest, she'd been inconsolable. School may have been safer than before, but Sandoval found it hollowed out and eerie. There was no one to talk to, and she no longer had the energy to try to make new friends. Her relationship with her parents had been strained, and she sensed that they still blamed her for getting involved with Carlos.

But her mother had her own reasons for feeling stressed. The Trump administration had announced plans to cancel temporary protected status for Salvadorans living in the US, including those who had bought homes, paid taxes, started families, and joined the legal workforce. The president was also canceling TPS for 60,000 Haitians who'd lived in the US since a 2010 earthquake, and for 2,500 Nicaraguans who'd arrived in 1999 following Hurricane Mitch. The Salvadoran population was the largest by far, some 200,000 people, most of whom had been living in the US for twenty years. Among them were parents of roughly 190,000 children who, like Sandoval, were American citizens.

Sitting on a bench toward the back of the courtroom, Sandoval tried to focus on what the judge was saying. He spoke fast and used technical words. Then, suddenly, she heard him utter her name.

A few days later, a social worker she knew received a copy of an ICE memo in which Sandoval was identified as the "girlfriend" of an MS-13 member who was "currently incarcerated after being convicted of murder." This designation appeared in a broader document that ICE had been keeping on Jorge. Its title was "Alien File Regarding Gang Affiliation." In the file, the government listed three reasons why agents were certain that Jorge belonged to MS-13. The first was that he'd been wearing a Brooklyn Nets hat, which, according to a school resource officer cited in one of the documents, was "indicative of membership in a gang," because "MS-13 members currently wear Chicago Bulls or Brooklyn Nets hats." The second was that someone had seen him "performing a gang handshake," although no further details were given. The final piece of evidence was taken as the most damning: at school, he had been observed in the company of two people on ICE's radar. One of them was a "confirmed gang member" whose name was redacted; the other was Sandoval. After she escaped from her ex-boyfriend, the local police knew that she'd been kidnapped and abused. It didn't matter that she had done nothing wrong. What she had suffered turned into an indelible mark that she didn't realize she was carrying. She was a "gang associate," and anyone close to her was an object of suspicion.

38.

Los Nerds

On January 12, 2017, at Guatemala's Health Ministry, a room had been set up for a press conference, with a table and chairs at the front and a reporters' scrum at the back. Lucrecia Hernández Mack was sitting next to the president, the cameras on her. "Corruption is synonymous with death," she said calmly into a microphone. Historically, the ministry was a morass of kickback schemes, aborted projects, and jobs hatched to pay off political favors. For a decade, funds in the ministry's annual budget had been allocated for a hospital in the department of Huehuetenango that consisted of nothing but a shell of outer walls; it had never been built. Other facilities, such as a dialysis clinic in Guatemala City, were short on staff and equipment because officials were siphoning off money; several patients died. Lucrecia was wearing a cream-colored blazer over a striped blouse, looking around the room while she spoke. "Corruption cases directly threaten the lives of the public when it comes to the Ministry of Health," she said.

Five months before, she had become health minister, the first woman to hold the position in the country's history. But she was serving an unlikely principal. The president sitting next to her, Jimmy Morales, was a former comedian who'd surprised everyone by winning the 2015 election on an anti-corruption platform. "I'm not of the right or of the left," he'd told Lucrecia, when they first spoke. His flexible ideology was one reason he had appointed her. But the core

Lucrecia Hernández Mack during an interview with the newspaper El Faro *in Guatemala City, Guatemala, September 6, 2018.*

of his administration included advisers and officials from the right, and many of them had ties to the military. When Helen Mack learned from her niece that Lucrecia had been approached to work in the government, she said, "How could you go with those military assholes? Those are the guys who ordered your mother killed!" Eventually, Helen came to accept the decision—not that Lucrecia ever fully assuaged her own doubts. She was forty-two years old and entering politics for the first time, tasked with cleaning up the government's most dysfunctional department.

TO BE A MACK in Guatemala was to be beloved by the left and reviled by the right. Since her mother's death, Lucrecia was struck by how many people would stop her aunt on the street to shake her hand and express their support. The milieu of Lucrecia's life had always been intellectual, passionately charged, international. The Myrna Mack Foundation had become a prestigious beacon for human rights advocacy in Central America, and, in 2011, Helen had served on a presidential commission on police reform. Growing up as the heir apparent to two leftist legends generated its own pressures. Lucrecia battled the anxiety of seeming like a *mala copia*, or cheap imitation, of her mother and aunt. By the late 1990s, she was alienated from the newly reconfigured Unidad Revolucionaria Nacional Guatemalteca, the left's political answer to the peace accords. Medicine, her lifelong calling, no longer struck her as the surest way to "be useful."

The realization came while she was doing her medical residency near the Honduran border, in one of the poorest areas of the country, populated by an Indigenous group called the Chorti. The parallels to Myrna's life were uncanny. Lucrecia was a mother now herself, to a baby boy whom she'd leave with family while setting out to do her work in the field. She would take a bus to tiny villages made up of clusters of hovels without running water or steady sources of food, then spend days on end encouraging the residents to seek medical treatment. In 1998, Hurricane Mitch had devastated southeastern Guatemala. In the area around Chiquimula, where Lucrecia was working, roadways had been washed away; the entire local economy, which depended on coffee and tobacco, simply ceased to exist. People were starving.

Guatemalans in the eastern part of the country were often too poor to emigrate; the farthest most of them could go were the larger towns in the department or the streets and shanties around Guatemala City. Tens of thousands of other Guatemalans who were slightly better off left the country for the US or Mexico. As a highly educated professional, Lucrecia had options herself, but decided to stay. The problems she witnessed didn't have immediate medical solutions. "A doctor isn't really devoted to health," she concluded. "She's devoted to illness." Lucrecia wanted to pursue something less reactive and more structural, so she gave up medicine and decided to study public health policy. She'd had a second son, who was less than a year old when she enrolled in a graduate program. After beginning work on a doctorate, in Mexico, she took jobs with the United Nations Development Programme and taught courses at a Guatemalan university. Myrna had had the social-science organization called AVANCSO; Lucrecia was part of a group of doctors and health specialists known as the Alianza por el Acceso Universal y Público a la Salud, or ACCESA.

At the end of the war, half of Guatemala lacked medical care, and the government did not have the means or the inclination to provide it. A patchwork of NGOs and third-party contractors emerged instead, heavily concentrated in the rural areas where La Violencia had left the most lasting damage. It was inevitable that Lucrecia would work in some of the same places that Myrna had. In Myrna's time, the highlands were hollowed out by mass migration to Mexico or forced relocations to "model villages." In the 2000s, the residents who had departed for the United States left behind signs of faraway prosperity: cinder-block houses that were slowly being constructed with the money they sent home.

In 2013, members of the Guatemalan Assembly passed a law curbing the role of NGOs in providing medical care because of complaints about poor coverage and persistent graft. But no alternative system had been prepared to fill the void. The Health Ministry itself was in shambles. In 2014 and 2015, amid shortages of vaccines and medicines, there were renewed concerns about the outbreak of preventable illnesses such as measles, polio, and HPV. The vaccination rate, particularly among children, had fallen to levels not seen since the late war years of the 1990s.

The health emergency was the capstone to a political crisis finally coming to a head. It followed the ineluctable question raised by Helen Mack's campaign for justice: Could Guatemala run itself? Getting a Guatemalan court to convict one of the military officers involved in her sister's murder had taken twelve years, roughly $3 million in legal expenses, and consistent pressure from the Inter-American Court of Human Rights. And, in the end, he had still gotten away. Several years later, after a three-judge panel convicted General Ríos Montt of crimes against humanity for his role in the genocide perpetrated in the early 1980s, the country's top court overturned the verdict within ten days. Another telling moment came in 2004, when the liberal government of Óscar Berger took office. The vice president, Eduardo Stein, a well-regarded diplomat who'd helped negotiate regional peace accords in the 1980s and '90s, sought out Helen Mack. "I need you to help me because we're having problems governing," he told her. Specifically, the issue was a shadow government of private interests run by ex-military officers and corrupt lawmen.

In 2007, at the behest of Guatemalan human rights advocates, including Helen Mack, the United Nations established the International Commission against Impunity in Guatemala (CICIG), an independent anti-corruption body, to investigate criminal groups that had come to dominate the country after three decades of civil war. It was a radical international experiment. The CICIG's mandate was to work directly with national institutions, such as the police, the Public Ministry, and the existing court system. But this presented an immediate problem because many of these offices were controlled by organized crime.

The commission's inaugural chairman was a Spaniard named Carlos Castresana, who lived in a secured villa in Guatemala City that had once been the headquarters for the US Marines. A foiled assassination plot forced him to sleep in a room above his office. "When you come to a country with such extended levels of corruption, it doesn't matter if you have built a good case," he later told the journalist David Grann. "Guatemala's institutions must be purged from the inside—they need an exorcism." The commission went on to create new institutions that could withstand corrosive influences. One was a special prosecutor's office that operated within the Public Ministry; another was a set of courts that handled complex investigations. Democrats and Republicans in the US Congress, who saw political corruption as a major driver of drug trafficking and migration, would give close to $45 million to the CICIG in the first twelve years of its existence.

By 2015, the legal fight against corruption was reaching its high-water mark. That April, the country's attorney general, Thelma Aldana, together with the CICIG, announced a criminal investigation into the president and vice president, accusing them of running a huge smuggling operation through the customs offices. The vice president resigned the following month; at one of her legal hearings, prosecutors played a wiretapped phone call that directly implicated the president in the bribery-and-kickback scheme. Thousands took to the streets to call for his ouster, and he was eventually arrested. Later that year, Jimmy Morales, who had no prior public-service experience, won the presidential election by campaigning on the slogan "Neither corrupt, nor a thief."

Lucrecia watched the protests from Mexico, where she was living with her two boys, who were now fifteen and seventeen, and their father, the sociologist she'd met in college, who had since become an academic eminence. She was restless to return to Guatemala and to align herself with the burgeoning anticorruption movement. Growing up with her father in Mexico and her mother in Guatemala, she had often lamented her "family diaspora," with each member pursuing noble causes in disparate places. Her boys were now settled and happy in Mexico; it was a "better" country for them—which was why she felt she had to leave it. She returned, alone, to a house in Zone 11 with a small garden and cool stone floors.

In 2016, an emissary of Morales's government approached Lucrecia to offer her a job. She immediately planned with the others at ACCESA and countered with a list of conditions. Her first was that she would choose her own team; she and her colleagues were skeptical of Morales and his inner circle, but unanimous in agreeing to work for the government if they could join it together. "We will be the outsiders of the outsiders," she said. Talks with the administration accelerated from there, and when Morales came to a final agreement with

Lucrecia he called a press conference that same day. Lucrecia's friends at ACCESA—university types, technocrats, "*los nerds*," politically and sartorially unpolished—had to rush to buy suits and ties before the event.

MORALES MET WITH LUCRECIA each week, surprising her with his pledges of support. The progressive left had always regarded him as a mediocrity surrounded by dangerous right-wing schemers. His power base ran through the Evangelical Church, which connected him to a host of conservative causes that were anathema to people like Lucrecia. But as far as she could tell, he seemed genuine about his campaign slogan. Among the conditions she had given for accepting the job was that she would have a direct line to the Finance Ministry for her budget; there could be no pressure from the executive to favor certain businesses or special contracts. Morales not only honored the terms but also made a show of cleaning up the ministry.

The press conference in January 2017 was held to commemorate a deal between the Health Ministry and the CICIG. While Lucrecia spoke, Thelma Aldana, the attorney general, looked on; she was sitting next to the chairman of the commission, a Colombian attorney named Iván Velásquez, who had taken over from Castresana's successor in 2013. They were beginning an investigation into some $4.8 million worth of illicit deals that had run through the ministry between 2012 and 2014. These consisted of bogus construction and remodeling contracts for hospitals in El Quiché, Chiquimula, and Antigua Guatemala, as well as 450 schemes involving kickbacks and monthly payments tied to a large group of legislators.

The headquarters of the Ministry of Health were in a crowded, teeming complex across the street from one of Guatemala City's busiest and most chaotic hospitals, the Roosevelt. Food vendors crammed along the road, doing brisk business while patients and their families pushed their way past the snarled traffic of motorcycles and buses. The ministry building itself was a drab, boxy structure of yellow stucco with an ocher trim. The office of the minister was accessible through a special parking lot, where a tile walkway fringed with thick palms led to a back stairway.

On Lucrecia's first day, a tower of business cards—more than sixteen hundred in all—waited for her on her desk, each one left by a different government official calling dibs on some contract. Lucrecia mentally divided the special interests into two camps—those bearing down on her from the inside and those from the outside. There were fifty-four different unions, in various stages of recalcitrance and bloat, representing some twenty-five thousand full-time ministry employees. (Another thirty-five thousand staff worked as independent contractors, a patronage system by which influential people secured jobs for cronies and supporters.) Union leadership was used to having a say in the top decisions of the ministry, including hiring for the staff positions around the minister, and they smarted when Lucrecia brought in her own people. Anytime they wanted to make a point, these stalwarts detonated a series of work stoppages and strikes, forcing Lucrecia to perform endless triage. Then there were the businessmen, lobbyists, and lawmakers who were used to wringing benefits out of the department. Their preferred tools were the weapons of the legislature. By law, Lucrecia had to appear in the Assembly when a legislator made a formal request, called a *citación*. Soon, she had ten *citaciones* each day, and she was constantly shuttling back and forth between the Ministry and the Assembly.

Conservative lawmakers accused Lucrecia of committing every manner of malfeasance, vilifying her in the newspapers and online. This was the dawn of a new age of digital harassment, in which opponents launched their attacks on social media. Lucrecia was uninitiated in the practice of all-out political warfare; going to speak to the press felt to her like "facing the firing squad." Among reporters, she developed a reputation for aloofness. But how else could she respond to calculated lies? At one point, Lucrecia was accused of pocketing almost half of the entire ministry's budget. "They've been asking me for your head from day one," Morales told her.

The country's forty-four hospitals had only 70 percent of the necessary medicines and supplies when Lucrecia and her team took over. Some clinics had already shut down due to budget shortfalls. Restoring primary-care services, particularly in the interior, was an immediate priority. But Lucrecia understood the task more broadly than her predecessors. For decades, doctors and nurses trained in Western medicine had been dismissive of whole categories of diagnoses that predominated among the Indigenous population. Villagers would often visit healers and shamans who treated ailments such as *mal de ojo* (evil eye), *pérdida del alma* (loss of the soul), and *el susto* (the fright). Some of these afflictions dated to pre-Columbian times and went by a range of different names. *El susto*, the anthropologist Linda Green wrote, was "understood by its victims to be the loss of the essential life force as a result of fright." In more conventional terms, its symptoms included depression, lethargy, insomnia, nightmares, diarrhea, and vomiting. To anyone mindful of La Violencia of the war years, the connection to post-traumatic stress was unavoidable. These conditions were, as Green put it, "social memory embodied."

In the summer of 2016, the Health Ministry announced that it would open clinics and hire personnel to treat seven different types of "ancestral maladies" that were contributing to high mortality rates in the countryside. "Independently of whether you believe it or don't believe in this, we have seen that it's necessary to be vigilant," Lucrecia told one newspaper.

Lucrecia had started the job with the confidence that she would have roughly four years to carry out her agenda. Then rumors began to circulate that Morales was thinking about expelling the CICIG from Guatemala, and everything started to change. In September 2016, the commission's chair, Iván Velásquez, opened an investigation into Morales's son and brother, stemming from a suspicious twenty-three-thousand-dollar payment made in 2013, in which they'd allegedly falsified an invoice filed to a government agency. The president cooperated with the early stages of the investigation, and his son and brother reported to the attorney general to be interviewed. But in January 2017, they were charged, jailed for a month, and eventually put under house arrest.

Velásquez was the third international jurist to lead the commission, and he had a reputation for unaccommodating probity. In Guatemala, his first quarry had been an army captain named Byron Lima, who was serving a twenty-year prison sentence for killing Bishop Juan Gerardi in 1998. Since his conviction, Lima had built a sprawling criminal empire from his cell at the Pavón Prison, in Guatemala City. Working with the Public Ministry, Velásquez dismantled Lima's crime ring and charged the director of the prison system for his complicity. Then the CICIG busted the customs scheme that led to the downfalls of the president and vice president.

The CICIG could be bold because being an international body supposedly secured its freedom from domestic political pressures. But the CICIG worked directly with Guatemalan institutions and investigated national politicians. Its authority therefore depended on the government's continued support. Both ardent backers of the CICIG, Helen and Lucrecia felt Velásquez was embarking on a righteous crusade. The issue with Morales's son involved a relatively small sum of money. At the Health Ministry, Lucrecia was learning about cases involving millions of quetzales transacted illegally to finance hospitals that were never constructed. Velásquez may have been technically right to flag misdeeds for investigation, yet the longevity of the CICIG could not rely solely on the logic of a prosecutor. This was the flip side of the problem of Guatemalan justice raised by Helen's activism. Maybe the country couldn't police itself, but principled outsiders didn't necessarily share the same national long view or sense of realpolitik.

In August 2017, the Public Ministry was preparing to argue before the country's Supreme Court that Morales should be stripped of his legal immunity as president. It had found evidence of campaign finance violations from his 2015 campaign, amounting to some eight hundred thousand dollars. On a Monday morning later that month, Lucrecia had her regular meeting with Morales. He seemed undistracted. They discussed a recent shooting by a disgruntled employee at the Roosevelt hospital. After leaving, Lucrecia learned that the foreign minister was furiously trying to persuade Morales not to expel the CICIG.

For the next few days, with the commission's fate in the balance, Lucrecia and her vice ministers gathered to game out their options. If the president moved against the CICIG, they felt they had no choice but to resign. The dilemma for Lucrecia was especially acute given her family's history of fighting government impunity.

At the end of the week, Morales traveled to New York for a meeting at the United Nations, where he was expected to announce his decision to terminate the CICIG. By Saturday, he hadn't, and Lucrecia began to relax. But around dawn on Sunday morning, a friend called her at home to share the news. Morales had just released a video declaring Iván Velásquez a persona non grata in Guatemala. The next day, after a year and a half in government, Lucrecia resigned.

39.

La Pastora

In the rising morning heat, Keldy Mabel Gonzáles Brebe de Zúniga walked through a blaze of red sand and desert scrub, trailed by her sons Erick and Patrick, who were now thirteen and fifteen. She wore a light-colored, flowing dress with a thin cotton shawl that covered her shoulders and back. Her broad, billowing garments resembled sacramental robes, giving her the aura of a mystic. In the towns along her route through Guatemala and Mexico, perfect strangers sought her out, drawn in by her intense eyes, magnified by square-framed glasses, and her maternal warmth. Because her dresses covered her legs down to her feet she didn't seem to walk so much as to float through space. Everywhere she went, people called her *la pastora*. Wandering through the desert, with her boys huddled close, she resembled a sage followed by two disciples.

The entire time that they had been alone in the desert, Keldy had kept watch for the white-and-green pickup trucks of the US Border Patrol. They had crossed where they could and planned to turn themselves in. An elderly couple she had met at a church in Janos, Mexico, drove them to a town along the border called Puerto Palomas. They began hiking from there. In a small knapsack, Keldy carried a sheaf of documents held together with rubber bands—police reports, notarized court papers, newspaper clippings—which she believed would make their asylum case clear and irrefutable. By noon, after several hours of walking, a roadway came into view. It was State Highway 9, in New Mexico.

When she spotted the first two trucks, she waved her arms and shouted, but the patrolmen drove past. The third one stopped, and an agent dressed in an olive-green uniform got out. In fluent Spanish, he asked if they were US citizens and whether they had any valid legal papers. Erick and Patrick avoided the eyes of this strange new man, even as he loaded them into the back of his vehicle. Their experience crossing borders made them distrustful of government agents. Four years before, they had fled with their parents to Mexico but were arrested. For a week, they were held in a jail called Siglo XXI, or Century Twenty-one, the largest immigrant detention center in Latin America. Once they were deported to Honduras, they went into hiding again, in a town farther east called Nueva Esperanza.

The rest of the family was now scattered. Keldy's husband, Mino, had left first, in 2016, and was already in the US, working on a dock in East Texas. Their oldest son, Alex, who was eighteen, had traveled with Keldy and his brothers to Northern Mexico, but decided to cross with his uncle. Keldy and the younger boys had a better chance of clearing the US border if they moved together as a unit. In the summer of 2015, a US federal district judge in California had ruled that the government could no longer detain families with children because it would violate the terms of the Flores agreement. Word spread throughout the region, and parents with no awareness of the ruling itself nevertheless knew what to do. As a legal adult, Alex was in a different category. The uncle he was crossing with had somehow acquired Mexican papers; this gave them a better shot at avoiding deportation to Honduras if they were caught. Keldy's adopted infant daughter, Dana, who had severe autism, was with Keldy's mother, Amanda, in Tapachula, Mexico, just north of the Guatemala border. The rest of the journey was strenuous and risky, so they waited to see how Keldy and the others did, staying in a small apartment financed by Mino's American wages.

The highway extended before Keldy and her sons in an infinite line. When they arrived at the station, in Deming, New Mexico, two hours had passed. A few agents booked them into custody. "We're going to deport you," one of them told Keldy, loudly enough for her children to hear. She was surprised by how good his Spanish was. "You're crazy, aren't you," he said. "How could you come with your children all this way?" Patrick was a rangy, taciturn boy, who tended to shy away from confrontation. But he was becoming visibly upset, his face flushed. "We should have stayed home, even if they were trying to kill us there," he said. "They would have treated us better in Honduras."

Keldy, Erick, and Patrick were given consecutive alien numbers, which, along with fingerprints and basic biographical information, were entered into the government's database. They spent the afternoon and night pressed together in a cold holding cell with a hard concrete floor. There wasn't much to cover themselves with, just a square silver Mylar blanket that crinkled when touched. Later that evening, after a shift change, one of the agents reassured them. "We're going to request that they prepare some papers for you so that you can leave and see the rest of your family," he said. When Keldy thanked him, she made sure to call him "sir."

The next day, it seemed like the agents were preparing to release them when yet another agent came over and said, "Wait a second, *señora*. We're seeing something here." Another night passed in the cell. By their second day in custody, the faces of the different agents were blurring together. This time, when one of them asked to speak with her privately, away from her children, she couldn't recall if he was the same person from the night before.

"What we're going to do is this," he began. "We're going to send you to prison for five days, and while that happens we're going to send your children to a shelter in El Paso. When you get out of prison, you'll be able to join them."

There wasn't time for Keldy to formulate a question. She began to stammer. The agents seemed uncertain themselves. But they were hustling her along, leading her back to the cell to grab her belongings and say goodbye to her children.

Erick and Patrick stood up and clung to the bars of the cell. Keldy tried to explain to them what had just been explained to her, taking short pauses to calm herself. Her boys were crying. They grabbed at their mother to try to keep her from the agents. Everyone was shouting. Keldy stood still while her body was fought over. The agents were yanking her out of the cell and away from her kids, but her eyes remained fixed on the taut, trembling fingers of her boys, who clutched her clothes until their grips broke.

LA PASTORA

◇—◇

In the late winter of 2017, after the presidential inauguration but before photos of Donald Trump and Mike Pence were officially hung on the walls of government offices, lawyers in the US Attorney's Office for the Western District of Texas received an email from the El Paso Border Patrol. The sector was suspending its "family unit policy." Laws on the books made illegal entry a misdemeanor and reentry a felony. Yet the agents rarely charged a parent with either offense because it would mean separating her from her children. The email suggested prosecuting parents anyway. "History would not judge [this] kindly," responded Richard Durbin, the acting US attorney based in San Antonio. He was a career prosecutor who would be replaced in a few months by a political appointee. For now, Durbin proposed a narrower approach. "We should be looking at each individual," he went on. "If culpability is very low and they have their own children we don't need to prosecute."

On Valentine's Day 2017, there was a meeting at the headquarters of Customs and Border Protection in Washington, on the fourth floor of a large graystone conference center and office hub called the Ronald Reagan Building. At a long conference table sat the agency's acting commissioner, Kevin McAleenan, a career DHS employee. He was a fit attorney with the posture of a cadet and an exacting manner. A former college football player, at Amherst, he went to law school at the University of Chicago, and after a stint in private practice, he joined CBP in 2006, overseeing security at the Los Angeles International Airport. Colleagues considered him conservative on issues related to enforcement, but also uncommonly analytical, with a head for data and the diplomatic polish of a seasoned public servant. McAleenan was hardly an ideologue. But in the early days of the new administration, there was a sense of opportunity that could appeal to career officials, too.

The top item on the day's agenda was ending catch and release. Some of the officials at the meeting raised the possibility of separating parents from their children at the border. Many attendees were surprised that such an extreme proposal had come up at all. It still wasn't clear whether it was merely theoretical. The policy had been broached before in brainstorming exercises, but it was always considered beyond the pale.

A few weeks later, in early March, the secretary of Homeland Security, John Kelly, went on CNN to describe the new administration's approach to immigration enforcement at the border. "I would do almost anything to deter" migrants from coming, he said. When asked if that would mean separating children from their parents, he replied, "I am considering exactly that. They will be well cared for as we deal with their parents." There was an immediate national outcry, and Kelly publicly backtracked. But that same month, in the El Paso sector, Border Patrol had already started referring parents for prosecution. Plans to extend the policy were underway in certain quarters of the new administration.

Hastening them along was the attorney general, Jeff Sessions. On April 11, 2017, he called for increased criminal prosecutions at the southern border, ordering US attorneys to develop "district-specific guidelines" for bringing charges against first-time border crossers. Federal rules prohibiting the prolonged detention of immigrant children, he said, were nothing more than "loopholes" used by families to game the system at the border. "After their release, many of these people simply disappeared," he later said. "President Trump is going to fix that."

Many US attorneys were uneasy about their new boss's instructions to prosecute parents. They all knew what the consequences would be. When the attorneys submitted their responses to the attorney general later that month, they tried to hedge, accepting prosecutions in certain cases but not as a blanket policy. Only the US Attorney's Office in Arizona granted the attorney general's instruction; prosecutions quietly began there, and the separation of families followed in the Border Patrol sector around Yuma. Sessions was furious that the wider response was so tepid. "It was almost as if no one paid attention," one of his top advisers complained.

Meanwhile, the El Paso Border Patrol sector was pressuring the US attorneys in New Mexico and West Texas to start prosecutions, and their bullishness was yielding results. Fragmentary details emerged of young children being ripped from their parents' arms before disappearing into the vast and separate shelter system set up for unaccompanied minors. Word started coming back to lawyers working in the US Attorneys' Offices after the adults appeared in court, begging for information about their children. Agents at the El Paso Border Patrol insisted that they had no choice. "It is always a difficult decision to separate these families," one of them wrote to government lawyers in West Texas. "It is the hope that this separation will act as a deterrent to parents bringing their children."

The justification was deterrence, but the policy itself remained secret. Jeff Sessions came to Texas twice in 2017, and not once did he mention the pilot program to his subordinates in the US Attorney's Office. It would take Durbin another full year before he learned that he had been part of an official experiment. How could migrants discern the contours of a new deterrence policy if the government's own employees weren't sure what was happening? In August, an official in the West Texas office wrote to a colleague:

> We have now heard of us taking breast feeding defendant moms away from their infants, I did not believe this until I looked at the duty log and saw the fact we had accepted prosecution on moms with one and two year olds. The next issue is that these parents are asking for the whereabouts of their children and they can't get a response, the courts are turning to us for help.

Lawyers working in the different US Attorneys' Offices tried to create criteria for prosecutions. Yet they could only accept or reject cases that Border Patrol referred, and the El Paso sector was flooding them. The standards reflected that pressure: they were designed to stave off the most egregious separations, while accepting the overall premise dictated by Border Patrol. In the US Attorney's Office in New Mexico, one criterion for prosecution was that the child in the family unit was "at least 10 years old." This was supposed to ensure that the child was verbal, so that eventually he could explain his situation to the government after it separated him from his family.

Keldy was transferred to a county jail before she could make any phone calls. Cuffed and shackled, she was a criminal defendant, charged with a misdemeanor. She had committed two phone numbers to memory—the first for Mino in East Texas and the second for her sister Claudia, who was living in Philadelphia, an asylum seeker herself. As soon as she was granted her phone call, she frantically dialed each of them on a blocky metal phone with a hefty receiver. Detainees were given only a few minutes on the line, so she had to speak quickly. Since Mino still had no immigration papers, Claudia would have to sponsor Erick and Patrick to get them out of custody. Keldy couldn't speak to them because, in the government's databases, her file was severed from those of her children.

Patrick and Erick were listed as "unaccompanied alien minors" who had arrived at the border alone and been transferred to the Department of Health and Human Services. HHS would take up their case from scratch, vetting relatives in the US. Keldy was part of a different system run by DHS. According to ICE's records, she had traveled to the US as a single adult. There was nothing in their files to link the boys to the nine-digit number that corresponded to their mother, and nothing in hers that led back to them.

Within a week, Keldy was back in the custody of DHS, this time at a detention center run by ICE on Montana Avenue in El Paso, a complex of low-slung buildings that resembled a cross between a prison and a military barracks. The closer you got to the front parking lot the more impregnable the space became, with thick doors under lock and key and long hallways of cinder block and Plexiglas. Deeper inside, past a small library with a lone computer and a bank of phones, were dormitory blocks with dozens of bunk beds. The rooms opened onto the yard, a square plot of asphalt ringed by high walls, where the detainees were given an hour each day for "recreation."

On the morning of October 4, one of the guards brought Keldy to a small room with bare walls. On a metal table was a phone. Someone identifying himself as Officer Su came on the line. He spoke in English, followed by another voice piped in from somewhere else, which translated everything into Spanish. Su, who belonged to a division of asylum officers at an agency called Citizenship and Immigration Services, which conducted preliminary interviews, was sitting at a cubicle in an office building in Arlington, Virginia. He wore a headset, and all around him snippets of other conversations droned in and out of range. For the next two hours, Keldy would answer questions to establish whether she had a "credible fear" of persecution in her home country. It was the first hurdle to clear for asylum. The second was an actual hearing before an immigration judge.

"Please remember to speak clearly and loudly, and also take frequent pauses so the interpreter can accurately tell me everything you say," Su told her. "Before we continue, I'm going to put you under oath." The guard was gone, and Keldy was completely alone in the interview room. Facing in the direction of the phone, and blinking hard at the emptiness before her, she raised her right hand and swore to tell "the truth, the whole truth, and nothing but the truth."

Keldy had spent months back in Honduras gathering evidence for asylum. But speaking to a disembodied voice on the phone, she stumbled through the story. Certain details didn't line up with the pointed sequence of questions. The asylum officer needed to establish specific facts. Why did Keldy leave Honduras? Who murdered her four brothers? "We never knew the names," she replied. "It was between 2006 and 2012. The last death was July 2012. That one brought my entire family a lot of consequences as far as persecution."

These killings took place "five years ago," Su pointed out. Was there still a threat to her personally? "Yes, but we've been in different parts of Honduras," she replied. He returned to the issue of who had killed Keldy's family, but she was trying to finish her earlier answer. The timeline was jumbled because the threats had come in waves: there were her siblings' killings, then the fallout after Keldy testified against their killers in court. The interpreter stopped translating and tried to get Keldy to respond to the officer's question, but she was getting nervous. "Ma'am, stop," Su interjected. "We're already an hour into this interview, and I haven't gotten any information I need."

The interview concluded at 1:46 p.m. "Is there any other reason you fear returning to Honduras?" Su asked. "I have nowhere to go in Honduras. My family is all in Mexico or the United States," Keldy answered.

It was another week before she learned that she had passed. This was excellent news, which nevertheless seemed to have no immediate bearing on her situation. Ordinarily, asylum seekers who cleared this first test could be released on bond to wait for their subsequent court dates. But increasingly the government was detaining asylum seekers through the entirety of their legal proceedings. In one case, a Haitian schoolteacher had won asylum in an immigration court yet was kept in ICE detention while the government appealed the case. It was two years before he was eventually released. On the initial form that came back to Keldy, with a box checked to indicate that she had "demonstrated a credible fear of persecution or torture," she was ordered to appear before a judge in a separate room at the facility on Montana Avenue, where she was already being held. The two blank lines reserved for the date and time of this court hearing read: "To be determined."

BY THE LATE FALL of 2017, the pilot program in El Paso was starting to attract more attention. A senior staffer at the Department of Health and Human Services noticed a pattern and emailed McAleenan, at CBP. Not only was the department running out of bed space for unaccompanied children in government shelters, he pointed out, but a significant share of the children entering HHS custody didn't appear to be unaccompanied at all. That fall, Miguel Torres, a magistrate judge in El Paso, voiced his own misgivings in open court. "I've probably done thousands of these [illegal entry] cases," he told lawyers one morning. "This is a newer phenomenon."

In November, four parents and a grandmother from Honduras and El Salvador appeared before Torres for criminal sentencing. Each had been charged with a misdemeanor for illegal entry, but none of them seemed to care about the outcome of the case. They claimed that the Border Patrol had taken their children, and that they had no idea where they were. Their lawyer was a public defender from Mexico City named Sergio Garcia, who had first come to the US in 1981, to study English at the University of Utah. His clients were so desperate to reunite with their children that they were willing to plead guilty to anything. "Instead of giving them due process rights to a hearing on asylum, or refugee status," he told Torres, "the government is just kidnapping their children." For weeks, Torres had been seeking an explanation for why so many parents seemed to be getting separated from their children and then kept in the dark on their whereabouts. The government prosecutors insisted that nothing was out of the ordinary. From the bench, Torres disagreed, saying, in reference to the parents, "I would be very worried as well if it was me."

Keldy had been one of the first parents to be separated from her children under the initiative, but there were some 280 others. Having twice been denied bond, she was still in detention on November 18, waiting for her hearing before an immigration judge, when McAleenan ended the El Paso pilot. Stopping the pilot had a perverse consequence for Keldy. Without a scandalous new policy to concentrate public attention, she was just another single adult from Central America languishing in ICE detention.

On Montana Avenue, Keldy was assigned to a dormitory block known as 8D, with about thirty other women who were given orange jumpsuits and strict instructions. Each group of detainees moved through the space as a unit. They ate together, shared a recreation hour, and lounged around the dorm and talked. Contact with the other groups was forbidden. Sometimes, they would pass one another in the hall, or overlap briefly in the commissary. When a woman lingered over her food and tried to make conversation, a guard was usually on hand to shout a reprimand: "You're here to eat, not to socialize."

40.

Stay at Your Own Risk

On the evening of November 27, 2017, a Bolivian risk-management consultant named José Luis Contreras was charging up the stairs of a hotel in Tegucigalpa. An organ of the government known as the electoral tribunal had rented out the building as its headquarters, and dozens of foreign contractors were stationed there, hired to monitor and tabulate the early results of the Honduran national elections. In Contreras's hand was a small plastic badge that gave him special access to a room full of computers on the third floor. Inside, graphs and pie charts flashed with updates displaying the vote tallies. What they showed was shocking. Despite being the heavy favorite, Juan Orlando Hernández, the president of Honduras, was losing.

Staring at the screens that night, Contreras couldn't understand why the government wasn't making any announcements. His main job was to take snapshots of the returns as they came in—samplings of the vote known as the "quick count." The plan was to share the findings in a press conference at around eight thirty p.m. Based on the early tallies, it didn't matter how Contreras parsed them. Every projection showed Hernández behind. But the nation's electoral tribunal, which certified the final results, remained silent. As far as Contreras was concerned, the data was in, and it was incontrovertible.

Contreras was a methodical man with a deep voice bearing the faint trace of a stutter. His area of expertise was insurance. He frequently worked with a friend from Peru named Theodore Dale, who was a software engineer and ran a firm specializing in election administration. Earlier that fall, the two had been preparing for another auditing job in Honduras when their plans abruptly changed. The company the government had hired to administer the elections was accused of having ties to the ruling party. When opposition politicians, threatening legal action, said they wouldn't recognize the results, the electoral tribunal rushed to hire another company. Overnight, Dale received a new charge. Rather than audit the elections, he was now being asked to help run them.

Hernández was already preparing for certain victory. Every aspect of political life in Honduras depended on him and his party. Not only had Hernández already appointed all five judges to the country's Supreme Court; he and the National Party controlled the legislature, the military, and the electoral tribunal. Recognizing their steep odds, his opponents formed a broad coalition called the Alliance against the Dictatorship. The alliance's own candidate was a former sportscaster in late middle age named Salvador Nasralla, who spoke with "the cadence of the game-show host he was once," as one journalist put it. He was charismatic, even charming, but had been cast in the role of inevitable loser.

By midnight, there still hadn't been a public announcement. On the second floor of the hotel, where the electoral tribunal had set up a media gallery, foreign election monitors from the European Union and the Organization of American States were milling around, waiting for a press conference that kept getting delayed. Outside, small groups of Nasralla supporters were shouting about fraud. Contreras was in a control room on the third floor, where he could see the latest vote tallies. They confirmed his quick count. With 57 percent of the vote in, Nasralla was leading by five points.

Sometime the next morning, one of the tribunal's magistrates let slip to a local reporter that the outcome appeared to be "irreversible." Soon afterward, everything went dark. The electoral tribunal halted the count and claimed the army had to bring, by truck, tens of thousands of outstanding ballots from the countryside. Contreras and Dale oversaw the software used to process the ballots once they were electronically scanned into the system, but they couldn't control the rest of the process. On Monday, the day after the election, the incoming electronic scans had slowed to a trickle. The data was not getting entered into the system. On Tuesday evening, the computers crashed; no one could say why. When they came back online a few hours later, the electoral tribunal announced that the five-point Nasralla lead had turned into a 1.2 percent advantage for Hernández.

A US ally in the Americas was stealing an election in plain sight. The foreign election monitors raised objections, and the Organization of American States issued an immediate report detailing "irregularities, mistakes, and systemic problems." Its top official called on the Honduran electoral tribunal not to announce a winner until all "the serious doubts" were resolved. When the tribunal went ahead anyway and declared Hernández the victor, the Organization of American States called for new elections.

The country with the greatest ability to stop the fraud had the strongest sense of loyalty to the fraudster. At first, the US refused to intervene. Eventually, it backed the electoral tribunal. On the same day that the vote count was halted—just before the computers mysteriously crashed—the secretary of state signed a document confirming that the Hernández government had qualified for more aid money. There were twelve conditions that had to be met for such a document to be signed, including that Honduras "combat corruption" and "protect the right of political opposition parties and civil society activists."

In the next month, as Hernández made a show of vetting the election results, the government flouted the conditions in spectacular fashion. During large public protests over the election, security forces killed twenty-two demonstrators. By the middle of December 2017, the results were officially certified. Honduras had a newly reelected president.

The six-month period after the election revealed the American position for what it was. Outright fraud followed by mass protests had barely registered as a cause for concern in Washington. Members of the Trump administration needed to portray Honduras as a success story. Doing so freed up the anti-immigration stalwarts to end temporary protected status for the sixty thousand Hondurans living legally in the US for more than a decade, whom they now wanted to send home once and for all.

The scheme wasn't isolated to Honduras. A broader effort was underway at DHS to whitewash the conditions in multiple countries over the objections of career officials at the State Department. The aim, according to the then acting head of DHS, was to "send a clear signal that TPS in general is coming to a close." Staffers were tasked with finding "positive gems" about individual countries that could be used as an excuse to end TPS protection for more than three hundred thousand of their citizens who were currently living in the US. Honduras was a critical case for the administration because DHS could hold up Hernández as an ally who was making progress in combating crime. The country was "on the cusp of a lot of change and positive development," one official said in a closed-door deposition. "I'm generally encouraged about the future prospects of those countries and about their current conditions."

Election theft could be ignored, but not the prospect of more immigrants. In early April 2018, a caravan of twelve hundred Hondurans traveling through Guatemala caused a panic at the White House. The images first appeared on a Fox News broadcast one Sunday morning. Families with small children were gathering south of the Mexican border, on their way to the United States to seek asylum. They were more than a thousand miles from the US, and moving on foot, with their belongings packed in sacks and bags strapped to their backs. Watching the segment from the White House, Trump started tweeting. "Border Patrol Agents are not allowed to properly do their job at the Border because of ridiculous liberal (Democrat) laws like Catch & Release," he began. "Republicans must go to Nuclear Option to pass tough laws NOW."

Inside his administration, staffers scrambled to prepare for the president's latest pronouncements. He wanted more money for his "big, fat, beautiful" border wall. The Republican Congress was already funding it, just not to the degree Trump had demanded. He called for federal troops to stand watch in South Texas. It didn't matter that border crossings were at their lowest point since 1971, or that officials at DHS were in the middle of delicate negotiations over security and trade with Mexico. Members of the administration now had to explain to their foreign counterparts that the president's Twitter fusillade had no bearing on their painstaking, months-long talks.

Lost in the din coming out of Washington were the words of the migrants themselves. One of them was Maria Elena Colindres, a former member of the national legislature in Honduras. She had served in public office until January 2018, when her term expired. In the controversial elections held at the end of the previous year, a rival from the National Party had unseated her. Reuters reporters found her among the families making the journey north. "We've had to live through a fraudulent electoral process," she said. "We're suffering a progressive militarization and lack of institutions. They're criminalizing those who protested." Colindres was planning to apply for political asylum, she said, as a persecuted political opponent of Juan Orlando Hernández.

The other migrants couldn't claim to be recognizable rivals of a corrupt and vindictive president. But Hernández's election theft was unignorable. The first time Hernández won a presidential election, the National Party had secretly funded his campaign by stealing more than $3 million from the country's health-care program. (Another $290 million was siphoned off through subsequent kickbacks, fraudulent contracts, and graft, all associated with the ruling order.) Thousands of people with treatable illnesses died because of drug shortages. Some hospitals had replaced prescription drugs with sugar and water. What would happen now? More to the point: Who wanted to wait around long enough to find out?

In Washington, the Sessions cabal was trying to revive the El Paso pilot and expand it across the entire southern border. The machinations were the work of two officials in their early thirties—one of them well-known to the public, the other a mystery. At the White House, Stephen Miller was already an internet meme, a public scourge, and a catchall symbol of the racism and malice of the Trump government. In a cast of exceptionally polarizing officials, he had embraced the role of archvillain. The other, Gene Hamilton, a lawyer at the Justice Department, was the antithesis of the snarling provocateur. Even his detractors admitted that he seemed like a "pretty nice guy."

Each one of the president's signature anti-immigration initiatives bore Hamilton's fingerprints, even if it was Miller who earned the notoriety. They worked together and were in constant contact. Sometimes, when other officials had questions or raised objections with Hamilton, he would call Miller directly on his cell phone so the two could respond together. In the first nine months of 2017, Hamilton occupied a senior perch at DHS, where he reported directly to John Kelly. Where Miller was brash and controlling, Hamilton exercised his influence at a decidedly lower key, and never challenged Kelly openly. Instead, he made himself indispensable. Kelly wasn't an expert. Hamilton was on hand to supply answers to any questions. By the end of his time at the department, Hamilton had amassed a stunning list of accomplishments. Working with Miller, he had drafted the Muslim ban, outmaneuvered top officials at the State and Defense departments to lower the refugee cap, and written the memo ending DACA. When he rejoined Sessions at the Justice Department, in late 2017, almost no one outside the closed circles of government knew what the young lawyer looked like.

Since December 2017, Hamilton had been spreading the word that the El Paso experiment was successful in reducing the number of migrants arriving at the border. There was scant evidence for this, so he created it. Solid information did exist about the rollout, which Hamilton ignored. At CBP, agents had described chaos in an after-action report that went straight to top officials at the agency. Their software and data-entry programs had immediately faltered when the separations began. Border Patrol agents had to type information about the families into spreadsheets. Typos led to cascading problems. Of the 280 families separated during the pilot, seven were misidentified when agents input the wrong alien number in government databases. Another thirty-three parents had nothing in their immigration files indicating that their children were also in custody. ICE and HHS did not know where Border Patrol had separated the families, so it became virtually impossible to reunite them.

Miller's plans were quietly falling into place. Having become the president's chief of staff the previous summer, John Kelly was no longer serving at DHS. His handpicked replacement had been his own chief of staff at the department, a smart but obscure attorney named Kirstjen Nielsen. She had served in the Bush administration but was noticeably underqualified for the top job; her shaky standing inside DHS made her vulnerable to attacks from all sides. She wasn't experienced enough to inspire the backing of career officials, and she'd already earned the enmity of the president's most rabid political appointees. Their vitriol had an unmistakable tinge of misogyny. Qualms they were too nervous to voice about Kelly when he was secretary were imputed to her instead. It didn't help that Trump never liked Nielsen, either. She hadn't served on his campaign, and her two biggest benefactors, aside from Kelly, were prominent Never Trumpers.

A department led by Nielsen was one Miller could control from the White

House. That left the Justice Department, which was Sessions's domain. After a group of US attorneys voiced concerns to Hamilton about the prosecution policy, Sessions convened a conference call on May 11. "We need to take away children," he told them. According to the attorneys' contemporaneous notes from the call, Sessions added, "if care about kids, don't bring them in [*sic*]; won't give amnesty to people with kids."

In April 2018, the images of the migrant caravan provided the sparks that administration ideologues needed to inflame the president. One reason the caravan upset Trump was its timing. Earlier in the year, the arrests made at the southern border were increasing, reaching fifty thousand per month that spring. Experts in and out of the government considered the uptick to be inevitable and unsurprising. Only the president was shocked, and he blamed Nielsen. "If I lose the election," he shouted at her during one meeting, "it's because of you."

The Fox News broadcast aired on a Sunday. The following Tuesday, Miller and Hamilton drafted a forceful statement for Sessions to read the next day, linking the caravan to calls for the criminal prosecution of border crossers. While Sessions was delivering the speech before the cameras, Miller and Hamilton were composing the memo that would become the president's "zero tolerance" policy. This was the basis for expanding the El Paso program, and Miller bolstered it by writing a new directive for the president to sign at the same time. It called for the end of catch and release.

On April 23, Nielsen received a document bearing the signatures of her department's three most important agency heads overseeing immigration: Thomas Homan at ICE, Kevin McAleenan at CBP, and Francis Cissna at Citizenship and Immigration Services. Their memo outlined several possible strategies for dealing with Central Americans at the southern border. The government could try to prosecute all single adults for illegal entry, or it could coordinate with DOJ prosecutors to target a certain percentage of these adults. But what they advised was something else entirely. The "most effective" way to stem the recent crossings, they wrote, was to prosecute parents who were trying to enter the country with their children. Each official was signing his name to a policy of family separation at the border.

For two weeks, the document sat on Nielsen's desk unsigned. Until she authorized it, DHS could not move forward. Trump called her five times a day to berate her. Miller and Hamilton timed their own hectoring phone calls for nights after eleven p.m. On May 4, Nielsen capitulated. But leadership at DHS still hadn't addressed any of the problems reported during the El Paso pilot program. Despite their obvious lack of preparation, officials at CBP were sending estimates of the number of people the new policy was due to affect to the Office of Management and Budget. Between May and September 2018, the government planned to separate twenty-six thousand children from their parents.

41.

Do I Have to Come Here Injured or Dead?

By April 2018, six months had passed since Keldy's preliminary asylum screening, yet she was still in detention, waiting for a hearing before a judge. Mino had put money on her phone so that she could call her sons every week, at a rate of eighty-five cents per minute. From their short, awkward calls—full of silences, monosyllables, repressed sobs—she could tell they were floundering without her.

Each morning, she woke around four to pray, then got back into bed and waited for the guards to rouse everyone for breakfast. The cafeteria was a large, open space with dozens of flags ringing the perimeter, each one from a different country represented among the ranks of the detainees. These symbols of foreign places seemed to be a source of institutional pride—an immigration jail styled as a model UN at mealtime—but the women were scolded if they tried to share food or hazard a conversation among themselves.

Of all the places in the US where Keldy could have applied for asylum, El Paso was one of the worst. On average, 40 percent of asylum seekers were given relief in immigration courts across the country, but immigration judges in El Paso had granted asylum just 3 percent of the time between 2013 and 2017. One judge, speaking from the bench, called the city's immigration court system the "bye-bye place." There was a gauntlet of other restrictions that blocked Keldy before she had a chance to make her case. According to one special bench ruling that applied only in El Paso, Keldy couldn't post bond until she submitted the full body of legal evidence for her asylum claim; another local rule forbade her to submit more than a hundred pages of materials in her own defense. When a judge ruled on her request for bond, it was denied based on the low statistical odds that she would eventually get asylum, rather than on the standard criteria of whether she was a flight risk. Unlike criminal defendants, immigrants aren't automatically granted a lawyer. The longer she remained in custody, the harder it was to find someone who could help her get out.

Occasionally, the other detainees would see Keldy crying softly to herself or staring off into space with bloodshot eyes. But she never seemed despairing. "God is the only one who can help us," she told one of them. Coming from someone else, that may have sounded fatalistic or zealous, but because Keldy spoke the words, the other women took them as a sign of spiritual vigilance. The detainees wanted to be around *la pastora*. She prayed for them and led prayer sessions each day in the yard that grew in popularity. Dozens of women joined her. They approached her to ask if she saw them in her dreams. Some of them called her *la profeta*, the prophet.

Two female guards watched Keldy with growing annoyance. One of them had red hair, the other blond. The detainees called each guard La Miss, attaching the Spanish article to the English honorific. But they secretly nicknamed the blond La Chucky, because her swept bangs resembled those of the murderous horror-film villain. Both guards found endless excuses to sanction Keldy. They confiscated her Bible, barked at her in front of the others, and cut her prayer services short. At night, lying on their cots in the barracks where they slept, Keldy and the others speculated in hushed voices about why these two guards were so fixated on her. The harsher they were, the more Keldy stood out as an undimmable force. After a few months, even detainees who weren't religious or whose Spanish was weak stayed close to her.

Toward the end of April 2018, Keldy started to notice more women claiming to have been separated from their children. There were several each week; by the start of May, she counted around twenty mothers in and around her unit. All of them were inconsolable, too traumatized to speak in full sentences. They sat off by themselves, moaning.

It would be several days, at least, before they had any inkling of where their children were. Keldy knew enough not to talk the mothers down. She sat and cried with them. Some of the women knew about her own children, but many didn't. She volunteered the information only if asked. To everyone, though, she said the same thing: "Someone will come and help us. I'm going to make sure of it."

Inside the facility, the women were not allowed to have notebooks or to carry around files, so Keldy obtained loose sheets of paper. At first, she took down the names of the separated mothers in her own unit, section 8D. The columns were neatly ordered, the penmanship careful. Her plan was to mail the list to lawyers, ICE officials, and public figures who might be able to help. There had been scattered news reports about family separation, but very little public awareness of the true dimensions of the situation. On the sheet were each woman's name, alien number, country of origin, and her children's names and ages. As word of Keldy's list got around, women from other units began to contact her. There were furtive handoffs of information in the hallways and in the cafeteria, as women from different units passed each other to sit down. Keldy would receive strips of paper with the information she needed. Other times, she would go to the library, where there was a desktop computer and a printer, and leave the list there for other women to add to when they could. "I finally realized that no one from the government was going to help us find our kids," she said. "We have to do it on our own."

Mary Kay Mahowald was a Franciscan sister from Minnesota in her sixties, with short gray hair, bright eyes, and a serene Midwestern accent. She was a regular presence at the ICE detention facility on Montana Avenue. Her job was to conduct outreach as a staffer at a small nonprofit across town called Las Americas Immigrant Advocacy Center. The guards at the facility were strict about visitors' appointments. They kept detailed logs and followed elaborate protocol. No one was allowed in without the full name and alien number of a detainee, and they turned away anyone who arrived without prior approval.

In a setting like this, Mahowald knew that her appearance could be usefully disarming. Behind her benign, grandmotherly facade was an activist's razor-sharp mind. Each time the guards waved her in for client visits, she lingered in the warren of meeting rooms and cells. She never broke any of the visiting rules. She learned how to finesse them to maximize her time with the detainees and gather as much information as she could. Because Keldy had been one of the first mothers to be separated under the Trump administration, she wasn't just a victim of the policy but also a singular witness to its accumulating horrors. Mahowald became her go-between: Keldy's link to the lawyers outside the jail, and their link to the reality of what was unfolding within.

Mahowald began to encourage Las Americas' clients to collect more details about the separated mothers. When she returned, Mahowald made sure those women received the necessary forms to sign so that they could get lawyers to represent them. She then made a formal request, through the jail authorities, to meet with them herself. It was a slow, arduous process. One meeting with a Guatemalan woman lasted an hour, most of it filled with moans and unintelligible stammers. Mahowald tried to stay focused. There would be time afterward to cry, she told herself. First, she needed information that she could share with the lawyers. Another woman panicked when Mahowald shared the form necessary for her to gain legal counsel. "What I am signing? Are you trying to keep my child?" the woman asked.

On May 20, in one of the facility's white cinder-block visiting rooms, Keldy gave her list to Mahowald. As a precaution, she had also mailed a copy to the office at Las Americas, whose address she found on a bulletin board with numbers to call for legal representation. On the top left corner of the envelope, for her return address, Keldy put her full name and alien number. There were ten names on the list, including her own.

THE DAY AFTER THE HANDOFF, Keldy had her first and only asylum hearing, in one of the large halls of the detention center that were used for court appearances. The room was virtually empty, with heaps of chairs scattered toward the back. Near the front, two plastic tables were angled before a slightly raised podium, where the judge, William Abbott, sat in a black robe. He rejected nearly 90 percent of the claims he heard—not the highest rejection rate in the district, but close. The outcome of a case often depended on the mood of an immigration judge. On May 21, 2018, Abbott struck Keldy as aloof and impatient, and the proceedings moved quickly.

Keldy didn't have a lawyer to represent her, so she sat alone at her table, waiting for her turn to speak. To one side was the ICE attorney arguing for her deportation; behind the two of them, a lone guard stood facing the door. The only other person in the room was a translator. The whole proceeding was over in less than an hour. Her asylum claim was denied.

Keldy was not the type to wallow after bad news, but for the next week she was too stunned to plot her next steps. She had amassed documents and papers to present in her own defense, yet after waiting eight months to address a judge, the moment came and went without the chance to explain the information in any of them. Abbott had kept returning to details that struck her as irrelevant. He seemed fixated on the fact that her brothers had been killed by different people, for different reasons, as though this proved some inconsistency in her own account. There was a gulf she couldn't understand between the reality of her life and the tight, legible plotlines Abbott seemed to be expecting.

On June 8, she went to the library to write a plea to an official inside the Montana Avenue facility who was managing the timing and paperwork of her eventual deportation. "Good morning and blessings to you, *señor deportador*," she began. "The reason for my note is that the judge has denied my asylum claim because he says I don't have evidence and that I'm lying." In the next two paragraphs, she begged the deportation officer for his help. There was no one to go home to in Honduras. The *sicarios* who'd tried to kill her once would be waiting. At the same time, she went on, "I've spent almost nine months here, and I can't stand it anymore not to be able to see my children." She was "sick," she wrote, and "getting worse." "I don't know what to do, but I am sure that it's not worth appealing the ruling because the judge, without even looking at my evidence, says that I'm lying." The letter was forceful but formal, and she left a line for her own signature at the bottom. After printing it out, she took her pen and went back over one line, drawing a circle around it for emphasis: "What is it that you all need for someone to get asylum? Do I have to come here injured or dead?"

42.

The Highlands at the Border

One morning in June 2018, Emily Kephart, a program coordinator at an immigrants' rights group called Kids in Need of Defense, set out to find a six-year-old Guatemalan girl who'd been separated from her father a month before. He was in a detention center in Arizona, on the verge of being deported. He begged the officials in the jail not to put him on a plane until he contacted his daughter, so that they could at least be deported together. But the ICE officials could only guess at where she might be. The government records were indecipherable. The administration was separating thousands of families without a plan for how to reunite them.

Kephart had received a tip from another nonprofit in Guatemala. Its staff had gotten involved only because the girl's father, from inside the Arizona detention center, had called some enterprising relatives in Huehuetenango, in the country's western highlands. They were all missing the single piece of information that could help Kephart narrow her search: the girl's alien number assigned to her when she and her father were first arrested.

Working from a small office in Baltimore, Kephart hit the phones. She had the girl's name and birth date on a scrap of paper. The first number she tried was an 800 hotline set up by the Office of Refugee Resettlement (ORR), which the government was telling separated parents to call. But the wait times were long—up to thirty minutes per caller—and if parents were inside a detention center, they frequently got cut off. There was no way to leave a callback number. For families calling from abroad the connection rarely worked, and the international rates were impossibly expensive. Kephart managed to get someone on the phone, but she hit an immediate dead end without the girl's alien number. The person she spoke with decided to make a note in the file of another girl, whose profile was similar but inexact: her first name was spelled differently, and her date of birth was a month off.

With the father's deportation rapidly approaching, Kephart pursued a final lead. The family in Guatemala had somehow managed to get the number of an ORR shelter from a neighbor of theirs in Huehuetenango. The neighbor had herself been separated from her child at the US border, and through a stroke of luck had managed to locate her child there. The number had a Chicago area code. Kephart called it. The girl wasn't there. But this time, the staffer on the line told her about a young girl at a different shelter nearby. Apparently, no one could figure out where her parents were. Kephart quickly called a case manager at this other shelter. "Look, I have this situation. I think you have a girl there," she began. The woman on the other end of the line interrupted her. "Oh, my God, yes!"

In the center of Climentoro, a town in Huehuetenango, a dozen large white houses rose above the village's traditional wooden huts like giant monuments. The structures were made of concrete and fashioned with archways, colonnaded porches, and elaborate moldings; some even boasted facades decorated with paintings of American flags. Their owners, who lived in the US, had sent money home to build American-inspired houses for when they returned, but few did. One three-story house with a faux-brick chimney was empty. The family of twelve had migrated a few years ago, leaving the vacant construction behind. *Vecinos fantasmas,* Feliciano Pérez, a local farmer, called them—ghost neighbors.

Pérez, who was thirty-five, was short and lean, with dark, weathered skin and metal caps on his front teeth. He wore a baseball cap mottled with camouflage and emblazoned with the words "Proud Marine Dad." Around 2013, he had noticed that weather had started to change. Climentoro had always been poor. Residents depended on the few crops that could survive at an elevation of more than nine thousand feet, harvesting maize to feed their families and selling potatoes for a small profit. But the changing climate was wiping out the region's crops. "In the higher part of town, there have been more frosts than there used to be, and they kill an entire harvest in one fell swoop," he said. "In the lower part of Climentoro, there's been much less rain and new sorts of pests." Farmers were abandoning their land.

An unfinished house built by remittance money sent from migrants living in the United States. Todos Santos Cuchumatán, Guatemala, February 6, 2019.

The western highlands cover roughly 20 percent of Guatemala and contain a large share of the country's three hundred microclimates, from dank, tropical locales near the Pacific coast to the arid, alpine reaches of the department of Huehuetenango. For decades, people's livelihoods were almost exclusively agrarian. The malnutrition rate, which hovered around 65 percent, was among the highest in the Western Hemisphere. In 2014, a group of agronomists and scientists, working on an initiative called Climate, Nature, and Communities in Guatemala, produced a report that cautioned lawmakers about the region's susceptibility to a new threat. The highlands region, they wrote, "was the most vulnerable area in the country to climate change."

In the years before the report was published, three hurricanes had caused damage that cost more than the previous four decades' worth of public and private investment in the national economy. Extreme weather events were just the most obvious climate-related calamities. There were increasingly wide fluctuations in temperature—unexpected surges in heat followed by morning frosts—and unpredictable rainfall. Almost half a year's worth of precipitation might fall in a single week, which would flood the soil and destroy crops. Grain and vegetable harvests that once produced enough to feed a family for close to a year now lasted less than five months. "Inattention to these issues," the report's authors wrote, can drive "more migration to the United States" and "put at grave risk the already deteriorating viability of the country."

In 2018, fifty thousand Guatemalan families were apprehended at the border, twice as many as the year before. The number of unaccompanied children also increased: American authorities recorded twenty-two thousand children from Guatemala, more than those from El Salvador and Honduras combined. Much of this migration was coming from the western highlands, which received not only some of the highest rates of remittances per capita but also the greatest number of deportees. Of the ninety-four thousand immigrants deported to Guatemala from the US and Mexico in 2018, about half came from the region.

The Trump administration's zero tolerance policy was calamitous to immigrants everywhere along the US border, but its effects were uniquely devastating in the Guatemalan highlands. Half of the parents who were deported without their children under the zero tolerance policy were Guatemalan; between 10 and 20 percent came from departments where the majority of the population was Indigenous: Huehuetenango, El Quiché, San Marcos. Only six hundred thousand Mam speakers existed in the world, but it was the ninth most common language spoken in US immigration courts, outranking French.

The dirt roads of Climentoro brought the area's shifting demographics into view. Small children milled around a wooden shack selling candy, and women wrapped in embroidered dresses and carrying pots of water to their houses stepped past wandering flocks of chickens and sheep. There were few families, fewer men, and more houses than there were people to populate them. Some were half built, others finished but abandoned. They were known as *casas de remesa*, or remittance houses, financed by immigrants living in the US. More than half of the residents were gone.

Pérez stayed in Climentoro to work on a project known as a "seed bank." In a small shed in a corner of town, shelves of large containers lined the walls; inside each was a particular type of maize seed—black, yellow, red, white—from successive years going back more than a decade. The idea was to create a repository of extra seeds so that farmers wouldn't go hungry when their crops were destroyed by an unexpected frost, a rainstorm, or a new strain of fungus. But under famine-like conditions it was an imperfect stopgap. One afternoon, a neighbor had approached Pérez to ask for work. "You don't have to pay me," the man said. "Just give me breakfast and lunch." A few weeks later, the neighbor and his family were gone.

The village of Quilinco was about ten miles from Climentoro, connected by a rocky, twisting road that demanded four-wheel drive. A few small houses were tucked away on the side of a mountain, which was dotted with thick patches of foliage and undulating strips of soil. Esvin Rocael López, who was thirty-four and oversaw Quilinco's seed bank, was shucking maize, raking the corn into metal pails. His burliness was accentuated by a snug-fitting Dallas Cowboys T-shirt. Typically, maize was planted in April, prior to a period of extended rain; in 2018, however, both May and June were dry. "No one knows whether to plant their crops or not," López said. "When do you do it? If the rains don't come at a predictable time, how do you know? These crops are for survival. If there aren't crops, people leave."

In places like these, the question was no longer if someone would emigrate but when. Extended periods of heat and dryness, known as *canículas*, had increased in four of the past seven years. Yet even measurements of annual rainfall, which was projected to decline over the next fifty years, obscured the effects of its growing irregularity on agriculture. At the border, American officials often spoke in seasonal generalities: more immigrants arrived in the spring when the weather was mild, fewer attempted the journey in the summer heat. But in the spring and summer months of 2018, the deterrent effects of zero tolerance were moot where people were starving.

In the distance, about ten thousand feet above sea level, rose a belt of craggy peaks. At these heights, the impact of a changing climate was especially dire: increasing aridity was exacerbating an already limited water supply. By the side of a road near the hamlet of La Capellania, groups of women carted piles of laundry in wheelbarrows and in baskets balanced on their heads to small drainage ditches where they washed their families' clothes with bars of soap, scrubbing them clean on flattened stones. They had set out with flashlights before dawn, wearing hats and jackets to withstand the freezing temperatures; the earlier the women arrived, the less likely it was that the water would be full of suds from prior use.

In another hamlet, Agua Alegre, fresh water for cooking and drinking was available only from a small communal tap. Some sixty families lived in the houses nearby, and long lines formed as the women filled plastic jugs to carry away. Five years before, when local authorities started rationing the supply during the summer, residents were told that they could draw water at any time of day they wanted, but only on certain days of the week; three years before, the schedule was limited to specific hours on consecutive days. Now water was available only on Wednesdays and Saturdays, between the hours of three in the afternoon and five in the morning. The shortages were the worst in March, April, and May.

◇—◇

The Trump administration spent the better part of the spring and summer of 2018 denying reports that it was separating children from their parents at the border. But the news accounts were growing more specific and damning. *The New York Times* published leaked DHS records showing hundreds of documented cases. At immigration courts in Arizona and Texas, where proceedings were open to the public and widely attended by reporters, parents described how agents of US Border Patrol had kidnapped their children. None of them could say where they were.

New tragedies were coming to light each day. One involved a Honduran father named Marco Antonio Muñoz, a thirty-nine-year-old with short dark hair and a thin mustache; a small hoop earring in his left ear gave his face a dash of youthfulness. He was apprehended with his wife and three-year-old child in Granjeno, Texas, a tiny town of some three hundred residents. Border Patrol agents brought all three of them to a large processing center in McAllen, then followed the dictates of the newly sanctioned zero tolerance policy. "They had to use physical force to take the child out of his hands," a Border Patrol agent later told *The Washington Post*. "The guy lost his shit." The agents threw Muñoz into a small cell with chain-link walls, but he began slamming his body into the metal. He never threatened the agents themselves. But according to an incident report, they considered him to be "pre-assault," which one of them later clarified to mean that "he had the look of a guy at a bar who wanted to fight someone." He was shackled—kicking and screaming—and driven in a van to a local jail about forty miles away that had a padded isolation cell where Border Patrol could hold him. Every half hour guards checked on him. Late the next morning, one of them entered to find him lying in a heap on the floor, bloody and unresponsive. A piece of clothing was twisted around his neck. He had hanged himself.

On June 18, at a White House press briefing, a reporter took out her phone and, on live television, played for the press secretary a recording obtained by the news outlet ProPublica. It was audio from a CBP holding cell in South Texas, where dozens of separated children were wailing and screaming for their parents. "Here we have an orchestra," a Border Patrol agent could be heard saying derisively on the recording. Inside the White House, a few of the president's advisers, including his own daughter and wife, were growing uneasy and urged him to end the family separation policy. Undeterred, Miller defended it. Voters would eventually support the White House on family separation "90–10," he insisted. For all his bravado, Miller was much savvier than his critics often realized when it came to knowing when to recede from view or to underplay his responsibility for policies that went hideously awry. But this time he redoubled his arguments, with the backing of the attorney general. Sessions was giving speeches in which he described the separated parents as being the "smugglers" of their own children.

The matter was more complicated for Nielsen at DHS. She had been reluctant to authorize the policy but now had to defend it. Her agencies and their staff were doing the actual physical work of separating the families at the border. All the concerns that had delayed her signing the zero tolerance memo were bearing out. She tried to save herself with legalistic misdirection. "We do not have a policy of separating families at the border. Period," she tweeted at one point. In other words, the government had a policy of prosecuting criminals, but not of deliberately breaking up families in the process. To make this argument, she had to pretend that the separations were an unintended (and unforeseen) consequence, which was wrong. At the same time, she reiterated the importance of imposing harsh penalties at the border to send a clear message to other immigrants.

"There are some who would like us to look the other way when dealing with families at the border," she said. "Past administrations may have done so, but we will not."

The script was jumbled, and Nielsen's advisers knew it. When Sarah Huckabee Sanders, the White House press secretary, suggested Nielsen give her own press conference on the situation, they pleaded with her to decline. Officials at the White House had a different objective. They wanted to protect the president and his inner circle and knew that Nielsen was susceptible to certain kinds of pressure. One reason she'd agreed to sign the memo in the first place was the possibility that zero tolerance might work and earn the president's favor; Nielsen didn't want Sessions to get the credit for it. All the White House had to do was imply that her loyalty to the president seemed to be wavering. A group of senior DHS officials overheard Sanders telling Nielsen, "The president is getting killed on this, and it's your department. How are you not going to go out there?"

43.

We Need Concrete Information

From the Montana Avenue facility, Keldy found a lawyer named Linda Rivas at Las Americas, the local nonprofit. A young mother herself and the organization's executive director, Rivas inherited Keldy's case file, but by the time she got involved, in the late spring of 2018, the window for a legal appeal had already closed. The only option was to buy time by filing a motion to reopen the case. Keldy, meanwhile, continued building her list of separated mothers. There were now more than twenty women whose information she had compiled, and every few days Mahowald would receive in the mail a thick cream-colored envelope with the recognizable nine-digit alien number in the top left corner.

On Wednesday, June 20, Trump beat one of the first retreats of his presidency. Overtaken by criticism from Republicans and Democrats, he issued an executive order ending the outright separation of families at the border. It was a significant concession that nevertheless sounded more consequential than it was. For the thousands of separated families, nothing immediately changed.

Early the following Friday, Irma Whiteley, a staff investigator at the El Paso public defender's office, got in her car and drove thirty miles north to Otero, a private prison in the New Mexico desert. ICE used a small portion of the space, with the US Marshals Service and the Bureau of Prisons overseeing the rest. Whiteley was going to see a group of mothers who were still in the custody of the Marshals, waiting to be sentenced before the government transferred them back to ICE to be deported. Whiteley's boss, the public defender, had received news hours earlier from John Bash, the US attorney for West Texas, that the government would cease prosecuting families for illegal entry because it was running out of detention space.

After stepping through a metal detector and signing a visitors' log, Whiteley entered a small room with a glass partition and a two-way telephone. Almost all the women she'd come to see were from Honduras and El Salvador. But the first to emerge was a Brazilian mother named Wesliane Souza, who was waiting for information about her thirteen-year-old son. Her skin was pale, and there were dark rings under her eyes; she gazed at Whiteley with a vacant stare. "So listen," Whiteley told her, speaking in Spanish, which Souza could mostly understand. "It looks like some of these criminal cases might get dismissed." She took out a few pieces of paper with numbers Souza could call once she was transferred to ICE detention and a script, in English and Spanish, that the mothers could use once they arrived in the new facility. It read: "I was separated from my child. I want to know where my child is, and I want to speak with my child. I want to be reunified with my child."

Whiteley held up the papers. "Keep them close," she said, before asking a guard to let her through a locked door to hand them off. Once the US attorneys dropped their prosecutions, the role of the public defender's office would be over. The lawyers Whiteley worked with could only represent someone charged with a crime. After the women were transferred to ICE they would have to find immigration lawyers to represent them. That took time, however, and most of the women were using every available second to locate and communicate with their children. The news of the abandoned prosecutions was good, Whiteley explained, but it belied this more complicated development. "There seems to be a good chance these cases get dismissed," she told Souza. "But now we don't know, and so I want you to be prepared."

A few days later, a more definitive turn of events took place in a courtroom in San Diego, where a federal judge named Dana Sabraw was presiding over a class action lawsuit filed by the American Civil Liberties Union. The case had been gathering momentum for months. In February, lawyers for the ACLU appeared before Sabraw on behalf of a Congolese asylum seeker whom CBP had separated from her seven-year-old daughter at the port of entry between San Diego and Tijuana. By the time the first briefs were submitted, three months had passed since the mother had last seen her daughter. "There is overwhelming medical evidence that the separation of a young child from her parent will have a devastating negative impact on the child's wellbeing," the lawyers wrote, in their initial filing. "This damage can be permanent." To protect the mother's identity, the lawyers called her Ms. L.; she became the basis for an entire class of parents who had been separated from their children at the border.

On June 26, 2018, Sabraw issued an injunction ordering the government to reunite the families. He set two deadlines: July 10 for the administration to reunite children under the age of five, and July 29 for everyone else. The order called for the reunification of some 2,900 children, but there wasn't any comprehensive list that either he or the advocates could rely on. The government had several partial lists, marred by omissions, gaps, and erroneous information. Every few days leading up to the deadlines, Sabraw demanded regular status reports with an updated accounting of where the government stood in identifying families eligible for reunification. These appeared in a series of tables with numbers that the ACLU lawyers—and by extension the broader public—could begin to scour for answers.

A few days before the first deadline, lawyers from the Justice Department and the ACLU arrived in Sabraw's court for a hearing. The judge wanted to know how many children the government planned to reunite, but the DOJ attorney couldn't give him an answer. The numbers, she replied, "are sort of always a little bit in flux." What was more, she added, some of the parents were no longer in government custody, including many who'd already been deported. Finding them was difficult, and reuniting them with their children would be impossible by the deadline. In the next hour, the extent of the government's disorganization grew increasingly clear.

The lead ACLU lawyer, Lee Gelernt, was a veteran litigator in his fifties, portly and plainspoken with a rumpled look and a steely manner. He'd spent the early days of the Trump administration in a state of ceaseless activity, filing lawsuits to block the travel ban, appearing on the television news, building cases. When friends asked him what they could do to help from New York, he joked that they should be sending white dress shirts to his hotel in

California; he had no time to wash his shirts in between marathon court hearings.

Gelernt left the hearing that day with a sense of urgency that bordered on alarm. It was Friday, July 6, and they were due back in court on Monday. "We need concrete information," he said. "The government's tracking system is not even close to acceptable."

Later that afternoon, Gelernt spoke with a group of advocates to devise a plan. The closest thing the government had to a comprehensive count of separated children came from ORR records. The advocates would assemble their own lists to make sure that the Justice Department wasn't leaving eligible families out when it submitted its numbers to Sabraw. One of the advocates, Michelle Brané, the executive director of the Women's Refugee Commission, had been carefully tracking abuses by Border Patrol for years. She had warned the Obama administration that DHS lacked the capacity to keep track of families who were separated while in government custody. Brané told the others that, based on her sources along the border, the government had begun making a list only *after* Sabraw's June order. The administration was taking the ORR records of children currently in their care and working backward to look for their parents, who were in the custody of DHS. But because DHS hadn't made its own lists of separated parents, Brané knew that the government's list would be incomplete.

The advocates split into two groups. One, led by Brané, focused on DHS; the other, led by Wendy Young, the president of Kids in Need of Defense, concerned itself with ORR. A network of other organizations—including the Vera Institute of Justice, Catholic Charities, RAICES, and the Florence Project—had access to parents and children in government custody. They shared information about their clients with Brané and Young, and the groups eventually collated their findings. The goal by the end of the weekend was to have a spreadsheet that the ACLU could bring to court. "We were doing what the government should have been doing all along," Young said.

On the night of Saturday, July 7, the advocates compared their own lists with a preview of the government's. They had 102 names of children under the age of five—ten more than what the Justice Department was bringing to the judge. The tallies were still so jumbled that these discrepancies generated more questions. Gelernt asked Brané, "Are you one hundred percent sure there's nothing weird about these cases to explain why they're not on the government's list?"

No one could be sure of anything. While the lawyers reconvened in court, Brané and the others were exchanging messages on Signal and WhatsApp, trying to investigate whether the government was leaving names off its list. One of Brané's biggest concerns was that whole categories of eligible families were being missed because the children had already been released to different family sponsors, such as aunts or uncles. If that were the case, and the children weren't currently in the custody of ORR, it would be up to DHS to report information about their parents.

Michelle Brané had never met Keldy, but she had the kind of profile that worried Brané the most. Erick and Patrick had been released to Keldy's sister Claudia, so they hadn't been in ORR custody since the fall of 2017. The government had separated Ms. L. from her daughter in November of that year, more than a month after Keldy's separation; Keldy had been separated so long ago that she didn't appear in the ACLU's initial records for the Ms. L. class. Keldy had spent her time in El Paso creating her own lists of names to share with lawyers outside the Montana Avenue jail, but now, with the judge's deadline nearing, she was in danger of not being counted herself.

The activists weren't the only ones scrambling in the days before Sabraw's first deadline. On July 3, the deportation officer to whom Keldy had written her beseeching note the previous month called her into an interview room, where he pulled out a piece of paper. It was a document written mostly in English, with a title Keldy couldn't understand: "Separated Parent's Removal Form." In the top right corner was the DHS crest, an eagle with outstretched wings. Below it were a few paragraphs of English text, untranslated save for certain Spanish words that prompted Keldy to fill in her personal information: *nombre de padre*; *país de ciudadanía*; *el centro de detención*; *nombre de hijo*. There were also blank lines asking for a *firma*, or signature. The officer translated parts of the document aloud.

Its stated purpose was to reach parents who were members of the Ms. L. lawsuit but also had so-called final orders of removal filed against them by ICE. This was the first time Keldy had seen any trace of the class action.

In Sabraw's court, lawyers from the Justice Department acted overwhelmed by the task of finding all the separated families under a tight deadline. Behind the scenes, however, officers at ICE were trying to pick off parents before the judge could force the government to reunite them with their children. Keldy had a choice, the deportation officer said, leading her down the page. Because she had lost her asylum case, she had an order of removal against her. She could either be deported with her children—or alone.

She signed next to the option that read: "I am affirmatively, knowingly and voluntarily requesting to return to my country of citizenship without my minor children who I understand will remain in the United States to pursue available claims of relief."

44.

The Caravan

At four-thirty on the morning of October 25, 2018, the streets of Mapastepec, a small city in Chiapas, Mexico, were already full of people on the move. Three weeks earlier, six hundred migrants had gathered in San Pedro Sula, Honduras; since then, the group had grown to more than five thousand. They had crossed into Guatemala and then Mexico, traveling roughly thirty miles a day. In the predawn darkness, mothers pushed strollers down pocked, unlit alleyways. Young men with backpacks shouted *vámonos* to their friends, while families who'd spent the night sleeping in a downtown park readied their belongings—a rumpled plastic bag with a change of clothes, a drawstring sack stuffed with an extra pair of shoes—to join the clusters of people drifting toward the highway.

The caravan's large size afforded some protection from both Mexican immigration agents and criminal syndicates along the route, which often abused, extorted, and kidnapped vulnerable travelers. These modest advantages, however, brought their own complications. The president of Honduras, Juan Orlando Hernández, claimed that the caravan was fueled by opposition politicians, a position that was adopted by the US State Department. Donald Trump called the migrants "gangsters" and "unknown Middle Easterners," accused the Democrats of encouraging them, and threatened to end aid to Central American governments. That morning, while the migrants were still more than a thousand miles from the US, James Mattis, the US defense secretary, was reportedly planning to send more federal troops to guard the US-Mexico border. The president was considering an executive order to close it entirely.

In Mapastepec, the migrants mobilized without any formal direction. They decided it would be too risky for individuals to assume leadership roles: criminals might kidnap them for leverage over the group. Among members of the caravan, details about the trip were passed by word of mouth, and occasionally someone would volunteer to walk through the streets with a megaphone to offer a final reminder about the next day's start time and destination. The previous night, hours before people scattered to find places to sleep, everyone already knew the next stop was Pijijiapan, a town thirty miles away.

On a street corner, a young couple hunched over the jammed back wheel of a stroller holding their two small children. The mother, a twenty-three-year-old from Colón, Honduras, named Jandy Reyes, wore a striped T-shirt and pink jeans. Her face was tight with exhaustion. Two weeks before she joined the caravan, a group of gangsters had arrived at the small housing complex where she lived with her husband, Carlos Flores, and their two sons, who were five and nearly two. The gang imposed a tax, called an *impuesto de guerra*, on a small food stall the couple owned. When Flores refused to pay it, the gangsters beat him badly and threatened to kill them both. Reyes and Flores hid out with family members and tried to plot an escape. "I returned, quickly, to get some things from my house, but everything was gone," she said. The gangsters had ransacked it. "The only things left were the walls, which they would have taken, too, if they could have moved them."

Colón was a nine-hour drive from San Pedro Sula. Reyes first heard about the caravan on Facebook, from a group called Unidos sin Fronteras. She texted a contact number on WhatsApp, and someone—she wasn't sure who—responded with a request for her personal information, including her name, ID, and the number of family members who would be traveling with her. When she learned that the group planned to meet in San Pedro Sula, she didn't bother to wait for further messages before setting off with her husband, children, sister, and niece. "I was going to have to leave the country anyway," she said. "Then I saw this about the caravan and figured I'd just do it now."

She walked toward the edge of Mapastepec, where the crowds grew denser. A large, semi-paved road intersected the path, with trucks and large vans streaming past, their headlights blinding in the dark. Small green taxis poked through the traffic, carrying migrants who could afford to pay, and a bottleneck formed as some of the others, on foot, veered into the road, positioning themselves between the trucks and the taxis to try to hitch a ride. On a dusty curb, near vendors hawking cigarettes and tamales, several young women changed their babies' diapers.

Migrant caravans had formed before. In the 1990s, groups of Honduran mothers set out in search of children who'd disappeared along the migratory route in Guatemala or Mexico. Traveling alone or in small groups was too dangerous, as evidenced by the fates of their sons and daughters. Sometimes different constituencies assembled, not just for the sake of safety but for the benefit of bringing visibility to a cause. In 2015, a group of disabled asylum seekers made the trip, calling themselves *La caravana de los mutilados*, or the Caravan of the Mutilated. It was the third attempt to reach the US for one member, a twenty-nine-year-old named José Luis Hernández. On his second journey, he had fallen from the freight train known as the Beast and lost an arm, half of one leg, and part of his left hand. He was deported to Honduras, where he spent two years recovering in a hospital. "If we don't risk anything, we don't live," he said. "There aren't any other options." He added, "No one ever wants to migrate. The whole thing is a fight not to become invisible."

Size and timing distinguished the caravan that formed in the fall of 2018. In some of the towns where it stopped in southern Mexico, there were more migrants than residents. The travelers didn't realize it, but the US was also preparing for midterm elections, the first referendum on Trump's presidency. Their progress thus became partisan fodder in the American campaign season.

Many US commentators assumed that the migrants knew exactly where they were going, but in fact, many of them hadn't thought that far in advance. For the first few weeks of the trip, there was a single, obvious route for the caravan through the small towns dotting the southern tip of Mexico. Beyond that, the travelers were basically improvising. When it came to the US, the preponderant view—that Donald Trump would not let them into the country—did not seem to slow anyone down. "We'll do what we can for now, then wait and see," said Daniel Jiménez, a thirty-year-old who had joined the caravan with six friends from his hometown in Honduras. That could mean trying to reach the US to seek asylum, or staying in Mexico to look for work, but the most important thing was to leave Honduras. "You just can't live there anymore."

As the sun rose around seven o'clock, about half of the migrants were walking along the shoulder of the highway. The rest were either sleeping on the side of the road or had caught rides on the backs of passing trucks. The air was humid and filled with flies, and the road baked in the mounting heat. Along the way, a Honduran man named José Tulia Rodríguez was carrying a giant white flag made from two large sticks and a piece of cloth. "Peace and God Are with Us," it read. It was a message to Mexico, he said, "to apologize for what we may be causing here, and to show we're grateful." He had no money, water, or food; the night before, he had slept on the street of Mapastepec, where locals had packed him off with tortas to eat on his walk. His plan was to keep moving until he saw a chance to find work to support his family. "I have two daughters at home in Honduras, plus my wife," he said. "I can't make enough money working in Honduras to buy shoes for my girls to wear to school." He learned about the caravan from a television news program. "People say this caravan is about politics?" he said. "Well, sure, if by politics you mean hunger."

Amanda, Keldy's mother, had been watching footage of the approaching caravan from Tapachula. She and Dana, Keldy's adopted daughter, had been waiting for a clear path to emerge through Mexico. At seventy-three years old, Amanda was vivacious and strong-willed, but she recognized her limits. There were dangers in Mexico for an elderly woman traveling alone with a disabled child. At the US border, government agents often treated relatives traveling with children harshly, on the assumption that smugglers posed as aunts, uncles, grandparents, or other guardians. By the middle of October, Amanda didn't have to rely solely on news reports to track the caravan's progress. Her grandson Osmán was on it. He messaged the family updates on Facebook, and when it passed through Tapachula, Amanda joined him with Dana.

On October 26, after reaching a town called Arriaga, at the northern tip of Chiapas, the caravan arrived at a crossroads. The migrants had to decide whether to continue west through Oaxaca, or to head north to Veracruz. Both routes were considerably more dangerous than Chiapas, and it was still not clear whether the caravan would proceed intact. Already, it was starting to thin, as some people found rides to cover more ground, making the caravan less of a monolith than a patchwork of smaller groups moving in loose coordination.

Positioned between the Mexican states of Chiapas and Oaxaca, Arriaga was a transit hub for Central American migrants heading north. The network of freight trains crisscrossing the country effectively began in Arriaga, and railroad tracks, littered with trash and surrounded by tall brush, framed the western edge of a derelict downtown. The city had been transformed into a de facto refugee camp, its streets lined with families sleeping on cardboard boxes and tattered blankets, the main park covered in pitched tarps and lean-tos. Migrants bathed with pails and bars of soap by an open water tank. Moving amid the swarm was Daniel Jiménez bare-chested, in jeans and a baseball cap; he was approaching other migrants, shaking hands, asking if they had any information about the next stage of the trip. There were all sorts of theories and speculation about the best route to take, but Jiménez was trying to cut through the gossip. "Every conversation starts with people saying, 'I hear this; I heard that.' It's all secondhand," he said. Jiménez and his friends tended to travel slightly ahead of the larger group to survey the scene at each destination, and then wait for the others to arrive with word of where they planned to travel next.

Members of the migrant caravan hitch rides in the back of a truck while leaving the town of Pijijiapan, in Chiapas, Mexico, October 25, 2018.

A few details about the group's plans emerged that afternoon. Oaxaca seemed like the most likely destination. But, for the time being, the caravan could not board the freight trains. Part of the railway had been destroyed by a series of storms, and there was a general concern that the trip would be too dangerous for families with small children. Around five thirty, a trim young man began walking around with a megaphone, trailed by a cluster of migrants. He'd just arrived from Tijuana, where he worked with Pueblo sin Fronteras, the organization that had coordinated the last major migrant caravan, in April. It was unclear how, or when, the group had linked up with the caravan, but its members occasionally acted as unofficial field marshals inside Mexico. "The next stop is San Pedro Tapanatepec, Oaxaca," he told everyone. "We'll go up through Oaxaca a little bit, and eventually head to Mexico City." People peeled off to tell their families. He went on, "We're going to see how the women and children feel, if we should wait a day and rest or push on tomorrow." The decision would be made, he said, at a meeting in the park at seven o'clock.

Hundreds of people began converging on the park an hour before the meeting was supposed to start. At six thirty, speeches began, amplified by a microphone hooked up to a speaker system. There were calls for strength and solidarity, punctuated by rants against Donald Trump and Enrique Peña Nieto, the Mexican president. Earlier that afternoon, Peña Nieto had announced a plan, called Estás en Tu Casa (Make Yourself at Home), to offer work permits to the migrants, but only if they agreed not to leave the states of Chiapas and Oaxaca. Irineo Mujica, a Mexican American activist from Pueblo sin Fronteras, led the crowd in a crescendo of rhetorical questions. Was the caravan going to let Peña Nieto dictate their fates? Was everyone determined to keep going? Were they fed up with the corruption and violence at home?

The topic turned to the next day. It was decided, Mujica said, that the caravan would set out for Oaxaca at three a.m. There were cheers and shouts of approval. No one could say who, exactly, had made the decision. When one woman was asked if she knew, she replied, "Everyone." She continued, "This caravan is ours, from Honduras, but Pueblo sin Fronteras is helping now. We have Pueblo sin Fronteras because we don't have a country."

Amanda and Osmán had their own plans. They would stay with the caravan until it reached the US, then break away to approach the border near Sonoyta, the Mexican border town close the Organ Pipe Cactus National Monument, in Arizona. On Facebook, Amanda posted a message on the page of a group called Hondureños Indignados. "I have left behind everything. Everything," she said. "I come from La Ceiba, a charmed city but these days one that's been trampled on by four more years of politics, without anything changing my fate."

45.

Solidarity 2000

None of Keldy's boys had ever been to court, and they weren't sure what to wear on the morning of August 6, 2019, when they were due to appear before a judge in Philadelphia. They arrived at the courthouse shortly before nine, in street clothes. Erick, now fifteen, was the youngest of the three but the tallest by a foot and the heaviest by fifty pounds. He wore cargo shorts and a T-shirt. At seventeen, Patrick had thin wisps of a mustache but the same boyish, wiry frame of his youth. He chose faded jeans and a navy blue polo shirt with a red insignia that accented his sneakers, a pair of Air Jordans. The oldest and shortest of the trio, with a husky build and narrow, watchful eyes, Alex dressed in black jeans, a black T-shirt, and white high-tops.

Waiting for them on the crowded city block in front of the court building was their lawyer, Karenina Wolff, a local attorney with short hair and a navy blue skirt suit. She was pacing, but stopped with a grin when the three brothers came into view. A lot was riding on the outcome of the morning's proceedings. But the boys didn't seem nervous, just quiet and somewhat withdrawn. Erick and Patrick let Alex do the talking. After mumbling a soft greeting, he said very little, and followed Wolff as she guided them through security and up the stairs to a waiting area outside the courtroom. Officially, the hearing had nothing to do with their immigration status; it was a family matter. Alex, who was twenty-one, was petitioning to become the legal guardian of his two younger brothers. To do so, he had to sue his own parents for custody.

The past two years had been exceptionally hard on the three siblings. Alex was working long hours as a builder at construction sites on the outskirts of Philadelphia, and had moved into a cramped house with roommates in a rundown, dangerous neighborhood in the city's north end. There were nightly shootings and steady foot traffic from street-corner drug deals. Glass vials crunched underfoot on the sidewalks, and many of the neighborhood's most familiar pedestrians were men in the throes of addiction.

Erick and Patrick were living nearby with their aunt and her children, and had enrolled in school. Erick began in the seventh grade, where his classmates were sometimes hostile but mainly indifferent to him and his halting English. High school, where Patrick went, was a far more treacherous place. Of the three brothers, he was struggling the most with Keldy's absence. He rarely spoke about it, but he loped around in a trance, his eyes downcast, often on the verge of tears. He was too depressed to conceal his vulnerability, which made him into an immediate target. At school, some members of a Dominican gang began to bully him. He came home with scuffs and bruises, frequently winded from having had to sprint away from fights in which he was always outnumbered.

Life with their aunt Claudia was also growing strained. She was an asylum seeker herself and had come to the US in 2016 after her husband was murdered. Her oldest daughter, who was twenty-three and pregnant when Claudia left Honduras, traveled to the US separately, and eventually joined her mother in a row house in Philadelphia. By the summer of 2019, they were both waiting for their immigration hearings, still more than a year off.

Unlike Keldy, they had crossed the border at an opportune moment. The Trump administration hadn't yet started overhauling US asylum policy. A shortage of immigration judges available to hear a rising number of asylum claims caused a backlog of more than a half million cases. The most common outcome was for asylum seekers to be released with distant future court dates. When Erick and Patrick were stuck in detention, in the fall of 2017, Claudia had immediately volunteered to take them in. But her own children and grandchildren were living with her now. She'd just lost her job in the kitchen of a local restaurant. She couldn't afford to house, feed, and clothe her nephews.

Alex floated the idea of bringing his younger brothers to live with him. He was a legal adult, and Erick's and Patrick's immigration cases were already in the care of another lawyer, who'd applied on their behalf for a status known as "special immigrant juveniles," a path to legalization for undocumented minors who'd been abused or neglected. The finances would be tight, but the plan was simple: the boys would be together and could look out for one another. Their parents liked the idea. Alex kept them each updated on WhatsApp—Mino in East Texas, Keldy in southern Mexico. Mino sent them money for a lawyer.

Wolff sat between the boys in a waiting area under a muted TV on the sixth floor of the court building. She was voluble and cheerful but radiated a nervous energy. Any minute the judge would call them in, she told them, in a commiserating voice. "You should be prepared." The procedure would be straightforward, she explained: an official sign-off on a transfer that had, in essence, already been approved. Wolff would present the case, and at various points Alex would have to stand up and affirm that his lawyer was accurately representing his request. A translator would be on hand.

The legal premise of the hearing was that Keldy and Mino had essentially failed, as parents, to care for their own children; that was why Alex needed to intercede. Wolff had prepared documents for Keldy and Mino to sign, acknowledging the morning's court hearing and recognizing that, by not appearing, they were ceding their guardianship of Erick and Patrick to Alex. "Mother and Father have abandoned and neglected the children," Wolff had written in the original complaint. "Reunification with Mother and Father is not viable." When Wolff ran through this language with the boys one last time, they blinked through her explanation and remained silent. Aloofness had become their armor. At one point, Wolff gently repeated herself, because it was hard to tell, from their blank expressions, if they understood her. A few minutes later, the doors to the court swung open, and a security guard dressed in blue called them in. They rose without hesitating.

⋄—⋄

A few nights before the boys appeared in the Philadelphia court, ten Honduran migrants gathered for a meeting with their pastor in the basement of a housing complex called Solidarity 2000, in the city of Tapachula, Mexico. The units were a cluster of weathered brick buildings set off from the roadway, about thirty minutes by car from the city's downtown. A small food stall built from gnarled wood marked the entrance to the complex. In the back, accessible by a dirt path spotted with trash, a field of overgrown grass was interrupted by a basketball court, where a group of little children ran around in circles. The room where the Hondurans were meeting was small and lit by a single exposed bulb hanging from the ceiling.

Several times a week, to keep their spirits up while they bided their time before heading north, the Hondurans convened around sunset for an informal religious service that was part mass and part group therapy. Their pastor, in a belted print dress and pink blouse, was Keldy.

"You have to say, 'I'm not going to let anything bad overtake me,'" she began, sitting at the fulcrum of a half circle of plastic lawn chairs. There were murmurs of agreement. They prayed, and Keldy encouraged them by talking about how her belief in God was making her stronger. Within a few minutes, the group began to chat in a relaxed, open way. These temporary residents of Solidarity 2000 called themselves Keldy's "congregation."

In attendance was Keldy's nephew Osmán, a twenty-one-year-old with dark curly hair and muscled arms that bulged under a tight T-shirt. He and his grandmother had attempted to enter the US late the previous year. She and Dana eventually made it to Philadelphia. Osmán was deported in the summer of 2019. Next to him was Luis Bonilla, a talkative man in his forties, who looked tired but resolute beside his wife. He'd been transferred among detention centers in Arizona, Texas, South Carolina, and Georgia. After falling gravely ill while in custody, he signed a "voluntary departure" form to abandon his asylum claim and commence his immediate deportation. He kept lifting his shirt to display a jagged surgical scar across his belly. "I couldn't take it anymore," he said. "And now, I have to go back! It gives me the chills. It enrages me. But I can't stay at home."

They all knew this swath of international terrain like it was an old neighborhood. But they could never stay in any one place for long. They took the same buses through Guatemala, were stopped at the same checkpoints, had to pay the same bribes to the same outfit of corrupt police officers. There was the same wait at the Mexican immigration office in Tapachula, the same stress over qualifying for temporary visas, the same pressures of scant work in Chiapas and wages kept low by opportunistic employers. It was more likely that they would get deported from Mexico than from the US. The likelihood of deportation from *either* Mexico or the US was much greater than their chances of making it through. When they were finally deported to Honduras, they would spend a week or two there, just long enough to raise the money to leave again.

Keldy occasionally interjected to share an anecdote or exhortation, but she spent most of her time listening. Each speaker angled his body in her direction. When any of them mentioned God, she leaned forward and said, "Amen." A chorus of amens would follow.

They revered her and placed her on a pedestal. Their respect came from the fact that she'd been through the same thing they had. When Keldy had emerged from the plane in San Pedro Sula, following her deportation, she'd had nowhere to go; her family had all fled. But there was a Honduran woman named Karla, whom she had met in the ICE jail on Montana Avenue. Karla arrived months after Keldy entered detention but was deported first. They maintained close contact over Facebook. When Keldy arrived, Karla and her mother gave her a spare corner of their house. She stayed for a week, too scared to walk the streets. After receiving a Western Union wire from Mino, Keldy boarded a bus for Guatemala.

In Tapachula, she lived in rented rooms amid a community of people she already knew. In addition to Osmán there were a dozen other women deported from El Paso. Just before setting out for Solidarity 2000 that evening, Keldy had left her small apartment on the corner of Fourth Avenue South, a little gated home pressed between clothing stores and a gas station, with her phone, a giant Samsung the size of a tablet, pinging incessantly in her purse. Her network had grown vast. Dozens of women who had been with her in the ICE jail messaged her each day asking for advice or benedictions. Some called from the far-flung places to which they'd been deported (Brazil, Senegal, El Salvador), others from US locales. Keldy wasn't associated with a brick-and-mortar church. She was a one-woman ministry. Her main chapel was Facebook Live, where she held daily prayer sessions. With the Messenger app, she blessed and counseled each parishioner privately, in a steady stream of texts and audio messages. She fielded these consultations for a few dedicated hours every morning and again sporadically throughout the day, in between house calls and trips to local migrant shelters where she volunteered. One woman wanted to update her on the food stall she was trying to open in San Salvador. Another texted with news of a pregnancy. "You're the only person who I can go to when I'm doing badly," one of the messages from that evening read. "You are an instrument of God." "I'll pray for you," Keldy replied.

The session at Solidarity 2000 lasted two hours, and at the end the group gathered by a stairwell, where the light was best, for Keldy to snap a photo to post on her Facebook page. When she walked out to the roadway, the sky was dark, and a light rain was falling. Osmán joined her while she waited for a ride. He was beginning to have problems with some neighbors who were accusing him of various absurd things. It was all pretense to extort him. "We're going to have to move you," Keldy told him, gravely. "Remember how I said to you that those guys were going to be a problem? Remember how I'd had a dream about them?" "It's true," Osmán replied. He lowered his head like he'd done something wrong.

A FEW DAYS LATER, he was gone—off to Ascensión, Chihuahua, in the northern part of the country. From there, he'd try to cross into the US once more. Watching as he and the others from Tapachula started to drift north, Keldy was getting restless herself. She knew she was trapped south of the US border. Because she'd been convicted once for crossing illegally, a future attempt could result in extended prison time. Keldy was tempted to try anyway, but the memory of the nearly two years she'd spent in an immigration jail made her reconsider. In the meantime, the one thing she could do was shorten the distance to her family. In Ciudad Juárez, she would be closer to her children, and closer to the border separating them. A sense of possibility could exist there.

Keldy had a new lawyer: Linda Corchado, the legal director of Las Americas. There wasn't much Corchado could do to help Keldy legally. She did have one idea, a lark that seemed worth a try. Dana needed to have a medical operation to correct a cleft palate. Keldy stood no chance of gaining full entry into the US because her asylum case had already been adjudicated, but she could apply for a form of temporary parole that would allow her to stay with Dana after the surgery.

Corchado, the daughter of Mexican parents, had grown up in El Paso. She'd seen how family members built their lives between two countries. It was a future that she tried to imagine for Keldy. If Keldy could establish legal status in Mexico, there might be a way for her to travel to the US to see her family, albeit impermanently.

Corchado's advice was not to rush north. Tapachula was a grim place, but less violent than Ciudad Juárez. Keldy had managed to obtain a humanitarian visa to stay in Mexico, which afforded her a significant measure of protection. By June, the Mexican government had already arrested more than ninety thousand migrants that year, deporting close to 80 percent of them. Keldy didn't have to stay in Tapachula forever, but if she waited a little longer it would buy Corchado time to prepare the case for her American parole. Keldy heeded her lawyer's advice for a few weeks. Then, in August, she couldn't stand to wait any longer.

46.

Remain in Mexico

The Pan de Vida migrant shelter, in Ciudad Juárez, Mexico, housed two hundred asylum seekers in a cluster of yellow cabins half an hour's drive from the nearest port of entry, in downtown El Paso. The surrounding streets were unpaved, with a few small houses made of cinder block dotting the roadside. On a sweltering afternoon in August 2019, none of the residents were comfortable going outside, not even in broad daylight. "It's just too dangerous," said Denis, a thirty-eight-year-old from Honduras. He was with his daughter and son, ages thirteen and seven. A few nights earlier, a truck full of armed men in masks had circled the grounds of the shelter a few times, then left. No one knew who they were, what they were looking for, or when they might return.

Denis was especially nervous. A few months earlier, his wife had left San Pedro Sula with two of the couple's children, including the eldest, a seventeen-year-old who was being targeted to join a local gang. Denis stayed behind to earn more money before following with the other two children. When his wife arrived in El Paso, immigration agents allowed her and the children to enter the US with a court date for a future asylum hearing. Denis planned to use the same process. But shortly after he and the two children reached Juárez, in mid-August, a group of local criminals kidnapped them and held them for five days in an abandoned church on the outskirts of town. They eventually escaped and traveled directly to the nearest US port of entry.

The asylum process had changed by the time they arrived in El Paso. Denis and his children were briefly detained, given a court date in December, and sent back to Mexico to wait, under a new policy called the Migrant Protection Protocols (MPP). For Central Americans trying to obtain asylum in the US, MPP now required them to stay in Mexico for the duration of their legal proceedings, which could last several months. When it was time to appear before a US immigration judge, asylum seekers had to travel back to a port of entry and reenter custody; at the end of the day's proceedings, a bus would take them back to Mexico, where they would wait until their next court date. Denis didn't understand all the details, just that he and his family were being shunted back to where they'd been kidnapped. He begged the US officials to put him in prison but to let his children through. He would do anything, he told them. "In Mexico, they'll rape my daughter."

A few weeks later, the three of them had grown restless at Pan de Vida and decided to walk to a supermarket a few hundred yards from the shelter, to get ingredients for dinner. In the parking lot, they saw one of their kidnappers standing next to a truck. Denis froze. Everything about him announced that he wasn't Mexican: his jumpy posture, accent, and dazed look. He drew stares from people who passed him on the street. But the kidnapper hadn't spotted them. Denis steered his children back to the shelter and made plans to leave Juárez. "It's better just to thank God that nothing worse happened," he told himself. A relative knew someone with a room in Monterrey, a less dangerous city around seven hundred miles south. They took a bus there a few days later. There were still two months before they were expected back in El Paso for a preliminary hearing that typically lasted an hour.

The seed of what became MPP was first planted in 2014. At the time, it was not an actionable policy, or even a full-fledged proposal, but an idea for a paradigm shift. Officials at DHS imagined a pilot program that the US could develop with the Mexican government. Together they would set up a shelter system in Northern Mexico with the help of international relief organizations. The population of people would be small, somewhere between five hundred and a thousand asylum seekers. They would receive housing, food, and legal services while in Mexico, then cross the border for hearings before an immigration judge. The scheme was never seriously considered—it was still too open-ended—but it wasn't shot down. Four years later, it was reborn, with only a faint resemblance to the earlier idea.

In July 2018, a group of government officials began to gather each week at the headquarters of Customs and Border Protection, in Washington, DC, to discuss what to do in the aftermath of the president's failed zero tolerance policy. None of the attendees expressed any contrition. The overall lesson, one said afterward, wasn't that the administration had gone too far in separating families, but, rather, that "we need to be smarter if we want to implement something on this scale again." Sitting around the table were representatives from the Department of Justice, the Office of Management and Budget, the Department of Defense, and the Department of Homeland Security. But Stephen Miller was the main force behind the conversations. He wanted multiple governmental agencies to "map out" a way to detain asylum seekers as they waited for their hearing before an immigration judge.

The job was to model all the steps in the process. If the government went after families, where would it detain them? Which resources would be needed at each step? To Miller, the status quo of catch and release was intolerable, a legal "loophole" so vast that it amounted to "open borders." It was now up to these officials to devise new ways for asylum seekers to be locked up or kept out. Forcing them to languish south of the border was seen as the best option.

Mexico was going through its own immigration crisis, and it had a new leader to meet the moment. Andrés Manuel López Obrador, who assumed the presidency in December 2018, was, at first blush, an unpromising partner for the Trump administration. A left-wing populist in his midsixties, López Obrador was a self-styled everyman, with a flair for championing the poor and lambasting the political establishment. He liked to forgo the plush accoutrements of higher office. When he traveled, he flew in coach with a small entourage. One of his first acts as executive was to auction off the presidential plane. As mayor of Mexico City in the early 2000s, he had proudly driven around in an old Nissan. Over the years, he had become a fixture of a sort—a fiery but familiar outsider who had twice run for president and nearly won. In 2006, after losing by less than a percentage point to the conservative Felipe Calderón in an election clouded by allegations of fraud, he and his supporters held a symbolic swearing-in ceremony in the Zócalo, the giant public square in the middle of Mexico City. Six years later he ran again and lost.

During his 2018 campaign, López Obrador crisscrossed the US to address eligible Mexican voters living in major American cities like Chicago and Los Angeles, where he challenged the racist US president. "Trump and his advisers speak of the Mexicans the way Hitler and the Nazis referred to the Jews," he declared at one campaign stop. A compilation of his speeches, which doubled as a kind of political autobiography, was titled *Oye, Trump*. López Obrador vowed not to do the US's "dirty work" when it came to immigration. He spoke with directness, even eloquence, about the fellowship Mexicans should feel with Central American migrants and promised to turn Mexico into a "country of refuge."

In the fall of 2018, López Obrador was not yet in office as thousands of Hondurans on the migrant caravan passed through Mexico. He announced that his incoming administration would grant them work visas and include them in a redevelopment agenda for the southern part of Mexico. "The plan is that no one be forced to emigrate," he said at the time. "If they make the decision to do so they should have options in Mexico." Thousands of expectant Central Americans began traveling to Mexico to find legal avenues for work. Officials inside the Trump administration, who expected the Mexican government to arrest and deport migrants, felt that this permissiveness would only encourage them to continue north, and made sure to convey their displeasure. The two countries had several sizable economic agreements on the line, and Trump was willing to use any leverage he had to get what he wanted on immigration policy.

What proved even more persuasive was the Mexican public's response to the caravans. The backlash started with isolated grievances in small towns along the route, first in the south and then farther north; there were allegations that members of the caravan were committing crimes and disrespecting the hospitality of their hosts. Eventually, the mayor of Tijuana expressed the mood just weeks before López Obrador was sworn in. "These people arrive in an aggressive, rude way, chanting, challenging the authorities, doing what we're not accustomed to doing in Tijuana," he said. "I don't dare to say that it is all the migrants but there are some who are bums, pot smokers, they're attacking families." For years, Mexico had been a "transit country," one through which migrants crossed to reach the US. But with their numbers increasing, and the US more determined than ever to turn them away, Mexico was becoming a terminus. Immigration was morphing into a toxic political issue in Mexico, a subject of resentment and contention. Leaders had to recalibrate.

With an ambitious domestic agenda to protect, López Obrador changed his priorities. Officials within Mexico's Interior Ministry, which included the National Immigration Institute and the Commission for Refugee Assistance, were opposed to MPP. They pointed to a lack of resources and concerns about the welfare of asylum seekers who would get stranded between the two countries. But López Obrador's team at the foreign office overrode them. Because the Americans were involved, the issue was less a question of national policy than of diplomatic necessity. The center of gravity inside the Mexican administration shifted to the foreign minister, Marcelo Ebrard, a veteran politico with presidential ambitions of his own. When the MPP agreement was announced, in December, the Mexican government presented the deal as a unilateral American move that they had little choice but to accommodate. In fact, there had already been strong buy-in from the upper tiers of the government, including from López Obrador himself.

MPP went into effect in January 2019, in Tijuana. The Department of Homeland Security extended it, city by city, to locations along the entire US-Mexico border. In mid-March, it came to Mexicali and Juárez. In July, MPP was instituted in the state of Tamaulipas, on the Gulf of Mexico, a stronghold for criminal cartels. Close to fifty thousand asylum seekers were returned to Mexico, where many of them faced extreme levels of violence. On August 3, cartel members arrived at a shelter in the border city of Nuevo Laredo, demanding that the pastor in charge hand over a group of Cubans to be ransomed; when he refused, he was abducted, never to be seen again. Later in the summer, a few miles away, a dozen asylum seekers who'd just been returned to Mexico were kidnapped. "The people in migration"—Mexican immigration authorities—"turned us over to the cartels," one of the victims later told *Vice News*. "They know what they are doing. They don't care if you're killed or not."

Nearly everyone at Pan de Vida had been placed in MPP, including a few people who were no longer sure where they stood in the process. A Honduran named Gabriel, who was sleeping in the same cabin as Denis, along with fifteen other people, kept a small slip of paper from his wallet, an artifact of the period before MPP was instituted in the El Paso area. At the time, Customs and Border Protection agents "metered" migrants at the ports of entry, using an informal system in which migrants were given a number on a waiting list and told to come back when it was their turn. Since March, while asylum seekers from other countries continued to be on the waitlist, Central Americans had to go through MPP. Gabriel didn't realize it, but the five-digit number on his slip of paper corresponded to the old system. The next time he went to the port of entry, he was put into MPP, and the waiting began again.

The residential cabins at Pan de Vida were on the perimeter of a large, dusty plot, where a makeshift soccer pitch and playground were hemmed in by a wall made of rubber tires. A mess hall with an open kitchen and long tables sat at the front of the compound. Outside, a weathered blue pickup truck was filled with trash bags, which the shelter's director drove to a nearby dump. Sitting at a table in the mess hall was a sharp-faced mother in her thirties named Dilcea. She was from Honduras and traveling with her twelve-year-old son, Anthony. The two had been in Juárez since June and had their first court hearing in mid-August. "There were so many people in the courtroom that I wasn't given a chance to say anything to the judge," she said. She had wanted to explain to him that she had diabetes and was running out of insulin.

When Keldy arrived in Ascensión, Chihuahua, at the end of August, she entered a world apart. The town was a way station on the path to a bigger way station: Juárez, where thousands of Central American migrants were stuck in MPP. The policy didn't affect her because her case had already been denied. But she started hearing stories of whole families who were now marooned. The region's shelters were filling to capacity, and those who couldn't find space there sought out churches. The rest were forced to squat in overcrowded encampments along the border.

During her first few days in Ascensión, Keldy stayed in the home of a religious leader she'd met on Facebook named Isela. When the two of them went to a local church so Keldy could present herself to the congregants, an older pastor demanded proof of her religious credentials from Honduras. Keldy pulled from her purse a national ID and pastoral certificate issued by the state, but the man was unconvinced. "This woman is a witch and a charlatan," he shouted. Keldy left the church and decided to hold small payer meetings at Isela's home instead. Within a few weeks, she continued to Juárez and took a room in the apartment of an acquaintance.

In Juárez, Keldy devoted herself to the city's population of migrants. Recently deported families would call her with the rough coordinates of where they were—highway mile markers, descriptions of intersections—and Keldy would take a taxi and bring them someplace they could sleep. She was a regular presence at the Pan de Vida migrant shelter, delivering sermons and benedictions. Ministering to this population, Keldy encountered a universe of migrants living underground. An elaborate system of abuse included the very people who were supposedly keeping the peace. It wasn't just criminal cartels who brutalized the Central Americans stuck in Juárez; it was also the police.

Earlier that spring, a twenty-year-old Honduran woman named Tania and her fourteen-year-old sister were separated at an El Paso port of entry. Her sister was sent to a children's shelter run by the Department of Health and Human Services and eventually placed with their mother, who lived in Boston. Tania spent six days in detention in the US before Mexican immigration agents picked her up and took her back across the border, into Mexico. They dropped her off at a migrant shelter that was already full. She roamed the streets, looking for another place to stay. Her tattered clothes and accent marked her as foreign, and her race—she was black and belonged to an Indigenous community called the Garifuna—led to several episodes of public abuse. On the street, people spit at her and yelled taunts.

Somehow, she had made it to her first court date, in El Paso. Dozens of other asylum seekers joined her; there were no lawyers present, and the judge read everyone their rights before sending them back to Mexico with a future court date. People had warned her that the legal proceedings were a sham, but now she felt she knew for herself. Back in Mexico, she decided that it was pointless to wait any longer. She and another woman from Honduras hired a smuggler to help them cross into the US. The smuggler was in league with a cadre of Mexican federal policemen. For two nights, Tania and the other woman were driven to different stash houses along the border. On the last night before they expected to cross, they were taken to yet another house, where there were four other women and a group of armed men, including policemen in uniforms, keeping watch. One of the policemen held a gun to Tania's head and ordered her to perform oral sex on him. She could hear the other women getting beat up in the other rooms. Early the following morning, Tania and another woman were transported to a separate location, where they were repeatedly raped. A week passed before local authorities found them and took them to a hospital.

Ever since the administration announced the end of its family separation policy, almost a year before, more and more Central American asylum seekers had arrived at the US border. In a rage stoked by Stephen Miller, the president had fired Kirstjen Nielsen in April 2019, along with at least two other agency heads who were otherwise in excellent standing with congressional Republicans. Trump was "pulling the rug out from the very people that are trying to help him accomplish his goal," Chuck Grassley, the former chairman of the Senate Judiciary Committee, lamented to the press.

It was a purge born of desperation. Customs and Border Protection was making more than a hundred thousand arrests each month, the most in a decade. This was a double blow to the administration's hardliners: efforts to deter migrants had not only failed, but backfired. When border policy changed in frequent and conspicuous ways, news spread through Central America. For the DHS establishment, the aim was to avoid dramatic, precipitous shifts like the zero tolerance policy, when the government adopted a position of unprecedented harshness only to publicly reverse itself a month and a half later.

Department officials felt that they knew how to manage the border crisis. They just needed more resources to house families and children. But Miller was contemptuous of conventional wisdom. If the federal courts issued injunctions blocking them, he argued, the Justice Department could appeal those decisions to the Supreme Court. Why place two justices on the bench if the White House didn't use them? The president had appointed more than a hundred judges to the federal judiciary. Before long, Miller believed, the benefits would pay off—all the more reason not to dilute the White House's agenda for the sake of prevailing in court. Miller's idea was to use executive actions as a battering ram against the lower courts. In July 2019, the president issued a new regulation in that spirit, banning asylum for anyone who traveled through another country to reach the US. When it got tied up with an injunction, the Justice Department appealed. This time, the Ninth Circuit narrowed the injunction while the parties argued it out in court; it was a partial but striking victory for the president.

If Miller was impatient with the courts, he was incensed by the bureaucratic hierarchy. As with any federal department, DHS staff took orders from the senior leadership at each of its component agencies. Those agency officials, in turn, took their cues from the top DHS brass. To rewire the chain of command, Miller made what others began to describe as calls "deep in the building." He would ring lower-level officials and give orders directly to them. Not only did he refuse to loop in their bosses; he also instructed the junior officials to shield their activities from the department's leadership. When he found people he could trust, or bully, Miller would enlist them as informers. Every Friday, he convened a meeting at the Eisenhower Executive Office Building, next to the White House, to discuss the ways in which federal bureaucrats were falling short of implementing Trump's agenda. Eventually, career officials stopped attending, and Miller's audience became the political appointees who were already aligned with him. Often, he harangued them anyway. Since Miller had inserted himself into DHS's policymaking process, officials felt obliged to keep their work from him. At one point, to prevent Miller from discovering the details of a policy discussion, Nielsen's replacement, Kevin McAleenan, held meetings in a classified security bunker, known as a SCIF, where cell phones were prohibited and strict rules of confidentiality were in effect. Convinced that a deep-state cabal was trying to thwart Trump's agenda, Miller forced officials to go underground in their own agencies.

IN SEPTEMBER 2019, the Department of Homeland Security opened two tent courts along the border, in Laredo and Brownsville, where as many as four hundred asylum seekers in MPP could be processed each day. People who showed up at ports of entry for their hearings were sent directly to these makeshift courts. The rationale, according to a report in *The Washington Post*, was for US authorities "to give asylum seekers access to the U.S. court system without giving them physical access to the United States." The serial dislocations of MPP—the staggered, piecemeal hearings; the long waits; the improvised courtrooms—achieved the government's desired effect: only 1 percent of all completed cases ended in relief. In these instances, DHS filed appeals. "We are bringing integrity to the system," Kevin McAleenan declared.

Another migrant shelter Keldy frequently visited in Juárez was called Buen Pastor, a complex of white buildings arranged around a small square paved in asphalt and surrounded by iron gates. The space was designed to accommodate sixty people. But by the summer of 2019, Juan Fierro, a pastor who ran the shelter, was housing between 100 and 130 migrants at a time. The day the Mexican government announced that MPP was coming to Juárez, he received a call from Mexican immigration agents known as Grupos Beta. They wanted to know how many people he could take in. Fierro received no additional financial support from the Mexican government to deal with the influx. He used donations from locals and NGOs to invest in the construction of a separate facility across the street.

There were more than a dozen migrant shelters in Juárez, many of which were run by different church dioceses. Buen Pastor was smaller than Pan de Vida, but larger than some others, which ranged from actual facilities—with beds, showers, and dining areas—to church basements. The city's best-known shelter, Casa del Migrante, was already at capacity. The municipal government announced a plan, called the Juárez Initiative, to repurpose an old export factory, or *maquiladora*, as a holding station for asylum seekers who were returned under MPP.

Buen Pastor wasn't just holding migrants who were in MPP. There was a large contingent of people from Uganda and a few Brazilians. None of them were covered by MPP, but they still faced long waits in Juárez, because each day, US immigration agents were interviewing fewer asylum seekers at the ports of entry. Almost all their attention was devoted to maintaining MPP. Several days would pass without CBP accepting anyone else at a port of entry. At the shelter each morning, asylum seekers would pack their bags and say goodbye to Fierro, expecting their numbers to be called, only to return later in the evening.

Originally, MPP was meant for migrants from Honduras, Guatemala, and El Salvador, the three countries in the region with the highest levels of immigration to the US. But the scope of MPP expanded in the summer of 2019. In June, Trump boxed in López Obrador with a threat. If the Mexican president failed to curb the numbers of new arrivals at the border, the US would impose tariffs. They would begin at 5 percent but could escalate to 25 percent by the fall.

López Obrador couldn't tell if Trump was bluffing, and he wasn't willing to gamble. Tariffs of any sort would plunge the Mexican economy into a free fall; it was already contracting in the early months of 2019, and the peso had declined in value. The fallout from a trade skirmish with the Americans could mar López Obrador's entire legacy. Marcelo Ebrard cut a deal that allowed both parties to claim victory. The Mexicans would have forty-five days to further demonstrate their commitment to blocking regional migration. If at the end of that period the situation hadn't changed, López Obrador would agree to a more radical arrangement. While Trump touted a "new deal with Mexico," in which "we got everything we wanted," López Obrador held a rally in Tijuana to celebrate an agreement that he claimed had averted a catastrophe. The Mexicans sent more troops to police the border and revised the terms of MPP. The new version of the program would cover anyone from a Spanish-speaking country.

One morning at Buen Pastor, a thirty-four-year-old teacher from Cuba named Dani Torres sat in the mess hall and watched as a group of children played with small toys. Back home, the country's intelligence agency had tried to compel Torres and her sister to share information about their mother, who belonged to a political opposition group called the Damas de Blanco. Torres's sister left for Panama, and Torres traveled through nine countries to reach the US. When she arrived in Juárez, in May, the port of entry was blocked because of metering. She was given a waitlist number: 18,795. She initially planned to wait her turn but changed her mind when she learned that MPP was being expanded to include Cubans. One day, she had what she considered a *chancecito*, a fleeting opportunity to try to cross the river. Border Patrol agents immediately apprehended her and put her into MPP. At her first court hearing, she was determined to expedite her case. She knew that many others would arrive in court without the necessary documentation. That wouldn't be her fate; she planned to beat the system by anticipating each of its arcane and onerous demands. In the courtroom, surrounded by dozens of other asylum seekers, who looked lost and unprepared, she raised her hand. "I have my forms and my petition for asylum," she told the judge. Through a translator, he responded that she could bring them to her next hearing, which was scheduled for five months in the future.

Fierro kept track of everyone's court dates on a spreadsheet on his desktop computer. Every Tuesday, at the Casa del Migrante, a fleet of buses would leave for Honduras, Guatemala, and El Salvador, carrying asylum seekers who had given up and opted for "voluntary departure." Those who had decided to leave Buen Pastor appeared in yellow on Fierro's sheet; they accounted for about a third of the names. From July to August 2019, in Juárez alone, Mexican authorities bused more than 550 asylum seekers back to Central America. Thousands of others, in border cities from Tijuana to Matamoros, likely left on their own, without bothering to alert national authorities.

Each morning, Keldy kept a daily ritual. Rising before dawn, she walked toward the border, where four bridges led into the US, and visualized herself on the other side. She prayed that the border would open for a moment, just long enough so that she could finally see her children. Then, just as resolutely as she had walked to the bridge, she turned and walked away, into the teeming, perilous city, where she knew she was needed.

47.

Rewriting Asylum

In the spring of 2019, Kevin McAleenan, the acting head of DHS, thought of himself as a technocrat working against the odds. Trump had railed against the governments of El Salvador, Honduras, and Guatemala and cut international aid to the region out of spite. From his years at CBP, McAleenan knew that individual policies at the border were stopgap measures that failed to address emigration at its source. He wanted to restart US aid money to the region, while also rewiring the asylum system to account for what he viewed as an unstoppable exodus.

He called his plans "asylum cooperative agreements," but they were also known as "safe-third-country" deals. The principle was that migrants had to apply for asylum in the first country they reached after fleeing their own, provided that the country had a working asylum system. A version of this sort of arrangement existed in parts of the European Union, and the US had already implemented a similar accord with Canada starting in 2004. If an asylum seeker showed up at a Canadian port of entry, the authorities would send her back to the US to pursue her claim there.

McAleenan sought to apply the model to Central America. Any asylum seeker who reached the US border after having crossed through El Salvador could be sent back. The same would be true for migrants who traveled through

Honduras and Guatemala. Mexico was always willing to do the US's bidding when it came to immigration enforcement. The only line it refused to cross was to sign a safe-third-country deal because it would force the country to offer asylum to everyone trying to reach the US. As a result, to stem Central American migration in particular, Guatemala was the keystone of McAleenan's plan. Farther south, in El Salvador and Honduras, governments would receive asylum seekers coming from South America. The overall effect would be an expanding web that caught everyone who moved through the region. No country would be forced to take back its own migrants, just those from other countries. But the US would have the power to send back whomever it wanted once they reached its southern border, on the grounds that such people had passed through one of the countries that were party to the deals.

The first of many problems with the plan was that none of the three countries of the Northern Triangle could be described as "safe." El Salvador didn't have an asylum system. Guatemala did, but it was minuscule. Then there was the bigger issue of how many people were already fleeing these three countries in the first place, a stark indication of the reality on the ground. Ninety-two percent of everyone arrested at the US southern border were from the Northern Triangle. Two hundred and seventy thousand Guatemalans tried to reach the US in 2019. What did that say about the stability of the country for the 261,000 Hondurans who entered it while heading north, or for the 92,000 Salvadorans?

Most of the migrants would lose their cases for asylum once they reached the US, which was proof to McAleenan that the system was being misused. "Only ten to fifteen percent of the Central Americans seeking asylum in the U.S. actually get it," he said in a meeting in Guatemala, during the summer of 2019. If the government didn't try to "curb the flow," authorities at the border would continue to be overwhelmed by more migrants than the system was designed to handle. McAleenan embodied a version of what had become a respectable American position. "The short-term goal" of the safe-third-country deals, he went on to say, "is deterrence," but "the long-term goal is to set the stage for investment and development in the region. There has to be a way for people to live in the hemisphere. It can't just be the U.S. and Canada."

For fifteen years, beginning around 2004, a laboratory on the border of Colombia and Venezuela churned out cocaine at a clip that eventually reached between three hundred and five hundred kilograms per month. The product was 99 percent pure, and it was costly—ten thousand dollars per kilogram. Packages went out regularly by planes, high-speed motorboats, and, on one occasion, a submarine. Some of the routes led to a ranch in Copán, Honduras, near the ruins of a ninth-century Maya acropolis with stone temples and the remnants of two pyramids. From there, traffickers fanned out into Guatemala and Mexico, where the Sinaloa cartel took control of the shipments, eventually smuggling them into the United States. The cocaine was packed in bulky rectangles that looked like bulging white bricks. On each block of tightly wrapped product were the two interlocking initials of its proprietor: "TH." The letters corresponded to the first and last name of Tony Hernández, a Honduran national congressman and a brother of the president.

In the fall of 2018, as hundreds of Honduran families from the migrant caravan reached the US border, Tony Hernández touched down in Miami, where agents from the DEA arrested him. The charges included trafficking more than 185,000 kilograms of cocaine, paying bribes to politicians up and down his drug routes, and selling weapons. Juan Orlando Hernández denied any knowledge of his brother's activities, but by the summer of 2019 evidence linking him to drug money was being made public. At the start of August, a forty-four-page court filing against Tony Hernández, in New York, referred to a certain "co-conspirator four." The person was unnamed, but clearly identifiable: "CC-4 was elected President of Honduras in late 2013." According to the filing, Juan Orlando Hernández was the subject of other DEA investigations as well. Some $1.5 million in contributions to his campaign came from drug sales, and "El Chapo" Guzmán, the head of the Sinaloa cartel and the world's most notorious drug kingpin, had once met with Tony Hernández personally in order to deliver a million dollars meant for Juan Orlando.

US officials were at cross purposes when it came to Hernández, but they tolerated him as president. He was a security partner who cooperated on drug interdictions and extraditions, and everything he said about limiting immigration and curbing crime was designed to appeal to his defenders in Washington. John Kelly, who had led the US military's Southern Command before joining the Trump administration, called Hernández a "great guy" and a "good friend." After meeting with him in March 2017, Hernández described Kelly as "someone who opens many doors."

At DHS, McAleenan took a utilitarian view. Hernández would sign the immigration pact because his own fate depended on it, especially with a possible indictment in his future. Privately, McAleenan was clear-eyed about Hernández: he was doing "the right thing" for the "wrong reasons." Publicly, he split the difference, calling Hernández "a strong partner" who was trying to "combat irregular migration and transnational criminal organizations."

Around the time McAleenan was developing his asylum agreements, a new president entered office in El Salvador. Nayib Bukele was thirty-seven—the youngest leader in Latin America—and had billed himself as an outsider and anti-corruption reformer. Maintaining a good relationship with the United States wasn't just a political imperative but an economic one. Twenty-two percent of the Salvadoran economy consisted of remittances sent by immigrants living in the US. Shortly after winning the presidential election in February 2019, Bukele traveled to Washington for a series of speeches and interviews. One of his first addresses was at the Heritage Foundation.

Trump was the screaming id of American self-interest, which made it easy for Bukele to maneuver. All Trump cared about was immigration enforcement; Bukele planned accordingly. He was so eager to comply with McAleenan's proposed deal that his advisers emailed a signed copy of the agreement straight to the Department of Homeland Security. US officials had to call them back to explain that the protocol was more involved, requiring signing and countersigning the document in public. Once the Salvadorans gave the White House what it wanted, Bukele could ask his own favor in return. He was trying to build a tourist attraction on beachfront real estate along the Pacific, and he wanted the US State Department, which issued routine travel advisories for Americans going abroad, to lower the country's threat level.

In July 2019, McAleenan was sitting with Bukele in San Salvador, discussing the asylum deals, when a White House staffer shared the latest report on border arrests with Trump. It showed that Honduras had surpassed Guatemala as the country with the most migrants apprehended by Border Patrol the previous month. Enraged, Trump demanded to speak with McAleenan, who was pulled out of his meeting with Bukele to take the call. Trump wanted to impose sanctions immediately, but McAleenan asked for two weeks, vowing to get the Honduran government to sign one of the asylum agreements. It would have no impact on Hondurans traveling north, but the president's fury could serve as leverage. Trump needed reassurance that the Honduran government took the immigration problem seriously. The next day, McAleenan and his team flew to the Soto Cano Air Base, in Honduras, to meet with Juan Orlando Hernández, whose first question was: "What do we get in return?"

For all McAleenan's shuttle diplomacy that summer, Guatemala consumed most of his time and attention. It would have been difficult to find a more pliant partner than the country's outgoing president, Jimmy Morales, who had a few months left in his term.

In late February 2017, Morales and a group of political aides and influential businessmen had met at a condominium in Guatemala City to hatch plans for attacking the reputation of the CICIG, the anti-corruption body, in the US. Within a few months, this group had expanded to include members of the Guatemalan National Congress. According to an investigation by Nómada, a Guatemalan news site, they began paying tens of thousands of dollars each month to the American lobbying firm Barnes & Thornburg, which was managed by a major fundraiser for Vice President Mike Pence. Another interest group opposing the CICIG retained the firm Greenberg Traurig, which had offices in Florida, the home state of Republican senator Marco Rubio. By April 2018, congressional Republicans were holding hearings on potential investigatory abuses committed by the CICIG; in the Senate, Rubio and the Utah Republican Mike Lee led a push to suspend US aid to the group.

After Morales expelled the CICIG, the US government remained silent, despite having once supported it. Morales had earlier earned praise from the Trump administration on another issue: two days after the White House moved the US embassy in Israel from Tel Aviv to Jerusalem, Morales had followed suit. Israel's ambassador to the US took aside Guatemalan officials in Washington and told them, "You now have two ambassadors in Washington."

In Guatemala, the immigration accords received significant media attention. They were wildly unpopular and had the rare effect of galvanizing both the political left and right against the government. But Morales was preparing for his life after the presidency; casting his lot with the Americans was his insurance policy. He sent his interior minister, Enrique Degenhart, to the US capital to work out the terms of the deal. Degenhart had made his first visit earlier that spring, just after McAleenan became acting secretary. McAleenan was still unpacking his new office when the two met. They knew each other from McAleenan's time as head of CBP. "We're here at the orders of our president to see how we can help," Degenhart said. "We give you our borders."

Throughout the spring and summer, Degenhart made several trips to Washington. By late July, everything was ready, and the Guatemalans were preparing to sign off when the Constitutional Court, the country's highest judicial body, interceded. Morales could not sign such a substantial international compact without congressional approval, according to the judges. Their ruling came the night before he was supposed to travel to Washington. His plans were canceled. Instead of the triumphant meeting he and the Americans had planned, a harried delegation went in his place—a cleanup crew. They met at the White House with McAleenan and Stephen Miller.

"I need the US to hit us with a big stick," Degenhart told the Americans at the meeting. He was a tall, imposing man with short gray hair and a doughy face. Morales needed a pretext to ignore the court's decision. "Let's scare our people into agreeing with this," Degenhart said.

A plan took shape: They would get Trump to issue a wrecking ball of a tweet, something that could, as Degenhart suggested, "get people to realize there's no other option." It would seem credible because everyone knew Trump would impose massive sanctions if he could. The only way to avert an economic catastrophe would be for the Guatemalan government to sign the asylum deal. At the end of the meeting, a photograph was taken in the Diplomatic Reception Room of the Eisenhower Executive Office Building. Under a gilt chandelier, against a backdrop of light pink walls trimmed in gilt fixtures, Degenhart stood beside McAleenan and Miller, with a smile on his face.

Several days later, Trump fired off his tweet, and the campaign in Guatemala began in earnest. Morales blamed the Constitutional Court for putting the country on a collision course with Trump. Guatemala's main business association, called the CACIF, an influential body of the wealthiest families who'd initially opposed the safe-third-country deal, came out in support of it. Trump's tweet had imperiled their bottom line. Tensions were already building between the Constitutional Court and the private sector. Several cases had come before the judges involving mining interests and hydroelectric projects. The court was seen as the final check on some highly lucrative concerns.

Members of the bench faced frequent threats and harassment, and the court was at an institutional crossroads. The judges surveyed the cases before them and tried to prioritize which ones were worth risking the court's future legitimacy. Incurring any more public opposition put all the cases at risk, because there was no institution left in the country that could defend the judges or vouch for their impartiality. Part of their calculus was grappling with the uncomfortable fact that Morales would likely defy some of their rulings anyway. Where would that leave them? Several weeks later, they quietly lifted the injunction against the immigration deal. By the fall, the Americans had signed agreements from the governments of Guatemala, El Salvador, and Honduras.

Part 4

48.

The Heart Doctor

On a bright April day in 2015, an old man in black, unbelted slacks and a button-down shirt walked in a daze through the deportation wing of the San Salvador airport. Another plane had just touched down, returning more people to their new old lives. This deportee stood out in the crowd. He was older than the others—balding and bespectacled—and in his hands was a ziplock bag with his passport and medication. His name was Carlos Eugenio Vides Casanova. He was seventy-seven years old.

I first heard the name Juan Romagoza when Vides Casanova was deported. The news of a high-profile deportation didn't strike me as an immigration story at first. I was focused on the theme of historical memory and accountability. These subjects had a way of sounding abstract until a geriatric ex–minister of defense wound up on an ICE plane, followed nine months later by his eighty-two-year-old predecessor—General José Guillermo García.

In the fall of 2015, I was researching a strange incident that was making me doubt whether the line between past and present even existed at all. A human rights clinic at the University of Washington, in Seattle, had just reported the theft of a computer and an external hard drive. There was sensitive information on both stolen devices about a pending public-records lawsuit against the Central Intelligence Agency and about a former Salvadoran colonel with ties to the US. The director of the clinic was working with advocates in El Salvador to obtain US government documents about the war years. In place of the computer on her desk was a hand-carved wooden cat about three inches long with its front paws extended and its back arched. The cat used to sit on the top of her computer monitor—a trinket brought back from a trip to Mexico—but whoever moved it had taken some care. It was angled to face her chair as though to suggest surveilling eyes.

The mystery of the theft went unsolved. But it prompted me to go to El Salvador, where I confronted the ex-colonel, Sigifredo Ochoa Pérez, over coffee at a McDonald's. He was accused of commanding a unit of troops that massacred hundreds of innocent villagers in a town called Santa Cruz, in the fall of 1981. I say "confronted," but I was shaky and confused through our whole conversation. He was so completely unrepentant and self-secure—a study in impregnability—that I left wondering if maybe I'd gotten some of the facts wrong.

At other times, I felt like I was trapped in a parable with a voided moral. One of the most fearsome figures in the Salvadoran high command was an officer named Nicolas Carranza, who was a point of contact between the military and the death squads. He became a US citizen in the late 1980s—most likely with the help of the CIA, where he'd been on the payroll—and worked as a security guard at an art museum in Memphis. I visited him one afternoon, showing up unannounced at his tan-colored suburban house with green shutters and a narrow front porch. Next to the front door was a small wooden plaque that read "Bienvenido." When I rang the bell, his wife answered the door. He stood behind her in an olive-colored fleece, light blue jeans, and loafers, cradling a barking chihuahua in his arms. He had Alzheimer's and could barely speak. The past was a wordless sphinx.

Like many others who followed the news of Vides Casanova's deportation, I started researching the backstory, and learned that Juan had been the lead plaintiff in what *The Washington Post* called "the case against the generals." He had testified against Vides Casanova twice in court. The first time was in West Palm Beach in the summer of 2002; the second was in Orlando in the spring of 2011. In between those two appearances, on November 14, 2007, Juan addressed a US Senate subcommittee on the subject of "accountability for human rights violators in the United States." "Two of the men responsible for my tortures . . .

are permanent residents here," he said. They "live comfortably, legally, and openly in South Florida." Referring to his role in the case five years earlier, he said that "having to confront my torturers in a legal tribunal" was among "the most difficult and important things I've done in my entire life, one of the moments when I was most proud." The West Palm Beach trial had generated most of the headlines, but the one in Orlando sealed Vides Casanova's fate. Considering the evidence submitted against him in the earlier case, the Department of Homeland Security eventually initiated deportation proceedings. Juan, who was fifty-nine at the time, told his story again. In West Palm Beach, a jury had decided on civil damages. In Orlando, the proceedings took place before an immigration judge.

On the day Vides Casanova was deported, large crowds of protesters had assembled at the San Salvador airport. In El Salvador, he was protected from further prosecution by an amnesty law, which had been passed a few months after the end of the war. A car idled out front, waiting to whisk him away. As he walked toward it, he spotted Juan. At least that's how Juan remembers it. Vides Casanova is unreachable, so it's impossible to know for sure. But Juan wouldn't have missed the moment for anything. A cousin had driven him up from Usulután. Shouting along with a chorus of others, he held a homemade sign, which he would later describe as "the famous sign," because, as he recalls, it made Vides Casanova stop to look. On one side of it was the word *Asesino*; on the other, the question *Donde están los desaparecidos?*

Half a decade would pass before Juan and I spoke. It was early May 2020, and the two of us were stuck inside. In New York, the death toll from the COVID-19 pandemic was still unrelentingly high, and I was barely leaving the house. In his childhood home in Usulután, Juan had even less freedom. He was allowed out only two days each week, during specific hours. El Salvador's president, Nayib Bukele, had imposed draconian requirements for a national quarantine. Those who violated its terms were arrested and sent to "containment centers." In theory, these were reserved for Salvadorans who'd been traveling abroad during the early days of the pandemic and needed to be tested. But they soon became de facto jails, where anyone accused of ignoring the rules was held indefinitely, in some cases for months on end.

By then I had read and reread the transcripts of Juan's testimony and decided that I had a sufficiently pointed question to ask him. On that dark, far-off morning in 1980, when he'd been chained to the floor and blindfolded in El Paraíso, how did he realize that the voice of one of his interrogators belonged to Vides Casanova? Was the connection he made instantaneous, or did the clarity come in retrospect? This wasn't the kind of thing you could put to someone you'd never met, but there was time.

I'd wondered about these questions ever since I started following the case. But the world had also changed radically since 2015, and it made me think about Juan differently as well. I'd considered him a survivor, a witness to history, an activist, and a doctor. But I had first learned about him only after he had returned to El Salvador. What I'd taken for granted was that for a third of his life, he'd been an immigrant in America, an identity he'd never shed. From the beginning of Donald Trump's presidency to its anarchic end, I covered immigration full time as a journalist. It was a four-year-long tornado of legal and humanitarian emergencies that spun me across the US, the borderlands, and Central America. I was studying the history of the immigration system at a moment when it was being dismantled. Juan had lived through the years of its construction.

Journalists can't be too mystical about the dynamics of human interaction. Usually, people speak to you for any number of rational reasons: a belief that something will come of it, a need to unburden themselves, a desire to be seen or heard. Juan made a different impression. To talk to him was to enter a flow of unselfconscious reflection. I was asking the questions, but he invited me in. His voice was warm and accented with an *Usuluteco* lilt—swallowed syllables and slanted vowels. Our first conversation lasted an hour, longer than either of us anticipated. We wound up in unexpected places: Cuernavaca, Mexico, at the church of an old lefty known as the Red Bishop; in San Francisco and Washington; then back in Santiago de María, where Óscar Romero had come for Sunday lunch. There were no linear or chronological paths to the conversation at first. Later, I'd try and fail to impose them. Juan spoke in concentric circles, telling and retelling an anecdote until it broke through to another, and another. I came to regard the knowing, unrushed voice on the other end of the line as the sound of history itself—following its own course, patient with my questions but not always responsive to them.

For a full year, we spoke every day except weekends, for a little over an hour, starting at four o'clock my time, two o'clock his. The following year, as life became more normal and a good deal busier for the both of us, we spoke two or three times a week. It was always at the same hour and always punctuated by the same valediction: *Nos vemos*, see you soon. Because of their regularity, Juan playfully called the conversations his "therapy," joking that he had an authentic New York analyst.

One day, deep into a story, he paused to ask *me* a question for a change. His sister in San Francisco had wondered why he was blocking off the same hour every day, he told me, and he realized he couldn't easily answer her. Could I remind him: What was this all about? I had told him about the book multiple times. But it had been at the start, when I was still introducing myself; now we were more than a year into our *pláticas*, or chats. For my part, I lost track of the original question I'd planned to ask him about Vides Casanova.

There were times when I shared his sense of disorienting absorption in our strange ritual. Usually, I put my phone on speaker, turned on a recorder, and jotted down notes to stay focused on every detail. (Later, I'd have many of the recordings transcribed, and I'd read and annotate each one.) But sometimes I stopped taking notes and talked to him while lying on the floor or pacing around. On one occasion, I was reporting a story at a church in Bay Ridge, Brooklyn, too far from home to make it back in time. So, at four o'clock, I snuck into the empty pews and called him from there. No notes, no recording. Just two people keeping a date.

About three or four months into our conversations, I learned an important lesson: ask him about everything at least twice, if not three or four times, because new details would almost always emerge. When they did, I'd gasp and say, "Juan, you never told me that!" Unfailingly he'd reply, "Well, you never asked." Eventually, Juan told his sister that this project was like a pregnancy that grew slowly over time. But in this case, he added, rather than nine months, the *embarazo* might last a few years.

49.

The Wuhan of the Americas

By the winter of 2020, Trump could duly claim to have curbed immigration in all forms, his biggest campaign promise of 2016. His administration had done it through brash executive action, relentless politics, and bureaucratic sleight of hand. The federal courts, which his allies had diligently filled with loyal judges, were increasingly fending off legal challenges. As they did, the administration pushed on. One of the lawsuits, brought against the Department of Homeland Security in April 2019, called for a halt to the MPP policy of shunting asylum seekers into Mexico. The program was briefly blocked, then reinstated. In the White House, Stephen Miller told officials, "Don't waste time trying to anticipate the risk of litigation. Everything will get challenged in the lower courts anyway. We'll win at the Supreme Court."

While the lower courts went back and forth on MPP, the Department of Homeland Security expanded it. On July 9, DHS started implementing the program in Laredo, Texas; on July 19, in Brownsville; on October 28, in Eagle Pass. On January 2, 2020, when MPP came to Nogales, Arizona, the administration reached a milestone: the policy now covered the entirety of the US-Mexico border. By March, sixty-four thousand asylum seekers had been enrolled in MPP, and 517 of them had been granted some form of legal relief. Thousands of asylum seekers abandoned their cases. Among those waiting in MPP, there were more than fifteen hundred documented cases of murder, rape, assault, and kidnapping, according to Human Rights First. In El Paso, the wait time for an initial court hearing was about five months, while the Mexican government was providing temporary work visas that lasted six months. DHS could say that it was giving migrants a chance to seek asylum, and that immigration judges were ruling against most applicants. But the actual situation was much more troubling. Of the thirty-two thousand removal orders issued by judges, 88 percent were delivered in absentia: the migrants whose asylum cases were being rejected weren't even there.

For as long as Stephen Miller had been in the White House, he harbored the ultimate ambition of closing the border entirely to asylum seekers. MPP was effective, but people still made it through. Miller wanted a policy free of exceptions and legal qualifications. The key was to portray immigration as a direct threat to American public health. It had long been a talking point on the far right—immigrants brought diseases—but Miller sought to convert the claim into an actual policy prerogative. In 2018, when a large group of migrants in federal detention became gravely ill, including two small children who died, Miller felt the president should take advantage of the opportunity to seal the border. Immigrants, he liked to say, were "vectors of disease." During the caravans that same year, Miller tried to find evidence that their participants were sick and contagious. He pressed local communities for information to see if any recently arrived immigrants had introduced new illnesses. In 2019, he called for Trump to invoke public health when a mumps outbreak hit some sixty immigration detention facilities. Each time, Miller encountered resistance from government lawyers and cabinet officials. But in March 2020, COVID changed the legal and political rationale.

An obscure authority was buried in the US legal code as part of the 1944 Public Health Service Act. One provision, known as Title 42, stated that the Centers for Disease Control and Prevention could authorize the federal government to block travel at the border in the event of an emergency involving communicable diseases. There was no evidence that asylum seekers were transmitting COVID-19 at high rates, and the disease was already spreading rapidly inside the United States. The head of the CDC's Division of Global Migration and Quarantine refused to sign off on the policy because, as the Associated Press reported, he thought that "there was no valid public health reason" for it.

But after Vice President Mike Pence called Robert Redfield, the head of the CDC, and ordered him to issue the authorization, the agency complied.

COVID complicated logistics at the border. What was the best way to hold large numbers of immigrants arriving in the middle of a pandemic? How should tests for the virus be administered? Other nations, too, paused their asylum processing during the pandemic. But within several months, many of them had restarted, at least in some measure. In the US, that was never the intention; under Title 42, the government was expelling all asylum seekers, including unaccompanied children, into Mexico. The Trump administration also froze visa processing at foreign embassies, tightening earlier restrictions with renewed justification. Citizenship and Immigration Services, the DHS agency in charge of administering the legal immigration system, was on the verge of a shutdown. Its funding relied entirely on fees from applications, but the administration had been starving the agency of applicants. The backlog of unprocessed citizenship applications had now reached 675,000; another 110,000 people had had their applications approved but were stuck because the agency had ended in-person naturalization ceremonies. With a budget shortfall of more than $1 billion, 70 percent of agency staff faced the prospect of mass furloughs. One of them told a reporter for the *Los Angeles Times*, "Not even my dystopian mind envisioned this."

ON MARCH 28, two days after he was deported to Guatemala from a detention center in Arizona, a twenty-nine-year-old man from a village in the country's western highlands became known as Patient 36. Up to that point, there had been thirty-five registered cases of COVID-19 in Guatemala, and Patient 36 was the first returning deportee to test positive for the illness. He had been put on a plane—part of a deportation fleet known as ICE Air—with forty other passengers, most of whom, like him, had spent several weeks in detention. After landing, they were briefly held in Guatemala City and evaluated, but because the authorities claimed that he showed no symptoms, he was allowed to travel to his family's home, in Momostenango, Totonicapán, where six other relatives, including a nine-month-old baby, lived. By the time he got there, he had a fever and a cough. A local health official told the newspaper *elPeriódico* that the man's wife had known that he was ill before he left the capital. She alerted a medical clinic in town, which tested him. Almost a week later, the Guatemalan government announced that another deportee—a thirty-one-year-old man from Mazatenango, about fifty miles south of Momostenango—had also tested positive, making him Patient 49.

Guatemala had only two large urban hospitals and a regional patchwork of smaller medical facilities; its capacity to contain a virulent pandemic was limited. The government of President Alejandro Giammattei, who was a trained surgeon, suspended international flights into the country, and border transit largely ceased. But could the government persuade the Trump administration to help it limit the spread of the coronavirus? The United States was fast becoming the global epicenter of the pandemic. As of late April, there were some five thousand Guatemalans in US immigration detention, and every week the Department of Homeland Security was sending between one and five flights to Guatemala City, each carrying up to 135 deportees.

Other countries in the region were forced to deal with deportees infected with the virus, including Colombia, Honduras, El Salvador, Mexico, and Haiti, many of which had fragile health care systems, scant hospital space, and a dearth of ventilators. The United States deported eighteen thousand people in March, and nearly three thousand in the first eleven days of April. In multiple cases, US officials knew that they were spreading COVID but didn't seem to care. A twenty-six-year-old Haitian man who'd become infected in a Louisiana detention center was put on a plane despite two positive tests; he claimed to know four others from the jail who were also sick but getting deported with him.

The irony was not lost on Central Americans. In the 1990s and early 2000s, during earlier waves of mass deportations, US and Latin American law enforcement personnel resorted to metaphor to describe what was happening: the gangs were replicating and expanding through the region like a virus. In 2020, the deportations were spreading an actual virus.

By mid-April, there were more than six hundred thousand known cases in the United States, compared with a total of less than eight hundred in El Salvador, Honduras, and Guatemala combined. Nevertheless, after the Guatemalan government suspended the arrival of some deportation flights, buying time to test other deportees, Trump signed an order threatening to impose a raft of sanctions on countries that "denied" or "delayed" the reception of deportees. "The US was being heavy-headed, and the Guatemalans didn't want to pay too high a price," said a person advising the Guatemalan government. "They don't want the wrath of the US right now."

The flights resumed, and a few days later Guatemala's health minister, Hugo Monroy, announced that between 50 and 75 percent of deportees who had just arrived in the country were found to be infected. In mid-April, the authorities said that seventy-four cases had originated from just two deportation flights. US officials considered this an exaggeration and sent scientists from the CDC to conduct tests. The results confirmed the Guatemalan government's analysis: when twelve deportees were selected at random, they all tested positive. By the end of the month, roughly 20 percent of the nearly seven hundred confirmed cases of COVID in Guatemala were people who had been deported from the US. "We must not stigmatize," Monroy said. "But I have to speak clearly. The arrival of deportees who have tested positive has really increased the number of cases." The United States, he added, had become "the Wuhan of the Americas."

ICE officials never had a clear sense of how widely the disease was spreading among those in custody, but its population was vast and conspicuously unprotected. Some thirty thousand people were being held in substandard conditions that heightened the risk of contagion. Testing was virtually nonexistent during the spring and summer months of 2020. Many detainees across the country launched hunger strikes and staged protests; some secretly uploaded videos to YouTube to plead for help and broadcast urgent messages, such as "We want to get out of here alive." An asylum-seeking Cuban doctor who was being held in a privately run facility in Louisiana told the *Mississippi Free Press*, "There's no way to 'distance' here. We sleep in bunk beds on top of each other, in columns with less than a [few feet] between us, head to toe. We use the same cafeteria as those in quarantine with no cleaning in between.... My medical opinion is that many people will die."

In early April, the agency began bussing and flying dozens of immigrants held in the Northeast to a detention center across the country, apparently to try to limit density in centers with known cases; among those transferred, however, twenty-one were already infected. By the end of the month, ICE reported that 449 people in detention had COVID-19. On May 31, having tested 2,781 detainees, it registered 1,461 positive cases. About half of all the people tested in custody were infected, meaning that there could have already been more than fifteen thousand detainees exposed to the virus. In early June, ICE transferred seventy-four detainees from Arizona and Florida to a facility in Farmville, Virginia. The alleged reason was that the Arizona and Florida facilities were overcrowded, but a DHS official admitted to *The Washington Post* that the detainees were moved so that ICE agents could contravene department rules on travel and secretly hitch a ride on the planes to help police Black Lives Matter protesters in Washington, DC. A super-spreader event followed, in which some three hundred immigrants in the Virginia facility contracted the virus. After one of them died, an ICE official conceded, "The rights and interests of detainees were not a factor. You had the department making up a reason to move them."

The high rates of infection among deportees returning to Guatemala briefly made international headlines, but that was primarily because the government had tried to stand up to Washington. Coming from Giammattei, a conservative who was sworn in as president in January, the move was unexpected. El Salvador and Honduras also had citizens held in US detention centers. Those governments allowed deportation flights to continue. In late April, both Nayib Bukele and Juan Orlando Hernández received a political boost from the Trump administration: large shipments of ventilators, accompanied by enthusiastic presidential tweets. Each was also granted a one-on-one telephone call with Trump. Giammattei was not.

The Guatemalan government began holding all deportees in quarantine for evaluation, even those without symptoms. Groups of angry residents in the western highlands, fearful of the coronavirus, threatened to set fire to the shelters and attack newly returned immigrants and their families. One deportee, a nineteen-year-old man from a village near Lake Atitlán, was confronted by a mob after several residents saw footage of him on a television broadcast as he was being transported into the town by ambulance. "They threatened to set my family on fire," he said later. "I was really afraid and I could only think about leaving the village so that I wouldn't cause any more trouble."

50.

Eddie and Juan

On the day of the 2020 US presidential election, Juan Romagoza was at home with COVID. He suffered a few days of flu-like symptoms, then was mainly restless. He had been in and out of the hospital to see one of his sisters, who was visiting from San Francisco but got sick in Usulután. Her oxygen levels dropped to dangerous levels, and the situation was grave before it finally cleared, a few weeks later; she returned to Juan's house for a slow convalescence. During that time, we had missed some of our regular conversations. A couple of days after the vote, when the returns were in, I received a text from Juan. His messages tended to be short and slightly formal. Sending them wasn't easy; they required a physical dexterity that he'd never fully recovered. This message read: *Felicidades, se va para fuera Trump, pero no quiere aceptar*—"Congratulations, Trump is out, but he doesn't want to accept it."

Juan was among the most political people I had ever met. Every aspect of his life radiated *militancia*, or activism. It could make our discussions of history tilt toward the abstract: he took credit for nothing, emphasized the collective struggle over individual action, and spoke indefatigably about organizing. In hundreds of our conversations, he somehow never failed to state, and restate, the central conviction of his adult life: that medical care was a human right and should be free.

But when it came to pure power politics—the brute, fascistic excesses of Trump, the authoritarianism of Bukele—Juan became more parsimonious. He spoke his mind, to be sure, and made plain that he had no patience for demagogues and strongmen. Yet he rarely wasted time stating the obvious. Venting his distaste for these men wasn't exactly cathartic.

Early the previous summer, when police had cleared Black Lives Matter protesters from the streets of Washington so that Trump could make his infamous appearance with a Bible at St. John's church, next to the White House, Juan shared his own memories of the place. He'd been there multiple times for hunger strikes. Trump's appearance was an abomination, but Juan spent less time lamenting it than recalling the dignity of the church. To him, it had offered refuge and solidarity. Some of this, I realized later, was for my benefit. Juan was steering me away from the desecration, and toward a sense of purpose.

Could Juan do the same when he contemplated El Salvador? He had served as the chief medical officer in Usulután during the country's two FMLN presidencies. The second FMLN leader, Salvador Sánchez Cerén, who took over from Mauricio Funes, was the first ex-guerrilla to be president. The insurrectionists of the past were the institutionalists of the present. Juan was in his late sixties by the end of Cerén's term; he finally decided to retire. His eight years in government had been eventful and productive. The number of health clinics had grown, from thirty-four to eighty-nine; their quality had improved; and the government had added four mobile clinics, equipped with maternity wards and staffed by social workers, psychologists, and specialized doctors. Juan traveled across the department overseeing facilities and recruiting patients who'd never had access to public health services. He led meetings with war veterans from both sides of the conflict, guiding them in conversations about trauma and loss. Many of these men were maimed, paralyzed, blinded, or brought low by ghastly wounds and crippling solitude. Some of them started spending holidays at Juan's house and came to consider him not just a doctor but a friend.

The work made Juan extremely proud, and although he'd invested most of his professional life in La Clínica, which was perhaps the crowning achievement of his career, his stint in the Usulután government carried special weight. It represented the continuation of his earliest days of activism. The war years had given way to the gang years—the period of Mano Dura and Super Mano Dura. Juan had inevitable run-ins and scares; on a couple of occasions, gangsters followed him on his rounds. A few of them made idle threats. But eventually, they came to his clinics and sought medical treatment like everyone else. When they did, he dispensed it without hesitating. In the gang parlance, the leader of a clique was known as a *palabrero*, or keeper of the word. Once the gangsters recognized Juan as a doctor with the fervor of a high priest, they gave him an honorific nickname: the *palabrero de salud*.

By 2019, however, the FMLN had all but failed as a party and as a principle. Since the late 1980s, along with ARENA, the two parties had governed the country without interruption; it was a period of chronic poverty, corruption, violence, and mass emigration. Mauricio Funes, whose election brought Juan his job in Usulután, had been living in exile in Nicaragua since 2016; he had fled after being convicted of charges that included money laundering, embezzlement, illicit association, and bribery. Three years later, state prosecutors brought new charges against Funes for tax evasion.

Bukele's candidacy was predicated entirely on the rejection of *bipartidismo*, or the two-party system. Three of his most recent predecessors had been either arrested or indicted, and all of them came from El Salvador's two main political parties. When Bukele announced his bid for the presidency, he'd been a mayor twice, first of a town of fewer than ten thousand people, called Nuevo Cuscatlán, and later of the capital. His campaign slogan—"There's enough money to go around as long as no one steals"—was a line he'd used almost as long as he'd been in public life. It was partly a promise and partly a rebuke. "I did not live the war," he said in one television interview. "I'm of the post-war generation, a generation that has *nuevas ideas*."

During the years of his ascent, Salvadorans heard from him constantly—on Twitter, on Facebook, and in a continual procession of ribbon cuttings and public acts. The son of a wealthy Muslim businessman, Bukele dropped out of college to run his father's public relations firm, whose main client was the FMLN. There were only two parties at the time, so in 2011, when he ran for mayor of Nuevo Cuscatlán, an old ARENA stronghold, it was on the FMLN ticket. He generated buzz as a reformer with a businessman's acumen. The FMLN needed a charismatic candidate for the mayoralty of San Salvador, which was widely regarded as a stepping stone to the presidency, and party elders picked Bukele because they thought his growing popularity would give them an additional edge in their races for the Assembly.

On the bigger stage of the nation's capital, Bukele's profile grew. He cleaned up parts of the city's ramshackle downtown, renovated a trio of historic plazas, and opened a high-end market, which had escalators and rooftop restaurants. At one point, he unveiled a $24 million public works project called 100% Iluminado, to install lamps on every street corner of the capital. "You can call it PR if you want to be a little cynical. But I'm talking about inspiration," he said in 2016. "I'm talking about something sublime." When critics disagreed, he tended to take it personally. To preempt any bad press, he started to build an alternate media landscape to support his cause: TV programs, a network of trolls on Twitter, an army of YouTubers, and several publications that pumped out pro-Bukele stories on Facebook. Eventually, he broke with the FMLN and founded a party of his own, which he called Nuevas Ideas.

Juan was skeptical of Bukele's personality, which he recognized as a type: charismatic, overpowering, conniving. He'd heard soaring promises before and was wary of Bukele's claim that he could deliver single-handedly where others had failed. He looked at Bukele and saw the past dressed up as the future—in a leather jacket and a backward cap, with a goatee and gelled hair. But his misgivings put Juan in the minority. When Bukele was elected president, in February 2019, he embodied a new national beginning. At his inauguration, his heavily pregnant wife stood beside him while he instructed crowds of ecstatic voters to raise their hands along with him after he swore the oath of office.

EDDIE ANZORA WAS LIVING in San Salvador at the time, and had recently had a second son. English Cool continued to operate—sometimes just barely, it seemed. Fast Eddie looked older. His buzz cut receded at the temples. There were new creases under his eyes. His youthful muscle was tipping into middle-aged bulk. But he kept up the hustle, and his endless ventures and side projects helped him bring his family up a few rungs into a more stable existence that resembled life in the middle class. They went out for dinner once or twice a week, and on weekends would take the bus to the beach.

The new president appealed to him. If Juan looked at Bukele and saw the past, Eddie glimpsed the future. When I texted him in early 2020 to ask about the gangs, he replied, "We're not really talking about that anymore." Bukele was promoting tourism on the Pacific coast with newly refurbished beaches that he was calling Surf City. He was seeking tech investment and making a name for himself on the world stage with savvy stunts like taking a selfie in the middle of an address to the UN General Assembly. He was a public relations guy, like Eddie, and Eddie could appreciate someone who knew how to generate press.

One night, over pizza in a mall in San Salvador, he told me about his latest project, called Salvy Life. It was part public relations hub, part news site, and part fashion line, with a slogan meant to sell the possibilities of life in El Salvador: *Playa, Ciudad, Campo,* or Beach, City, Countryside. His model was all the magazines he'd read growing up in California—*Vice, Mad, LA Weekly*. He wanted dynamic, engaging stories about El Salvador that could open it up both to foreigners and to residents who could stand to see their home with new eyes. Gesturing toward me, he said, "I read all you university writers to see how you do it. I want to give it that tone. And I don't want to use words that are too Latino-ish, too Chicano-ish."

At English Cool, he was giving his students a new assignment for them to practice their language skills: they were to write short pieces about some aspect of El Salvador that they liked or found interesting. He would post the best entries on the website of Salvy Life, which he had designed himself, using a template from GoDaddy. "I'll figure out how to get something cool from them," he said.

For the first time in a while, it seemed to Eddie like El Salvador had a place in the world, and that corresponded to a new chapter in his own life. He was no longer in limbo. It may not have been what he envisioned growing up, but in El Salvador he was home. "When I got here, everyone thought it was shit," he told me. "But I knew: someone out there is living a good life."

Eddie Anzora (right) with a student at his language school, English Cool, in San Salvador, El Salvador, 2013.

51.

Keldy

One morning in April 2021, Keldy Mabel Gonzáles Brebe de Zúniga received a text message from her immigration attorney, in El Paso. In February, barely two weeks after assuming office, Joe Biden had signed an executive order to create a federal task force charged with reunifying families that had been separated under Trump's zero tolerance policy. The details of how the order might affect Keldy's case weren't yet clear. But government sources were telling her lawyer, Linda Corchado, that the reunification process could begin before the fall. A week later, Corchado sent another message: "Keldy, do you know where you can get passport photos taken in Juárez?" The next series of messages came faster; Corchado was receiving more information from the Department of Homeland Security. Keldy was sitting in her room one morning, having just returned from her morning ritual of praying at one of the international bridges, when Corchado texted a date and time: she was scheduled to cross into El Paso on Tuesday, May 4, at eight in the morning.

"Something different is passing over me now," Keldy said. I'd known her for three years, since meeting her at the ICE detention center on Montana Avenue; I'd visited her in Mexico. But hearing her now felt like I was listening to someone else. Her voice was clearer and brighter. She was only thirty-seven years old, and for the first time in dozens of hours of conversation, she sounded like it. "I'm returned to life," she said.

Still, she was nervous that something might go wrong, and decided not to share the news with her children. Instead, she texted her niece a video from the Juárez side of the Paso del Norte bridge. "Blessings to you," she began, barely suppressing a smile. She was wearing tinted glasses and a gray, black, and white checkered flannel shirt. Her hair, freshly cut, whipped in the wind. "I'm going over there," she said. "I'm going all the way up until I'll be with my children." Then she swore her niece to secrecy. If the international bridges connecting Juárez to El Paso were a symbol of hope, they were also a reminder of the greatest trauma of her life. Waiting on the American side were agents from Customs and Border Protection. At one point, she texted Corchado, "They're not going to set a trap for me, are they?"

For more than a year after the government instituted its zero tolerance policy, the Trump administration lied about how many families had been affected. In the summer of 2018, the Department of Justice was forced to acknowledge having separated roughly twenty-seven hundred children, but the actual number was more than fifty-six hundred. It took months of litigation to dislodge the accurate tally, because the earlier count had deliberately left out most of what had happened in 2017. The first separations began in two waves that year, and they'd never entirely stopped. There was the El Paso pilot that swept up Keldy, as well as another one, begun slightly earlier, in Yuma, Arizona. That policy, called the Criminal Consequence Initiative, was responsible for the separation of 234 families between July 1 and December 31, 2017. In March 2019, Judge Sabraw expanded the number of eligible class members in the suit, and once he did, the government had no choice but to go back through its data and reconstruct the complete lists of everyone it had separated. The result was that there were now two official troves of names. One was from the summer of 2018, when Sabraw first ruled on the case; the other, which was much more recent, included a fresh accounting of the families separated in 2017. Keldy's name was on the second list.

One lawyer had become obsessed with filling in the gaps in the government's records: Ann Garcia, a bright, diligent woman in her early thirties who lived in Denver, where she worked out of coffee shops and public libraries for an organization called the Catholic Legal Immigration Network. ("I was working remotely before everyone was working remotely," she said.) Garcia wanted to consolidate the data collected by nonprofits and legal-service providers along the border to create detailed accounts of the separated families whose whereabouts, in hundreds of cases, remained completely unknown. Mostly this consisted of spending the better part of 2019 pleading with other lawyers to share information about their old clients, running their alien numbers through a government hotline for updates, then cold-calling them with mixed success.

Garcia first spoke to Keldy in the summer of 2019, after reaching her on Facebook, and they'd stayed in close contact ever since. Keldy tended to have that effect on people: when she recognized goodness, she latched on, and won the person over with her resoluteness. Garcia was Keldy's match in persistence, but she didn't have much to offer in the way of practical solutions. Although Keldy believed a judge should reopen her asylum case, the only legal mechanism left was to argue that the conditions in Honduras had gotten worse since she first applied. She sent Garcia news clips about violence in La Ceiba and urged her to talk to local professors and journalists whose contact information she found on social media. "From Keldy's view, the judge made a mistake," Garcia said. "From a judge's view, the thinking was, 'When a place is on fire, how do you prove that the fire is getting worse?'" Garcia ran down every lead Keldy shared with her, but she started to take a longer view: only if Trump lost could there be a full reckoning.

On the campaign trail, Biden lambasted Trump for his inhumanity, directing his outrage at the administration's family-separation policy. It was "criminal," "abhorrent," and "violates every notion of who we are as a nation," he said. In October 2020, at the final presidential debate, the issue got prime billing as the two candidates sparred over asylum policy. Trump attacked Biden for Obama's response to the unaccompanied-minors crisis in 2014. "Who built the cages, Joe?" he asked. "Who built the cages?" Biden countered with a reference to MPP: "This is the first president in the United States of America that said anybody seeking asylum has to do it in another country." Then he seized on a filing in Sabraw's court from a few days earlier. The latest status report indicated that the parents of 545 children still could not be found. "Their kids were ripped from their arms and separated," Biden said. "Those kids are alone. Nowhere to go. Nowhere to go."

When, as president, Biden created the task force at the Department of Homeland Security, its executive director was Michelle Brané, from the Women's Refugee Commission. The advocates were coming in from the cold. Ready to build a master list of families the government could reunite, Brané went to Lee Gelernt, at the ACLU, and Gelernt went to a group of other lawyers that included Garcia. "Who are you in touch with?" he wanted to know. The idea was to find parents who'd been deported, and to begin to bring them across the border. It was March 2021. For two years, Garcia had been toiling in obscurity; now she was cast in a central role, connecting the families and their immigration lawyers to a government body that could finally help. Keldy was one of the first names she handed over.

On Tuesday, May 4, 2021, half an hour before she was due at the bridge, Keldy began wheeling two suitcases to the border. Corchado was meeting her on the Mexican side so that they could cross together. Biden's task force had planned for the exchange to go smoothly. Keldy was entering the US with a special status known as humanitarian parole, which would grant her work authorization and a reprieve from deportation for three years. A minute before eight o'clock, she took her first steps in El Paso, which Corchado captured with a photograph. Keldy posed for the camera, twirling in a blue dress and black shoes, with her arms outstretched to the sky.

Three other separated parents were traveling to the US that week to be with their children, the first of hundreds of reunifications that the Biden administration planned to orchestrate over the next several months. According to Michelle Brané, the executive director of the task force, more than a thousand families remained separated. The administration, she said, "is in the process of reviewing additional files to determine if there are more. Finding every family and giving them an option to reunite and heal from this process is our mandate." The first group of parents were already in Northern Mexico and had lawyers who could assist with their crossings. Keldy was the first among them to make it across the border.

The rest of her day was spent in transit—a plane to Dallas, a connecting flight to Philadelphia. When she touched down, just after seven o'clock in the evening, the husband of one of her nieces, a large, gregarious man named Fredy, came to get her in a black pickup truck. Keldy wanted to surprise her sons, but she needed an excuse to get the whole family together without creating suspicion. A team of Australian documentarians, whom Keldy had met in Juárez, would be on hand. Fredy and his wife, Viviana, who was also in on the secret, told everyone that the journalists were part of a news crew that would be conducting interviews about Keldy's legal case. The family, which included more than a dozen people—Keldy's three sons, her mother, her two sisters, their children and grandchildren, those children's spouses—had made posters ahead of time, some with words of encouragement ("We miss and love you") and others with a message for President Biden ("We're asking that you help").

Keldy Mabel Gonzáles Brebe de Zúniga in Philadelphia, Pennsylvania, May 16, 2021.

By the time Keldy collected her suitcases at the airport, the family was gathering at Fredy and Viviana's place, a small brick row house in North Philadelphia. The film crew came through the door just after eight. Tucked behind them was Keldy. There were fifteen people crowded in the front of the house. For a full second after Keldy emerged, there was silence. Then, a jolt, less a sound than a low rumble, as Keldy's sons rushed to her. Her sisters and nieces collapsed in on them. Keldy disappeared, the circle of family members tightening around her. Someone turned up a Christian rock song on a speaker system. In the split seconds when Keldy's sons readjusted their grip around their mother, I caught glimpses of their faces, soaked in tears and flushed a deep red. Amanda, who was thin and frail, held her arms up to the ceiling like someone at a revival meeting. The volume of the music was so high that the room was both loud

Keldy Mabel Gonzáles Brebe de Zúniga reunites with her sons at a relative's home in Philadelphia, Pennsylvania, May 4, 2021.

and strangely still. Then the speakers cut out, and the house filled with the sound of Keldy and her three children wailing.

Standing on the fringes of the group, near the door, was Lee Gelernt, who'd come from New York to congratulate Keldy and her children. The government and the ACLU were in settlement negotiations over what the separated parents deserved going forward. "I've been doing this since 2017, and I don't see it ending very soon," Gelernt said. "Like all big civil rights cases, it ultimately comes down to a long grind."

Possible forms of restitution—beyond securing parole and making travel arrangements—included access to medical and mental-health services and possible financial compensation. But the most important question was whether the separated families would receive permanent legal status. The parole that Keldy had received could be renewed after three years, but as a form of protection, it was provisional. What she needed was a pathway to a green card.

There were signs that the Biden administration was taking the settlement negotiations seriously. On Tuesday, Biden's secretary of Homeland Security, Alejandro Mayorkas, said that the week's reunifications were "a source of pride, because it's just the beginning." He referred to the separated parents and their children as "victims." The implication was that the previous administration had deliberately mistreated them, which raised questions of redress. "We recognize that we need to do more, that humanitarian parole does not provide a stable basis to remain in the US for an extended period of time," he said. "We're looking at the legal authorities that we have."

On that May night, at the house in Philadelphia, future legal issues were still a distant concern. The mood gradually loosened, and food started to come out of the kitchen. A dining table filled with large platters of rice and beans, carne asada, pico de gallo, and cups of horchata. Keldy and her sons sat around

Keldy Mabel Gonzáles Brebe de Zúniga with members of her family in Philadelphia, Pennsylvania, May 4, 2021.

the table, laughing and sharing photos on their phones. A toddler fell asleep on the couch; the older kids drifted to the porch. Someone rolled out what looked like a birthday cake with the words "Welcome Home" written in icing.

Keldy's eldest son, Alex, quietly took it all in. He was the most stoic of her children, short and stocky, with watchful eyes. As the night wore on, Alex kept up his usual reserve, but a look of relief had settled on his face. At one point, Keldy took him aside. "Thank you for everything you did for your brothers," she said. "I'm so proud of you."

52.

Lucrecia

Trump sought to hide the asylum crisis south of the border. Biden started paying an immediate price for bringing it back into view. The Central American exodus had never really ceased. MPP and the use of Title 42 covered over the reality in Northern Mexico. The pandemic brought new spells of desperation, as did two hurricanes that struck the region in the fall of 2020, displacing tens of thousands of people. Inside the new administration, a common refrain was that "all the options are bad." Biden's advisers had criticized Trump for using Title 42 for political rather than public-health reasons. Yet the administration did not want to relinquish what seemed like a useful tool in an unpredictable time: under Title 42, the government could continue to expel people en masse. While DHS tried to restore its capacity for processing new arrivals, the president was desperate to manage the increasing number of migrants. The politics were obliterating. The border dominated his first press conference as president, in March 2021. "What we're doing right now is attempting to rebuild the system that can accommodate what is happening today," Biden said. "It's going to take time."

Republicans had a slogan ready—"Biden's Border crisis"—which network news mostly adopted. As usual, the Democrats were divided, so the president was largely on his own. The White House had called for an immediate winddown of MPP, and a team went to work on the complex logistical operation of locating people enrolled in the program and "paroling" them into the country. Title 42 remained in place, with one exception. Whereas Trump used the policy to exclude unaccompanied children, Biden allowed them in. The partial policy shift, however, meant that the number of children admitted at the border increased substantially. In late March, there were eighteen thousand unaccompanied migrant children in US custody, including more than five thousand who were held in overflow cells at the border. Officials had to resurrect temporary shelters run by the Department of Health and Human Services. When members of the progressive left saw that Biden was using some of the same facilities from the Trump era—albeit for different purposes—they attacked him for "putting kids in cages."

Of the three consecutive US presidents who faced humanitarian emergencies at the southern border, Biden was playing a recurring role. In 2015, the Obama administration had recognized the need to invest in Central America and sent Biden there to manage the situation. He made trips to Mexico City, Guatemala City, San Salvador, and Tegucigalpa. He urged the region's leaders to reach benchmarks on fighting corruption, stimulating the economy, and supporting the justice system. As president, six years later, Biden deputized his vice president, Kamala Harris, to do the same.

Harris regarded the job as a trap. She became an instant Republican target, and because the most viable policy proposals for the region required years, if not more, to register demonstrable effects at the border, there was no immediate way to repel the attacks. At a meeting in April 2021, Biden mentioned to leaders of the Congressional Black Caucus that Harris was working on immigration for the new administration. She cut in to correct him: "the Northern Triangle—not immigration," she said.

In an uncanny reprise of the 1980s, Central America was once again a place of high peril for US politicians. If Harris was supposed to fly to the region for meetings, where should she go? There were no interlocutors left who could speak in good faith. Years of American interventionism, followed by many more years of indifference, made old allies suspect and new ones impossible to find.

In the winter of 2015, when Biden was vice president, he had spoken in Guatemala City at a summit for regional leaders, where he joked about how close Juan Orlando Hernández was with John Kelly, then head of the US military's Southern Command. Addressing Kelly in front of the crowd, he said, "I keep talking to the president of Honduras to make sure he doesn't have you move your headquarters to Honduras." For Harris, though, Hernández was now off-limits. His ties to drug traffickers could no longer be ignored. By the spring of the next year, in an extraordinary turn of events, he was extradited to the US, in a state of visible shock that his old protectors had turned on him.

In El Salvador, Bukele was in direct conflict with the Biden administration. His new party had won a supermajority in the Assembly a month after Biden entered the White House. On the same day that they were sworn in, the new representatives fired all the judges on the country's Supreme Court, then ousted the sitting attorney general. Bukele had a grudge against the judges: he'd declared a state of legal exception at the start of the pandemic, which they invalidated as unconstitutional. Their replacements were friendlier, allowing Bukele to skirt a constitutional prohibition that had kept past presidents from running for a second term. Trump wouldn't have cared, but the Biden State Department did. Bukele smarted. Within a few months, members of his administration appeared on US lists of corrupt officials whose visas were being revoked.

That left Guatemala as the Biden administration's only passable partner, so Harris planned to fly there. But first, she held a meeting in Washington about the rule of law with four Guatemalan jurists and lawyers, all women, who'd been forced into exile for their work. One of them, Thelma Aldana, had been attorney general during the heyday of the CICIG, the anti-corruption body, and later became a leading presidential candidate, in 2019, before an opposition campaign forced her to quit and leave the country. Another was a judge whom the ruling party in Congress had refused to seat on the Constitutional Court, in 2021, despite her legitimate election. The State Department, which was trying to repair the damage left by Trump, gave awards to Guatemalan legal figures and issued strong statements of support.

"At this table are attorneys who have prosecuted drug traffickers and organized crime," Harris said. "At this table are judges who have advocated for an independent judiciary and the rule of law; leaders who have taken on corruption, who have taken on violence." She added that "injustice is a root cause of migration" and "corruption is preventing people from getting basic services." Afterward, Aldana tweeted, "There is hope for Guatemala."

These were the right things for the US government to say and to do, and it mattered that the message came from the top of the administration. The trouble was that the influence of the US was waning. Top Guatemalan officials now feared the US less than they did the sprawling network of corrupt homegrown players. Harris traveled to Guatemala and said her piece to President Alejandro Giammattei, who countered that the corruption investigations were the partisan fixations of an overzealous left. In conspicuously perfunctory terms, he vowed to cooperate with Washington, then proffered a sharp criticism. Biden, he said, needed "to send more of a clear message to prevent more people from leaving."

In the American press, the narrative surrounding the visit reverted to the parsing of a cliché. At one point, following a hackneyed script, Harris told migrants, "Don't come." This became the top-line review of her visit, the quote that summarized the summit. The right called her ineffectual, the left inhumane. A week after she returned, a thirty-nine-year-old lawyer named Juan Francisco Sandoval, who was the head of Guatemala's elite Special Prosecutor's Office against Impunity (FECI) at the Public Ministry, was fired for insubordination. He fled to El Salvador in the middle of the night to avoid arrest. The Biden administration could not protect him at home. All it could do was welcome him with an asylum application once he reached the US.

THE FIRST WEEK OF March 2022, I found Lucrecia Hernández Mack in Guatemala City, in a small second-floor office on a busy commercial street around the corner from the National Assembly. She was a congresswoman now, with an upstart leftist party called Semilla. The room was simple and unadorned—a wood desk with two chairs, several potted plants pressed up against a large window, and a sign strung together from multiple sheets of printer paper that faced the street and read, *Renuncia Giammattei*: "Resign, Giammattei." Lucrecia was there often but never for long. One morning, she came in late, around eleven, because a meeting at the Education Ministry had been delayed. The minister never showed, sending the vice minister in her stead. After two years of the pandemic, the government was finally bringing students back to the classroom. Lucrecia, along with other members of the Semilla delegation, had been making visits to primary schools to inspect the conditions before the students returned. She arrived back at her office *desconcertada*—uneasy—about the lack of progress, but she didn't have time to dwell on it. She was due at the Assembly for a plenary session.

I joined her on the walk over, as she described her party's latest maneuvers while meandering through traffic. Two men in late middle age stopped her to shake her hand and send their best to her aunt. Another passerby nodded respectfully, recognizing her from television. In the front hallway of the Assembly building, a camera crew was waiting for her to comment on the national vaccination policy, which she did in tight, forceful paragraphs before proceeding into the chamber. A couple of blocks away was the downtown intersection where her mother had been murdered. There was a memorial tile midway down the street at the site of the stabbing; at the corner was a plaque renaming the street Calle Myrna Mack Chang.

Three decades after the murder, the specter of her mother still followed Lucrecia around. The country was ignoring the message that Myrna had been trying to send. Lucrecia's worst experience as a newcomer to politics, she told me, was a moment during the campaign in 2019 when she had traveled with other Semilla candidates to Huehuetenango. Speaking in Spanish, she found herself addressing a group of Indigenous women in a language they didn't understand. A translator stood next to her, but the crowd was slipping away. What could she offer them anyway? The mayoral candidates were handing out soft drinks and pieces of candy. The visiting presidential candidates promised schools, hospitals, and new roadways. "A congressional candidate can offer laws, and that's with luck," she told me. The more established political parties distributed cash and held cookouts. Semilla couldn't afford that, and in any case Lucrecia refused to buy anyone off. Her ex-husband, who went with her on these trips, said, "The campaign is very different where there's no highway and only dirt roads."

Even the paved streets of the capital were full of obstructions. The week I visited in March was typical for Lucrecia and her party—another series of fights that they could draw out but never win. A few days earlier, the Assembly had passed a vaccination law that Lucrecia had been working on since she'd served as Minister of Health. Of 160 lawmakers, 106 voted for it, but the president issued a veto, citing "inconsistencies" in the law. No one could say for sure what his real reasons were. Guatemala didn't have a law that required the government to provide the public with vaccines, and without one the state lacked a compelling incentive to ensure that there were enough to meet even the most basic needs.

Lucrecia was also outspoken about a campaign being waged by the country's Public Ministry. Ever since the CICIG had been forced out of the country, in 2018, the attorney general, an arch conservative named María Consuelo Porras, had been charging and arresting lawyers who'd been involved in the fight against corruption. Twenty-two judges and anti-corruption prosecutors had been forced into exile. The claims against them were baseless; in many cases, private lawyers with ties to vested interests brought highly dubious charges that the ministry used as pretexts to launch formal investigations. The State Department issued sanctions against Consuelo Porras, but she wasn't deterred.

Officials who crossed special interests in Guatemala had always been targeted with bogus lawsuits, arbitrary firings, or physical threats. But the campaign against these former prosecutors and judges was intensifying and driving away dozens of the top legal minds in the government. One former official called it the "Guatemalan judiciary and ministry in exile," which raised the question of who might be left to defend those who remained.

On a rainy Thursday afternoon in the spring, I met one group of the exiles at a row house in Washington. Others were living in Mexico, El Salvador, and Spain, but the largest share was concentrated in and around DC. Juan Francisco Sandoval, short and bespectacled, with a wry sense of humor, was the group's social center. Forty years old and considered one of the brightest minds of his generation, he'd always dreamed of serving as the country's attorney general. Instead, he was taking English classes every afternoon, contributing op-eds from afar, and setting up a WhatsApp chat thread for his colleagues who were adapting to their new lives as immigrants in Washington. The newest addition to the group was a judge named Erika Aifán, one of the most revered jurists in the country, who'd arrived in the US with a single suitcase. "I've asked myself, 'Why didn't they just kill us?'" she said. "They've followed us. They've demonstrated that we're vulnerable. They've recorded us. But they need us alive precisely to discredit us. They're turning us into criminals. They need to change the public opinion. Exile is a form of death; it's just a kind of civil death. It's a way to disappear us from the national context."

Semilla held a total of seven seats in an Assembly dominated by conservatives. The party was a gadfly at best, but Lucrecia was certain that congress was where she had to be. "As a minister, I was a piñata," she once told me. "I was on the other side of the line." When she left the government, in 2017, she had assumed, wrongly, that the attacks against her would stop. Not only did they continue; they almost thwarted her legislative career before it could start. The same group of conservative opponents who harassed her as minister tried to block her from assuming office on a technicality after she won election, in 2019. Her aunt gave her legal advice, and she filed a court petition that staved off the effort. As a member of Semilla, she was surrounded by a group of reformers and up-and-comers, some still in their early twenties. She felt, for once, that her "political orphanhood" had ended.

Her party had limited power when it came to votes and coalitions in the Assembly, but at least Lucrecia could engage on the ground level. It was the political equivalent of hand-to-hand combat. To do anything but fight was to do nothing at all, and so that's what she did, like it was the most natural thing in the world.

It was in this same unsentimental spirit—matter-of-fact, devoid of drama to the point of aridity, just as I always imagined her mother had been—that Lucrecia told me about the state of her own health. We were in the car, on the way to Zone 2 one afternoon for lunch. In the fall of 2020, she was diagnosed with cervical cancer, and she announced that she would undergo treatment and take a brief leave from the Assembly. The process was slow and painful, but within a year the cancer had appeared to go into remission. On her return to the body, she had introduced a piece of legislation that would improve treatment for Guatemalan cancer patients. But now, she said, the cancer was back. Her sons and ex-husband were in Guatemala. Helen was around. She'd be with them and take a trip with her boys at the end of the summer. Without using the word *hope*, or any loose synonym, she allowed that maybe the disease would slow; in any case, she seemed at peace.

When she told me she was unafraid of dying, I believed her. We were nearing her childhood neighborhood. The family's former house had been converted into an office of some sort, and the roadway next to it had become a major thoroughfare clogged with semitrucks. The church where Bishop Gerardi had been murdered remained intact, though, and after lunch we rode over to the campus of the University of San Carlos. She pointed out her mother's name on a monument called the Wall of University Martyrs, which honored hundreds of students and faculty who'd been killed during the war years.

Back in the car, on the way to her apartment in Zone 11, she excused herself to answer the phone. It was a reporter calling with questions about the vaccine law. There were still some details she felt it was important for the public to get right.

53.

Simply Not Who We Are

In the final weeks of December 2021, after ten months of negotiations, the Biden administration withdrew from settlement talks with the ACLU to provide financial compensation to the families separated at the border. The move was a shock even to administration officials. Previously, the president had left little room to doubt what he thought of the Trump administration's zero tolerance policy. In November, he had said of the parents, "You deserve some kind of compensation, no matter what." What had changed his mind?

In October, *The Wall Street Journal* reported that advocates were asking the government to consider giving $450,000 to each family member who had been separated. This number wasn't final; the DOJ hadn't agreed to it, and the government's opening bid in the negotiations was substantially lower. But the GOP wasted no time using the figure to attack Biden. Already, Republican attorneys general in several states had filed lawsuits to block every immigration initiative that the president had issued since taking office. In virtually all cases, they were succeeding. An executive action to reinstate priorities for ICE enforcement was blocked in a conservative federal court. The Biden administration began to wind down MPP in February 2021, using the president's parole authority to bring in thirteen thousand migrants stuck in Mexico, but another lawsuit froze the entire effort in August. Even the administration's more technocratic reforms, such as a DHS regulation to put asylum officers in charge of hearing asylum cases instead of overextended judges, were halted.

On November 3, a Fox News reporter asked Biden about the *Wall Street Journal* story at a press conference. It was "garbage," Biden replied, dismissing the reports as inaccurate. But the figure *had* come up in the settlement talks. A few days later, Biden corrected himself. He reasserted his belief that the families separated by Trump should receive some form of compensation; he just wasn't sure what an appropriate amount might be. Privately, though, officials at the White House argued that moving ahead with a settlement had become a greater political liability than any potential fallout from a broken promise.

A broader retreat was beginning to cloud the president's agenda at the border. Members of the Biden transition team had decided to leave Title 42 in place, continuing to refuse entry to asylum seekers while working on a new system to scale up capacity. The hope was to pause asylum in order to save it. Title 42, one administration official said, would be "a deterrence tool while getting the asylum system up and running. There were regular conversations about how it wasn't going to exist forever."

To anyone determined to keep immigration out of the news, however, Title 42 could seem like a useful tool for clearing the border. Its seductiveness as a policy was a trap. Instead of setting goals for expanding asylum access, or bringing some order to ports of entry, the government resorted to an ad hoc approach of expelling as many migrants as it could. Andrea Flores, who worked on border policy at Biden's National Security Council before resigning, summarized the thinking on Title 42 to me one day in the late fall of 2021. "We don't want to have to process people at all. Can't we just turn them away? That's the Title 42 process."

That September, thirty thousand Haitians had arrived at the border seeking asylum, about half of them setting up a makeshift camp under the Del Rio International Bridge. Members of the US Border Patrol, some on horseback, were photographed menacing migrants with whips on the northern banks of the Rio Grande. From the south, Mexican law enforcement agents swept through the border town of Ciudad Acuña, arresting as many Haitians as they

Migrants camp out next to the Del Rio International Bridge after crossing the Rio Grande into the US. Del Rio, Texas, September 19, 2021.

could. Eventually, a fleet of planes flew Haitians from Texas to Port-au-Prince, until the camp was cleared. The patrolmen on horseback were "beyond an embarrassment," Biden said. They were "simply not who we are." He said nothing about Title 42, which remained in effect; without it, the government couldn't have deported the Haitians so easily.

The administration's plans to lift Title 42 were repeatedly delayed. When it finally announced the end of the policy, in the spring of 2022, there was strong opposition, including, most tellingly, from Democrats. Many feared that ending Title 42 would unleash an emergency at the border. In two short years, it had become the status quo. The debate was rendered moot weeks later when a federal judge blocked Biden yet again.

Central Americans were still coming to the border in large numbers. But now a different population was overwhelming the US government: Venezuelans, Nicaraguans, and Cubans. DHS could not expel them using Title 42 because none of these countries' governments would accept deportation flights from the US. Mexico was increasingly unwilling to take the migrants. A deal brokered by DHS led to a provisional solution. In exchange for allowing thirty thousand migrants from these countries to enter the country each month with temporary work visas, the US would deport the rest. By then, many of the president's top immigration advisers at DHS and the White House had quietly left the administration. A new team was tasked with preparing for the spring of 2023, when Title 42 had to be lifted once and for all because the government had declared the public health emergency over. Among the first ideas floated by the administration was a policy that barred migrants from asylum if they crossed through another country in the region to reach the US.

54.

Home

I met Juan for the first time on a scorching Sunday morning in April 2022. The main plaza in Usulután was teeming with people. Street vendors sold food and knickknacks under umbrellas, and children bobbed and darted among the crowds. At the center of the activity was the church. All white and free of decorative flourishes, it was plain but grand, with two sets of columns chiseled in light relief on the facade; a bell tower rose on each side. Jutting from the top of the building's front pediment was a large iron cross. People were already inside for mass, and some of the churchgoers spilled onto the front steps. Outside, a calmness hung around the place like a force field, holding everyone—the vendors, the children, the passersby—in a loose communal orbit.

Juan was waiting for me in a gazebo beside the church, in front of a walkway lined with tree-shaded benches. This was where the village *señoras* had once sat, on election night in 1968, when the troops showed up and Juan had to hustle everyone to safety. He was seventy now, about five and a half feet tall, with a thick barrel chest that bulged under a pink T-shirt and sparse gray hair. His skin was dark, his teeth a bright white. Neither of us had ever been in a position quite like this one: we were celebrating a reunion two years in the making that was also a first encounter. It was relaxingly anticlimactic. We relieved the residual awkwardness by setting out for some horchata. A woman sold large plastic bags of it from the back window of her house, though she refused to let Juan pay. Along the way, he nodded greetings to people and called out to friends by name. When their eyes politely but quizzically fell on me, he said, "This is Jonathan. We used to steal chickens together."

Two weeks before, the government had declared a state of exception after members of MS-13 killed eighty-seven people in the span of seventy-two hours. The authorities could arrest anyone they considered suspicious. Detainees were not entitled to a legal defense. The right to gather in groups larger than two was suspended, and all minors would be tried as adults. Nine thousand people had already been arrested; within a few months, the number would grow to fifty thousand. On his Twitter account, Bukele shared a running tally of the arrests along with scabrous commentary, posting photographs of tattooed men in handcuffs and underwear ("little angels"), some of whom appeared to have been roughed up ("He must have been eating fries with ketchup"). Critics of the new policy—whether common citizens, journalists, or foreign governments—supported "the terrorists," he wrote. Each morning, mothers and wives gathered outside the jails to plead for information about their sons and husbands, insisting on their innocence. Bukele conceded that 1 percent of the roundups might result in wrongful arrests, but the public could only take his word for that figure. "As we continue arresting more gangsters, more people are going to protest," Bukele said. "Because there will always be a mother of a gangster, a family member, or a friend who isn't going to like that we are cleansing that cancer."

It was an echo of the war years, but Salvadoran voters, who loved the president and despised the gangs, supported the policy by an overwhelming margin. Enforcement consisted of crackdowns in mostly poor neighborhoods, populated with people who were seen as having *dudosa confiabilidad*, or questionable trustworthiness. As one human rights advocate told me, "You hear people say, 'Surely they must have been doing something if they're being taken away.'" Prior to the state of exception, Bukele's government, like its predecessors, had also secretly negotiated with imprisoned gang leaders. When the talks failed, however, the force of Bukele's response forestalled the criticism that he had mismanaged the situation. Everyone who was arrested faced a minimum of six months in prison, but most languished longer, often without being charged. Innocent people were being swept up in large numbers. Jealous neighbors called in tips; bread sellers working in gang-controlled neighborhoods were locked up because they were found with small amounts of cash. Dozens of people died in custody. When the prisons were filled, Bukele built another one, which he called the Center for the Confinement of Terrorism, with a capacity of forty thousand.

The state of exception would outlive its name—a year later, it would remain in effect, with the Salvadoran Congress renewing the terms each month. "During the war, we lived with a state of exception," the country's vice president told me when I interviewed him one morning in April 2022. There was "nothing strange" about doing it again. In Spanish, the state of exception was called *el regimen de excepción*; the journalist Julia Gavarrete started calling it *la normalidad excepcional*. Outside of a small but vocal group of human rights advocates, journalists, and opposition figures, fewer and fewer Salvadorans objected. Bukele had managed to do what no other recent president could: after several months, he had severed the ties between gang leaders in prison and their foot soldiers outside. As one Salvadoran news outlet put it, "The gangs do not exist in this moment as El Salvador knew them for decades."

There were military convoys on the road outside Usulután when I arrived, but the main streets of the city were clear of troops. Juan's house was bigger than I had imagined it: two floors of white stucco, with arched windows, a tile roof, and a bougainvillea tree on the balcony. Inside was a colonnaded hallway that opened onto a lush interior garden, surrounded by bedrooms and an open kitchen. A lone chicken prowled around.

Juan's home in Usulután, El Salvador, April 2022.

I rarely see the homes of the people I write about. Often, my subjects are fleeing them, as in Keldy's case; other times, they are expelled from them, as Eddie had been. I could never experience the LA of Eddie's youth, or La Ceiba as Keldy had known it; those places no longer exist. A sense of loss permeates much of what remains. In Juan's case, the world outside the house had transformed radically, but inside its walls everything was intact. The air was damp but cool, and in the rooms were framed photographs of his family, an honorific citation he'd received from the Salvadoran legislature, and paintings of the saints. He'd even mounted a piece of the building's old facade, which collapsed during Hurricane Mitch, in 1998. The date of its construction—1824, when Juan's family first moved in—was scrawled across the cornice.

The only conspicuous snag in the internal continuity of the house was that it was getting packed up. Juan was finally selling the place. Within the month, he would move to a new house in a rural canton, in a district called Santa María, about twenty minutes away. Some of the rooms were nearly empty, and boxes had begun to pile up.

Juan at home in Usulután, El Salvador, April 2022.

"It's not easy, but it's time," he told me. We were each reclining in a hammock, drinking our horchatas. Juan rocked back and forth in his; I wobbled in mine. During the early months of the pandemic, he'd taken our calls in these hammocks, alternating between the ones in the hallways of the first and second floors. They were a pocket of comfort and security. As a boy, when it was too hot in the bedroom he shared with his three other siblings, he'd sneak out and sleep in a hammock in the garden. When he returned to El Salvador and began treating patients again, he opened a small clinic with money from an award he'd received from the Robert Wood Johnson Foundation. It was on a beach in a town called El Espino. Patients called it *la clínica de las hamacas*, the hammock clinic, for its distinguishing feature.

I thumbed through an old binder that Juan's mother had kept until her death. It was crammed with newspaper articles about his work in the US, from a range of local, state, and national outlets, some in English and some in Spanish. The clippings went back to his first days in California. There were old photographs of him—handsome, daring-looking, with a pencil mustache and a cowboy hat. He was marching, shouting, carrying signs, leading crowds. The captions on these alternated between calling him Juan and Juan Pérez, the name he had used in his undocumented days. The Washington years began a quarter of the way into the binder and predominated. Gone were the mustache and long hair, the tight T-shirts and work boots. A photograph of Juan in a gray suit showed him posing with Barack Obama; another included a note from Hillary Clinton. While I paged through, Juan spoke at his usual pitch, drifting toward his favorite subjects. "The one thing that's been a constant in all my years practicing medicine," he was saying, "is that people want to talk. Their symptoms are only half of it."

He was gazing off into the garden. Still standing, unbowed by time, was the mango tree where Juan had hidden the night before he left the country, in 1981, when he was kept awake by thoughts of where he might be going.

Acknowledgments

Allowing someone else to tell your story involves a major leap of faith. My biggest and profoundest thanks go to the people who took that chance on me. The list is long and spans years. They invited me into their lives and showed me great trust, often at extremely trying moments and on exceedingly sensitive subjects. Above all, I am grateful to Juan Romagoza, Eddie Anzora, Lucrecia Hernández Mack, and Keldy Mabel Gonzáles Brebe de Zúniga. As I wrote, I kept a pink Post-it note on my computer with a phrase from Juan: *una cucharita de justicia*, "a small spoonful of justice." It's what these four were seeking for years, each in a different way. For me, these words were a charge to act with the greatest possible care—to do some small measure of justice to these lives of fortitude, resilience, and humility. I can't possibly thank them enough for everything they have taught me. It goes well beyond the contents of this book.

As the manuscript went to press, I received the news that Lucrecia Hernández Mack had just died. The cause was the cancer she'd been fighting since 2020. Because it was Lucrecia, I half expected the disease to give up before she ever would. And for a while that eventuality didn't seem so far-fetched. In March 2022, she had told me the prognosis was several months at the most. Then a year passed. By the start of July 2023, however, Lucrecia's condition had become grave. She didn't expect to make it to August 20, the date of the second and final round of Guatemala's presidential elections. To everyone's shock and delight, Semilla, the party Lucrecia had helped create, was still in the running. Its candidate, Bernardo Arévalo, the son of the first democratically elected president in the country's history, was gaining momentum in the polls. But

Lucrecia's health was worsening. There was no trace of self-pity or fear in her voice when she told me that she was getting her affairs in order; to the contrary, public health was on her mind to the end. She left me a message about how telling her story might help destigmatize illness and increase cancer awareness. She died seventeen days after Arévalo won. It is a small consolation given the enormity of her loss. But it is a consolation: Lucrecia got to see this one through.

Doris Meissner and Cecilia Muñoz spent many hours talking me through granular issues of policy and politics, all while being gracious about my stubborn fixation on their own individual roles in the broader history. Scott Mechkowski was exceptionally candid and showed real grace in speaking with me in the knowledge that we didn't share the same views. My marathon interview sessions with John Fife helped me reenter the spiritual dimension of the early 1980s. If the past is a different country, I couldn't have made my way around without Peggy Hutchison, Charles Kamasaki, Eileen Purcell, Alma Hamar, Carmelina Cadena, Allan Burns, Miguel Salat, and Jim McGovern.

Patty Blum helped make this book possible. With an assist from Almudena Bernabeu, she made sure that I could get in touch with Juan, then shared her vast expertise and gave me legal and historical documents that were invaluable. Matt Eisenbrandt, himself an author of a great book on the US and El Salvador, was amazingly generous. Joshua Phillips wrote a piece about Juan for *The Washington Post* in 2002 that made an indelible impression on me. When I got in touch, back in 2016, he treated me like an old friend; the rest was history.

Muz Chishti, one of the sharpest minds out there on immigration, has talked me through endless subjects over the years. Each conversation felt revelatory. For their direction on different facets of immigration policy and politics, I owe special thanks to David Martin, Lee Gelernt, Michelle Brané, Ann Garcia, Andrea Flores, Amit Pandya, Andrew Selee, Alex Aleinikoff, Stephanie Leutert, Lucas Guttentag, Marshall Fitz, Adam Goodman, Frank Sharry, Jeh Johnson, Janet Murguía, Tatiana Brofft, Anya McMurray, Angela Kelley, Tonatiuh Guillén, Jennifer Nagda, Maria Woltjen, Marc Rosenblum, Sabrina Teichman, Mike Fisher, and the teams at Safe Passage Project and Make the Road New York. There are a number of people who must remain anonymous. Without them, I would have been flying blind while trying to understand what was happening in the upper reaches of government, from Washington to San Salvador.

El Salvador was where the idea for this book first cohered. I was honored to have help from Gabriel Labrador of *El Faro*, a fiercely diligent and talented reporter and an even more generous colleague. My dear friend Julia Gavarrete is part journalist, part magician. She generated ideas and found leads that never would have occurred to me, including her suggestion that, at the end of a long reporting day in February 2016, I get a drink with a guy by the name of Eddie Anzora. Thanks to Victor Peña, Fred Ramos, Carlos Dada, and Juan José Martínez d'Aubuisson. For advice on knotty historical questions, I was lucky to have the input of Héctor Lindo, Héctor Dada, and Charlie Goff. Carlos García is one of the great authorities on all things related to Central American gangs. During these last several years, I would have been lost without him.

One of the guiding premises of this book is that every locale in Central America is a portal: step across a threshold in San Salvador or in the Guatemalan highlands and you might find yourself in Houston, Mt. Pleasant, or Suffolk County. I've learned the most about my own country by entering (and exiting) it through these sorts of trick doors. Many people have opened them for me: Feride Castillo, Joel Orozco, Walter Barrientos, Willy Barreno, Kate Doyle, Javier Zamora, and Angelina Godoy.

In Guatemala, Sebastian Charchalac, whom I'm proud to call a friend, was an immensely knowledgeable source and guide through the western highlands. For depth, context, and access on matters big and small, I relied on Helen Mack, Rachel Nolan, Enrique Recinos, Luis Arreaga, Richard Lee Johnson, Cindy Espina, Edwin Castellanos, Francisco Villagrán, Juan Francisco Sandoval, Álvaro Montenegro, Irma Alicia Velásquez Nimatuj, Silvia Monterroso, Yarsinio Palacios, Jean-Marie Simon, Anita Isaacs, Laura Fabiola Marroquín, Enrique Naveda, Lilian Cruz, and Danilo Enrique Villagrán. The community of Paraje León—so kind and open to me in so many ways—introduced me to the work of Humberto Ak'abal, a lasting gift.

Honduras has always been a particularly opaque country for a foreign journalist to try to penetrate. Whatever progress I made in understanding it, I attribute to Dana Frank, Darío Euraque, Amelia Frank-Vitale, and Laura Blume.

Since 2013, El Paso has been a hub for much of the work I've done along the border. As that work clarified over the last several years, a number of people were indispensable: Linda Corchado, Linda Rivas, Connie Gutiérrez, Molly Molloy, Patrick Timmons, Erik Hanshew, and Irma Whiteley.

The New Yorker has been my professional home for the last decade, first as a fact-checker and then as a writer. I've been schooled by the very best and consider it the highest privilege to call some of my favorite writers, journalists, editors, and staffers there my colleagues and friends. Thanks to David Remnick and Michael Luo for making all my work possible. I'm especially grateful to Willing Davidson and Rob Fischer, my two brilliant editors whom I would go on thanking for another twenty pages if I didn't have their voices in my ear telling me not to overwrite this. Virginia Cannon, Daniel Zalewski, Eric Lach, and Peter Canby were instrumental in so much of my work. And I owe my thanks to Patrick Radden Keefe, William Finnegan, Jon Lee Anderson, Daniel Alarcón, Evan Osnos, Gerry Cadava, Carla Blumenkranz, Graciela Mochkofsky, Rozina Ali, Camila Osorio, Teresa Mathew, Micah Hauser, Anakwa Dwamena, Danielle Mackey, Stephania Taladrid, and of course Bruce Diones.

Edward Orloff, my agent, was a master conceptualizer and editor from the early days of this project, luring me to the starting line with one of his famous "Dear Edward" emails and shaping the original proposal with the greatest skill. At Penguin, my editor, Will Heyward, was a constant and unwavering companion from the drop. His belief in this project, and in me, kept me believing. Many thanks to Natalie Coleman, who expertly steered this book to the finish line, and to Ann Godoff and Scott Moyers for making it all happen. Jackson Vail and Inés Rénique fact-checked the text and were truly essential partners in scouring the manuscript from every angle. Thea Traff elevated the book immeasurably with her exceptional eye and nuanced grasp of its contents.

A number of institutions supported me so that I could do this work. I was an Emerson fellow at New America, where I'm indebted to Awista Ayub and Sarah Baline in particular. They created a real sense of community for me and my wonderful cohort; at a time when Zoom fatigue was real, I genuinely looked forward to each and every session we had from 2020 to 2021. At Emerson, thanks are due to Patrick D'Arcy, Amy Low, and Megan Dino. The Robert Silvers Foundation supported my writing and research, as did the Pulitzer Center on Crisis Reporting.

Thanks also to Mark Krotov, Karla Cornejo Villavicencio, Eleanor Martin, Rachel Arons, Ruben Reyes Jr., Verónica Reyes-Escudero, Sebastían Escalón, Julie Gonzales, *el verdadero* David Brooks, Mauricio Lima, Adriana Zehbrauskas, Hannah Yoon, Susan Meiselas, Harry Mattison, Luz Gioia, Steven Dudley, Daniel Dale, Vicki Gass, Luis Cortes, and Michelle Mittelstadt.

A core group has already been name-checked above in relation to their specific expertise. But their support was so total that I need to reiterate just how thankful I am: Rachel Nolan, Adam Goodman, Ann Garcia, Rob Fischer, Andrea Flores, and Patty Blum.

This is a book about home, and I dedicate it to the people who have made one for me: my parents, Bob and Edlyn Blitzer, my greatest supporters always; my wife, Alexandra Schwartz; and our son, Benjamin. Alex, you are everything to me—including my favorite writer, and the reader I trust the most. *Quiero respirar el aire que respiras tú.*

Note on Sources

The material in this book is the result of hundreds of interviews conducted in English and Spanish between 2016 and 2023. For the four main subjects, there were too many encounters and conversations to fully cite in the Notes. I've been in close contact with Juan Romagoza since May 2020, Eddie Anzora since February 2016, Keldy Mabel Gonzáles Brebe de Zúniga since June 2018, and Lucrecia Hernández Mack since May 2019. Unless otherwise noted, personal and biographical information about them and their experiences came from our extensive conversations. The same principle holds true for all other figures in the book. Where I reported details, conversations, and dialogue directly from interactions or firsthand experience, I have not included additional notes. In instances where it was possible to provide further information—particularly when speaking to government sources or subject-matter experts—I have tried to do so. Many people who appear in the book granted multiple interviews over the course of several months. They include John Fife, Doris Meissner, Scott Mechkowski, and Cecilia Muñoz. Only in very rare cases did I conduct a single interview with any given person; in virtually every case, there were multiple follow-up conversations. However, in the Notes, for the sake of concision, I have provided the date of the first or most thorough interview.

Throughout the book, I have used my subjects' real names unless they specifically requested a pseudonym for their own protection. Chapter 37 ("Killing Fields") is the only section where subjects go by pseudonyms, and I have indicated each instance in the notes. When I cite legal documents (affidavits, transcripts, government files) for subjects with pseudonyms, everything but their names is consistent with the original sources. That includes dates, titles of government memoranda, and any specific passages quoted. In Chapter 46 ("Remain in Mexico"), I have used people's first names but not their last names. This was at their explicit request. Dozens of other sources throughout the text worked for the US and foreign governments. In most of these cases, they agreed to speak on "background" or "deep background," meaning I could use the material on the condition that I maintain their anonymity.

Notes

CHAPTER 1: THE HEART DOCTOR

9 **house with his parents:** All material related to Juan Romagoza is the result of extensive interviews with the author from 2020 to 2023; Juan Romagoza Arce v. José Guillermo García, United States District Court, Southern District of Florida, Northern Division, trial transcript, June 24, 2002, at 68.
9 **around the corner:** *Arce v. García*, trial transcript, June 24, 2002, 69.
9 **when Juan was thirteen:** *In the Matter of Carlos Eugenio Vides Casanova*, transcript from removal hearings, April 19, 2011, 331.
10 **watched his fifty-two-year-old grandfather:** *Arce v. García*, trial transcript, June 24, 2002, 70.
10 **mother was a seamstress:** *Arce v. García*, trial transcript, June 24, 2002, 68.
10 **wound up lasting ten:** *Arce v. García*, trial transcript, June 24, 2002, 71; transcript from removal hearings, 335.
10 **closing for months:** *Arce v. García*, trial transcript, June 24, 2002, 71.
10 **like Usulután and Sonsonate:** *Arce v. García*, trial transcript, June 24, 2002, 71–73; transcript from removal hearings, 337.
11 **old but charming:** The hospital was subsequently destroyed in an earthquake. Descriptions come from archival photographs, courtesy of El Salvador Ministry of Health.
11 **assisted with the surgery:** *Arce v. García*, trial transcript, June 24, 2002, 83; transcript from removal hearings, 341–46.

CHAPTER 2: THE TRUE IDENTITY OF THE PEOPLE OF GOD

13 **armed with machetes and hoes:** Jeffery M. Paige, *Coffee and Power: Revolution and the Rise of Democracy in El Salvador* (Cambridge, MA: Harvard University Press, 1997), 103.
13 **had been in public hands:** Paige, *Coffee and Power*, 106.
13 **auctioning off:** Héctor Lindo-Fuentes, *Weak Foundations: The Economy of El Salvador in the Nineteenth Century 1821–1898* (Berkeley: University of California Press, 1991), 147.
13 **more general value:** Paige, *Coffee and Power*, 105.
13 **treated like slaves:** Roque Dalton, *Miguel Mármol*, trans. Kathleen Ross and Richard Schaaf (Evanston, IL: Curbstone Press, 1987), 287.
14 **rounded up prisoners:** Michael McClintock, *The American Connection, Volume I: State Terror and Popular Resistance in El Salvador* (London: Zed Books, 1985), 112.
14 **"paranoiac fear":** Thomas Anderson, *Matanza: El Salvador's Communist Revolt of 1932* (Lincoln: University of Nebraska Press, 1971), 158.
14 **"born half dead":** Roque Dalton, "Todos," in Roque Dalton, *Las historias prohibidas del pulgarcito* (Siglo XXI, Ciudad de México, 1974).
14 **seventy-five people:** Raymond Bonner, *Weakness and Deceit: America and El Salvador's Dirty War* (New York: OR Books, 2016), 21.
15 **taxonomy of uniforms:** Bonner, *Weakness and Deceit*, 45; Héctor Lindo, interview with author, June 15, 2023.
15 **"in support of the state":** McClintock, *American Connection, Volume I*, 22.
15 **"opposition to an existing government":** McClintock, *American Connection, Volume I*, 30.

16 **Their candidate:** This was José Napoleón Duarte.
16 **one guerrilla organization:** Bonner, *Weakness and Deceit*, 137.
16 **"associations of teachers":** Bonner, *Weakness and Deceit*, 73.
18 **close personal friend:** Matt Eisenbrandt, *Assassination of a Saint: The Plot to Murder Óscar Romero and the Quest to Bring His Killers to Justice* (Berkeley: University of California Press, 2017), 45.
20 **on a transistor radio:** Roberto Morozzo della Rocca, *Óscar Romero: Prophet of Hope* (London: Dartmon, Longman & Todd, 2015), 90.
20 **"the people of God":** Óscar Romero, "La pobreza de las bienaventuranzas, fuerza de la verdadera liberación del pueblo," February 17, 1980. The full audio of the sermon is available at www.romerotrust.org.uk/homilies-and-writings/homilies/poverty-beatitudes-force-true-liberation-people.
21 **159 in October:** William Stanley, *The Protection Racket State: Elite Politics, Military Extortion, and Civil War in El Salvador* (Philadelphia: Temple University Press, 1996), 166, 206.
21 **on the payroll of the CIA:** Bonner, *Weakness and Deceit*, 138.
23 **direct aid to the military:** Bonner, *Weakness and Deceit*, 137.
23 **theologian Reinhold Niebuhr:** Elizabeth Drew, "Human Rights," *New Yorker*, July 8, 1977.
24 **called it "the Carter":** Bonner, *Weakness and Deceit*, 297.

CHAPTER 3: THE GENERAL AND HIS BOOTS

26 **"moderate solution":** Raymond Bonner, *Weakness and Deceit: America and El Salvador's Dirty War* (New York: OR Books, 2016), xxi.
26 **"military solution":** Expert Report of Professor Terry L. Karl, *In the Matter of: José Guillermo García-Merino, in Removal Proceedings*, Executive Office for Immigration Review, October 2, 2014, 33. In the countryside, according to Karl, the military had different names for its strategy: "total war," "scorched earth," and "cleansing."
26 **left for dead:** Juan Romagoza Arce v. Jose Guillermo García, United States District Court, Southern District of Florida, Northern Division, trial transcript, June 24, 2002, 78–79.
26 **"your future life expectancy":** William Stanley, *The Protection Racket State: Elite Politics, Military Extortion, and Civil War in El Salvador* (Philadelphia: Temple University Press, 1996), 210.
27 **nine hundred civilians:** Bonner, *Weakness and Deceit*, 143.
27 **"domesticate" the party:** Stanley, *Protection Racket State*, 184.
27 **started the job:** Christopher Dickey, "The Nun Murders and the Presidential Transition Team," *Daily Beast*, April 13, 2017.
28 **"major immediate threat":** *Arce v. García*, trial transcript, June 24, 2002, 204.
28 **stiflingly hot:** John Quinn, "A Personal Story of Death in a Cathedral Square," *San Francisco Chronicle*, April 6, 1980.
28 **Tens of thousands:** Joseph B. Treaster, "26 Salvadorans Die at Bishop's Funeral," *New York Times*, March 31, 1980; Greg Grandin, "Remembering Those Murdered at Oscar Romero's Funeral," *The Nation*, March 25, 2015.
29 **so many people inside:** Quinn, "A Personal Story of Death in a Cathedral Square."
30 **"Death to White":** Eileen Markey, *A Radical Faith: The Assassination of Sister Maura* (New York: Nation Books, 2016), 243.
30 **"we will begin":** Markey, *A Radical Faith*, 250.
30 **decided to negotiate:** William LeoGrande, *Our Own Backyard: The United States in Central America 1977–1992* (Chapel Hill: University of North Carolina Press, 1998), 59.
30 **"explicitly rejected dialogue":** Stanley, *Protection Racket State*, 211.
31 **list of five suspects:** Tim Weiner, *Enemies: A History of the FBI* (New York: Random House, 2012), 348–55.
31 **a CIA cable:** "Involvement of Col. Oscar Edgardo (Casanova) Vejar in Murder of American Nuns," CIA.gov, August 6, 1984, www.cia.gov/readingroom/docs/DOC_0000049092.pdf.
32 **"by the sword":** "Cauldron in Central America: What Keeps the Fire Burning?" *New York Times*, December 7, 1980.
32 **"clearly not just nuns":** "The Murder of US Churchwomen That Exposed a Government Coverup," Retro Report, November 10, 2014, transcript, www.retroreport.org/transcript/a-search-for-justice/.
33 **Juan's shoes:** Trial transcript, June 24, 2002, 102.
33 **threatening to throw:** *Arce v. García*, trial transcript, June 24, 2002, 104–5.
34 **"best hotel in El Salvador":** *Arce v. García*, trial transcript, June 24, 2002, 111.
34 **grew more elaborate:** *Arce v. García*, trial transcript, June 24, 2002, 115.
34 **a man of high rank:** *Arce v. García*, trial transcript, June 24, 2002, 140–45.
35 **green eyes:** Ross Gelbspan, *Break-ins, Death Threats and the FBI: The Covert War against the Central America Movement* (Boston: South End Press, 1991), 48.
35 **"been running this country":** Testimony of Terry Karl, April 20, 2002, *Arce v. García*, 510–13.
35 **know about his family:** *In the Matter of Carlos Eugenio Vides Casanova*, transcript from removal hearings, April 19, 2011, 376.

36 **Worms emerged:** *Arce v. García*, trial transcript, June 24, 2002, 142.
36 **a few coffins:** *In the Matter of Carlos Eugenio Vides Casanova*, transcript from removal hearings, April 19, 2011, 383.

CHAPTER 4: SPANISH FOR VIETNAM

37 **behavior was "disloyal":** "Cowan Is Fired as Chief of Manzo Council," *Arizona Daily Star*, April 11, 1976.
37 **give her thirty days:** Julie Gonzales, "From the Barrios to the Border" (Double Senior Thesis for Departments of History and Race, Ethnicity, and Migration, Yale University, April 4, 2005), 21.
37 **state of panic:** Lupe Castillo, interview with author, October 6, 2020.
37 **boxes of documents:** Judy Donovan, "Telephone Calls from Worried Clients Flood Manzo Council," *Arizona Daily Star*, April 13, 1976; John Rawlinson, "Manzo Council Could Be Shut in Alien Dispute," *Arizona Daily Star*, April 13, 1976.
37 **eight hundred client files:** Donovan, "Telephone Calls from Worried Clients Flood Manzo Council"; Gonzales, "From the Barrios to the Border," 22.
37 **sweeping stray papers:** Castillo, interview, October 6, 2020.
38 **presidency of Gerald Ford:** Gonzales, "From the Barrios to the Border," 10–13.
38 **held a walkout:** Lupe Castillo, interview with author, June 15, 2020, October 6, 2020; Margo Cowan, interview with author, October 8, 2020, October 12, 2020.
39 **"who or where they are":** John Crewdson, *The Tarnished Door: The New Immigrants and the Transformation of America* (New York: Crown, 1983), 14.
39 **forty dollars a month:** Crewdson, *Tarnished Door*, 7.
39 **"person of Mexican ancestry":** United States v. Brignoni-Ponce, 422 U.S. 873 (1975).
39 **"invasion of illegal aliens":** Douglas S. Massey and Karen A. Pren, "Unintended Consequences of US Immigration Policy: Explaining the Post-1965 Surge from Latin America," *Population and Development Review* 38, no. 1 (2012): 1–29.
39 **"a greater threat":** Crewdson, *Tarnished Door*, 17.
40 **twenty-five applications:** Gonzales, "From the Barrios to the Border," 26.
40 **single week to finalize:** Judy Donovan, "Agents Using Manzo's Files against Aliens," *Arizona Daily Star*, August 27, 1976; Donovan, "Telephone Calls from Worried Clients Flood Manzo Council."
40 **deported fifty people:** Donovan, "Agents Using Manzo's Files against Aliens."
40 **"nonviolence from Cesar":** Ben MacNitt, "Margo Cowan, the Advocate," *Tucson Citizen*, January 11, 1978.
41 **Manzo tried to convince:** Cowan and Castillo, interviews.
41 **"It was inevitable":** MacNitt, "Margo Cowan, the Advocate."
41 **formal certification:** Ann Crittenden, *Sanctuary: A Story of American Conscience and the Law in Collision* (New York: Grove, 1988), 27.
42 **twelve hundred dollars a head:** Miriam Davidson, *Convictions of the Heart: Jim Corbett and the Sanctuary Movement* (Tucson: University of Arizona Press, 1988), 7.
43 **"something bad":** Crittenden, *Sanctuary*, 4.
44 **main source of information:** Castillo, interview, October 6, 2020.
44 **perched on a small hill:** Castillo and Cowan, interviews.
44 **Quiñones offered them food:** Crittenden, *Sanctuary*, 133–37; Davidson, *Convictions of the Heart*, 38–39.
44 **"OK, they're gone":** Castillo, interview, October 6, 2020.
44 **locate Mexican documents:** Castillo, interview, October 6, 2020.
44 **had a heart condition:** Castillo, interview, June 15, 2020.
44 **A&W Root Beer stand:** Cowan, interview, October 8, 2020.
45 **no paperwork at the office:** Ron Colson, interview with author, September 10, 2020; Mike Fischer, interview with author, September 4, 2020.
45 **improvised assembly line:** Colson and Fischer, interviews.

CHAPTER 5: SOMETHING IMMIGRANT AND HUNGRY

47 **a million refugees:** Gary MacEoin and Nivita Riley, *No Promised Land: American Refugee Policies and the Rule of Law* (Boston: Oxfam America, 1982), 14.
47 **38,000 Hungarians:** "White House Statement on the Termination of the Emergency Program for Hungarian Refugees," December 28, 1957, The American Presidency Project, www.presidency.ucsb.edu/documents/white-house-statement-the-termination-the-emergency-program-for-hungarian-refugees.
47 **240,000 Cubans:** Jorge Duany, "Cuban Migration: A Postrevolution Exodus Ebbs and Flows," Migration Policy Institute, July 6, 2017.
47 **1,500 Ugandans:** Deborah Anker and Michael Posner, "The Forty Year Crisis: A Legislative History of the Refugee Act of 1980," *San Diego Law Review* 19, no. 1 (1981).

47 **nearly 80,000:** Mark Tolts, "A Half-Century of Jewish Emigration from the Former Soviet Union: Demographic Aspects" (paper presented at the Seminar on Russian and Eurasian Jewry, Davis Center for Russian and Eurasian Studies, Harvard University, November 20, 2019).
47 **130,000 Vietnamese and Cambodian refugees:** *Evacuation and Temporary Care Afforded Indochinese Refugees: Operation New Life, Report to the Congress by the Comptroller General of the United States*, Government Accountability Office, June 1, 1976, www.gao.gov/assets/id-76-63.pdf.
47 **pass an "adjustment act":** Dave Martin, interview with author, May 14, 2020.
48 **Several such acts followed:** Doris Meissner, interview with author, May 14, 2020. Doris Meissner sat for three extended interviews on November 27, 2019, January 13, 2020, and May 14, 2020.
48 **ninety thousand refugees:** Average is based on the total admissions from 1975 to 1980. The data was provided by the US Department of State, Bureau of Population, Refugees, and Migration (PRM), Refugee Case Management System, www.wrapsnet.org/archives/.
48 **unqualified advance:** Philip Schrag, *A Well-Founded Fear: The Congressional Battle to Save Political Asylum in America* (Oxford, UK: Routledge, 2000), 26–29.
48 **"rather than ideology":** Anker and Posner, "The Forty Year Crisis."
49 **managing a political campaign:** Martin Tolchin, "Woman in the News; Immigration Expert Who Takes Broad Approach—Doris Marie Meissner," *New York Times*, June 20, 1993.
50 **in a single year:** Meissner, interviews.
50 **"every boat in South Florida":** John Crewdson, *The Tarnished Door: The New Immigrants and the Transformation of America* (New York: Crown, 1983), 51.
50 **dinghies to cabin cruisers:** Crewdson, *Tarnished Door*, 52.
50 **arrived in Key West:** Meissner, interviews.
51 **Orange Bowl stadium:** Crewdson, *Tarnished Door*, 67.
51 **watched in astonishment:** Meissner, interview, May 14, 2020.
51 **policy paradox:** Meissner, interviews.
51 **had criminal records:** Crewdson, *Tarnished Door*, 70.
51 **escaping down the road:** "Last Cubans to Leave Fort Chaffee," *United Press International*, February 3, 1982; Jana K. Lipman, "A Refugee Camp in America: Fort Chaffee and Vietnamese and Cuban Refugees, 1975–1982," *Journal of American Ethnic History* 33, no. 2 (2014): 57–87; William LeoGrande, "From Havana to Miami: U.S. Cuba Policy as a Two-Level Game," *Journal of Interamerican Studies and World Affairs* 40, no. 1 (1998): 67–86.
51 **"refugees are just thugs":** Steve Brewer, "First Transferees to Arrive at Fort Chaffee," Associated Press, September 25, 1980.
52 **failing to "stand up":** "Last Cubans to Leave Fort Chaffee."
52 **"undesirable immigrants":** Emma Kaufman, "Segregated by Citizenship," *Harvard Law Review* 132, no. 5 (2019), https://harvardlawreview.org/print/vol-132/segregation-by-citizenship/; "Cuban Refugee Crime Troubles Police across U.S.," *New York Times*, March 31, 1985.
52 **"something very feral":** Lawrence Grobel, "Reflections on Scarface," *Empire*, May 9, 2011, www.empireonline.com/movies/features/reflections-scarface/.
52 **"Remember Fort Chaffee":** LeoGrande, "From Havana to Miami."

CHAPTER 6: PRO BONO COYOTES

53 **85 percent:** Kristina K. Shull, "Nobody Wants These People: Reagan's Immigration Crisis and America's First Private Prisons" (PhD diss, University of California, Irvine, 2014), 81.
53 **two hundred bunk beds:** El Centro Report to Senator Dennis DeConcini, October 29, 1981, cited in Shull, "Nobody Wants These People," 81.
53 **rate of fifty per hour:** Shull, "Nobody Wants These People," 79.
54 **talk over the din:** Margo Cowan, interview with author, October 10, 2020.
54 **would take two full hours:** Ann Crittenden, *Sanctuary: A Story of American Conscience and the Law in Collision* (New York: Grove, 1988), 45.
54 **"picks a fight with you":** Margo Cowan, interview with author, October 12, 2020.
54 **"to stop everything":** Cowan, interview, October 12, 2020.
54 ***Basta con la migra***: Cowan, interview, October 12, 2020.
54 **Golden West:** Crittenden, *Sanctuary*, 44.
54 **sixty volunteers rotated:** Crittenden, *Sanctuary*, 46.
55 **stave off deportation:** Lupe Castillo, interview with author, June 15, 2020.
55 **sign a G-28:** Castillo, interview.

55 names of future clients: Crittenden, *Sanctuary*, 45.
55 more than ten thousand: Crittenden, *Sanctuary*, 55.
56 "authorities in El Salvador": Gary MacEoin and Nivita Riley, *No Promised Land: American Refugee Policies and the Rule of Law* (Boston: Oxfam America, 1982), 75–76.
56 "asylum to win": Cowan and Castillo, interviews.
56 at conspicuous odds: Cowan and Castillo, interviews.
57 "Upon careful review": MacEoin and Riley, *No Promised Land*, 86.
57 "everyone in the world": Susan Bibler Coutin, "Falling Outside: Excavating the History of Central American Asylum Seekers," *Law & Social Inquiry* 36, no. 3 (2011): 569–96.
57 "run these forms off": Margo Cowan, interview with author, October 8, 2020.
57 "moving people off": Cowan, interview, October 8, 2020.
57 150 asylum seekers: Crittenden, *Sanctuary*, 46–47.
58 "dressed in clerical drag": Crittenden, *Sanctuary*, 5.
58 tenets of liberation theology: John Fife, interview with author, March 24, 2020. Fife sat for three extended interviews on March 24, 2020, April 10, 2020, and January 21, 2021.
58 high school with Fife's son: Crittenden, *Sanctuary*, 53.
58 "we have political asylum": Fife, interviews.
58 release them from custody: Fife, interviews.
59 back of the church building: Miriam Davidson, *Convictions of the Heart: Jim Corbett and the Sanctuary Movement* (Tucson: University of Arizona Press, 1988), 57–58.
59 Castillo showed him: Castillo, interview October 6, 2020.
59 Padre Jaime: Davidson, *Convictions of the Heart*, 40.
59 all of them were being rejected: Fife, interviews.
60 three thousand dollars: Crittenden, *Sanctuary*, 53.
60 according to Johnston: Davidson, *Convictions of the Heart*, 46.
60 pro bono coyote operation: Fife, interviews; Crittenden, *Sanctuary*, 54.
60 the idea that October: Fife, interviews.
60 Twenty-one Salvadorans: Crittenden, *Sanctuary*, 55.
60 "I don't think": Fife, interviews.
60 "to happen on our border": Fife, interviews.

CHAPTER 7: WE CAN'T STOP, BUT DO WE HAVE ANY OTHER CHOICE?

61 "strategic choke point": William LeoGrande, *Our Own Backyard: The United States in Central America, 1977–1992* (Chapel Hill: University of North Carolina Press, 1998), 74, 80.
62 invoked emergency provisions: LeoGrande, *Our Own Backyard*, 70; Raymond Bonner, *Weakness and Deceit: America and El Salvador's Dirty War* (New York: OR Books, 2016), 197; Michael McClintock, *The American Connection, Volume I: State Terror and Popular Resistance in El Salvador* (London: Zed Books, 1985), 288.
62 military didn't split: LeoGrande, *Our Own Backyard*, 69.
62 cut power lines: LeoGrande, *Our Own Backyard*, 134.
62 "sitting in garrisons": LeoGrande, *Our Own Backyard*, 135.
63 "that fucking island": William LeoGrande and Peter Kornbluh, *Back Channel to Cuba: The Hidden History of Negotiations between Washington and Havana* (Chapel Hill: University of North Carolina Press, 2015), 225–67.
63 "dry up the ocean": McClintock, *American Connection, Volume I*, 307.
63 "tougher than lizard lips": Bonner, *Weakness and Deceit*, 285; McClintock, *American Connection, Volume I*, 307.
63 annihilated multiple villages: Unfinished Sentences, *God Alone Was with Us: The Massacre of Santa Cruz*, video, 18:33 (Seattle: University of Washington, Center for Human Rights, 2015). Personal diaries of Philippe Bourgois. (He was a graduate student conducting field work at the time and had arrived in the village of Peña Blanca days before the massacre; he fled with the residents.)
63 assigned at least ten: Mark Danner, *The Massacre at El Mozote* (New York: Vintage, 1994), 119.
63 morning of December 8: McClintock, *American Connection, Volume I*, 308.
64 "a hotshot strategist": Danner, *Massacre at El Mozote*, 39.
64 978 people: Nelson Rauda Zablah, "El estado hace oficial el número de víctimas en El Mozote: 978 ejecutados, 553 niños," *El Faro*, December 4, 2017.
65 hadn't bothered to bury: Danner, *Massacre at El Mozote*, 101.
65 "effort to comply": Danner, *Massacre at El Mozote*, 102.
66 "not possible to prove": Danner, *Massacre at El Mozote*, 110.

66 **"no evidence" of a massacre:** Danner, *Massacre at El Mozote*, 127.
66 **ordered Bonner back:** Danner, *Massacre at El Mozote*, 137.
66 **Patricia Derian:** Elizabeth Drew, "Human Rights," *New Yorker*, July 18, 1977.
67 **José Rosales:** Center for National Security Studies, *Salvadorans in the United States: The Case for Extended Voluntary Departure* (New York: American Civil Liberties Union, 1984). This report includes the full affidavit of José Rosales.
68 **urgency of the mission:** John Fife, interviews with author, March 24, 2020, April 10, 2020, and January 21, 2021.
68 **"were easy to fool":** Margo Cowan, interview with author, October 12, 2020.
69 **Chevy LUV pickup:** Ann Crittenden, *Sanctuary: A Story of American Conscience and the Law in Collision* (New York: Grove, 1988), 57.
69 **"what you're doing":** Miriam Davidson, *Convictions of the Heart: Jim Corbett and the Sanctuary Movement* (Tucson: University of Arizona Press, 1988), 65.
69 **"We can't stop":** Fife, interviews.
69 **arrests in churches, schools, or hospitals:** Fife, interviews.
69 **"the church is a sanctuary":** Davidson, *Convictions of the Heart*, 67.
69 **church as a public platform:** Fife, interviews.
70 **"that's a great idea":** Fife, interviews.
70 **the proposition passed:** Davidson, *Convictions of the Heart*, 67.
70 **"violation of the 1980 Refugee Act":** Crittenden, *Sanctuary*, 74.
71 **The *Tucson Citizen*:** Crittenden, *Sanctuary*, 72; Davidson, *Convictions of the Heart*, 69.

CHAPTER 9: THE GUATEMALAN SOLUTION

77 **"an invisible government":** Stephen Schlesinger and Stephen Kinzer, *Bitter Fruit: The Story of the American Coup in Guatemala* (Cambridge, MA: Harvard University Press, 2005), 80–81.
77 **Árbenz was a Communist sympathizer:** Árbenz, who idolized Franklin Delano Roosevelt, passed an agrarian reform law to convert unused private land into smaller plots for peasants. The aim was to address the country's rampant inequalities, including its feudal labor system, but the Americans counted it as another mark against him. As the historian Nick Cullather writes, "by attaining its short-term goal" of removing Árbenz, the CIA "thwarted the long-term objective of producing a stable, non-Communist Guatemala." Nick Cullather, *Secret History: The CIA's Classified Account of Its Operations in Guatemala, 1952–1954* (Redwood City: Stanford University Press, 1999), 116–17.
78 **four thousand members:** Schlesinger and Kinzer, *Bitter Fruit*, 59.
78 **"a prototype area":** Cullather, *Secret History*, 35.
78 **"packaged by Bloomingdale's":** Schlesinger and Kinzer, *Bitter Fruit*, 123.
78 **"grave presumption of dangerousness":** Michael McClintock, *The American Connection, Volume II: State Terror and Popular Resistance in Guatemala* (London: Zed Books, 1985), 33.
79 **US intelligence report:** Greg Grandin, Deborah T. Levenson, and Elizabeth Oglesby, eds., *The Guatemala Reader: History, Culture, Politics* (Durham, NC: Duke University Press, 2011), 256–58.
79 **"use of terror":** Virginia Garrard-Burnett, *Terror in the Land of the Holy Spirit: Guatemala under General Efraín Ríos Montt, 1982–1983* (Oxford, UK, and New York: Oxford University Press, 2010), 31.
79 **country's sovereignty:** McClintock, *American Connection, Volume II*, 50.
79 **bases in Panama:** Susanne Jonas, *The Battle for Guatemala: Rebels, Death Squads, and US Power* (Boulder, CO: Westview Press, 1991), 70.
80 **syringes were collected:** Adam Diamant, "Pavon Was a Riot Waiting to Happen," *Christian Science Monitor*, April 3, 1989.
80 **"Guatemalan solution":** Juan Romagoza Arce v. Jose Guillermo García, United States District Court, Southern District of Florida, Northern Division, testimony of Terry Karl, April 20, 2002, 549.
80 **worked intermittently:** Garrard-Burnett, *Terror in the Land of the Holy Spirit*, 44.
81 **"only political corpses":** Jean-Marie Simon, *Guatemala: Eternal Spring, Eternal Tyranny* (New York: W. W. Norton & Company, 1987), 72.
81 **three guerrillas walked:** Francisco Goldman, "The Girls of Guatemala," *Esquire*, March 1981.
81 **60 percent:** Jonas, *Battle for Guatemala*, 105.
82 **killing several dozen people:** Garrard-Burnett, *Terror in the Land of the Holy Spirit*, 46.
82 **Nearly everyone inside was killed:** Garrard-Burnett, *Terror in the Land of the Holy Spirit*, 47; Jonas, *Battle for Guatemala*, 128–29; McClintock, *American Connection, Volume II*, 140.
83 **Cherokee Chief:** Simon, *Guatemala*, 71.

CHAPTER 10: THE RED BISHOP

88 **a large can:** Jennifer Scheper Hughes, *Biography of a Mexican Crucifix: Lived Religion and Local Faith from the Conquest to the Present* (Oxford, UK, and New York: Oxford University Press, 2010), 152.
88 **songs from Latin America:** Charlie Goff, "Second Vatican Council," *The News*, November 13, 2012.
89 **"true pilgrimage":** Gabriela Videla, *Sergio Méndez Arceo: Un señor obispo* (Sucre, Chuquisaca: Correo del Sur, 1981), 52; Hughes, *Biography of a Mexican Crucifix*, 131–70.
89 **"guerrilla infrastructure":** Susanne Jonas, *The Battle for Guatemala: Rebels, Death Squads, and US Power* (Boulder, CO: Westview Press, 1991), 164.
89 **bishop in Chiapas:** Renny Golden and Michael McConnell, *Sanctuary: The New Underground Railroad* (Ossining, NY: Orbis Books, 1986), 120.
92 ***la situación*:** Virginia Garrard-Burnett, *Terror in the Land of the Holy Spirit: Guatemala under General Efraín Ríos Montt, 1982–1983* (Oxford, UK, and New York: Oxford University Press, 2010), xii.
92 **the Maya Q'anjob'al:** Comisión para el Esclaracimiento Histórico, *Guatemala: Memoria del silencio* (Guatemala City: U.N. Office of Project Services, 1999).
92 **"blindness and madness":** Garrard-Burnett, *Terror in the Land of the Holy Spirit*, 86.
93 **"great Indian masses":** Greg Grandin, Deborah T. Levenson, and Elizabeth Oglesby, eds., *The Guatemala Reader: History, Culture, Politics* (Durham, NC: Duke University Press, 2011), 389.
93 **changes in rainfall:** Jonas, *Battle for Guatemala*, 149.
93 **"total kill":** Garrard-Burnett, *Terror in the Land of the Holy Spirit*, 87.
93 **"move to villages":** Kate Doyle, ed., "The Final Battle: Ríos Montt's Counterinsurgency Campaign," National Security Archive, May 9, 2013, 8, https://nsarchive2.gwu.edu/NSAEBB/NSAEBB425/.
93 **"kill one's own brother":** Garrard-Burnett, *Terror in the Land of the Holy Spirit*, 8.

CHAPTER 12: SMUGGLERS WITH A CONSCIENCE

99 **Peggy Hutchison was tugging:** Peggy Hutchison, interview with author, September 13, 2020.
100 **motion sensors:** Timothy Dunn, *The Militarization of the U.S.-Mexico Border, 1978–1992* (Austin: CMass Books, 1996), 216.
101 **"discernment process":** Catholic Social Service, San Francisco, "Sanctuary: The Discerning Process for a Faith Community"; interview with Eileen Purcell.
102 **150 congregations:** Marshall Ingwerson, "More US Churches Join Effort to Harbor Central Americans," *Christian Science Monitor*, July 25, 1984; Peter Applebome, "Sanctuary Movement: New Hopes after Trial," *New York Times*, May 6, 1986.
103 ***60 Minutes*:** Hilary Cunningham, *God and Caesar at the Rio Grande: Sanctuary and the Politics of Religion* (Minneapolis: University of Minnesota Press, 1995), 36.
103 **"Phoenix anti-smuggling unit":** Ann Crittenden, *Sanctuary: A Story of American Conscience and the Law in Collision* (New York: Grove, 1988), 104.
103 **"going off the wall":** Robert Tomsho, *The American Sanctuary Movement* (Austin: Texas Monthly Press, 1987), 86.
103 **thirty thousand copies:** Crittenden, *Sanctuary*, 90.
104 **politicizing the work:** John Fife, interviews with author, March 24, 2020, April 10, 2020, and January 21, 2021.
104 **"uncover and name":** Simon Behrman, *Law and Asylum: Space, Subject, Resistance* (Oxford, UK: Routledge, 2018), 142.
104 **"proper analysis of the conflict":** Fife, interviews.
105 **a group of Nicaraguan men:** Hutchison, interview.
105 **"Low-risk" migrants:** Miriam Davidson, *Convictions of the Heart: Jim Corbett and the Sanctuary Movement* (Tucson: University of Arizona Press, 1988), 82.
105 **with a pad and pen:** Hutchison, interview.

CHAPTER 13: STEPSISTER OF THE GOVERNMENT

107 **"no win issue":** Thomas Maddux, "Ronald Reagan and the Task Force on Immigration, 1981," *Pacific Historical Review* 74, no. 2 (2005): 195–236.
107 **"may be more detrimental":** Daniel J. Tichenor, *Dividing Lines: The Politics of Immigration Control in America* (Princeton, NJ: Princeton University Press, 2001), 376–77.
107 **Philadelphia police department:** Maddux, "Ronald Reagan and the Task Force," 209.
107 **"could keep illegals out":** Maddux, "Ronald Reagan and the Task Force," 222.
107 **well-connected California farmer:** Maddux, "Ronald Reagan and the Task Force," 218.

108 "pattern of employment": Tichenor, *Dividing Lines*, 376.
108 "Good Lord": Maddux, "Ronald Reagan and the Task Force," 224.
108 **failed to make**: Charles Kamasaki, *Immigration Reform: The Corpse That Will Not Die* (Simsbury, CT: Mandel Vilar Press, 2019), 3.
109 "contribution to the debate": Kamasaki, *Immigration Reform*, 61–62.
109 "closing the back door": Kamasaki, *Immigration Reform*, 62.
109 **through Ellis Island**: Kamasaki, *Immigration Reform*, 118.
110 "own political future": Maddux, "Ronald Reagan and the Task Force," 214.
111 **twenty-five thousand more**: Adam B. Cox and Cristina M. Rodríguez, *The President and Immigration Law* (New York: Oxford University Press, 2020), 57.
111 "tripled the black population": Maddux, "Ronald Reagan and the Task Force," 214–15.
111 "sudden influxes of foreigners": Jean v. Nelson, 711 F.2d 1455, (11th Cir., 1983).
111 "held in custody": Jenna M. Loyd and Alison Mountz, *Boats, Borders, and Bases: Race, the Cold War, and the Rise of Migration Detention in the United States* (Berkeley: University of California Press, 2018), 61.
111 "really quite the opposite": *Jean v. Nelson*, 11.
111 **policy of mass detention**: César Cuauhtémoc García Hernández, *Migrating to Prison: America's Obsession with Locking Up Immigrants* (New York: New Press, 2019), 46–47.
111 "pulling this all together": *Jean v. Nelson*.
112 "good, sane immigration policy": Robert Pear, "Smith Urges Miami Businessmen as Head of Immigration Service," *New York Times*, June 13, 1981; Robert Pear, "Immigration Post Loses Its Nominee," *New York Times*, November 13, 1981.
112 **Alan Nelson**: "Reagan to Choose Californian to Run Immigration Services," *New York Times*, November 18, 1981.
112 "moment of truth has arrived": Gary MacEoin and Nivita Riley, *No Promised Land: American Refugee Policies and the Rule of Law* (Boston: Oxfam America, 1982).
113 **lasted twenty minutes**: MacEoin and Riley, *No Promised Land*, 16–17.
113 "couldn't get there": MacEoin and Riley, *No Promised Land*.
113 "determined to deport": MacEoin and Riley, *No Promised Land*, 20.
113 **thirty-three different districts**: US General Accounting Office, Immigration and Naturalization Service: Overview of Management and Program Challenges; Testimony Before the House Committee on the Judiciary, Subcommittee on Immigration and Claims, House of Representatives (Washington, DC, July 29, 1999) (statement of Richard M. Stana, associate director, Administration of Justice Issues, General Government Division).
113 **district directors**: Doris Meissner, interviews with author, November 27, 2019, January 13, 2020, and May 14, 2020.
113 **delivered on INS letterhead**: Government Accountability Office, *Asylum: Uniform Application of Standards Uncertain—Few Denied Applicants Deported* (Washington, DC, 1987), 9–10.
114 **crisscross the country**: Doris Meissner, interviews.
114 "deep six it": Ann Crittenden, *Sanctuary: A Story of American Conscience and the Law in Collision* (New York: Grove, 1988), 61.

CHAPTER 14: THE HEART DOCTOR SPEAKS

117 "I strongly recommend": Miriam Davidson, *Convictions of the Heart: Jim Corbett and the Sanctuary Movement* (Tucson: University of Arizona Press, 1988), 111.
117 **file of press clippings**: Davidson, *Convictions of the Heart*, 111.
117 "to take them to court": Davidson, *Convictions of the Heart*, 158.
117 **Wienerschnitzel International**: Ann Crittenden, *Sanctuary: A Story of American Conscience and the Law in Collision* (New York: Grove, 1988), 114.
118 "continues to spread": Robert Lindsey, "Aid to Aliens Said to Spur Illegal Immigration," *New York Times*, December 23, 1985.
118 **two hundred dollars**: Crittenden, *Sanctuary*, 110.
118 "just didn't fit": Davidson, *Convictions of the Heart*, 88.
119 "transporting illegal aliens": Wayne King, "Two Go on Trial in Houston for Illegally Helping Aliens," *New York Times*, February 19, 1985; Teresa Godwin Phelps, "No Place to Go, No Story to Tell: The Missing Narratives of the Sanctuary Movement," *Washington and Lee Law Review* 123 (1991): 131.
119 **Jack Elder**: King, "Two Go on Trial in Houston"; Phelps, "No Place to Go."
119 **Phil Conger**: Crittenden, *Sanctuary*, 98.
120 **grew tenfold**: Mary Helen Johnson, "National Policies and the Rise of Transnational Gangs," Migration Policy Institute, April 1, 2006.
120 "heart of the Western Hemisphere": William LeoGrande, *Our Own Backyard: The United States in Central America, 1977–1992* (Chapel Hill: University of North Carolina Press, 1998), 201.
120 **displaced by 1984**: Susan Bibler Coutin, "Falling Outside: Excavating the History of Central American Asylum Seekers," *Law & Social Inquiry* 36, no. 3 (2011): 569–96.

CHAPTER 15: A PARK CALLED PAIN

124 **housing Chilean refugees**: Eileen Purcell, interview with author, November 18, 2020.
125 **"blame the leftists"**: Dennis J. Opatrny, "Archbishop Returns from San Salvador," *San Francisco Examiner*, April 1, 1980.
125 **"men, women, and children"**: Fahizah Alim, "Prelate Says US Returning Refugees to Near-Certain Death in El Salvador," *Sacramento Bee*, January 22, 1982.
126 **twenty-three hundred Americans**: Tim Weiner, *Enemies: A History of the FBI* (New York: Random House, 2012), 349–50.
126 **two hundred reported cases**: Ross Gelbspan, *Break-ins, Death Threats and the FBI: The Covert War Against the Central America Movement* (Boston: South End Press, 1991), 1.
126 **international "terrorist support" groups**: United States Congress, Senate, The FBI and CISPES, *Report of the Select Committee on Intelligence, United States Senate, Together with Additional Views*, 101st Congress, 1st Session, July 1989 (Washington, DC: US Government Printing Office, 1989), www.intelligence.senate.gov/sites/default/files/publications/10146.pdf; Weiner, *Enemies*, 352–53; Gelbspan, *Break-ins, Death Threats and the FBI*, 42.
127 **wanted to hear**: José Artiga, interview with author, December 2, 2020.
128 **had first appeared**: Allan Young, *The Harmony of Illusions: Inventing Post-Traumatic Stress Disorder* (Princeton, NJ: Princeton University Press, 1995), 111–13.
128 **streets parted**: José Allen, interview with author, May 29, 2020.
130 **"two-track" approach**: William LeoGrande, *Our Own Backyard: The United States in Central America, 1977–1992* (Chapel Hill: University of North Carolina Press, 1998), 221.
130 **administration's internecine struggles**: LeoGrande, *Our Own Backyard*, 220.
130 **forty-two thousand**: Charles Briscoe, "Special Forces History, San Miguel: The Attack on El Bosque," *Veritas* 3, no. 3 (2007).
130 **"salvage the situation"**: LeoGrande, *Our Own Backyard*, 226.
130 **more than three hundred**: Karen DeYoung, "Salvadoran Land Reform Imperiled, Report Says," *Washington Post*, January 25, 1982.
131 **"no power, no authority"**: LeoGrande, *Our Own Backyard*, 228.
131 **"voice a suspicion"**: LeoGrande, *Our Own Backyard*, 230.
131 **visited Southside Presbyterian church**: Dennis DeConcini, interview with author, September 9, 2020.
132 **"really need to listen"**: Miguel Salat, interview with author, September 10, 2020.
132 **"One thing Congress can't resist"**: LeoGrande, *Our Own Backyard*, 224.
133 **"fleeing Communist oppression"**: Norman Sandler, "President Reagan Warned Wednesday That 100 Million People Face Communist Enslavement, Chaos, and Anarchy," United Press International, May 9, 1984.

CHAPTER 16: SANCTUARY GOES TO TRIAL

134 **seventy-one counts**: Beth McCorkle, "A Federal Grand Jury Has Indicted 16 People," United Press International, January 14, 1985.
134 **deportation proceedings**: Miriam Davidson, *Convictions of the Heart: Jim Corbett and the Sanctuary Movement* (Tucson: University of Arizona Press, 1988), 94; W. Gardner Sel, "Activists 'Ride Herd' on Security," *Washington Post*, February 4, 1985.
135 **At the conference**: Gary MacEoin, ed., *Sanctuary: A Resource Guide for Understanding and Participating in the Central American Refugees' Struggle* (Harper & Row: New York, 1985).
135 **"Woe to our society"**: Ann Crittenden, *Sanctuary: A Story of American Conscience and the Law in Collision* (New York: Grove, 1988), 202; MacEoin, *Sanctuary: A Resource Guide*, 7–13.
135 **contingent from San Francisco**: Eileen Purcell, interview with author, November 18, 2020; MacEoin, *Sanctuary: A Resource Guide*.
136 **"protect the people who are still there"**: Purcell, interview.
137 **the power to admit**: Davidson, *Convictions of the Heart*, 108–9.
137 **"only real defense"**: Davidson, *Convictions of the Heart*, 108–9.
138 **Alejandro Rodríguez**: The account of this moment in the trial comes from reporting by Miriam Davidson, in *Convictions of the Heart*. Rodríguez was a pseudonym.
138 **after four months**: Davidson, *Convictions of the Heart*, 123.
139 **before he could finish**: Davidson, *Convictions of the Heart*.
140 **"young male case"**: Susan Bibler Coutin, "Falling Outside: Excavating the History of Central American Asylum Seekers," *Law & Social Inquiry* 36, no. 3 (2011): 569–96.
140 **the young men's identity alone**: Marc Van Der Hout, interview with author, September 4, 2020; Patty Blum, multiple interviews with author.
140 **momentum for similar challenges**: Lucas Guttentag, interview with author, September 9, 2020.
140 **"were not trained"**: Coutin, "Falling Outside"; Guttentag, interview.

141 **two arguments:** Carolyn Patty Blum, "The Settlement of American Baptist Churches v. Thornburgh: Landmark Victory for Central American Asylum Seekers," *International Journal of Refugee Law* 3, no. 2 (1991): 351.
141 **"It's not enough":** "No Hiding Place Here," *Newsweek*, March 4, 1985.
141 **the grant rate:** Crittenden, *Sanctuary*, 21.
141 **3 percent:** Blum, "The Settlement of American Baptist Churches," 350; Government Accountability Office, *Asylum: Uniform Application of Standards Uncertain—Few Denied Applicants Deported* (Washington, DC: 1987).
141 **"It works slowly":** Davidson, *Convictions of the Heart*, 155.
141 **September 1989:** Blum, "The Settlement of American Baptist Churches," 352. The class also consisted of Salvadorans and Guatemalans who had been denied other forms of legal protection, such as extended voluntary departure and withholding of deportation.
142 **"a double standard":** Robert Pear, "US Issues Asylum Rules Praised as Fairer to Aliens," *New York Times*, July 19, 1990.
142 **allowing some three hundred thousand:** Library of Congress, Research Guides, "1991 American Baptist Churches (ABC) v. Thornburgh," https://guides.loc.gov/latinx-civil-rights/abc-v-thornburgh.

CHAPTER 17: NOTHING MORE PERMANENT THAN A TEMPORARY IMMIGRANT

143 **cities across the country:** Board of Supervisors Document, Memo to Human Services Committee, December 18, 1985, City of San Francisco.
143 **months of intense lobbying:** San Francisco Sanctuary Covenant, "Campaign for City of Refuge," *Planning Documents* (1985). Materials provided by Eileen Purcell.
143 **"Juan (pseudonym)":** Special Hearing of the Human Services Committee, S.F. Board of Advisors, "Resolution to Declare San Francisco a City of Refuge for Guatemalan and Salvadoran Refugees," December 18, 1985.
144 **"invasion of feet people":** Charles Kamasaki, *Immigration Reform: The Corpse That Will Not Die* (Simsbury, CT: Mandel Vilar Press, 2019), 272.
144 **"forty wars raging in the world":** Mark Robert Schneider, *Joe Moakley's Journey: From South Boston to El Salvador* (Boston: Northeastern University Press: 2013), 152.
144 **"nothing more permanent":** Kamasaki, *Immigration Reform*, 272.
145 **two new provisions:** Kamasaki, *Immigration Reform*, 287.
145 **"like Rasputin":** Kamasaki, *Immigration Reform*, 290.
145 **"whole bill is dead":** Schneider, *Joe Moakley's Journey*, 148. Kamasaki, *Immigration Reform*, 293.
145 **"most comprehensive reform":** "President Reagan's Remarks at Signing Ceremony for Immigration Reform and Control Act in Roosevelt Room," November 6, 1986, Records of the White House Television Office, video, www.youtube.com/watch?v=FvZ0QHpxmRs; full transcript, www.reaganlibrary.gov/archives/speech/remarks-signing-immigration-reform-and-control-act-1986.
145 **"a deal going with Iran":** "President Reagan's Remarks at Signing Ceremony."

CHAPTER 18: THE DOCTOR AND THE GENERAL

147 **how to persuade him:** Mark Silverman, interview with author, May 1, 2020.
147 **issued a decree:** Marcia Bernbaum, "La Clínica del Pueblo: An Immigrant Community Health Center of the People, for the People, Case Study Reference Document," 8–9.
148 **three-story row house:** For further context on La Clínica, I spoke extensively with Peter Shields (June 1, 2020), Catalina Sol (June 8, 2020), and Alma Hamar (July 10 and July 17, 2020).
149 **A Salvadoran friend:** Sylvia Rosales-Fike, interview with author, August 16, 2021.
149 **based on family ties:** Lourdes Vides, Application for Naturalization, March 25, 1988, US Department of Justice, Immigration and Naturalization Service.
149 **"can't classify him":** William Stanley, *The Protection Racket State: Elite Politics, Military Extortion, and Civil War in El Salvador* (Philadelphia: Temple University Press: 1996), 152.
150 **"ferocious kind of look":** Ross Gelbspan, *Break-ins, Death Threats and the FBI: The Covert War Against the Central America Movement* (Boston: South End Press, 1991), 48.
150 **their own *tandas*:** Expert Report of Professor Terry L. Karl, *In the Matter of: José Guillermo García-Merino, in Removal Proceedings*, Executive Office for Immigration Review, October 2, 2014, 30; Charles Mohr, "Salvador Army: Its Adaptability Is a Key to War," *New York Times*, August 19, 1983.
150 **alliances with members of the *tandona*:** Stanley, *Protection Racket State*, 153.
151 **August 21, 1989:** Videotaped Deposition of the Defendant, Carlos Eugenio Vides Casanova, November 19, 1999, Ford v. García, US District Court Southern District of Florida, 8.
151 **waiting for him:** Vides Casanova Deposition, November 19, 1999, Ford v. García, 7; Lourdes Vides, Application for Naturalization, March 25, 1988.
151 **early afternoon in October:** José Guillermo García, Request for Asylum in the United States, February 9, 1990, US Department of Justice, Immigration and Naturalization Service.
151 **first among the travelers:** Fabio Andrade, interview with author, summer 2020.

CHAPTER 19: HALF ANTHROPOLOGIST, HALF WANNABE HOOD

157 **The Naked Jungle**: Ioan Grillo, *Gangster Warlords: Drug Dollars, Killing Fields, and the New Politics of Latin America* (New York: Bloomsbury, 2016), 201.

CHAPTER 20: GANG WARS

159 **more than a third**: Steven Dudley, *MS-13: The Making of America's Most Notorious Gang* (New York: Hanover Square Press: 2020), 69, 79, 105.
159 **"jumping in"**: Samuel Logan, *This Is for the Mara Salvatrucha: Inside the MS-13, America's Most Violent Gang* (New York: Hyperion: 2009); Ricardo Pollack, *18 with a Bullet*, PBS documentary (2006).
159 **Arapahoe and South Bonnie Brae**: Dudley, *MS-13*, 79.
159 **started small**: Carlos Martínez and José Luis Sanz, "El origen del odio," *El Faro*, August 6, 2012.
160 **reject anyone who wasn't Mexican American**: Martínez and Sanz, "El origen del odio."
160 **La Grandota**: Martínez and Sanz, "El origen del odio."
160 **devil's horns**: Dudley, *MS-13*, 43.
160 **named after streets or intersections**: Martínez and Sanz, "El origen del odio."
161 **gain some ground**: Carlos García, "MS-13 Sureña: La consolidación de una pandilla chola," in *Mara Salvatrucha 13: El retrato histórico e internacional de una pandilla* (forthcoming).
162 **"Gangville"**: Joel Orozco, interview with author, October 2, 2021.
163 **"overdosed on oratory"**: "New Drug Law: The Senate's Duty; The House Offers Only Empty Promises," *New York Times*, October 4, 1988.
163 **target Black suspects**: Donna Murch, "Crack in Los Angeles: Crisis, Militarization, and Black Response to the Late Twentieth-Century War on Drugs," *Journal of American History* 102, no. 1 (2015).
163 **"taken out and shot"**: Ronald J. Ostrow, "Casual Drug Users Should Be Shot, Gates Says," *Los Angeles Times*, September 6, 1990.
165 **shifts and break times**: Victoria Marin, interview with author, November 2019.
165 **"you could flip them off"**: Orozco, interview.
165 **thirty or forty guys strong**: Orozco, interview.
166 **nineteen inmates had been stabbed**: Chris Blatchford, *The Black Hand: The Bloody Rise and Redemption of "Boxer" Enriquez, a Mexican Mob Killer* (New York: HarperCollins, 2008), 7.
166 **18th street gang aligned itself**: See also Rich Connell and Robert J. Lopez, "An Inside Look at 18th St.'s Menace," *Los Angeles Times*, November 17, 1996; Robert J. Lopez and Rich Connell, "Gang Turns Hope to Fear, Lives to Ashes," *Los Angeles Times*, November 18, 1996; Robert J. Lopez and Jesse Katz, "Mexican Mafia Tells Gangs to Halt Drive-Bys," *Los Angeles Times*, September 26, 1993.
167 **"pack of wild animals"**: John L. Mitchell, "The Raid That Still Haunts L.A.," *Los Angeles Times*, March 14, 2001.
167 **were left homeless**: Lou Cannon, *Official Negligence: How Rodney King and the Riots Changed Los Angeles and the LAPD* (New York: Times Books, 1997), 17.
167 **"gang associate"**: Elana Zilberg, *Space of Detention: The Making of a Transnational Gang Crisis between Los Angeles and El Salvador* (Durham, NC: Duke University Press, 2011), 91.
167 **no such thing**: Tom Hayden, *Street Wars: Gangs and the Future of Violence* (New York: New Press: 2004), 4.
168 **"anti-insurgency run amok"**: John Buntin, "What Does It Take to Stop Crips and Bloods from Killing Each Other?" *New York Times Magazine*, July 10, 2013.
168 **"We were not sure"**: Ana Muñiz, *Police, Power, and the Production of Racial Boundaries* (New Brunswick, NJ: Rutgers University Press, 2015), 39.
168 **Mara Salvatrucha in Hollywood**: Dudley, *MS-13*, 75.
168 **six ounces of weed**: Cannon, *Official Negligence*, 17.
169 **seventy-five active gangs**: Martínez and Sanz, "El origen del odio."
169 **Gringo Battalion**: Dudley, *MS-13*, 88; Carlos García, "Guerras Civiles," in *Mara Salvatrucha 13: El retrato histórico e internacional de una pandilla* (forthcoming).
169 **"obliterate violence by gangs"**: Jerry Belcher, "Police Target Aliens in Gangs for Deportation," *Los Angeles Times*, September 5, 1986.
170 **anyone with a criminal record**: Tom Diaz, *No Boundaries: Transnational Latino Gangs and American Law Enforcement* (Ann Arbor: University of Michigan Press, 2009), 113.
170 **By early 1989**: Stephen Braun, "US-LA Task Force Deports 175 with Ties to Drug, Gang Activity," *Los Angeles Times*, April 12, 1989.

CHAPTER 21: LA CLÍNICA DEL PUEBLO

173 **direct American aid**: William LeoGrande, *Our Own Backyard: The United States in Central America, 1977–1992* (Chapel Hill: University of North Carolina Press, 1998), 577.
174 **"punched-out prizefighters"**: LeoGrande, *Our Own Backyard*, 555.

484 NOTES

174 **$90 million a year:** LeoGrande, *Our Own Backyard*, 567.
174 **$1 billion:** LeoGrande, *Our Own Backyard*, 565.
175 **understated but firm quality:** Jonathan Blitzer, "Field Notes: Meeting Alfredo Cristiani," Pulitzer Center, March 14, 2018, https://pulitzercenter.org/stories/field-notes-meeting-alfredo-cristiani.
175 **thirteen thousand died:** Steven Dudley, *MS-13: The Making of America's Most Notorious Gang* (New York: Hanover Square Press: 2020), 92.
176 **constituent meeting in Jamaica Plain:** Miguel Salat, interview with author, September 10, 2020.
177 **fibs to trick Salvadoran officials:** Jim McGovern, interview with author, January 30, 2020.
177 **"not the final curtain":** Mark Robert Schneider, *Joe Moakley's Journey: From South Boston to El Salvador* (Boston: Northeastern University Press: 2013), 173.
177 **"at a standstill":** Charles Kamasaki, *Immigration Reform: The Corpse That Will Not Die* (Simsbury, CT: Mandel Vilar Press, 2019), 347.
178 **"fixing IRCA's loose ends":** Kamasaki, *Immigration Reform*, 340.
178 **there were 459,000:** Marcela Valdes, "Their Lawsuit Prevented 400,000 Deportations. Now It's Biden's Call," *New York Times Magazine*, April 7, 2021.
178 **"no fucking bill":** Schneider, *Joe Moakley's Journey*, 182.
179 **sitting along the periphery:** Frank Sherry, interview with author, February 7, 2020; Cecilia Muñoz, interview with author, December 6, 2019. See also Kamasaki, *Immigration Reform*, 347–50.
179 **"putting teeth":** Kamasaki, *Immigration Reform*, 349.
179 **others went underground:** Cecilia Menjívar, "Liminal Legality: Salvadoran and Guatemalan Immigrants' Lives in the United States," *American Journal of Sociology* 111, no. 4 (2006): 999–1037.
179 **A quarter:** D'vera Cohn, Jeffrey S. Passell, and Kristen Bialik, "Many Immigrants with Temporary Protected Status Face Uncertain Future in U.S.," Pew Research Center, November 27, 2019.

CHAPTER 22: HISPANICS VERSUS BLACKS VERSUS WHITES

180 **with Quicken:** Peter Shields, interview with author, June 1, 2020; Manny Fernandez, "New Home Attests to Community's Health," *Washington Post*, April 5, 2003.
181 **training course:** Marcia Bernbaum, "La Clínica del Pueblo: An Immigrant Community Health Center of the People, for the People, Case Study Reference Document," 18.
181 **foreign-born Latino:** Audrey Singer, "Latin American Immigrants in the Washington, DC Metropolitan Area: History and Demography" (paper prepared for Latin American Immigrants: Civic and Political Participation in the Washington, DC-Metro Area, Woodrow Wilson International Center for Scholars, November 1, 2007). Census figures are widely understood to undercount immigrants who are undocumented.
181 **second largest:** Terry A. Repak, *Waiting on Washington: Central American Workers in the Nation's Capital* (Philadelphia: Temple University Press: 1995), 1.
181 **one or the other:** Robert L. Jackson, "Washington Mayor Imposes Curfew," *Los Angeles Times*, May 8, 1991.
181 **locked file cabinets:** Interview with Peter Shields, June 1, 2020.
181 **arrived after that date:** Patrick Scallen, "The Bombs That Drop in El Salvador Explode in Mt. Pleasant" (PhD diss., Georgetown University, 2019).
181 **"don't know where to go":** Carlos Sanchez, "Salvadorans Fearful of Deportation," *Washington Post*, May 26, 1987.
182 **dignified and galvanizing name:** Bernbaum, "La Clínica del Pueblo," 19.
182 **receiving special funds:** Bernbaum, "La Clínica del Pueblo," 23.
182 **part-time nurse:** Bernbaum, "La Clínica del Pueblo," 18.
183 **bottles of beer:** Linda Feldmann, "Mt. Pleasant Residents Join Hands to Shake Riots' Stigma of Violence," *Christian Science Monitor*, May 29, 1991.
183 **paper go-cup:** Mount Pleasant Riot Oral History Project, interview with Alice Kelly, January 10, 2018, https://digdc.dclibrary.org/islandora/object/dcplislandora%3A42734.
184 **Fourteenth Street and Columbia Road:** Mount Pleasant Riot Oral History Project, interview with Pedro Avilés, November 15, 2017, https://digdc.dclibrary.org/islandora/object/dcplislandora%3A42728.
184 **"Hispanics versus Blacks versus whites":** Linda M. Harrington and Mitchell Locin, "DC Imposes Curfew a 2nd Night Community Leaders Blame City Government Unrest," *Chicago Tribune*, May 8, 1991. For a general breakdown of the demographics of Mount Pleasant, see Repak, *Waiting on Washington,* 61–69.
184 **"attract more Americans":** Feldmann, "Mt. Pleasant Residents Join Hands."
184 **hundred spoke Spanish:** Harrington and Locin, "DC Imposes Curfew a 2nd Night."
184 **7-Eleven on Mount Pleasant Street:** Annotated Maps, *Washington Post*, May 7, 1991.
184 **set up a loose cordon:** Mount Pleasant Riot Oral History Project, interview with Alice Kelly.
185 **Black agitators:** Scallen, "Bombs That Drop in El Salvador," 228–35; Rene Sanchez and Debbi Wilgoren, "DC Police Consulted INS During Disturbance," *Washington Post*, May 11, 1991.

NOTES

185 **Within three days:** Rene Sanchez, "Curfew Leaves Mount Pleasant Area Quieter," *Washington Post*, May 8, 1991.
185 **More than two hundred:** Emily Friedman, "Mount Pleasant Riots: May 5 Woven Into Neighborhood's History," WAMU 88.5, May 5, 2011.
186 **police-Latino community relations:** Sharon Pratt, "Lessons from a D.C. Riot," *Washington Post*, August 12, 2011.
186 **knew very little:** Catalina Sol, interview with author, June 8, 2020.

CHAPTER 23: WAR ZONES

191 **tripled its vote share:** William LeoGrande, *Our Own Backyard: The United States in Central America, 1977–1992* (Chapel Hill: University of North Carolina Press, 1998), 575.
195 **fifty-six blows:** Los Angeles Times, *Understanding the Riots: Los Angeles before and after the Rodney King Case* (Los Angeles: Los Angeles Times, 1992), 33.
195 **"repetitively use excessive force":** Report of the Independent Commission on the Los Angeles Police Department, 1991, https://michellawyers.com/wp-content/uploads/2010/06/Report-of-the-Independent-Commission-on-the-LAPD-re-Rodney-King_Reduced.pdf.
195 **wave of street protests:** Lou Cannon, *Official Negligence: How Rodney King and the Riots Changed Los Angeles and the LAPD* (New York: Times Books, 1997), 265.
195 **hadn't spoken for a full year:** Cannon, *Official Negligence*.
196 **close to $250 million:** Los Angeles Times, *Understanding the Riots*, 95.
196 **recently dispatched to Panama:** Los Angeles Times, *Understanding the Riots*, 98.
197 **joined the mobs:** Óscar Martínez and Juan José Martínez, *The Hollywood Kid: The Violent Life and Violent Death of an MS-13 Hitman* (London and Brooklyn, NY: Verso, 2019), 73–75.
197 **"the police is tied up":** Carlos García, *Los LA Riots y la Mara Salvatrucha* (unpublished monograph), 4.

CHAPTER 24: OPERATION BLOCKADE

198 **toilets would be clogged:** Fabio Andrade, interview with author, summer 2020.
198 **happening at major American airports:** Doris Meissner, interview with author, November 27, 2019; David A. Martin, "Making Asylum Policy: The 1994 Reforms," *Washington Law Review* 70 (1995): 725–55.
198 **passports "flushers":** Patrick Radden Keefe, *The Snakehead: An Epic Tale of the Chinatown Underworld and the American Dream* (New York: Doubleday, 2009), 105.
199 **steady asylum applications:** Martin, "Making Asylum Policy," 730.
199 **expanded protections for Chinese:** Keefe, *Snakehead*, 99.
199 **a hundred thousand cases:** Martin, "Making Asylum Policy," 731.
199 **Carmelina Cadena:** Carmelina Cadena, interview with author, February 25, 2020.
199 **twenty thousand Indigenous Maya:** Allan F. Burns, *Maya in Exile: Guatemalans in Florida* (Philadelphia: Temple University Press: 1993), 28.
200 **"a good omen":** Larry Rohter, "In a Florida Haven for Guatemalans, Seven Deaths Bring New Mourning," *New York Times*, October 24, 1991.
200 **"speaking in tongues":** Allan F. Burns, "Indiantown, Florida," in *The Maya Diaspora*, eds. James Loucky and Marilyn M. Moors (Philadelphia: Temple University Press, 2000), 166.
200 **the Cuchamatán mountains:** Leon Fink, *The Maya of Morganton: Work and Community in the Nuevo New South* (Chapel Hill: University of North Carolina, 2003), 39.
200 **"I need a good work":** Burns, *Maya in Exile*, 28.
200 **only fourteen asylum petitions:** Burns, *Maya in Exile*, 23.
200 **103,000 additional:** David A. Martin, "Making Asylum Policy: The 1994 Reforms," *Washington Law Review* 70 (1995): 725–55.
200 **"earlier stream of 'war refugees'":** Fink, *Maya of Morganton*, 39.
201 **"Work Authorization (political asylum)":** Martin, "Making Asylum Policy."
201 **added hundreds of thousands:** In 1997, Congress passed the Nicaraguan Adjustment and Central American Relief Act. One of its articles allowed Salvadorans and Guatemalans who were members of the *ABC v. Thornburgh* class action to reapply for asylum by canceling past deportation orders. Some 120,000 Salvadorans eventually obtained legal status in the US through the act, along with roughly 24,000 Guatemalans. See Sarah Grammage, "El Salvador: Despite End to Civil War, Emigration Continues," Migration Policy Institute, July 26, 2007; Susanne Jonas, "Guatemalan Migration in Times of Civil War and Post-War Challenges," Migration Policy Institute, March 27, 2013.
201 **backlog had grown:** US Department of Justice, Immigration and Naturalization Service, "Asylum Reform: Five Years Later," news release, February 1, 2000, www.uscis.gov/sites/default/files/document/news/Asylum.pdf.

202 **fifteen hundred people:** "Haiti: Background to the 1991 Overthrow of President Aristide," Congressional Research Service, October 22, 1993.
202 **"first few days":** Timothy McNulty, "Clinton Reverses Course on Haitians," *Chicago Tribune*, January 15, 1993.
202 **twelve hundred new boats:** Ben Barber, "Haitians, Hopeful, Building Boats in Anticipation of Clinton Welcome," *Baltimore Sun*, January 17, 1993.
202 **had recently revealed:** Ruth Marcus and Michael Isikoff, "Clinton Withdraws Baird's Justice Nomination," *Washington Post*, January 22, 1993. Baird had previously disclosed information about the hiring to Clinton, the FBI, and Republican and Democratic members of the Senate Judiciary Committee. David Johnston, "Clinton's Choice for Justice Dept. Hired Illegal Aliens for Household," *New York Times*, January 14, 1993.
203 **thirty thousand dollars:** Keefe, *Snakehead*, 18.
203 **"packed its bag":** Keefe, *Snakehead*, 100.
203 **three major components:** Meissner, interviews.
204 **"Dead man":** Ron Fournier, "The Fish Rots from the Head in Chicago," *National Journal*, December 2, 2015; Elizabeth Bumiller, "The Brothers Emanuel," *New York Times Magazine*, June 15, 1997.
204 **"something about the border":** Meissner, interviews.
204 **four hundred agents:** Timothy Dunn, *Blockading the Border and Human Rights: The El Paso Operation That Remade Immigration Enforcement* (Austin, University of Texas Press; 2009); Adam Goodman, *The Deportation Machine: America's Long History of Expelling Immigrants* (Princeton, NJ: Princeton University Press, 2020), 173–76.
205 **268 miles:** U.S. Customs and Border Protection, El Paso Sector Texas, www.cbp.gov/border-security/along-us-borders/border-patrol-sectors/el-paso-sector-texas.
205 **75 percent Hispanic:** Dunn, *Blockading the Border*, 120.
205 **Operation Blockade:** "Blockade" was eventually considered a misnomer, because it was impossible to literally shut down the border. The policy was therefore renamed Operation Hold the Line.
205 **they saw the results:** Joel Brinkley, "A Rare Success at the Border Brought Scant Official Praise," *New York Times*, September 14, 1994.
205 **"prevention through deterrence":** Dunn, *Blockading the Border*, 96, 205–28; William Branigin, "Border Patrol Reinforcements to be Sent to Porous Sections," *Washington Post*, October 8, 1997.

CHAPTER 25: ABOVE THE REST

207 **"going to get eaten up":** Joel Orozco, interview with author, October 2, 2021.
208 **areas hit hardest:** Elana Zilberg, *Space of Detention: The Making of a Transnational Gang Crisis between Los Angeles and El Salvador* (Durham, NC: Duke University Press, 2011), 60.
208 **"Whites pointed at Blacks":** Zilberg, *Space of Detention*, 63.
210 **"This is for *la raza*":** Robert J. Lopez and Jesse Katz, "Mexican Mafia Tells Gangs to Halt Drive-bys," *Los Angeles Times*, September 26, 1993.
210 **thirty-eight thousand dollars:** Josh Meyer, "Van Nuys: 5 Tagging Suspects Arrested in Raids," *Los Angeles Times*, April 14, 1994.
210 **Kill 'Em Quick:** "Exploring an Abandoned Juvenile Detainee Camp," YouTube video, 6:36, posted by "POV LA," February 21, 2018, https://www.youtube.com/watch?v=tXteO0mXcPc.
211 **sheet of scrap metal:** Orozco, interview.
211 **fly to Central America:** Zilberg, *Space of Detention*, 131.

CHAPTER 26: THE THIRD RAIL OF AMERICAN POLITICS

213 **"ultra centrist":** Janet Murguía, interview with author, January 30, 2020.
214 **forceful campaign slogans:** Jason DeParle, *American Dream: Three Women, Ten Kids, and a Nation's Drive to End Welfare* (New York: Penguin, 2004), 101–3.
214 **"cut to the right":** Murguía, interview.
214 **"end of welfare reform":** Andrew Wroe, *The Republican Party and Immigration Politics: From Proposition 187 to George W. Bush* (London: Palgrave Macmillan, 2008), 140.
214 **"sack of shit":** John F. Harris, *The Survivor: Bill Clinton in the White House* (New York: Random House, 2005), 238.
214 **slashed the welfare rolls:** Charles Kamasaki, *Immigration Reform: The Corpse That Will Not Die* (Simsbury, CT: Mandel Vilar Press, 2019), 366.
215 **pregnant with her second child:** Cecilia Muñoz, interview with author, December 6, 2019. Muñoz sat for extended interviews on December 6, 2019, January 10, 2020, January 24, 2020, February 13, 2020, and April 10, 2023.
215 **"If we do end up in a war":** Kamasaki, *Immigration Reform*, 337.
215 **"family unity" policy:** Kamasaki, *Immigration Reform*, 336–38.
216 **"speaking Mexican":** Muñoz, interviews.

NOTES

216 **conduit into the administration:** Muñoz, interviews.
216 **in the haggling:** Murguía, interview.
216 **"deeply disappointed":** Bill Clinton, "Remarks on Welfare Legislation," August 1, 1996, www.nytimes.com/1996/08/01/us/text-of-president-clinton-s-announcement-on-welfare-legislation.html.
217 **"Cecilia's Moments of Joy":** Muñoz, interviews.
217 **"third rail of American politics":** Jonathan Weisman, "GOP Finds Hot Button Issue in Illegal Immigration," *Washington Post*, October 23, 2007.
217 **shouted "goal":** Thomas Homan, interviews with author, August 21, 2018, and July 16, 2020.
217 **"get results within sixty days":** Bill Ong Hing, "The Dark Side of Operation Gatekeeper," *U.C. Davis Journal of International Law and Policy* 7, no 2 (2001): 3.
218 **Her recommendations included:** Kamasaki, *Immigration Reform*, 363–68.
218 **"infiltrate the judiciary committees":** Deepa Fernandes, *Targeted: Homeland Security and the Business of Immigration* (New York: Seven Stories, 2007), 216–18.
218 **until four days before:** Jake Bernstein, "Lamar's Alien Agenda," *Texas Observer*, October 25, 2002.
219 **"problem of illegal immigrants":** Dara Lind, "The Disastrous, Forgotten 1996 Law That Created Today's Immigration Problem," Vox, April 28, 2016.
219 **"a single goal":** Lind, "The Disastrous, Forgotten 1996 Law."
220 **"record deportations":** Lind, "The Disastrous, Forgotten 1996 Law."

CHAPTER 27: FAST EDDIE

222 **joined the INS:** Scott Mechkowski, interview with author, July 26, 2019. Mechkowski sat for extended interviews on July 26, 2019, September 15, 2019, September 22, 2019, October 6, 2019, November 17, 2019, and December 8, 2019.
224 **"apparent extreme hardship":** Janet Reno to Doris Meissner, "Re: Guidelines for Use of Prosecutorial Discretion in Removal Proceedings," November 4, 1999, https://big.assets.huffingtonpost.com/Smith_to_Reno_1999.pdf.
224 **Ninety-one percent:** Jake Bernstein, "Lamar's Alien Agenda," *Texas Observer*, October 25, 2002.
227 **by US mail:** Eric Schmitt, "Congress Set to Break Up Beleaguered Agency," *New York Times*, April 10, 2002.
227 **138,000 immigrants:** United States Congress, House, Committee on the Judiciary, Subcommittee on Immigration, Border Security, and Claims, *War on Terrorism: Immigration Enforcement since September 11, 2001: Hearing before the Subcommittee on Immigration, Border Security, and Claims of the Committee on the Judiciary, House of Representatives*, 108th Congress, 1st Session, May 8, 2003 (Washington, DC: US Government Printing Office, 2003), 3.
227 **April 17, 2003:** Rachel L. Swarns, "Aftereffects: Immigrants; Illegal Aliens Can Be Held Indefinitely, Ashcroft Says," *New York Times*, April 26, 2003.
227 **case involving David Joseph:** Bob Herbert, "Ashcroft's Quiet Prisoner," *New York Times*, August 13, 2004.
227 **"a perception in Haiti":** Bob Egelko, "Many Illegals Can Be Jailed Indefinitely: Ashcroft Rules That Granting Bail Could Threaten National Security," *San Francisco Chronicle*, April 25, 2003.
228 **"services to legal immigrants":** Eric Schmitt, "Vote in House Strongly Backs an End to I.N.S.," *New York Times*, April 26, 2002.
229 **more than doubled:** Douglas Massey, "Chain Reaction: The Causes and Consequences of America's War on Immigrants," IZA, Julian Simon Lecture Series no. 8 (2011); Charles Kamasaki, *Immigration Reform: The Corpse That Will Not Die* (Simsbury, CT: Mandel Vilar Press, 2019), 366.
230 **30 percent of arrests:** Margot Mendelson, Shayna Strom, and Michael Wishnie, *Collateral Damage: An Examination of ICE's Fugitive Operations Program* (Washington, DC: Migration Policy Institute, February 2009).
230 **instituted the annual arrest quotas:** Mendelson, Strom, and Wishnie, *Collateral Damage*.
230 **only 17 percent:** Mendelson, Strom, and Wishnie, *Collateral Damage*.

CHAPTER 28: THE SISTERS

235 **different ideological paths:** Helen Mack, interview with author, March 16, 2022.
235 **"to be stigmatized":** David Gonzalez, "The Saturday Profile: Finding Despair, Then Faith, in a Sister's Murder," *New York Times*, September 21, 2002.
236 **staunch anti-communist:** Gonzalez, "Saturday Profile"; Lucrecia Hernández Mack, interview with author, August 11, 2021.
236 **a student of leftist causes:** Lucrecia Hernández Mack, interview.
236 **"we're most needed":** Lucrecia Hernández Mack, interview.
236 **preserving their identity:** Lucrecia Hernández Mack, interview.
237 **"military and police operations":** Susanne Jonas, *The Battle for Guatemala: Rebels, Death Squads, and US Power* (Boulder, CO: Westview Press, 1991), 158.

NOTES

238 **another fifteen thousand:** Communities of Population in Resistance of the Sierra, "We Are Civilians," in *The Guatemala Reader: History, Culture, Politics*, eds. Greg Grandin, Deborah Levenson, and Elizabeth Oglesby (Durham, NC: Duke University Press 2011), 427.
238 **"war of extermination":** Elizabeth Oglesby, "An Arc Bent toward Justice: How Myrna Mack's Research Helped Prove Genocide in Guatemala Decades after Her Murder," *Latin American Studies Association Forum* 51, no. 1 (2020): 25–29.
238 **Two dozen of them:** Jean-Marie Simon, *Guatemala: Eternal Spring, Eternal Tyranny* (New York: W. W. Norton & Company, 1987), 235.
238 **one hillside hamlet:** Simon, *Guatemala*, 236.
238 **"chickens in a coop":** Myrna Mack, "Assistance and Control," in *The Guatemala Reader: History, Culture, Politics*, eds. Greg Grandin, Deborah Levenson, and Elizabeth Oglesby (Durham, NC: Duke University Press 2011), 422.
238 **pack a bag:** Paula Worby, Diane Nelson, and Liz Oglesby, "Huellas," in *Myrna, Décimo aniversario del asesinato de Myrna Mack*, ed. Fundación Myrna Mack (Guatemala City: Fundación Myrna Mack, 2000), 14.
239 **"waving a red flag":** Worby, Nelson, and Oglesby, "Huellas," 13.
239 **to present themselves:** Inter-American Court of Human Rights, Case of Myrna Mack Chang v. Guatemala, Judgment of November 25, 2003.
239 **"Assistance and Control":** Mack, "Assistance and Control," 422–24.
239 **risk of being attacked:** Expert report of Elizabeth Oglesby, 2013 Rios Montt Genocide Trial. Available at www.plazapublica.com.gt/content/peritajes-en-el-juicio-por-genocidio.
239 **Georgetown University funded much:** *Case of Myrna Mack Chang v. Guatemala*.
239 **a certain "Chinese woman":** *Case of Myrna Mack Chang v. Guatemala*, 30.
239 **she was being followed:** *Case of Myrna Mack Chang v. Guatemala*, 32.
240 **had been selling newspapers:** *Case of Myrna Mack Chang v. Guatemala*, 32.
240 **political assassinations had increased:** Jonas, *Battle for Guatemala*, 163.
240 **Myrna called Lucrecia:** *Case of Myrna Mack Chang v. Guatemala*, 33.
240 **Forty-five minutes:** The attack began at 6:45 p.m. *Case of Myrna Mack Chang v. Guatemala*, 35.
241 **The white dress:** Lucrecia Hernández Mack, interview with author, March 4, 2022.
241 **Escobar's government sources:** *Case of Myrna Mack Chang v. Guatemala*, 40.
241 **after the murder:** Helen Mack, interview.
241 **"had the *desconfianza*":** Helen Mack, interview.
241 **"recognized the terror":** Gonzalez, "Saturday Profile."
241 **In August 1991:** Francisco Goldman, *The Art of Political Murder: Who Killed the Bishop?* (New York: Grove, 2007), 43; *Case of Myrna Mack Chang v. Guatemala*, 40–41.
242 **apparently by mistake:** Helen Mack, interview.
242 **an immigration infraction:** "Fugitive in Guatemalan Slaying Is Captured," *Los Angeles Times*, December 6, 1991.
242 **government prosecuted Beteta:** See also *Informe N. 10/96, Sobre Admisibilidad*, Caso 10.636, Guatemala, March 5, 1996.
242 **"amid the contradictions":** Gonzalez, "Saturday Profile."
242 **The threats came:** Helen Mack, interview; *Case of Myrna Mack Chang v. Guatemala*.
242 **novel legal tool:** Helen Mack, interview.
242 **suppressed police report:** *Informe N. 10/96, Sobre Admisibilidad*.
242 **an unexpected place:** Kate Doyle, "Justice in Guatemala," *Nation*, October 17, 2002, www.thenation.com/article/archive/justice-guatemala/.
243 **Thomas Stroock:** "Selective Violence Paralyzes the Left," Department of State, Secret Cable, May 10, 1991, https://nsarchive2.gwu.edu/NSAEBB/NSAEBB11/docs/doc26.pdf.
244 **"I'll pay for you":** Lucrecia Hernández Mack, interview.
244 **"logic was protection":** Helen Mack, interview.
244 ***silencios* and *reclamos*:** Helen Mack, interview.
244 **acted as an *oreja*:** Helen Mack, interview.
245 **killed a year later:** Frank Smyth, "The Untouchable Narco-state," *Texas Observer*, November 18, 2005.
245 **an assassination plot:** Lawyers Committee for Human Rights, *A Test of Justice in Guatemala: The Myrna Mack Murder Trial* (New York, 2003), 23; Helen Mack, interview.
246 **government recognized:** A few years after the government accepted responsibility for the murder, it reversed itself. At another hearing in San José, Helen Mack ran after the Guatemalan delegation, in tears, when they walked out of the courtroom in protest. "It was an abiding image of the trial," a reporter wrote in *The Christian Science Monitor*. Helen Mack had to fight to get the Guatemalans to San José, then had to plead with them to stay in their seats. See Bryan Kay, "After Her Sister's Murder Helen Mack Chang Became a Reformer," *Christian Science Monitor*, January 27, 2015.

246 **the Guatemalan high court:** *Case of Myrna Mack Chang v. Guatemala*, 41–42; Goldman, *Art of Political Murder*, 173.
246 **known as the *cofradía*:** This was an appropriation of a Maya term that described a town's elders.
246 **the late 1990s:** Smyth, "Untouchable Narco-State."
246 **"preferred transit point":** Smyth, "The Untouchable Narco-State."
247 **three hundred people:** Grandin, Levenson, and Oglesby, eds., *Guatemala Reader*, 386.
247 **facts of the conflict:** Comisión para el Esclaracimiento Histórico, *Guatemala: Memoria del silencio* (Guatemala City: U.N. Office of Project Services, 1999).
247 **could not name:** Goldman, *Art of Political Murder*, 5.
247 **Sometimes they were held:** Lucrecia Hernández Mack, interview, March 4, 2022.
248 **The report was explosive:** Goldman, *Art of Political Murder*, 22.
248 **in angry silence:** Goldman, *Art of Political Murder*, 55.
248 **special auditorium:** Lawyers Committee for Human Rights, *Test of Justice in Guatemala*, 24–27; Enrique Recinos, interview with author, August 26, 2022.
248 **"better be frightened":** Lawyers Committee for Human Rights, *Test of Justice in Guatemala*, 35.
248 **"open season":** Lawyers Committee for Human Rights, *Test of Justice in Guatemala*, 24–25.
249 **The verdict came:** Recinos, interview; Lawyers Committee for Human Rights, *Test of Justice in Guatemala*, 25–33; Lucrecia Hernández Mack, interview; Helen Mack, interview.
249 **let out a sob:** Enrique Recinos, interview.
249 **"partially satisfied":** "Guatemalan Ex-Officer Is Convicted in Murder," *Washington Post*, October 4, 2002.
249 **nine thirty p.m.:** Recinos, interview; Lucrecia Hernández Mack, interview.

CHAPTER 29: THE TRIAL

250 **focused on his lawyer:** Juan Romagoza Arce v. Jose Guillermo García, United States District Court, Southern Florida, Northern Division, trial transcript, June 24, 2002, at 67.
251 **"Where else":** Joshua E. S. Phillips, "The Case against the Generals," *Washington Post*, August 17, 2003.
251 **She had called:** Shawn Roberts, interview with author, July 18, 2020.
251 **"command responsibility":** Beth Van Schaack, "Command Responsibility: The Anatomy of Proof in Romagoza v. García," *U.C. Davis Law Review* (2003). See also Patty Blum, interviews with author, July 22, 2020, and August 20, 2020.
251 **"Litigation can be horrible":** Roberts, interview.
251 **was adamant:** Blum, interview, July 22, 2020.
251 **Ford had convinced:** Scott Greathead and Michael Posner, "Bill Ford, Remembered," *Nation*, June 18, 2008.
251 **bumped into his torturer:** Jonathan Blitzer, "My Only Friend Is My Conscience," *New York Review of Books*, December 7, 2017.
252 **lack of living victims:** Blum, interviews; Roberts, interview.
252 **Neris González and Carlos Mauricio:** *Arce v. García*, trial transcript, June 27, 2002, and July 2, 2002.
253 **a military dictatorship:** *Arce v. García*, trial transcript, July 17, 2002, 102.
253 **"Unified" and "consolidated":** *Arce v. García*, trial transcript, June 25, 2002, 72–78.
255 **"familiar with military boots":** *Arce v. García*, trial transcript, June 24, 2002, 82.
258 **"Let me turn back":** *Arce v. García*, trial transcript, July 17, 2002, 58.
258 **$54 million in damages:** Manuel Roig-Franzia, "Torture Victims Win Lawsuit Against Salvadoran Generals," *Washington Post*, July 24, 2002; David Gonzalez, "Torture Victims in El Salvador Are Awarded $54 Million," *New York Times*, July 24, 2002.

CHAPTER 30: HOMIELAND

259 **twenty-two thousand Salvadorans:** "Latest Data: Immigration and Customs Enforcement Removals," TRAC Immigration Database, Syracuse University, https://trac.syr.edu/phptools/immigration/remove/. In 2007, ICE removed 21,892 Salvadorans; the previous year, it removed 11,334.
261 **a government psychologist wrote:** Roberto Valencia, *Carta desde Zacatraz* (Madrid: Libros del K.O., 2018), 36.
262 **whom the government named:** Héctor Silva Ávalos, *Infiltrados: Crónica de la corrupción en la PNC 1992–2013* (San Salvador: UCA Editores, 2014), xiii.
262 **Between 1993 and 1996:** Valencia, *Carta desde Zacatraz*, 35.
262 **robberies, kidnappings, and homicides:** Larry Rohter, "In U.S. Deportation Policy, a Pandora's Box," *New York Times*, August 10, 1997.
262 **old pistols and nightsticks:** Rohter, "In U.S. Deportation Policy."
262 **"a very serious problem":** Rohter, "In U.S. Deportation Policy."

262 **"Piecemeal neighborhood gangs"**: Juan José Martínez d'Aubuisson, *A Year Inside MS-13: See, Hear, and Shut Up* (New York: OR Books/Counterpoint, 2015), 7.
262 **hanging around**: Valencia, *Carta desde Zacatraz*, 57.
263 **the first spin-offs**: Martínez d'Aubuisson, *A Year Inside MS-13*, 8.
263 **"southern pacts"**: Martínez d'Aubuisson, *A Year Inside MS-13*, 73.
263 **"Where do you come from"**: Juan José Martínez, "Los Sureños, los otros pandilleros de El Salvador," *InSight Crime*, December 23, 2014.
263 **more obscure offshoots**: Luis Enrique Amaya and Juan José Martínez, "Sureños en El Salvador: Un acercamiento antropológico a las pandillas de deportados," *Realidad y Reflexión* 14, no. 39 (2014): 7–49.
263 **"deportation and abandonment"**: Amaya and Martínez, "Sureños en El Salvador."
264 **separate facilities**: Valencia, *Carta desde Zacatraz*, 347–54.
265 **low operating costs**: Jonathan Blitzer, "Called Away," *New Yorker*, January 22, 2017.
265 **"very loyal"**: Tim Johnson, "For Deportees to El Salvador, Call Centers Become a Refuge," McClatchy, July 11, 2015.
265 **What differentiated them**: Juan José Martínez, interview with author, April 27, 2016.
265 **in English, as "homeland"**: Emerson Portillo, interview with author, April 25, 2016.

CHAPTER 31: THE REFORMERS

270 **arrived early**: Cecilia Muñoz, interview with author, January 10, 2020.
271 **no longer a sponsor**: Shari Robertson and Michael Camerini, "Last Best Chance," *How Democracy Works Now* (New York: Epidavros Project, Inc., 2010), https://www.howdemocracyworksnow.com/story/last-best-chance.
271 **phone lines crashed**: Muñoz, interview; Frank Sharry, interviews with author.
271 **the far right**: Mike Allen, "Talk Radio Helped Sink Immigration Reform," *Politico*, August 20, 2007; Nicole Hemmer, *Partisans: The Conservative Revolutionaries Who Remade American Politics in the 1990s* (New York: Basic Books, 2022), 27–81; Robertson and Camerini, "Last Best Chance."
271 **food stamps restored**: Charles Kamasaki, *Immigration Reform: The Corpse That Will Not Die* (Simsbury, CT: Mandel Vilar Press, 2019), 369.
272 **policy sanctioning ruses**: John Torres, acting director of ICE, "Use of Ruses During Arrest Operations," memorandum, August 15, 2005; John Torres, "Use of Ruses in Enforcement Operations," memorandum, March 6, 2006; Marcy Forman and John Torres, "Use of Ruses in ICE Enforcement Operations," memorandum, August 22, 2006. These documents were made public as a result of Freedom of Information Act requests filed by Immigrant Defense Project, Center for Constitutional Rights, and Hispanic Interest Coalition of Alabama in 2013. Files available at www.immigrantdefenseproject.org/raids-foia/#memos.
272 **a common ploy**: Bess Chiu et al., *Constitution on ICE: A Report on Immigration Home Raid Operations*, Kathryn O. Greenberg Immigration Justice Clinic (2009); Joel Rubin, "It's Legal for an Immigration Agent to Pretend to Be a Police Officer outside Someone's Door. But Should It Be?" *Los Angeles Times*, February 20, 2017.
272 **thirteen hundred people**: "Arrest Totals from December 12 Swift Raids," Associated Press, September 11, 2007, www.denverpost.com/2007/09/11/arrest-totals-from-dec-12-swift-raids/.
272 **"enforcement stuff"**: Shari Robertson and Michael Camerini, "Brothers and Rivals," *How Democracy Works Now* (New York: Epidavros Project, Inc., 2010), www.howdemocracyworksnow.com/shop/dvd-brothers-and-rivals.
272 **until he wasn't**: Shari Robertson and Michael Camerini, "Sam in the Snow," *How Democracy Works Now* (New York: Epidavros Project, Inc., 2010), www.howdemocracyworksnow.com/story/sam-in-the-snow.
272 **by his explicitness**: Cecilia Muñoz, interview.
273 **"I have a job to do"**: Robertson and Camerini, "Last Best Chance."
273 **few trademark formulations**: Muñoz, interview.
274 **"this is my guy"**: Muñoz, interview.
274 **from the outside**: Muñoz, interview.
274 **"communities are terrorized"**: "Obama Addresses the National Council of La Raza," *Washington Post*, July 15, 2008.
275 **"This is Barack Obama"**: Muñoz, interview.
277 **permanent offices**: Mary A. Clark, "The New Left and Health Care Reform in El Salvador," *Latin American Politics and Society* 57, no. 4 (2015): 97–118.
277 **"We don't want revenge"**: Blake Schmidt and Elisabeth Malkin, "Leftist Party Wins Salvadoran Vote," *New York Times*, March 16, 2009.
277 **Alianza Ciudadana contra la Privatización**: Clark, "The New Left and Health Care Reform"; Mary Clark, "El cambio sí llegó al Sistema de salud," *El Faro*, Feb. 2, 2017.
277 **public-health experts**: Clark, "The New Left and Health Care Reform."
277 *promotores de salud*: Clark, "The New Left and Health Care Reform."

CHAPTER 32: THE VOICE OF GOD

281 **Eleven thousand people:** Hurricanes: Science and Society, University of Rhode Island Graduate School of Oceanography, "1998-Hurricane Mitch," www.hurricanescience.org/history/storms/1990s/mitch/.
282 **"country of the seventies":** Walter LaFeber, *Inevitable Revolutions: The United States in Central America* (New York: W. W. Norton & Company, 1984), 178.
282 **$750,000 a day:** LaFeber, *Inevitable Revolutions*, 330–32.
283 **"zero tolerance" for crime:** Adrienne Pine, *Working Hard, Drinking Hard: On Violence and Survival in Honduras* (Berkeley: University of California Press, 2008), 61.
283 **"mandate of the people":** Pine, *Working Hard, Drinking Hard*, 62.
283 **"illicit association":** Pine, *Working Hard, Drinking Hard*, 63.
283 **"to exterminate":** Alberto Arce, *Honduras a ras de suelo: Crónicas desde el país más violento del mundo* (Mexico City: Ariel, 2015), 136–37.
285 **twenty-eight cars:** Óscar Martínez, *The Beast: Riding the Rails and Dodging Narcos on the Migrant Trail* (London and Brooklyn, NY: Verso, 2010), 51–52.
287 ***golpe profiláctico*:** William Finnegan, "An Old-Fashioned Coup," *New Yorker*, November 22, 2009.
287 **a grocery store:** Recepción de Denuncia, Ministerio Público, Atlántida, La Ceiba, March 14, 2013.
287 **in a confidential cable:** Hugo Llorens, "Open and Shut: The Case of the Honduran Coup," US Embassy Tegucigalpa, July 24, 2009.
288 **slush fund:** Dana Frank, *The Long Honduran Night: Resistance, Terror, and the United States in the Aftermath of the Coup* (Chicago: Haymarket Books, 2018), 138–39.
288 **white motorcycle:** Recepción de Denuncia, Ministerio Público, Atlántida, La Ceiba, November 1, 2011.
288 **"asking the authorities":** Recepción de Denuncia, Ministerio Público, Atlántida, La Ceiba, June 20, 2012.

CHAPTER 33: DEPORTER IN CHIEF

290 **more than the funding:** Doris Meissner et al., *Immigration Enforcement in the United States: The Rise of a Formidable Machinery* (Washington, DC: Migration Policy Institute, 2013).
290 **nearly doubled:** Muzaffar Chishti, Sarah Pierce, and Jessica Bolter, "The Obama Record on Deportations: Deporter in Chief or Not?" Migration Policy Institute, January 26, 2017.
290 **"outlier with an advantage":** Cecilia Muñoz, interview with author.
291 **"doesn't make any sense":** Muñoz, interview.
291 **"overshooting the runway":** Muñoz, interview.
291 **six hundred thousand jobs:** Bureau of Labor Statistics, *Current Employment Statistics: Highlights, April 2009*, May 8, 2009.
291 **supposed to pass:** Muñoz, interview.
291 **"the National Guard":** Muñoz, interview.
291 **At a staff meeting:** Muñoz, interview.
292 **secretary emphasizing:** Julia Preston, "Deportations from U.S. Hit a Record High," *New York Times*, October 6, 2010.
292 **federal program:** Known as 287(g) agreements, the policy was codified by the Illegal Immigration Reform and Immigrant Responsibility Act of 1996. Another, related program, called Secure Communities, was instituted in the final months of the George W. Bush administration. When the 9/11 Commission published its final report, in 2004, the section on immigration enforcement recommended "a growing role for state and local law enforcement agencies . . . so that they can cooperate more effectively with those federal authorities in identifying terrorist suspects." See Muzaffar Chishti and Jessica Bolter, "Two Decades after 9/11, National Security Focus Still Dominates U.S. Immigration system," Migration Policy Institute, September 22, 2021.
293 **In Las Vegas:** Randy Capps et al., *Delegation and Divergence: A Study of 287(g) State and Local Immigration Enforcement* (Washington, DC: Migration Policy Institute, 2011).
293 **The groupings:** John Morton, assistant secretary, ICE, "Civil Immigration Enforcement: Priorities for the Apprehension, Detention, and Removal of Aliens," memorandum, June 30, 2010.
293 **sharpened the terms:** John Morton, director, ICE, "Civil Immigration Enforcement: Priorities for the Apprehension, Detention, and Removal of Aliens," memorandum, March 2, 2011.
293 **three million were prioritized:** Marc R. Rosenblum, *Understanding the Potential Impact of Executive Action on Immigration Enforcement* (Washington, DC: Migration Policy Institute, 2015).
293 **trial and error:** John Sandweg, interview with author, March 10, 2017.
294 **affirmative-action hire:** Cecilia Muñoz, *More Than Ready: Be Strong and Be You . . . and Other Lessons for Women of Color on the Rise* (New York: Seal Press, 2020), 55.
294 **"If they call Rahm":** Muñoz, interview.

294 **"above and beyond":** "Remarks by the President on Comprehensive Immigration Reform in El Paso, Texas," May 10, 2011, transcript, https://obamawhitehouse.archives.gov/the-press-office/2011/05/10/remarks-president-comprehensive-immigration-reform-el-paso-texas.
295 **fell to her:** David Nakamura, "White House Immigration Adviser Cecilia Muñoz Is Taking the Heat for Obama," *Washington Post*, September 8, 2014.
295 **"the human cost":** Ginger Thompson and Sarah Cohen, "More Deportations Follow Minor Crimes, Records Show," *New York Times*, April 6, 2014.
295 **end of the day:** Janet Murguía, interview with author, January 30, 2020.
295 **"were being balanced":** Murguía, interview, July 5, 2023.
295 **"return to her roots":** Peter Wallsten, "Activists Say Obama Aide Cecilia Muñoz Has 'Turned Her Back' on Fellow Hispanics," *Washington Post*, November 9, 2011.
295 **"She should take a stand":** Wallsten, "Activists Say Obama Aide."
295 **the same in private:** Evan McMorris-Santoro and Kate Nocera, "The Rough Road for Cecilia Muñoz, Defender of Obama's Immigration Policy," *BuzzFeed News*, August 3, 2014.
296 **"You need people":** Muñoz, interview.
297 **Two teams:** Muñoz, interview; Janet Napolitano, interviews with author, 2017–2020; Felicia Escobar, interview with author, 2017.
297 **Beginning in 1981:** Department of Justice, Memorandum Opinion for the Secretary of Homeland Security and the Counsel to the President, November 19, 2014, www.justice.gov/file/179206/download.
297 **but also wary:** Napolitano, interview; Muñoz, interview; Escobar, interview.
298 **"even a blind person":** Author interview with a former White House official, February 21, 2020.
298 **"fastest-growing demographic":** Obama interview with editorial board of *Des Moines Register*, October 23, 2012.
298 **Obama to keep his distance:** Ryan Lizza, "Getting to Maybe," *New Yorker*, June 17, 2013. In mid-February, an administration source leaked the details of the White House plan to the press, prompting Marco Rubio, a Republican in the Gang of Eight, to declare Obama's bill "dead on arrival" (Alan Gomez, "White House Immigration Plan Offers Path to Residency," *USA Today*, February 16, 2013).
298 **"target practice":** Muñoz, interview.
298 **"the most ambitious effort":** Julia Preston, "Besides a Path to Citizenship, a New Path on Immigration," *New York Times*, April 16, 2013.
299 **A week before:** Alec MacGillis, "How Republicans Lost Their Best Shot at the Hispanic Vote," *New York Times Magazine*, September 15, 2016.

CHAPTER 34: BORDER EMERGENCY

300 **returning from California:** Jeh Johnson, interview with author, November 16, 2020.
300 **a $175 million program:** Lauren Markham, *The Far Away Brothers* (New York: Crown, 2017), 85. This was the program's budget at the Department of Health and Human Services in 2013. It nearly doubled the next year. (By 2017, it exceeded a billion dollars.)
301 **"too big to downplay":** Jeh Johnson, interview with author, November 16, 2020; Cecilia Muñoz, interview with author.
301 **69,000 unaccompanied children:** U.S. Customs and Border Protection, "Southwest Border Unaccompanied Alien Children FY 2014," www.cbp.gov/newsroom/stats/southwest-border-unaccompanied-children/fy-2014.
301 **33,000 children:** Julia Preston, "New US Effort to Aid Unaccompanied Child Migrants," *New York Times*, June 2, 2014.
301 **six thousand and eight thousand children:** Dara Lind, "The 2014 Central American Migrant Crisis," *Vox*, October 10, 2014.
301 **A naval base:** Matt Hansen, "Lawmakers, Community Leaders Tour Base, Rally for Detained Minors," *Los Angeles Times*, July 8, 2014.
301 **base in San Antonio:** Alex Ura, "State, Waiting for Feds, Providing Vaccines for Child Detainees," *Texas Tribune*, June 26, 2014.
302 **"pushing amnesty":** Erica Werner, "Cantor Mailer Takes Aim at Amnesty for Undocumented Immigrants," Associated Press, May 27, 2014.
302 **blocked by a crowd:** Matt Hansen and Mark Boster, "Protesters in Murrieta Block Detainees' Buses in Tense Standoff," *Los Angeles Times*, July 1, 2014.
302 **At DHS headquarters:** Jeh Johnson, interview with author, November 16, 2020.
302 **"send up" a list:** Author interviews with two former DHS officials, March 13, 2020, and July 19, 2020.
302 **not fatal:** Interviews with two former DHS officials.
302 **immediately shot down:** Interviews with two former DHS officials.
303 **A few advisers:** Interviews with two former DHS officials.

NOTES

303 **"We simply cannot"**: Julia Preston, "Hope and Despair as Families Languish in Texas Immigration Centers," *New York Times*, June 14, 2015.
303 **less like prisons**: Preston, "Hope and Despair."
304 **"keep it together"**: Muñoz, interview.
304 **Earlier that day**: Alec MacGillis, "How Republicans Lost Their Best Shot at the Hispanic Vote," *New York Times Magazine*, September 15, 2016.
304 **June 30, 2014**: The account of this scene is reconstructed through multiple interviews with Cecilia Muñoz, Frank Sharry, Marielena Hincapié, Angelica Salas, and Gustavo Torres. For a partial account of this meeting, see also Major Garrett, "Behind the Scenes of Obama's Sudden Immigration Reversal," *Atlantic*, July 7, 2014.
305 **"deporter in chief"**: Eyder Peralta, "National Council of La Raza Dubs Obama 'Deporter in Chief,'" National Public Radio, March 4, 2014.
305 **"Sorry about that"**: Garrett, "Behind the Scenes."
305 **conversation turned to the border**: Garrett, "Behind the Scenes."
306 **"when my family and I"**: Muñoz, interview.
306 **"You know what"**: There was no transcript of this meeting. This quotation was reconstructed from interviews with five people present, some of whom took contemporaneous notes.

CHAPTER 35: MEMORY CARD

307 **Juliana Ramírez grew up**: The names of the immigrants who appear in this section have been changed for the subjects' protection and at their request.
307 **in a black mask**: Juliana Ramírez, interview with author, August 29, 2017.
307 **three years old**: Ramírez, interview; affidavit in support of asylum, April 25, 2017.
307 **refusing to pay**: Interview with Juliana Ramírez's mother, Ramona, August 29, 2017; affidavit in support of asylum, April 28, 2017.
308 **"What I need"**: Transcript of recorded phone call, Application for Asylum, April 28, 2017. "Lo que necesito ahorita es un dinero para pagar el abogado de una gente que está afectada por lenguas suya . . . La gente del cantón la conozco. Yo conozco a su familia, a sus hijos, a su hija, la conozco."
308 **consulted Michael Chertoff**: Jeh Johnson, interview with author, November 16, 2020.
308 **"on the railcars"**: Sarah Stillman, "Where Are the Children?" *New Yorker*, April 27, 2015.
309 **40,000 unaccompanied children**: US Customs and Border Protection, *United States Border Patrol Southwest Family Unit Subject and Unaccompanied Alien Children Apprehensions Fiscal Year 2016*, www.cbp.gov/newsroom/stats/southwest-border-unaccompanied-children/fy-2016.
309 **42,000 Salvadorans**: "Latest Data: Immigration and Customs Enforcement Removals," TRAC Immigration Database, Syracuse University, https://trac.syr.edu/phptools/immigration/remove/.
312 **two big classrooms**: Marvin Carias, interview with author, April 27, 2016.
312 **some four hundred**: Laura Andrade and Adilio Carrillo, *El Sistema Penitenciario Salvadoreño y Sus Prisiones* (San Salvador: Instituto Universitario de Opinión Pública, Universidad Centroamericana José Simeón Cañas, 2015), xii–10. By December 2021, there would be 636 inmates at the facility: "Resumen de Información de Penales (RIP) Periodo desde las 140010DIC021 hasta las 140011DIC021," Fuerza Armada de El Salvador, December 11, 2021.
312 **in front of prison guards**: Óscar Martínez et al., "Gobierno negoció con pandillas reducción de homicidios," *El Faro*, March 14, 2012.
312 **Sector 6**: Daniel Castro, "The Truce," *Harper's*, May 2019.
313 **"the US capital"**: Hannah Stone, "El Salvador Gets 'Tough' Amid Worsening Crime," *Christian Science Monitor*, February 6, 2012.
313 **vowed to unleash**: José Luis Sanz and Carlos Martínez, "Entrevista: 'Aplicaremos el método de pacificación que se usa en las favelas de Río,'" *El Faro*, January 26, 2012.
313 **in exchange for perks**: Carlos Martínez, Óscar Martínez, and Efren Lemus, "Munguía Payés justifica haber sacado de máxima seguridad a líderes pandilleros," *El Faro*, March 16, 2012.
313 **the first meeting**: Castro, "The Truce"; Carlos Martínez and José Luis Sanz, "La nueva verdad sobre la tregua entre pandillas," *El Faro*, September 15, 2012; Martínez, Martínez, and Lemus, "Munguía Payés justifica."
313 **the negotiator reminded him**: Castro, "The Truce."
313 **"army of seventy thousand"**: Carlos Martínez and José Luis Sanz, "La nueva verdad sobre la tregua entre pandillas."
314 **M16s and a Claymore mine**: Castro, "The Truce."
314 **"transnational criminal organization"**: U.S. Department of Treasury, "Treasury Sanctions Latin American Criminal Organization," news release, October 11, 2012.
314 **"At no time"**: Elisabeth Malkin, "El Salvador Cracks Down on Crime, but Gangs Remain Unbowed," *New York Times*, August 11, 2015.

314 **arresting government officials:** Alberto Arce, "El Salvador Throws Out Gang Truce and Officials Who Put It in Place," *New York Times*, May 20, 2016.
314 **sixty thousand gangsters:** Óscar Martínez et al., "Killers on a Shoestring: Inside the Gangs of El Salvador," *New York Times*, November 20, 2016.
315 **half the minimum wage:** Martínez et al., "Killers on a Shoestring."
316 **Christmas raids:** Josh Gerstein and Seung Min Kim, "Obama Administration Kicks Off Family Deportation Raids," *Politico*, January 4, 2016; Jerry Markon and David Nakamura, "U.S. Plans Raids to Deport Families Who Surged across Border," *Washington Post*, December 23, 2015.

CHAPTER 36: TRUMP

319 **"being provocative":** Jonathan Blitzer, "Donald Trump in Patchogue," *New Yorker*, April 16, 2016.
319 **"an immigration problem":** John Jay LaValle, interview with author, April 2016.
319 **"beaner hopping":** "Climate of Fear: Latino Immigrants in Suffolk County, N.Y.," Southern Poverty Law Center, September 1, 2009.
319 **federal government intervened:** Kirk Semple, "Latino Drivers Report Thefts by Officers," *New York Times*, March 2, 2014. Following an investigation by the Justice Department, hundreds of Latinos in Suffolk County went on to file a class action lawsuit against the county police department. Officers were accused of systematically stopping Latino drivers for supposed traffic infractions, then frisking them and stealing their cash. The scheme was known as "stop and rob." See Liz Robbins, "Latinos, in Class-Action Case, Accuse Suffolk County Police of Bias and Harassment," *New York Times*, April 29, 2015.
320 **"we are nationalists":** Steve Kornacki, *The Red and the Blue: The 1990s and the Birth of Political Tribalism* (New York: Ecco, 2018), 155–57.
321 **tried to recruit:** Joshua Green, *Devil's Bargain: Steve Bannon, Donald Trump, and the Storming of the Presidency* (New York: Penguin Press, 2017), 184.
321 **descend the escalator:** "That's Hitler," Bannon had thought, in respectful awe, according to an account in Jeremy W. Peters, *Insurgency* (New York: Crown, 2022), 187.
321 **"for our ideas":** Green, *Devil's Bargain*, 185.
321 **"Good Housekeeping":** Mark Krikorian, interview with author, October 29, 2019.
322 **first nominee:** Elaina Plott, "The Fall of Jeff Sessions, and What Came After," *New York Times Magazine*, June 30, 2020.
322 **In a memo titled:** Jeff Sessions, "Immigration Handbook for the New Republican Majority," memorandum, January 2015.
322 **the family moved:** Jean Guerrero, *Hatemonger: Stephen Miller, Donald Trump, and the White Nationalist Agenda* (New York: William Morrow, 2020), 18–22.
322 **"angry all the time":** Guerrero, *Hatemonger*, 59.
322 **was a teenager:** Julia Ioffe, "The Believer," *Politico Magazine*, June 27, 2016.
323 **"like a rash":** Jonathan Blitzer, "Get Out," *New Yorker*, March 2, 2020.
323 **"Islamo-Fascism Awareness":** McKay Coppins, "Trump's Right-Hand Troll," *Atlantic*, May 28, 2018.
323 **"without a soul":** Stephen Miller, "America: The Forgotten Campus Culture," *The Chronicle*, November 20, 2006.
323 **quadrupled in Alabama:** Jason DeParle, "How Stephen Miller Seized the Moment to Battle Immigration," *New York Times*, August 17, 2019.
323 **"rule of law":** Sasha Aslanian, "Immigration Lurks, But Not Discussed, in 6th District Race," Minnesota Public Radio, October 11, 2010; Stephanie Akin, "The Other 'Steve' in the White House," *Roll Call*, February 13, 2017.
323 **the Heritage Foundation:** Blitzer, "Get Out."
323 **emails about immigration:** Blitzer, "Get Out."
324 **"master's degree":** Author interview with Senior House Republican staffer, December 2, 2019.
324 **"The laws need to change":** Author interview with DHS official, November 15, 2019.
325 **"deepest levels":** Nick Miroff and Josh Dawsey, "The Adviser Who Scripts Trump's Immigration Policy," *Washington Post*, August 17, 2019.
325 **"miraculous intervention":** Jeff Sessions, "Speech at Executive Office for Immigration Review," Department of Justice, October 12, 2007, video, www.c-span.org/video/?435666-1/attorney-general-jeff-sessions-asylum-policies.
325 **"How do you maneuver":** Julie Hirschfeld Davis and Michael D. Shear, *Border Wars: Inside Trump's Assault on Immigration* (New York: Simon & Schuster, 2019), 51.
326 **"has two impulses":** Blitzer, "Get Out."
326 **"new world order":** Davis and Shear, *Border Wars*, 76.
327 **"walking encyclopedia":** Maggie Haberman and Katie Rogers, "Still Standing, Jared Kushner and Ivanka Trump Step Back in the Spotlight," *New York Times*, July 28, 2018.

328 **In attendance:** Jonathan Blitzer, "How Stephen Miller Single-Handedly Got the U.S. to Accept Fewer Refugees," *New Yorker*, October 13, 2017.
328 **intercepting documents:** Blitzer, "How Stephen Miller Single-Handedly."
328 **cost-benefit calculation:** Julie Hirschfield Davis and Somini Sengupta, "Trump Administration Rejects Study Showing Positive Impact of Refugees," *New York Times*, September 18, 2017.
329 **"DACA with heart":** Jonathan Blitzer, "Donald Trump Holds Dreamers' Future in His Hands," *New Yorker*, September 3, 2017.
329 **"replace existing demographics":** Michael Edison Hayden, "Miller Dismisses DACA in Emails, Mirroring Anti-Immigrant Extremists' Views," Southern Poverty Law Center, January 14, 2020.

CHAPTER 37: KILLING FIELDS

330 **learned about the crime:** Michael Scherer, "2016 Person of the Year: Donald Trump," *Time*, December 7, 2016.
330 **seventeen killings:** Timothy Sini, "Testimony Regarding MS-13," United States Senate Committee on Homeland Security and Governmental Affairs, May 22, 2017, 1, www.hsgac.senate.gov/wp-content/uploads/imo/media/doc/Testimony-Sini-2017-05-241.pdf.
330 **eighty-nine gang members:** Sini, "Testimony Regarding MS-13," 4.
330 **four hundred people:** Sini, "Testimony Regarding MS-13," 3.
331 **"You don't feel":** Steve Bellone, interview with author, June 2017.
331 **Steve Levy:** "Climate of Fear: Latino Immigrants in Suffolk County, N.Y.," Southern Poverty Law Center, September 1, 2009; David Freedlander, "Long Island's O.G. Anti-Immigrant Politician," *Daily Beast*, August 9, 2017.
331 **pollster in New Jersey:** Adam Geller, interview with author, November 3, 2017; Jonathan Blitzer, "How the Gang MS-13 Became a Trumpian Campaign Issue in Virginia," *New Yorker*, November 6, 2017.
332 **Sini had been there:** Jonathan Blitzer, "The Gang MS-13 Is a Real Problem, but Does Trump Have Any Answers?" *New Yorker*, May 9, 2017.
332 **"compete with that noise":** Timothy Sini, interview with author, April 2017.
332 **began his career:** Thomas Homan, interviews with author, August 21, 2018, and July 16, 2020.
333 **1.4 million people:** Marc R. Rosenblum, *Understanding the Potential Impact of Executive Action on Immigration Enforcement*, Migration Policy Institute (2015).
333 **dropped substantially:** Kristen Bialik, "Most Immigrants Arrested by ICE Have Prior Criminal Convictions, a Big Change from 2009," Pew Research Center, February 15, 2018; Bryan Baker, *Immigration Enforcement Actions: 2016* (Washington, DC: Department of Homeland Security, Office of Immigration Statistics, 2017), 4; www.dhs.gov/sites/default/files/publications/Enforcement_Actions_2016.pdf.
333 **in late January:** Homan, interview, August 21, 2018.
333 **raid in Las Cruces:** Greg Ewing, interview with author, March 11, 2017; see Jonathan Blitzer, "After an Immigration Raid, a City's Students Vanish," *New Yorker*, March 23, 2017.
334 **had been abandoned:** Julie Kirkes, interview with author, March 14, 2017.
334 **"laws on the books":** Tal Kopan, "ICE Director: Undocumented Immigrants 'Should Be Afraid,'" CNN, June 16, 2017.
334 **"off the table":** Jonathan Blitzer, "In Calling for Politicians' Arrest, an ICE Official Embraces His New Extremist Image," *New Yorker*, January 4, 2018.
335 **traffic court:** "Climate of Fear."
335 **a policeman in El Salvador:** Jonathan Blitzer, "Trapped," *New Yorker*, January 1, 2018.
340 **"We automatically notify":** Sini, "Testimony Regarding MS-13."
340 **involved with the gang:** Sarah Gonzalez, "MS-13 Gang Crackdown Relies on 'Questionable' Evidence from Schools," National Public Radio, August 7, 2017; Sarah Gonzalez, "Undocumented Teens Say They're Falsely Accused of Being in a Gang," National Public Radio, August 17, 2017.
340 **Bellport High School:** Victor Manuel Ramos, "Lawyer: Students at Bellport High Wrongly Accused of MS-13 Ties," *Newsday*, June 23, 2017.
340 **"I'm scared":** Sarah Gonzalez, "Undocumented Teens Say They're Falsely Accused of Being in a Gang," National Public Radio, August 17, 2017.
340 **ICE identified someone:** Julia Edwards Ainsley, "US Immigration Raids to Target Teenaged Suspected Gang Members," Reuters, July 21, 2017.
341 **Angel Melendez:** Angel Melendez, interview with author, August 23, 2017.
341 **Jorge's case:** Jonathan Blitzer, "How Gang Victims Are Labelled as Gang Suspects," *New Yorker*, January 23, 2018.
342 **twenty years:** Robert Warren and Donald Kerwin, "A Statistical and Demographic Profile of the US Temporary Protected Status Populations from El Salvador, Honduras, and Haiti," *Journal on Migration and Human Society* 5, no. 3 (2017): 578. The majority of Hondurans who were granted TPS in the late 1990s, because of Hurricane Mitch, had also lived in the US for twenty years.

342 **broader document:** "Memorandum for: Alien File Regarding Gang Affiliation," from Daniel Loechner through Celestino J. Martinez, supervisory Special Agent, Intel, July 3, 2017.

CHAPTER 38: LOS NERDS

343 **"synonymous with death":** Comisión Internacional contra la Impunidad en Guatemala (CICIG), Comunicado de Prensa 002, "Unidad especial investigará actos de corrupción en el ministerio de salud," January 12, 2017, https://www.cicig.org/comunicados-2017-c/unidad-especial-investigara-actos-de-corrupcion-en-el-mspas/.
343 **"not of the right":** Lucrecia Hernández Mack, interview with author, March 3, 2022.
345 **half of Guatemala:** "Country Profiles: Guatemala," *Epidemiological Bulletin* 25, no. 2 (June 2004), www3.paho.org/english/dd/ais/be_v25n2-perfil-guatemala.htm.
345 **the role of NGOs:** US Agency for International Development, "Guatemala: Health System Assessment 2015, Executive Summary," August 2015, https://2012-2017.usaid.gov/documents/1862/guatemala-health-system-assessment-2015-executive-summary.
346 **preventable illnesses:** Mack, interview.
346 **fallen to levels:** Mack, interview; World Bank Immunization Data, https://data.worldbank.org/indicator/SH.IMM.IDPT?locations=GT.
346 **$3 million:** T. Christian Miller, "Colonel Guilty in Murder of Anthropologist," *Los Angeles Times*, October 4, 2002.
346 **"to help me":** Sebastián Escalón, "Guatemala Pide Auxilio," February 22, 2021, in *El Experimento*, podcast, 32:58, www.no-ficcion.com/project/transcripcion-guatemala-pide-ayuda.
346 **The CICIG's mandate:** Escalón, "Guatemala Pide Auxilio"; Jonathan Blitzer, "The Exile of Guatemala's Anti-Corruption Efforts," *New Yorker*, April 29, 2022.
346 **the US Marines:** David Grann, "A Murder Foretold," *New Yorker*, April 4, 2011.
347 **$45 million:** "Guatemala: An Overview," Congressional Research Service, updated April 4, 2023, http://crsreports.congress.gov/product/pdf/IF/IF12340.
348 **honored the terms:** Mack, interview.
348 **$4.8 million:** CICIG, "Presentación del caso asalto al ministerio de salud pública," July 16, 2019, www.cicig.org/casos/caso-asalto-al-ministerio-de-salud-publica/.
349 **fifty-four different unions:** CICIG, "Presentación del caso asalto."
349 **thirty-five thousand staff:** CICIG, "Presentación del caso asalto."
349 **ten *citaciones*:** Author interview with staff secretary, Office of Minister of Health, March 2, 2022.
349 **accused of pocketing:** Mack, interview.
349 **"for your head":** Mack, interview; Gabriel Labrador, "Me decían: 'Aguantemos con Jimmy,'" *El Faro*, September 24, 2018.
349 **70 percent:** Asier Vera, "Los centros de salud de Guatemala atenderán el mal de ojo, la pérdida del alma, los sustos y los antojos," *El Mundo*, August 25, 2016.
350 **"the essential life force":** Linda Green, *Fear as a Way of Life: Mayan Widows in Rural Guatemala* (New York: Columbia University Press, 1999), 120–24.
350 **"necessary to be vigilant":** Vera, "Los centros de salud de Guatemala."
350 **opened an investigation:** CICIG, "Capturas relacionadas con fraude al registro de la propiedad," January 18, 2017, www.cicig.org/casos/capturas-relacionadas-con-fraude-al-registro-de-la-propiedad/; Héctor Silva Ávalos and Steven Dudley, "El 'pecado original' del presidente Jimmy Morales y de Guatemala," *InSight Crime*, August 23, 2018.
350 **they were charged:** "Detenidos hermano e hijo del presidente de Guatemala en investigación por corrupción," CNN Español, January 18, 2017; "El hermano y el hijo del presidente de Guatemala quedan bajo arresto domiciliario," CNN Español, February 23, 2017. In August 2019, a court acquitted Morales's brother and son on the grounds that it couldn't "prove participation or motive" in the commission of a crime. José Elías, "Guatemala absuelve al hijo y al hermano del presidente acusados de emitir facturas falsas," *El País*, August 19, 2019.
350 **unaccommodating probity:** As a young attorney in Medellín, Colombia, Velásquez had once refused a bribe from Pablo Escobar. To break the news to him personally, Velásquez traveled to La Catedral, the prison built by the government to house Escobar according to his own personal specifications. It was known as Hotel Escobar and had a soccer field, discotheque, and Jacuzzi; Escobar hosted weekly parties there, and installed a special telescope that allowed him to see Medellín from his room. "I don't accept money other than my salary," Velásquez told him. In July 1992, when the Colombian government tried to transfer Escobar to a different facility, he held Velásquez responsible. Velásquez received a call one day from Escobar's brother warning him that Pablo was furious and planned to kill him (Sebastian Escalón, "Iván el Terrible," August 8, 2022, *El Experimento*, podcast, 40:59).

CHAPTER 39: LA PASTORA

353 **State Highway 9:** US Department of Homeland Security, Arrest Report, September 20, 2017.
354 **"You're crazy, aren't you":** Keldy Mabel Gonzáles Brebe de Zúniga, interview with author, March 10, 2021.

NOTES

355 **before photos of Donald Trump:** Jacob Soboroff, *Separated: Inside an American Tragedy* (New York: Custom House, 2020), 30.
355 **"History would not judge":** Department of Justice, Office of the Inspector General, *Review of the Department of Justice's Planning and Implementation of Its Zero Tolerance Policy and Its Coordination with the Departments of Homeland Security and Health and Human Services* (January 2021), 14.
355 **"looking at each individual":** Department of Justice, *Review of the Department of Justice's Planning*, 15.
355 **Valentine's Day:** Soboroff, *Separated*, 28–30; Jonathan White, witness testimony, United States Congress, House, *Examining the Failures of the Trump Administration's Inhumane Family Separation Policy: Hearing Before the Subcommittee on Oversight and Investigations of the Committee on Energy and Commerce, House of Representatives*, 116th Congress, 1st Session, February 7, 2019, transcript, www.congress.gov/event/116th-congress/house-event/LC64497/text.
355 **raised the possibility:** Jonathan White, witness testimony; Soboroff, *Separated*, 31.
356 **"do almost anything":** *The Situation Room with Wolf Blitzer*, March 6, 2017; Mahita Gajanan, "Homeland Security Chief Says He's Considering Separating Immigrant Children from Parents," *Time*, March 6, 2018.
356 **already started referring:** Department of Justice, *Review of the Department of Justice's Planning*, 13.
356 **"Trump is going to fix that":** Lomi Kriel, "Trump Moves to End Catch and Release, Prosecuting Parents and Removing Children Who Cross the Border," *Houston Chronicle*, November 25, 2017.
356 **around Yuma:** Department of Homeland Security, Interagency Task Force on the Reunification of Families, *Initial Progress Report* (June 2, 2021), 22.
356 **"no one paid attention":** Department of Justice, *Review of the Department of Justice's Planning*, 11.
356 **yielding results:** The US Attorney's office in New Mexico had previously limited the number of prosecutions for illegal crossings that it would receive from the El Paso Border Patrol sector. On July 16, 2017, the acting US Attorney for the district "removed all restrictions," according to a report by the Government Accountability Office. US Government Accountability Office, "Unaccompanied Children: Agency Efforts to Reunify Children Separated from Parents at the Border," October 2018, 14, www.gao.gov/assets/gao-19-163.pdf.
357 **"It is the hope":** Department of Justice, *Review of the Department of Justice's Planning*, 15.
357 **"We have now heard":** Department of Justice, *Review of the Department of Justice's Planning*, 16.
357 **"at least 10 years old":** Department of Justice, *Review of the Department of Justice's Planning*, 15.
358 **another voice piped in:** US Department of Homeland Security Citizenship and Immigration Services, *Credible Fear Interview Notes*, Arlington Asylum Office, Interview Location: El Paso SPC (telephonic), October 4, 2017, Interviewing APSO: E. Su. (All quotes from the credible fear interview are drawn from this document, which contains a transcript of the proceeding.)
358 **office building in Arlington:** Author interview with USCIS official, March 15, 2021; *Credible Fear Interview Notes*, October 4, 2017.
359 **"under oath":** *Credible Fear Interview Notes*, October 4, 2017.
359 **a Haitian schoolteacher:** His name was Ansley Damus. He spent two years and twenty-seven days in detention, despite winning his asylum case twice. The government appealed each time.
360 **"To be determined":** Department of Homeland Security, *Notice to Appear, In the Matter of: Gonzales-Brebe de Zuniga, Keldy Mabel*, currently residing at c/o ICE Custody El Paso Processing Center, 8915 Montana Avenue, El Paso, TX, October 11, 2017.
360 **noticed a pattern:** Department of Justice, *Review of the Department of Justice's Planning*, 17.
360 **"done thousands of these":** Melissa del Bosque, "The El Paso Experiment," *Intercept*, November 1, 2020.
360 **named Sergio Garcia:** del Bosque, "The El Paso Experiment."
360 **"kidnapping their children":** Lomi Kriel, "Migrants Families Left Broken at the Border: Questionable Federal Policy Separates Parents and Children," *Houston Chronicle*, November 26, 2017.
360 **"I would be very worried":** Kriel, "Migrant Families Left Broken at the Border."
360 **280 others:** Department of Justice, *Review of the Department of Justice's Planning*, 15.

CHAPTER 40: STAY AT YOUR OWN RISK

362 **couldn't understand why:** José Luis Contreras, interviews with author, December 16–18, 2017, October 18, 2018, and April 21, 2021.
363 **was accused:** "Luis Zelaya: 'Mapas Soluciones tiene vínculos con el Partido Nacional,'" *Tiempo*, June 6, 2017; "TSA pagará millionaria cifra si cancela contrato a Mapa Soluciones," *Tiempo*, October 19, 2017.
363 **hire another company:** Marilyn Méndez, "La manejará Asica," *Diario La Prensa*, October 26, 2017; "Descodificando el fraude electora," *ContraCorriente*, December 14, 2017.
363 **"the game-show host":** Jonathan Blitzer, "A U.S. Ally Says He Won Honduras's Presidential Election. Hondurans Aren't So Sure," *New Yorker*, November 29, 2017.
363 **to be "irreversible":** Jonathan Blitzer, "In Honduras, Calls Rise for New Presidential Elections," *New Yorker*, December 19, 2017; "Magistrado dice que tendencia es irreversible mientras el pueblo se parte," *ContraCorriente*, November 28, 2017.

364 **twelve conditions:** Patricia Zengerle, "U.S. Document Certifies Honduras as Supporting Rights amid Vote Crisis," Reuters, December 4, 2017.
365 **"a clear signal":** Elaine Duke email to John Kelly, November 6, 2017.
365 **"positive gems":** Brandon Prelogar email to Kathy Neubel Kovarik, Kathryn Anderson, and Laurence Levine, October 13, 2017.
365 **"on the cusp":** Deposition of Gene Hamilton, October 20, 2017, Martin Jonathan Batallia Vidal et al. v. Elaine Duke, Acting Secretary, Department of Homeland Security et al., 16-CV-4756 (NGG) (JO) (E.D.N.Y. October 19, 2017).
365 **panic at the White House:** Jonathan Blitzer, "The Administration Is Rushing to Turn Trump's Latest Immigration Tweets into a Real Policy," *New Yorker*, April 5, 2018.
366 **"fraudulent electoral process":** Delphine Schrank and Mica Rosenberg, "Migrant Caravan Heading to U.S. Border Puts Mexico in Tough Spot with Trump," Reuters, April 2, 2018.
366 **$3 million:** Sarah Chayes, *When Corruption Is the Operating System: The Case of Honduras*, Carnegie Endowment for International Peace, May 30, 2017; Lauren Carasik, "Washington Complicit in Honduras Corruption Scandal," Telesur, June 5, 2015.
366 **"pretty nice guy":** Author interview with administration official, October 1, 2017.
366 **respond together:** Jonathan Blitzer, "How Stephen Miller Single-Handedly Got the U.S. to Accept Fewer Refugees," *New Yorker*, October 13, 2017.
367 **memo ending DACA:** Jonathan Blitzer, "A Trump Official Behind the End of DACA Explains Himself," *New Yorker*, November 10, 2017.
367 **he created it:** Dara Lind, "Trump's DHS Is Using an Extremely Dubious Statistic to Justify Splitting Up Families at the Border," *Vox*, May 8, 2018.
367 **after-action report:** Department of Homeland Security, Office of the Inspector General, *DHS Lacked Technology Needed to Successfully Account for Separated Migrant Families* (November 25, 2019), 15.
367 **vulnerable to attacks:** Jonathan Blitzer, "How the D.H.S. Secretary, Kirstjen Nielsen, Became One of President Trump's Fiercest Loyalists," *New Yorker*, March 1, 2018; Jonathan Blitzer, "Why Trump Is So Angry at His Homeland Security Secretary," *New Yorker*, May 17, 2018.
368 **"take away children":** Department of Justice, Office of the Inspector General, *Review of the Department of Justice's Planning and Implementation of its Zero Tolerance Policy and Its Coordination with the Departments of Homeland Security and Health and Human Services* (January 2021), 39.
368 **"If I lose the election":** Julie Hirschfeld Davis and Michael D. Shear, *Border Wars: Inside Trump's Assault on Immigration* (New York: Simon & Schuster, 2019), 267.
368 **to prosecute parents:** "Memorandum for the Secretary," from Kevin K. McAleenan, L. Francis Cissna, and Thomas D. Homan, Subject: Increasing Prosecutions of Immigration Violations, April 23, 2018.
368 **five times a day:** Author interview with senior DHS official, February 5, 2020; Jonathan Blitzer, "Get Out," *New Yorker*, March 2, 2020.
369 **hectoring phone calls:** Author interview with senior administration official, October 8, 2020.
369 **twenty-six thousand children:** Department of Homeland Security, *DHS Lacked Technology*, 17.

CHAPTER 41: DO I HAVE TO COME HERE INJURED OR DEAD?

370 **the "bye-bye place":** American Immigration Council, *Administrative Complaint Regarding El Paso Service Processing Center Immigration Court Judges* (April 3, 2019), 2.
371 **who could help:** Belky R., interviews with author, August 3, 2019, and March 21, 2021.
371 **La Miss:** Carla R., interview with author, March 11, 2021.
371 **stayed close:** Gloria H., interview with author, February 27, 2020.
373 **rejected nearly 90 percent:** "Judge-by-Judge Asylum Decisions in Immigration Courts FY 2015–2020," TRAC Immigration Database, Syracuse University, https://trac.syr.edu/immigration/reports/judge2020/denialrates.html.

CHAPTER 42: THE HIGHLANDS AT THE BORDER

375 **find a six-year-old:** Jonathan Blitzer, "The Government Has No Plan for Reuniting the Immigrant Families It Is Tearing Apart," *New Yorker*, June 18, 2018.
377 **"most vulnerable area":** Biota S.A. y Nature Conservancy, *Análisis de la vulnerabilidad ante el cambio climático en el altiplano occidental de Guatemala* (2014).
377 **three hurricanes:** Clima, Naturaleza y Comunidades en Guatemala, *Acciones exitosas de adaptación al cambio climático y reducción de la pobreza en el altiplano occidental de Guatemala* (2017), 11.
377 **flood the soil and destroy crops:** Edwin Castellanos, interviews with author, January 2019; Sebastian Charchalac, interviews with author, January–February 2019.
378 **"Inattention to these issues":** Clima, Naturaleza y Comunidades en Guatemala, *Acciones exitosas de adaptación*, 12.

378 **Half of the parents:** Rachel Nolan, "Language Barriers," *New Yorker*, January 6, 2020. Nolan details how a lack of translators speaking Indigenous languages systematically undermines the rights of asylum seekers who otherwise can't defend themselves in immigration proceedings. Lee Gelernt, the ACLU attorney challenging the Trump administration's family-separation policy, told Nolan, "The Indigenous population was likely the least able to understand their rights, and may therefore have been more susceptible to losing their children and waiving away their own asylum rights."

378 **ninth most common:** Two other Guatemalan Mayan languages were among the twenty-five most common languages spoken in American immigration courts: K'iche' and Q'anjob'al.

380 **leaked DHS records:** Caitlin Dickerson, "Hundreds of Immigrant Children Have Been Taken from Parents at U.S. Border," *New York Times*, April 20, 2018.

380 **Marco Antonio Muñoz:** Nick Miroff, "A Family Was Separated at the Border, and This Distraught Father Took His Own Life," *Washington Post*, June 9, 2018; Nick Miroff, "Honduran Father Who Died in Texas Jail Was Fleeing Violence, Consul Says," *Washington Post*, June 11, 2018.

381 **support the White House:** Julie Hirschfeld Davis and Michael D. Shear, *Border Wars: Inside Trump's Assault on Immigration* (New York: Simon & Schuster, 2019), 271.

382 **"the other way":** Davis and Shear, *Border Wars*, 275.

382 **get the credit:** Davis and Shear, *Border Wars*, 263.

382 **Sanders telling Nielsen:** Jonathan Blitzer, "Get Out," *New Yorker*, March 2, 2020.

CHAPTER 43: WE NEED CONCRETE INFORMATION

383 **Irma Whiteley:** Jonathan Blitzer, "How the Humanitarian Crisis on the Mexico Border Could Worsen," *New Yorker*, June 23, 2018.

385 **"overwhelming medical evidence":** Ms. L. and Ms. C. vs. US Immigration and Customs Enforcement, 2018, www.aclu.org/sites/default/files/field_document/2018.03.09_32_amended_complaint.pdf.

385 **comprehensive list:** Jonathan Blitzer, "The Activist Effort to Find the Children the Government Took from Their Parents," *New Yorker*, July 13, 2018.

385 **"little bit in flux":** Transcript from July 6, 2018, Status Conference, *Ms. L. v. ICE*, https://storage.courtlistener.com/recap/gov.uscourts.casd.564097/gov.uscourts.casd.564097.93.0.pdf.

388 **She signed next to the option:** US Immigration and Customs Enforcement. Enforcement and Removal Operations. Separated Parent's Removal Form. Certificate of Service, July 3, 2018.

CHAPTER 44: THE CARAVAN

389 **streets of Mapastepec:** Large portions of this chapter are drawn from Jonathan Blitzer, "On the Desperate and Uncertain Trail of the Migrant Caravan," *New Yorker*, October 26, 2018.

391 **"we don't risk":** Jonathan Blitzer, "Why the Trump White House Is Having a Meltdown over the Migrant Caravan," *New Yorker*, October 19, 2018.

391 **more migrants than residents:** Jonathan Blitzer, "A Small Town in Mexico Prepares to Double in Size with the Arrival of the Migrant Caravan," *New Yorker*, October 30, 2018.

392 **arrived at a crossroads:** Jonathan Blitzer, "The Migrant Caravan Reaches a Crossroads in Southern Mexico," *New Yorker*, October 27, 2018.

CHAPTER 45: SOLIDARITY 2000

402 **80 percent:** Antonio Flores, Luis Noe-Bustamante, and Mark Hugo Lopez, "Migrant Apprehensions and Deportations Increase in Mexico, but Remain below Recent Highs," Pew Research Center, June 12, 2019.

CHAPTER 46: REMAIN IN MEXICO

404 **imagined a pilot program:** Author interview with DHS official, July 19, 2020.

405 **"need to be smarter":** Jonathan Blitzer, "Will Anyone in the Trump Administration Ever Be Held Accountable for the Zero-Tolerance Policy?" *New Yorker*, August 22, 2018.

406 **"no one be forced to emigrate":** Alberto Nájar, "Caravana de migrantes: AMLO anuncia un inédito programa de visas de trabajo en México para tratar de contener la migración centroamericana a EE.UU," *BBC News*, October 18, 2018.

406 **"aggressive, rude way":** Sandra Dibble and Gustavo Solis, "A Fourth Wave of Central Americans Arrives in Tijuana," *San Diego Union-Tribune*, November 15, 2018.

407 **strong buy-in:** Author interviews with three former Mexican government officials, fall 2021.

407 **"turned us over":** Emily Green, "Trump's Asylum Policies Sent Him Back to Mexico. He Was Kidnapped 5 Hours Later by a Cartel," *Vice News*, September 16, 2019.

410 **Why place two justices:** Jonathan Blitzer, "Are the Courts Beginning to Move in Favor of Trump's Immigration Policies?" *New Yorker*, February 6, 2020.
411 **"deep in the building":** Nick Miroff and Josh Dawsey, "The Adviser Who Scripts Trump's Immigration Policy," *Washington Post*, August 17, 2019; Jonathan Blitzer, "Get Out," *New Yorker*, March 2, 2020.
411 **Every Friday:** Blitzer, "Get Out."
411 **classified security bunker:** Blitzer, "Get Out."
412 **"physical access":** Nick Miroff, "Along Texas Border, Trump Administration Sets Up Tent Courts for Virtual Asylum Hearings," *Washington Post*, September 18, 2019.
412 **only 1 percent:** American Immigration Council, "Fact Sheet: 'The Migrant Protection Protocols,'" January 7, 2022.
412 **130 migrants:** Jonathan Blitzer, "How the U.S. Asylum System Is Keeping Migrants at Risk in Mexico," *New Yorker*, October 1, 2019.
412 **Almost all their attention:** Author interview with senior Border Patrol official, August 30, 2019.
413 **would impose tariffs:** Jonathan Blitzer, "How Trump's Tariff Threat Could Outsource the Asylum Crisis to Mexico," *New Yorker*, June 19, 2019.

CHAPTER 47: REWRITING ASYLUM

416 **it was minuscule:** In 2018, the Guatemalan government approved just twenty asylum claims; its entire staff for processing applications consisted of twelve officials nationwide, only three of whom conducted actual interviews. See Eleanor Acer and Kennji Kuzuka, "Is Guatemala Safe for Refugees and Asylum Seekers?" Human Rights First, July 1, 2019, https://humanrightsfirst.org/library/is-guatemala-safe-for-refugees-and-asylum-seekers/.
416 **Ninety-two percent:** Jonathan Blitzer, "Does Asylum Have a Future at the Southern Border?" *New Yorker*, October 3, 2019.
416 **Two hundred and seventy thousand:** DHS Office of Immigration Statistics, *Fiscal Year 2020 Enforcement Lifecycle Report* (Washington, DC: December 2020), 6, www.dhs.gov/sites/default/files/publications/immigration-statistics/Special_Reports/Enforcement_Lifecycle/2020_enforcement_lifecycle_report.pdf.
416 **"ten to fifteen percent":** Blitzer, "Does Asylum Have a Future?"
416 **"short-term goal":** Blitzer, "Does Asylum Have a Future?"
417 **99 percent pure:** Government's Sentencing Submission, United States of America v. Juan Antonio Hernández Alvarado, March 16, 2021, S2 Cr. 379 (PKC) (S.D.N.Y. January 19, 2023), 6.
417 **Packages went out regularly:** "DEA Announces Arrest of Former Honduran Congressman and Brother of Current President of Honduras for Drug Trafficking and Weapons Charges," US Drug Enforcement Administration, November 26, 2018, www.dea.gov/press-releases/2018/11/26/dea-announces-arrest-former-honduran-congressman-and-brother-current.
417 **Sinaloa cartel took control:** Government's Sentencing Submission, *United States v. Alvarado*.
417 **forty-four-page court filing:** Jeff Ernst and David C. Adams, "President of Honduras Implicated in $1.5 Million Drug Money Conspiracy by New York Prosecutor," Univisión, August 3, 2019.
417 **"El Chapo" Guzmán:** Government's Sentencing Submission, *United States v. Alvarado*.
418 **"great guy":** Jake Johnston, "How Pentagon Officials May Have Encouraged a 2009 Coup in Honduras," *Intercept*, August 29, 2017.
418 **Hernández described Kelly:** Jonathan Blitzer, "A U.S. Ally Says He Won Honduras's Presidential Election. Hondurans Aren't So Sure," *New Yorker*, November 29, 2017; Garance Burke, Martha Mendoza, and Christopher Sherman, "Amid Corruption Concerns, Gen. Kelly Made Allies in Honduras," Associated Press, April 12, 2018; Allan Nairn, "US Spent Weeks Pressuring Honduras Opposition to End Protests Against Election Fraud," *Intercept*, December 22, 2017.
418 **"a strong partner":** Emily Palmer and Benjamin Weiser, "El Chapo Said to Have Given $1 Million to Honduran President's Brother," *New York Times*, October 2, 2019.
418 **Twenty-two percent:** World Bank, "Personal Remittances, received (% of GDP), El Salvador," https://data.worldbank.org/indicator/BX.TRF.PWKR.DT.GD.ZS?locations=SV.
418 **officials had to call:** Jonathan Blitzer, "Strongman of the People," *New Yorker*, September 12, 2022.
418 **sitting with Bukele:** Author interview with Trump administration official, December 29, 2020.
419 **investigation by Nómada:** "Jimmy, Baldizon, and These Business Executives Organized the Lobby against Todd and the CICIG," Nómada, October 20, 2018.
419 **Another interest group:** Colum Lynch, "Corrupt Guatemalans' GOP Lifeline," *Foreign Policy*, February 5, 2019.
419 **"two ambassadors in Washington":** Author interview with Trump administration official, February 20, 2023; author interview with Guatemalan official, March 3, 2023.
420 **"give you our borders":** Author interview with Trump administration official, December 29, 2020.
421 **Tensions were already building:** Author interview with Guatemalan official, June 6, 2021.

CHAPTER 48: THE HEART DOCTOR

425 **making me doubt**: Jonathan Blitzer, "'My Only Friend Is My Conscience': Face to Face with El Salvador's Cold Killer," *New York Review of Books*, December 7, 2017.
426 **I visited him**: Jonathan Blitzer, "Field Notes: Nicolas Carranza," Pulitzer Center, March 19, 2018, https://pulitzercenter.org/stories/field-notes-nicolas-carranza.
426 **"Two of the men responsible"**: United States Congress, Senate, *No Safe Haven: Accountability for Human Rights Violators in the United States*, Hearing before the Subcommittee on Human Rights and the Law of the Committee on the Judiciary, United States Senate, November 14, 2007, 110th Congress, 1st Session (Washington, DC: US Government Printing Office, 2008).

CHAPTER 49: THE WUHAN OF THE AMERICAS

430 **"Don't waste time"**: Jonathan Blitzer, "Are the Courts Beginning to Move in Favor of Trump's Immigration Policies?" *New Yorker*, February 6, 2020.
430 **granted some form of legal relief**: It took seven months for the first person enrolled in MPP—a thirty-year-old from Honduras—to actually win asylum. But when the immigration judge granted it, DHS decided to hold him in custody while government lawyers considered filing an appeal. Three months later, another person, a Venezuelan, won asylum but was sent back to Nuevo Laredo anyway. Only when a congressional office intervened did DHS allow him into the US (Lyndon B. Johnson School of Public Affairs, *Migrant Protection Protocols: Implementation and Consequences for Asylum Seekers in Mexico* [University of Texas at Austin, 2020], 21).
430 **more than fifteen hundred**: Muzaffar Chishti and Jessica Bolter, "Court-Ordered Relaunch of Remain in Mexico Policy Tweaks Predecessor Program, but Faces Similar Challenges," Migration Policy Institute, December 2, 2021.
431 **the wait time**: LBJ School of Public Affairs, *Migrant Protection Protocols*, 20. There was some delay before the Mexican government regularly started to issue these temporary visas. Eventually, according to the government agency responsible, the visas were valid for a period ranging from six months to a year. See "Preguntas frecuentes sobre la Clave Unica de Registro de Población Temporal para Extranjeros," April 3, 2019, www.gob.mx/segob/renapo/acciones-y-programas/preguntas-frecuentes-sobre-la-clave-unica-de-registro-de-poblacion-temporal-para-extranjeros.
431 **thirty-two thousand removal orders**: Chishti and Bolter, "Court-Ordered Relaunch of Remain in Mexico."
431 **actual policy prerogative**: Caitlin Dickerson and Michael D. Shear, "Before Covid-19, Trump Aide Sought to Use Disease to Close Borders," *New York Times*, May 3, 2020.
431 **refused to sign off**: Jason Dearen and Garance Burke, "Pence Ordered Borders Closed after CDC Experts Refused," Associated Press, October 3, 2020.
432 **Other nations**: Susan Fratzke, Migration Policy Institute, interview with author, October 4, 2021.
432 **"my dystopian mind"**: Molly O'Toole, "Trump Policy and Coronavirus Leave Agency Bankrupt, Tens of Thousands of Potential Voters in Limbo," *Los Angeles Times*, June 28, 2020.
432 **Patient 36**: Cindy Espina, "Paciente 36: El viaje y retorno de un migrante en medio de una pandemia," *elPeriódico*, May 26, 2020; Jonathan Blitzer, "The Trump Administration's Deportation Policy Is Spreading the Coronavirus," *New Yorker*, May 13, 2020.
433 **despite two positive tests**: Monique O. Madan and Jacqueline Charles, "He Says He Has Covid and Has Never Been to Haiti. But ICE Still Wants to Deport Him There," *Miami Herald*, May 8, 2020.
434 **"We must not stigmatize"**: Hedy Quino Tzoc, "Munroy: 75% en un vuelo de deportados dieron positivo por COVID-19," *La Hora*, April 14, 2020.
434 **"get out of here alive"**: Jonathan Blitzer, "The Private Georgia Immigration-Detention Facility at the Center of a Whistle-Blower's Complaint," *New Yorker*, September 19, 2020.
434 **"no way to 'distance' here"**: Ashton Pittman, "'They See Us as Disposable': ICE Detainees Plead for Release from Covid-19 'Breeding Ground,'" *Mississippi Free Press*, April 6, 2020.
435 **twenty-one were already infected**: Hamed Aleaziz, "ICE Moved Dozens of Detainees across the Country during the Coronavirus Pandemic. Now Many Have Covid-19," *BuzzFeed News*, April 29, 2020.
435 **449 people**: American Immigration Lawyers Association, "ICE Issues Guidance on COVID-19," September 25, 2020, www.aila.org/infonet/ice-issues-guidance-on-covid-19.
435 **super-spreader event**: Antonio Olivo and Nick Miroff, "ICE Flew Detainees to Virginia so the Planes Could Transport Agents to D.C. Protests. A Huge Coronavirus Outbreak Followed," *Washington Post*, September 11, 2020.
435 **"were not a factor"**: Blitzer, "The Private Georgia Immigration-Detention Facility."
435 **"set my family on fire"**: Sofia Menchu, "Maya Villages in Guatemala Spurn U.S. Deportees as Infections Spike," Reuters, May 1, 2020.

CHAPTER 50: EDDIE AND JUAN

438 **"I did not live the war"**: Geovani Galeas, *¿Quién es Nayib Bukele?* (San Salvador: Editorial La Red, 2018), 16.
438 **dropped out**: Gabriel Labrador, "Bukele, el autoritario cool," *El Faro*, September 29, 2021.
439 **"call it PR"**: Lauren Markham, "Prince of Peace," *Virginia Quarterly Review* 92, no. 4 (2016).

CHAPTER 51: KELDY

442 **Criminal Consequence Initiative**: Kevin Sieff, "The Trump Administration Used an Early, Unreported Program to Separate Migrant Families Along a Remote Stretch of the Border," *Washington Post*, July 9, 2021.
443 **with mixed success**: García's first major discovery was that almost a quarter of all the parents "reunited" with their children in the US had removal orders subjecting them to immediate rearrest and deportation. When ICE released them from borderland detention centers, none of the officials ever bothered to change the information on their court summonses. That meant that someone who left a jail in South Texas to live with family in Florida, for example, was still expected in immigration court at the border. Failing to show up triggered an automatic deportation order. This crisis wasn't even the most urgent one the advocates faced at the start of 2020—hundreds of parents had been deported without their children and still couldn't be found. Organizations like Justice in Motion, an American outfit with deep ties to local groups in Central America, were sending search parties to remote towns in the region.
443 **"made a mistake"**: Interviews with author, May 24, 2021, and June 8, 2021.
444 **wheeling two suitcases**: This is drawn from Jonathan Blitzer, "A Mother, Separated from Her Children at the Border, Comes Home," *New Yorker*, May 5, 2021.

CHAPTER 52: LUCRECIA

448 **"What we're doing"**: Joe Biden, "Remarks by President Biden in Press Conference," March 25, 2021, www.whitehouse.gov/briefing-room/speeches-remarks/2021/03/25/remarks-by-president-biden-in-press-conference/.
449 **exclude unaccompanied children**: A federal judge had ordered Trump to exempt child migrants from Title 42 in the fall of 2020, but his administration was slow to comply. Biden maintained that protecting children was the bare minimum. See Jonathan Blitzer, "Biden Has Few Good Options for the Unaccompanied Children at the Border," *New Yorker*, March 9, 2021.
449 **"the Northern Triangle"**: Jonathan Martin and Alexander Burns, *This Will Not Pass: Trump, Biden, and the Battle for America's Future* (New York: Simon & Schuster, 2022), 321.
450 **"I keep talking"**: Joe Biden, "Remarks by Vice President Biden at a Plenary with Central American Leaders," March 2, 2015, https://hn.usembassy.gov/remarks-vice-president-biden-plenary-central-american-leaders/.
450 **refused to seat**: The judge was Gloria Porras. See Lorena Arroyo, "Gloria Porras: 'Me preocupa cómo en Guatemala están utilizando las leyes para alcanzar objectivos aviesos," *El País*, April 13, 2021.
450 **"At this table"**: Kamala Harris, "Remarks by Vice President Harris Before Meeting with Guatemalan Justice Sector Leaders," May 19, 2021, www.whitehouse.gov/briefing-room/speeches-remarks/2021/05/19/remarks-by-vice-president-harris-before-meeting-with-guatemalan-justice-sector-leaders/.
451 **a sharp criticism**: Ed O'Keefe, "Guatemala's President Says Kamala Harris 'Doesn't Hold Back' Ahead of Immigration Talks," CBS News, June 6, 2021.
453 **prosecutors had been forced**: Jonathan Blitzer, "The Exile of Guatemala's Anti-Corruption Efforts," *New Yorker*, April 29, 2022.
453 **"judiciary and ministry in exile"**: Author interview with senior US official, April 29, 2022.
453 **"just kill us"**: Blitzer, "The Exile of Guatemala's Anti-Corruption Efforts."

CHAPTER 53: SIMPLY NOT WHO WE ARE

457 **in order to save**: For instance, a planning document from December 2020, which the author obtained, stated that thirty days into the Biden presidency the US would admit 3,000 asylum seekers each month; after 180 days, it would admit 12,000 a month.
457 **"a deterrence tool"**: Jonathan Blitzer, "How Biden Came to Own Trump's Policy at the Border," *New Yorker*, October 6, 2021.
457 **"We don't want"**: Jonathan Blitzer, "The Disillusionment of a Young Biden Official," *New Yorker*, January 28, 2022.

CHAPTER 54: HOME

461 **"cleansing that cancer"**: Casa Presidencial (@presidenciasv), Twitter, April 4, 2022, https://twitter.com/presidenciasv/status/1511140413884751880?s=12&t=Wm6s-3t0jGION3XDs-0flw.
461 **"You hear people say"**: Jonathan Blitzer, "Strongman of the People," *New Yorker*, September 12, 2022.
462 **"gangs do not exist"**: Carlos Martínez, Efren Lemus, and Óscar Martínez, "Régimen de Bukele desarticula a las pandillas en El Salvador," *El Faro*, February 3, 2023.

Bibliography

Anderson, Thomas. *Matanza: El Salvador's Communist Revolt of 1932.* Lincoln: University of Nebraska Press, 1971.
Andrade, Laura and Adilio Carrillo. *El Sistema Penitenciario Salvadoreño y Sus Prisiones.* San Salvador: Instituto Universitario de Opinión Pública, Universidad Centroamericana José Simeón Cañas, 2015.
Arce, Alberto. *Honduras a ras de suelo: Crónicas desde el país más violento del mundo.* Mexico City: Ariel, 2015.
Arzobispo de Guatemala, Oficina de Derechos Humanos, *Nunca más: Impacto de la violencia.* Informe Proyecto Interdiocesano de Recuperación de la Memoria Histórica, 1998.
Ávalos, Héctor Silva. *Infiltrados: Crónica de la corrupcíon en la PNC 1992–2013.* San Salvador: UCA Editores, 2014.
Behrman, Simon. *Law and Asylum: Space, Subject, Resistance.* Oxford, UK: Routledge, 2018.
Blatchford, Chris. *The Black Hand: The Bloody Rise and Redemption of "Boxer" Enriquez, a Mexican Mob Killer.* New York: HarperCollins, 2008.
Bonner, Raymond. *Weakness and Deceit: America and El Salvador's Dirty War.* New York: OR Books, 2016.
Brockman, James R. *Romero: A Life.* Ossining, NY: Orbis Books, 1989.
Burns, Allan F. *Maya in Exile: Guatemalans in Florida.* Philadelphia: Temple University Press, 1993.
Cannon, Lou. *Official Negligence: How Rodney King and the Riots Changed Los Angeles and the LAPD.* New York: Times Books, 1997.
Comisión de la Verdad para El Salvador. *De la locura a la esperanza: La guerra de 12 años en El Salvador.* March 15, 1993.
Comisión para el Esclarecimiento Histórico. *Guatemala: Memoria del silencio.* Guatemala City: U.N. Office of Project Services, 1999.
Cox, Adam B., and Cristina M. Rodríguez. *The President and Immigration Law.* New York: Oxford University Press, 2020.
Crewdson, John. *The Tarnished Door: The New Immigrants and the Transformation of America.* New York: Crown, 1983.
Crittenden, Ann. *Sanctuary: A Story of American Conscience and the Law in Collision.* New York: Grove, 1988.
Cullather, Nick. *Secret History: The CIA's Classified Account of Its Operations in Guatemala, 1952–1954.* Redwood City, CA: Stanford University Press, 1999.
Cunningham, Hilary. *God and Caesar at the Rio Grande: Sanctuary and the Politics of Religion.* Minneapolis: University of Minnesota Press, 1995.
Dalton, Roque. *Las historias prohibidas del pulgarcito.* Mexico City: Siglo XXI, 1974.
———. *Miguel Mármol.* Translated by Kathleen Ross and Richard Schaaf. Evanston, IL: Curbstone Press, 1987.
Danner, Mark. *The Massacre at El Mozote.* New York: Vintage, 1994.
d'Aubuisson, Juan José Martínez. *A Year Inside MS-13: See, Hear, and Shut Up.* New York: OR Books, 2015.
Davidson, Miriam. *Convictions of the Heart: Jim Corbett and the Sanctuary Movement.* Tucson: University of Arizona Press, 1988.
Davis, Julie Hirschfeld, and Michael D. Shear. *Border Wars: Inside Trump's Assault on Immigration.* New York: Simon & Schuster, 2019.
della Rocca, Roberto Morozzo. *Óscar Romero: Prophet of Hope.* London: Darton, Longman & Todd, 2015.
DeParle, Jason. *American Dream: Three Women, Ten Kids, and a Nation's Drive to End Welfare.* New York: Penguin, 2004.
Diaz, Tom. *No Boundaries: Transnational Latino Gangs and American Law Enforcement.* Ann Arbor: University of Michigan Press, 2009.
Dudley, Steven. *MS-13: The Making of America's Most Notorious Gang.* New York: Hanover Square Press, 2020.

Dunn, Timothy. *Blockading the Border and Human Rights: The El Paso Operation That Remade Immigration Enforcement.* Austin: University of Texas Press, 2009.

———. *The Militarization of the US-Mexico Border, 1978–1992.* Austin: CMass Books, 1996.

Eisenbrandt, Matt. *Assassination of a Saint: The Plot to Murder Óscar Romero and the Quest to Bring His Killers to Justice.* Berkeley: University of California Press, 2017.

Fernandes, Deepa. *Targeted: Homeland Security and the Business of Immigration.* New York: Seven Stories, 2007.

Fink, Leon. *The Maya of Morganton: Work and Community in the Nuevo New South.* Chapel Hill: University of North Carolina Press, 2003.

Frank, Dana. *The Long Honduran Night: Resistance, Terror, and the United States in the Aftermath of the Coup.* Chicago: Haymarket Books, 2018.

Galeas, Geovani. *¿Quién es Nayib Bukele?* San Salvador: Editorial La Red, 2018.

García, Carlos. *Mara Salvatrucha-13: Retrato histórico e internacional de una pandilla* (forthcoming).

Garland, Sarah. *Gangs in Garden City: How Immigration, Segregation, and Youth Violence Are Changing America's Suburbs.* New York: Nation Books, 2009.

Garrard-Burnett, Virginia. *Terror in the Land of the Holy Spirit: Guatemala under General Efraín Ríos Montt, 1982–1983.* Oxford, UK, and New York: Oxford University Press, 2010.

Gelbspan, Ross. *Break-ins, Death Threats and the FBI: The Covert War against the Central America Movement.* Boston: South End Press, 1991.

Golden, Renny, and Michael McConnell. *Sanctuary: The New Underground Railroad.* Ossining, NY: Orbis Books, 1986.

Goldman, Francisco. *The Art of Political Murder: Who Killed the Bishop?* New York: Grove, 2007.

Goodman, Adam. *The Deportation Machine: America's Long History of Expelling Immigrants.* Princeton, NJ: Princeton University Press, 2020.

Grandin, Greg. *The Blood of Guatemala: A History of Race and Nation.* Durham: Duke University Press, 2000.

———. *The Last Colonial Massacre: Latin America in the Cold War.* Chicago: University of Chicago Press, 2004.

Grandin, Greg, Deborah T. Levenson, and Elizabeth Oglesby, eds. *The Guatemala Reader: History, Culture, Politics.* Durham, NC: Duke University Press, 2011.

Green, Joshua. *Devil's Bargain: Steve Bannon, Donald Trump, and the Storming of the Presidency.* New York: Penguin, 2017.

Green, Linda. *Fear as a Way of Life: Mayan Widows in Rural Guatemala.* New York: Columbia University Press, 1999.

Grillo, Ioan. *Gangster Warlords: Drug Dollars, Killing Fields, and the New Politics of Latin America.* London: Bloomsbury, 2015.

Guerrero, Jean. *Hatemonger: Stephen Miller, Donald Trump, and the White Nationalist Agenda.* New York: William Morrow, 2020.

Harris, John F. *The Survivor: Bill Clinton in the White House.* New York: Random House, 2005.

Hayden, Tom. *Street Wars: Gangs and the Future of Violence.* New York: New Press, 2004.

Hemmer, Nicole. *Partisans: The Conservative Revolutionaries Who Remade American Politics in the 1990s.* New York: Basic Books, 2022.

Hernández, César Cuauhtémoc García. *Migrating to Prison: America's Obsession with Locking Up Migrants.* New York: New Press, 2019.

Hughes, Jennifer Scheper. *Biography of a Mexican Crucifix: Lived Religion and Local Faith from the Conquest to the Present.* Oxford, UK: Oxford University Press, 2010.

Jonas, Susanne. *The Battle for Guatemala: Rebels, Death Squads, and US Power.* Boulder, CO: Westview Press, 1991.

Jonas, Susanne, and Nestor Rodríguez. *Guatemala-US Migration: Transforming Regions.* Austin: University of Texas Press, 2014.

Kamasaki, Charles. *Immigration Reform: The Corpse That Will Not Die.* Simsbury, CT: Mandel Vilar Press, 2019.

Keefe, Patrick Radden. *The Snakehead: An Epic Tale of the Chinatown Underworld and the American Dream.* New York: Doubleday, 2009.

Kornacki, Steve. *The Red and the Blue: The 1990s and the Birth of Political Tribalism.* New York: Ecco, 2018.

LaFeber, Walter. *Inevitable Revolutions: The United States in Central America.* New York: W. W. Norton & Company, 1984.

Lakhani, Nina. *Who Killed Berta Cáceres? Dams, Death Squads, and an Indigenous Defender's Battle for the Planet.* London and Brooklyn, NY: Verso, 2020.

LeoGrande, William. *Our Own Backyard: The United States in Central America 1977–1992.* Chapel Hill: University of North Carolina Press, 1998.

LeoGrande, William, and Peter Kornbluh. *Back Channel to Cuba: The Hidden History of Negotiations Between Washington and Havana.* Chapel Hill: University of North Carolina Press, 2015.

Lindo-Fuentes, Héctor. *Weak Foundations: The Economy of El Salvador in the Nineteenth Century 1821–1898.* Berkeley: University of California Press, 1991.

Logan, Samuel. *This Is for the Mara Salvatrucha: Inside the MS-13, America's Most Violent Gang.* New York: Hyperion, 2009.

BIBLIOGRAPHY

Los Angeles Times, *Understanding the Riots: Los Angeles before and after the Rodney King Case*. Los Angeles: Los Angeles Times, 1992.

Loucky, James, and Marilyn M. Moors, eds. *The Maya Diaspora: Guatemalan Roots, New American Lives*. Philadelphia: Temple University Press, 2000.

Loyd, Jenna M., and Alison Mountz. *Boats, Borders, and Bases: Race, the Cold War, and the Rise of Migrant Detention in the United States*. Berkeley: University of California Press, 2018.

Luiselli, Valeria. *Tell Me How It Ends: An Essay in Forty Questions*. Minneapolis: Coffee House Press, 2017.

MacEoin, Gary, ed. *Sanctuary: A Resource Guide for Understanding and Participating in the Central American Refugees' Struggle*. New York: Harper & Row, 1985.

MacEoin, Gary, and Nivita Riley. *No Promised Land: American Refugee Policies and the Rule of Law*. Boston: Oxfam America, 1982.

Mahler, Sarah J. *Salvadorans in Suburbia: Symbiosis and Conflict*. Boston: Allyn and Bacon, 1995.

Manz, Beatriz. *Refugees of a Hidden War: The Aftermath of Counterinsurgency in Guatemala*. Albany: State University of New York Press, 1988.

Markey, Eileen. *A Radical Faith: The Assassination of Sister Maura*. New York: Nation Books, 2016.

Markham, Lauren. *The Far Away Brothers: Two Young Migrants and the Making of an American Life*. New York: Crown, 2017.

Martin, David A., ed. *The New American Asylum Seekers: Refugee Law in the 1980s*. University of Virginia: Springer-Science and Business Media, 1988.

Martínez, Carlos. *Juntos, todos juntos: Crónica del primer intento colectivo de saltar la frontera estadounidense*. La Rioja: Pepitas de Calabaza, 2019.

Martínez, Óscar. *The Beast: Riding the Rails and Dodging Narcos on the Migrant Trail*. Translated by Daniela Maria Ugaz and John Washington. London and New York: Verso, 2013.

———. *A History of Violence: Living and Dying in Central America*. Translated by John B. Washington and Daniela Ugaz. London and New York: Verso, 2016.

Martínez, Óscar, and Juan José Martínez. *The Hollywood Kid: The Violent Life and Violent Death of an MS-13 Hitman*. Translated by John B. Washington and Daniela Ugaz. London and New York: Verso, 2019.

McClintock, Michael. *The American Connection, Volume I: State Terror and Popular Resistance in El Salvador*. 2 vols. London: Zed Books, 1985.

———. *The American Connection, Volume II: State Terror and Popular Resistance in Guatemala*. 2 vols. London: Zed Books, 1985.

Menjívar, Cecilia. *Fragmented Ties: Salvadoran Immigrant Networks in America*. Berkeley: University of California Press, 2000.

Motomura, Hiroshi. *Immigration outside the Law*. Oxford, UK: Oxford University Press, 2014.

Muñiz, Ana. *Police, Power, and the Production of Racial Boundaries*. New Brunswick, NJ: Rutgers University Press, 2015.

Muñoz, Cecilia. *More Than Ready: Be Strong and Be You . . . and Other Lessons for Women of Color on the Rise*. New York: Seal Press, 2020.

Ngai, Mae M. *Impossible Subjects: Illegal Aliens and the Making of Modern America*. Princeton, NJ: Princeton University Press, 2004.

Paige, Jeffery M. *Coffee and Power: Revolution and the Rise of Democracy in Central America*. Cambridge, MA: Harvard University Press, 1997.

Peters, Jeremy W. *Insurgency: How Republicans Lost Their Party and Got Everything They Ever Wanted*. New York: Crown, 2022.

Pine, Adrienne. *Working Hard, Drinking Hard: On Violence and Survival in Honduras*. Berkeley: University of California Press, 2008.

Ponce, Matías. *CICIG: Misión posible*. Telaraña Group: Guatemala, 2021.

Pradilla, Alberto. *Caravana: Cómo el éxodo centroamericano salió de la clandestinidad*. Mexico City: Debate, 2019.

Ramji-Nogales, Jaya, Andrew I. Schoenholtz, and Philip G. Schrag. *Refugee Roulette: Disparities in Asylum Adjudication and Proposals for Reform*. New York: New York University Press, 2009.

Reichman, Daniel R. *The Broken Village: Coffee, Migration, and Globalization in Honduras*. Ithaca, NY: Cornell University Press, 2011.

Repak, Terry A. *Waiting on Washington: Central American Workers in the Nation's Capital*. Philadelphia: Temple University Press, 1995.

Schlesinger, Stephen, and Stephen Kinzer. *Bitter Fruit: The Story of the American Coup in Guatemala*, rev ed. Cambridge, MA: Harvard University Press, 2005.

Schneider, Mark Robert. *Joe Moakley's Journey: From South Boston to El Salvador*. Boston: Northeastern University Press, 2013.

Schrag, Philip G. *Baby Jails: The Fight to End Incarceration of Refugee Children in America*. Berkeley: University of California Press, 2020.

———. *A Well-Founded Fear: The Congressional Battle to Save Political Asylum in America*. Oxford, UK: Routledge, 2000.
Simon, Jean-Marie. *Guatemala: Eternal Spring, Eternal Tyranny*. New York: W. W. Norton & Company, 1987.
Soboroff, Jacob. *Separated: Inside an American Tragedy*. New York: Custom House, 2020.
Stanley, William. *The Protection Racket State: Elite Politics, Military Extortion, and Civil War in El Salvador*. Philadelphia: Temple University Press, 1996.
Tichenor, Daniel J. *Dividing Lines: The Politics of Immigration Control in America*. Princeton, NJ: Princeton University Press, 2001.
Tomsho, Robert. *The American Sanctuary Movement*. Austin: Texas Monthly Press, 1987.
Valencia, Roberto. *Carta desde Zacatraz*. Madrid: Libros del K.O., 2018.
Videla, Gabriela. *Sergio Méndez Arceo: Un señor obispo*. Sucre, Chuquisaca: Correo del Sur, 1981.
Weiner, Tim. *Enemies: A History of the FBI*. New York: Random House, 2012.
Wilkinson, Daniel. *Silence on the Mountain: Stories of Terror, Betrayal, and Forgetting in Guatemala*. Durham, NC: Duke University Press, 2004.
Wroe, Andrew. *The Republican Party and Immigration Politics: From Proposition 187 to George W. Bush*. London: Palgrave Macmillan, 2008.
Young, Allan. *The Harmony of Illusions: Inventing Post-Traumatic Stress Disorder*. Princeton, NJ: Princeton University Press, 1995.
Zilberg, Elana. *Space of Detention: The Making of a Transnational Gang Crisis between Los Angeles and El Salvador*. Durham, NC: Duke University Press, 2011.

Image Credits

Page 20: Susan Meiselas/Magnum Photos
Page 28 (top): Harry Mattison/Courtesy of the International Center of Photography
Page 28 (bottom): Etienne Montes/Gamma-Rapho via Getty Images
Page 35: Luis Romero/AP
Page 65: Susan Meiselas/Magnum Photos
Page 70: Peter Weinberger/USA Today Network
Page 92: Courtesy of Jean-Marie Simon
Page 129 (top): Courtesy of Cheryl Nuss
Page 129 (bottom): Juan Romagoza
Page 164 (top and bottom): Courtesy of Eddie Anzora
Page 182: La Clínica del Pueblo
Page 186: Courtesy of Nancy Shia
Page 196: ZUMA Press, Inc./Alamy Stock Photo
Page 232: Courtesy of Eddie Anzora
Page 237: Mack Family Collection/Fundación Myrna Mack
Page 257: Courtesy of the Center for Justice and Accountability
Page 288: Eduardo Verdugo/AP
Page 313: Courtesy of Fred Ramos
Page 315: Courtesy of Fred Ramos
Page 344: Víctor Peña/El Faro
Page 377: Courtesy of Mauricio Lima
Page 393: Courtesy of Adriana Zehbrauskas
Page 440: Courtesy of Eddie Anzora
Page 445: Matt Rourke/AP
Page 446: Courtesy of Hannah Yoon
Page 447: Courtesy of Hannah Yoon
Page 458: Adrees Latif/REUTERS/Redux
Page 462: Courtesy of the author
Page 463: Courtesy of the author

Index

Italicized page numbers indicate material in photographs or illustrations.

Abbott, William, 373–74
abolitionist movement, 60
Above Ground Entertainment, 231, 267
Abrams, Elliott, 66–67, 68, 103, 114, 141
ACCESA (Alianza por el Acceso Universal y Público a la Salud), 345, 347–48
AC/DC, 160
ACLU (American Civil Liberties Union), 218, 341, 444, 446, 456
    Immigrants' Rights Project, 139
    lawsuits challenging family separation policy, 384–88
Acuerdos de Paz, 313–14
Affordable Care Act, 201
AFL-CIO, 71
Agua Alegre, Guatemala, 380
Agua Prieta, Mexico, 38–39, 99–100
Akateko, 199
Alarcón, Antonio, 333
Aldana, Thelma, 347, 450
Alianza Ciudadana contra la Privatización, 277
Alianza Republicana Nacionalista (ARENA), 175, 263–64, 277, 438
Alliance against the Dictatorship, 363
Alta Verapaz, Guatemala, 82, 237, 239
Amaya, Rufina, 64–65
American Baptist Churches (ABC) v. Thornburgh, 142, 201, 253–54
American Baptist Churches in the USA v. Meese, 140–41, 179, 201
American Convention on Human Rights, 246
American Psychiatric Association (APA), 128
American Recovery and Reinvestment Act, 201
America's Voice, 304–5

"amnesty," 271, 368
Anderson, Thomas, 14
ANTEL, 86–87
Anti-Drug Abuse Act, 163
anti-gang policing, 167–68, 208, 211, 263–64
Anzora, Carlos, 156, 170, 188, 189–90
Anzora, Eddie
    arrest of, 220–21, 226, 232–34
    in El Salvador, 170, 188–91, 194, 196–97, 310–13, 314–17, 439–40, *440*
    call center work, 265–69, 310–12, 314–17, 439–40
    deportation, 220–21, 231–34, 259–69
    in Los Angeles, 155–58, 161–65, *164*, 168–70, 188–89, 206–12, 220–21, 231–32, *232*
    Mayra and, 310
    Uncle Jaime, 161–62
    Victoria and, 156, 157–58, 161–62, 164–65, 188–91, 221, 231, 264–65, 266
Anzora, Michael, 156, 170
Apfel, Ken, 216
Árbenz, Jacobo, 77–78, 235, 478*n*
Arcadia, Florida, 199–201
Arce, Manuel Rafael, 36, 72–73
Arévalo, Juan José, 78
Arias, Óscar, 174
Arizona Daily Star, 102
Arriaga, Mexico, 392–93
Artiga, José, 126–27
Aryan Brotherhood, 166
Ashcroft, John, 227–28
asylum, 1–4, 47–52, 55–60, 198–204, 403–5
    American Baptist Churches cases, 140–41, 142, 179, 201, 253–54

asylum (*cont.*)
  Biden White House and, 448–51, 456–59
  Clinton White House and, 201–4, 216–19
  Keldy case. *See* Zúniga, Keldy Mabel Gonzáles Brebe de
  Obama White House and, 300–306
  Reagan White House and, 103, 104–5, 107–14, 120, 127, 140–42
  Refugee Act of 1980, 48–52, 56, 57, 68, 70, 104–5, 112, 135–36, 137, 139, 140, 141–42, 199, 203, 327
  Trump White House and, 327–29, 397, 410–14, 418–19, 420–21, 430–32, 443–44
  waiving of rights, 55–56, 140
"asylum cooperative agreements," 415–16
Atlacatl Battalion, 63–64, 175–76, 193
ATR (Above the Rest), 206–10, 211, 233
AT&T, 265
authoritarianism, 2, 436
AVANCSO (Association for the Advancement of Social Sciences), 237–41, 345

Bachmann, Michele, 323
Baird, Zoë, 202
Bannon, Steve, 321
Barillas, 238–39
Barnes & Thornburg, 419
Barrientos, Walter, 335–36
Barrio Hollywood, 38–39
Bash, John, 384
Bellone, Steve, 330–31
Bellport High School, 340
Berger, Óscar, 346
Berlin Wall, 107, 175
Beteta Álvarez, Noel de Jesùs, 241–44, 249
Bias, Len, 163
Biden, Joseph
  election of 2020, 443–44
  immigration policy, 305, 441, 444–45, 446, 448–51, 456–59
Big Baby (boat), 50
Big Daddy Kane, 157
Bingaman, Jeff, 271
Bin Laden, Osama, 323
Black Guerrilla Family, 166
Black Lives Matter, 435, 437
Black Sabbath, 160
Blanche III (boat), 50
Blood In Blood Out (movie), 261
Bloods, 155, 197, 337
Blum, Carolyn Patty, 139–40, 253–54, 256, 258
Board of Immigration Appeals, 57
Boehner, John, 299, 304, 305
Bonilla, Luis, 399

Bonner, Raymond, 64–65, 66
border, 3, 38–39, 99–101, 115, 204–5, 246–47, 430–31, 457
  Cowan and Manzo Area Council, 37–46, 53–58, 68
  Fife and, 58–60, 68–77, 70
  Salvadoran refugees, 41–46, 53–58
  sanctuary movement and, 69–71, 70
border fencing, 51, 68, 99, 100, 274, 299
Border Patrol
  Brané and, 386–87, 444–45
  Cowan and Manzo Area Council, 37–42, 44–46, 56, 68
  Hutchison and, 99–106, 119
  merger with Customs, 228
  OTMs (other than Mexican), 44–46
  Reyes and, 204–5
  Trump White House and, 332–33, 355–57, 360–61, 365, 367, 380–81, 418–19
  United States v. Brignoni-Ponce, 39
border wall of Trump, 320, 324, 365
Bosques de la Paz, 268
Bossert, Tom, 326–27
Boston Celtics, 163
Boston Globe, 126
Boy Scouts, 33
Bradley, Tom, 195
Braman, Norman, 111–12
Brané, Michelle, 386–87, 444–45
Brecthel, John, 169–70
Breitbart News, 321, 323, 329
Brentwood, New York, 330–31, 334–42
Brentwood High School, 337, 339–40
Brooks, Jack, 179
Brown and Black Forum, 274
Brownback, Sam, 272
Brownsville, Texas, 119, 411–12
Buchanan, Pat, 320
Buen Pastor, 127, 412–14
Bukele, Nayib, 418–19, 427, 438–40, 450–51, 461–62
Bush, George H. W.
  election of 1988, 217
  election of 1992, 201–2, 204, 320
  foreign policy, 150–51, 173–76, 177, 196
  immigration policy, 142, 199, 201–2, 320
Bush, George W.
  immigration policy, 264, 270–74
  September 11 attacks, 226, 228

Cabañas Department, 63–65
CACIF Guatemala, 421
Cadena, Carmelina, 199–201

INDEX

Calderón, Felipe, 405–6
California caravans, *129*, 131, 132
California Governor's Prayer Breakfast, 125
California Proposition 187, 217
California Street Terrorism Enforcement and Prevention Act, 167–68
call centers, 265–69, 310–12, 314–17, 439–40
Cambodian refugees, 47
campesinos, 10, 14–19, 21, 97, 127, 148, 172–73, 181, 187
Cantor, Eric, 302, 304
Capone, Al, 52
caravans, 116, 128, 129, 365, 368, 389–95, *393*, 406–8, 415–16
Carnegie Endowment for International Peace, 201
Carranza, Nicolas, 426
Carrera, Juan Guillermo Oliva, 242
Carroll, Earl, 136–39, 141
Carter, Jimmy
　election of 1976, 23
　election of 1980, 29–30
　human-rights policy, 22–23, 30, 61–63, 93
　immigration policy, 22–24, 41, 48–52, 61–63, 111
Carter, Raymond, 166–67
"Carter, the," 24
Casa del Migrante, 412, 414
CASA de Maryland, 270–71, 305
Casa El Salvador, 125–26, 126–27, 130
Casa Óscar Romero, 119
Casa Presidencial, 10, 30, 35, 286
casas de remesa, 377, 378–79
Castillo, Leonel, 41, 110
Castillo, Lupe, 41, 42–46, 53–58, 100
Castillo Armas, Carlos, 78
Castresana, Carlos, 346–47, 348
Castro, Fidel, 50, 51, 112
"catch and release," 324–25, 355–56, 368, 405
Catholic Charities, 386
Catholic Legal Immigration Network, 443
Center for Constitutional Rights, 139
Center for Immigration Studies, 321–22, 323, 328
Center for Justice and Accountability, 251, 257
Center for the Confinement of Terrorism, 462
Central America. *See specific countries*
Central American migrant caravans. *See* migrant caravans
Central Juvenile Hall (Los Angeles), 163
Cerezo, Vinicio, 237, 240, 244
cerote, 160, 316–17
Chalatenango, El Salvador, 32–36, 72–73, 76, 95–98, 121, 193
Chamber of Commerce, US, 108
Chamizal National Memorial, 294

Chamorro, Violeta, 177
Chapman, Leonard, 39
Chapultepec Park, Mexico City, 87, 88, 94, 95, 194
Chavez, Cesar, 40, 56
Chávez, Hugo, 277
Chertoff, Michael, 273, 308
Chevy Caprice, 210–11
Chevy Monte Carlo, 156, 157
Chevy Tahoe, 231, 232
Chiapas, Mexico, 86, 89, 236, 389, 392–94, 399–400
Chicago Bulls, 340
Chicago Religious Task Force on Central America, 103–4, 117, 122, 135–36
Chicago Tribune, 202
children. *See* Dreamers; family separations; unaccompanied children
"Children's Story" (song), 206
Chile, 88
　coup d'état of 1973, 124
Chilean refugees, 124
Chinese immigrants, 199, 202–3
cholo fashions, 160, 189, 261, 263
Chorti people, 344–45
Christian Democrats (El Salvador), 22, 27–28, 30, 130, 132, 174–75, 237
Christian Science Monitor, 130, 137
Christians for Socialism, 88
Christmas raids, 316
Chuj people, 92
CIA (Central Intelligence Service)
　Chile and, 124
　El Salvador and, 21–22, 30–31, 177–78, 425–26
　Guatemala and, 43, 78–79, 236, 242–43
　Nicaragua and, 177
Cinco de Mayo, 183
Cissna, Francis, 368
citaciones, 349
citizenship, 144, 170, 271, 295, 432
　for Dreamers, 296–99
Citizenship and Immigration Services, 228, 368, 432
Ciudad Juárez, Mexico, 204–5, 294, 401–3
Clark, Anthony, 134
Clark, William, 129–30
Clarke, Maura, 31
Climate, Nature, and Communities, 377
climate change, 376–80
Climentoro, Guatemala, 376–79
Clinton, Bill
　election of 1992, 201–2, 204, 217
　election of 1994, 213–14
　election of 1996, 220

Clinton, Bill (*cont.*)
  governor of Arkansas, 51–52, 110
  immigration policy, 51–52, 110, 201–4, 216–18, 220, 261–62
  welfare reform, 214–16, 218–19
Clinton, Hillary, 274, 275, 464
Coalition for Humane Immigrant Rights of Los Angeles, 306
Coast Guard, 111, 202, 227, 228
cocaine, 161–65, 246–47, 417–18
coffee, 13, 14, 345
Coffin, William Sloane, 135
cofradía, 246
Colby, William, 39
Cold War, 5, 23, 47, 61, 78, 112, 282
Colindres, Maria Elena, 365–66
Colón, Honduras, 390–91
Colonia Búfalo, La Ceiba, 287
Columbus Boys, 165
Committee in Solidarity with the People of El Salvador (CISPES), 126
Communist Party of El Salvador, 13–14
Communist Party of Guatemala, 75, 77–78
Community Resources against Street Hoodlums (CRASH), 167
Community Tagger Task Force, 210
Comprehensive Immigration Reform Act of 2007, 270–74, 302, 304–5, 333
"conditional entry," 47
Conger, Phil, 119–20, 134
Congressional Black Caucus, 449
Consequence Delivery System, 4, 308
Consuelo Porras, María, 453
Contract with America, 213–14, 217–18
Contras, 145–46, 173–74, 213
Contreras, José Luis, 362–66
Convictions of the Heart (Davidson), 137, 138
Corbett, James, 59–60, 69, 70–71, 99–100, 102, 103–4, 117–20, 134, 135
Corchado, Linda, 401–2, 441–42, 444–45
CoreCivic, 303
Coronado Locos, 160
COVID-19 pandemic, 427, 431–37, 451–52
Cowan, Margo, 37–46, 53–58, 68, 69, 71, 100, 117
crack cocaine epidemic, 161–65
CRECE (Central American Refugee Committee), 127, 129, 143–44, 147–49, 239
crime, 219–20, 292–93
  Clinton and, 203–4, 223, 261–62
  El Salvador and, 264
  Guatemala and, 246–48, 346
  Honduras and, 283
  Los Angeles and gangs, 167–68, 170, 176, 211, 233
  Marielitos and, 51–52

MS-13 and, 330–32, 334–37
sanctuary jurisdiction claims, 131, 143–44, 147–48
Trump and, 318–20, 324–25, 330–31, 334, 389–90
Criminal Consequence Initiative, 442–43
Crips, 168, 197
Cristiani, Alfredo, 175–76, 177, 191–92, 194
Cruz, Jesus, 118–19, 138
Cruz, Ted, 321
Cuban refugees, 47, 48, 50–52, 110–11, 413–14, 434, 458
Cuban Revolution, 15
Cuernavaca, Mexico, 88–93
Cuevas, Kayla, 330, 336, 337, 338, 341
Cuomo, Andrew, 334–35
Customs and Border Protection (CBP), 3, 228, 290, 301, 355, 367–69, 408
Cypress Hill, 189, 261

Daily Californian, 128
Dale, Theodore, 363–64
Dallas Cowboys, 379
Dalton, Roque, 14
Damas de Blanco, 413–14
D'Aubuisson, Roberto, 150
Davidson, Miriam, 137, 138
DeConcini, Dennis, 131–32, 144–45, 178
dedos fregados, 91
Defense Department, US, 24, 51, 62, 129, 177, 178, 328, 367, 405
Deferred Action for Childhood Arrivals (DACA), 297–99, 329, 333, 367
Degenhart, Enrique, 420
Dell, 265
Del Rio International Bridge, 457–58, *458*
Deming, New Mexico, 353–54
Denver, Colorado, 199, 282–83, 285, 286, 287
deportations, 204–5, 227–30, 309–10, 458–59. *See also* Border Patrol; *and specific cases*
  COVID-19 pandemic and, 432–35
  Cowan at El Centro, 53–58, 60
  DACA and, 297–99, 329, 333, 367
  IIRIRA of 1996, 218–20, 223–24, 264, 324
  Obama as "deporter in chief," 290–99, 305
  Salvadoran migrants, 119–20, 125, 128, 131–32
  Title 42 expulsions, 431, 432, 448–49, 457–59
  "voluntary departure," 55–56, 70, 140, 144–45, 223, 399, 414
deportistas, 268–69
Deras, Ernesto, 169, 197
"development poles," 238
DHS (Homeland Security, US Department of)

INDEX

arrest quotas, 272
border emergency, 300–306
Brané at, 386–87, 444–45
budget, 290
Chertoff at, 273, 308
creation of, 228, 290
deportations, 292–94, 458–59
Guatemala City meeting, 3–4
immigration raids, 271–72
Johnson at, 300–301, 303, 308
Kelly at, 326–27, 333, 356, 366–67
Mayorkas at, 446, 457
McAleenan at, 355–57, 360–61, 411–12, 415–16, 418–19, 420
Mechkowski at, 228–29
Migrant Protection Protocols, 404, 407–8, 411–14, 430–31, 443–44, 448–49, 456–57
Napolitano at, 292–94, 297
Nielsen at, 364–65, 367–69, 381–82, 410
Diario Militar, 78, 236
Díaz-Balart, Mario, 304
Direct English, 310, 311–12
"discernment process," 101
Dobbs, Lou, 271
Dole, Bob, 214
Dolores Park (San Francisco), 124, 125–26
Domestic Policy Council (DPC), 297, 325, 328
Donovan, Jean, 30–31
"Dope Man" (song), 156
Dos Hermanos (boat), 50
Douglas, Arizona, 38–39, 45, 99–101
Doyle, Kate, 243
Dreamers, 290, 295–99, 329, 333, 367
Drug Enforcement Administration (DEA), 222, 246, 417–18
Duarte, José Napoleón, 132–33, 174–75
dudosa confiabilidad, 461
Duke University, 323
Durbin, Richard, 355, 357
Duvalier, François "Papa Doc," 112
Duvalier, Jean-Claude, 112

Ebrard, Marcelo, 407, 413
"economic migrants," 104–5, 200
18th Street Gang, 155–56, 159–60, 161, 166, 169, 190, 196, 207, 261–64, 312–16
Eisenhower, Dwight, 78, 297
el banco del calcetín, 184
El Centro Detention Center, 53–58, 60, 132
Elder, Jack, 119
El Diario de Hoy, 261
El Mozote massacre, 64–66, 65
Eloy Detention Center, 2
El Paraíso, 33–34, 96, 97, 130, 255, 428

El Paso, Texas, 51, 95, 204–5, 224, 294, 431
Keldy case, 370–74, 383–84, 387–88
pilot program, 357, 360–61, 366–69, 370–74, 442–43
El Paso Border Patrol, 355–57, 360–61, 497n
elPeriódico, 432–33
El Quiché, 82, 92–93, 237, 238, 239, 247, 348, 378
El Salvador
call centers, 265–69, 310–12, 314–17, 439–40
Civil War. See Salvadoran Civil War
coup d'état of 1979, 21–23, 35
Eddie Anzora in, 170, 188–91, 194, 196–97, 310–13, 314–17, 439–40
deportation, 220–21, 231–34, 259–69
election of 1972, 16
election of 2004, 264
election of 2009, 277–78
election of 2014, 314
election of 2019, 439
gangs, 262–64, 312–17, 313, 315, 439–40, 461–62
Juan Romagoza in. See Romagoza, Juan
La Matanza, 13–14, 35, 90
migrants. See Salvadoran migrants
Moakley in, 176–79
political history of, 11–36, 43, 61–68, 73–74, 85, 87–88, 130–31, 149–51, 174–76, 191–94, 277–78, 438–40, 461–62
Ramírez in, 307–9
"El Salvadorian Underground Railroad" (Rayburn), 116–17
el susto, 350
Elysian Park (Los Angeles), 209–10
Emanuel, Rahm, 204, 214, 216, 217, 220, 275, 291, 294, 298
Embassy of the United States (Guatemala City), 3–4
Embassy of the United States (San Salvador), 26, 29–30
English Cool, 310–12, 314, 439
English4CallCenters, 310–12
Escobar, Felicia, 298
Escobar, Pablo, 496n
Estás en Tu Casa (Make Yourself at Home), 394
Estrada, Doria Elia, 56
ES 503, 267
Ethiopia, 23
European Union, 363, 415
"exclusion hearings," 112–13
ExpressTel, 266
extreme weather events, 377–78
Ezell, Harold, 117–18

fábricas, 165
fall of Saigon, 49, 61
family detentions, 309–10
  border emergency, 300–306
family separations, 4, 360–61, 368–69, 380–88, 408–11, 441–43
  ACLU lawsuits challenging, 384–88
  Biden executive order, 441
  end of policy, 410–11
  Homan's initial idea of, 302–3
  Keldy case
    asylum case file, 383–84, 387–88, 401–2, 443
    asylum hearing, 370–74
    border crossing and arrest, 352–54
    children's hearing, 396–98
    humanitarian parole, 444–45, 446
    preliminary asylum screening, 357–60
    reunification with children, 445–47, 446, 447
    separation from children, 360–61, 370–73, 396–98, 441–44
  Kephart and, 375–76
  restitution, 446, 456–57
  reunifications, 385, 444–47
  Trump executive order, 383–84
"family unity" policy of Bush administration, 215
Farabundo Martí National Liberation Front (FMLN), 61–63, 73–74, 85, 127, 130, 175–76, 191–94, 277, 312–13, 314, 437–39
FBI (Federal Bureau of Investigation), 31, 126, 150, 242, 328
Federal Emergency Management Agency (FEMA), 51, 228, 301
Federation for American Immigration Reform (FAIR), 218
Fierro, Juan, 412, 413, 414
Fife, John, 58–60, 68–77, 70, 94–95, 100, 102–4, 114, 117, 131
  Sanctuary Movement, 69–71, 70, 134, 135
fincas, 13
First Amendment, 141
Flake, Jeff, 292
Florence Project, 386
Flores, Andrea, 457
Flores, Carlos, 390
Flores, Francisco, 263–64
Flores Agreement, 301, 353
"flushers," 198
Ford, Bill, 251
Ford, Gerald, 38
Ford, Ita, 31
Foreign Assistance Act, 62
Forester, Steve, 113
Form G-28, 45, 55, 59
Fort Bragg, 169

Fort Chaffee, 51–52, 110
Fort Huachuca, 100
Fourth Amendment, 316
Fox News, 323, 365, 368, 457
Francisco Marroquín University, 244
free trade, 265–66
Frente Democrático Revolucionario (FDR), 30–31
Fuerzas Armadas Rebeldes (FAR), 245–46
"fugitives," 228–30
Fulton Locos, 169, 197, 262
Fulton Locos Salvatrucha, 262
Funes, Mauricio, 277–78, 312–13, 438

Gaitán, Edgar Augusto Godoy, 242
Galdamez, Rodrigo, 311
Gang of Eight, 298–99
gangs. *See also specific gangs*
  of El Salvador, 262–64, 312–17, *313*, *315*, 439–40, 461–62
  of Los Angeles, 157–58, 167–68, 197, 206–13
Garbage Pail Kids, 156–57
Garcia, Ann, 442–43
García, Carlos, 197
García, José Guillermo, 22, 30, 150–51, 250–58, 425
García, Lucas, 82
Garrard-Burnett, Virginia, 93
Gates, Daryl, 195–96
Gavarrete, Julia, 462
Gelernt, Lee, 385–87, 444, 446, 499*n*
GEO Group, 303
Georgetown University, 31, 175, 239
George Washington University Hospital, 148, 172, 180
Gerardi, Juan, 247, 248, 350, 455
Giammattei, Alejandro, 433, 435, 451
Giffords, Gabby, 291
Gillespie, Ed, 331
Gingrich, Newt, 213–14, 217–18
Global Migration and Quarantine (DGQM), 431–32, 434
GoDaddy, 440
Golden Eagle, 267
Golden Venture (ship), 202–3
Golden West, 54
golpe profiláctico, 287
Gómez, Juan, 335–36
González, Neris, 252–58, *257*
González Dubón, Epaminondas, 245
graffiti, 163, *164*, 207, 209, 210
Graham, Lindsey, 326
Graham, Salomon, 118–19, 137
Grande, Rutilio, 18–19
Grann, David, 346–47

INDEX

Grassley, Chuck, 410
Great Recession, 285, 291
Greenberg Traurig, 419
Grijalva, Mercedes, 97–98
Grupos Beta, 412
Guadalupe, Morena, 74, 95, 251–52
Guatemala
  climate change impact in, 376–80
  corruption in, 82, 244–46, 343–51, 453–55
  coup d'état of 1954, 43, 236
  COVID-19 pandemic in, 432–35
  election of 1985, 236–37
  election of 1993, 244–45
  election of 2004, 346
  election of 2015, 343
  health emergency, 343–51
  indigenous peoples. *See* Indigenous Guatemalans
  Juan Romagoza in, 80–83
  Lucrecia Mack in. *See* Hernández Mack, Lucrecia
  Mack sisters in, 235–49
  political history of, 43, 77–79, 81–82, 92–93, 235–37, 449–55
Guatemala: Eternal Spring, Eternal Tyranny (Simon), 244
Guatemala: Never Again!, 247–48
Guatemala City, 3, 4, 75, 79–83, 235–49, 343–46, 350, 419, 451–55
Guatemala City earthquake of 1976, 80
Guatemala Health Ministry, 343–44, 348, 350, 351, 434
Guatemalan Labor Party, 82
Guatemalan migrants, 88–93, 94–95, 104, 113–14, 199–201, 378
guerra contra la delincuencia, 283
Guerrero, Jean, 322–23
Guillermoprieto, Alma, 64–65
Gullage, Dick, 50
Guttentag, Lucas, 139, 140

H-1B visas, 228
Haig, Alexander, 61–63
Haitian refugees, 110–13, 201–2, 227, 342, 433, 457–58
Hamilton, Gene, 326, 366–69
Harpys, the, 155–58
  Dead End, the, 155, 158
Harris, Kamala, 449–50
Harrison Locos Salvatrucha, 263
Hawks, Howard, 52
Hefner, Hugh, 225
Hernández, José Luis, 391
Hernández, Tony, 417–18
Hernández Mack, Lucrecia, 235–37, *237*, 243–46, *344*
  congressional career of, 451–55

  fight against corruption in Guatemala, 244–46, 343–45, 347–51, 453–55
  mother's murder, 240–44, 244, 249, 452
Hesburgh, Theodore, 108–9, 110
Heston, Charlton, 157
hieleras, 308
Hincapié, Marielena, 305
Hinojosa, Maria, 295–96
HIV/AIDS, 182
Hollywood Locos, 160
Hollywood Locos Salvatrucha, 262
Holocaust, 60, 135
Homan, Thomas, 302–3, 332–34
Homeland Security. *See* DHS
Homeland Security Act of 2002, 228
"homieland," 265–66
Honduran migrants, 1–2, 3, 309–10, 378, 398–401
  caravans, 364, 368, 389–95, 406–8
Honduras
  coup d'état of 2009, 286–88
  election of 2002, 283
  election of 2017, 362–66
  Hurricane Mitch, 281–83, 342, 463
  Keldy in, 281–89
  political history of, 43, 286–88, 362–66
Hotel El Presidente (San Salvador), 29–30
Hotels.com, 266, 267
Howard University, 276
Huehuetenango, Guatemala, 92, 199, 237, 343, 375, 376–80, 452
Huerta, Dolores, 40
humanitarian parole, 444–45, 446
Human Rights First, 431
Hungarian refugees, 47, 48
Hurricane Mitch, 281–83, 342, 345, 463
Hustler, The (movie), 225
Hutchison, Peggy, 99–106, 119, 134

ICE (Immigration and Customs Enforcement)
  arrest quotas, 230
  border emergency, 300–306
  COVID-19 and, 434–35
  creation of, 228
  deportations, 227–30, 290, 292–94, 341
  Detention and Removal Operations, 228
  Homan and, 302–3, 332–34
  immigration raids, 271–72, 316, 333–34
  Keldy case. *See* Zúniga, Keldy Mabel Gonzáles Brebe de
  Mechkowski at, 228–29
  Operation Raging Bull, 341
  Secure Communities, 293, 333, 491*n*
ICE Air, 432–33
Ice-T, 156

Illegal Immigration Reform and Immigrant Responsibility Act of 1996 (IIRIRA), 218–20, 223–24, 264, 290, 324, 491*n*
Immigrant Legal Resource Center, 147
Immigration Act of 1990, 4, 178–79, 215, 217–18
Immigration and Customs Enforcement. *See* ICE
Immigration and Nationality Act (INA) of 1965, 47–48
Immigration and Naturalization Service. *See* INS
immigration policy, 2–5, 47–52. *See also specific legislation and presidents*
    Gang of Eight and, 298–99
    Select Commission on Immigration and Refugee Policy, 108–9
Immigration Reform and Control Act (IRCA) of 1986, 109, 144–46, 163, 170, 178, 181, 215, 315
impuesto de guerra, 390
"I'm Your Pusher" (song), 156, 206
Indigenous Guatemalans, 81–82, 89, 90, 92–93, 104, 199–201, 238–39, 344–45, 349–50, 452
Inforpress Centroamericana, 236
Inman, Maurice, 114
INS (Immigration and Naturalization Service), 39, 112
    Anzora's arrest, 220–21, 226, 232–34
    asylum, 55–60, 103, 137, 140–42, 198–203
    budget, 107
    Castillo at, 41, 110
    Cowan and Manzo Area Council, 36, 41, 46, 56
    deportation process, 198–99
    El Centro Detention Center, 53–58, 60, 132
    Haitian refugees, 110–13
    lawsuits against, 139–42
    Los Angeles gang suspects, 169–70
    Mechkowski at, 222–24, 226–30
    Meissner at, 49–52, 110, 112, 201–4, 219–20
    Nelson at, 112, 144
    Operation Blockade, 205
    Operation Last Call, 224
    Operation Sojourner, 118
    restructuring of 2020, 227–28
    sanctuary movement and, 69–71, 101–6, 113–14, 126, 128
    trial, 134–39
Inter-American Court of Human Rights, 246, 346
Inter-American Development Bank, 278
"internally displaced," 238
International Commission against Impunity in Guatemala (CICIG), 346–51, 419, 450, 453
"invisible wall," 3
Iran-Contra Affair, 145–46, 173–74, 213
Iraq War, 276

Ixil people, 92
Ixil Triangle, 238–40

Jamaica Plain, 132, 176
James Monroe High School, 206, 207
Jarrett, Valerie, 292, 304–5
Jewell, Angela, 184
Jewish refugees, 23, 47
Jiménez, Daniel, 391–92, 393
Johnson, Jeh, 300–301, 303, 308
Johnson, Lyndon B., 38
Johnston, Bill, 58–60, 70
Joint Chiefs of Staff, 15, 63, 328
Jordan, Barbara, 218
Jordan, Michael, 163
Joseph, David, 227
José Simeón Cañas Central American University (La UCA), 175–76
Justice Department, US, 49, 110–13, 117, 129, 201, 227, 327, 366, 367, 368, 385–88, 405, 410, 411, 442
Juvenile Camp Louis Routh, 210

Kaibiles, the, 247
Kamasaki, Charles, 179
Kansi, Mir Aimal, 202
Karl, Terry, 253
Kazel, Dorothy, 30–31
Kelly, John, 326–27, 333, 356, 366–67, 418, 449–50
Kennedy, Edward "Ted," 142, 178, 271, 291, 298
Kennedy, John F., 15
Kephart, Emily, 375–76
K'iche' people, 92, 135
Kids in Need of Defense, 375–76, 386
Kill 'Em Quick, 210
King, Rodney, 194–96
Kirkes, Julie, 333
Kirkpatrick, Jeane, 31–32
Kodak, 266
Kolbe, Jim, 292
Krikorian, Mark, 321
Kris Kross, 189
Krome, 113

La Bestia (the Beast), 285
La Capellania, Guatemala, 379
La caravana de los mutilados, 391
La Ceiba, Honduras, 281–89, 395, 443, 462
La Clínica del Pueblo, 148–49, 171–74, 180–83, 182, 185, 254–57, 275–76
La Eme, 166, 209, 263
La Grandota, 160
La Limpieza, 78–79

INDEX

La Mano Dura, 283
land reforms in El Salvador, 18–19, 71, 130–31, 246
Langdon Avenue Elementary School, 162
Langdon Gang, 165, 207
La Palma, El Salvador, 193
la pastora, 352, 371
la raza, 210
Laredo, Texas, 411–12, 430
Las Americas Immigrant Advocacy Center, 372–73, 383, 401–2
Las Cruces, New Mexico, 333–34
Latino Civil Rights Task Force, 186
Latino drivers, 319, 332, 494*n*
LaValle, John Jay, 319
La Violencia, 92, 345, 350
Lawyers' Committee for Human Rights, 251
Lee, Mike, 419
Leeward Locos, 160
Legislative Assembly of El Salvador, 130–31, 345–46, 349, 438–39, 450, 451, 452, 454
LeoGrande, William, 174
Levy, Steve, 331
liberation theology, 58
Lima, Byron, 350
limpieza, 64, 78–79
Lind, Dara, 219
LL Cool J, 157
Lobo, Porfirio, 288
Lodi NewsSentinel, 128
London *Times*, 102
López, Esvin Rocael, 379
López Obrador, Andrés Manuel, 405–7, 413–14
Los Angeles
    Eddie Anzora in, 155–58, 161–65, *164*, 168–70, 188–89, 206–12, 220–21, 224–26, 231–32, *232*
    gang wars, 157–58, 167–68, 197, 206–13
    Juan Romagoza in, 115–16, 120–23
    riots of 1992, 194–97, *196*, 208
Los Angeles International Airport, 355
Los Angeles Marathon, 210
Los Angeles Olympic Games (1984), 160–61
Los Angeles Police Department (LAPD), 160–61, 163, 167–68, 176, 195–96, 208, 209–10
    Rampart scandal, 211
Los Angeles Times, 169, 208, 432
Los Muñecos (The Dolls), 42
los nerds, 348
"low-risk" refugees, 105
Lucas García, Fernando Romeo, 81, 82, 92–93
Lucero, Marcelo, 319, 320, 332
Lula da Silva, 277

McAleenan, Kevin, 355–57, 360–61, 411–12, 415–16, 418–19, 420
McAllen, Texas, 246–47, 300–301, 380
MacArthur Fellowships, 271, 296
MacArthur Park (Los Angeles), 116, 120–23, 144
McCain, John, 271, 274, 292, 326
McClatchy, 265
McGovern, Jim, 176
Mack, Helen, 235–49, *237*, 344, 346
    Myrna's murder, 240–43, 244–49, 344
Mack, Myrna, 235–49, *237*
    murder of, 240–43, 244–49, 452
Mack, Yam Jo, 235–36
McMaster, H. R., 327
Maduro, Ricardo, 283
Mahowald, Mary Kay, 372–73, 383
Make the Road, 336
mal de ojo, 349–50
Mano Dura, 263–64, 314, 437
Manzo Area Council, 37–46, 53–58, 117
maquiladora, 412
maras, 283
Mara Salvatrucha (MS), 157–58, 160–61, 165–69, 262–63, 307. *See also* MS-13
mariconada, 91
Mariel boatlift, 52, 110–11, 199, 202
Marielitos, 50–52
Mármol, Miguel, 13–14
Martínez, Carlos, 160
Martínez d'Aubuisson, Juan José, 262, 263
Maryknoll Sisters, 30–31
Mattis, James, 390
Mauricio, Carlos, 252–58, *257*
Maya Q'anjob'al people, 92–93
Maya Q'eqchi', 82
Mayorkas, Alejandro, 446, 457
Mazzoli, Romano, 109
MCP Gang, 163, 168–70
Mechkowski, Scott, 222–24, 226–30
Medicaid, 215
"medium-risk" refugees, 105
Megadeth, 160
Meissner, Doris, 117, 224
    background of, 48–49
    Carter White House, 49–52, 110
    Clinton White House, 201–4, 219–20
    Reagan White House, 110–14
Melendez, Angel, 341
Menchú, Rigoberta, 244
Méndez Arceo, Sergio, 88–91
Mendez v. Reno, 140
Mercury News, 128
Mérida Escobar, José, 241–42
Merkt, Stacey, 119

INDEX

Metropolitan Cathedral of San Salvador, 17–21, *20*, 28, *28*
Mexican Mafia, 156, 166, 197, 209–10, 263
Mexico
    election of 2006, 405–6
    election of 2018, 406
    migrant caravans through, 364, 368, 389–95, 406–8, 415–16
    political history of, 405–8, 413–14
Mexico border. *See* border
Miami Airport, 151
Miami Times, 112
Micheletti, Roberto, 287–88
Mickens, Nisa, 330, 336, 337, 338, 341
migrant caravans, 116, 128, 129, 365, 368, 389–95, *393*, 406–8, 415–16
Migrant Protection Protocols (MPP), 404, 407–8, 411–14, 430–31, 443, 448, 456
Military Veterans Association of Guatemala, 248
Miller, Stephen, 322–28, 366–69, 381, 405–6, 410–11, 420, 430–31
Mirada Locos 13, 263
missionaries murders of 1980, 30–31
Mississippi Free Press, 434
Moakley, Joe, 131–32, 144–45, 176–79, 191
"model villages," 238
Molina, Marta, 74
Monroy, Hugo, 434
Monterrosa, Domingo, 64
Morales, Jimmy, 343–44, 347–51, 419–21
Moran, Tyler, 298
Morazán Department, 63–64, *65*
Morazán Park (Guatemala), 235–36
Morrison & Foerster, 253–54
Moscow Olympic Games (1980), 160
Most Holy Redeemer Church (San Francisco), 127, 147
Mount Pleasant, 148, 173, 192, 255, 275–76
    riots of 1991, 183–87, *186*
Movimiento Estudiantil Revolucionario Salvadoreño (MERS), 11
MS-13, 165–67, 169–70, 197, 207, 261–64, 308, 309, 312, 313, 314–15, 330–32, 334–37, 461
Mujica, Irineo, 394–95
Munguía Payés, David, 312–13
Muñoz, Cecilia
    background of, 215
    Bush and, 270–75
    Clinton and welfare reform, 215–19
    at La Raza, 215, 217, 218, 274, 291, 294, 304–5
    in Obama White House, 290–98, 301–2, 304–6, 333
    in Trump White House, 325–26

Muñoz, Ignacio, 216–17
Muñoz, Marco Antonio, 380–81
Murguía, Janet, 213–18, 271, 295, 304–5
Muslim ban, 326–27, 367
Myrna Mack Foundation, 244–45, 344

Naked Jungle, The (movie), 157
Napolitano, Janet, 292–94, 297
Nasralla, Salvador, 363–65
National Association of Latin American Health Professionals, 182
National Autonomous University of Mexico, 79
National Conference of Catholic Bishops, 125
National Council of La Raza, 215, 217, 218, 274, 291, 294, 304–5
National Fugitive Operations Program, 272
National Guard of El Salvador, 15, 16, 22, 31, 34, 67, 72, 74, 103, 126, 149–50, 172, 175, 196, 250–56, 291
National Immigration Forum, 218
National Immigration Law Center, 304–5
National Party of Honduras, 283, 288, 363, 365–66
National Police of El Salvador, 15
National Rifle Association (NRA), 331
National Sanctuary Defense Fund, 135
National Security Archive, 243
National Security Council (NSC), 63, 78, 129–30, 302, 328, 457
National Security Entry-Exit Registration System (NSEERS), 227
National Women's Political Caucus, 49
naturalization ceremonies, 432
Nelson, Alan, 112, 144
Newman, Paul, 225
Newsweek, 102, 163
New York Times, 64–65, 66, 109, 163, 202, 262, 291, 295, 298–99, 304, 380
Nicaragua, political history of, 23–24, 61, 62, 88, 105, 114, 129–30, 145–46, 173–74, 177
Nicaraguan Adjustment and Central American Relief Act, 485*n*
Nicaraguan migrants, 105, 342, 458
Nicaraguan Revolution, 23–24, 62, 146
Nicgorski, Darlene, 134
Niebuhr, Reinhold, 23
Nielsen, Kirstjen, 367–69, 381–82, 410
Nike Air Jordans, 396
Nike Cortez, 191, 207, 263, 341
9/11 attacks (2001), 226–27, 264
Nixon, John, 138
Nixon, Richard, 38, 39, 48, 61
Nobel Peace Prize, 244
Nogales, Arizona, 44–46, 59, 68–69, 99–100, 119, 430

INDEX

Noriega, Manuel, 177, 196
Normandie Locos, 160
Northern Triangle, 3, 308, 416, 449
North Korea, 227
notarios, 200–201
notice to appear in court (NTA), 223
Nuestra Familia, 166
Nuevo Cuscatlán, 438
Nuevo Laredo, Mexico, 286, 407
NumbersUSA, 323
N.W.A, 156

Obama, Barack, 464
   election of 2008, 274, 276
   election of 2012, 298, 322, 331
   immigration policy, 4, 272–74, 290–99, 327, 333, 449
      border emergency, 300–306
      "deporter in chief," 290–99, 305
Ochoa Pérez, Sigifredo, 63–64, 426
O'Currance Call Center, 315–17
Office of Legal Counsel, 297
Office of Management and Budget (OMB), 216, 328, 369, 405
Office of Refugee Resettlement (ORR), 301–3, 375–76, 386–87
Olavarria, Esther, 298
O'Neill, Thomas "Tip," 163
Operation Blockade, 205
Operation Gatekeeper, 205
Operation Hammer, 167
Operation Hold the Line, 486n
Operation Just Cause, 177
Operation Last Call, 224
Operation Raging Bull, 341
Operation Rescue, 63–64
Operation Rio Grande, 205
Operation Safeguard, 205
Operation Sojourner, 118
Operation Wetback, 111
opioid epidemic, 321
Orantes, Hugo, 43
Orantes-Hernandez v. Smith, 140
ORDEN, 21
Organization of American States, 246, 313, 363, 364
Organ Pipe Cactus National Monument, 41–42, 58, 395
Orlando Hernández, Juan, 2, 362–66, 389, 417, 419, 435, 449–50
Orozco, Joel, 207, 210, 211, 221, 225, 231
Ortega, Daniel, 174
Ortíz, Margarita, 75, 80–81, 83, 85, 91
Osorio, Juan Valencia, 242, 249

Otero Prison, 383–84
OTMs (other than Mexican), 44–46
Oye, Trump (López Obrador), 406

Pacheco, Maria Gabriela, 295
Pacino, Al, 52
Pacoimas 13, 263
Panama, 3, 79, 132, 177, 196, 413
Pan-American Highway, 83
Pan de Vida, 403, 404, 407–8, 409, 412
pandilleros, 283–84, 285
Panetta, Leon, 219
Parque Libertad (San Salvador), 263
Partido de Conciliación Nacional (PCN), 16
Patchogue, New York, 318–20
Patient 36, 432–33
Patriot Act of 2001, 227
Pavón Prison, 79–80, 350
Peasant Unity Committee (CUC), 82
Peña Nieto, Enrique, 394
Pence, Mike, 355, 419, 432
People (magazine), 117
pérdida del alma, 350
Pérez, Feliciano, 376–79
Personal Responsibility and Work Opportunity Act of 1994, 214–16, 223
Pew Research Center, 178
Photoshop, 267
Pierce College, 225
Pima County Sheriff, 43
Pimentel, Stanley, 31
Pinochet, Augusto, 124
Playboy Gangster Crips, 168
Playboy Mansion, 225
Podesta, John, 275
Policía de Hacienda (PH), 15
Pollo Campero, 313
Pontieri, Paul, 318–20
"Post-Vietnam syndrome," 128
Presente.org, 295
Presidential Security Department, 242, 249
PricewaterhouseCoopers, 333
promotores de salud, 181–82, 277–78
PTSD (post-traumatic stress disorder), 128
Public Health Service Act of 1944, 431–32
Pueblo sin Fronteras, 394
Puerto Palomas, Mexico, 352–53
Purcell, Eileen, 136
Purcell, Juan, 136

Quilinco, Guatemala, 379
Quinn, John, 125
Quiñones, Ramón Dagoberto, 44, 45–46, 59, 68, 99–100, 119, 134

RAICES, 386
Ramírez, Juliana, 307–9
Ramírez, Ramona, 307–8, 309
Rampart scandal, 211
Rayburn, James, 116–18, 137–38
Reader's Digest, 39
Reagan, Ronald, 322
 election of 1980, 29–30
 election of 1984, 133
 foreign policy, 30, 31–31, 62, 65–67, 93, 120, 131, 132–33
 Iran-Contra Affair, 145–46, 173–74, 213
 immigration policy, 65–67, 103, 104–5, 107–14, 141, 144–46, 163, 199
Red Cross, 167
Redfield, Robert, 432
Reed, Bruce, 214, 216, 217
Refugee Act of 1980, 48–52, 56, 57, 68, 70, 104–5, 112, 135–36, 137, 139, 140, 141–42, 199, 203, 327
Reid, Harry, 298
"removables," 1–2
Reno, Donald, Jr., 137–39
renta, 262, 336
Republican Party, 108, 215–16, 218–19, 291, 299, 304, 321, 322, 324, 365, 448–49, 456. *See also specific members*
 Contract with America, 213–14, 217–18
Reyes, Jandy, 390
Reyes, Silvestre, 204–5
Right Livelihood Award, 244
Ríos Montt, Efraín, 93, 346
Rivas, Linda, 383
Roberts, Shawn, 251, 255–56, 258
Rodríguez, Alejandro, 138–39
Rodríguez, José Tulia, 392
Romagoza, Enrique, 73, 75
Romagoza, Juan
 asylum claim of, 120, 143, 147, 149, 192
 author's interviews with, 427–29, 436–37, 460–61, 462–64
 border crossing of, 115–16
 California caravans, *129*, 131, 132
 cancer diagnosis of, 275–76
 COVID diagnosis of, 436–37
 early life and education of, 9–12
 in El Salvador, 72–76, 460–64, *462*, *463*
  arrest and torture, 33–36, 72, 75, 79, 122–23, 250–51, 252–53, 426–28
  Chalatenango, 32–36, 72–73, 76, 95–98
  Laura and, 27, 36, 95–98, 192–93
  return to, 192–94, 275–78, 436–38, 460–64
  Usulután, 9–10, 14–17, 73–74, 98

 El Salvador political history and, 14–16, 17–21, 25–27, 32–36, 73–74, 85, 87–88, 191–92, 277–78, 461–62
 escape plan of, 75–76
 in Guatemala, 80–83
 in Los Angeles, 115–16, 120–23
 Méndez Arceo and, 88–91
 in Mexico City, 84–88, 94–95, 98
 Romero and, 17–21, 25–26, 29, 428
 Sanctuary trial and, 135
 in San Francisco, 124–29, *129*, 143–44, 147–48
 trial of Vides Casanova and García, 250–58, *257*, 426–28
 in Washington, DC, 147–49, *182*, 185, 186–87
  La Clínica, 148–49, 171–74, 180–83, *182*, 185, 192, 256–57, 275–76
  riots of 1991, 185, 186–87
Romagoza, Maria, 98, 192–93, 252, 257
Romero, Óscar, 17–23, *20*, 58, 88, 105, 428
 assassination of, 24–26, *28*, 28–29, 31–32, 132, 150, 175, 251
Romney, Mitt, 298, 322
Roosevelt, Franklin Delano, 478*n*
Roosevelt Hospital, 348, 351
Rosales, José, 67–68
Rosales-Fike, Sylvia, 181
Ross Center, 337
Rouse, Pete, 292, 294
Rubio, Marco, 419
Ruiz, Samuel, 89

Sabraw, Dana, 384–88, 442
Saca, Antonio, 264, 265
Sacramento Bee, 102–3
St. Augustine Cathedral (Tucson), 135
St. John's Episcopal Church (Washington, DC), 174, 437
St. Teresa of Avila church (San Francisco), 127, 129
Salas, Angelica, 306
Salt-N-Pepa, 157
Salvadoran Civil War, 11–13, 17–22, 25–36, 120, 131–32, 191–94, 262
Salvadoran Independence Day, 260
Salvadoran migrants, 16–118, 120–21, 159–60, 181, 309–10, 342, 378
 deportations, 119–20, 125, 128, 131–32, 378
 El Centro Detention Center, 53–58, 60
salvaje, 157–58
Salvy Life, 440
Sánchez Cerén, Salvador, 314, 437
sanctuary jurisdictions (cities), 131, 143–44, 147–48
sanctuary movement, 69–71, *70*, 100, 101–6, 113–14, 126, 128
 trial of, 134–39

INDEX

Sanctuary of Our Lady of Guadalupe (Nogales), 44, 59, 99–100, 105, 119, 134
Sanders, Sarah Huckabee, 382
San Diego, 51, 53, 115–16, 119, 205, 217, 384–85
Sandinistas, 23–24, 61, 62, 88, 105, 114, 129–30, 146, 173–74, 177
Sandoval, Elena, 337–40, 341–42
Sandoval, Juan Francisco, 451, 453–54
San Francisco
    Romagoza in, 124–29, 143–44, 147–48
    as sanctuary jurisdiction, 139–40, 143–44, 147–48
San Francisco Chronicle, 128
San José Las Flores, El Salvador, 193–94
San Juan de Aragón, Mexico, 84–85, 86–87
San Matteo Ixtatán, Guatemala, 238–39
San Pedro Sula, Honduras, 283, 284, 390, 403–4
San Rafael National Hospital (Santa Tecla), 11–12, 26
Sansivar Locos Salvatrucha, 262–63
Santa Monica High School, 323
Santiago de María, El Salvador, 9, 17–18, 428
Sanz, José Luis, 160, 169
Saravia, Mauricio Pérez, 194
Saturday Night Massacre, 48, 61
Scarface (movie), 52
Second Vatican Council, 88
Secret Service, 228
section 8D, 361, 372
Secure Communities, 293, 333, 491*n*
seed banks, 378–79
Select Commission on Immigration and Refugee Policy, 108–9
Semilla (political party), 451–53, 454
September 11 attacks (2001), 226–27, 264
Serrano, Jorge, 244–45
Service Employees International Union, 304–5
Sessions, Jeff, 321–25, 329, 332, 356–57, 366–68, 381, 382
Shalimar 13, 263
Sharry, Frank, 305
Shields, Peter, 180–83
Shoe War, 166
Shultz, George, 130
Siglo XXI, 353
Silverman, Mark, 147, 149
Simon, Jean-Marie, 244
Simpson, Alan, 109, 144, 178–79, 218–19
Sini, Timothy, 332, 339–40
60 Minutes (TV show), 103, 117
Slattery, Jim, 213
Slattery, William, 203
Slick Rick, 206
Smith, Lamar, 218, 224

Smith, William French, 107–8
Smyth, Frank, 246–47
Social Security, 121, 127, 221
Socorro Jurídico, 19
Sol, Catalina, 186–87
Solidarity 2000, 1–2, 398–401
Somoza, Anastasio, 24
Sonderling Center, 337
Sonoyta, Mexico, 42, 286, 394–95
Soto Cano Air Base, 419
South Central Los Angeles, 156, 162–63, 166–67
SOUTHCOM, 15
"southern pacts," 263
South Los Angeles, 155–58
Southside United Presbyterian Church (Tucson), 58–59, 69–71, *70*, 102, 118–19, 131
South Texas Family Residential Center, 303
Souza, Wesliane, 384
Soviet Jewish refugees, 47
Soviet Union, 23
Soyapango, El Salvador, 170, 189, 260
Special Prosecutor's Office against Impunity (FECI), 451
Stash, The (magazine), 231
State Department, US
    Bureau of Human Rights, 56, 114
    Chile and, 124
    El Salvador and, 177–78, 314
    Guatemala and, 77–78, 242–43
Stein, Eduardo, 346
"strategic hamlets," 238
Street Fighter (video game), 165
Strom, Cordia, 218
Stroock, Thomas, 243
Suffolk County GOP, 318–19
Suffolk County Police Department, 319, 330–31, 340
Super Mano Dura, 264, 437
Surf City, 440
Sylmar Juvenile Hall, 210
Syrian refugees, 326, 327

TACA Airlines, 151, 198–99
tagging, *164*, 170, 194, 209, 210
Tamaulipas, 285–86, 407
tandas, 150–51, 252
tandona, 150
Tanton, John, 218
Tapachula, Mexico, 1–2, 4, 353, 392, 398–402
tariffs, 413
Tea Party, 304
Teleperformance, 266

temporary protected status (TPS), 178–79, 337, 342, 364–65, 365
Texas Observer, 218, 246–47
Texas Rangers, 68
Tijuana, Mexico, 95, 115–16, 217, 385, 394, 406, 407, 413, 414
Tillerson, Rex, 327
Time (magazine), 163
Title 42, 431, 432, 448–49, 457–59
TJ Locos, 165
Torres, Dani, 413–14
Torres, Gustavo, 305
Torres, John, 229
Torres, Miguel, 360
Total Resources against Southeast Hoodlums (TRASH), 167
Tower, John, 111
Treasury Department, US, 314, 315
Treasury Police of El Salvador, 15
Trejo, Danny, 231
Trump, Donald
　election of 2016, 318–20, 324–26, 331
　election of 2018, 391–92
　election of 2020, 430, 436–37, 443–44
　immigration policy, 4, 325–29, 364–69, 378, 380–84, 389–92, 397, 410–14, 418–19, 420–21, 430–31, 432, 434, 435, 442–44, 449, 457. *See also* family separations
　border wall, 320, 324, 365
　Consequence Delivery System, 4, 308
　crime allegations, 318–20, 324–25, 330–31, 334, 389–90
　as election issue, 430, 318–21, 324–25, 391–92, 443–44
　El Paso pilot program, 355–57, 360–61, 366–69, 370–74, 442–43
　MPP, 404, 407–8, 411–14, 430–31, 443, 448, 456
　refugee cap, 327–29
　TPS, 337, 342, 364–65, 365
　"zero tolerance," 325, 368, 378–82, 405, 410, 441, 442, 456
　Muslim ban, 326–27, 367
　photo op at St. John's church, 437
Tucson Citizen, 41, 71
Tucson Ecumenical Council, 59, 69–71
Tucson Metropolitan Ministry, 119

Ugandan refugees, 47, 412
unaccompanied children, 300–301, 303, 309–10, 330, 332, 338, 340, 356–57, 358, 360, 378, 443, 449
underground railroad, 60, 102
"undue hardship," 219, 224

Unidad Revolucionaria Nacional Guatemalteca (URNG), 245–46, 344
Unidos sin Fronteras, 390
Unión Nacional Opositora, 16
United Farm Company, 77–78
United Farm Workers, 40
United Methodist Church, 99–100
United Methodist Reporter, 102
United Nations Commission for Historical Clarification, 247
United Nations Development Programme, 345
United Nations High Commissioner for Refugees, 105, 138
United Nations Protocol Relating to the Status of Refugees, 57
United States
　election of 1976, 23
　election of 1980, 29–30
　election of 1984, 133
　election of 1992, 201–2, 204, 320
　election of 1994, 213–14
　election of 2008, 274, 276
　election of 2012, 298, 322, 331
　election of 2014, 322
　election of 2016, 318–20, 324–26, 331
　election of 2020, 430, 436–37, 443–44
United States-Mexico border. *See* border
United States Mission to the United Nations, 328
United States v. Brignoni-Ponce, 39
United We Dream, 296–97
University of California, Berkeley, 128, 139, 253–54
University of California, San Diego, 208
University of Chicago, 355
University of El Salvador, 10–11
University of Maryland, 163
University of Notre Dame, 108
University of San Carlos, 82, 243–44, 245, 455
University of Texas, 58
University of Washington, 425
University of Wisconsin, 49
Uruguay, 23
Usulután, El Salvador, 36, 84, 85, 87, 91, 92, 94–95, 120, 121, 122, 124, 182, 190, 193, 194, 250, 255, 276, 427, 436–38, 460, 462
　Juan Romagoza in, 9–10, 14–17, 73–74, 98

Van Der Hout, Marc, 139–40
Varelli, Frank, 126
VDARE, 323
"vectors of disease," 431
Velásquez, Iván, 348, 350–51, 496*n*

Venezuela, 277, 286, 417
Venezuelan migrants, 458
Vera Institute of Justice, 386
Verapaces people, 92
Vermont Avenue Elementary School, 157
verticalismo democrático, 245
Victoria 82, 93
Vides Casanova, Carlos Eugenio, 35, 72, 126, 175
  emigration to US, 149–51
  lawsuit of, 250–58, 425–27
  Romagoza interrogation, 34–36
  Salvadoran Civil War, 22, 31, 34–36
Vietnamese refugees, 47, 49
Vietnam War, 15, 23, 49, 61, 79, 128, 163
Violent Crime Control and Law Enforcement Act of 1994, 203–4, 223
Virgin of Guadalupe, 32
Vogel, William, 41
"voluntary departure," 55–56, 70, 140, 144–45, 223, 399, 414

Wall Street Journal, 456, 457
War on Poverty, 38
Washington, DC
  Juan Romagoza in, 147–49, 171–74, 180–83, 182, 185, 186–87
  riots of 1991, 183–87, 186
Washington Post, 64–65, 66, 102, 130, 181, 251, 325, 380, 412, 426, 435
Watergate, 23, 48, 163
Weinberger, Caspar, 35, 129–30
Western Union, 264–65
WhatsApp, 387, 390, 398, 453
White, Frank, 51–52
White, Robert, 27–28, 30, 253
Whiteley, Irma, 383–84
Wienerschnitzel International, 117–18
Wiesel, Elie, 135
Wilson, Pete, 217
Wolff, Karenina, 396–98
Women's Refugee Commission, 386, 444
Wood, Kimba, 202
workplace raids, 272, 292
work visas, 406, 431, 458–59
World Bank, 49

World Trade Center bombing of 1993, 202, 203
World War II, 77, 124
"Wuhan of the Americas," 434

Yakuza, 315
Yaroshefsky, Ellen, 139, 140
Young, Neil, 321
Young, Wendy, 386–87

Zacatecoluca Prison, 312
Zamora, Mario, 27–28
Zelaya, Manuel, 286–88
"zero tolerance," 283, 325, 368, 378–82, 405, 410, 441, 442, 456
Zetas cartel, 247, 286
Zilberg, Elana, 208
Zúniga, Alex, 284, 289, 353, 396–98, 445–47, 447
Zúniga, Erick, 284, 352–54, 357–60, 370, 387
  family hearing, 396–98
  family reunification, 445–47, 446
Zúniga, Keldy Mabel Gonzáles Brebe de, 445
  Amanda and, 282, 283, 284, 285, 353, 392, 394–95, 445
  asylum case file, 383–84, 387–88, 401–2
  asylum hearing, 370, 372, 373–74
  asylum screening, 357–60
  border crossing and arrest, 352–54
  Carlos and, 285, 337–39, 341–42
  Claudia and, 286, 357–58, 387, 397
  Dana and, 353, 392, 399, 401–2
  deportation to Mexico, 373–74, 387–88, 399–401, 408–10, 412, 414
  in Honduras, 281–89
  humanitarian parole, 444–45, 446
  Luis Fernando and, 282–83, 284, 285, 288
  Nelsin Obed and, 287
  Osmán and, 392, 394–95, 399, 400, 401
  reunification with children, 445–47, 446, 447
  separation from children, 360–61, 370–73, 396–98, 441–44
Zúniga, Mino, 284–88, 289, 304, 353, 357–58, 370, 398, 400
Zúniga, Patrick, 284–85, 352–54, 357–60, 370, 387
  family hearing, 396–98
  family reunification, 445–47, 446